The Games of Anatoly Karpov

To Erjflaoc and Emiliana

The Games of Anatoly Karpov

Kevin J. O'Connell, Jimmy Adams

B. T. Batsford Limited *London*

First published 1974
© Kevin J. O'Connell, Jimmy Adams 1974
ISBN 0 7134 2849 X

Printed and bound in Great Britain by
Cox & Wyman Ltd,
London, Fakenham and Reading
for the publishers

B. T. Batsford Ltd.
4 Fitzhardinge Street, London W1H OAH

Contents

Preface

In the short period December 1971 to December 1973 Anatoly Karpov grew in stature and reputation from a strong grandmaster to come to be regarded, throughout the world, as the Soviet Union's real hope to wrest the World Championship title from Robert Fischer.

This book gives all the games (347) to which we have had access, and chronicles Karpov's development to the point of his semi-final Candidates' match.

In this volume we have attempted to incorporate several improvements on its predecessor (*The Games of Robert J. Fischer*):

(a) many more games have been annotated; almost every game has some notes, and about half of them are deeply annotated.

(b) surveys of most of the tournaments are given at the beginning of each chapter.

(c) a concise list of biographical details has been included (p. xiii).

(d) the index of openings is very detailed and includes Karpov's results with each opening variation.

(e) an index of annotators and sources.

KJO'C, JBA
London, February 1974

Acknowledgements

We wish to thank the following:

Anatoly Karpov	for checking, at Bath, the details of his tournament and match record
Charles de Villiers	for assistance in the annotation of games
Mike Wills	for translation of much material from Russian sources
M. Blaine	for translation from *Magyar Sakkelet*
R. G. Wade	for the use of his library
Peter Markland	for the loan (in perpetuity) of his bulletins of Graz
Alan Perkins	for his help in tracing two games from Graz which did not appear in the bulletins

Sources of annotations will be found acknowledged in some detail in the index, but here we would like especially to acknowledge and thank: Tony Gillam and *The Chess Player* B. H. Wood and *Chess*, Brian Reilly and the *British Chess Magazine, Chess Life and Review*, and, of course, all the Russian chess newspapers and magazines without which this book would be far less complete than it is.

Foreword

'Fischer got the title . . . I don't see why, in another six years, Karpov should be in a different position.'

Dr Mikhail Botvinnik, Skopje 1972

There is a lot of propaganda about you as a challenger to Fischer. Does that bother you?

'I don't think about it. I hope to play Fischer in three or four years.'

Anatoly Karpov, San Antonio 1972

Karpov's Elo Rating

1971	2540	
1972	2630	World No. 7=
1973	2660	World No. 2=

Symbols

+	Check
+ +	Double check
±	Some advantage for White
∓	Some advantage for Black
±	Clear advantage for White
∓	Clear advantage for Black
± ±	White has a won position
∓ ∓	Black has a won position
=	Balanced position
!	Good move
!!	Excellent move
!?	Interesting move
?!	Doubtful move
?	Inferior move
??	Losing move
(s)	Sealed move
TN	Theoretical novelty
1–0	Black resigned
0–1	White resigned
½–½	Draw agreed

Tournament and Match Record

			+	=	−
1965	All-Union Schoolboys, Moscow (4½/8)		.	.	.
	9 Spartakiad USSR Juniors, Harkov (7)		.	.	.
1966	All-Union Schoolboys, Moscow (5½/9)	5–6=	.	.	.
	Masters v. Candidate Masters		5	10	0
	USSR Junior Team Ch		1	.	.
	USSR Juniors–Scandinavia Juniors		1	1	0
1966/7	Trinec	1	9	4	0
1967	World Junior, USSR qualifying event	5	3	1	3
	All-Union Schools Spartakiad (?/10)		.	.	.
	RSFSR Spartakiad		1	.	.
	USSR Junior Team Ch		.	.	0
1967/8	Groningen	1	6	8	0
1968	USSR–Yugoslavia		3	1	0
	USSR Juniors–Scandinavia Juniors	bd. 2	0	1	1
	Moscow University Ch	1	7	6	0
	6 USSR Team Ch	bd. 6	9	2	0
1969	Leningrad Match-Tournament	1	5	5	2
	USSR Juniors–Yugoslavia Juniors		2	2	0
	'Red Armies', Warsaw	res	1	0	0
	USSR Armed Forces Team Ch	bd. 2	5	1	1
	World Junior Ch, Stockholm	1	12	5	0
	Hungary–RSFSR, Budapest		0	2	2
1970	RSFSR Ch, Kuibyshev	1	8	9	0
	San Antonio	1–3=	7	7	1
	Caracas	4–6=	8	7	2
	38 USSR Ch, Riga	5–7=	5	14	2
1971	39 USSR Ch, Daugavpils ½-final	1	9	8	0
	Student Olympiad, Mayaguez	bd. 3	7	1	0
	USSR Armed Forces Team Ch	bd. 1	3	3	1
	USSR Team Ch, Rostov-on-Don	bd. 6	6	1	0
	39 USSR Ch, Leningrad	4	7	12	2
	Alekhine Memorial, Moscow	1–2=	5	12	0
1971/2	Hastings	1–2=	8	6	1
1972	USSR Olympiad, Moscow	bd. 2	4	3	2
	Student Olympiad, Graz	bd. 1	5	4	0
	20 Olympiad, Skopje	1st res	12	2	1

			+	=	—
1973	Budapest	2	4	11	0
	USSR National Teams Match-Tournament	bd. 1	2	2	0
	Leningrad Interzonal	1–2 =	10	7	0
	European Team Ch, Bath	bd. 4	4	2	0
	41 USSR Ch, Moscow	2–6 =	5	11	1
	Madrid	1	7	8	0
1974	Candidates ¼-final v. Polugayevsky	Won	3	5	0
	Candidates ½-final v. Spassky	Won	4	6	1
			203	**190**	**23**

Biographical Details

Anatoly Evgenyevich Karpov

date of birth	23.5.1951
place of birth	Zlatoust, Southern Urals
mother	Nina Grigorievna
occupation	Housewife?
father	Evgeny Stepanovich
occupation	Chief engineer of a Tula factory

chess career

learnt chess	1955	age	4
3rd category	1958		7
2nd category	1960		9
1st category	1960		9
candidate master	1962		11
master	1966		15
international master	1969		18
grandmaster	1970		19
World Championship candidate	1973		22

education

school	Zlatoust, School No. 3
	Tula, ?
university	Moscow State University 1968–1969
	Leningrad State University 1969–

personal

height (12.71)	5 ft 7½ in.
weight (12.71)	7 stone 12 lbs
colour of hair	Brown
colour of eyes	Green
family moved to Tula	1965

1 EARLY YEARS

In 1965 Karpov, at thirteen, was the youngest player in the All-Union Schoolboys and, at fourteen, had his first game published in *Shakhmatny Bulletin*. In the same year he also played in the 9th Spartakiad of Schoolboys at Harkov – on board three for the RSFSR, he won the board prize jointly with D. Kudishevich. In 1966 Anatoly played in a candidate master *v.* master event at Leningrad, and as a result of his excellent score he was awarded the master title. He thus became the youngest master in the Soviet Union. Also in 1966 he played in the All Union Schoolboys' event in January, in which he placed 5th–6th equal, the USSR Junior Team Championship in July, and a junior team match, USSR-Scandinavia, in Stockholm 27–28 August, scoring 1½/2 on board six against the Norwegian player Hatlebakk.

Karpov's international début was made at the end of 1966 under very strange circumstances. The Soviet Chess Federation received an invitation to send two players to an international junior tournament. The choice fell on Anatoly and Viktor Kupreichik. When Karpov and his companion arrived in Czechoslovakia it turned out that an error had been made – the tournament turned out to be not at all for juniors, but for adults. There was nothing to be done, willy nilly it was necessary to include the two youngsters in the tournament. The result was stunning; Karpov took first place without losing a single game.

The results of this tournament, the annual new year event at Trinec, were: 1 Karpov 11, 2–3 Kupka and Kupreichik 9½, 4 Smejkal 8½, 5–6 E. Nowak and Sikora 8, 7 Augustin 7½, 8 Schoupal 5½, 9–11 Blatny, Kornasiewicz and Maroszczyk 5, 12 V. Nowak 3, 13 Rutka 1½. Asked about his results at Bath, Karpov recalled that he had drawn with Kupka, E. Nowak and Maroszczyk and thought that his other draw had been against Blatny. Unfortunately neither a complete tournament table nor any of the games were reported in *Ceskoslovensky Sach* nor, surprisingly, in the Soviet chess press.

In 1967 Karpov played in the USSR Junior Championship, the RSFSR Spartakiad, the USSR Junior Team Championship, and also a little-known match tournament to decide who would be the Soviet representative at the 1967 World Junior Championship in Jerusalem, but following the Six Day War, no more was heard of this. By the end of the year he was already well known inside the Soviet Union and was preparing for Groningen, the event which was to make him known to the rest of the world for the first time.

The games in this section do not provide a complete coverage of these years, but only the most interesting games were selected for publication in the Soviet chess magazines.

0101 K-Orekhov: USSR
Armed Forces zonal 1965

French

1 P–Q4   P–K3

A useful move which keeps open possibilities of entering the Nimzo-Indian, Queen's Indian, Dutch, Benoni, Queen's Gambit Declined and French – or perhaps a stew containing two or more of these ingredients. It was at one time a great favourite with Keres who would answer 2 P–QB4 with his own 2 . . . B–N5+. Though he played this pet line against such giants as Alekhine, Capablanca, Euwe and Flohr, the Estonian grandmaster seldom included it in his repertoire after the war. An attempted revival in the Piatigorsky Cup, Los Angeles 1963, only resulted in a severe defeat at the hands of Miguel Najdorf. America also witnessed the downfall of an alternative idea, 2 . . . P–QB4, played in the last round at San Antonio 1972 in a game Portisch–Larsen – a victory which enabled the Hungarian grandmaster to share first prize with Karpov and Petrosian.

2 P–K4

It's interesting that in the European Team Championship, Ober-hausen 1961, Portisch, an exclusively QP player, also chose this move going over to a K-side opening against Tal. There was, however, a special reason for this in that Portisch himself was a regular user of the French defence and, after some analysis at home, could find no satisfactory antidote to the variant 1 P–K4 P–K3 2 P–Q4 P–Q4 3 N–Q2 N–KB3 4 P–K5 KN–Q2 5 P–KB4! He hoped that the ex-World Champion would show him the best procedure for Black, but alas the question remained unanswered as Tal went under to a K-side attack! The years have gone by and Portisch is still waiting: in the 1972 Olympiad the Swiss Junior World Champion, Hug, was also crushed after the same ill-fated invitation to a French.

2 . . .   P–Q4

Larsen prefers 2 . . . P–QB4 here as he also does against 2 P–QB4.

3 N–Q2

The invention of Dr Tarrasch which has the advantage over 3 N–QB3 of not allowing the pin 3 . . . B–N5 and of keeping the QBP free to advance to QB3 to support the centre after Black's inevitable . . . P–QB4. The disadvantage is that the knight obstructs the QB thereby delaying somewhat Q-side development. Though Karpov has also played 3 N–QB3 the game against Enevoldsen (2311) shows that this, at least, of his teenage preferences is still with him.

3 . . .   N–KB3

The principal alternative is 3 . . . P–QB4, which is the habitual choice of Korchnoi; it leads to active piece play and open lines as compensation for an isolated QP. Hübner, the most successful top board at the Skopje Olympiad, prefers the more closed positions arising from 3 . . . N–QB3 – the Guimard variation.

4 P–K5   KN–Q2

4 . . . N–N1!? has also been tried; White should continue his piece development with 5 B–Q3, and not play 5 P–KB4 when after 5 . . . P–KR4! Black is all set to ride his KN to the fine post at KB4.

5 B–Q3   P–QB4
6 P–QB3   N–QB3
7 N–K2

So that the two knights do not tread on each other's toes; thus 7 . . . Q–N3 8 N–B3.

7 . . .   P–B3

Black begins an assault on e5. The alternative is 7 . . . Q–N3, hitting d4.

8 KP × P

Karpov's tendency is to play the openings simply, avoiding theoretical arguments. The books recommend 8 N–KB4 Q–K2 and then 9 KP × P, but Karpov is a practical player not a chess library. 8 P–KB4 would be bad on account of 8 . . . QBP × P 9 BP × P P × P 10 QP × P (10 BP × P? N × QP!) 10 . . . B–B4.

8 . . .   N × BP

8 . . . Q × P 9 N–B3 P × P 10 P × P B–N5 + is a comfortable method of equalizing.

9 N–B3

Black's intended liberation of his QB with . . . P–K4 must be continually watched.

9 . . .   B–Q3
10 0–0   0–0
11 N–N3

Karpov is unravelling his pieces with his eyes set on the K-side.

11 . . .   Q–B2

An immediate 11 . . . P–K4 leads to a double-edged position e.g. 12 P × KP N × P 13 N × N B × N 14 P–KB4 B–B2 15 P–B5 B × N 16 P × B N–K5 17 B × N P × B 18 Q–N3+ K–R1. An alternative 13 B–B5 B × B (13 . . . N × N+ 14 Q × N N–K5 15 B × P+!) 14 N × B N × N+ 15 Q × N N–K5 leads to nothing for White. In such circumstances White would have to play energetically, otherwise Black would just complete his development.

12 B–KN5   B–Q2

12 . . . P–K4 was still possible.

13 Q–N1

The more natural 13 Q–B2 would allow 13 . . . P–B5 and if 14 B × N BP × B. Now, however, 14 B × N and 15 B × P + is a threat.

13 . . .   P–KR3

Should Black play 13 . . . R–B2 (to answer 14 B × N with 14 . . . P × B) White has the interesting move 14 B–R4, intending 15 N–N5. 13 . . . B–K1 with the same idea leads to difficult problems after 14 B × N P × B 15 R–K1. Naturally 13 . . . P–KN3 is not possible because of the bishop sacrifice.

14 B × N   R × B
15 N–R5   R–B2 (*1*)

15 . . . R3–B1 was also to be considered as after 16 B–R7+ K–R1 17 N × P is unsound because of 17 . . . B–QB1! and 16 N–R4 can be answered by 16 . . . B–K1. But Black prefers to have his rook protecting his KNP and, soon, his KP.

| 16 B–N6 | R–K2 |
| 17 N–R4 | |

Karpov is taking full advantage of the weaknesses in Black's K-side: he now threatens 18 B–R7+ K–B2 (else 19 N–N6+ wins the exchange) 19 Q–N6+ K–B1 20 N×P R×N 21 Q–B6+ R–B2 22 Q–R8+ K–K2 23 N–N6 mate. Black therefore has no time for the quick snack of 17 . . . B×P+ after which White would have, in addition to the above threat, the menace of 18 P–KN3 winning the bishop.

| 17 . . . | B–K1 |
| 18 P–KB4 | |

From the start Karpov has made it clear that he is striking out for a K-side offensive, and this move prepares the entry of the KR, via KB3, into the theatre of war. This pawn move also holds up . . . P–K4 and shuts out the threat of . . . B×P+.

18 . . .   **P×P**

The price for the aforementioned privileges.

19 K–R1

Ruling out the possible check on move 20 which would force the exchange of queens.

| 19 . . . | P×P |
| 20 P×P | Q–Q2 |

Black fears 21 B×B R1×B 22 Q–KN6 R–KB1 23 QR–K1 Q–Q2 24 R–K3 with a tremendous attack, so he prepares to answer 21 B×B

with 21 . . . Q×B barring the white queen's entry.

If 20 . . . P–K4 21 B×B R1×B 22 Q–KN6 R–KB1 23 N–B5 wins.

21 Q–Q3

Preventing 21 . . . P–K4 and freeing the QR for action.

21 . . .   **B–KB2**

Preparing . . . P–K4 again.

22 R–B3

More troops are coming to pummel Black's K-side; 23 R–N3 would be mighty hard to meet, so a counter-action is vital . . .

22 . . .   **P–K4**

23 R–N3   **B×B**

If Black eats the poisoned pawn by 23 . . . P×P he dies as follows 24 B×B+ R×B 25 R×P+ K–B1 (25 . . . R×R 26 N–B6+) 26 N–N6+ K–K1 27 R–K1+.

24 Q×B   **R–KB1**

Directed against 25 N–B6+ and 25 N–B5.

25 P–B5

Black can see the coming holocaust but cannot do anything about it.

25 . . .	P–K5
26 P–B6	R2–B2
27 N–B5 (2)	

Though piling up on pawns is a frequent tactic of Karpov, he is unlikely to excel the absolute maximum treatment that he is now giving the KNP.

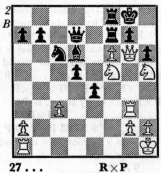

27 . . .   **R×P**

Snatching the white rook would lead to the following demonstration: 27 ... B×R 28 N×RP+ K–R1 29 N×R+ R×N (29 ... Q×N 30 P×P+) 30 P×P+ R×P (30 ... K–N1 31 Q–R6!) 31 Q–R6+ K–N1 (31 ... R–R2 32 Q–B8 mate) 32 N–B6+.

28 N×R+	R×N
29 Q×NP+	Q×Q
30 R×Q+	K–R1
31 R–Q7	R×N
32 R×B	

After a forced series of moves Black finds himself with knight and pawn for rook, but his extra pawn cannot be maintained, so Black stakes all on his passed KP which could be a tricky customer ...

| 32 ... | P–K6 |
| 33 R–K6 | |

Karpov did not have much appetite for Black's KRP even though it was with check: 33 R×RP+ K–N2 34 R–K6 N–K4 35 R–K1 K–B2 36 R–Q6 N–Q6 or 35 K–N1 K–B2 36 R–Q6 N–Q6 again with the same result – problems for White.

| 33 ... | N–K4 |
| 34 K–N1 | |

Stopping this embarrassing business of back rank mates.

| 34 ... | K–N2 |
| 35 R–K1 | K–B2 |

If an immediate 35 ... N–B5 then 36 R–K7+ K–B3 (36 ... R–B2 37 R×R+ K×R and White easily wins the ending) 37 R×NP N–Q7 38 P–KR3! but not 38 R×RP? P–K7!

36 R×RP	N–B5
37 R–R3	R–K4
38 R–B3+	K–K3
39 K–R1	

A funny move, probably played to safely arrive at the time control.

39 ...	R–K5
40 P–KR3	K–K4
41 P–N4	

The beginning of the final stage: White's connected K-side pawns are decisive, and Karpov shows fine technique in cashing in on his assets.

It is of interest to note that if Karpov's king was still on N1 Black still could not make the combination 41 ... N–Q7 42 R3×P N–B6+ 43 K–B2 N×R 44 R×N since the K+P ending is won for White.

41 ...	P–Q5
42 R–B5+	K–K3
43 P×P	R×QP
44 R–B8	P–N4
45 P–N5	R–Q2
46 K–N2	P–R4
47 P–KR4	P–N5
48 P–N6	P–R5
49 P–R5	

With the black king cut off the going is easy.

49 ...	R–Q4
50 P–R6	R–KN4+
51 K–B1	R×P
52 P–R7	R–R3
53 P–R8=Q	R×Q
54 R×R	P–N6
55 P×P	P×P
56 K–K2	P–N7
57 R–K8+	K–Q4
58 R×P	

Karpov has calculated exactly to the end.

58 ...	N×R
59 K×N	K–B5
60 K–Q2	K–N6
61 R–QN1	K–R7
62 K–B2	1–0

The first game Karpov had published in *Shakhmatny Bulletin*.

0102 AK–Lilein: All Union Schoolboys, Moscow, January 1966:

Sicilian

1 P–K4 P–QB4 2 N–QB3 N–QB3 3 P–KN3 P–KN3 4 B–N2 B–N2 5

N1–K2 P–Q3 6 0–0 P–K3 7 P–Q3 R–N1 8 B–K3 N–Q5 9 Q–Q2 P–QN4 10 N–Q1 P–N5 11 P–KB4 N–K2 12 P–N4 P–B4 13 P–KR3 Q–R4 14 N–N3 Q–R5 15 P–B3 NP×P 16 QNP×P N–B7 if 16 ... N–N6 17 Q–QB2 **17 R–B1 N×B 18 N×N 0–0** *(3)*. **19 NP×P KP×P 20 P×P N×P 21 N/N3×N B×N 22 N×B R×N 23 B–K4 R–R4 24 K–R2 R–KB1 25 R–KB2 B–R3 26 P–B4 Q–Q2 27 B–N2 R4–B4 28 R1–B1 Q–K2 29 B–Q5+ K–R1 30 Q–N2+ B–N2 31 Q–K2 Q–R5 32 Q–N4 Q×Q 33 P×Q R×P 34 R×R B–K4 35 K–N2** if 35 K–N3 P–N4 **35 ... B×R 36 R–QN1** ½–½

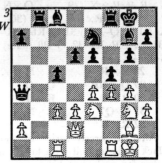

Masters v. Candidate Masters

Leningrad, June 1966

Candidate Masters	Masters	AK v. Masters			
Karpov 10/15	I. Zaitsev 12	1½	½	½	½
M. Mukhin 6	Chistiakov 10½	2½	1	1	½
Zotkin 5½	Alexeyev 9½	1½	½	½	½
Menkov 5	Noakh 7½	2½	1	1	½
Shakhtakhtinsky 2	Ravinsky 7	2	1	½	½

Each player played three games against each player of the other category. Karpov exceeded the master norm by two points.

0103 Grigory Ravinsky–AK:

Ruy Lopez

1 P–K4	**P–K4**

In his younger days Karpov always answered the KP this way. More recently he has added the Sicilian to his repertoire.

2 N–KB3	**N–QB3**
3 B–N5	**P–QR3**
4 B–R4	**N–B3**
5 0–0	**B–K2**
6 Q–K2	

This is the Worrall Attack, one-time favourite of Alekhine, Keres and Spassky. The idea is to protect the KP with the queen, to allow the KR to back up the advance P–Q4 from Q1. The fact that two moves are required for this means that White's Q-side development is very late getting started.

The only move ever likely to supersede the trustworthy 6 R–K1 is the Delayed Exchange Deferred (6 B×N). This has been extensively analysed in a new book by the English theoretician L. M. Pickett, who feels forced to conclude that 'it is so strong for White that the Closed Morphy Defence has lost its viability'.

6 ...	**P–QN4**

White threatened to win the KP; e.g. if 6 ... 0–0? 7 B×N QP×B 8 N×P Q–Q5 9 N–KB3 Q×KP? 10 Q×Q N×Q 11 R–K1 wins a piece.

7 B–N3	**P–Q3**

The alternative is 7 ... 0–0 8 P–B3 P–Q4 since if 9 P×P B–KN5! 10 P×N P–K5 gives Black a strong attack.

8 P–B3	

8 P–QR4 is countered by 8 ...

B–N5! 9 P–B3 (9 P × P N–Q5) 9 . . .
0–0! as after 10 P × P P × P 11 R × R
Q × R 12 Q × P N–R2! Fine-Keres,
AVRO 1938.

| 8 . . . | 0–0 |
| 9 R–Q1 | |

An immediate 9 P–Q4 allows 9 . . .
B–N5 10 R–Q1 P × P 11 P × P P–Q4
12 P–K5 N–K5 with equal chances,
but now if 9 . . . B–N5 10 P–Q3!
followed by P–KR3 leaves the bishop
misplaced.

9 . . .	N–QR4
10 B–B2	P–B4
11 P–Q4	Q–B2

To defend the KP which is the
strong point of Black's rugged
defence.

12 P–KR3

Black threatened 12 . . . BP × P 13
P × P B–N5! 14 N–B3 P–N5, or 14
B–Q3 N–B3 with a powerful game in
both cases.

| 12 . . . | R–K1 |

White's queen was not only a
liability because of the aforementioned bishop pin, but also now due
to the masked attack by the black
rook.

13 P × KP

By this exchange White puts a stop
to any tactical opening up of the
centre and leaves the black KR in a
dead-end street. However, a better
way of doing this was by 13 P–Q5
which would give better chances of a
K–side attack. Anyway White could
not have continued his development
with 13 QN–Q2 because of 13 . . .
BP × P! and Black wins a pawn
because of the unprotected bishop.

| 13 . . . | P × P |
| 14 QN–Q2 | R–Q1 |

Black has time in hand for this
rook readjustment, which contributes
to his observation of the d5 square;
there have been many brilliant
White wins in the Lopez based on a

knight thrust at this weak point with
a subsequent activation of the
Spanish prelate should the knight be
captured.

| 15 N–B1 | R × R |

This immediate exchange forces
an awkward recapture by White,
who really would like his other rook
on Q1 – this problem dates back to
his slow Q-side development.

| 16 Q × R | P–B5 |

Making space for himself on the
Q-side and at the same time cramp-
ing White on this wing.

17 B–N5

Continuing his mobilization and,
in certain cases, intending B × N
followed by N–K3–Q5.

| 17 . . . | B–K3 |

Again watching the d5 square.

18 Q–K2

White anticipates an attack on his
queen by . . . R–Q1. The variation
18 B × N B × B 19 N–K3 R–Q1 20
N–Q5 B × N 21 P × B Q–B4 22
B–K4 P–N3! followed by . . . B–N2
and . . . P–B4 loses for White.

| 18 . . . | N–N2 |

This knight is aiming to improve
its status by taking up the attractive
post at c5 – striking at White's weak
d3 square and keeping White's Q–
side under restraint. Anyway 19 P–
QR4 was menaced, when 19 . . .
N–N2 is not playable because of 20
P × P.

19 N–N3

Perhaps White feared for the
safety of his KP, or perhaps intended
to crush his young opponent on the
K-side, but really 19 N–K3 would
have left open more options for
the knight which now gets rather
shut out of the game by Black's next
move.

| 19 . . . | P–N3 |
| 20 R–Q1 | R–Q1 |

Black is quite happy to exchange,

thereby diminishing any attacking potential of his opponent.

21 R×R+   B×R
22 Q–K3 *(4)*

Welcoming the black knight to c5 when 23 N×P! Q×N 24 B–B4 wins at least a pawn.

22 . . .   N–Q2

Further liquidation before proceeding with the Q-side offensive: because of his 16 . . . P–B5 Black has room to dig himself in on this flank – the knights in particular have got it made in view of the semi-blocked pawn framework.

23 B×B

An attempt to keep the bishop on the board with 23 B–R6 could be met by 23 . . . P–B3 stopping 24 N–N5 and also giving added protection to the KP; then if, for example, 24 Q–R7 N/N2–B4 and if queens are exchanged Black's Q-side attack comes in fast, and of course 25 Q–R8?? N–N3 wins the queen; finally the K-side thrust 24 P–KR4 N–Q3 25 P–R5 is not without its dangers e.g. after 25 . . . N–B2 26 P×P P×P 27 N–R4 P–N4! wins.

23 . . .   N×B

23 . . . Q×B 24 Q–R7 N/Q2–B4 25 N×P Q–Q7 was also possible, but Karpov has his future well under control by a solid, steady improvement of his piece placement.

24 Q–R6

Ravinsky, on the other hand, still shows his enthusiasm for tactical niceties: he now intends 25 N–N5 N–B1 (25 . . . N–KB3 26 N–B5! P×N 27 Q×N wins) 26 N–B5 P–B3 (26 . . . P×N 27 P×P B–Q4 28 P–B6) 27 N×B N/B1×N 28 N–K3 with 29 N–Q5 to follow.

24 . . .   P–B3

Preventing 25 N–N5 and preparing to drive away the queen with . . . N–B2.

25 Q–K3

The queen leaves quietly.

25 . . .   P–QR4

Black has a real future on the Q-side, but White will come up against a brick wall on the K-wing.

26 P–KR4

If 26 P–QR3 to stem the black pawns then 26 . . . Q–B4! 27 Q×Q (27 Q–Q2 N–B3 and 28 . . . P–N5) 27 . . . N×Q followed by 28 . . . N–B3 and 29 . . . P–N5.

26 . . .   P–N5
27 P–R5   K–N2

No entry!

28 B–Q1

Anticipating a possible . . .P–N6.

28 . . .   N–B2

Karpov has mapped out in advance the best squares for his knights, and indeed every one of his men.

29 RP×P   RP×P
30 N–Q2 *(5)*

Since his K-side ambitions are over White gets ready to meet the coming invasion.

30 . . .   N–B4

With the clever threat of 31 . . . N–Q6 32 P–N3 BP×P! 33 Q×N P×RP and the pawn queens. If 31 B–K2 to stop the entry at d3 then 31 . . . N–R5 is just as devastating.

31 P–N3   BP×P
32 RP×P

If 32 N×P N×N 33 B×N B×B 34 P×B P×P wins.

32 ...   **Q–N3**

A refinement which allows Black to recapture on b4 with the queen if necessary, so as to increase pressure on the weak QNP and occupy the weak squares with pieces.

33 N3–B1   **N–Q3**

With the mighty threat of 34 ... P×P 35 Q×P N–N4 36 Q–K3 N–Q5 with the QNP getting the full Karpov pile-up technique.

34 P–QB4   **Q–B3**

Preparing his next move with gain of time by the threat to the KP.

35 B–B2   **P–R5**

36 P×P

Otherwise 36 ... N×NP 37 N×N P×N 38 B×P N×BP.

36 ...   **B×P**

37 N–KN3

37 N×B N×N 38 Q–K2 N–R6 winning easily.

37 ...   **B–B2**

Not 37 ... N×RP? 38 Q–R7+ – another Ravinsky trap.

38 P–R5   **Q–N4**

With the capture of the RP the win will be easy in view of Black's tremendous passed pawn.

39 P–B4

Desperation – now Karpov finishes in style.

39 ...   **Q×P**

40 P×P   **Q–R8+**

41 K–B2

If 41 K–R2 Q×P 42 N–B3 then 42 ... N–B4! is a nice move.

41 ...   **Q×P**

42 N–B3   **Q–N7**

43 Q×N   **P–N6**

44 N–Q4   **P×B**

0–1

For if 45 Q×P Q×N+ or 45 N×P N–B5! winning a piece either way.

0104 AK–Mikhail Noakh:

Petroff

1 P–K4 P–K4 2 N–KB3 N–KB3 3 P–Q4 N×P 4 P×P P–Q4 5 P×Pep B×P 6 B–K2 0–0 7 N1–Q2 B–KB4 8 0–0 N–QB3 9 N×N B×N 10 N–N5 B–N3 11 B–Q3 Q–B3 12 B×B Q×B 13 P–QB3 QR–Q1 14 Q–N3 P–N3 15 N–B3 KR–K1 16 B–N5 N–R4 17 Q–N5 P–KB3 18 B–R4 Q–B2 19 KR–Q1 Q–B5 20 Q×Q N×Q 21 P–QN3 N–K4 22 N–Q4 P–QR3 23 B–N3 P–N3 24 K–B1 K–B2 25 R–Q2 P–QB4 26 N–K2 B–B2 27 R1–Q1 R×R 28 R×R P–KN4?! (6)

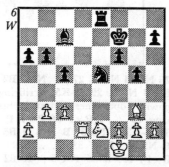

29 P–KB4 N–N3 30 R–Q7+ R–K2 31 R×R+ K×R? 31 ... N×R 32 P×P B×B 33 P×P B×P 34 P×N B–K4! 32 P×P B×B 33 P×P+ K×P 34 P×B! K–K4 35 N–N1 K–K5 36 K–K2 N–K2 37 N–R3 N–Q4 38 N–B2+ K–B4 39 K–Q3 P–KR4

40 P–R4 P–N4 41 P×P P×P 42
P–B4 P×P+ 43 K×P N–K6+ 44
K×P K–K3 45 P–QN4 K–Q2 46
N–K4 1–0

0105 AK–Alexander Chistiakov:

Sicilian

1 P–K4 P–QB4 2 N–QB3 3 P–
KN3 P–Q3 4 B–N2 N–B3 5 N1–K2
P–KN3 6 0–0 B–N2 7 P–Q3 P–KR4
8 P–KR3 B–Q2 9 K–R2 N–K4 10
P–B3 10 P–B4!? 10 . . . Q–B2 11
B–N5 B–B3 12 Q–Q2 N–R2 13
B–B4 P–R5 14 QR–N1 P×P+ 15
B×P N–B3 16 P–B4 N4–Q2 17
P–N4 P×P 18 R×P N–R4 19 B–B2
R–QB1 20 P–Q4 P–N3 21 R–B4 Q–
N1 22 P–Q5 B–N2 23 R×R+
Q×R 24 B–Q4 B–QR3 25 R–B3
P–B3 (7)

26 N–N3 N×N 27 R×N K–B2 28
B–B3 N–B1 29 P–K5 sacrificing a
pawn to open lines against the black
king. 29 . . . QP×P 30 P×P P×P
31 B–K3 R–R5 32 B–N4! Q–B5 33
B–N5 R×B If 33 . . . R–R1 34
B×P! K×B 35 P–Q6+ K–B2 36
P–Q7 N×P 37 Q×N+ K–B1 38
R–B3+ K–N1 39 B–K6+ wins.
34 R×R Q–B2 35 N–K4 K–N1 36
P–Q6 P×P 37 Q–Q5+ Q–B2 38
Q×Q+ K×Q 39 N×P+ K–N1 40
R–QR4 B–K7 41 R×P N–K3 42
B–K3 B–B6 43 N–K8 B–KR1 44

N–Q6 P–K5 45 R–R8+ K–R2 46
N–B7 B–B3 47 R–K8 N–B2 48
R–QB8 N–Q4 49 N–N5+ K–N2 50
N×B P×N 51 B–Q2 B–K4+ 52
K–N1 B–Q5+ 53 K–B1 K–B2 54
R–QR8 K–K3 55 P–B4 N–K6+ 56
B×N B×B 57 R–R3 B–B4 58 R×P
K–K4 59 R–Q3 K–K5 60 K–K2
P–KN4 61 R–Q5 B–K2 62 K–Q2
B–N5+ 63 K–B2 B–K2 64 K–N3 K–
B5 65 K–R4 K–N6 66 R–Q3+ K–
N7 67 K–N5 B–B4 68 P–QR4 B–B7
69 P–B5! P×P 69 . . . B×P 70 P–R5
70 P–R5 P–B5 71 K×P B–N8 72
P–R6 B–N3 73 K–N5 B–N8 74 K–
B6 B–R2 75 K–N7 1–0.

0106 Alexander Chistiakov–AK:

White has the better development
and a splendid knight on Q4. White
played **19 N–B2** to liquidate Black's
one advantage – the bishop pair. A
critical moment of the game has
arisen. Clearly after 19 . . . B–K3
there follows 20 N×B P×N 21 Q–
N4 N×P 22 B×P with a fierce
attack. After long thought Karpov
decided that his only chance lay in
tactical complications with **19 . . .
B–N4!** 20 R–K2 N×P indirectly
defending the bishop: 21 N×B
B×P+ 22 R×B Q×N 23 Q–K2 R–
K1 21 B×P RP×B 22 N×B N–K5
23 N–N5 Q–K2 24 N×B N×N
White can win material but his

position is uncomfortable. Now 25
... Q–K5 is threatened. **25 Q–Q5
KR–Q1 26 Q–N2 R–Q6 27 N×P
R–B2 28 P–K4** A blunder in a
difficult position. **28 ... Q–B4+** and
White soon resigned.

0107 Igor Zaitsev–AK:

Petroff

**1 P–K4 P–K4 2 N–KB3 N–KB3 3
P–Q4 N×P 4 B–Q3 P–Q4 5 N×P
N–Q2 6 N×P** (*9*)

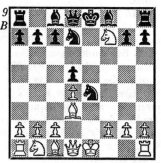

Now Anatoly chose, in preference
to the natural 6 . . . K×N, the
counter-attacking **6 . . . Q–K2 7
N×R N–B6+ 8 K–Q2 N×Q 9
R–K1 N×BP 10 B×P N–K5+** Still
it was not too late for Black to remain
with extra material and . . . run into
an attack after 10 . . . N–K4 11 R×N
B–K3. **11 R×N P×R 12 B–N6+
K–Q1 13 N–B7+ K–K1 14 N–
Q6++ K–Q1 15 N–B7+** ½–½.

USSR Junior Team
Championship

Vladimir, 5–14.8.1966
Asked about this event (at Bath),
Karpov thought he won a board
prize.

Only one game from this event,
limited to players between the ages of
12 and 18, is available:

0108 D. Kudishevich–AK:

Ruy Lopez

This game was annotated by
Anatoly Karpov in 'Youth Lectures'
in the Latvian magazine *Sahs* in
1970. The comments in quotes are
taken from that article.

'. . . a stubborn, tense, it cannot be
said faultless, struggle developed. At
one moment it seemed that Black
was near to victory. He seized the
centre and gradually gave up his
pawns to the enemy. But there
followed White's own counter-stroke
and the struggle flared up with
renewed strength. Time-trouble gradually approached (and this is a very
fearsome thing for a chessplayer –
avoid time-trouble!) and Black
again succeeded in seizing the initiative. The white pieces found themselves in a tangle from which they
were unable to emerge.'

1 P–K4	P–K4
2 N–KB3	N–QB3
3 B–N5	P–QR3
4 B–R4	N–B3
5 0–0	B–K2
6 R–K1	P–QN4
7 B–N3	P–Q3
8 P–B3	0–0
9 P–KR3	N–QR4
10 B–B2	B–N2

A refreshing change from the usual
10 . . . P–B4. This bishop move helps
to promote an early . . . P–Q4 in
many lines. The Soviet grandmaster
Lutikov achieved considerable success with it in the sixties, but the 1967
Interzonal game Fischer–Stein put
the brakes on its chances of catching
on further.

11 P–Q4	N–B5

11 . . . P–B4 12 P–Q5 B–B1 13
QN–Q2 P–B5 14 N–B1 N–N2 15
P–KN4! gave White a lasting

initiative in Spassky–Olafsson, Moscow 1959.

'In my remarks concerning . . . (Karpov–Zhelyandinov, game 1002) . . . I said that White often bases his play on the knight at QR5. Thus the idea of this variation consists in the redeployment of the knight away from its unfortunate position on a5. At the same time, Black hinders for a while the emergence of the white QN. It is now disadvantageous for White to play 12 QN–Q2 as Black replies 12 . . . N×N and gets rid of one of the most dangerous members of the Spanish inquisition.'

12 P–QN3

An immediate 12 QN–Q2 justifies Black's method of development after 12 . . . N×N 13 B×N P–Q4!

12 . . .   N–N3

As in the Alekhine, a black knight has been given the run-around before settling down on QN3 – a square from which it is ready for any action that might arise in the centre.

13 QN–Q2

'It is obvious that in the variation 13 P×P P×P 14 Q×Q QR×Q 15 N×P or 14 N×P Black wins back the pawn by the move . . . N×P and gets a good game.'

13 . . .   N/B3–Q2

Stein moved his QN for the fifth(!) time with 13 . . . N/N3–Q2 but after 14 P–QN4! P×P 15 P×P P–QR4 16 P×P P–B4 17 P–K5! QP×P 18 P×KP N–Q4 19 N–K4 N–N5 20 B–N1 R×P 21 Q–K2 N–N3 22 N3–N5 B/N2×N 23 Q×B P–N3 24 Q–R4 P–R4 25 Q–N3 N–B5 26 N–B3 K–N2 27 Q–B4 R–KR1 28 P–K6 P–B4 29 B×P!! the game found its way into Bobby's *My 60 Memorable Games.*

14 N–B1   P–QB4
15 P–Q5

'Leads to very sharp play. A quieter continuation for White was 15 N–K3. Black accepts the challenge.'

This move is not so strong as when Spassky played it as Karpov soon demonstrates; 15 N–K3 P–N5 (to gain control over d4) 16 P×KP QP×P 17 P–B4! would have left White with a clear initiative.

15 . . .   P–B4

Quite in the hypermodern tradition: White's proud pawn centre is to be wiped out with blows from the flanks.

16 P×P

16 Q–K2 to prevent the demolition after 16 . . . P×P 17 B×P N–B3 18 P–B4 would have instead been answered by 16 . . . P–KB5! with strong K-side attacking potential, just like favourable King's Indian positions: after preparation Black would advance his K-side pawns using White's KR3 as a means for opening a file for an invasion of heavy artillery.

16 . . .   B×P

Mission accomplished: soon black pawns will stand where white ones once stood. . . .

'An inaccuracy. Better was 16 . . . N×P 17 P–B4 N–N5 with fully satisfactory play. But during the game I was afraid that White would be able, successfully, to organize a central blockade and therefore I did not want to allow P–QB4.'

17 P–QR4

Threatening 18 P–R5 B×N 19 Q×B winning a piece.

17 . . .   B–QB3
18 N–K3

The start of a deep plan to meet Black's coming central pawn-roller; 18 P–R5 N–Q4! 19 B–Q2 N–B5! 20 N–N3 B–B3 or 19 P–B4 N–N6! 20 Q–Q2 P–N5 21 B–N2 P–K5 22 N3–R2 R×P both leave Black in charge.

'A very original and interesting position arises. On the one hand Black has a pawn preponderance in the centre, on the other hand his K-side is somewhat weakened and White threatens, by the moves P–QB4, P–QR5 and N–Q5, to blockade the pawns and transform Black's strength into a weakness. There is one defence to these plans. ...'

18 ...   **P–K5**

Not 18 ... P–Q4 at once because of 19 P–R5.

19 N–Q2

If 19 N–R2 then Black plays 19 ... P×P 20 P×P P–QR4! (to prevent the nagging P–QR5 and threaten ... P–Q4) 21 P–QB4 N–K4! when Black's active pieces can hammer the weak white pawns.

19 ...   **P–Q4**

Fulfilment of a prophecy made on move 16.

'At first sight it seems that Black has obtained an excellent position, but by some energetic moves, White shows that this is not quite so.'

20 P–R5   **N–B1**

21 P–QB4!

All part of the plan; the anti ... P–Q5 move, 21 B–N2, would have been destroyed by 21 ... B–B3!

'A blow struck at the centre. It turned out that Black was in all one tempo short for fortifying his better pawn centre (. . . N–KB3). Now Black is thrown headlong into a whirlpool of complications.'

21 ...   **P–Q5**

22 N–Q5

Like a human hand-grenade, the knight is thrown into the enemy camp to cut off fuel for the terrible twins. To back out now with 22 N–N4 would allow 22 ... P–R4 23 N–R2 P–Q6 24 B–N1 N–Q3 25 Q×P (25 P–B3 B–R5) 25 ... R×P

26 Q–Q1 (26 Q–N6 B–B3 27 R–R2 R–N4) 26 ... B–B3 27 R–R2 B–Q5 28 N–N4 Q–R5 with an overwhelming attack.

22 ...   **B×N**

23 P×B   **P–Q6**

24 B–N1

'The black pawns are far extended and they greatly restrict the opposing pieces, but at the same time they are vulnerable to immense danger. The question arises – how are they to be defended. After 24 ... B–B3 25 R–R2 N–K4 26 N×P Q×QP 27 P–B4 the QP is lost. More complicated is the variation 24 ... N–B3 25 N×P N×N 26 R×N N–Q3 27 R–KN4 P–B5 28 P×P P×P 29 B–R2 R×P 30 B–R3 and now against 30 ... R×QP follows 31 R×BP! N×R 32 B×N±. Having calculated these variations I decided to play the move. ...'

24 ...   **N–K4**

White's plan to win the KP was a success, but there is a hitch. ...

25 N×P

If 25 R×P then 25 ... Q×QP 26 B–N2 B–B3∓∓.

25 ...   **Q×QP**

26 B–N2

The beginning of a second long combination by White – of course if Black is permitted ... P–B5 without hindrance White has no chance against the connected passed pawns; 26 P–B4 is not possible because of 26 ... Q–Q5+ picking up the rook.

'An inaccuracy. It was better to play immediately 26 N–B3 Q–Q5 27 B–N2 B–B3 28 R–R2! with great advantage to White. Possibly my opponent did not see 28 R–R2! and therefore chose a different order of moves. Now I succeeded in evading this extremely unpleasant variation.'

26 ...   **P–B5** (*10*)

27 N–B3

'Here White had at his disposal the very interesting and seemingly very strong move 27 P×P! At the board I didn't much like Black's position, specifically because of this move. The following variations arise:

(a) 27 . . . P×P 28 B–R2 and now against 28 . . . R×P follows 29 N–N3 and against 28 . . . B–N5 29 N–B3 Q–Q3 30 Q–R4±;

(b) 27 . . . N×P 28 B–B3 P–N5 29 P–B6! and wins.

'Only at home, in calm surroundings, did I find the satisfactory continuation 27 . . . P×P 28 B–R2 N–Q3! (It is difficult to play such a move at the board because all the pieces in the centre are 'hanging'). White cannot win a pawn after 29 N×N B×N 30 B×N B×B 31 Q–N4 QR–B1 32 B×P Q×B and against 29 N–B3 there is the reply 29 . . . Q–N2 with the threats . . . Q×B and . . . R×P.'

27 . . .   Q–B4
28 N–R4

From here on comes an extended series of tactics, counter-tactics and counter-counter-tactics – a sequence which lasts for the next fourteen moves!

'Better was to transpose into the variations given above, because against 28 N–K4 Black cannot play 28 . . . Q–B2 because of 29 P–B4.

After the text move Black seizes the initiative.'

28 . . .   P×N

'Who could have foreseen that this pawn would decide the outcome of the game.'

29 R×N   Q–B2
30 P×BP   B–B3

The point! 31 R–K2 is out.

31 Q×QP

The last of the brave trio of pawns is executed – but the three brothers did not die in vain. . . .

31 . . .   R–N1

Diamond cut diamond. If 31 . . . B×R 32 Q–Q5+ Q–B2 33 B×B with some real headaches for Black. The move played eliminates the queen fork on d5 and, moreover, underlines the awkwardness of White's piece placement.

32 Q–Q5+   K–R1
33 B–Q4

After 33 B–B3 Black could play the spectacular 33 . . . R–N4! as on 34 P×R Q×B or 34 Q–K4 R×R or 34 P–B5 B×R 35 B×B Q×BP 36 Q×Q R×Q White is always lost.

33 . . .   N–K2
34 Q–K4

34 R×N Q×R 35 B–B2 KR–Q1 36 B×B Q×B wins and of course if 34 Q–B5 then simply 34 . . . Q×Q.

34 . . .   N–B3

Threatening both rook and bishop.

35 R–B5 (*11*)

White is just about keeping his balance despite the treacherous situation. 35 P–B4 would have been defeated by 35 . . . N×B! 36 Q×N KR–Q1 37 Q–K4 R–Q8+ 38 K–R2 B×R 39 P×B P–R6! and the threat of . . . P–R7 wins at once.

35 . . .   Q–R2

'Having seized the initiative, Black accurately conducts this phase of the game. The white pieces mutually

11
B

protect each other and any move brings with it material loss.'

Pin and counter pin! After 35 . . . B×B White plays not 36 R×N Q–Q2 37 P–B6 P–N3 38 R–R3 R×B+ 39 Q×R Q×R but 36 Q×B! KR–Q1 (36 . . . N×Q 37 R×Q) 37 Q–N4 Q–K2 38 R×N Q–K8+ 39 K–R2 Q–K4+ 40 P–N3 Q×R 41 P–B6! which is very dangerous e.g. 41 . . . P×P 42 B×P!!

36 B–K3

36 B×B Q×R 37 B–B3 was a good

try, but Black has the beautiful defence 37 . . . R–N6!! when 38 B–Q2 Q–Q5! or 38 Q–B2 N–Q5! (not 38 . . . Q×QBP 39 B×P+) 39 B×N (or 39 Q–Q2 R×B!) 39 . . . Q×B 40 R×P R–N7 both win nicely.

36 . . .	**B×R**
37 P–B6	

Mate threat!

37 . . .	**P–N3**

Not 37 . . . P×P 38 R–R5!

38 R×N	**Q–Q2**
39 B–B2	**P–R6**

No sense in losing the pawn now.

'A second queen is on the way, and not a single white piece can do anything about it.'

40 B–R6	**R×P**
41 R×R	**B×R**
42 Q–B4	

The last of the white tactics – a double attack.

42 . . .	**Q–Q1**
0–1	

A wonderful example of Karpov's tactical ability – he had an answer to everything!

World Junior Qualifying Event May/June(?) 1967

This event was won by Andrei Lukin. Two preliminary groups were held with the first three in each progressing to the final. The result of Karpov's preliminary group: 1 L. Grigorian 5½/7; 2 Bokuchava 5; 3–4 Lukin and Timoshenko 4½; 5 Karpov 3½; 6–7 Dvoretsky and Vaganian 2; 8 Palatnik 1.

Karpov's victory over Lukin and loss to Timoshenko follow. He also defeated Vaganian and Palatnik, but scored only half a point from his games against Grigorian, Bokuchava and Dvoretsky.

0109 Andrei Lukin–AK:
Nimzo–Indian

1 P–Q4	**N–KB3**
2 P–QB4	**P–K3**
3 N–QB3	**B–N5**
4 B–N5	

A move with which Spassky has had a good deal of success. It combats Black's basic strategy of controlling e4 by means of the pin on the knight. If Black breaks this pin by means of . . . P–KR3 and . . . P–KN4,

he will have severe K-side weaknesses to worry about instead.

    4 . . .   **P–KR3**
    5 B–R4   **P–B4**

The standard treatment. Black
takes advantage of the absence of
White's QB from the Q-side to
launch a counter-offensive there.

    6 P–Q5   **B×N+**

The main alternative to this move
is to play 6 . . . P–QN4, gambiting
a pawn to gain the initiative in the
centre after 7 QP×P BP×P 8 P×P
with 8 . . . P–Q4. Karpov chooses a
line more in keeping with his style.
He makes the capture now because if
6 . . . P–Q3 first, White can play 7 R–
B1 and then build up a strong centre
without making any concessions
in return; while if 6 . . . 0–0 then
7 P–Q6 will make life difficult for
Black.

    7 P×B   **P–Q3**
    8 P–B3

Both preparing P–K4 and provid-
ing a retreat for the bishop.

    8 . . .   **0–0**
    9 P–K4   **R–K1**

Black does best to maintain the
central tension. After 9 . . . P–K4
White will simply castle and start an
attack with P–B4.

    10 B–Q3!

Lukin offers a pawn on the
strength of the line 10 . . . P×P 11
BP×P P–KN4 12 B–N3 N×QP 13
N–K2! when 13 . . . N–K6 14 Q–Q2
N×P+ 15 K–B2 gives White a very
strong attack, and any retreat of the
knight allows White to regain the
pawn (Q6) or go for a direct K-side
attack which is also very promising
. . .

    10 . . .   **QN–Q2**

But Karpov is not interested

    11 P×P

A critical point. White decides
to keep the black knight off e5 at the
expense of a couple of tempi and his
trusty pawn at Q5. However, Black
can obtain very good play because he
is well ahead in development. A
sounder plan would have been
simply to complete his development
by 11 N–K2 and 12 0–0 before
aiming for P–B4.

    11 . . .   **P×P**
    12 P–B4   **Q–B2?**

While this is quite a good move on
positional grounds, White's over-
ambitious play called for a more
energetic counter, and this is to be
found in 12 . . . P–QN4! If then 13
P×P Black continues 13 . . . P–B5!
14 B–QB2 (14 B×P? Q–B2 15 Q–K2
P–Q4∓) and now 14 . . . Q–B2 gives
plenty of play for the pawn, with the
miscellaneous threats of . . . B–N2,
. . . P–K4 and . . . P–Q4. White
probably does best to decline the
pawn, but the threat of 13 . . . P×P
14 B×P P–Q4 is very awkward to
meet.

    13 N–B3   **P–QN4**

Now White has time to consolidate
in the centre.

    14 B×N   **N×B**
    15 P–K5   **QP×P**
    16 P×KP   **N–Q2**
    17 0–0

In deciding on 12 . . . Q–B2
Karpov may have overlooked that he
cannot now capture on e5: 17 . . .
N×P? 18 N×N Q×N 19 B–N6
winning material.

    17 . . .   **B–N2**
    18 B–B2!

Again the weakness of Black's
K-side is used to provide an indirect
defence for the KP. Now the idea is
18 . . . N×P? 19 N×N Q×N 20
Q–Q3 and wins, or 18 . . . B×N 19
Q×B and:

(a) 19 . . . Q×P 20 Q–Q3 N–B3 21
R×N P×R 22 Q–R7+ K–B1 23
B–N6 wins.

(b) 19 . . . N×P 20 Q–K4 P–N3 21
QR–K1 with a very strong attack

18 . . .   **P×P**
19 Q–K2   **B–Q4**

Black wants to preserve this pawn
and follow up with . . . Q–R4
counter-attacking the Q–side pawns.

20 QR–K1

Now every white piece is in action
and he is ready to start his attack.

20 . . .   **Q–R4** *(12)*

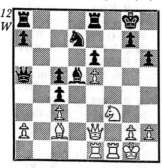

21 N–N5!   **Q×BP**

He cannot play 21 . . . P×N 22
Q–R5 N–B1 23 R–B2 followed by
R1–KB1 and a capture on f8.

22 B–R7+   **K–R1**
23 B–N1

White improves the position of his
bishop so as to free the queen to go
to KR5. Now if Black tries to
exchange some rooks with 23 . . . R–
KB1 White will win with 24 N–B7+
K–N1 25 Q–R5 Q–Q7 26 R–K2 Q–
Q5+ 27 K–R1 when there is nothing
to be done against the threat of
28 N×P+ P×N 29 Q–N6+ mates.

23 . . .   **R–K2!**

Black is now ready to meet 24 N–
B7+ K–R1 25 Q–R5 with 25 . . .
R–KB1 when he has both rooks
taking part in the defence.

24 Q–R5

Apparently the strongest, with its
threat of 25 Q–N6, but Black can still
hold on.

24 . . .   **Q–Q5+**
25 K–R1   **B×P+**
26 K×B   **Q–Q7+**
27 K–R1   **Q×N**
28 Q–B3

Still the best, as it not only attacks
the rook but also prepares to come in
on the weakened diagonal leading to
h7. However, Black finds himself
three pawns up for the moment and
can prepare to give up a rook for the
bishop that has been making all the
trouble.

28 . . .   **R–QN1**
29 Q–K4   **P–N3!**

First Karpov prepares a safe
square for the king on g7. Since the
ending would be lost for White after
the exchange of queens he must
allow Black to carry out his idea.

30 R–KN1

If White tries 30 Q×BP then
30 . . . R–N5 brings the rook into
action so that it can be hoisted over
to the K-side, and Black remains two
pawns up.

30 . . .   **Q–B4**
31 Q–K3 *(13)*

He cannot now take the BP
because of 31 . . . Q–B6+ 32 R–N2
R–N7 when the initiative passes over
completely to Black.

31 . . .   **R×B**

Black must now give up the exchange to avert the imminent

destruction of his K-side, but in so doing he breaks White's attack and consolidates his own position, remaining with three scattered pawns as quite adequate compensation.

32 R×R

Not 32 Q×RP+? R–R2 and Black wins.

32 ...   K–N2

White has no more attacking chances and must start worrying about his own exposed king as well about his weak KP.

33 QR–K1   R–B2
34 Q–K2

After 34 R/N1–B1 Q–R4 (not so clear is 34 . . . Q×R+ 35 R×Q R×R+ 36 K–N2 R–B4 37 Q–QR3) White's remaining pieces will be tied to defending the KP and Black can expect to win in due course. But the text move makes it even easier for Black.

34 ...   Q–Q6
35 R–N3   Q–Q4+
36 Q–KN2

White's king is too exposed to allow him to keep the queens on, so he forces their exchange in the hope that Black's pawn weaknesses will give him technical problems in the ending.

36 ...   Q×Q+
37 K×Q   R–B4
38 R–QR3

Passive defence of the KP allows Black to prepare the advance of his king.

38 ...   N×P
39 R×P+   K–B3
40 R–KB1   N–Q6

Threatening to exchange rooks and queen the BP.

41 R–R4   N–N7
42 R–R5   N–Q6
43 R–R4   K–K4

Black must give up a pawn to make progress.

44 R×P   K–Q4
45 R–QB2   R–N4+

Up to now Black has not exchanged rooks because to do so would have brought White's king towards the BP, but now he decides to keep his rook on the board both to take part in threats against the white king, and to stop the QRP if necessary.

46 K–B3   K–Q5
47 P–KR4   R–K4

Cutting the king off again.

48 R–Q1   P–B5
49 P–R4   R–KB4+
50 K–N3

Not 50 K–K2?? R–B7 mate.

50 ...   R–QR4
51 R–QR2   P–B6
52 R–KB1   N–B4
53 R–B4+   K–Q6
54 R–R3

Allowing a neat finish.

54 ...   R×P!
55 R–B3+

Or 55 R4×R N×R 56 R×N P–B7 leading to an ending which Black wins by simply allowing the White king to get to e5 before playing . . . P–N4!

55 ...   K–Q7

And the pawn is immune because of the knight fork on e4. White tries one more trick.

56 R–B2+   K–Q8
57 R–B1+   K–B7
58 R–B1+   K–N7!
0–1

0110 Gennady Timoshenko–AK:

Bishop's Opening

1 P–K4 P–K4 2 B–B4 N–KB3 3 P–Q4 P×P 4 N–KB3 N×P Safer is 4 . . . P–Q4 5 P×P B–QN5+ 6 P–B3 Q–K2+ 7 B–K2 P×P 8 P×P (8 N×P!?) 8 . . . B–QB4 9 0–0 0–0 10 P–B4 and now 10 . . . R–K1=

(Hooper) or 10 . . . B–KN5=
Vinogradov–Rovner, Leningrad Ch
1956. Also 4 . . . B–B4!? **5 Q×P N–
KB3 6 N–B3 P–B3** The alternative is
6 . . . N–B3 7 Q–R4 and now either
7 . . . B–N5 or 7 . . . B–K2 is allright
for Black. **7 B–KN5 P–Q4 8 0–0–0
B–K2 9 KR–K1** 9 Q–R4!? **9 . . . B–
K3** 9 . . . 0–0!? 10 Q–R4 B–K3 is
roughly equal. **10 Q–R4 QN–Q2 11
B–Q3 P–B4?** This is too weakening,
though the alternatives are not very
appetizing: 11 . . . Q–R4±; 11 . . .
N–B4 12 N–Q4 N3–Q2!? (12 . . .
N–N1 13 B×B±) 13 B×B Q×B 14
Q×Q+ K×Q 15 P–B4± Neish-
tadt–Volkovich, Moscow Ch 1958.
**12 N–K5 N×N 13 R×N P–Q5 14
P–B4 N–Q2** 14 . . . P×N? 15 B–
N5+ N–Q2 (15 . . . B–Q2 16 B×B/
K7!) 16 B×N+!±± is hopeless
for Black. **15 B–N5 B×B 16 P×B Q–
B2 17 B×N+ K×B 18 Q–K4**
(*14*)

Black's difficulties are shown in the
variation 18 . . . P–QN3 (seemingly
consolidating his pawn chain) 19
N–N5 Q–B3 20 N×QP! and now:
(a) 20 . . . Q×Q 21 N×B+ K–K2
22 R×Q P×N 23 R1–K1±;
(b) 20 . . . P×N 21 R×P+ K–B2 22
R×B! Q×R (22 . . . P×R 23 R–B4
Q×R 24 Q×Q+ gives White a
winning ending) 23 R–B4+ K–N1

24 Q–B4+ K–N2 25 R–B7+ K–
R3 26 Q–QR4 mate.

But Black could have tried 18 . . .
QR–Q1 19 N–Q5 Q–Q3 20 P–B3
K–B1.

In the game Karpov continued
with the outright blunder **18 . . .
Q–B3?** which allowed the beautiful
19 R×BP! and Black's position is
completely wrecked, e.g. if 19 . . .
Q×R 20 Q×NP+ K–Q3 21 N–
K4+, or 20 . . . K–Q1 21 Q×R+
also winning. Therefore Karpov
tried **19 . . . Q×Q 20 N×Q KR–
QB1 21 R×P+ K–K2** and lost the
ending because of his pawn minus
and inactive pieces: **22 P–QR4
P–QN3 23 R×R R×R 24 K–Q2
B–B4 25 P–B4 R–B3 26 N–N3 B–K3
27 K–B3 B–B4 28 P–R4 P–KR3 29
P–N4 R–B1 30 N–K4 P–B4 31 N–
B2 P×P 32 P×P R–KR1 33 N–R3
B–Q2 34 P–N5 R–R4 35 K–N4 R–
R1 36 P–R5 B–K3 37 P–R6 B–B2
38 K–B3 P–N3 39 K–N4 R–QB1 40
N–B4 R–B4 41 N–Q3 R–B1 42
P–B5 P×P+ 43 N×P B–K1 44
P–N3 R–B2 45 R–Q1 R–B1 46 R–
K1+ K–Q3 47 N–N7+ K–Q2 48
R–K3 B–B2 49 R–Q3+ K–K2 50
R–QB3 R×R 51 K×R B–Q4 52
K–Q4 B–N7 53 K–B5 B–B8 54 N–
R5 1–0**

RSFSR Spartakiad 1967

The following game is from this
event, but no other details are
available.

0111 Vladimir Antonishin–AK:

Queen's Indian

**1 P–Q4 N–KB3 2 P–QB4 P–K3
3 N–KB3 P–QN3 4 N–QB3 B–N2 5
P–QR3 B–K2 6 P–Q5 0–0** Better
6 . . . P–Q3 7 P–K4 P–B3 8 P×KP
P×P 9 N–KN5 B–QB1 10 P–B4 0–0

11 B–Q3 P–K4 12 P–KB5± Petrosian–Keres, Zürich 1961 **7 P–K4 P–Q3 8 B–Q3** Or 8 B–K2 P–B3 9 P×KP P×P 10 0–0 P–B4 11 N–KN5 Q–Q2 12 P–K5! P×P 13 Q×Q QN×Q 14 N×KP± Uhlmann–Kluger, Budapest 1961. **8 . . . QN–Q2 9 0–0 N–K4?! 10 N×N P×N 11 P–B4 N–Q2 12 Q–N4 B–B4+ 13 K–R1 Q–K2 14 Q–N3 B–Q5 15 N–N5 P×QP 16 KP×P± P–QB3 17 P–Q6 Q–Q1 18 N×B P×N 19 P–KB5 P–B3 20 B–R6 R–B2 21 QR–K1 N–B4 22 B–N1 Q–Q2 23 P–N4 N–R5 24 P–B5 N–B6 25 B–Q3 P–R4 26 B–Q2 N–Q4 27 R–K4 RP×P 28 RP×P R–R7 29 Q–K1 B–R3?! 30 B×B R×B/3 31 R–K8+ R–B1 32 Q–K6+! Q×Q 33 R×R+ K×R 34 P×Q±± P–QN4 35 P–N4 R–R7 36 P–N5! R×B 37 R–R1 P–N3 38 P×P** (*15*) **1–0**

15
B

USSR Junior Spartakiad

Leningrad 1967

1	RSFSR	×	5½	4½	3	6	6½	25½
2	Moscow	2½	×	4½	4½	5½	5½	22½
3	Ukraine	3½	3½	×	5	5½	5	22½
4	Georgia	5	3½	3	×	4½	5	21
5	Byelorussia	2	2½	2½	3½	×	4½	15
6	Moldavia	1½	2½	3	3	3½	×	13½

The teams in this event were composed of six boys and two girls.

Karpov played board two for RSFSR behind Gennady Timoshenko. Seiran Chechelyan (board two for Georgia) had the absolute best result with 8½/9 (there were four preliminary rounds), his only draw being against Karpov.

None of Karpov's games are available from this event.

	1	2	3	4	5	6	7	8	
1 **Karpov**	×	½	1	1	½	1	½	1	5½
2 Jocha	½	×	½	1	1	1	½	½	5
3 Lewi	0	½	×	1	0	1	1	1	4½
4 Timman	0	0	0	×	½	1	1	1	3½
5 Zara	½	0	1	½	×	0	½	1	3½
6 Hostalet	0	0	0	0	1	×	1	0	2
7 Ligterink	½	½	0	0	½	0	×	½	2
8 Moles	0	½	0	0	0	1	½	×	2

The Preliminaries were held in the form of a single seven-round Swiss: 1 Jocha 5; 2–6 Hostalet, Karpov, Lewi, Ligterink, Timman 4½; 7–8 Zara, Moles 4; 9 Jacobsen 3½; 10 Boersma 3; 11–14 Dudek, Maeder, Schaufelberger, Tate 2½; 15–16 Fučak, Meulders 2.

0201 AK–Heinz Schaufelberger:
PR1: 27 December:

Sicilian

1 P–K4   P–QB4
2 N–QB3

As a teenager Karpov never made an extensive study of sharp and complicated opening variations like many youngsters do. He preferred to rely on solid systems, avoiding theoretical arguments. The Closed Sicilian was his favourite choice for many years, though today he confidently plays the usual 2 N–KB3 followed by 3 P–Q4.

2 . . .   N–QB3

Throughout Sicilian history this move had been regarded as the natural answer, contributing as it does to restraint of P–Q4 by White. However, in the 1968 Candidates matches future World Champion Spassky had so incisively demolished both Geller and Larsen after their 2 . . . N–QB3 that Korchnoi decided he had better shop around for something else before his turn came; the result was a valuable contribution to theory after 2 . . . P–K3! – the 5th match game continuing 3 P–KN3 P–Q4 4 P×P P×P 5 B–N2 N–KB3 6 KN–K2 P–Q5 7 N–K4 N×N 8 B×N N–Q2! 9 P–Q3 N–B3 with an easy game. Such was the impact of Korchnoi's idea that Spassky declined to use the Closed Sicilian at all in his title-winning match against Petrosian the following year.

3 P–KN3   P–KN3
4 B–N2   B–N2

More black power on d4.

5 P–Q3

Before Spassky it was Smyslov who was the publicity agent for the Closed Sicilian, and it was he who introduced the strong innovation 5 P–Q3 P–K3 6 B–K3 N–Q5 7 N3–

K2! for if 7 . . . N×N 8 N×N B×P 9 R–QN1 Q–R4+ 10 B–Q2 Q×P 11 R×B! Q×R 12 B–QB3 wins. After White's fifth move Black must take counter-measures against the intended sequence of B–K3, Q–Q2 N–Q1 P–QB3, N–K2 and, at last P–Q4.

5 . . .	**P–Q3**
6 KN–K2	

Spassky's successful system was 6 P–B4 followed by 7 N–B3 and 8 0–0, a line which brought Geller down three times in the match – all to K-side assaults in which the white pieces and pawns co-operated well in storming the black fortress.

6 . . .	**Q–Q2**

Black has in mind a very interesting mode of development; in the 1954 world title match, Botvinnik chose 6 . . . P–K4 which to this day is still regarded as a powerful equalizer.

7 B–K3	**P–N3**
8 P–B4	**B–N2**

Now the idea is clear – Black intends to castle long to sidestep the fury of a K-side offensive.

9 0–0

It is interesting to note that an almost identical position (with the white KN on f3 instead of e2) occurred in the game Bernstein–Fischer, Netanya 1968. Interesting because that game was played a few months later – possibly Fischer had seen this game and decided that he could pick up some tips from Schaufelberger on how to combat the Closed Sicilian.

9 . . .	**N–Q5**

In his position Fischer continued with 9 . . . P–B4! and after 10 Q–Q2 N–B3 11 K–R1 0–0–0 12 QR–K1 K–N1 13 B–N1? P×P 14 P×P B–QR3 had a won position already; it does seem that the Swiss champion should have adopted the same move

– an example of the need for clairvoyancy in chess . . .

10 Q–Q2	**P–KR4**

Intending 11 . . . P–R5 with . . . N–R3–N5 to follow.

11 P–KR3

To answer 11 . . . P–R5 with 12 P–KN4 P–B4 13 NP×P P×P 14 B–B2! as in the game.

11 . . .	**P–B4**

Aiming once again for . . . P–R5 now that P–KN4 is not possible.

12 B–B2

A dual purpose move:
(a) to discourage 12 . . . P–R5 when 13 NP×P! and Black must lose time to recover the pawn e.g. 13 . . . N×N+ (if 13 . . . B–KB3 at once then 14 N×N! with the same formula as in the game) 14 Q×N B–KB3 15 Q–K1±
(b) to threaten 13 N×N, which if played at once would lose a piece after 13 . . . P×N.

12 . . .	**0–0–0**

Better was 12 . . . N×N+ 13 Q×N and only then 13 . . . 0–0–0, though White still keeps the initiative with 14 P–QR4.

13 N×N!	**B×N**

Black realizes that he must swap the dark squared bishops as after 13 . . . P×N 14 N–K2 P–K4 15 P–B3 QP×P 16 N×P N–K2 17 P–QR4! White serves up a tremendous Q-side attack in which White's QB plays a leading role.

14 B×B	**P×B**
15 N–K2	**P–K4** (*16*)

Karpov has gone out of his way to help Black build up a pawn centre – so that he can bring it tumbling down!

16 P–B3!

Now Black has real problems e.g. if 16 . . . QP×P 17 Q×P+ Q–QB2 (17 . . . K–N1 18 BP×P) 18 QR–B1 Q×Q 19 R×Q+ K–N1 20 KP×P

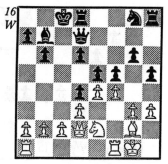

16
W

gives Black dangerous counter-chances against White's weakened K-side.

22 ... **P–Q5**
23 Q–Q2 (*17*) **R×P?**

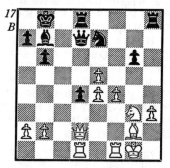

17
B

NP×P 21 P×P P×P 22 R×P winning, or 16 . . . Q–N2 17 QBP×P KP×QP 18 Q–N4 and the QP is lost.

16 ... **P–R5**
True to his lively style Schaufelberger tries an enterprising counter.

17 QBP×P **RP×P**
If 17 . . . KP×QP 18 N×P RP×P 19 Q–B3+ K–N1 (19 . . . Q–QB2 20 Q×Q+ K×Q 21 N–K6+) 20 N–B6+ wins the exchange.

18 QP×P **N–K2**
The best defence, threatening 19 . . . QP×P 20 Q–B3+ N–B3!, for if 18 . . . QP×P 19 Q–B3+ Q–QB2 20 QR–B1 Q×Q 21 R×Q+ K–N1 22 KP×P KP×P (22 . . . NP×P 23 P×P) 23 P×P with a technically won game.

19 Q–B3+ **K–N1**
19 . . . Q–B2 20 QR–B1 Q×Q 21 R×Q+ K–N1 22 KP×QP R×QP 23 N×P or 19 . . . N–B3 20 P–Q4! both leave White set for victory.

20 N×P
20 KP×BP? would be a big mistake e.g. 20 . . . N×P 21 P–Q4 B×B 22 K×B N–K6+ 23 Q×N Q×P+ 24 K–N1 Q–R7 mate.

20 ... **BP×P**
20 . . . R–QB1 allows 21 Q–Q4!

21 QP×P **P–Q4**
If 21 . . . P×P 22 Q×P+.

22 QR–Q1
22 P×P B×P! 23 QR–Q1 Q–K3

Throughout the game Schaufelberger had used his imagination to the full – perhaps now he had run out of ideas; but instead of this easily refutable sacrifice he could have continued with 23 . . . Q–K3 when despite the two pawns deficit the game is by no means over.

24 B×R **Q×B**
25 Q–N2 **Q–R5**
Aiming for 26 . . . N–B4! which would ruin everything for White.

26 R–B3!
The idea being to play 27 K–B2 and 28 R–KR1.

26 ... **R–R1**
Naturally 26 . . . N–B4 is no good now after 27 P×N.

27 R×P **N–B4**
And it's still no good . . .

28 P×N **P×P**
Or 28 . . . B×R 29 Q×B Q–R7+ 30 K–B1 and no more checks.

29 R4–Q3 **R–N1**
30 Q–R2 **1–0**
A good example of Karpov's style as a junior faced by an opponent who was at that time one of the leading young players in Western Europe.

0202 AK—Karl–Heinz Maeder:
PR2: 28 December:

Sicilian

1 P–K4 P–QB4 2 N–QB3 N–QB3
3 P–KN3 P–KN3 4 B–N2 B–N2 5
P–Q3 P–Q3 6 KN–K2 P–K4 7 N–
Q5 KN–K2 8 N–K3 B–K3 9 0–0 0–0
10 N–B3 R–N1 11 N/B3–Q5 B×N
12 P×B N–Q5 13 P–QR4 with the
threat of 14 P–KN4 and 15 P–QB3
winning the knight 13 . . . N5–B4 14
N–B4 P–KR4 15 B–Q2 N–R3 16
P–QN4 N–N5 17 R–N1 N–KB3 18
B–N5 P×P 19 R×P Q–Q2 20
B×N B×B 21 P–R5 (*18*)

21 . . . P–R5 22 P–QB3 K–N2 23
Q–N3 R–KR1 24 R–N1 P×P 25
RP×P Q–B4 26 N×QP Q×QP 27
N×NP R/N1–QB1 28 P–QB4 Q–K7
29 N–Q6 R/B1–Q1 30 N–K4 Q–R4
31 Q–KB3 1–0

0203 Andras Jocha–AK:
PR3: 28 December:

Ruy Lopez

1 P–K4 P–K4 2 N–KB3 N–QB3
3 B–N5 P–QR3 4 B×N QP×B 5
0–0 B–KN5 6 P–KR3 P–KR4 7 P–
B3 Q–Q6 8 P×B P×P 9 N×P B–
Q3 (*19*)
10 N×Q 10 N×NP? N–B3 11
N×N+ P×N 12 Q–N4?? R–R8+
13 K×R Q×R mate, or 12 P–K5∓.
10 . . . B–R7+ ½–½

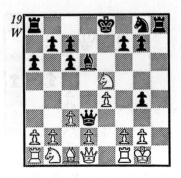

0204 AK–Gert Ligterink:
PR4: 29 December:

Sicilian

1 P–K4 P–QB4 2 P–KN3 P–Q4 3
P–Q3 P×P 4 P×P Q×Q+ 5
K×Q N–QB3 6 B–K3 P–QN3 7
N–Q2 P–N3 8 P–QB3 B–KN2 9 P–
B3 N–B3 10 N–R3 0–0 11 K–B2 B–
N2 12 R–Q1 KR–Q1 ½–½

0205 Dan Zara–AK:
PR5: 30 December:

Petroff

1 P–K4 P–K4 2 N–KB3 N–KB3
3 N×P P–Q3 4 N–KB3 N×P 5
Q–K2 Q–K2 6 P–Q3 N–KB3 7 B–
N5 N1–Q2 8 N–B3 P–KR3 9 B–R4
Q×Q+ 10 B×Q B–K2 11 0–0–0
P–R3 12 KR–K1 0–0 13 B–B1 R–
K1 14 N–K4 K–B1 15 N×N B×N
16 R×R+ K×R 17 R–K1+ K–B1

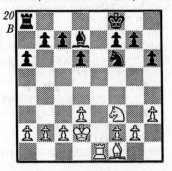

18 B×B N×B 19 P–KR3 B–Q2 20 K–Q2 *(20)* ½–½

0206 Jan Timman–AK:
PR6: 30 December:

QP – Torre

1 P–Q4 N–KB3 2 N–KB3 P–K3 3 B–N5 P–Q4 4 QN–Q2 QN–Q2 5 P–K3 B–K2 6 B–Q3 0–0 7 Q–K2 P–B4 8 P–B3 P–QN3 9 N–K5 N×N 10 P×N N–Q2 11 B×B Q×B 12 P–KB4 P–B4 13 P×Pep R×P 14 P–K4 B–N2 15 0–0 R1–KB1 *(21)*

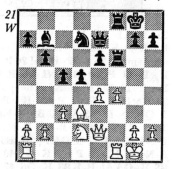

16 P×P B×P 17 QR–K1 R×P 18 B×P+ ½–½ 18 . . . K×B 19 Q–R5+ and 20 Q×B.

0207 AK–Pedro Hostalet:
PR7: 1 January:

QP – Torre

1 P–Q4 N–KB3 2 N–KB3 P–Q4 3 B–N5 P–K3 4 QN–Q2 QN–Q2 5 P–K3 B–K2 6 B–Q3 P–B4 7 P–B3 P×P 8 KP×P Q–B2 9 0–0 0–0 10 R–K1 P–QR3 11 N–B1 P–N4 ½–½

0208 Dan Zara–AK:
FR1: 2 January:

Queen's Indian

1 P–Q4 N–KB3 2 N–KB3 P–K3 3 P–KN3 P–QN3 4 B–N2 B–N2 5 0–0 B–K2 6 P–B4 0–0 7 N–B3 P–Q4 8

N–K5 Q–B1 9 P×P N×P 10 N×N P×N 11 B–B4 Q–K3 12 R–B1 12 Q–B2 P–B3 13 P–K4! ± – Bronstein. 12 . . . B–Q3 13 N–Q3 N–Q2 14 Q–N3 KR–K1 15 P–K3 P–QB3 16 B×B Q×B 17 R–B2 N–B1 18 R1–B1 N–K3 19 Q–N4 Q×Q 20 N×Q N–Q1 21 B–B1 P–QR4 22 N–Q3 P–B3 23 R–B3 B–R3 24 N–B4 B×B 25 K×B K–B2 *(22)*

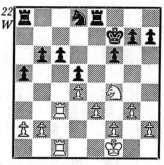

26 R×P N×R 27 R×N R/K1–QB1 28 R×NP QR–N1 29 N×P R×R 30 N×R R–B7 31 N–R4 P–B4 32 P–R4 P–R3 33 P–R3 P–N4 34 P×P P×P 35 K–N2 P–N5 ½–½ Black could still try for a win by moving his king over to the Q-side.

0209 AK–John Moles:
FR2: 3 January:

Ruy Lopez

1 P–K4 P–K4 2 N–KB3 N–QB3 3 B–N5 P–QR3 4 B–R4 N–B3 5 Q–K2 B–K2 6 P–B3 P–QN4 7 B–N3 P–Q3 8 P–QR4 B–N2 9 0–0 0–0 10 P–Q3 P–R3 11 R–K1 N–KR2 12 P–Q4 N–N4 13 B×N P×B 14 P–Q5 If 14 RP×P RP×P 15 R×R Q×R 16 Q×P N–R4 with good compensation e.g. 17 B–B2 R–N1 with the idea 18 Q–Q3 B–R3. 14 . . . N–R2 15 R–Q1 P–KN5 16 N–K1 B–B1 17 P×P N×P 17 . . . P×P!? and then 18 Q–K3 B–N4 19 P–B4 B×P 20

Q–B2 Q–N4 21 N–B2 P–N6∓ but 18 N–R3!±. Karpov proceeds, systematically to pile up on Black's QRP – the results are shattering: **18 B–B4! B–Q2 19 N–B2! Q–B1 20 N–Q2 P–N3 21 N–N4 B–N4 22 R–R5! Q–N2 23 N–N3 K–N2 24 R1–R1** Now the pressure is just too much – call Karpov a bully if you will, but his system brings results. The isolani is now lost, so Black tries a desperate attack: **24 . . . P–KB4 25 N×P Q–N3 26 B×N P×P** (*23*)

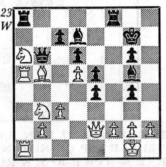

27 P–QB4! R×P 28 P–B5 R×Q 29 P×Q B–K6+ 30 K–R1 B×B 31 P–N7 R–R1 32 P–N8=Q R×Q 33 N×R B–QB5 34 R5–R3 R×QNP 35 N–R5 R×N 36 N×B B–Q5 37 R–Q1 R–N5 38 N–K3 R–N4 39 P–N3 R–B4 40 K–N2 R–N4 41 R–QB1 **1–0**

0210 Jerzi Lewi–AK:

FR3: 3 January:

English

1 P–QB4 P–K4 2 N–QB3 P–Q3 3 P–KN3 P–KN3 4 P–Q4 N–QB3 5 P×P P×Q 6 Q×Q+ N×Q 7 N–B3 B–Q3 8 N–QN5 B–Q2 9 N×B+ P×N 10 P–N3 P–B3 11 B–QR3 N–B2 12 R–Q1 K–K2 13 B–KN2 B–B3 14 0–0 P–B4 15 N–K1 N–B3 16 N–B2 KR–Q1 17 N–N4 QR–B1 18 R–Q2 P–K5 19 P–B3 K–K3 20

R1–Q1 N–K4 21 R–Q4 P×P 22 N×B R×N 23 P×P R–R3 24 B–N4 R×P (*24*)

25 R–K1 25 R×P+ R×R 26 R×R+ K–B2 27 B–B3= White wants more. **25 . . . P–KN4! 26 P–B4 P×P 27 P×P R–KN1 28 R–Q2 R×R 29 B×R N–K5** The point. **30 R×N P×R 31 P×N K×P 32 B–QB3+ K–B5 33 K–B2 P–K6+ 34 K–B1 K–K4 35 B–Q5 R–N4 36 B–N4 K–K4 37 B–QB3+ K–B5 38 B–N4 R–N3 39 P×P K–K4 40 B–B6 K–Q5 41 B–KB3 K–Q6 42 B–K2+ K–K5 43 B–Q1 R–B3+ 44 K–K1 K–Q5 45 B–R3 K–B6 46 B–B1 K–Q6 47 B–K2+ K–K5 48 B–B1 R–B7 49 B–B4 R×P 50 K–Q1 K–Q5 51 B–K2 P–Q4 52 B–R3 K–B6 53 B–B3 P–Q5 54 B–B5 R–KB7 0–1**

0211 AK–Jan Timman:

FR4: 4 January:

English

1 P–QB4 P–K3 2 N–QB3 N–KB3 3 N–B3 B–N5 4 Q–N3 P–B4 5 P–QR3 B–R4 6 P–K3 0–0 7 B–K2 P–Q4 8 0–0 N–B3 9 N–QR4 Q–K2 10 Q–B2 N–Q2 11 P–Q4 QP×P 12 P×P P–K4 13 P–K4 N–Q5 14 N×N P×N 15 B×P N–K4 16 P–QN4 B–B2 17 B–Q5 P–Q6 18 Q–Q1

B–N5 19 P–B3 B–KR4 20 R–R2 K–R1 (*25*)

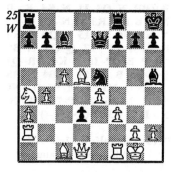

Karpov proceeds first to trap a piece in characteristic style: **21 P–N4 B–KN3 22 P–B4 N×P** The best chance, as 22 . . . N–Q2 23 P–B5 is hopeless. **23 Q×N P–B4** Black's idea consists in maintaining his passed QP. **24 P×P B/N3×P 25 Q–B3 QR–Q1 26 N–B3 Q–B3 27 R–KN2!** Karpov is already preparing a counter-attack: of course 27 . . . Q×N now loses to 28 B–N2. **27 . . . Q–Q5+ 28 K–R1 R–B3 29 B–Q2** Blockading the dangerous passed pawn and protecting the knight. **29 . . . R–KR3** Now it looks like Black is getting some real play with a threatened entry on KR6 but Karpov makes a nice combination which spins the attack round to him! **30 Q–B2! R×B 31 R–K1!** Threatening a back rank mate which cannot be stopped by 31 . . . R–Q1 because of 32 Q×Q or 31 . . . B–K3 32 Q×Q R×Q 33 P–B5 or 31 . . . K–N1 32 Q×Q R×Q 33 R–K7 – so Black tried **31 . . . R–K3** But now there follows a forcing sequence of moves which ends in catastrophe for Black. **32 N×R Q×N 33 R×R B×R 34 K–N1** 34 . . . B–R6 was menaced, so White breaks the pin on his rook. **34 . . . Q–N6** To stop 35 B–B3, exploiting the weak g7 square: this

was the essence of Karpov's plan, started on move 30, and he plays on this theme until Black is battered into submission. **35 Q–K1!** Renewing the threat. **35 . . . K–N1** To answer 36 B–B3 with 36 . . . P–KN3. **36 P–B5! B–B2 37 B–R6 P–KN3 38 Q–R1!** The climax of Karpov's exquisite queen manoeuvre begun with 30 Q–B2. **38 . . . B–K4 39 Q×B Q–Q8+ 40 K–B2 Q–B7+ 41 K–N3 1–0** A nice lesson in how to convert material advantage into attack.

0212: Pedro Hostalet–AK:
FR5: 5 January:

Nimzo–Indian

1 P–Q4 N–KB3 2 P–QB4 P–K3 3 N–QB3 B–N5 4 P–K3 0–0 5 Q–B2 P–B4 6 P–QR3 B×N+ 7 Q×N N–B3 8 B–Q3? 8 P×P is the right course. **8 . . . P×P 9 P×P P–Q4 10 N–K2 P×P 11 B×BP** (*26*)

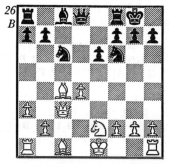

When it comes to punishing an opponent for leaving his king in the centre, Karpov can be really violent. It is hard to believe that White's resignation is forced after only seven more moves, yet such is the impact of Karpov's play that this is exactly what happens.

11 . . .   P–K4!
Immediately underlining White's backward development, for if 12

P×P N–K5! 13 Q–K3 Q–R4+ 14 N–B3 N×N 15 P×N N×P.

12 B–K3

Protecting the QP.

12 . . .   **N–K5**
13 Q–N3   **Q–R4+**
14 K–B1

As 14 N–B3 allows 14 . . . P×P White's king is now very definitely held in the centre for good.

14 . . .   **N×QP**
15 N×N   **P×N**
16 P–B3

Not 16 B×QP N–Q7+ winning the queen.

16 . . .   **P×B**
17 P×N   **Q–Q7!**
0–1

It is a forced win for Black after 18 B–K2 B–N5! 19 R–K1 QR–B1 20 Q–Q1 R–B8! 21 Q×R B×B+ 22 K–N1 B–B6!

0213 AK–Andras Jocha:
FR6: 6 January:

Sicilian

1 P–K4 P–QB4 2 N–QB3 N–QB3 3 P–KN3 P–KN3 4 B–N2 B–N2 5 P–Q3 P–Q3 6 KN–K2 P–K4 7 N–Q5 KN–K2 8 B–N5 P–KR3 9 B–B6 0–0 10 N×N+ N×N 11 B×B K×B 12 Q–Q2 B–K3 13 P–KB4 Q–Q2 14 0–0 P–B3 15 R–B2 QR–Q1 16 R1–KB1 P–N3 ½–½

0214 Gert Ligterink–AK:
FR7: 8 January:

Queen's Gambit Declined

1 P–Q4 N–KB3 2 P–QB4 P–K3 3 N–QB3 P–Q4 4 B–N5 B–K2 5 P–

K3 0–0 6 N–B3 QN–Q2 7 R–B1 P–B3 8 B–Q3 R–K1 9 0–0 P×P 10 B×BP N–Q4 11 N–K4 B×B 12 N4×B P–KR3 13 N–K4 Q–K2 14 N–N3 N4–N3 15 B–Q3 P–K4 16 B–N1 P×P 17 Q–Q3 N–B1 18 N×P B–Q2 19 P–K4 QR–Q1 20 Q–QB3 B–B1 21 P–B4 N–R5 22 Q–K3 Q–N5 23 N4–B5 Q×NP 24 B–B2 N–B6 25 P–K5 B×N 26 N×B Q–N3 27 Q×Q ½–½

0215: Dragoljub Ćirić–AK:
simultaneous: 6 January:

Ruy Lopez

This game was one of a ten-board simultaneous display given by the Yugoslav grandmaster in the afternoon after the sixth round of the finals, played that morning! Ligterink won, Maeder, Schaufelberger and Timman drew and Ćirić won the other five.

1 P–K4 P–K4 2 N–KB3 N–QB3 3 B–N5 P–QR3 4 B–R4 N–B3 5 0–0 B–K2 6 R–K1 P–QN4 7 B–N3 P–Q3 8 P–B3 0–0 9 P–KR3 N–QR4 10 B–B2 B–N2 11 P–Q3 P–B4 12 QN–Q2 R–K1 13 N–B1 Q–B2 14 N–N3 P–N3 15 B–R6 N–Q2 16 N–N5 N–B1 17 P–N4 P×P 18 P×P B×N 19 B×B N–B3 20 Q–Q2 N–Q5 21 B–Q1 N5–K3 22 B–R6 QR–B1 23 N–K2 P–Q4 24 Q–K3 Q–Q3 25 P–R3 P×P 26 P×P R–B5 27 P–B3 N–Q5 28 N×N R×N 29 B–K2 N–K3 30 Q–B2 Q–Q2 31 P–KR4 R–Q3 32 B–K3 N–Q5 33 B–KB1 ½–½

A lightning tournament, held on December 31st, was won by Karpov with 13½/16 followed by Jocha 12½, Lewi 12, Timman 10½ etc.

3 TWO MATCHES

USSR-Yugoslavia 30½–17½   Sochi, 21.6–2.7.1968

1 Geller	½ ½ ½ ½	Gligorić	7 Gurgenidze ½ ½ ½ 1	Nikolić
2 Bronstein	½ 1 1 ½	Ivkov	8 Ranniku 1 1 0 0	Liliak
3 Holmov	½ ½ ½ ½	Matulović	9 Alexandria 1 1 0 0	Jivković
4 Sakharov	1 1 1 ½	Ostojić	10 Konopleva 1 ½ 1 1	Belamarić
5 Platonov	½ ½ 0 ½	Minić	11 Steinberg 1 0 1 ½	Fucak
6 I. Zaitsev	1 1 ½ ½	Bukić	12 **Karpov** 1 1 1 ½	Vujaković

The composition of the teams was boards 1–7 men, 8–10 women, 11–12 juniors.

0301 Vujaković–AK: (R1):

Ruy Lopez

1 P–K4 P–K4 2 N–KB3 N–QB3 3 B–N5 P–QR3 4 B–R4 N–B3 5 P–Q4 P×P 6 0–0 B–K2 7 P–K5 N–K5 8 N×P N×N 9 Q×N N–B4 10 N–B3 0–0 11 B–K3 N×B 12 Q×N P–Q4 13 P×Pep B×P 14 B–B4 B×B 15 Q×B B–K3 16 KR–K1 Q–Q2 17 QR–Q1 Q–B3 18 R–Q3 QR–K1 19 R3–K3 P–B3 20 P–KR4 B–Q2 21 Q–Q4 R×R 22 R×R B–K3 23 P–R5?! P–R3 24 R–N3 R–B2 25 Q–

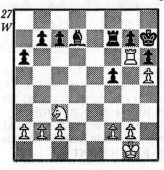

```
27
W
```

Q8+ K–R2 26 Q–Q3+ P–B4 27 R–N6? unnecessarily entombing the rook **27 ... Q–Q2 28 Q×Q B×Q** (27) **29 N–Q5? P–B5 30 P–KN3 P×P 31 R×P/N3 R–B4 32 N×P R–B4! 33 R–QB3 R×R 34 P×R B–N5 35 K–N2 B×P 36 N–K6 B–B2 37 N–B5 B×P 0–1**

0302 AK–Vujaković: (R2):

Pirc

1 P–K4 P–Q3 2 P–Q4 N–KB3 3 N–QB3 P–KN3 4 P–B3 P–B3 5 B–K3 P–QN4 6 Q–Q2 N1–Q2 7 N1–K2 B–KN2 Black should try to exploit the Q-side: 7 ... N–N3 8 P–QN3 Q–B2 9 P–KN4 P–K4 10 B–N2 P–N5 11 N–Q1 P–QR4 12 0–0 P–B4∓ Hennings–Smyslov, Havana 1967. **8 P–KN3 0–0 9 B–N2 N–N3 10 P–N3 P–QR4 11 0–0 Q–B2 12 P–KR3 B–N2 13 N–B4 KR–Q1 14 Q–B2 QR–B1 15 N–Q3 N/B3–Q2 16 QR–Q1 P–N5 17 N–K2 P–QB4 18**

P–KB4 B–QR3 19 P–B5 R–B1 20
R–Q2 BP×P 21 B×P B×N 22
P×B B×B 23 N×B Q–N1 24 P–
KR4 N–B3 25 B–R3 R–B4 26 Q–
K3 N/N3–Q2 27 N–K2 Q–B2 28 P–
N4 (*28*)

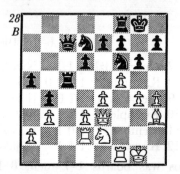

28 . . . R–B7? leaves the N/Q2 unde-
fended 29 R×R Q×R 30 P–N5 N–
R4 31 P×P N–K4 32 P×RP+
K×P 33 P–Q4 N–QB3 Or 33 . . .
N–N3 34 B–N4 N–N2 35 P–R5
N–R1 (35 . . . N–R5 36 Q–R3) 36 P–
N6+ K–N1 37 Q–R6±± 34 R–
B1 1–0

0303 Vujaković–AK: (R3):

Ruy Lopez

1 P–K4 P–K4 2 N–KB3 N–QB3
3 B–N5 P–QR3 4 B–R4 N–B3 5 P–
Q4 P×P 6 0–0 B–K2 7 P–K5 N–K5
8 N×P 0–0 9 N–B5 P–Q4 10 B×N
P×B 11 N×B+ Q×N 12 R–K1 B–
B4 13 P–KB3 N–B4 14 P–QN3 N–
K3 15 B–R3 P–B4 16 N–B3 P–QB3
17 Q–Q2 KR–Q1 18 N–R4 Q–R2 19
Q–B2 P–B5 20 N–B5 B×P 21 QR–
B1 if 21 Q×B N×N 22 P×P
N–Q6+ P×P 22 P×P B–N3 23
P–B4 N×N 24 B×N Q–Q2 25 P–
R3 R/Q1–N1 26 R–B3 (*29*) ½–½
White has a strong initiative for the
pawn.

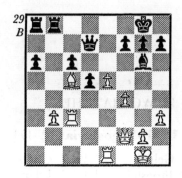

0304 AK–Vujavković: (R4):

Pirc

1 P–K4 P–Q3 2 P–Q4 P–KN3 3
N–QB3 N–KB3 4 P–KR3!? B–N2 5
B–K3 0–0 6 Q–Q2 P–B3 7 P–KN4
P–K4 8 0–0–0 Q–K2 9 P–Q5 P–
B4 10 N1–K2 N–R3 11 N–N3
N–B2 12 K–N1 N3–K1 13 B–K2 R–
N1 14 QR–N1 P–QN4 15 P–KR4
P–N5 16 N–Q1 N–N4 17 P–R5 P–
B5 18 Q×P N1–B2 19 Q–Q2 B–Q2
20 P–QB3 P–R4 21 K–R1 P–R5 (*30*)

22 N–B5 B×N If 22 . . . P×N 23
NP×P K–R1 24 R×B! K×R 25 P–
B6+ Q×P 26 B–N5±± 23 NP×B
P–R6 24 RP×P QRP×P+ 25
N×P BP×P 26 P×P R–R1 27
B×P R–R6 28 B–R6 P×P 29 R×P
R–B5 30 R1–KN1 1–0

USSR Juniors–Scandinavia Juniors   Tallinn, 17–19.8.1968

1 Miklyaev ½ 1 Andersson ½ 0;   2 **Karpov** 0 ½ Jacobsen 1 ½;
3 Sveshnikov ½ 1 Angantysson;   4 Umansky 1 1 Turunen;
5 Chechelyan 0 1 Heim;   6 Lebovich 1 1 Asplund;   7
Makarichev ½ ½ Bille;   8 Belyavsky 1 1 Ristoia;   9 Mechitov
1 1 Harestad;   10 Berkovich 1 0 Svensson;   11 Petrosian 1 1
Kvist;   12 Pushkansky 1 ½ Bostrom;   13 Meiran 0 0 Shonsby;
14 Veingold ½ ½ Ornstein;   15 Peshina ½ 1 Pedersen. 20½–9½.

0305 AK–Bo Jacobsen: R1:

Dutch

1 P–QB4 P–KB4 2 P–KN3 N–
KB3 3 B–N2 P–KN3 4 N–QB3 B–N2
5 N–B3 0–0 6 0–0 N–B3 7 P–Q4
P–Q3 8 P–Q5 N–K4 9 N×N P×N
10 P–K4 P–B5 11 P–N3 P–KN4 12
P–B3 Q–Q3 13 P–KN4 P–KR4 14
P–KR3 P×P 15 BP×P B–Q2 16
P–QR4 Q–N3+ 17 K–R2 K–B2 18
B–B3 R–R1 19 K–N2 R–R5 20
P–R5 Q–B4 21 B–R3 Q–K6 *(31)*

22 Q–K1 B×P 23 P×B if 23 B×B
N×B 23 . . . N×NP 24 R–R1 R×R
25 Q×Q Not 25 Q×R Q–B7+ 26
K–R3 Q–N6 mate, nor 25 K×R
R–R1+ 26 K–N2 R–R7+. 25 . . .
N×Q+ 26 K×R P–N5 27 B–K2
P–B6 28 B–B5 If 28 B–KB1 P–N6
with the idea of . . . P–N7+ if 29
B–Q3 P–B7 with . . . R–R1 mate to
follow; also 28 B–Q1 P–B7 with the
idea of 29 . . . R–R1 mate. **28 . . . B–**

R3 29 R–K1 If 29 B×N B×B threat
mate. **29 . . . P–N3 30 B×BP** Or
30 B×N B×B 31 B×P R–R1+ 32
K–N2 P×B+ 33 K×P B–Q7 wins.
**30 . . . QNP×B 31 B–Q1 K–N3 32
N–N5 B–B5 33 R×N** if 33 K–N1
P–N6 with . . . R–R1–R7 to follow
**33 . . . B×R 34 N×BP R–R1+
35 K–N2 R–R5 36 P–R6 B–
B5 37 K–N1 P–N6 38 B–B3 R–R7
39 B–N2 K–B2 40 K–B1 R–R3 41
K–K2 R–QN3 0–1**

0306 Bo Jacobsen–AK: R2:

Bird

1 P–KB4 P–Q4 2 N–KB3 P–KN3
3 P–KN3 B–N2 4 B–N2 N–KB3 5
0–0 0–0 6 P–Q3 P–N3 7 P–K4 B–N2
8 P–K5 N–K1 9 P–KN4 P–KB3
Q–K1 P–K3 11 N–B3 P–KB4 12
P×P NP×P 13 K–R1 P–Q5 14 N–
K2 P–B4 15 R–KN1 N–QB3 16
B–Q2 P–QR4 17 P–QR3 P–R5 18

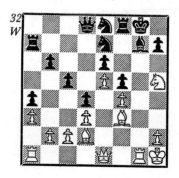

N–N3 N–K2 19 N–R5 B×N 20 B×B R–R2 (*32*)

21 R×B+ N×R 22 N–B6+ K–B2 If 22 . . . K–R1 23 Q–R4±± 23 Q–N3 R–KR1 24 R–KN1 Q–KB1 25 Q–N5 N–N3 26 P–R4 N–K1 27 P–R5 Q–K2 Not 27 . . . N–K2 28 P–R6 N–N3 (28 . . . N×N 29 Q×N+ K–K1 30 Q×KP!±±) 29 N×P R×N (29 . . . Q–N1 30 N–B6!) 30 Q×N+ K–K2 31 Q×R+ Q–B2 32

Q×Q+ K×Q 33 P–R7±± 28 N× N Or 28 P×N+ P×P+ 29 K–N2 N×N 30 P×N Q×P and Black is alive and kicking. 28 . . . K×N 29 P×N P×P+ 30 K–N2 Q×Q+ 31 P×Q R–QB2 32 R–KR1 R–N1 33 R–R4 K–B2 34 R–R7+ R–KN2 35 R–R8 R–KN1 36 R–R7+ R–KN2 37 R–R4 R–N1 38 B–Q1 K–N2 39 K–B2 R–Q1 40 B–K2 R2–Q2 ½–½

4 MOSCOW UNIVERSITY CHAMPIONSHIP 1968–1969

		1	2	3	4	5	6	7	8	9	0	1	2	3	4	
1	**Karpov**	×	½	1	½	1	½	½	½	½	1	1	1	1	1	10
2	Ageichenko	½	×	0	½	1	1	1	0	½	1	1	1	½	1	9
3	Gik	0	1	×	1	½	1	0	½	½	1	1	1	½	1	9
4	Vatnikov	½	½	0	×	1	0	1	½	1	0	½	1	1	1	8
5	Vibornov	0	0	½	0	×	1	½	1	0	1	1	1	1	1	8
6	Skvortsov	½	0	0	1	0	×	0	1	½	1	1	1	1	1	8
7	Krasnov	½	0	1	0	½	1	×	0	1	½	0	1	1	1	7½
8	Lepeshkin	½	1	½	½	0	0	1	×	½	½	½	½	½	1	7
9	Estrin	½	½	½	0	1	½	0	½	×	½	½	0	1	1	6½
10	Bitman	0	0	0	1	0	0	½	½	½	×	0	1	1	1	5½
11	Sukhanov	0	0	0	½	0	0	1	½	½	1	×	1	0	0	4½
12	Hramtsov	0	0	0	0	0	0	0	½	1	0	0	×	1	1	3½
13	Zilbert	0	½	½	0	0	0	0	½	0	0	1	0	×	½	3
14	Pronin	0	0	0	0	0	0	0	0	0	0	1	0	½	×	1½

Winning this tournament is the only recorded achievement of Karpov's year at Moscow University. During the summer vacation(?) he transferred to the Faculty of Economics, University of Leningrad.

The tournament was played over a period of several months. At one stage Karpov scored six straight wins.

0401 AK–Gik:

Sicilian

1 P–K4 P–QB4 2 N–KB3 P–Q3 3 P–Q4 P×P 4 N×P N–KB3 5 N–QB3 P–KN3 6 B–K3 B–N2 7 P–B3 0–0 8 B–QB4 N–B3 9 Q–Q2 Q–R4 10 0–0–0 B–Q2 11 P–KR4 N–K4 12 B–N3 KR–B1 13 P–R5 N×RP 14 K–N1 was played in Spassky–Stein, RSFSR–Ukraine 1967, when Black obtained counterplay with the exchange sacrifice 14 ... R×N 15 Q×R Q×Q 16 P×Q R–QB1 17 K–N2 P–R4. In the last Student Team Tournament in Austria (Ybbs) the German (West German

– eds) players succeeded in strengthening White's play and the variation has again gained attention. So White doesn't have to waste a tempo with his king ... 14 B–R6 B×B

14 ... N–Q6+ brings about an extremely sharp situation: 15 K–N1 N×P (not 15 ... B×N 16 N–Q5!) 16 K×N B×B 17 Q×B and now:
(a) 17 ... Q×N+? 18 K–N1 P–R4 19 R–Q3 Q–N5 20 P–R3 Q–N3 21 P–N4 P–R5 22 P×N P×B 23 N×P P–Q4 24 RP×P Q×P 25 Q–R2 K–B1 26 R×P±±
(b) 17 ... R×N (variously given!!, ! or !?) 18 P–N4 N–B3 19 P–K5! R×B+ 20 RP×R P×P 21 N–K2

B–K3 22 N–B3!± Mecking–Joksić, Vrsac 1971.

15 Q×B R×N 16 P×R Q×BP? Better 16 . . . N–KB3 or 16 . . . R–QB1! **17 N–K2!**± *(33)*

33
B

17 . . . **Q–B4** If 17 . . . N–Q6+? 18 R×N Q–R8+ 19 K–Q2 Q×R 20 P–N4 N–N6 21 Q×Q N×Q 22 K–K3! and the knight is caught. **18 P–N4 N–KB3 19 P–N5 N–R4** Here I was about to play 20 N–N3, but noticed that after 20 . . . B–N5! White's queen is shut out of play. If 21 N–B5 then there follows 21 . . . B×N 22 P×B Q–K6+ 23 K–N1 Q–B5 and there is no continuation of the attack in sight. **20 R×N!** The only way forward! **20 . . . P×R 21 R–R1 Q–K6+ 22 K–N1 Q×BP** Clearly not 22 . . . Q×N because of 23 Q×P/R5 and mate is inevitable. **23 R×P P–K3** 23 . . . Q×P does not work on account of 24 P–N6! when the brave pawn comes under four threats but remains inviolate! Possibly better chances of salvation are to be found in 23 . . . N–N3 24 Q×P+ K–B1 25 R–R6 P–K3 26 R×N P×R 27 Q×B Q×N. **24 P–N6! N×P** Forced as on 24 . . . BP×P 25 Q×RP+ K–B1 26 Q–R8+ K–K2 27 R–R7+ N–B2 28 Q×R Q×N 29 Q×NP±± **25 Q×P+ K–B1** *(34)*

34
W

26 R–B5! This blow was not expected by my opponent. 26 . . . P×R is not possible in the face of mate, so Black gives up the queen for rook and bishop. **26 . . . Q×B+ 27 RP×Q P×R 28 N–B4 R–Q1** If 28 . . . N×N then, of course, 29 Q–R8+ and 30 Q×R. **29 Q–R6+ K–K1 30 N×N P×N 31 Q×P+ K–K2 32 Q–N5+ K–K1 33 P×P R–B1 34 Q–N8+ K–K2 35 Q–N7+ K–Q1 36 P–B6 1–0**

0402 AK–Sukhanov:

Sicilian

1 P–K4 P–QB4 2 N–QB3 N–QB3 3 P–KN3 P–KN3 4 B–N2 B–N2 5 P–Q3 N–B3 6 B–K3 P–Q3 7 P–KR3 N–Q5 8 N3–K2 Q–N3 9 P–QB3 N×N 10 Q×N B–Q2 11 N–B3 Q–R3 12 N–R4 B–B3 13 Q–B2 P–Q4 14 P–K5 N–Q2 15 P–KB4 B–N4 16 B×QP B×QP 17 Q–N2 0–0–0 18 R–Q1 P–B5 19 P–N3 P–K3 20 B×BP B×B 21 P×B Q×BP 22 Q–K2 Q×Q+ 23 K×Q P–B3 *(35)*

24 P×P B×P 25 N–B3 P–K4 26 P×P N×P 27 B×P QR–K1 28 N×N B×N 29 K–Q3 29 K–B3 R/R1–B1+ 30 K–N2 B×BP 31 R–QB1 R–K7+ 32 K–N1 R–B6+ **29 . . . B×NP 30 KR–B1 R–K3?** Now White penetrates to the seventh. Simple and good was 30 . . .

R–K2. **31 B–Q4 R–Q1 32 R–B7
P–R4 33 R–QN1 P–N3 34 P–QR4
B–B2 35 K–B4 R–QB3+ 36 K–N5
K–N2 37 R–K1 R–Q4+ 38 K–N4
R–KB4 39 R×R P×R 40 K–N5
R–Q3 41 K–B4 R–N3 42 R–K7 K–
B3 43 R–R7 P–B5 44 R×P P–B6 45
K–Q3 R–N7 46 R–KB5 R–QR7 47
R×P R×P 48 P–R4 R–R4 49 R–
B6+ K–N2 50 R–R6 R–KB4 51
K–K4 R–B8 52 K–Q5 R–B4+ 53
K–K6 R–B6 54 P–R5 K–B3 55 R–
B6 R–R6 56 P–R6 B–Q1 57 R–N6
P–N4 58 K–B7+ K–Q4 59 K–N7
P–N5 60 P×P K×B 61 R–Q6+
K–K4 62 R×B R–KN6+ 63 K–R8
K–B3 64 P–R7 K–B2 65 R–Q1 R–
N6 66 R–KB1+ K–K2 67 R–B4 1–0**

0403 Krasnov–AK:

Queen's Gambit Declined

**1 P–Q4 N–KB3 2 P–QB4 P–K3 3
N–KB3 P–Q4 4 N–B3 B–N5 5 B–
N5 P–KR3 6 B×N Q×B 7 P–K3
0–0 8 B–K2 P×P 9 B×P P–QN3 10
0–0 B–N2 11 R–B1 P–B4 12 N–QN5
P–R3 13 N–Q6 B×N 14 P×B** If 14
Q×B Q×Q 15 P×Q P×P with the
idea of 16 . . . R–Q1. **14 . . . P×P 15
N–K4 Q–K4** 15 . . . Q–N3+!? 16
K–R1 P×P is unclear. **16 P×P
Q–B5 17 P–Q5 P–QN4 18 B–N3 N–
Q2 19 P×P N–K4 20 P×P+
K–R1 21 K–N2 N–N3 22 N–N3** (*36*)

22 . . . **QR–Q1 23 Q–K2** Otherwise
23 . . . N–R5+ wins. **23 . . . Q×R 24
R×Q N–B5+ 25 K–B1 N×Q 26
N×N R–B1 27 R–R1 B–Q3 28 P–
B4 P–N3 29 K–N2 B–K2 30 K–B3
KR–Q1 31 P–B5 P–N4** if 31 . . .
P×P 32 R–KN1! and 33 R–N8+
**32 N–N3 R–Q6+ 33 K–N2 K–N2
34 N–R5+ K–B1 35 R–K1 P–R4
36 P–B6 B–N5 37 R–K4 R×B**
White's idea was 38 N–N7 and 39 R–
K8+, so Karpov returns the ex-
change. **38 P×R K×P 39 R–K5
R–B4** This cuts the bishop off from
K2, but 39 . . . R–QN1 is hopelessly
passive. **40 R–K7+ K–N3 41 N–N3
K×P 42 R–K2 R–K4 43 R–B2
R–K3 44 K–B3 K–K4 45 R–B8 R–
KB3+ 46 K–K2 R–Q3 47 P–B3 R–
B5 48 N–K4 B–N5** If 48 . . . R–R5 at
once, then 49 R–K8+ K–Q4 50 R–
Q8 wins **49 K–K3 R–R5 50 R–K8+
K–B4 51 N–N3+ K–B3 52 R–QN8
R×P 53 R–N6+ K–B2 54 R×NP
R×P 55 K–K4 R×P 56 N–B5
P–R5 57 N–Q4 R–N7 58 R–N7+
K–K1** If 58 . . . K–N3 59 R–N6+
K–R4 60 N–B5 wins. **59 N–B6 B–B6
60 R–QR7 R–QR7 61 K–B5 P–
R6 62 R–K7+ K–B1 63 K–N6 R–
Q7 ½–½** White draws by perpetual
check after 64 R–KB7+ K–K1 (not
64 . . . K–N1 65 N–K7+ K–R1 66
R–R7 mate) 65 R–K7+.

0404 AK–Pronin:

Franco–Sicilian

1 P–K4	P–K3
2 P–Q4	P–QB4

The Franco–Sicilian as Gunderam labels it in *Neue Eröffnungswege*. Indeed in his book there are many black successes to illustrate how recommendable this variation really is. As in the opening to Karpov–Orekhov (0101), transpositional possibilities are ever-present.

3 P–Q5

Gaining ground in the centre and definitely giving the game a QP flavour.

3 ...	P×P
4 P×P	P–Q3

Setting up the Benoni pawn formation.

5 N–KB3

After 5 P–QB4 Black can fianchetto his KB and develop his KN to e7 with possibilities of going to f5 and d4 – a manoeuvre seen in Petrosian's games.

5 ...	P–QR3

5 ... N–KB3 6 N–QB3 B–K2 is a position frequently obtained by Larsen who has won many games from it; Hamilton–Larsen, Lugano 1968, continued 7 B–K2 0–0 8 0–0 N–R3 9 B–KB4 N–B2 10 P–QR4 P–QN3 11 B–B4 P–QR3 12 Q–Q3 R–K1 13 QR–N1 Q–Q2! 14 P–R3 Q–B4 15 B–KN3 Q×Q 16 B×Q B–N2 17 B–QB4 B–KB1 18 QR–Q1 B–B1 19 KR–K1 B–B4 20 R–Q2 R×R+ 21 N×R R–K1 22 K–B1 B–Q2 23 B–K2 P–R3 24 B–B3 P–QN4! This game clearly demonstrates the winning formula in the Danish grandmaster's home-made opening:
(a) development of pieces;
(b) piece pressure on White's temporarily isolated QP;
(c) occupation of, and later ex-

change of heavy pieces on, the open K-file;
(d) use of the free squares e5, e4, f6 and f5 for manoeuvring;
(e) eventual Q-side attack with . . . b5 when White's pawns will be weakened because of the need:
(e1) to support the isolani at d5 and
(e2) to stop an invasion of black pieces on the numerous empty squares in and around White's centre.

In the 1950's the Hungarian grandmaster Barcza also used to get the position after White's sixth move e.g. Filip–Barcza, Sofia 1957, which continued 6 . . . B–N5 7 B–K2 B×N 8 B×B B–K2 9 0–0 0–0 10 B–B4 QN–Q2 11 R–K1 N–K1 12 B–K2 P–QR3 13 P–QR4 B–N4 14 B–N3 B–B3 15 B–B1 B–K4 16 B×B N×B 17 P–R5 N–KB3 when Black's strategy of becoming master of the dark squares was realized.

It is amusing to see the 1970 Lugano tournament bulletin in which the very knowledgeable editor (the late Mr Kühnle-Woods, manager of *Chess Express*) headed the first round game Unzicker–Larsen a Benoni. That game was naturally Larsen's pet line, and the great Dane lost no time in gently reminding the editor that the opening was not a Benoni but a Barcza–Larsen defence. A correction duly appeared in the second round bulletin to this effect! What gives this variation its own character is its non-fianchetto of the KB which is standard practice in the Modern Benoni.

In the game Gligorić–Barcza, Büsum 1969, the Hungarian played 5 . . . B–N5 6 B–K2 B×N 7 B×B B–K2 8 0–0 N–KB3 9 N–R3! 0–0 10 N–B4 QN–Q2 11 P–QR4 (11 R–K1! is best according to Gligorić) 11 . . . N–K4! 12 N×N P×N=. Of course this game has an affinity with Filip–Barcza above, while Larsen's approach is quite different: 'Si duo faciunt idem non est idem' – Cicero.

6 P–QR4

To restrain 6 . . . P–QN4.

6 . . .   B–N5

The Barcza half of the defence.

7 B–K2   B×N

Black exchanges at once, consistent with his plan of getting on to e5.

8 B×B   P–QN3

To answer 9 P–R5 with 9 . . . P–QN4, but being rather casual about getting his pieces moved off the first rank.

9 0–0   B–K2
10 N–Q2!

Following the recipe of Gligorić, who got to c4 via a3.

10 . . .   N–Q2
11 R–K1

Setting a devilish trap and just willing the black knight to e5.

11 . . .   N–K4 *(37)*

The alternative 11 . . . KN–B3 12 N–B4 0–0 13 B–B4 N–K1 14 Q–K2 B–B3 15 R–R3! P–QN4 16 N×P N×N 17 B×N R–K1 (17 . . . B×P 18 R–K3!) 18 R–K3 R×R 19 Q×R with a winning position is an example of the difficulties Black finds himself in. However, the move played is nicely dealt with by Karpov.

12 R×N!

A beautiful sacrifice which makes the absolute maximum of the natural resources in the position.

12 . . .   P×R
13 P–Q6

The start of something big – this pawn goes down in a blaze of glory to open not only the bishop's diagonal but also the file for the queen.

13 . . .   B×P

13 . . . R–B1 14 P×B Q×P 15 N–B4 or 13 . . . R–R2 14 B–B6+ are clearly good for White.

14 B–B6+

This zwischenschach puts out any ideas Black may have had of castling.

14 . . .   K–B1

14 . . . K–K2 would have enabled Karpov to show how rich in possibilities this deceptively simple position is e.g. 15 B×R Q×B 16 N–B4 Q–B3 17 Q–K2! and then:

(a) 17 . . . K–B3 18 P–QN3! N–K2 19 B–N2 N–N3 20 P–B4! R–K1 (20 . . . N×P 21 B×P+) 21 P×P+ N×P 22 R–KB1+;

(b) 17 . . . K–K3 18 Q–N4+ K–B3 19 Q–N5+ K–K3 20 Q×NP;

(c) 17 . . . P–B3 18 P–B4 and:

(c1) 18 . . . Q–Q4 19 N×NP Q–Q5+ 20 K–R1 N–R3 21 P–B3 winning the queen in mid-board.

(c2) 18 . . . K–K3 19 P×P B×P 20 B–B4 Q–B2 21 R–K1.

In every case the exposed black king, left in the centre because of Black's slow development, is the cause of the trouble.

15 B×R   Q×B
16 N–B4   B–B2

Forced, to cover the QNP, but now White gets ready to soften up the QBP.

17 B–K3!

Preparing his next move.

17 . . .   N–K2

17 . . . Q–B3 is nicely met by 18 P–QR5! P–QN4 19 N×P B×N 20 Q–Q8+ Q–K1 21 B×P+ N–K2 22 B×N+.

18 P–R5!

Black has already been severely punished for his time consuming and weakening eighth move which resulted in:

(a) a weakening of the h1–a8 diagonal;

(b) a retarded development with his king stuck in the centre; – and now we have

(c) the break up and destruction of the weakened Q-side pawn chain.

18 . . .   P×P

If 18 . . . P–QN4 (18 . . . Q–B3 19 P×P B×P 20 R×P wins at once) 19 N–N6! B×N (19 . . . Q–B3 20 B×P K–K1 – *not* 20 . . . *Q×B?? 21 N–Q7+* – still leaves Black helpless) 20 P×B P–B3 21 Q–Q7 K–B2 22 B×P R–K1 (or if here 22 . . . Q–Q1 23 R–Q1 Q×Q 24 R×Q R–K1 25 R×N+! and the QNP is decisive) 23 P–N7 Q–N1 24 R×P with 25 R–R8 to follow.

19 B×P   Q–B3?

A blunder, overlooking White's tactical reply, though Black is lost anyway as the following lines show:

(a) 19 . . . Q–B1 20 Q–Q5! K–K1 21 N–Q6+ B×N 22 Q×B N–B3 23 R×P!;

(b) 19 . . . Q–K1 20 Q–B3! K–N1 21 Q–N7 Q–B3 22 N×RP! Q×Q (22 . . . B×N 23 Q×N) 23 N×Q N–N3 24 R×P and the connected passed pawns are too strong.

20 N×KP!

For if 20 . . . Q×B 21 N–Q7+, or 20 . . . B×N 21 Q–Q8+ Q–K1 22 B×N+ and it's time to put the pieces back in their starting positions.

20 . . .   Q–K1

21 Q–Q4 (*38*)

Protecting his knight which was now threatened, and preparing the entry of the white rook.

21 . . .   P–R4

If 21 . . . B×N 22 Q×B and 23 R–K1 wins straightaway, but 21 . . . K–N1 was the best defence. Perhaps Black played his 21 . . . P–R4 to prepare 22 . . . K–N1 since he may have feared the possibility of 21 . . . K–N1 22 N–Q7 N–B3 23 N–B6+ P×N 24 Q–KN4 mate!, but really Black can easily stop this fantasy and White would continue in sober fashion with 22 B–N6! then:

(a) 22 . . . N–B3 23 N×N Q×N 24 R–K1 P–R3 (24 . . . B×B 25 Q×B!) 25 B×B Q×B 26 R–K8+ K–R2 27 Q–K4+ P–N3 28 R–K7;

(b) 22 . . . B–N1 23 Q–Q7 K–B1 (23 . . . Q×Q 24 N×Q and the Q-side pawns fall) 24 R–Q1 B×N (24 . . . Q×Q 25 N×Q+ wins the bishop) 25 Q×Q+ K×Q 26 R–Q8 mate.

(c) 22 . . . B×B 23 Q×B and again the doubled pawns will be wiped out.

22 R–K1   1–0

Setting up a double pin – if now 22 . . . K–N1 23 N–N6! P×N 24 R×N Q–KB1 25 R×B wins comfortably. A beautifully economical miniature.

The other games from this event are, regrettably, unavailable.

Karpov played for the Armed Forces team which came second with 72½/110 behind 'Burevestnik' (Students) with 78. The composition of teams was of ten players, in board order 6 seniors, 1 junior, 2 women and 1 girl. The Armed Forces team was: Geller, Vasyukov, Liberzon, Lein, Lutikov, Karpov; Gusev; Bilunova, Skegina; Sivamskaya. Reserve: Gufeld.

Karpov, then, received the considerable honour of playing on one of the senior boards (he was still, of course, a junior at this time) with a fully fledged international grandmaster as reserve, ready to deputize should young Anatoly be indisposed!

Karpov's result of 10/11 was the absolute best result of the event.

0501 Popov–AK:
  R1 v. Moldava:

Ruy Lopez

1 P–K4 P–K4 2 N–KB3 N–QB3 3 B–N5 P–QR3 4 B–R4 N–B3 5 0–0 B–K2 6 R–K1 P–QN4 7 B–N3 P–Q3 8 P–B3 0–0 9 P–Q4 B–N5 10 P–Q5 N–QR4 11 B–B2 P–B3 12 P×P If 12 P–KR3 B×N! is much better than 12 . . . B–Q2?! 13 N× P 12 . . . **Q–B2 13 P–KR3 B–R4 14 N1–Q2 QR–Q1 15 Q–K2 N×BP 16 N–B1 KR–K1 17 B–N5 N–Q2 18 B–K3 B–N3**= 19 **P–QR4 Q–N2 20 P×P P×P 21 R/K1–Q1 N–B3 22 B–N5 N–KR4 23 P–KN3 B×B 24 N×B N–B3 25 B–Q3 P–N5 26 N–B3 N–N1! 27 N1–Q2** (*39*)

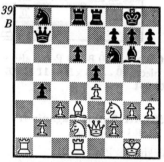

27 . . . **P–Q4 28 N–R4** If 28 KP×P P–K5 wins a piece. **28 . . . QP×P 29 B–N5 R–KB1 30 N×B RP×N 31 R–R4 P×P 32 P×P P–K6 33 P×P N–Q4** With the idea of 34 . . . N×BP with a family fork. **34 N–K4 N×KP**

35 R–N1 if 35 Q×N Q×B 35 . . . N–Q4 36 P–B4 N–K2 37 P–B5 N–B4 38 B–Q3 Q–Q4 39 B–B4 Q–Q2 40 B–N5 N–B3 41 B×N Q×B 42 R–R6 Q–B1 43 K–R2 R–Q5 44 R6–N6 R1–Q1 45 R1–N2 R5–Q2 46 P–R4 N–Q5 47 Q–K3 Q–R1 48 N–Q6 Q–Q4 49 R–N8 R×R 50 R×R+ K–R2 51 N–K4 P–B3 52 R–N2 R–R2 53 R–KB2 Q–R1! The threat is 54 . . . R–R6 55 Q–K1 (55 N–B3 Q–R4) 55 . . . N–B6+. **54 K–R3 R–R6 55 Q–K1 N–**

B4 56 P–R5? better 56 R–K2 **56 . . .
R–K6 57 N×P+ P×N 58 Q–Q1
R×P+ 59 K–R2 Q–K5 0–1**

0502 Sangla–AK:

R2 v. Kalev:

QP – Torre

**1 P–Q4 N–KB3 2 N–KB3 P–K3 3
B–N5 P–B4 4 P–B3 P×P 5 P×P
Q–N3 6 Q–N3 N–K5 7 B–B4 N–
QB3 8 P–K3 B–N5+ 9 N1–Q2?** 9
N3–Q2 was best. **9 . . . P–N4** (*40*)

10 B×P If 10 B–N3 P–N5 also wins
a piece. **10 . . . B×N+ 11 N×B Q–
R4 0–1**

0503 AK–Rafael Vaganian:

R3 v. Spartak:

Alekhine

**1 P–K4 N–KB3 2 P–K5 N–Q4 3
P–Q4 P–Q3 4 N–KB3 P–KN3 5 B–
K2 B–N2 6 P–B4 N–N3 7 P×P
BP×P 8 P–QN3 0–0 9 B–N2 N–B3
10 0–0 B–N5 11 P–KR3 B×N 12
B×B P–Q4 13 P–B5 N–B1 14 Q–
Q2 P–K3 15 P–QN4 P–QR3 16
P–QR4 N1–K2 17 N–R3 N–B4 18
N–B2 P–KR4 19 P–N5 N–R4 20 Q–
N4 N–B5 21 B–K2 P–R4 22 Q–B3
N×B 23 Q×N Q–N4 24 KR–Q1
P–K4 25 P×P N–R5 26 N–K1
B×P** (*41*)

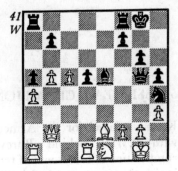

27 Q–B1 Cleverly saving the ex-
change. Not 27 R×P B×Q 28 R×Q
B×R. **27 . . . Q–B3 28 R–R2 B–Q5
29 N–Q3 KR–K1 30 R–B2 QR–B1
31 B–B1 N–B4** With the idea of
playing 32 . . . N–K6 33 P×N
B×KP+ 34 R–B2! when 34 . . . Q–
R5 and 34 . . . Q–Q5 are both awk-
ward for White. **32 K–R1 Q–R5 33
Q–Q2 B–N2 34 Q×P R–R1 35 Q–
N4 R×P 36 Q×Q R×Q 37 P–N3
R–QB5 38 R1–B1 R×R 39 R×R
N–Q5 40 R–B1 R–QB1 41 B–N2
N×P 42 R–QN1 N–B6 43 R×P
B–Q5** ½–½

0504 Nisman–AK:

R4 v. Trud:

Nimzo–Indian

1 P–QB4   N–KB3

Later Karpov showed a marked
preference for the line 1 . . . P–QB4 2
N–KB3 N–KB3 3 N–QB3 (or 3 P–
KN3) 3 . . . P–Q4 – a relatively
underexposed variation with which
he can be well satisfied resultwise, his
most illustrious victim being Viktor
Korchnoi in the Alekhine Memorial
1971.

**2 N–QB3   P–K3
3 P–Q4**

Allowing Black to go into a
Nimzo–Indian. Also possible was 3
N–B3 B–N5 4 Q–N3 P–B4 5 P–QR3

B–R4 6 P–K3 0–0 7 B–K2 P–Q4 8
0–0 N–B3 9 N–QR4! Q–K2 10 Q–
B2! N–Q2 11 P–Q4! Karpov–
Timman, Groningen 1967–8, with
a superior position for White. If
White instead tries to sidestep the
Nimzo–Indian by 3 P–K4 then 3 ...
P–B4 equalizes easily.

3 ...   B–N5

The Nimzo–Indian – an uncom-
promising set-up which secures a
rapid piece development whilst restraining White in the centre.
Though Botvinnik once said it is
doubtful whether there is a refutation, in practice such super-grand-
masters as Portisch and Gligorić
handle the white side of it so skilfully
as to win the vast majority of these
games.

Anyway such a sound defence is
well suited to Karpov's style and,
indeed, he was never one for gambl-
ing on sharper systems like the Modern Benoni or King's Indian – the
Queen's Gambit Declined yes!

4 P–QR3

The oldest living grandmaster,
Sämisch, introduced this line to the
chessworld some 50 years ago and it
bears his name to this day: the
names of so many opening variations
provide an everlasting memorial to
chess giants of yesteryear – the
sculptors of modern day chess.

4 ...   B×N+
5 P×B

With this recapture White adds
more support to his centre and this,
in conjunction with his two bishops,
can be converted into attacking
power in the centre and on the K-
side. Every advantage has a disadvantage, and the doubled QBPs can
be shown up as weak and an object
of counterattack.

5 ...   P–B4

Whilst making his first strike at the
centre, Black blockades and immo-
bilizes the QBPs.

6 P–K3

The main alternative is 6 P–B3
planning to build a concrete pawn
centre with 7 P–K4; Black can then
play 6 ... P–Q4 7 BP×P N×P with
a piece attack on the white centre, or
else continue 6 ... P–Q3 7 P–K4
0–0 8 B–Q3 N–B3 9 N–K2 P–
QN3 10 B–K3 B–R3 11 N–N3 N–
QR4 12 Q–K2 P×P 13 P×P R–B1
14 R–QB1 Q–K1 15 0–0 Q–R5 as in
Polugayevsky–Karpov,   Moscow
Blitz 1972.

6 ...   N–B3

An elastic move since this knight
can either aid a central pawn
advance with ... P–Q3 and ... P–
K4, or else attack the leading
doubled pawn from a5.

7 N–K2

Here, rather than to B3, as the
knight is heading for KN3 whence it
can observe the key e4 square.

7 ...   P–QN3

This is the way the QB gets to see
daylight.

8 N–N3   B–R3

An aggressive development which
initiates the attack on c4, but one
which is not without risk ...

9 B–Q3?

This is a mistake that should lose a
pawn. The critical variation is 9 P–
K4 0–0 (9 ... P–Q3? 10 Q–R4 wins;
9 ... N–QR4 10 P–K5 N–N1 11
N–K4±) 10 B–N5 P–R3 11 P–KR4!
P×P 12 P×P P×B 13 P×P P–N3
(the h5 square must be kept from the
white queen) 14 P–K5! N–R2 15
Q–N4! N×NP 16 N–K4 K–N2 (16
... N×N? 17 Q–R3) 17 N×N R–
R1 18 R×R Q×R 19 R–Q1 with a
dangerous attack.

9 ...   N–QR4
10 Q–K2   P–Q3?

10 ... P×P 11 BP×P R–QB1

wins the QBP straight off. It seems that neither player was acquainted with the intricacies of this variation!

11 B–N2   Q–Q2

Intending to occupy a4 to increase the pressure on c4. Now 11 . . . P×P 12 BP×P R–QB1 13 R–QB1 holds the pawn.

12 P–K4   0–0–0!

If 12 . . . Q–R5 13 P–K5 QP×P 14 P×KP N–Q2 15 N–K4! and White has all the chances.

13 P–QR4

Stopping 13 . . . Q–R5. Not now 13 P–K5? QP×P 14 P×KP Q×B.

13 . . .   P–R4!

14 0–0?

14 P–R4 was the only move, but then Black can proceed with 14 . . . P–K4 15 P–B3 (to stop 15 . . . Q–N5) 15 . . . P–N3! with . . . N–N1, . . . P–B3, . . . Q–KN2, . . . N–K2, . . . QR–N1 and . . . P–KN4 to follow. There really isn't much White can do about this K-side onslaught – he is in too much of a bind. But after the move played it's worse still.

14 . . .   P–R5

15 N–R1

What a disgrace.

15 . . .   P–K4 (42)

Preparing to take control of f4 and also opening the bomb bay doors for the black queen to blast the enemy king's fortress if necessary.

16 P–B4

Blocking the centre with 16 P–Q5 allows Black to display his attacking talent to the full e.g. 16 . . . N–R4! 17 P–N3 (to stop . . . N–B5 followed by . . . N×B and capture of the QBP; while if 17 B–B1 N–QN6 followed by . . . N×B and . . . N–B5) 17 . . . Q–R6 18 B–B1 P–B3! 19 B–Q2 (Or 19 P–N4 N–QN6 20 R–N1 N×B and 21 . . . N–B5, but not 19 . . . N–B5? 20 B×N P×B 21 P–B3! and 22 N–B2 winning the queen!) 19 . . . P–KN4 20 B–K1 QR–N1 21 R–R2 K–N1! 22 R–N2 B–B1! 23 R–R2 (Or 23 P–B3 N–B5 24 P×N NP×P+ 25 N–N3 RP×N and 26 . . . P–N7 winning) 23 . . . N–B5! 24 P×N NP×P+ 25 N–N3 Q×P!! 26 K×Q RP×N+ 27 K–N2 P×P+ 28 K×P R–R7+ 29 K–B3 B–N5 mate!

White not only has the K-side attack to worry about, but also the eternal problem of defending c4. White's text move prevents Black's plan of . . . N–R4–B5 at the cost of the exchange.

16 . . .   N–R4

17 BP×P

17 B–B1 N–QN6 18 R–R3 N×B 19 R×N N×P or 17 P–N3 RP×P 18 RP×P Q–R6 19 Q–N2 (19 R–B3 N×KBP!) 19 . . . Q×Q+ 20 K×Q B×P! both lose for White.

17 . . .   QP×P

18 P–Q5   N–B5

19 R×N

Forced, otherwise 19 . . . N×B and White's position falls apart at the seams.

19 . . .   P×R

20 P–K5

This position is what White wanted, but though it looks impressive Nisman is in for a disappointment.

20 . . .   P–R6

Gaining a few more inches to work in.

21 P–N4

Threatening to win the black queen with 22 B–B5. The alternative 21 P–N3 P×P 22 N×P K–N1 23 R–KB1 (23 N–K4 R–R5!) 23 . . . Q×RP 24 R×P B×P is hopeless for White.

21 . . .   K–N1

Preferring to stop the threat by tucking away his king rather than by transposing into the previous note by capturing en passant.

22 B–B1 (*43*)

Allowing a neat combination, but the obvious 22 N–B2 is dealt with by 22 . . . P–B6! 23 Q×P (23 Q–B1 Q–K1!) 23 . . . N×P! 24 B×N B×B 25 P–Q6 Q–K3 winning easily.

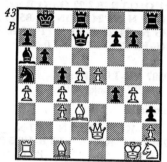

22 . . .   B×P!

23 B×B

If 23 B×P B×B 24 Q×B Q×QP 25 P–K6+ K–R1 decides.

23 . . .   N×B

24 Q×N

24 B×P still loses to 24 . . . Q×QP and 24 P–Q6 is 'bounced' by 24 . . . N×KP! 25 Q×N Q×NP+ 26 N–N3 (26 K–B2 Q–N7+ 27 K–K1 KR–K1 wins the queen) 26 . . . KR–K1 27 Q×KBP R–K8+ 28 K–B2 Q×Q+ 29 B×Q R×R with two pawns and two exchanges to Black's credit.

24 . . .   Q×NP+

25 N–N3

If 25 K–B2 Q–N7+

25 . . .   R–R5!

Not, of course, 25 . . . P×N?? – there are ranks as well as files in chess

26 Q×KBP

The best of three evils, the others being: 26 B×P P–KN4! and 26 Q–Q3 P×N 27 Q×P Q–K7! both of which are killing.

26 . . .   Q×Q

27 B×Q   R×B

28 R–Q1

Protecting d5 but since the QRP is now lost White could quietly resign.

28 . . .   P–N3

To play 29 . . . R×RP without allowing 30 N–B5.

29 R–Q2

If 29 P–R5 then simply 29 . . . P×P! and Black has a distant passed pawn with the white king shut right out of the game.

29 . . . R×RP 30 K–B2 Now at least the king can be centralized. **30 . . . R–QB5 31 R–Q3 P–R4 32 K–K3 R–K1 33 P–K6 P×P 34 P–Q6 R–Q1 35 N–K4 K–B1 36 N–B6 R–Q2!** White has done his best to make the most of his passed pawn, but his best just isn't good enough – d6 is as far as the pawn goes. **37 N×R K×N 38 K–Q2 R–KR5 39 K–B2 P–QN4 40 R–N3 K×P 41 R×NP R–KB5 42 K–N3 P–B5+ 43 K–R3 R–B6 44 K–N2 P–N5 45 P×P P×P 46 R–N4 K–Q4 0–1**

0505 AK–Peshina:

R5 v. Zhalgiris:

English

1 P–QB4 P–KN3 2 P–KN3 B–N2 3 B–N2 P–QB4 4 N–KB3 N–QB3 5 0–0 P–Q3 6 N–B3 P–KR4 7 P–Q3 N–R3 8 P–K4 0–0 9 P–KR3 R–N1

10 B–N5 P–R3 11 N–Q5 K–R2 12 R–B1 B–Q2 If 12 . . . B×NP 13 B×N! **13 P–R3 P–N4 14 P–QN4 P–B3?** This and his 17th move result in self-destruction of his pawn chain. **15 B–Q2 BP×P 16 RP×P P×P 17 P×P P–K3 18 N–B4** (*44*)

18 . . . **N×P 19 B×N R×B 20 Q×P R–N3 21 Q–R3 P–K4 22 N–Q5 R–B3 23 P–B5 P–R4 24 N–Q2 R–K1 25 N–QB4 B–KB1 26 N4–N6 N–N1 27 KR–Q1 B–K3** Black is hopelessly lost: his pieces are unable to co-operate and he has absolutely no counterplay. **28 Q×P Q–N1 29 N–N4 R–B2 30 N–R6 Q–R2 31 Q–N5 R1–B1** If 31 . . . R2–K2 32 P–B6 and 33 P–B7. **32 N/N6×R R×N 33 P–B6 1–0** Karpov really was just too strong for the majority of the other board six players.

0506 Kiprichnikov–AK:
    R6 v. Daugava:

Ruy Lopez

1 P–K4 P–K4 2 N–KB3 N–QB3 3 B–N5 P–QR3 4 B–R4 N–B3 5 0–0 B–K2 6 B×N QP×B 7 N–B3 N–Q2 8 P–Q4 P–B3 9 B–K3 Best is 9 N–K2! with the idea of using the knight on the K-side and making possible P–QB3 to bolster the centre. **9 . . . 0–0 10 Q–K2 Q–K1 11 N–KR4 P–KN3 12 N–B3 B–Q3 13 QR–Q1 R–B2 14**

N–Q2 P–QN4 15 P–B4 Assisting in the self-destruction of his pawn centre. **15 . . . P×QP 16 B×P P–QB4 17 B–K3 B–N2 18 P–QR4 P–N5** (*45*)

19 N3–N1 If 19 N–Q5 then 19 . . . P–B4 and White's position still falls apart. **19 . . . B×KP 20 N×B Q×N 21 Q–Q3 R–K2 22 Q×Q R×Q 23 B–Q2 N–N3 24 P–QN3 P–B5 25 P–R5 N–Q4 26 B–B1 N×P 27 K–B2 R1–K1 28 K–B3 N–K7 0–1**

0507 AK–Lisenko:
    R7 v. Lokomotiv:

Sicilian

1 P–K4 P–QB4 2 N–KB3 N–QB3 3 B–N5 P–KN3 4 P–B3 B–N2 5 0–0 N–B3 6 R–K1 0–0 7 P–KR3 Q–N3 8 N–R3 P–Q4 9 P–Q3 R–Q1 10 Q–K2 P–Q5 11 B×N P×B 12 P×P P×P 13 N–B4 Q–B2 14 B–Q2 P–QR4 15 R/K1–QB1 B–K3 16 Q–K1 A characteristic Karpov pile-up on a weak pawn, but Black fights his way out of trouble. **16 . . . B×N 17 R×B Q–N3 18 P–QN3 P–B4 19 R–R4 Q–N4** The counterattack on the QP saves Black. **20 N–K5 N–Q2 21 N–B4 N–K4 22 N×N B×N 23 Q–K2 B–B2 24 P–B4 Q–B3 25 R–QB1 Q–Q3 26 Q–B3 B–N3 27 P–B5 B–B2 28 K–B1** (*46*)
28 . . . **P×P** A surprising move, but Black still uses White's QP as a

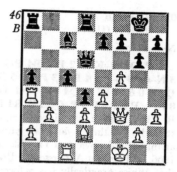

46
B

means of counterattack. 29 Q×P Q–
N6 30 Q–B3 Q×Q+ 31 P×Q B–
N3 32 K–B2 P–B3 33 R–KN1+ K–
B2 34 P–B4 P–K3 35 K–B3 P–B4 36
R–K1 K–B3 37 P×P P×P 38 P–R4
R–KN1 39 P–R3 R–R2 40 R–QB1
R1–QR1 41 P–R5 R–QB1 42 R4–
B4 R–K1 43 R–K1 R×R 44 B×R
R–QN2 45 P–N4 BP×P 46 P×P
P–R5 47 P–N5 P–R6 48 R–B2 R–R2
49 R–QR2 B–B4 50 P–N6 B×P 51
B–N4 R–R5 ½–½ After 52 B–Q6 (52
B×P? B–B4) and 53 R×P the
game is completely level.

0508 Tsikhelashvili–AK:
R8 v. Dinamo:

Vienna

**1 P–K4 P–K4 2 N–QB3 B–B4
3 Q–N4?** Apparently new at this
level – it must have been played
many times in games between rank
beginners. A similar line is known
with Black's KB on N5, then 3 Q–
N4!? N–KB3 4 Q×NP R–N1 5 Q–
R6 R–N3 6 Q–K3 N–B3 7 N–Q5
N–KN5 8 Q–Q3 B–B4 9 N–R3 P–
Q3∓ has made its way through the
hallowed portals of Keres' *Dreispring-
erspiel bis Königsgambit*, but the text
line is even weaker. **3 . . . N–KB3 4
Q×NP R–N1 5 Q–R6 B×P+ 6
K–Q1** Perhaps it would have been
better to get it over with: 6 K×B N–

N5+. **6 . . . R–N3 7 Q–R3 P–Q4 8
Q–Q3 B–N3 9 N×P N×N 10 Q×N
Q–B3 11 N–B3 N–B3 12 P–B3
B–N5** Already Black has a winning
position – not very surprising really.
**13 Q–Q3 Q–K2 14 P–KR3 B–Q2 15
P–KN4 0–0–0 16 Q–K2 P–KR4 17
P–N5 P–B4** (47)

47
W

**18 P–KR4 R–Q3 19 B–R3 P×P 20
Q×P B×B 21 R×B R–B1 22 P–
Q3 Q–Q2 23 R–N3 B–B7! 24 R–N2
R×P+ 25 N–Q2 R–K6 26 R×B
R×Q 27 R×R+ N–Q1 28 K–B2
R–K8 29 P–N3 P–K5 30 P–N6 Q–
N2 31 R×N+ K×Q 32 N×P
R×N 33 B–N5+ K–B1 34 R–Q1
P–N3 0–1**

0509 AK–Oleg Romanishin:
R9 v. Avangard:

QP – Richter–Veresov

**1 P–Q4 P–Q4 2 N–QB3 N–KB3 3
B–N5 P–B3 4 N–B3 N1–Q2 5 P–K3
P–KN3 6 B–Q3 B–N2 7 0–0 0–0 8
R–K1 R–K1 9 P–KR3 Q–N3 10
R–N1 P–KR4 11 B–K2 N–K5 12 B–
R4 P×P** An interesting possibility is
12 . . . N×N 13 P×N Q–R4!?
13 N×N P×N 13 . . . R×N!? was
worth considering. **14 N×P N–K4
15 P–QB4 P–QB4!?** With the idea
of freeing e6 for the use of his bishop

without allowing it to be exchanged e.g. 15 . . . B–K3 16 N×B R×N 17 P–QN4± But the text move weakens the Q-side and, especially, d5. **16 N–N5!** (*48*)

48
B

16 . . . B–K3 Probably better than 16 . . . P–QR3 when both 17 N–Q6!? and 17 N–B3 with N–Q5 to follow are good for White. **17 Q–R4 Q–B3** Threatening 18 . . . P–QR3 19 N–B3 N×P∓. **18 R/K1–QB1 P–KR3** Now 18 . . . P–QR3 19 N–B3 N×P meets with 20 B×N Q×Q 21 N×Q B×B 22 R×B P–N4 23 R×BP P×N 24 R–QR5±. **19 R–B2 P–N4 20 B–N3 R/K1–Q1 21 P–N4! P×P 22 Q×NP N–Q6 23 Q–R3 P–R3?!** Weakening b6. **24 N–B7 QR–B1 25 Q–R5 P–N4 26 N×B P×N 27 B–N4±± N–K4 28 B×N B×B 29 R1–QB1 R–Q3 30 P–N3** Creating an important flight square. **30 . . . Q–N3 31 Q–K1 P×P 32 R×P R×R 33 R×R Q–N2 34 Q–QB1 R–N3 35 R–B8+ K–N2 36 Q–B5 B–Q3 37 Q–B3+ P–K4 38 K–N2 R–N8 39 P–QR4** Preventing 39 . . . Q–N4 with 40 . . . Q–B8+ and 41 . . . Q–R8 mate to follow. **39 . . . Q–KB2 40 R–Q8 1–0** After 40 . . . B–K2 41 R–Q7 Q–B3 42 Q–B7 K–B1 43 Q–B8+ K–N2 44 Q–K8 Black has no way to continue his resistance.

0510 Reiman–AK:
   R10 v. IUD:

Nimzo–Indian

1 P–Q4 N–KB3 2 P–QB4 P–K3 3 N–QB3 B–N5 4 P–K3 P–B4 5 B–Q3 0–0 6 N–B3 P–Q4 7 0–0 N1–Q2 8 BP×P KP×P 9 P–QR3 B–R4 10 R–N1? Gligorić has since demonstrated in three famous games against Damjanović and Yanofsky in 1968, and against Andersson in 1971 that White practically has a forced win here e.g. Gligorić–Andersson, Berlin 1971, went 10 P–QN4! P×NP 11 N–QN5 P–QR3? (11 . . . N–N1 is a little better) 12 Q–N3! P×P 13 N–Q6 B–B2 14 B1×P B×N 15 B×B R–K1 16 KR–B1 17 R–K3 B–KB4! with a magnificent dividend already in sight for the paltry one pawn investment. **10 . . . B–B2 11 P–QN4 P×QP 12 P×P P–KR3 13 R–K1 R–K1 14 P–R3 R×R+ 15 Q×R N–B1 16 B–K3 B–Q2 17 Q–Q2 R–B1 18 N–K5 N–K3 19 B–B5 B×N 20 P×B P–Q5 21 P×NP P×B 22 Q×P Q×P 23 N–Q5 Q–Q1 24 R–Q1 P–QN3 25 N–B4 Q–K2 26 N–Q5 Q–K1 27 R–Q3 B–N4 28 Q–N3 Q–Q1 29 R–QB3 R×R 30 N×R B–B5 31 N–K4 B–Q4 32 N–B3 N–Q5 33 Q–K5?** (*49*) better 33 B–Q3

49
B

33 . . . B×P 34 K×B Q–N4+ 35 K–B1 N×B 36 Q–K4 Q–N3 37 Q–B3 0–1 (time)

0511 AK–Miklyaev:

R11 v. Burevestnik:

Ruy Lopez

1 P–K4 P–K4 2 N–KB3 N–QB3 3
B–N5 P–QR3 4 B–R4 P–Q3 5 P–B3
B–Q2 6 0–0 P–KN3 7 P–Q4 B–N2
8 P–KR3 N–B3 9 N1–Q2 0–0 10 R–
K1 R–K1 11 B–B2 P–R3 12 P–R3 K–
R2 13 N–B1 P–QN4 14 N–N3 N–
QR4 15 P–N3 P–B4 16 P–Q5 P–B5
17 P–N4 N–N2 18 B–K3 Q–B2 19 N–
R2 P–QR4 20 Q–Q2 R–R3 21 R–
KB1 R1–R1 22 QR–B1 P×P 23
RP×P N–N1 24 P–B4 P–B3 25 P–
R4 B–K1 26 N–N4 P–R4 27 N–R2
P×P 28 B×P N–Q1 29 Q–Q1 K–
R1 30 N–K2 N–B2 31 P–N4 N–K4
32 P×P P×P 33 N–N3 Q–B2 34
N–B3 N–N5 35 N–Q4 B–R3 36 Q–
Q2 B×B 37 Q×B N1–R3 38 N3–
B5 N×N 39 N×N Q–B1 40 B–Q1
N–K4 41 R–QB2 R–R7 42 R×R
R×R (*50*)

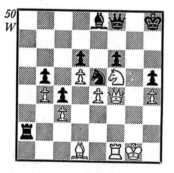

This position formed the subject of a
full-page article by Alexei Suetin in
the *Bulletin Tsentralnovo Shakhmatnovo
Kluba* (Central Chess Club Bulletin)
No. 11 1969, much of which appears
below.

43 N–N3!

The black pawns come under
heavy fire from the threats of 44
Q×P+ and 44 B×P.

43 . . .   Q–N2

The attempt to create something
on the back rank with 43 . . . R–R8
suffers a fiasco after 44 B×P R×R+
45 K×R and White wins easily.

All the same Black had an interesting possibility of creating counterplay with 43 . . . R–R6! immediately
attacking the vulnerable base of the
white pawn chain.

If White draws the queen off on
defence duty with 44 Q–Q2 then
Black immediately activates his
game by means of 44 . . . Q–N2!
threatening to seize the initiative.

The main variation occurs after 44
Q×P+ Q×Q 45 R×Q B–Q2!
(The first tactical nicety. 45 . . .
R×P is not so clear on account of 46
K–B2!) 46 R–R6+ (Enticing the
enemy king on to g8 or g7 where it
will come under fire from White's
knight.) 46 . . . K–N1 47 R×QP
R×P 48 N×P R–B8 49 N–B6+
K–B2!

An interesting tactical moment. In
case of 49 . . . K–N2 50 N×B R×B+
51 K–B2 P–B6 52 N×N P–B7 the
natural 53 N–Q3? is not good on
account of the unexpected combinational counter-stroke 53 . . . R–Q7+
and it becomes clear that White loses
after 54 K–K1 R×N as there is no
defence against the threat of . . . R–
Q8+ and . . . P–B8=Q. All the same
this line is inadequate for Black.
Instead of 53 N–Q3? White plays 53
R–QB6! P–B8=Q 54 R×Q R×R
55 K–K3 and the ending is lost for
Black.

50 N×B R×B+ 51 K–B2 K–K2!
(All this is forced. The analysis,
belonging to grandmasters Geller
and Furman, is correct.) 52 R–K6+
K×N (*51*)

53 K–K2!! (Already White has to
urgently think about his own salvation. 53 R×N is bad because of 53
. . . P–B6! and the pawn queens.)

51
W

53 . . . R–Q5 54 R × N P–B6 55 P–Q6 etc draws.

44 Q × P Q × Q 45 R × Q R–R8 46 R–B1 R–B8 47 N–K2! The start of the winning knight manoeuvre, gaining a tempo on its journey to f5. 47 . . . R–R8 48 N–Q4 K–N1 49 N–B5! R–R3 50 K–B2 And now the king successfully enters the action.

50 . . . B–N3 51 K–K3 B × N 52 P × B R–R7 53 K–Q4 R–R8 54 B–K2! R–R7 55 B × RP White already has a winning advantage. Black is defenceless against the advance of the KBP. 55 . . . R–R7 56 R–B4 R–Q7+ 57 K–K4 R–Q6 58 P–B6 R × BP 59 K–B5! An instructive moment in the realization of his advantage. The white king penetrates into Black's position and takes an active part in the decisive attack. 59 . . . R–K6 60 R–B1 N–Q2 61 R–KN1+ K–B1 62 R–QR1 R–K4+ 63 K–N6 R–K1 64 R–R7 R–Q1 65 R–B7! Indispensable accuracy. Karpov deprives his opponent of any hope of counterplay based on advancing his QBP. 65 . . . K–N1 66 K–N5 K–R1 67 B–N6 K–N1 68 P–R5 K–R1 69 P–R6 P–B6 70 R × P R–KB1 71 P–B7 1–0

	1						2						3						
1 **Karpov**	×	×	×	×	×	×	1	½	1	0	½	½	1	1	½	1	1	0	½	**7½**
2 Vaganian	0	½	0	1	½	½	×	×	×	×	×	×	½	1	½	0	1	½	**6**
3 Steinberg	0	½	0	0	1	½	½	0	½	1	0	½	×	×	×	×	×	×	**4½**

This event was held specifically for the purpose of determining who would represent the Soviet Union in the forthcoming World Junior Championship.

Karpov quite clearly established his superiority over his rivals.

The event took place in the Leningrad Palace of Pioneers 'imeni Zhdanova'.

0601 AK–Mikhail Steinberg:

Ruy Lopez

1 P–K4 P–K4 2 N–KB3 N–QB3 3 B–N5 P–QR3 4 B–R4 N–B3 5 Q–K2 P–QN4 6 B–N3 B–K2 7 P–B3 0–0 8 P–Q4 P–Q3 9 0–0 P×P?! 10 P×P B–N5 11 B–K3 N–QR4 If 11 ...N×KP 12 B–Q5! wins. 12 B–B2 N–B5 13 B–B1 P–B4 14 P–QN3 N–N3 15 B–N2 N/B3–Q2 16 P–QR4 NP×P?! 17 NP×P P–QR4 18 R–Q1 R–B1 19 N–R3 P–B5 20 B–B3 P–Q4 21 P–K5 B–N5 22 N–QN5 N–N1 23 P–R3 B–R4 24 Q–K3 White has been given enough rope ...he is using it to strangle Black. 24 ...N–B3 25 R–Q2 B×N 26 Q×B N–R1 27 R–QB1 N–B2 28 B–B5 N–K3 If 28 ...R–N1 29 N×N Q×N 30 Q×P wins. 29 Q–N4 Q–K2 30 P–B4 R–N1 31 K–R2 N–B2 32 N×N Q×N 33 Q–B3 N–K2 34 B–B2 P–B4 35 R–B1 Q–Q2 36 P–N3 Q–K3 37 R–N2 P–N3 38 P–N4 K–R1 39 R–N3 R–B2 40 Q–K3 R1–KB1 41 B–N2 Q–N3 42 R–N2 Q–QB3 43 R–B3 Q–K3 44 B–B1 Q–N3 45 K–R1 P×P? A remarkable move. His patience, waiting for the

end, must have been exhausted. 46 P×P N–B3 47 P–K6 R–K2 48 P–B5 Q×P 49 Q×Q+ N×Q 50 B–N2 P–B6 (52)

51 R×P! K–N1 52 R–K3 B–B4 53 R–K5 R–N1 54 B–B3 N×B 55 R×N P–Q5 56 B×RP B–Q3 57 R–Q5 1–0

0602 AK–Mikhail Steinberg:

Sicilian

1 P–K4 P–QB4 2 N–QB3 N–QB3 3 P–KN3 P–KN3 4 B–N2 B–N2 5 P–Q3 P–Q3 6 P–B4 P–K4 7 N–B3 N1–K2 8 0–0 0–0 9 K3 N–Q5 10 Q–Q2 N2–B3 11 QR–N1 B–N5 12 N–

Q5 N–K2 13 N5×N+ Q×N 14
P–B3 P×P? 15 B×P N×N+ 16
B×N B–K3 17 P–N3 QR–K1 18
R/N1–K1 P–N3 19 P–Q4 R–Q1 20
B–N2 P×P 21 P×P Q–Q2 22 Q–
N4 KR–K1 23 P–Q5 B–N5 24 R–B1
B–K4 25 R–B6 Q–K2 26 R1–B1
B×B 27 P×B Q–R5 28 Q–K1 Q–
B3 29 Q–Q2 Q–K2 30 R1–B3 R–
QB1 (53)

54
W

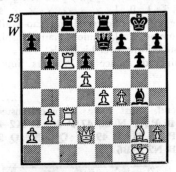

53
W

31 P–KR3! R×R If 31 ... B–Q2 32
R–B7. 32 P×R±± B–K3 33 R–Q3
R–Q1 34 K–R2 R–QB1 35 R×P Q–
B2 36 Q–Q4 Q–K2 37 K–N3 P–KR4
38 B–B1 P–R5+ 39 K–R2 Q–K1 40
Q–B6 Q–B1 41 P–K5 Q–K1 42
Q×RP K–N2 43 Q–B6+ 1–0

0603 AK–Mikhail Steinberg:

Sicilian

1 P–K4 P–QB4 2 N–QB3 N–QB3
3 P–KN3 P–KN3 4 B–N2 B–N2 5
P–Q3 P–Q3 6 P–B4 P–K3 Varying
with, as it turns out, good effect from
the previous game. 7 N–B3 N1–K2 8
0–0 0–0 9 B–K3 N–Q5 10 Q–Q2 P–
N3 11 QR–K1 B–N2 12 B–B2 Q–Q2
13 N×N If 13 N–Q1 Q–R5! is good
for Black. 13 ... P×N 14 N–K2 P–
K4 15 P–B3 QP×P 16 N×P QR–
Q1 17 K–R1 P–Q4 (54)
18 KP×P? Even worse than the
alternatives 18 Q–K2 QP×P 19

QP×P P×P 20 P×P Q–Q7!∓ and
18 BP×P P–Q5! both of which are
good for Black. 18...P×P 19 Q×P
N×P 20 Q–Q2 N×N 21 P×N B–
QR3 22 B–Q4 B×B 23 P×B Q×P
24 R–K7 B×P 25 R–Q1 Q–B3 26
R×RP B–K5 27 R–Q7 R×R 28
Q×R B–B4 29 Q–Q4 Q×Q 30
R×Q R–B1 31 P–KR4 R–B6 32
K–R2 R–R6 33 B–Q5 R–Q6 34 R×
R B×R 35 K–N2 K–N2 36 K–B3 B–
B4 37 K–B4 K–B3 38 P–N4 B–K3
39 P–N5+ K–K2 40 K–K5 B×B 41
K×B P–B4 42 K–K5 K–Q2 43 K–
Q5 K–B2 44 K–K5 K–B3 45 P–R5
P×P 46 K×P K–Q3 0–1
   The other three games against
Steinberg (in all of which Karpov
was   Black),   are   unfortunately
unavailable.

0604 Rafael Vaganian–AK: G1:

Queen's Indian

1 P–Q4 N–KB3 2 P–QB4 P–K3 3
N–KB3 P–QN3 4 P–K3 B–N2 5 B–
Q3 B–K2 6 0–0 P–B4 7 QN–Q2 P–
B3 8 P–QR3 P×P 9 P×P Q–Q4
10 P×P Q×P 11 B–B4 Q–Q3 12
N–N3 0–0 13 Q–K2 P–KR3 14 R–
Q1 KR–Q1 15 B–K3 QR–B1 16
QR–B1 N–Q4 17 B–Q2 P–QR4 18
R–B2 Q–N1 19 N–B1 N–N5 20
B×N Q×B 21 R2–Q2 B–B3 22 N–
Q3 Q–B2 23 N/Q3–K5 (55)

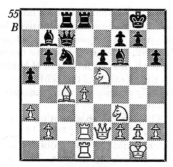

55
B

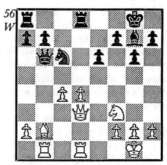

56
W

23 . . . N×P 24 R×N R×R 25 N×R Q×N 26 N–N5 Q×NP 27 N–Q6 Q×Q 28 B×Q R–B2 29 N×B R×N 30 P–QR4 R–B2 31 B– N5 R–B7 32 P–R3 P–N3 33 R–Q6 R–B8+ 34 B–B1 R–R8 35 R×NP R×P 36 P–N3 B–Q5 37 R–N8+ K– N2 38 B–K2 R–R7 39 K–B1 P–R5 40 R–N4 P–K4 41 R–N7 P–R6 42 R×P+ K–R1 43 R–B8+ K–N2 44 R–B7+ K×R 45 B–B4+ K–B3 46 B×R P–N4 47 P–B3 P–R4 48 K– K2 P–K5 49 P×P P–N5 50 P×P P×P 51 B–N3 B–K4 52 K–B2 K– K2 53 K–K3 B×P 54 K–Q4 B– K4+ **0–1** After 55 K×B P–N6 decides.

0605 AK–Rafael Vaganian: G2 :

Alekhine

1 P–K4 N–KB3 2 P–K5 N–Q4 3 P–Q4 P–Q3 4 N–KB3 P–KN3 5 B– K2 B–N2 6 0–0 0–0 7 P–QN3 N– QB3 8 P–B4 N–N3 9 P×P BP×P 10 B–N2 B–N5 11 Q–Q2 P–K3 12 N– R3 P–Q4 13 KR–Q1 P×P 14 N×PN×N 15 P×N Q–N3 16 QR– N1 B–B4 17 B–Q3 B×B 18 Q×B KR–Q1 (*56*)
19 P–Q5 B×B 20 Q–K2 P×P 21 P×P N–N5 22 R×B Q–B4 23 P– KR3 P–N3 24 P–Q6 R×P 25 R×R Q×R 26 Q–K4 N–Q4 27 R–Q2 R– Q1 28 N–K5 With the idea of 29 N– N4 and 30 R×N. 28 . . . Q–B4 29 Q–

B3 P–B4 30 P–KR4 R–Q3 31 R–Q1 K–N2 32 P–R5 K–B3 33 P×P P×P 34 Q–KN3 K–N2 35 Q–N5 R–K3 36 N–B3 N–B3 37 R–QB1 Q–K2 38 Q–B4 R–Q3 39 R–K1 N–K5 40 P– N4 Q–B3 41 P–N5 Q–K2 42 K–N2 K–N1 43 R–KR1 Q–KN2 44 R– QB1 Q–N2 45 R–KR1 ½–½ A most interesting position – Black is close to winning, but if he tries for the whole point he is liable to lose. Two intriguing variations are:
(a) 45 . . . N–Q7 46 Q×R Q×N+ 47 K–N1 (47 K–R2 Q×P+ 48 K– R3 Q–B6+) 47 . . . Q–Q8+ 48 K– N2 with perpetual, and
(b) 45 . . . R–Q6 46 Q–K5! Q–N2 47 Q–K8+ Q–B1 48 R–R8+ and White wins.

0606 Rafael Vaganian–AK: G3 :

Nimzo–Indian

1 P–Q4 N–KB3 2 P–QB4 P–K3 3 N–QB3 B–N5 4 P–K3 0–0 5 N–B3 P–B4 6 B–K2 P–Q4 7 0–0 QN–Q2 8 BP×P KP×P 9 Q–N3

A similar position arose in one of the games of the 1968 Candidates match between Korchnoi and Tal, in which White had developed his KB not on K2 but on Q3. Tal played 9 . . . N–N3 and after 10 N–K2 P–QR4 11 P×P N/N3–Q2 12 P–QR3 N×P 13 B×P+ White had the better position.

9 ...　　　　　　　　B×N

Black parts with the bishop, but in exchange secures control of the square e4 with gain of tempo. In the event of 10 P×B P–B5 the position takes on a closed character and White's two bishops cannot generate activity.

If Black, by analogy with the Korchnoi–Tal game, continues with 9 ... N–N3 then 10 N–N1 P–QR4 11 P–QR3 P–B5 12 Q–B2 B–Q3 13 N–B3 would have given White some advantage in connection with the weakening of his opponent's Q-flank.

10 Q×B　　　　　　N–K5
11 Q–B2　　　　　　P–QN3
12 P×P

After 12 P–QN3 B–N2 13 B–N2 R–B1 this move would have been forced.

12 ...　　　　　　　P×P
13 P–QN3　　　　　B–N2
14 B–N2　　　　　　R–B1
15 KR–Q1

A superficial move. 15 N–Q2, to exchange the active black knight and giving more room for the bishops, is stronger. If 15 ... P–B4 then there could have followed 16 P–B3 Q–N4 (as Karpov intended to play) 17 P–B4 with the better game for White.

15 ...　　　　　　　Q–K2
16 QR–B1　　　　　P–B4 (57)

57
W

17 N–K1?

An unfortunate move. White does not think about the initiative, but prepares, by means of P–KN3 and N–KN2, to set up a defensive barrier on the K-side with the aim of holding up the advance of the KBP. Karpov skilfully exposes the disadvantages of this plan.

The logical continuation was 17 P–QN4. After 17 ... P×P 18 Q–R4 Black would have been obliged to go over entirely to defence. The extra pawn does not play a significant role, and what is more it is impossible to keep it. For example 18 ... N2–B4 19 Q×RP R–R1 20 Q–N6 R×P 21 Q×P N×P 22 B–Q4, or 18 ... P–QR3 19 P–QR3.

Seemingly Black was compelled to reply 17 ... P–B5 against which 18 B–Q4 gives White quite good chances.

17 ...　　　　　　　Q–R5
18 P–N3　　　　　　Q–R3
19 N–N2　　　　　　K–R1!

Creating the threat 20 ... P–Q5. If then 21 P×P there follows 21 ... P×P 22 Q–Q3 N×BP 23 K×N Q×P 24 R–KN1 (24 B–KB3 N–K4) 24 ... N–K4 25 Q×QP N–N5+ 26 K–B1 R×R+ 27 B×R Q×P (threat 28 ... N–R7 mate) 28 B×N P×B+ 29 N–B4 B–R3+ wins.

20 Q–Q3　　　　　　QR–K1

Because White no longer has the move B–N5 Karpov develops the rook on to the K-file, again threatening the move 21 ... P–Q5. On 22 P×P there comes 22 ... N×BP 23 K×N Q×P 24 R–KN1 (or 24 B–KB3) 24 ... P–KB5! with a winning attack.

In the event of 21 B–KB3 Black continues just the same with 21 ... P–Q5 22 P×P B–R3 23 Q–B2 (or 23 Q–B3) 23 ... N–N4∓.

In order to liquidate the attack White should play 21 P–B4, abandoning the square e4 to the opposing knight, but Vaganian decides against this and prefers the following weakening of position which leads to bankruptcy.

21 P–B3   **N–N4** (*58*)

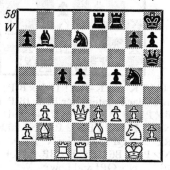

22 N–B4

Black's task would have been more difficult after 22 P–KR4. As the variations given below show, Black must still win: 22 . . . N–R6+ 23 K–B1 P–Q5 24 P×P (24 P–B4 Q–QB3) 24 . . . P–KB5.

How does White continue now? Let us say 25 P–KN4, but now 25 . . . R–K6 26 P–N5 (26 N×R Q×P and White cannot avoid mate) 26 . . . Q–R4 27 N×P R×N 28 Q×R B×P 29 K–K1 B×B wins.

If 25 QP×P there follows 25 . . . P×P and on 26 Q×N B×P is decisive. If instead 26 P–B6 B×P 27 R×B Q×R 28 Q×N then 28 . . . R×P+ 29 K–K1 R×B+ 30 K×R Q–K5+ and mates.

In the event of 25 P–Q5 P×P and White again cannot hold the position.

22 . . .   **P–Q5**
23 P–KR4

If 23 P×P Black sacrifices the exchange with 23 . . . R×B, obtaining a winning position. Thus 24 Q×R N×P+ 25 K–B1 N×RP+ 26 K–B2 N–B3 27 P–Q5 R–K1 28

N–K6 N7–N5+ 29 K–K1 (29 K–N1 R×N!) 29 . . . B×P 30 R×B Q–R8+ forces White's resignation.

23 . . . B×P 24 P×P N–R6+ 25 N×N B×B 26 Q–Q2 R–K6 27 K–R2 N–B3 28 N–B4 N–N5+ 29 K–N2 B–B6+ 30 K–N1 B×R 0–1

0607 AK–Rafael Vaganian: G4:

Alekhine

1 P–K4   **N–KB3**
2 P–K5

2 N–QB3 loses the initiative fast after 2 . . . P–Q4 3 P–K5 P–Q5.

2 . . .   **N–Q4**

The only move as everybody knows. But does everybody know what to do after 2 . . . N–K5? It goes like this 3 P–QN4! P–K3 4 P–QB3! Q–R5 5 Q–K2 P–KB4 6 P–Q3 N–N4 7 P–N3 Q–R3 8 B–B4! Q–N3 9 P–KR4 N–B2 10 P–R5 Q–N5 11 P–B3 – no comment!

3 P–Q4   **P–Q3**
4 N–KB3

Most modern masters tend to distrust the big pawn centre obtained after 4 P–QB4 N–N3 5 P–B4 though recently Velimirović, possibly the fiercest attacking player in the world, has dressed it up to make it look quite attractive (if you like that sort of thing): 5 . . . P×P 6 BP×P N–B3 7 B–K3 B–B4 8 N–QB3 P–K3 9 N–B3 B–K2?! 10 P–Q5! N–N5 11 R–B1! P–KB3 12 P–QR3 N–R3 13 P–KN4!?± Velimirović–Gipslis, Havana 1971.

4 . . .   **P–KN3**

In the last few years this has become at least as popular as the older 4 . . . B–N5.

5 B–K2

Later Karpov abandoned this for 5 B–QB4 as in his fine win against Grigorian in the 1971 USSR Ch.

5 . . .   **B–N2**

6 P–B4   N–N3

7 P×P

Black's pressure on the centre forces this exchange.

7 . . .   BP×P

Not 7 . . . KP×P when 8 B–N5! messes things up for Black after 8 . . . P–B3 or 8 . . . Q–Q2 and prevents castling on 8 . . . B–B3 9 B–R6.

8 P–KR3

To prevent 8 . . . B–N5 which puts more strain on White's defence of the centre. Browne–Fischer, Rovinj-Zagreb 1970, continued instead with 8 N–B3 0–0 9 0–0 N–B3 10 B–K3 B–N5 11 P–QN3 P–Q4 12 P–B5 N–B1! 13 P–KR3 (13 P–N4! is best) 13 . . . B×N 14 B×B P–K3 15 Q–Q2 N1–K2 16 N–N5? (16 N–K2) 16 . . . N–B4! 17 B–N4 P–QR3 18 B×N P×N! with a won position which clearly illustrates the strategy.

8 . . .   0–0

9 0–0   N–B3

10 N–B3   B–B4

For 10 . . . P–Q4 see the notes to game 0609.

11 B–B4

The Karpov variation.

11 . . .   P–KR3!

12 R–B1?

It was through the bad experience of this game that Karpov switched to 12 B–K3 in later games.

12 . . .   P–K4!

13 B–K3

13 P×P P×P 14 B–K3 N–Q5! is beautiful for Black.

13 . . .   P–K5!

14 N–Q2   R–K1 (59)

Black's clever idea is that if now 15 P–KN4 Q–R5! 16 P×B P×P leaves White in a jam e.g. 17 N–N3 P–B5 18 B–Q2 P–B6 19 B×BP P×B 20 Q×P N×BP with a winning position.

After 15 P–KN4 Q–R5! White can, instead of taking the bishop, try protecting his KRP with 16 K–R2

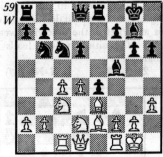

59
W

(If 16 K–N2 K–R2!! 17 P×B P×P and Black mates after both 18 P–B4 B×P! 19 B×B R–KN1+ and 18 N–N3 P–B5 19 B–Q2 R–KN1 20 K–R2 N×QP! 21 N×N B×N 22 N×P P–B6! 23 B×BP B–K4+) 16 . . . N×QP! and now:

(a) 17 B×N B×B 18 P×B B–K4+ 19 K–N2 (If 19 K–N1 Q×RP 20 P–B4 B–Q5+ wins) 19 . . . Q–N4+ 20 B–N4 (Or 20 K–R1 Q–B5!) 20 . . . P×P and Black wins.

(b) 17 P×B B–K4+ and then:

(b1) 18 K–N1 Q×RP 19 P–B4 KP×Pep 20 R×P (If 20 N×P Q–N6+ 21 K–R1 N×N∓∓) 20 . . . B–R7+ 21 K–B2 Q–R5+! 22 K–N2 N×R 23 N×N Q–N6+ 24 K–B1 R×B∓∓;

(b2) 18 K–N2 N×KBP! 19 Q–K1 (If 19 B×N Q–N4+ 20 B–N4 N–R5+ 21 K–R1 Q–B5 leads again to mate) 19 . . . N×B+ 20 P×N Q–N4+ 21 K–R1 Q×P and White will soon drown in a sea of pawns.

15 N–N3

Covering d4 and somewhat relieving the congestion.

15 . . .   P–Q4!

16 P×P

16 P–B5 would only leave Black's centre intact and consolidated. 16 N×QP transposes into the game continuation after 16 . . . N×N 17 P×N N–N5.

16 . . .   N–N5!

Black wants to blockade the isolated QP with a knight, not with the queen which could easily be driven away.

17 Q–Q2   N5×QP

17 . . . K–R2, safeguarding his KRP, was also quite playable, since 18 N×P N×RP!, but Vaganian is not noted for his lack of imagination and is always eager to sharpen the conflict at every available opportunity.

18 N–B5

Karpov does not care to try the free sample with 18 N×N N×N 19 B×P when 19 . . . P–K6! 20 B×P N×B 21 P×N B–R3 (21 . . . Q–N4 22 R–QB3 B×RP 23 B–B3! leads to nothing for Black) 22 R–QB3 R–QB1! 23 R–B3 B–K5 24 R–N3 Q–Q3 25 K–B2 P–B4! with . . . P–B5 to follow is very dangerous.

18 . . .   N×B!

Thereby weakening both White's K-side and the dark squares.

19 P×N   Q–N4

Using the threat of 20 . . . B×RP to gain time for some even more unpleasant tactics later.

20 K–R1

Not 20 K–R2 QR–Q1 21 R–QB2 B–K4+ 22 K–R1 Q–N6 23 R–B4 P–N4! winning.

20 . . .   QR–Q1

The QP is now menaced owing to the unprotected state of the white queen.

21 R–QB2

Breaking the pin on his KP and foreseeing that the rook could be useful on the second row in defending his king.

21 . . .   Q–N6

22 . . . B–K4 is the idea.

22 Q–B1

This time breaking the pin on the QP. Of course 22 Q–K1 loses a pawn, and then another pawn . . .

22 . . .   N–Q4!

23 N×N

If 23 N–Q1 to protect the KP then 23 . . . N–N5 24 R–QB4 B×RP! 25 P×B Q×RP+ 26 K–N1 Q–N6+ 27 K–R1 R–Q4 28 N–B2 R–N4! 29 B–N4 R1–K4!! 30 P×R B×P and it's all over.

23 . . .   R×N

Now the rook is in position to assist in wrapping up the game with 24 . . . B×RP 25 P×B Q×RP+ 26 K–N1 R–N4+ 27 K–B2 Q–N6 mate.

24 B–N5

Clearing the way for White's QR to stop the mate, 24 B–Q1 does not exactly serve the same purpose as 24 . . . B×RP! 25 P×B Q×RP+ 26 R–R2 Q×R/B8 mate.

24 B–B4 was another try but 24 . . . R×N! 25 B×P+ (If 25 P×R B–K4 26 K–N1 Q–R7+ 27 K–B2 B–N6+ 28 K–K2 Q×NP+ 29 K–Q1 Q×P and Black will prove that his pawns and bishops are too much for the white heavy brigade.) 25 . . . K×B 26 R×R B–KB1! 27 R–B7+ R–K2 28 Q–B4+ K–N2 and the everlasting . . . B–Q3 motif makes Black the winner again.

24 . . .   R–QB1

Itching to play 25 . . . P–N3.

25 B–R4

25 B–B4 still goes down to 25 . . . R4×N 26 B×P+ K×B 27 R×R R×R 28 Q×R Q×KP! with the bishops and the KP this time battering White to defeat. So the refugee KB wanders to a4 to save its skin.

25 . . .   P–N3! *(60)*

A good move – falling into a trap!

26 N×P

Neither 26 B–N3 R4×N! nor 26 N–R6 R×R 27 B×R B×RP was preferable.

26 . . .   B×N!

A case of the trapper being

60
W

trapped – Black allows his rook to be captured with check, but he has calculated right to the end.

27 R×R+ K–R2
28 R–QB2

Stopping the threatened disaster on g2 e.g. 28 R–N1 Q×RP mate, or 28 Q–Q2 Q×RP+ 29 K–N1 Q×R with a bishop bonus.

28 . . . R–KR4
29 K–N1 R×P
30 R×P

White has to do something about 30 . . . Q–R7+ 31 K–B2 Q×P+ and 30 R1–B2 is no good because of 30 . . . R–R7! 31 Q–Q2 Q–R6! 32 K–B1 (32 P×Q?? R–R8 mate) 32 . . . R–R8+ 33 K–K2 Q–N5+ 34 R–KB3 Q×P+ 35 R–B2 Q–N5+ and wins.

30 . . . Q–R7+ 31 K–B1 Q–R8+ 32 K–K2 Q×P+ 33 R–B2 If 33 K–K1 R–R8+ mates. **33 . . . Q–N5+ 34 K–Q2 R–R8** All this was forced, and so will Karpov's resignation very shortly since his queen is lost. **35 Q×R** Or 35 R–B1 Q–N7+ 36 K–B3 and 36 . . . Q×R/B8 decides. **35 . . . B×Q 36 B–N3 B–B6 37 B–K6 Q×B 38 B×B P–KN4 39 R–QB7 K–N3 40 R×P P–N5 41 R–B1 P–R4 42 R–R6 P–N6 43 P–R4 B–R3 44 R–B3 P–R5 0–1** A game of some interest!

0608 Rafael Vaganian–AK: G5: Nimzo–Indian

1 P–Q4 N–KB3 2 P–QB4 P–K3 3 N–QB3 B–N5 4 P–KN3 P–B4 5 P–Q5 N–K5 6 Q–B2 Q–B3 7 N–R3 N×N 8 B–Q2 N×QP 9 P×N B×B+ 10 Q×B P–K4 11 P–Q6 N–B3 12 B–N2 N–Q5 13 R–Q1 0–0 14 N–N5 Q–N3 15 N–K4 P–N3 16 P–K3 N–B3 17 N×P P×N 18 B×N *(61)*

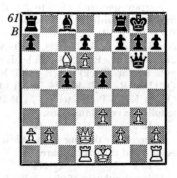

61
B

18 . . . R–N1 If 18 . . . P×B 19 P–Q7. 19 B–B3 Q–B4 20 B–K2 Q–R6 21 B–B1 Q–K3 22 P–N3 B–N2 23 B–B4 Q–R6 24 B–Q5 B–R3 25 R–QB1 KR–B1 26 Q–R5 B–Q6 27 Q–Q2 B–N4 28 P–B3 R–N3 29 B–B4 B×B 30 R×B R1–B3 31 Q–QB2 P–N3 Meeting the threat of 32 R–KR4. 32 K–B2 R×QP 33 R×P R/N3–B3 34 P–QN4 P–KR4 35 P–K4 P–R5 36 P–N4 R–B3 37 Q–K2 R×R 38 P×R Q×NP 39 R–QN1 Q–R6 40 K–K3 P–N4 41 R–N1 R–KN3 42 R–N4 K–B1 43 P–R4 R–QB3 44 Q–Q2 Q–B8 45 R×NP Q–QR8 46 K–B2 K–K2 47 R–B5 R–KN3 48 R×BP+ K×R 49 Q×P+K–B1 50 Q–Q8+ K–B2 51 Q–Q7+ K–N1 52 Q–Q8+ K–N2 53 Q–K7+ K–N1 ½–½

0609 AK–Rafael Vaganian: G6:

Alekhine

1 P–K4 N–KB3 2 P–K5 N–Q4 3
P–Q4 P–Q3 4 N–KB3 P–KN3 5
P–B4 N–N3 6 P×P BP×P 7 P–
KR3 His customary choice since
faring badly, though he eventually
drew, with 7 B–K2 B–N2 8 0–0 0–0 9
P–QN3 N–B3 10 B–N2 B–N5.
7 . . . B–N2 8 B–K2 0–0 9 N–B3 N–
B3 10 0–0 B–B4 11 B–B4 (*62*)

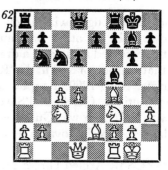

The Karpov variation. The previously known moves were 11 P–QN3
which wastes one tempo too many
and allows 11 . . . P–Q4! 12 P–B5
N–Q2 13 B–N2 B–K5 14 N–QR4
P–K4!∓ Minev–Bobotsov, Varna
1968, and 11 B–K3 P–Q4 12 P–B5
N–B5 13 B×N P×B 14 Q–R4 B–Q6
15 KR–Q1 when Black's safest is 15
. . . Q–R4 16 Q×Q N×Q=
Bouwmeester–Blau, Adelboden 1969.
The idea behind Karpov's move is
to maintain central tension for as
long as possible, and thus limit
Black's ability to inaugurate counterplay.
Theory has developed as follows:
11 . . . P–KR3! 11 . . . P–Q4 was
disastrous for Black in Karpov–
McKay, Stockholm 1969. **12 B–K3**
12 R–QB1 proved a tactical failure
in the sparkling fourth game Karpov–Vaganian, while 12 Q–Q2

P–N4! Adorjan–Eales, Groningen
1970, is quite satisfactory for Black.
12 . . . P–Q4 13 P–QN3 Here is the
substance of Karpov's idea. 13 P–B5
is also possible but failed rather
miserably in Stean–Timman, Isling-
ton 1970, its one outing so far.
13 . . . P×P 14 P×P R–B1 14 . . .
N–R4 seems to be inferior, though it
need not be quite so bad as in
Karpov–Neckar. **15 R–B1 N–R4 16
P–B5 N3–B5 17 B–B4 P–KN4**
Boleslavsky recommends 17 . . .
P–K4! as equalizing. **18 B–N3 Q–Q2
19 B×N** Karpov could have obtained some advantage with 19 R–
K1 followed by N–K5. **19 . . . N×B
20 Q–K2 Q–K3 21 KR–K1 Q×Q
22 R×Q P–K3 23 N–K4 B×N 24
R×B N–R4 25 B–K5 KR–Q1 26
R–N1 R–Q4 27 R–N5 P–N3** (*63*)

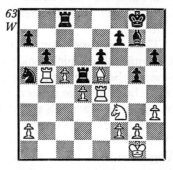

**28 B×B K×B 29 R–K5 N–B5 30
R×R P×R 31 P×P N×P 32 R–R5
R–B8+ 33 K–R2 R–B2 34 N–K5
K–B3 35 N–N4+ K–B4 36 R–B5
R–K2 37 N×P+ K–K5 38 R–B1
K–Q6** Not 38 . . . K×P?? 39 N–
B5+ **39 K–N3 P–B3 40 R–B6 R–K7
41 N–B5 R×RP 42 R×P R–N7 43
K–N4 P–R4 44 R–B7 N–B1 45 R–
B8 N–N3 46 R–B7 R×P 47 P–N3
N–B1 48 R–Q7 K–K5 49 R–QB7
R×N 50 R×N R–B8 51 R–QR8
R–QR8 52 K×P K×P 53 P–R4**
½–½

7 1969 MISCELLANY

This section contains games from three separate events: a match between junior teams of the USSR and Yugoslavia, the 'Red Armies' team tournament in Warsaw, and the USSR Armed Forces Team Championship.

The first two games are from the USSR-Yugoslavia match for juniors, played during April in Moscow. In the other two games from this event, Karpov, on board three, scored a win and a draw.

The third game is the only game that Karpov played in the 'Red Armies' team tournament in Warsaw, May 1969. Karpov was reserve for the Soviet team of Geller, Lutikov, Gufeld and Savon. The event was won by the USSR with 11½/12 (it was Gufeld who let the team down!) ahead of Poland 6, Czechoslovakia 4, and Cuba 2½.

The other three games are from the USSR Armed Forces Team Championship which took place at Leningrad in June(?). Karpov won the board prize for second board (Furman played on board one) ahead of three masters and four candidate masters. The event was won by Karpov's team: Leningrad.

The Official USSR ranking list appeared on the 1st of March 1969. This listed the top ten juniors: 1 Balashov, 2 Belyavsky, 3 Vaganian, 4 Karpov etc.

0701 Evrosimovsky–AK:

Hungarian

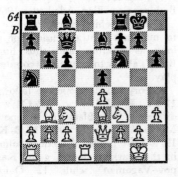

1 P–K4 P–K4 2 N–KB3 N–QB3 3 B–B4 P–Q3 4 P–Q3 B–K2 5 P–KR3 N–B3 6 N–B3 N–QR4 7 B–N3 0–0 8 0–0 P–KR3 9 B–K3 P–B3 10 P–Q4 Q–B2 11 P×P P P×P 12 Q–K2 P–QN3 13 KR–Q1 (*64*)

13 ... N–N2! 14 N–K1 N–B4 15 P–B3 In protecting K4 and making room for his queen on KB2 White weakens KN3. 15 ... B–R3 16 Q–B2

KR–Q1 **17 N–R4 N×N 18 B×N N–R4! 19 P–KN3** Another pawn move, this time to stop an entry at f4. **19 . . . R–Q3 20 R×R Q×R 21 P–B3** White wants to develop his rook on d1, but now d3 and half of b3 is left unprotected. **21 . . . Q–K3! 22 K–R2 B–B5! 23 P–R3** cuts off White's KB, while 23 P–QN4 loses the c4 square. The move played deserts b3. **23 . . . N–B3** Having done its duty on h5, the knight has further work to do in the centre. **24 R–Q1 N–K1 25 B–B2 N–Q3 26 N–Q3 P–KB4 27 N–N4 P×P 28 P×P R–KB1 29 Q–N2 N–B2! 30 B–Q3 B–KN4 31 B–KN1** If 31 B×B/N5 N×B, striking at the weaknesses at h3, f3 and e4. **31 . . . P–KR4! 32 Q–K2 B–N6** A reward for his 22nd move. **33 R–KB1 P–R5 34 P–N4** The unconditional surrender of f4. **34 . . . B–KB5+ 35 K–N2 R–Q1 36 B–K3** (*65*)

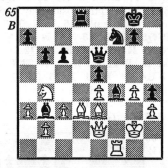

65
B

36 . . . P–B4 37 B×B P×B 38 N–Q5 An unfortunate necessity – White loses at once after 38 N–B2 P–B5 or 38 N–R6 N–K4. **38 . . . B×N 39 P×B Q×QP+ 40 B–K4 Q–Q7 41 R–B2 Q×Q 42 R×Q N–N4 43 P–B4** What has d4 done to deserve this? **43 . . . R–Q5 44 B–N7** Or 44 B–Q5+ R×B 45 P×R P–B6+. **44 . . . K–R2 45 R–K5 K–R3 46 R–Q5 R×P 47 R–Q6+ P–N3 48 B–R6**

P–B6+ 0–1 White has had enough – after 49 K–N1 R–B8+ 50 K–R2 (50 K–B2 N–K5+) 50 . . . R–B7+ 51 K–R1 N–K5 52 R–Q1 N–N6+ 53 K–N1 R–N7 mate.

0702 AK–Evrosimovsky:

English

1 P–QB4 P–KB4 2 N–QB3 N–KB3 3 P–KN3 P–K4 4 B–N2 N–B3 5 N–B3 B–K2 6 P–Q4 P–K5 7 N–KN5 0–0 8 0–0 Q–K1 9 P–B5 P–KR3 10 N–R3 P–Q4 11 R–N1 N–Q1 12 P–QN4 P–B3 13 B–B4 P–KN4 14 B–K5 Q–R4 15 P–B4 P–N5 16 N–B2 Q–N3 17 Q–N3 P–KR4 18 B×N B×B 19 P–K3 P–R5 20 KR–B1 K–N2 21 P–N5 R–R1 22 P–R4 Q–R4 23 N–K2 N–K3 24 N–R1 R–R2 25 K–B2 B–Q2 26 Q–R2 Q–B2 27 R–N1 P–R6 28 B–B1 K–R3 29 P–N6 (*66*)

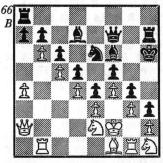

66
B

What crime did Black's light-squared bishop commit to merit such a fate? **29 . . . P×P 30 R×P R–R2 31 Q–N3 B–B1 32 Q–N4 B–Q1 33 P–R5 B×R 34 RP×B R–R7 35 K–K1 B–Q2 36 N–B2 Q–B1 37 N–B1 R–R8 38 K–Q2 Q–QR1 39 N–Q1** The charge of the light brigade was never like this; this is more like a dressage event. **39 . . . R–R1 40 N–B3 Q–R6 41 Q×Q R×Q 42 K–B2 R1–R1 43 B–K2 K–N2 44 K–N2 K–B3 45 N–**

N3 B–K1 46 R–QB1 K–K2 47 B–Q1 B–Q2 48 R–R1 R×R 49 N×R N–N2 50 B–N3 R–R4 51 B–B2 N–R4 Suddenly a threat. **52 N–K2 N–B3 53 B–N3 B–K3 54 B–Q1 N–Q2 55 N–N3 R–R1 56 N–B3 N–N1 57 N–B1 N–R3 58 N–R4 N–N1 59 K–R3 N–Q2** Also playable, strictly for fun, is 59 . . . B–B1 followed by 60 . . . K–K1! **60 K–N4 N–B1 61 N–N3 N–N3 62 N–Q2 N–R5 63 N–B1 N–B6 64 B–B2 K–B3 65 B–N1 B–Q2 66 B–B2 N–K8 67 B–N1 R–K1 68 K–B3 K–N3 69 N–Q2 K–R4 70 N–B1 R–QR1 71 K–N4** $\frac{1}{2}$–$\frac{1}{2}$

The other two games from the same match are, unfortunately, unavailable.

0703 AK–Konikowski:
Catalan

1 P–Q4 N–KB3 2 N–KB3 P–Q4 3 P–QB4 P–K3 4 N–B3 B–K2 5 P–KN3 0–0 6 B–N2 QN–Q2 7 0–0 P×P 8 P–K4 P–B3 9 P–QR4 P–QR4 10 Q–K2 N–N3 11 R–Q1 N/B3–Q2 12 B–B4 B–N5 13 N–Q2 Q–K2 14 B–K3 R–Q1 15 N×P N×N 16 Q×N N–N3 17 Q–N3 B–Q2 18 N–R2 P–QB4 19 N×B RP×N If 19 . . . BP×N there follows 20 P–Q5! N–B1 21 P–Q6! with the idea that if 21 . . . N×P White gets a decisive advantage from 22 B–B5 B–B3 23 P–K5. **20 P×P N×P** (67)

67
W

21 P–K5! R/Q1–N1 Nor are the alternatives very palatable:
(a) 21 . . . N×BP 22 B×N Q×B 23 R×R R×R 24 R×B±±
(b) 21 . . . Q–K1 22 P–B6! B×P 23 R×R!±±
(c) 21 . . . B–K1 22 R×R R×R 23 R×N±±

22 P–B6! B×P 23 B×B P×B 24 R×N P–QB4 25 R×R R×R 26 Q–B4 1–0

0704 AK–E. Kogan:
Sicilian

1 P–K4 P–QB4 2 N–KB3 N–QB3 3 B–N5 P–KN3 4 0–0 B–N2 5 P–B3 N–B3 6 R–K1 0–0 7 P–KR3 P–QR3 8 B–B1 P–QN4?! However 8 . . . P–Q3 9 P–Q4 P×P 10 P×P P–K4 11 N–B3±, **9 P–QR4 P–N5 10 P–Q3 P–Q3 11 QN–Q2 N–Q2 12 P×P N×P 13 P–R5 B–N2 14 N–B4 B–QB3 15 B–Q2 B–N4 16 P–Q4±** Black's attempted Q-side play begins to look a little silly. **16 . . . N–QB3 17 P–Q5 N3–K4 18 N3×N N×N 19 N–N6 R–R2 20 B–B3 N–Q2 21 N–B4 B×B 22 P×B B×N 23 B×B N–K4 24 B–B1 P–B5 25 Q–Q4** Making the advance P–KB4 safe. **25 . . . R–N2 26 R–R4 R–N4 27 R1–R1 R–B4** (68)

68
W

28 P–B4 N–Q6 29 R×P! R×R 30 Q×R N–B4 31 Q–N4 Q–B2 32 R–

N1 R–B1 33 K–R2 Q–Q2 34 B–K2
P–R4 35 Q–Q4 Q–R5? 36 Q × Q
N × Q 37 B × QRP R–R1 38 R–QR1
Of course. 1–0 on time.

0705 AK–Nebolsin:

Sicilian

1 P–K4 P–QB4 2 N–KB3 N–QB3
3 B–N5 P–KN3 4 0–0 B–N2 5 P–B3
P–QR3 6 B × N 6 B–R4 P–QN4 7
B–N3 P–K4 8 P–Q4 is a sharp
alternative. Karpov prefers the line
with a clear strategic plan. 6 . . .
QP × B 7 P–Q3 N–B3 White now
does best to restrict the mobility of
Black's KB and to fix Black's Q-side
weaknesses e.g. 8 P–QR4 P–QR4 9
N–R3 0–0 10 R–K1 P–N3 11 Q–K2
Q–B2 12 P–K5 N–Q4 13 P–R3 P–R3
14 N–B2 K–R2 15 P–B4 N–N5 16
P–QN3 N × N 17 Q × N R–Q1 18
B–N2 B–B4 19 QR–Q1 R–R2 20 N–
R4 with White making plans for a
K-side attack, and Black . . . planning passive defence – he has absolutely no counterplay either in the
centre or on the Q-side, Dzhindzhikhashvili–Taimanov, Spartakiad 1967.
But Karpov doesn't seem to have
been aware of this game. 8 P–KR3
0–0 9 Q–K2 P–QR4 10 B–B4 P–R5
Apparently Nebolsin has seen the
game! 11 N–R3 R–K1 12 KR–Q1
N–Q2 13 P–Q4 P × P 14 P × P Q–R4
15 QR–B1 N–N3 Black is beginning
to sneak round the edges. 16 B–B7
Q–R3 17 Q–K3 P–KB4!? (*69*)

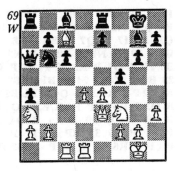

18 P–Q5? Better 18 B × N! Q × B 19
N–B4 with quite a good position.
18 . . . KBP × P 19 B × N P × N 20
P–Q6 Q–K7 21 P–Q7 B × P 22
R × B Q × Q 23 P × Q B × P The
point. 24 R–B4 B × N 25 R × NP
P × P 26 K × P B–Q3 27 R × BP
R/K1–QB1 28 B–B7 P–R6 29 K–B3
R–R4 30 P–K4 R–KN4 31 B × B
Black was threatening to creep round
to QR8 and then start a war on c7.
31 . . . R × R 32 B × KP R–B6+ 33
K–B4 R–N7 34 B–B6 R × KRP 0–1

0706 Ritov–AK:

Alekhine

1 P–K4 N–KB3 unusual for
Karpov 2 N–QB3 P–Q4 3 P–K5 N–
K5 4 N × N This leaves White's KP
subject to agrophobia. Better is 4
QN–K2 followed by the ejection of
the black knight. 4 . . . P × N 5 P–Q4
P × Pep 6 B × P N–B3 7 N–B3 7
B–KB4 of Mieses–Helling, 1930,
preserves the KP. 7 . . . B–N5 8 P–
KR3 B × N 9 Q × B Q–Q5 10 0–0
Q × KP 11 B–KB4 Q–B3 The pawn
has been dipped in curare – 11 . . .
Q × P 12 QR–N1 Q–B3 13 R × P
with the deadly threat 14 B–QN5.
12 QR–Q1 (*70*)

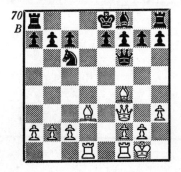

12 . . . P–KN4 13 B×BP Q×Q 14 P×Q B–N2 15 B–B5 0–0 16 B–K4 QR–B1 17 R–Q7 N–K4 18 B×N B×B 19 R×NP R–B2 20 R–N5 B–B5 21 R–Q1 P–K3 22 P–B3 P–B4 23 B–B2 K–B2 24 K–B1 K–B3 25 K–K2 P–KR4 26 R–Q4 R/B1–B2 27 B–Q3 P–R5 28 P–R4 R/KB2–Q2 29 R×R R×R 30 P–R5 R–Q4 31 P–N4 P–N5 32 BP×P P×P 33 P×P P–R6 34 R×R P×R 35 K–B3 K–N4 36 P–N5 P–R7 37 K–N2 K×P 38 B–K2+ K–B4 39 B–B3 K–K3 40 K–B1 B–B2 41 P–N6 P×P 42 P–R6 B–N1 43 K–K2 P–N4 ½–½

The other four games, from the same event, are, unfortunately, unavailable. It is not known against whom they were played or what the results of them were, though it is quite possible that Karpov won them all.

Stockholm, 10–30.8 1969

	1	2	3	4	5	6	7	8	9	0	1	2	
1 Karpov	×	½	1	½	1	1	1	1	1	1	1	1	10
2 Adorjan	½	×	1	½	½	½	1	1	½	½	0	1	7
3 Urzica	0	0	×	1	½	1	½	1	½	1	½	1	7
4 Kaplan	½	½	0	×	½	1	1	1	½	½	0	1	6½
5 Andersson	0	½	½	½	×	0	½	½	1	½	1	1	6
6 Neckar	0	½	0	0	1	×	1	½	1	1	½	0	5½
7 Juhnke	0	0	½	0	½	0	×	½	1	1	1	1	5½
8 Vujačić	0	0	0	0	½	½	½	×	½	1	1	½	4½
9 Vogt	0	½	½	½	0	0	0	½	×	½	1	1	4½
10 Diaz	0	½	0	½	½	0	0	0	½	×	1	1	4
11 McKay	0	1	½	1	0	½	0	0	0	0	×	1	4
12 Castro	0	0	0	0	0	1	0	½	0	0	0	×	1½

Preliminary Group 2

	1	2	3	4	5	6	7	
1 Karpov	×	½	1	½	½	1	1	4½
2 McKay	½	×	0	1	½	1	1	4
3 Payrhuber	0	1	×	½	0	1	1	3½
4 Torre	½	0	½	×	½	1	1	3½
5 Hug	½	½	1	½	×	0	½	3
6 Sznapik	0	0	0	0	1	×	1	2
7 Fridjonsson	0	0	0	0	½	0	×	½

Also there was a lightning tournament, entitled by the tournament book 'The Unofficial World Junior Championship in Lightning Chess!':

Preliminary Group 2: Karpov 5/5, Vujačić 4, Torre, 3, Ogaard 2, Bellon 1, Seret 0.

Final A: Adorjan 10½/11, Karpov 9, Andersson 7½, Kaplan 7, Ligterink 6, Torre 6, Vujačić 5½ Neckar, 5½ Hug 4½, Diaz 3, Meulders 1, Weber ½.

We Have Waited 14 Years For This Day

A discussion with GM Semyon Furman, trainer of A. Karpov. This article appeared in *Shakhmatisti Rossii* October 1969.

I became acquainted with Anatoly Karpov at the end of last year on the eve of the USSR Team Championship. The army chess players were taking part in a training conference in which Anatoly, representing the team on the first junior board, took part.

A lean, pale-faced youth, in appearance somewhat phlegmatic. It even seemed that it was with difficulty he moved the chess pieces. Was it possible that such a one was capable of the highest sporting achievements?

When Eduard Gufeld caught sight of Anatoly for the first time he said 'this little boy will never be a grandmaster, he is too thin'.

To which Efim Geller, standing beside him, remarked, not without irony, 'Well, of course everyone judges by his own standards, you, for example, Edik became a grandmaster when your weight reached 100 kilogrammes'.

Nature did not endow Anatoly Karpov with a gigantic frame, but it conferred upon him a rare chess talent and strength of will, and also modesty and a love of hard work.

When I began to concern myself with Karpov I immediately understood that this was a very able chess player with great prospects. And I was not mistaken. In the USSR Team Championship Anatoly scored 10/11, conceding to all his young adversaries only two half points.

From this moment I, as trainer of the army chess players, took charge of Anatoly, and now I have been helping him prepare for competitions for almost a year.

In order to win the right to take part in the World Junior Championship, Anatoly had to show his superiority over two other candidates; Rafael Vaganian and Misha Steinberg. This match-tournament of the young chess players took place in the spring of last year in Leningrad and ended in a convincing victory for Karpov.

We regard the World Junior Championship very seriously. Anatoly realized his great responsibility on behalf of millions of Soviet chessplayers. Fourteen years have passed since the time that Boris Spassky for the first (and last) time won for our country the title of World Junior Champion. It is time, it was already time long ago, for this title to return to the country of the chess champions.

The preparations for the World Championship consisted of various aspects. Most of all it is very important for every chessplayer to know himself; this is not so easy, especially at a youthful age. During work with Karpov we succeeded in bringing to light the strong and weak sides of his game and in completely assessing his capabilities. Thus, for example, it transpired that Anatoly is somewhat at odds with the theory of the openings, but this circumstance even pleased me. This problem was easy to settle and we liquidated this fairly rapidly. It is true that Karpov's opening repertoire remained somewhat limited, but we did not try to broaden it. At that moment our main task consisted of achieving success in a concrete tournament and I endeavoured to deepen Karpov's knowledge of specific opening systems.

The natural feature of Karpov's chess talent delighted me; a fine positional sense. That is a special intuition which always characterized the great chessplayers. I also paid attention to Karpov's masterly conduct of endgames and overall accuracy of technique.

But how to take the most logical advantage of these strong sides of Karpov's chess talent in the forthcoming tournament?

On studying the games of Karpov's future opponents I formed the impression that the foreign juniors were in general good tacticians but weak strategists. As a rule they searched for a suitable moment to deliver a tactical blow, and rarely concerned themselves with the game as a strategic whole. Therefore we decided that Karpov would choose those openings which would not give his opponents opportunities to sharpen the game without retribution. Running in advance I remark that this line of attack proved the most expedient and completely justified itself.

It was also necessary to pay attention to Anatoly's physical preparation. Daily morning gymnastics were prescribed for him. During the training period Anatoly often played badminton and table tennis and went boating. At first we relaxed near Moscow, at Bakovka, and then we moved to Zelenogorsk, near Leningrad, with its almost Scandinavian climate. This change of venue was very expedient because the Junior Championship would take place at Stockholm and it was essential for Anatoly to become acclimatized.

Were we confident of final success?

I must say frankly that I did not have 100% confidence in Karpov's victory. Firstly many Soviet juniors had returned from previous championships on the shield. Secondly I was not exceptionally well acquainted with the play of Anatoly's future opponents, indeed the final composition of the tournament only became known on the eve of the first round. True, I knew Karpov's strength extremely well, knew what he was capable of. But you know, everything is relative and is seen only in comparisons.

As for Anatoly himself, in general he knows his own strengths and limitations. It seems to me that before Stockholm his confidence in victory matched his strength (! – eds).

We arrived in Sweden several days before the start of the Championship in order to better to acclimatize to and acquaint ourselves with the conditions. We were shown the tournament hall, in which we had to pick our way through a forest of scaffolding and step-ladders. We were not even certain whether all the repair work would be finished before the opening of the tournament, but our fears proved to be groundless; the Swedes tried not to grieve us with troubles.

This place was received by the Stockholm Chess Federation from the municipal authorities very recently. The money for the repairs was given by chess patrons; it was even necessary to open a special fund. Now the chessplayers will have their own central club. It was fairly spacious for a club, but was most unsuitable for holding a major tournament, There was no big hall and in the oblong rooms where the Junior Championship took place it was very cramped, especially for the spectators (the converted building had been an ancient debtors' prison – eds.). Our TsShK (Moscow Central Chess Club; formerly the house of the Tsarist Civil Governor of Moscow – eds.) certainly would have been more suitable and spacious, but by Swedish standards even the Stockholm club was good enough.

Of course for adults to play in such conditions would have been significantly tougher, but the youngsters did not complain. True, many of them were tired out towards the end of the tournament, but I think it was the strict tournament schedule which was to blame for this. Playing off the adjourned games took place in the mornings, and only one rest day in the whole month (20 days – eds) could not have helped anyone. The only consolation was the weather. The Swedes said that they could not remember such a good summer for a long time.

During our preparation for the Championship, we had calculated that Karpov's chief rivals would be the Hungarian Adorjan, the Swede Andersson and the Scotsman McKay, but at the very last moment the Puerto Rican, Kaplan, winner of the previous

World Championship, arrived in Stockholm and it became clear that he was the number one rival.

The 1969 World Junior Championship attracted a record number of participants. The Championship was contested by 38 youths from 37 countries (the Swedes were represented by two players according to the host nation's rights). True, it was unclear whether it was possible to consider England and Scotland as separate countries. However, seeing as in other forms of sport (e.g. football) they each field their own teams no one felt able to challenge this tradition.

The participants were divided into six preliminary groups, from each of which the two winners were to make up the main final.

The system of division into such small groups involves many surprises and is fundamentally shameful. It turned out that by no means the strongest participants won through to the final. Thus the American Rogoff and the Philippino Torre failed to reach the main final, while the Colombian Castro, who reached the final, was considerably weaker than them.

In the preliminary group Karpov was noticeably nervous. At first his rivals forged ahead and it was not clear whether Anatoly was in a position to concede any draws, or was absolutely obliged to go all out for the win. Thus, playing sharply for the win against Torre and the Swiss player Hug, Anatoly stood on the verge of defeat in these games. And in general I noticed that in the preliminaries the especially nervous ones were those participants who had every ground for aspiring to the leading places in the final.

But everything turned out favourably. Karpov did not lose a single game and even took first place in his section.

I was happy with Anatoly from the very beginning. I clearly saw his prospects in the final, and I knew that there he would play very differently, that under unworried conditions he could show his best qualities.

My forecasts were fulfilled. In the finals he played a completely different game. Karpov began to win game after game. Karpov's victories affected the play of his rivals in a fatal manner. Realizing that by 'normal play' it was impossible to catch up with Karpov, certain participants began to take too many risks and this turned out badly for them. Anatoly was able to pull ahead of his rivals. Two rounds before the end of the tournament he had assured himself first place irrespective of the outcome of the remaining games.

Of course no one could have foreseen that Karpov would succeed in winning eight consecutive games in the final. No one set him such a target and even he himself had not counted on such a series of wins. Even so, this was not fortuitous – we had succeeded in accurately defining what tactics Anatoly should follow in order to achieve maximum success. Karpov showed himself to be a remarkably able student. He succeeded in creatively developing the ideas which I showed him during the preparation for the tournament. Even those ideas which did not arise out of the given concrete opening Karpov took advantage of during the other stages of the game.

At this point the game Juhnke-Karpov is given with notes by Furman.

I have already remarked that the main strength of the foreign juniors was in tactical play, therefore the task in front of Karpov consisted of obtaining positions such that tactical contrivances by his opponents would be doomed to failure. This meant that the position must be reliable and a plan of campaign logically flow out of the requirements of the position itself.

Now part of the game Karpov–Andersson appears.

The attack in this game was carried out by Karpov on a firm positional base and was prepared for by consistently planned play. All the same, certain chess-players sometimes succeeded in complicating the play and 'luring' Anatoly into the realms of tactical struggles. But then they turned out to be in unfavourable conditions because they were acting anti-positionally, for example the Colombian Castro risked using the King's Gambit against Karpov and paid heavily for it.

Castro–Karpov.

On the basis of this game it's possible to judge Karpov's tactical ability. Therefore the 'course of solidarity' is explained not by any weakness of Karpov's combinational vision, but by expediency and safety.

Karpov's magnificent play and his modest disposition aroused the regard and sympathy of the Swedish chesslovers; the local inhabitants turned to us with good wishes for success, and later with congratulations. During the period of the Championship Anatoly had a bit of a cold: the Swedes were very concerned and literally overwhelmed him with medicines, and one of them brought a thermos flask of hot tea to Anatoly at his hotel. Anatoly quickly got better, and it seemed to me that his recovery was helped not so much by the hot tea as by the warmth of the local hospitality.

The Swedish press, radio and TV publicized the Championship widely. Of course the Swedes were rooting for their own Ulf Andersson, undoubtedly a very talented player. While Ulf was still in with a chance it was impossible to get near his board. Later the spectators' interest turned to Karpov. I even recall an occasion when, under the onslaught of the public who had climbed on to the windowsill in order to get a better view of Anatoly, the radiator was torn away from the wall. Once again the repair brigade had to be brought in. . . .

On one of the days Boris Spassky and Bent Larsen, who were staying in Stockholm, visited the tournament. The famous grandmasters were themselves juniors not long ago, each of them in his time carried off the title of World Junior Champion (Larsen never won the title – he was 5th in 1951 and 8th in 1953 – eds). This symbolic meeting made an indelible impression on the youngsters.

The closing ceremony of the Championship took place in the picturesque park of lake Skansen. The deputy mayor of Stockholm laid on a ceremonial lunch for the participants. There the prizes were distributed.

And so Anatoly Karpov won the title of World Junior Champion. In accordance with the FIDE rules he was awarded the title of international master. And what next? How will the sporting fate of the young player work out? Many grandmasters of high reputation were Junior Champions in the past, will Karpov join their ranks?

Anatoly, in my opinion, will undoubtedly become a grandmaster. When? I think a year or two, but this depends not only on his training but also on his opportunities of participating in big tournaments. The sooner that Anatoly starts to meet top-flight masters the sooner he will become a grandmaster.

Semyon Furman was talking to V. Henkin.

0801 Julius Fridjonsson–AK:
PR1: 10 August:

Ruy Lopez

1 P–K4 P–K4 2 N–KB3 N–QB3 3
B–N5 P–QR3 4 B–R4 N–B3 5 Q–K2
P–QN4 6 B–N3 B–B4 7 P–B3 Or 7
P–QR4 R–QN1 8 P×P P×P 9 N–
B3 0–0 and Black is well on his way
to equalizing e.g. 10 P–Q3 P–Q3 11
B–N5 P–R3 12 B×N Q×B Bogol-
jubow–Eliskases, match 1939. 7 . . .
P–Q3 8 P–KR3?! Unnecessary,
better 8 0–0. 8 . . . 0–0 9 0–0 Q–K2 10
P–Q3 P–R3 11 QN–Q2 N–KR4!
Already eyeing White's K-side weak-
nesses; White must do something
about 12 . . . N–N6, and also 12 . . .
N–B5. 12 P–Q4 N–B5 13 Q–K3 B–
N3 The uncertainty of his oppon-
ent's play somewhat dulls Karpov's
vigilance. Here 13 . . . B–R2 was
more accurate since the bishop will
subsequently be in need of defence
here. 14 R–Q1 N–QR4 15 B–B2 Q–
B3 Another possibility was 15 . . . P–
QB4. 16 K–R2 P–B4 17 P–Q5 R–N1
To prepare . . . P–B5. 18 N–KN1 Q–
N3 19 P–KN3? (*71*) 19 Q–N3 would
be better, but White is probably lost
anyway.

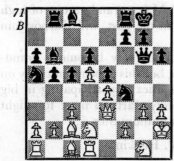

19 . . . N×QP! Fridjonsson must
have been reckoning on 19 . . .
N×RP 20 N×N Q–R4 21 P–KN4.
20 Q–K2 N–K2 21 P–KB4 P×P 22

P×P Q–B3 23 N/Q2–B3 N–N3 24
P–K5 P×P 25 P×P B–B2 0–1 It
is fitting that White's sole surviving
K-side pawn will be the one on
KR3 – the one that caused all the
trouble.

0802 AK–Werner Hug:
PR2: 11 August:

Sicilian

1 P–K4 P–QB4 2 N–KB3 N–KB3
3 P–K5 N–Q4 4 P–Q4 Less energetic
than 4 N–B3 P–K3 5 N×N P×N 6
P–Q4 N–B3 7 P×P B×P 8 Q×P Q–
N3 9 B–QB4 B×P+ 10 K–K2 0–0
11 R–B1 B–B4 when 12 N–N5! now
looks like a refutation, e.g. 12 . . . N–
Q5+ 13 K–Q1 N–K3 14 N–K4! P–
Q3 15 P×P B×P? 16 N×B R–Q1
17 B–B4! N×B 18 Q×BP+ K–R1
19 Q–N8+ 1–0 Unzicker–Sarapu,
Siegen 1970. 4 . . . P×P 5 Q×P P–
K3 6 B–K2!? A novelty. 6 . . . N–
QB3 7 Q–K4 P–Q3 8 0–0 P×P 9
N×P N×N 10 Q×N/K5 Q–Q3 11
B–QN5+ B–Q2 12 B×B+ Q×B 13
P–QB4 Q–B2 14 Q–K2 N–B3 15 N–
B3 P–QR3 16 B–N5 B–K2 17 B×N
B×B 18 N–Q5 Q–Q1 19 QR–Q1
0–0 20 N×B+ Q×N 21 R–Q7 P–
QN3 22 R/B1–Q1 QR–Q1 23 P–
KN3 P–KN3 24 P–QN4 R×R 25
R×R R–Q1 26 R–B7 Q–QB6 27 P–
B5 P×P 28 P×P Q–Q6 (*72*)

29 Q–K5?? Q–Q8+?? 29 . . . Q–KB6 wins very easily – both players seem to have been under considerable tension. **30 K–N2 Q–Q4+ 31 Q×Q R×Q 32 K–B3 K–N2 33 K–K3 K–B3 34 P–B4 P–R3 35 P–QR4 P–N4 36 P–R3 P×P+ 37 P×P R–R4 38 K–Q4 R–R5** ½–½

0803 Eugenio Torre–AK:
PR3: 12+13+14 August:

Ruy Lopez

1 P–K4 P–K4 2 N–KB3 N–QB3 3 B–N5 P–QR3 4 B–R4 N–B3 5 0–0 B–K2 6 P–Q4 P×P 7 P–K5 N–K5 8 P–QN4?! 8 N×P is normal and good, though it does not promise White anything much. **8 . . . N–B6 9 N×N P×N 10 P–QR3 0–0 11 Q–Q5 P–QN4 12 B–N3 P–QR4 13 B–K3** Of course the QNP is indirectly protected by . . . B–R3. **13 . . . B–N2 14 QR–Q1 P×P 15 Q×QP Q–B1 16 P–K6 BP×P 17 P×P K–R1 18 B×P Q×Q 19 R×Q B–B1 20 R×P B×B 21 R×N B–B5 22 R–N1 B–R7 23 –Q1 B×P 24 P–R3 R/B1–B1 25 R×R+ R×R 26 R–R1 B–B5 27 N–K5 B–Q4 28 R–N1 B–R6 29 R×P B–K5 30 B–Q4 P–R3 31 R–N3 B–N7 32 N–Q3 B–R8 33 R–R3 B×N 34 R×B B×P 35 R–R7** 35 R–QB1 is also equal. **35 . . . R–KN1 36 P–R4 K–R2 37 B×BP P–R4 38 P–B3 B–B4 39 K–B2 K–N3 40 K–K3 B–K3 41 K–K4 B–B1 42 R–QB7 R–K1+ 43 B–K5 B–B4+ 44 K–B4 B–K3 45 R×P+ K–R3 46 P–N4 P×P 47 P×P R–KB1+ 48 K–N3 R–B2** (73) **49 R–N5** Or 49 R×R B×R 50 B–B4+ K–N2 51 P–R5 B–B5 (51 . . . K–R2 52 K–R4) 52 P–N5 B–Q6= (Tarrasch, in 1921, demonstrated the draw here with the white bishop on K3), while if 49 R–N8 not 49 . . . R–KR2?? 50 B–B4 mate, but simply 49

73
W

. . . R–B6+ 50 K×R B×R 51 B–B4+ K–R2 52 P–R5 B–N6 53 K–N3 B–B7=. 49 . . . R–QR2 50 B–Q4 R–R6+ 51 K–B4 R–R5 52 K–K5 B–N6 53 R–R5+ K–N3 54 R–N5+ K–R3 55 K–B6 R–R3+ 56 K–B5 R–R4+ 57 B–K5 B–B7+ 58 K–B6 R–R3+ 59 K–K7 R–R2+ 60 K–Q6 R–R3+ 61 K–B5 R–R5 62 R–N8 B–R2 63 R–N5 B–B7 64 B–B3 B–Q8 65 B–N4 B–K7 66 R–R5+ K–N3 67 R–K5 B–B6 68 P–R5+ K–N2 69 R–K6 K–B2 70 R–KN6 B–K7 71 R–N5 R–R1 72 K–Q5 R–KN1 73 R–B5+ K–N2 74 B–B3+ K–R3 75 R–B6+ K–N4 76 P–R6 R–Q1+ 77 K–Q6 ½–½ The white pawns never reach the all-important sixth rank.

PR4: 13 August – Karpov had a free day.

0804 AK–Klaus Payrhuber:
PR5: 14 August:

King's Indian Attack

1 P–K4 P–QB4 2 N–KB3 P–KN3 3 P–KN3 N–KB3 4 P–Q3 N–B3 5 B–N2 P–Q3 6 0–0 B–N2 7 R–K1 The well known game Smyslov–Botvinnik, USSR Ch 1955, went 7 QN–Q2 0–0 8 P–QR4 N–K1 (A safer treatment would be 8 . . . R–N1 followed by Q-side expansion) 9 N–B4 P–K4 10 P–B3 P–B4!? 11 P–QN4! QBP×P 12 BP×P P×P 13 P×P B–K3 14

N–K3 N×P 15 R–N1 P–QR4 16
B–QR3 N–B2 17 B×N P×B 18
R×P B–R3 19 R–N6! and Black's
position soon collapsed in sympathy
with the QP. **7 . . . 0–0 8 P–B3 N–K1
9 N–R3** Karpov follows a different
course – he wants all his pieces to see
the light of day as simply as possible
9 . . . P–B4?! Payrhuber seems to be
unfortunately influenced by his
knowledge of Botvinnik's manoeuvre
– here this just creates weaknesses.
**10 N–KN5 N–B2 11 Q–N3+ K–R1
12 P×P B×KBP 13 N–B7+ R×N
14 Q×R P–K3** (74)

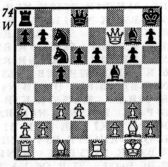

And White's queen is trapped. Very
clever, but . . . **15 B–N5** . . . it isn't,
so . . . **1–0**

0805 Roderick McKay–AK:
PR6: 15 August:

Ruy Lopez

**1 P–K4 P–K4 2 N–KB3 N–QB3 3
B–N5 P–QR3 4 B–R4 N–B3 5 0–0
B–K2 6 Q–K2 P–QN4 7 B–N3 0–0 8
P–B3 P–Q3** Or 8 . . . P–Q4 9 P–Q3
R–K1 10 R–K1 B–N2 11 QN–Q2
Q–Q2 12 N–B1 QR–Q1=. **9 P–Q4
P×P 10 P×P B–N5 11 R–Q1
P–Q4 12 P×P** 12 P–K5 is the
alternative. **12 . . . N–QR4! 13 B–B2
R–K1 14 Q–Q3** 14 N–B3 B–N5
15 Q–Q3 B–R4∓ was Antoshin–
Smyslov, Moscow 1955. **14 . . . B–R4**

**15 B–N5 B–N3 16 Q–Q2 N–B5 17
Q–B1 B×B∓ ½–½**

0806 AK–Alexander Sznapik:
PR7: 16 August:

Sicilian

**1 P–K4 P–QB4 2 N–KB3 P–Q3 3
P–B3 N–KB3 4 B–Q3 N–B3 5 0–0
P–KN3 6 B–B2 B–N2 7 P–KR3 0–0
8 R–K1 N–K1 9 B–N3 N–K4** 9 . . .
P–K4 = Ruy Lopez!? **10 P–Q3
N×N+ 11 Q×N N–B2 12 P–QR4
B–Q2 13 N–Q2 R–N1 14 N–B1 P–
N3 15 N–K3 P–QR3 16 N–Q5 N–
K3 17 Q–N3 P–QN4 18 P×P P×P
19 R–R7± P–N5 20 B–QB4 P×P
21 P×P R–N8 22 P–B4 K–R1** (75)

23 Q–B2! If immediately 23 P–B5
B–K4 24 Qany N–N2 is surviving.
Now the threat of P–B5 is very
serious. **23 . . . B–QB3 24 N×P
B×BP** Threat 25 . . . R×B and 26
. . . B–Q5, but this is easily parried.
**25 N×B Q–N3 26 R–R6 Q–N2 27
B–Q2 N–Q5 28 B×B 1–0**

0807 AK–Lubomir Neckar:
FR1: 18 August:

Alekhine

**1 P–K4 N–KB3 2 P–K5 N–Q4 3
P–Q4 P–Q3 4 N–KB3 P–KN3 5 P–
B4 N–N3 6 P×P BP×P 7 P–KR3
B–N2 8 N–B3 0–0 9 B–K2 N–B3 10**

0-0 B-B4 11 B-B4 P-KR3! 12 B-K3 P-Q4 13 P-QN3 P×P 14 P×P N-R4 For 14 . . . R-B1 see game 0609. 15 P-B5 N/N3-B5 16 B-B4 P-KN4 17 B-N3 Q-Q2 18 R-K1! P-N3 19 P×P P×P 20 N-K5!± N×N 21 P×N Q-K3 Better 21 . . . KR-Q1. 22 B-B3 QR-Q1 23 B-Q5 Q-B1 24 Q-B3 P-K3 25 B-K4 N-B5 26 QR-B1 N-Q7 27 Q-R5 Q-R3 27 . . . N×B 28 N×N would be unduly generous. 28 B×B P×B 29 P-KR4± P-B5 (76)

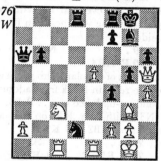

76
W

30 B-R2? Simply 30 P×P gives White a winning attack. **30 . . . Q-Q6 31 P×P Q-B4 32 N-K2 P-B6?** Now it's Black's turn. He should have played 32 . . . B×P and if 33 Q×RP then 33 . . . Q-N5 with a good game. **33 N-N3± Q×NP 34 Q×Q P×Q 35 N-B5 P×P 36 K×P R-Q6? 37 N-K7+ K-R2 38 R-KR1±± B-R3 39 B-N3 N-K5 40 R-B6 P-B3 41 N-B5 K-N3 42 N×B N×B 43 P×N R-Q7+ 44 K-B3 R×P 45 N-N4 R-R6+ 46 N-K3 P-N5+ 47 K-K4 R-R5+ 48 R-B4 P-B4+ 49 K-B4 R×R+ 50 N×R P-N4 51 N-Q6 R-QR1 52 P-K6 1-0**

0808 Borivoje Vujačić–AK:
    FR2: 19 August:

Ruy Lopez

1 P-K4 P-K4 2 N-KB3 N-QB3 3 B-N5 P-QR3 4 B-R4 N-B3 5 Q-K2

P-QN4 6 B-N3 B-B4 7 P-B3 P-Q3 8 P-Q3 P-KR3 9 QN-Q2 0-0 10 N-B1 N-KN5 11 B-K3 B×B 12 P×B N-R4 13 N-N3 N×B 14 P×N P-N3 15 P-N4 Q-K2 16 0-0 P-KR4 (77)

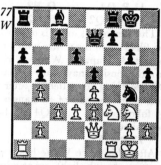

77
W

17 P-R3 N-R3 18 P-Q4 B-N2 19 P-Q5 P-QB3 20 P×P B×P 21 N-Q2 Q-N4 22 Q-B2 K-N2 23 QR-Q1 QR-Q1 24 N-K2 P-B4 25 N-B3 Q-K2 26 P×P N×P 27 N-N3 N-R3 28 P-K4 P-R5 29 N-K2 B×P 30 Q×P Q×Q 31 N×Q R×R+ 32 K×R B-N2 33 N-B3 N-B4 34 R-R1 R-KB1 35 K-N1 N-K6 36 N-N5 K-R3 37 P-R4 N×P 38 R-KB1 R×R+ 39 K×R K-N2 0-1

0809 AK–Ulf Andwesson:
    FR3: 20 August:

Ruy Lopez

1 P-K4 P-K4 2 N-KB3 N-QB3 3 B-N5 P-QR3 4 B-R4 N-B3 5 0-0 B-K2 6 R-K1 P-QN4 7 B-N3 0-0 8 P-B3 P-Q3 9 P-KR3

This is usually played before P-Q4 since otherwise the pin by . . . B-N5 can be disturbing.

| 9 . . . | N-QR4 |
| 10 B-B2 | P-B4 |

All part of the standard (and much overlooked) strategy of this variation; Black gains a little space on the

Q-side and prepares to defend e5 with his queen, thus removing her from a file which may one day be inhabited by ferocious rooks. Meanwhile he retains options of play on the QB-file.

11 P–Q4	**Q–B2**
12 QN–Q2	**B–N2**

The idea of this move is to provoke the blocking of the centre which now follows. Attempts by White to maintain the tension may result in Black's QB becoming very effective after the freeing manoeuvre of exchanges on d4 followed by . . . P–Q4 has been carried out.

13 P–Q5

After this move White has a permanent, though slight, space advantage.

13 . . .

There is no longer any reason to keep the bishop on b7. The loss of two tempi is insignificant since nothing very sudden can happen in this blocked position.

14 N–B1	**B–Q2**
15 P–QN3	**N–N2**

White's plan is to reduce Black's Q-side play to a minimum before committing himself to the K-side attack which is his objective. Since he cannot keep all the Q-side lines permanently closed, he aims to limit Black to one open file, and to maintain equality of space on that side.

16 P–B4	**KR–N1**
17 N–K3	**B–KB1**
18 N–B5	

It is unfavourable for Black to exchange this knight since then White will occupy e4 with the other knight and conduct a pawn-storm with P–KN4–N5 and so on.

18 . . .   **N–Q1**

Both to clear the QN-file and to bring the knight over to the defence of the K-side – from f7 eventually.

19 N–R2

Karpov's conduct of this game is typical of his style. A more direct approach involving P–KN4, K–R2, R–KN1 and doubling rooks on the KN-file would eventually run into a solid black defensive position, when White would have to justify his build-up by a sacrifice. Instead of such a speculative, though often employed, plan, Karpov uses his pieces in front of his pawns to create the most favourable conditions possible for an eventual breakthrough by first forcing weaknesses in Black's K-side.

19 . . .   **N–K1**

20 P–KR4

All part of the plan. This pawn will help to restrain Black from adopting a solid set-up based on . . . P–B3, . . . P–N3, with the KB on B1 and knights on KB2 and KN2.

20 . . .	**P–B3**
21 P–R5	**N–B2**
22 R–K3	

If White can now force . . . P–R3, he will have an overall light square bind which will considerably help his attack.

22 . . .   **N–N4**

23 N–R4

Preventing . . . P–N3.

23 . . .	**Q–Q1**
24 R–N3	**N–QB2**
25 N2–B3	**P–R3** *(78)*

78
W

Black couldn't really avoid this as after 25 . . . B–K2 26 P–R6! was very strong e.g. 26 . . . P–N3 loses a pawn to 27 N×N P×N 28 N–B3 P–KN5 29 N–R2.

26 N–N6 **P–R4**
27 P–R4!

Otherwise Black gets two open files with 27 . . . P–R5.

27 . . . **P×BP**
28 P×P

White's first priority is now to cover all the entry-points on the QN-file so that the black rooks cannot penetrate.

28 . . . **N–R3**
29 Q–K2 **R–R2**
30 B–Q2 **R2–N2**

30 . . . R–N7 of course achieves nothing – the boarder is repelled by 31 B–B3.

31 B–B3 **N–N5**

This attempt at repetition of moves gets him nowhere. Sooner or later he will have to try . . . R–N5, with the intention of recapturing with the QBP and thus obtaining some positional advantages as compensation for the exchange. However, White need not accept the rook until it actually succeeds in threatening something, and can meanwhile continue cheerfully with his own plans.

32 B–Q1 **N–R3**
33 N–Q2

Avoiding the repetition while still covering the b1 square.

33 . . . **N–N5**
34 R–K3 **B–K1**
35 N–B1 **Q–B1**
36 N–N3 **B–Q2**
37 Q–Q2 **N–R2**
38 B–K2 **K–B2**

With the rather half-hearted idea of heading for points West. But he soon decides that he may as well have his king available to defend the weaknesses in his K-side. He is strategically lost anyway.

39 Q–Q1 **B–K2**
40 N–B1

Over the last few moves White has been preparing an exchange of light-square bishops by B–KN4. This knight is about to lend a hand from KR2. Once this exchange has been achieved he will simply place his knights on g6 and f5, then play P–N3 and P–B4 with a position that wins itself.

40 . . . **B–Q1**

Black's last, though very limited, chance of breaking out was to play 40 . . . P–B4 or the same on his 41st.

41 N–R2 **K–N1**

He might as well have continued with his plan (now that the QRP is protected) of playing . . . N–R3 and . . . R–N6, but was probably oppressed by a sense of the futility of the whole business.

42 B–N4 **N–N4**

After 42 . . . B×B 43 N×B N–B7? 44 N×RP+ White picks up a pawn.

43 B×B **Q×B**

The first piece exchange of the game!

44 N–B1 (*79*)

Now he goes for f5. In desperation Black tries his last remaining chance. 'The positional advantage is on White's side – he controls more space, Black's light squares are weak, and his bishop has no prospects. White intends to seize the point f5 with the aid of the manoeuvre N/B1–N3–B5 followed by the pawn-storm P–N3 and P–B4. Not wishing to be a passive observer of the onslaught being prepared, Andersson tries to free himself from White's grip on the position.'

44 ...	**P–B4**
45 P×P	**Q×BP**
46 N–N3	**Q–B2**

This move loses without a fight. He had to try 46 . . . Q–B7 to keep chances, e.g. 47 Q–N4 R–KB2!

'Against 46 . . . Q–B7 47 P–B4 would have followed and 47 . . . P×P is not possible because of 48 R–K8+. The struggle which follows revolves around the advance P–B4.'

47 Q–K2

'Renewing the threat.'

47 ...	**B–B3**
48 R–KB1	**Q–Q2**

'Black can no longer prevent the opening up of the position.'

49 P–B4!

The decisive break-up.

49 ...	**P×P**
50 R×P	**B×B**
51 R×B	**R–K1**
52 R–K3	**R2–N1**
53 Q–KB2!	

Still Black cannot capture on e3.

53 ...   **N–R2**

'Defending the f8 square because 53 . . . R×R was no good on account of 54 R–B8+.'

54 N–B5

The horses are showing their teeth!

54 ...	**R×R**
55 Q×R	**N–KB3**

To give his king a square.

'If 55 . . . R–K1 then 56 N5–K7+, but now White wins in a different way.'

56 N6–K7+   **K–R1**

Or 56 . . . K–R2 57 Q–KN3.

'In the event of 56 . . . K–R2 White would have continued, as in the game, 57 N×RP, and against 56 . . . K–B2 the simple 57 Q–KN3 is decisive.'

57 N×RP

The end.

57 ...	**R–K1**
58 N–B7+	**K–R2**
59 R–K4!	**R×N**
60 R×R	**1–0**

'The attack in this game was carried out by Karpov on a firm positional base and was prepared for by consistently planned play.'

The comments in quotes are by GM Semyon Furman.

0810 Oscar Castro–AK:

FR4: 21 August:

King's Gambit

1 P–K4 P–K4 2 P–KB4 'Certain of Anatoly's rivals naïvely thought that it was possible to unnerve him in this way.' **2 . . . P×P 3 B–B4 N–KB3 4 N–QB3** 'Against this somewhat harmless move theory recommended the reply 4 . . . P–B3, however Karpov wanted to lead his opponent away from well-trodden paths and played a different move.' The theory referred to is 4 . . . P–B3 5 Q–B3 P–Q4 6 P×P B–Q3 7 P–Q3 B–KN5 8 Q–B2 0–0 9 B×P – Freeborough and Ranken, and now 9 . . . R–K1∓ – Keres. **4 . . . B–N5** 'This move is also known to theory, but it turned out not to be known to Castro.' **5 P–K5** 'Now a sharp tactical skirmish, somewhat better for Black who has a lead in development, is brought about. 5 KN–K2 would have led to the better game for White.' Alekhine's recommendation was 5 KN–K2 P–Q4 6 P×P P–B6 7 P×P 0–0 8 0–0

P–B3 9 P×P N×P 10 P–Q4 B–KR6
11 R–B2±. **5 ... P–Q4 6 B–N5+ P–
B3 7 P×N P×B 8 P×P** A game
Paulsen–Kolisch went 8 Q–K2+ B–
K3 9 Q×P+ N–B3 10 N–B3 (if
10 Q×NP N–Q5 – Freeborough and
Ranken) 10 ... Q×P 11 Q×NP R–
QB1 12 N×P Q–B4 13 N–B7+
R×N 14 Q×R Q–K5+ 15 K–Q1
0–0 16 P–Q3 Q–N3 17 Q×P/B4±.
**8 ... R–N1 9 Q–K2+ B–K3 10
Q×P+ N–B3 11 Q×NP** 'Realizing
that the strategic battle has been
lost, Castro tries to grab as many
pawns as possible.' **11 ... R–QB1 12
N–B3 R×P 13 0–0 B–KR6 14 R–
K1+** 'Otherwise g2 cannot be
defended; if 14 R–B2 B–QB4.'
14 ... K–B1 15 R–K2 B–N5! (*80*)

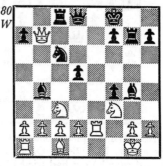

16 **R–B2** Not 16 K–R1 B/KN5×N
17 P×B R–B2 and 18 ... Q–N4
with mate to follow. **16 ... B–QB4 17
P–Q4 N×P 18 N×N B×N 19
B×P B×R+ 20 K×B R–N3!
21 K–N1! P–Q5 22 R–KB1 Q–Q2
23 Q–N4+ K–N1 24 N–K4 Q–Q4
25 Q–K7 Q–K3 26 Q–N7 B–K7 27
R–K1 R×BP 28 N–N5 Q–B4**
Furman terminates the game score
here, but the tournament book gives
the further **29 B–K5 R×N** An
amusing finish would be 29 ...
Q×B?? 30 Q×BP+ K–R1 31 Q–
B8+ R–KN1 32 N–B7 mate. **30 P–
KR4 Q×B 0–1**

0811 AK–Roderick McKay:
  FR5: 22 August:

Alekhine

1 **P–K4 N–KB3 2 P–K5 N–Q4 3
P–Q4 P–Q3 4 N–KB3 P–KN3 5 P–
B4 N–N3 6 P×P BP×P 7 P–KR3
B–N2 8 N–B3 0–0 9 B–K2 N–B3 10
0–0 B–B4 11 B–B4 P–Q4? 12 P–B5
N–B5 13 P–QN3 N/B5–R4 14 R–B1
P–N3 15 P×P P×P 16 Q–Q2 N–
N2 17 N–QN5 R–B1 18 R–B3 Q–Q2
19 R1–B1 P–B3** (*81*)

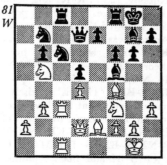

20 B–B7! Black is lost. **20 ... N/B3–
Q1** If 20 ... R×B 21 N×R Q×N 22
R×N±±. **21 B×P R×R 22 R×R
P–K4 23 P–QR4 N–B3 24 P–QN4
P–K5 25 N–R2 R–B1 26 P–R5 B–
B1 27 R–QN3 P–K6 28 Q×P
N×NP 29 N–N4 Q–N2 30 R–B3 P–
R4 31 R×R B×R 32 Q–K8 B–KB4**
Not 32 ... B–Q2? 33 N×P+ Q×N
34 Q×B/7 **33 N–K3 B–Q2 34 Q–N8
B–B3 35 N–R7 Q–Q2 36 P–R6 N–
Q3 37 B–B5 1–0** Since it was
Black's turn to move and he couldn't
move anything.

0812 Jürgen Juhnke–AK:
  FR6: 23 August:

Ruy Lopez

1 **P–K4 P–K4 2 N–KB3 N–QB3 3
B–N5 P–QR3 4 B–R4 N–B3 5 P–Q4**

P×P 6 0–0 B–K2 7 P–K5 N–K5 8
N×P 0–0 Also possible is 8 . . .
N×N 9 Q×N N–B4 10 N–B3 0–0 11
B–K3 N×B 12 Q×N P–Q4! 13
P×Pep B×P 14 QR–Q1 B–Q2 15
Q–Q4 B–KB4 ½–½ Jezek–Z. Nilsson,
corres 1958–9. **9 N–B5 P–Q4 10
B×N P×B 11 N×B+ Q×N 12 R–
K1** 'This is a well-known theoretical
position in which the move 12 . . . P–
B3 is recommended, but in one of the
semi-finals of the USSR Champion-
ship I played here, against master
Korelov, 12 . . . R–K1 and obtained
the advantage. During the prepara-
tion I showed Karpov this move and
Anatoly was able to use it.' **12 . . . R–
K1!** Keres states the previous
theory: 12 . . . P–B3 13 P–KB3 N–N4
14 N–B3 B–B4 15 P×P Q×P=.
13 P–KB3 'This is precisely the
natural reply that Black was counting on. But even in the event of 13
P–QN3 P–B3 14 P–KB3 N–Q3! 15
B–N2 N–B2 16 P–KB4 P×P 17
P×P B–B4 and Black's position is
preferable.' 13 N–B3!? is worth considering. **13 . . . N–Q3 14 P–QN3 N–
B4 15 B–R3** 'Or 15 B–N2 B–N2
followed by . . . P–QB4.' **15 . . . Q–
N4 16 B–N2?** 16 Q–Q2 is better –
Nilsson. **16 . . . N–R5 17 Q–K2 P–B3
18 Q–B2 B–R6!** 'Not immediately
18 . . . P×P because of 19 P–KB4.'
19 P–KN4 P×P *(82)*

20 N–Q2? 20 Q–N3 holds out longer.
'A blunder, but White's position was
already hopeless.' **20 . . . Q×N 0–1**

0813 AK–Lothar Vogt:
FR7: 24 August:

Pirc

**1 P–K4 P–KN3 2 P–Q4 B–N2
3 N–KB3 P–Q3 4 P–B3 N–KB3 5
B–Q3 0–0 6 0–0 QN–Q2 7 QN–Q2
P–K4 8 R–K1 P–B3 9 P–QR4 Q–
B2 10 B–B1 P–Q4?!** Spirited but
inadequate, 10 . . . R–K1 is better.
**11 QP×P N2×P 12 N×N Q×N 13
P×P Q×QP** *(83)*

Now White's pieces pour out into
the attack. **14 B–B4 Q–QR4** In the
second round Vogt had tried 14 . . .
Q–QB4 against Juhnke: 15 Q–N3
R–N1 16 N–K4 N×N 17 R×N B–
B4 18 B–K3 Q–Q3 19 B–B4 Q–B3 20
B×R B×R 21 Q×P±±. The
'improvement' lasts nine moves
longer than the Juhnke game.
**15 N–N3 Q–B2 16 Q–B3 B–N5 17
Q–B4 Q–B1 18 P–R3 B–Q2 19 B–
K3 B–K3 20 B×B Q×B 21 N–B5
Q–B1 22 B–Q4! N–Q4 23 Q–Q2
R–Q1 24 B×B K×B 25 P–QB4
N–B3 26 Q–B3± Q–B4** The only
way to meet the threats of R–K7 and
N–K4. **27 R–K5! Q–B5 28 R–K7
K–N1** Otherwise 29 N–K6+ would
have been quite a large family fork.

29 N×P R–Q7 30 R–KB1 R–N1 31 P–KN3 Q–Q5 Not 31 . . . Q–N4? 32 P–R4±±. **32 Q×Q R×Q 33 P–N3±± K–B1 34 R1–K1 R–K5 35 R1×R N×R 36 R–B7! P–QB4 37 K–N2 P–QR3 38 P–R5 N–Q7 39 N×P N×NP 1–0** Black suddenly realized that 40 N×N?? is not forced and that 40 N–Q7+ is stronger.

0814 Aurel Urzica–AK:
FR8: 25 August:

Four Knights

1 P–K4 P–K4 2 N–KB3 N–QB3 3 N–B3 N–B3 4 B–N5 B–N5 5 0–0 0–0 6 P–Q3 P–Q3 7 B–N5 B×N 8 P×B B–Q2 9 P–Q4 P–KR3 10 B–KR4 R–K1 11 R–K1 P–QR3 12 B–Q3 B–N5 13 P–Q5 N–N1 14 P–KR3 B×N 15 Q×B QN–Q2 Black stands a little better – his knights can cope more easily with the closed position. **16 B–N3 N–B4 17 P–B4 Q–K2 18 R–K3 N/B3–Q2 19 P–KR4 R/K1–N1 20 Q–K2 P–QN3 21 P–R3** *(84)*

Karpov brings out the dynamic possibilities in the position: **21 . . . N×B 22 R×N N–B4 23 R3–Q1 P–QB3!** Revealing his plan: the QB-file is to be opened for the black heavy pieces in order to set up a counter-offensive against the white QBPs. **24 P–R4** If 24 P×P R–QB1!–

B3 as in the game. **24 . . . P×P 25 R×P** A proud rook, but now the QBPs are left to their fate, although 25 BP×P Q–Q2 26 Q–B4 Q–N5! 27 R–K1 P–B4 or 26 P–R5 P×P! 27 R×P R–N7 and the open b+c–files give Black a strong attack. Now, however, the game is quickly decided **25 . . . R–QB1! 26 P–KB3** To cover the KP and to bring the QB back from oblivion. **26 . . . R–B3 27 P–R5 P×P! 28 R×RP Q–B2 29 B–K1 N–K3!** The double threat of 30 . . . N–B5 and 30 . . . R×P is killing. **30 P–N3 R×P 31 Q–Q3 R×BP 32 R×RP R×R 33 Q×R N–Q5 34 Q–Q3 Q–R2! 35 K–B1 R–B8 0–1** The pinned bishop will soon be lost.

0815 AK–Andras Adorjan:
FR9: 26 August:

Ruy Lopez

1 P–K4 P–K4 2 N–KB3 N–QB3 3 B–N5 P–QR3 4 B–R4 N–B3 5 0–0 B–K2 6 R–K1 P–QN4 7 B–N3 P–Q3 8 P–B3 0–0 9 P–KR3 N–QR4 10 B–B2 P–B4 11 P–Q4 Q–B2 12 QN–Q2 N–B3 13 P×KP P×P 14 N–B1 B–K3 15 N–K3 QR–Q1 16 Q–K2 P–B5! Much better than the older 16 . . . P–N3. **17 N–B5 B×N 18 P×B P–R3!?** 18 . . . KR–K1 is the main line. The text is an idea of Igor Zaitsev. **19 N×P N×N 20 Q×N B–Q3 21 Q–K2 KR–K1** *(85)*

Black has sufficient compensation for the pawn. **22 B-K3 N-Q4 23 Q-B3 N×B 24 R×N R×R 25 Q×R B-B4 26 Q-K2 Q-B5 27 R-Q1 R×R+= ½-½**

0816 Julio Kaplan-AK:
FR10: 27 August:

King's Gambit

1 P-K4 P-K4 2 P-KB4 P×P 3 N-KB3 P-KN4 4 B-B4 B-N2 5 P-Q4 P-Q3 6 0-0 N-QB3 7 P-B3 P-KR3 8 P-KN3 P-N5 9 N-R4 P-B6 10 Q-N3 10 N-Q2 is regarded as more logical, and gives White good attacking chances. **10 . . . Q-Q2?** 10 . . . Q-K2 retaining confrol of f5 is better. **11 N-Q2** Missing his chance for 11 N-B5! **11 . . . N-R4 12 Q-B2 N×B 13 N×N N-K2 14 N-K3 Q-B3** Everything is under control again. **15 P-Q5 Q-B4 16 K-R1 B-Q2 17 B-Q2 P-QR4 18 Q-Q3 P-R4 19 QR-K1 B-K4 20 N-B4** (86) ½-½

0817 AK-Joaquim Diaz:
FR11: 28 August:

King's Indian

1 P-QB4 N-KB3 2 N-QB3 P-B4

3 N-B3 P-KN3 4 P-KN3 N-B3 5 B-N2 B-N2 6 0-0 0-0 7 P-Q4 P×P 8 N×P N×N 9 Q×N P-Q3 10 Q-Q3! Probably the strongest, though Fischer's new idea (10 B-N5) will bear further investigation. **10 . . . B-B4 11 P-K4 B-K3 12 P-N3 N-Q2 13 B-N2** 13 B-K3 Q-R4 14 QR-B1 QR-B1 15 Q-Q2 KR-Q1 16 P-B4 N-B3 17 P-KR3 B-Q2 18 P-KN4 led to an unclear struggle in Suetin-Shamkovich, Leningrad 1967 However, White does not need to play so sharply, and a quiet positional line suited Karpov well. **13 . . . N-B4 14 Q-Q2 Q-Q2 15 QR-B1 P-QR3 16 KR-Q1 KR-Q1 17 N-K2 B×B 18 Q×B** As so often in this line White has built up a very solid position generating strong pressure against Black's constricted set-up. **18 . . . P-B3 19 N-B4 B-B2 20 Q-K2 P-K4?** (87)

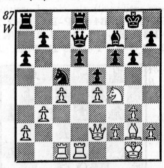

Black's QP is condemned without trial. **21 B-R3! P-B4 22 N-Q3 N×N 23 R×N QR-B1 24 R/B1-Q1 P-QN4 25 KP×P KNP×P 26 R×P Q×R 27 R×Q R×R 28 B×P R-B4 29 Q-K3 R/Q3-QB3 1-0**

Our Young Champion   V. Tumanov

If at the World Junior Championship in Stockholm a special prize had been awarded for modesty and serious application to chess then, together with title of Champion, it would have gone to Anatoly. In the course of the three weeks he sat at the board calmly and in a business-like manner and pulled off one victory after another.

'Everything depends on the finish' he replied to the importunate questions of Swedish correspondents, although it was obvious that everything was virtually decided already. Eight consecutive victories in the final made his position unassailable. And it was only in the ninth round when the Hungarian Andras Adorjan, having drawn with Karpov, shook his hand and said 'Congratulations, you are the Champion' that Anatoly's face lit up in a broad grin.

Many had believed in Karpov's victory. The ex-World Champion Mikhail Botvinnik, a man of high principle and guarded in his judgements, had spoken highly of Anatoly's play. And Boris Spassky, on the eve of Anatoly's departure for Stockholm, had announced 'I am convinced that Karpov will repeat my success of fourteen years ago and become the World Junior Champion'.

On what was based the faith of the Soviet chess-players in the success of their representative? – an analysis of Anatoly's short but impressive sporting career.

Karpov was five years old when he became acquainted with chess. He lived at the time in Zlatoust, a small town in the Urals, far from the chess centres. Anatoly soon stood out in the All-Russian Schools Championships, and at the age of eleven obtained the rank of candidate master. Quite a lot of attention was focused on the able young boy. Mikhail Botvinnik began to concern himself with him. Even then there was already an uncommonly striking tenacity and purposefulness in Karpov's play. It was strange to observe how, scarcely noticeable behind the chess pieces, the small boy sat, not stirring for five hours at a time, absorbed only by his will to win.

At the age of fifteen Anatoly became a master, the youngest chess master in our country. And now, at eighteen, he is World Junior Champion. Isn't it a fact that the sporting biographies of

Anatoly Karpov and Boris Spassky are surprisingly similar, and is there not a special significance in this?

When Anatoly flew into Moscow from Stockholm not one correspondent was able to extract an interview from him. It was not at all because Karpov had not yet learnt to give them, it was simply that he did not have the time. Evgeny Stepanovich Karpov, chief engineer of one of the Tula factories, drove his son, straight from the airport, back to Tula for 'repairs'. Anatoly certainly needed as much rest as possible because before him stretched a whole year of studies at the Moscow State University (MGU).

And so I was chatting to Anatoly. The World Junior Champion visited the central house of culture of the Railwaymen (Moscow – eds) where the 37th USSR Championship was taking place. He looked with interest at the games played by the young débutants in the event.

'I thought' said Anatoly, 'that Volodya Tukmakov would show up best of all, but then I was mistaken'.

The conversation turned to Anatoly's chess career.

'Up to the age of twelve' said Karpov, 'I had a very confused understanding of chess theory. I had read, all in all, two chess books, the titles of which I cannot now remember.

'When I was included in the junior *Trud* school where M. Botvinnik directed the studies, the ex-champion of the world, on becoming acquainted with my knowledge, exclaimed "he doesn't understand anything about chess". Understandably Mikhail Moiseyevich, not wanting to insult me, did not say this to my face, but I was later informed that this was the first thing he ever said about my play.

'The studies with M. Botvinnik did me a lot of good, especially the homework which he gave out. This homework taught me to work independently, forced me to sit down to work at chess books.

'Now my trainer is grandmaster Semyon Furman. He helped me to win in Stockholm and I am very grateful to him. I shall be glad if Semyon Abramovich continues to work with me. He is splendid both as a man and as a chessplayer.'

And which chessplayers have had the greatest influence on your play?

'Capablanca and Botvinnik.'

It frequently happens that parents are unhappy about the extra-curricular activities of their children, fearing that these will interfere with their studies. What was the attitude of Karpov's parents to his chess?

'They had no reason to be worried' said Anatoly, 'I always got an "excellent" for my studies, and I finished school with the gold medal, and now I am taking the first course of the Economics Faculty of the MGU.'

Well, what are your interests apart from chess?

'I like pop music, Lermontov and I collect stamps.'

Anatoly looked searchingly at me, expecting some further questions, but I well realized that he had long been wanting to go to the tournament hall where it was much more interesting.

Karpov, playing on the top junior board, did not get the results to match his newly acquired title of World Junior Champion. The Hungarian team of Portisch, Lengyel, Barcza, Barczay, Forintos and Csom, *Women*: Bilek, Veroci, Karakas and Ivanka, *Juniors*: Adorjan and Ribli proved too strong for the Russian Soviet Federative Socialist Republic team of Polugayevsky, Geller, A. Zaitsev, Antoshin, Averkin and Yuferov, *Women*: Bilunova, Tsifanskaya, Skegina and Alekhina, *Juniors*: Karpov and Sveshnikov, winning 27–21.

0901 AK–Andras Adorjan:

King's Indian

1 P–Q4 P–KN3 2 P–QB4 B–N2 3 N–QB3 P–Q3 4 N–B3 N–KB3 5 P–KN3 0–0 6 B–N2 QN–Q2 7 0–0 P–QR3!?

This unusual move was introduced into master praxis by Navarovszky. It can be justified with the following tactical points: 8 P–K4 P–B4 and:
(a) 9 P–Q5 P–QN4! 10 N–Q2 N–N3! 11 P×P P×P 12 N×P B–QR3 13 Q–K2 Q–Q2 and Black wins.
(b) 9 P–K5 N–K1 10 KP×P N×P 11 P×P N2×P 12 B–K3 B×N! 13 P×B Q–B2 and Black is better.

If White tries to hinder Black's Q-side opportunities with 8 P–QR4 then 8 . . . P–QR4! could be an answer. Although this is a loss of tempo, after . . . P–QB3 and . . . P–K4 White's dark square weaknesses provide ample compensation.

These motifs are the main characteristic of the type of position that Black has built up, especially advantageous in that it tests the opponent with new ideas, and as chess is played with a time control this is very important.

8 P–K4 P–B4 9 R–K1 P×P 10 N×P N–B4

This position is reminiscent of the Sicilian Dragon. On the other hand, the QN has moved to B4 (instead of the usual B3), where it is in readiness to execute the most important strategic aim of exchanging itself, when it moves to R5, for White's N/QB3. If that is achieved then the weakness of d5 ceases, and the remaining black knight has a larger role to play – it facilitates the possibility of doubling rooks on the QB-file apart from the very important manoeuvre . . . N–Q2–K4.

11 P–KR3

Another variation would have been 11 P–N3 B–Q2 12 B–N2 R–B1 13 P–QR4? (13 Q–K2 P–QN4! 14 P×P P×P 15 N4×P N3×P! 16 N×N B×N 17 Q×B B×B with even chances; in this variation 15

N3 × P is not good because of 15 . . .
P–K4! 16 N–B2 N4 × KP! 17 P–QR4
R–K1! 18 N2–R3 P–Q4) 13 . . . N–
N5! 14 P–KR3 N–K4 15 B–KB1 N–
B3! with advantage for Black.
**11 . . . B–Q2 12 B–K3 R–B1 13 R–
QB1 Q–R4!**
This prepares . . . P–QN4. The
immediate 13 . . . P–QN4 would be
disadvantageous because of 14 P × P
P × P 15 P–QN4! N–R3 16 P–R3.
On the other hand, if White tries to
prevent this move then the plan of
exchanging knights and playing . . .
P–K4 would be possible
14 P–R3 N–R5! 15 P–QN4!?
A move that could be argued
about, because of the weakening of
White's pawn at c4 it allows Black
Q-side play. It is true that it only
hangs by a thread that White's plan
of P–QB5 is unsuccessful.
After the less demanding variation
15 N × N B × N 16 P–N3 B–K1! 17
P–QR4 N–Q2 Black's game is easy –
he has no problems.
**15 . . . N × N 16 R × N Q–R5! 17 Q–
N1 R–B2 18 R1–QB1 R1–B1 19
Q–Q3 B–K1!!** (*88*)

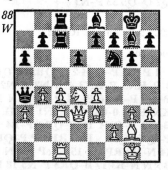

88
W

The best move of the whole game,
and a very difficult decision. Only
after considering a lot of pros and
cons was I able to convince myself
that the evergreen motifs in the game
(e.g. . . . P–K4 followed by the

breakthrough . . . P–Q4, possibly
with . . . P–QN4, . . . P–QR4 and . . .
B–K3! combinational-wise) were
valid – in the absolute it is not
enough for a combinational decision.
On the other hand the text move
allows 20 . . . N–Q2–K4 against
which there is no defence.
20 B–B3
The aforesaid threat could be
parried by 20 P–B4 but the answer
20 . . . N–R4! 21 P–N4 (21 K–R2 P–
K4! 22 P × P B × P) 21 . . . N × P! 22
B × N P–K4 23 B–K3 P × N 24 B × P
B × B 25 Q × B P–QN4! would be to
Black's advantage.
20 . . . N–Q2! 21 B–Q1?
21 Q–B1 was better, which, as
against the game, would have saved
a tempo: 21 . . . N–K4 22 B–K2 Q–
Q2 and:
(a) 23 R3–B2 P–QN4! 24 P × P
R × R 25 R × R R × R 26 N × R
P × P 27 N–Q4 Q–N2! 28 B × P N–
B6+! 29 N × N B × N 30 Q–N1 Q–
R1! 31 B–B1 P–Q4! 32 N–Q2 P × P
33 N × P Q–Q4!∓∓
(b) 23 P–B4 N–B3 24 R–Q1 N × N
25 B × N Q–K3 26 B × B K × B 27 B–
B–N4 P–B4 28 P × P P × P 29 B–
K2 P–N4!∓
(c) 23 P–B5 N–B3 24 R–Q1 N × N
25 B × N Q–R5∓
21 . . . N–K4 22 Q–B1
22 B × Q N × Q 23 R × N B × B 24
R3–B3 B–Q2 25 K–R2 P–B4! 26
P × P P × P gives Black a decisive
advantage because of the threats of
. . . P–Q4 and . . . P–K4.
**22 . . . Q–Q2 23 P–B5 P–QN4! 24
B–N3 P × P 25 R × P R × R 26 P × R
N–B5!**
This little combination results in a
winnable position. To my great surprise Karpov, a good defensive
player, defends rather poorly and
with his next hastens the end.
27 B × N B × N 28 R–Q1 P–K4 29

B×B P×B 30 B–Q5 R×P 31 R×P
Q–B1! (89)

89
W

32 P–KR4 R–B7! 33 P–K5?

This results in the loss of a pawn
without compensation. He should
have tried 33 P–R5!?

**33 ... Q–B6! 34 R–Q3 Q×KP 35
Q–N2**

Or 35 R–K3 Q×B 36 R×B+
K–N2 37 Q–R1+ P–B3 38 R–K7+
K–R3 39 P–N4 R–Q7 40 P–N5+
K–R4! 41 R×P+ K–N5 ∓ ∓

35 ... K–N2

It's a pity that 35 . . . P–N5?!
doesn't work – 36 P×P? Q–K8+ 37
Q–B1 Q×Q+ 38 K×Q B–N4 ∓ ∓,
but after 36 Q–K4! the win would
be very difficult.

36 Q–B3?

Loses instantly. White could have
prolonged the game with 36 Q–K4
Q×Q 37 B×Q B–B3! 38 B×B
R×B, but without much hope.

**36 ... Q–K8+ 37 K–N2 R–B8 38
P–N4**

Or 38 K–R3 B–Q2+ 39 P–N4 P–
B4!

**38 ... Q–R8+ 39 K–N3 R–KN8+
40 K–B4 Q–R7+ 41 K–K4 Q×RP
0–1**

0902 Andras Adorjan–AK:

Ruy Lopez

1 P–K4 P–K4 2 N–KB3 N–QB3
3 B–N5 P–QR3 4 B×N QP×B 5
0–0 P–B3 6 P–Q4 B–KN5 7 P–B3
B–Q3 8 B–K3 Q–K2 9 QN–Q2
0–0–0 10 Q–B2 P–KR4 11 P–KR3
B×N 12 N×B P–KN4 13 P×P
B×P 14 N×B P×N 15 QR–Q1
R×R 16 R×R P–N5 17 Q–Q3 N–
R3 18 B×N R×B 19 Q–K3 R–Q3
20 R×R P×R 21 P×P P P×P (90)

90
W

22 Q–R6 Q–KB2 23 P–QN3 K–B2
24 Q–N5 Q–Q2 25 Q–N6 P–Q4
With the creation of a strong QP,
Karpov achieves enough counterplay to draw this inferior position.
26 Q–B6 Q–Q3 27 Q–N7+ K–N3
28 P×P P P×P 29 Q×KNP P–Q5 30
P×P P×P 31 Q–K2 P–Q6 32 Q–
Q2 Q–Q5 33 P–N3 ½–½

0903 AK–Zoltan Ribli:

Sicilian

1 P–K4 P–QB4 2 N–QB3 N–QB3
3 P–KN3 P–KN3 4 B–N2 B–N2 5
P–Q3 P–K3 6 P–B4 P–Q3 7 N–B3
KN–K2 8 0–0 0–0 9 R–N1 R–N1 10
B–Q2 P–QN4 11 P–QR3 P–B4 12
P–QN4 QBP×P 13 RP×P P–QR4
14 N–R2 RP×P 15 N×P N×N 16
B×N N–B3 17 B–QR3 P–N5 18 B–
N2 P–K4 19 KP×P B×P 20 N–
Q2 Q–Q2 21 N–B4 B–N5 22 Q–Q2
P×P 23 B×B K×B 24 R×BP P–
Q4 25 R×R R×R 26 N–K3 B–B6
27 R–KB1 B×B 28 R×R K×R 29
Q×B N–K2 (91)

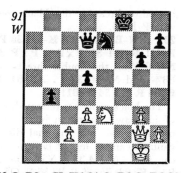

91
W

30 Q–B3+ K–K1 31 Q–B6 Q–R2 32
Q–K5 P–R4 33 P–Q4 Q–N2 34 K–
N2 K–Q2 35 K–B3 P–N6! Ridding
himself of one weakness 36 P×P
Q×P 37 K–B4 Q–R7 38 K–N5 Q–
Q7!? 39 P–R3 N–B4 40 Q×P+
K–B2 41 Q–B7+ K–B1 42 K×NP
N×N 43 Q–K6+ K–B2 44 Q–K5+
K–Q2 45 K×P Q–K7+ 46 K–N5
Q–B6 47 Q–B4 Q–Q4+ 48 K–N6
Q–B3+ 49 K–N7 N–Q4 50 Q–
B5+ K–Q1 51 P–N4 N–K2 52 Q–
B6 Q–K5 53 P–N5 K–Q2 54 P–N6
Q–Q4 55 P–R4 Q–KR4 56 Q–N5 Q–
Q8 57 Q–N5+ K–Q1 58 Q–K5 At
last White is ready to push the RP **58
... Q–N5 59 P–R5 Q–Q2 60 Q–R5+
K–K1 61 Q–K5 K–Q1 62 K–R8 Q–
R6** (92)

92
W

63 K–R7 The unpleasant threat was
63 ... N×P+ **63 ... Q–Q6 64
K–N7 N–B4+ 65 K–B8 Q–KB6 66
Q–B6+ K–Q2 67 P–Q5** Something

had to be done about 67 ... Q–R1+
68 K–B7 Q–K1 mate **67 ... Q×RP
½–½** White has perpetual check starting with 68 Q–B6+.

0904 Zoltan Ribli–AK:

Ruy Lopez

**1 P–K4 P–K4 2 N–KB3 N–QB3 3
B–N5 P–QR3 4 B–R4 N–B3 5 P–Q4
P×P 6 0–0 B–K2 7 R–K1**
One and a half decades ago the
candidate master Laszlo Alfoldy, a
known chess writer, believed and
ascertained that this position must be
won for White. Unfortunately no one
believed him at the time. However,
this is now one of Ribli's favourite
lines.
7 ... P–QN4 8 P–K5 N×P 9 R×N
According to theory this exchange
holds more chances for Black. However, 9 N×N P×B 10 Q×P 0–0 11
Q×RP R–N1 gives Black a good
game.
9 ... P–Q3
This is necessary, according to
theory, because the immediate 9 ...
P×B is good for White: 10 N×P 0–0
11 N–QB3 R–K1 12 B–N5 B–N2 13
N–B5. This assertion is based on the
following move order: 13 ... B–KB1
14 R×R Q×R 15 B×N P×B 16 Q–
N4+ K–R1 17 Q×P Q–K4 18
Q×QP St. Szabo–Balanel, Bucharest
1954. On the other hand, in the
game Barczay–Antoshin (from this
match), Black, instead of capturing
on move 15, continued 15 ... Q–K3
16 B×P Q×N 17 B×B R×B 18
Q–Q3 Q×Q 19 P×Q B–B3 20 R–
Q1 R–Q1 21 R–Q2 K–B1 22 P–B3
K–K2 23 K–B2 ½–½.
10 R–K1
That this variation is good for
Black is based upon 10 R–N5? P×B
11 R×P N–R4! of Reshevsky–Euwe,

Dubrovnik 1950. Instead of the decentralization of the rook, the retreat to K1 is much healthier. Now the weakened black pawn formation gives White's minor pieces good opportunities. We shall see on move 12 why the build-up of the White position is successful.

10 . . . P×B 11 N×P B–Q2 12 Q–B3! 0–0 13 N–B6! B×N 14 Q×B R–K1

Because of the B/K2 this move is a necessary preamble to . . . Q–Q2, and it is only this tempo that ensures that White, with some positional advantage, should regain the temporarily sacrificed pawn.

15 N–B3 Q–Q2 16 Q×Q N×Q 17 N×P B–B3 18 B–Q2 R–K3 19 QR–Q1 R1–K1 20 K–B1 K–B1 21 P–QN3 R×R+ 22 B×R!

The R/Q1 will still play a part in the undermining of Black's Q-wing. It would be a pity to exchange it.

22 . . . R–K4 23 P–QB4 P–N3 24 B–N4

There is a time when it is more important to make sure that the opponent cannot do something than do something ourselves. This move thwarts, for the moment, Black's . . . N–B4.

24 . . . R–KB4?

This attacking gesture is easily countered. On the other hand, Black is worried that the well-placed white minor pieces do not allow Black much counterplay. At this moment 24 . . . P–KR4 would have been a cold-blooded waiting game.

25 B–Q2! B–Q5 26 B–R6+ B–N2 27 B–K3

This type of build-up is more uncomfortable for Black than one with B–N4.

27 . . . N–K4 28 P–KR3!

This not only hinders . . . N–N5,

but also threatens the black rook with P–KN4.

28 . . . N–B3 29 P–B5 K–K2 30 P–KN4! R–K4 31 P×P+ P×P 32 N–N6 With the double threats N–B8+ and N–B4. **32 . . . B–B1 33 B–B4 R–K3 34 R–B1!**

The black army has retreated, the Q-side pawn formation is catastrophically weak and material disadvantage can no longer be avoided, e.g. 34 . . . N–K4 35 B–N5+ (35 R–B7+ K–B3) 35 . . . P–B3 36 N–Q5+ K–B2 37 R–B7+ is decisive. This motif recurs in other variations as well. The ensuing pawn sacrifice is therefore a positional necessity.

34 . . . P–Q4 35 N×P+ K–Q2 36 N–B7! R–K5 37 B–N3 P–B4

Another compulsory sacrifice because after 37 . . . P–QR4 38 N–Q5 not only does 39 N–B6+ win the exchange but 39 N–N6+ is threatened with annihilation as well. These two threats can only be parried by the hopelessly passive . . . R–K3.

38 P×P P×P 39 N×P P–B5 40 B–R4 R–K4 41 R–B4! R–KB4

On 41 . . . R–QR4 42 R×P followed by 43 B–N3 would save the knight, but the three pawns would quickly decide the issue.

42 P–N4! K–Q3 (*93*)

It looks as if the position has eased slightly for Black, as apparently

. . . K–Q4 is threatened. But oh no, the following clever move thwarts this last hope.

43 P–N5! R ×P 44 R ×P B–N2 45 R–B7 B–K4 46 R ×P R–R4 47 N–N4! The bone-crusher **47 . . . N ×N**

48 B–K7+ K–K3 49 B ×N R ×P 50 B–B5 B–B5 51 K–N2 R–B7 52 B–N6 R–N7 53 B–Q8 B–K4 54 B–R4 1–0 The game was adjourned here, but next day Black resigned without resuming play.

No details concerning this event are available, other than the fact that it was played in Leningrad (we are grateful to Karpov for pointing this out). The two games that appear in this section are probably from the Leningrad event, though it is possible that one or both of them could be from the USSR Armed Forces Team Championship zonal event, played in Riga earlier in 1970. No reference has been found to indicate that Karpov played in this latter event, but in the Latvian magazine, *Sahs* No. 12/1970, there is a photograph of the event in progress, and this shows Karpov strolling between the chess tables!

1001 Rafael Vaganian–AK:

Queen's Indian

1 P–Q4 N–KB3 2 P–QB4 P–K3 3 N–KB3 P–QN3 4 P–QR3 I used Tigran Petrosian's system for the first time very recently against Victor Korchnoi in the Grandmasters v. Young Masters tournament in Sochi; throughout that game I had a pretty good position. **4 ... B–N2 5 N–B3 P–Q4 6 B–N5 B–K2 7 P–K3 QN–Q2 8 P×P P×P** 8 ... N×P was not so good: 9 B×B Q×B 10 N×N B×N 11 R–B1 with the freer game for White. **9 B–Q3 0–0 10 0–0 N–K5 11 B–KB4 P–QB4 12 R–B1** On 12 P×P could follow 12 ... N×N 13 P×N N×P and Black stands well, but not 13 . . . P×P because of 14 B×P+ K×B 15 Q–N1+. **12 ... P–QR3** In my opinion an important loss of tempo. Bearing in mind that Black is preparing to play ... P–B4 it was essential to take the king off the dangerous diagonal

with 12 ... K–R1. **13 Q–B2 P–B4 14 P×P P P×P 15 KR–Q1** Black has a difficult game: 16 B×N BP×B 17 N×KP! P×N 18 N–K5 B–B1 19 Q×KP R–R2 20 N–B6 is already threatened. **15 ... Q–B1 16 P–QN4?** It's possible that the position does not demand such a radical solution but I wanted to get down to concrete operations. Not bad also was the quiet 16 B–B1. **16 ... P×P 17 P×P B×P** (*94*)

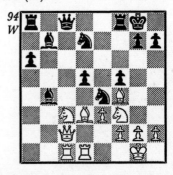

18 N–R2 Originally I had planned

to play 18 Q–N3 B×N 19 B×N BP×B 20 R×B N–B4 21 Q–R3 (against 21 Q–N6 N–R5 is good) 21 ... P×N 22 R×N, but here my opponent would have had at his disposal the unpleasant thrust 22 ... Q–N5. **18 ... B–R6** 18 ... Q×Q 19 R×Q B–R4 was stronger, although after 20 B–B7 White would have for the pawn a position rich in possibilities. **19 Q–N1! B×R 20 R×B N2– B4** if 20 ... N5–B4 then simply 21 B×BP R×B 22 Q×R Q–B1 23 Q–N1 **21 B×N QP×B 22 N–Q4 B–Q4 23 N–N4 Q–N2** Probably the only way to escape from the pin. **24 R×N KR–B1?** The losing move. It was still possible to hold on by means of 24 ... QR–B1 25 R×B Q×N 26 Q–Q1 Q–R5 27 N–K2 when, at the end, White does not have such an enormous advantage. **25 R×B Q×N 26 Q–Q1!** 26 R– Q8+ K–B2 27 Q–R2+ Q–B5 was weaker. **26 ... Q–R5 27 R–Q8+ K– B2 28 Q–R5+ 1–0** (Notes by Vaganian)

1002 AK–Zhelyandinov:
Ruy Lopez

The notes to this game that appear within quotation marks are by Karpov from 'Youth Lectures' in the Latvian magazine *Sahs*.

'In the game a variation put into practice by V. Smyslov is met.

'What is characteristic for this variation?

'As is usual in the Spanish (Ruy Lopez), White attempts to play in the centre and on the K-side, while Black organizes counterplay on the Q-side.

'And it is necessary to say straight out – concrete ways have not yet been found which allow White to obtain any advantage in the opening stage. The difficulties of the struggle

are carried over into a long and sophisticated middle-game. The following game is no exception.'

1 P–K4	P–K4
2 N–KB3	N–QB3
3 B–N5	P–QR3
4 B–R4	N–B3
5 0–0	B–K2
6 R–K1	P–QN4
7 B–N3	P–Q3
8 P–B3	0–0
9 P–KR3	P–R3
10 P–Q4	R–K1
11 QN–Q2	B–B1
12 N–B1	B–Q2

'Another possible continuation is 12 ... B–N2.'

13 N–N3	N–QR4
14 B–B2	P–N3

After this the black QN, up until the end of the game, is unable to get into play. 14 ... N–B5 15 P–N3 N– N3 getting the knight closer to the centre held out better prospects.

'Other continuations are 14 ... N–B5 or 14 ... P–B4. Against 14 ... P–B4 White replies 15 P–N3 N–B3 16 P–Q5 N–K2 17 N–R4 with advantage. I decided to lead play into the position that would have arisen from that variation.'

15 P–N3

'This move limits the field of operations of the knight on QR5. Very often White bases his play on utilizing the bad position of this knight. In the text game, the black knight retreats to the square b7, but even there it remains rather out of play. 15 N–R2 followed by P–KB4 deserves consideration.'

15 ...   P–B4

16 P–Q5

White blocks the centre and play is transferred to the flanks. It is clear that White will aim for a K-side offensive, while Black will go for a Q-side counter-attack. As soon becomes clear White has the better chances; in no small measure thanks to Black's passive QN.

| 16 ... | B–N2 |
| 17 B–K3 | N–R2 |

'Black adopts an interesting plan. He attempts first to restrict White's K-side play and then to start his Q-side counterplay. In the game Black did not completely succeed in effecting this idea. In the middle of the game he starts to change plans and suffers defeat.'

| 18 Q–Q2 | P–R4 |
| 19 N–R2 | N–N2 |

'Now and on the next moves the continuation P–KB4 and then P–B5 would have led to very sharp play.'

It is interesting that a similar position, but on move 22 and with the black queen on K2, arose in Stein-Geller, 37 USSR Ch. Stein effected the advance 22 P–KB4 and after 22 ... P×P 23 B×KBP had the initiative. All the same Geller brought about considerable complications with a pawn sacrifice.

Karpov chooses another plan. He carries out a regrouping manoeuvre in order to make the advance P–KB4 with the greatest possible effect. Above all he reduces to a minimum Black's freedom of action on the Q-side and only then gets down to his attack.

| 20 QR–B1 | P–R4 |
| 21 P–R3 | |

'The idea of the text move is clear – White intends, at an appropriate moment, to close the Q-side, and also to play P–QN4 to bury the black knight on b7.'

Now on 21 ... P–QR5 there will follow 22 P–N4.

| 21 ... | Q–N3 |

Later on the queen will go to K2, losing several tempi *en route*. Better 21 ... Q–K2 at once.

In the Chigorin systems Black usually operates on the lines of ... Q–B2, ... P–KB3 and ... N/QN2–Q1–B2. In the given case, Black's position has been weakened by ... P–KR4 and the advance ... P–B3 would make the position of the black king difficult. One gets the impression that White's plan, in conjunction with the move P–Q5, is very unpleasant for Black.

| 22 K–R1 | |

'White intends to prepare and carry out the advance P–KB4. Therefore it is useful to remove the king from the g1–a7 diagonal.'

| 22 ... | P–N5 |
| 23 RP×P | RP×P |

'23 BP×P BP×P 24 P–QR4 and the re-development of a knight on QB4 was possible, but at the time of the game I intended the plan with P–KB4 and I did not want to give it up. And so White succeeded in closing the Q-side, but at the same time conceded the QR-file. In the outcome it transpires that the QR-file does not give Black sufficient counterplay.'

| 24 P–QB4 | |

Now Black's Q side counterplay is finished. The incursion of the rooks along the open QR file is of a purely symbolic character.

24 ...	R–R7
25 Q–Q1	R1–R1
26 R–B1	Q–Q1
27 N–K2	

'Here I intended the re-deployment of knight on Q3 and bishop on QN2 and then the move P–KB4. Black prevented the re-deployment B–QN2, but all the same the white knight occupied the Q3 square.'

| 27 ... | B–KB3 |

The game is given in *Shakhmaty v SSSR*, where it was annotated by Magergut, as continuing 27 ... Q–K2 28 R–QN1 B–KB3 29 N–B1 R7–

R6 30 N–B3 K–R1 thus rejoining the game score (followed by Karpov) given in the column.

'Black loses the thread of the game. He makes all the subsequent moves in random order. Now if Black had decided to exchange the dark-squared bishops then a better way to do this was by 27 . . . Q–KB1 and 28 . . . B–R3.'

28 N–B3

'Preventing . . . B–KN4.'

28 . . .   K–R1?

'After White carries out his plan with P–KB4 it becomes clear that the king ought to be on KN1 in order to defend the f7 square.'

29 R–QN1	Q–K2
30 N–B1	R7–R6
31 N–Q3	B–N2
32 N–Q2

'White is unable to transfer the bishop to QN2 because of . . . P–B4.'

32 . . .   Q–B1

33 P–B4

White finally realizes this important advance.

33 . . .   P×P

It is not possible to maintain the centre, since on 33 . . . P–B3 there follows a double capture on K5.

34 B×KBP   Q–K2

Now Black's position falls apart. 34 . . . P–B3 is no help, e.g. 35 B–N3 and if 35 . . . Q–K2 (the threat was 36 P–K5) then 36 N–B4 N–B1 37 P–K5 with a strong attack.

35 N–B3

'Now White wants to carry out the advance P–K5. If he can achieve this then the black position collapses.'

35 . . .   R–R7

If 35 . . . P–B3 to prevent P–K5 then 36 B–B1! with N–B4 to follow.

'Against 35 . . . P–B3 White plays 36 B–R2 and then N–B4 and P–K5.'

| 36 P–K5 | B–B4 |
| 37 R–K1 |

'White breaks through in the centre, after which all his pieces spring to life. At the same time the black pieces are strewn all over the place and cannot organize effective resistance.'

| 37 . . . | Q–B2 |
| 38 R–QB1 | K–N1 (*95*) |

'See, he's got to put the king back. But there now follows a combination and White wins quickly.'

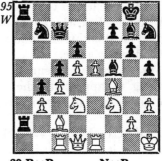

39 P×P	N×P
40 N×NP!	P×N
41 B×B	B–B6

'On 41 . . . P×B follows 42 P–B5.'

| 42 B–N1 | R–R8 |
| 43 R–K2 | 1–0 |

'It is typical that after the logical culmination of the plan, White succeeded in finishing the game with a little combination.'

Interview With Anatoly Karpov

This interview appeared in the magazine *Sahs* (No. 10/1970) in conjunction with the 'Youth Lectures' article (see the introduction to the previous game).

Q: Three or four years ago in the Republic's youth newspaper the headline was published *15-year-old Master*. It was devoted to you. Is it true that you were the youngest master in the Soviet Union?

AK: Yes, but not for long. Soon after the fourteen-year-old Ukraine player Misha Steinberg became a master.

Q: And how old were you when you became a candidate master?

AK: Eleven. This was in 1962.

Q: Who introduced you to chess and where did you get your first training?

AK: My father taught me to play. He did not have a grading, he just loved the game. I also started to love it and I started to go to the chess classes in the Metallurgists' Palace of Sport, we then lived in Zlatoust, and I was soon given a 3rd category rating.

Q: Who was your first trainer?

AK: The leader of the section in the Palace of the Metallurgists, Alexander Pak. He taught the section general opening play, was a great chess enthusiast, and succeeded in inspiring in his students a love for this game.

Q: It must be assumed that in those days you were still too young to appreciate the real beauty of chess. Who or what prompted you to be seriously immersed in chess culture as you now are?

AK: Capablanca. When I came across one of his games I began to study it with great interest, then a second and a third. I could sit out the evenings at these studies without getting bored.

And later something else happened: I landed up at Botvinnik's school; four times a year we went to Moscow and spent a whole week there. Mikhail Moiseyevich set homework and then went through it with us. This was very interesting. Undoubtedly it was there that I began to apply myself more seriously to chess.

Q: Which of the two events – the USSR junior selection tournament, or the World Junior Championship itself – do you consider was the more difficult for you?

AK: It was more difficult for me in the World Junior.

Q: Notwithstanding your good result?

AK: Yes. I was under constant tension.

Q: Your favourite opening for White?

AK: 1 e4. Most of all I like to play the Spanish (Ruy Lopez).

Q: Who is your favourite grandmaster?

AK: Spassky – I am all the time afraid of him.

Q: What are your immediate chess plans?

AK: To play well in the semi-final of the USSR Championship and to get into the final.

Q: And if we are not speaking about chess?

AK: To finish my studies at the Faculty of Economics, Leningrad University.

Q: Who is your trainer at the moment?

AK: Grandmaster Semyon Abramovich Furman.

Q: At the age of eleven you became a candidate master, at fifteen a master, and at eighteen an international master. When do you reckon to get the grandmaster title?

AK: It is still early to think about this question. I have played very few games with grandmasters. Now the important things are training and more encounters with strong chessplayers.

11 KUIBYSHEV 7.5.–2.6.1970

RSFSR Championship and 38 *USSR Championship semi-final*

	1	2	3	4	5	6	7	8	9	0	1	2	3	4	5	6	7	8	
1 **Karpov**	×	1	½	½	½	½	1	½	1	1	1	½	½	½	1	1	½	1	**12½**
2 Krogius	0	×	½	½	1	½	½	½	1	½	1	1	½	½	1	½	½	1	**11**
3 Antoshin	½	½	×	½	½	1	½	½	0	½	0	½	1	1	1	½	1	1	**10½**
4 Dementiev	½	½	½	×	½	1	½	½	½	½	½	½	½	1	1	½	½	1	**10½**
5 Doroshkevich	½	0	½	½	×	1	0	½	½	½	1	½	1	0	½	1	1	1	**10**
6 Averkin	½	½	0	0	0	×	1	1	0	½	1	½	1	½	0	1	1	+	**9½**
7 A. Zaitsev	0	½	½	½	1	0	×	1	0	1	½	1	0	½	½	½	1	1	**9½**
8 I. Kopilov	½	½	½	½	½	0	0	×	½	½	1	1	1	½	½	½	1	½	**9½**
9 Pozdnyakov	0	0	1	½	½	1	1	½	×	1	0	½	0	½	0	1	1	½	**9**
10 Rashkovsky	0	½	½	½	½	½	0	½	0	×	½	½	½	1	1	½	1	1	**9**
11 Chernikov	0	0	1	½	0	0	½	0	1	½	×	1	½	1	1	½	½	1	**9**
12 Anikayev	½	0	½	½	½	½	0	0	½	½	0	×	1	½	0	1	½	1	**7½**
13 Zhukhovitsky	½	½	0	½	0	0	1	0	1	½	½	0	×	½	1	½	½	½	**7½**
14 Tseshkovsky	½	½	0	0	1	½	½	½	½	0	0	½	½	×	1	0	½	1	**7½**
15 Shestakov	0	0	0	0	½	1	½	½	1	0	0	1	0	0	×	½	1	½	**6½**
16 Pavlyutin	0	½	½	½	0	0	½	½	0	½	½	0	½	1	½	×	½	0	**6**
17 Tarasov	½	½	0	½	0	0	0	0	0	0	½	½	½	½	0	½	×	½	**4½**
18 Sergievsky	0	0	0	0	0	–	0	½	½	0	0	0	½	0	½	1	½	×	**3½**

Karpov had number four in the draw and his opponents in rounds one to four were Krogius, Chernikov, Sergievsky and Doroshkevich, but it is not possible to work out with any certainty in what order he played the others.

Five games are available from this event

1101 AK–Pozdnyakov:

Sicilian

1 P–K4 P–QB4 2 N–KB3 P–K3 3 P–Q4 P×P 4 N×P P–QR3 5 B–Q3 P–Q3 6 0–0 P–KN3?! 7 B–K3 B–N2 8 P–KB4 N–QB3 9 N×N P×N 10 P–B3 N–K2 11 N–Q2 R–QN1 12 R–N1 0–0 13 Q–K2 P–QR4 14 P–QR4 P–KB4 15 K–R1 Q–B2 16 N–B3 P×P 17 B×P P–B4 18 B–Q3 B–Q2 19 B–N5 N–Q4 20 N–N5 P–R3 21 B×B Q×B 22 N–K4 *(96)*

22 . . . R–N3 23 R–R1 Q–K2 24 R–B2 KR–N1 25 B–B1 N–B3 26 N–N3 Q–KB2 27 P–B4 P–R4 28 R–B3 P–R5 29 N–B1 P–Q4 30 Q–K1 P×P 31 Q×QRP Q–K2 32 Q–K1 N–Q4 33 Q–K4 P–B6 34 P×P B×P 35 R–R2 Q–B3 36 P–R5 R–N8 37 Q–B2 B–Q5 38 P–R6 R8–N3 39 B–Q2 R–R1 40 Q–B4 N–N5 41 B×N R×B 42 Q–B2 Q–B4 43 Q–Q2

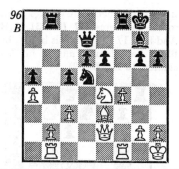

96 B

Q–K5 44 P–R3 R–N8 45 Q–R5 P–B5 46 Q–KN5 Q–B4 47 Q×RP P–B6 48 Q–K7 B–B3 49 Q–QB7 Q–QN4 50 K–R2 Q–Q4 51 R–N3 P–N4? 52 R–R5! Q×R 53 Q×Q P–B7 54 R×P+ B×R 55 Q×B+ K–R2 56 Q–R5+ K–N2 57 Q–K5+ **1–0** Black cannot prevent White from checking either on c7 or on the b1–h7 diagonal.

1102 AK–Nikolai Krogius:

French

1 P–K4 P–K3 2 P–Q4 P–Q4 3 N–Q2 P–QB4 4 KN–B3 N–QB3 5 KP×P KP×P 6 B–N5 Q–B3 7 0–0 KN–K2 8 P×P B×BP 9 N–N3 B–N3 10 R–K1 0–0 11 B–K3 B–N5 A safer equalizing method is 11 ... B × B! 12 P×B B–N5 =. **12 B×B** If White ignores the pawn offer, Black secures an easy game. **12 ... Q×B 13 B×N N×B 14 Q×P N–N5 15 Q–K4 B×N 16 P×B P–QR4 17 P–QR3** Krogius suggests as better 17 N–Q4. **17 ... N–B3 18 Q–K3 Q–N4 19 P–QR4 Q–R4 20 Q–K4 Q–KN4+ 21 K–R1 Q–B3 22 N–B5 QR–Q1?** 'After 22 ... Q×NP 23 N–Q7 KR–Q1 24 QR–N1 Q–Q5 the position is considerably simplified, and chances would have been level. However I renounced that line, over-estimating Black's attacking possibilities.' Krogius. **23 P–B3! P–QN3 24 N–Q3**

P–R3 25 P–KB4 R–Q2 26 R–K3 R/B1–Q1 27 R–KN1 N–K2 28 N–K5 R–Q8 29 R/K3–K1 R×R 30 R×R N–B4 31 N–N4 Q–N3 32 N–K5 Q–R4 33 Q–B3 Q–R5 34 N–B4 Q–B3 35 P–R3 N–R5 36 Q–K4 N–N3? The decisive mistake. 36 ... N–B4 was necessary. **37 P–B5!** Now White seizes the f5 square. **37 ... N–R5 38 N–K3 K–R1 39 R–K2!** Q–N4 40 K–R2 P–R4 41 P–KB4 Q–R3?! 41 ... Q–B3!? is probably rather better. **42 K–N3!** P–KN4 43 P×Pep N×P 44 N–B5 Q–B1 45 Q–B3 K–N1 46 Q×P R–Q6+ 47 K–N4 Q–R1 48 N–Q4 R–Q8 49 N–B3 R–Q4 50 N–N5 Q–QB1+ 51 K–N3 R–KB4 52 Q–R7+ K–B1 53 Q–R6+ K–N1 (97)

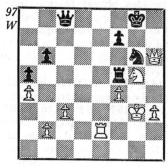

97 W

54 N–K6! 1–0

1103 AK–Alexander Zaitsev:

Caro Kann

1 P–K4 P–QB3 2 P–Q4 P–Q4 3 N–QB3 P×P 4 N×P N–Q2 5 N–KB3 Another possibility, which keeps more pieces on the board, is 5 B–QB4 KN–B3 6 N–N5 P–K3 7 Q–K2. Karpov's line is a solid one with a good reputation. **5 ... KN–B3 6 N×N+ N×N 7 N–K5 B–B4 8 P–QB3** More usual here is 8 B–QB4, but Karpov has an experiment in mind. **8 ... P–K3 9 P–KN4!?** Here

it is. This idea (to gain space on the K-side and embarrass the black QB) has been tried before after 8 B–QB4, but in that case Black has a good defence in 9 . . . B–K5 10 P–KB3 B–Q4! and if 11 B–Q3 Q–N3! or 11 B–K2 P–QN4. In the present position, Black cannot, of course, bring the bishop to d5 since then P–QB4 would win it at once. Zaitsev could now play 9 . . . B–K5 10 P–B3 before retreating to N3, but he quite justifiably decides to preserve this option for later use.

9 . . . B–N3 10 P–KR4 B–Q3 Now 11 P–R5 fails to 11 . . . B–K5 12 P–B3 B×N. **11 Q–K2 P–B4!? 12 P–R5?** 12 B–N2 should have been played. **12 . . . B–K5 13 P–B3 P×P!** The idea behind Black's eleventh move is now apparent. The bishop on e4 has an ideal retreat square at d5, and the immediate 14 P×P? is very bad because of 14 . . . B–N5+ and 15 . . . Q×P.

14 Q–N5+ N–Q2! An interesting, possibly strong, alternative was 14 . . . B–B3 15 N×B P×N 16 Q×BP+ K–K2! with attacking chances against the exposed white king. **15 N×P!** The best practical chance. The alternatives are all clearly in Black's favour:

(a) 15 N×N B–B3!;
(b) 15 Q×N+ Q×Q 16 N×Q B×P;
(c) 15 P×B B B×N.

15 . . . B–N6+ 16 K–K2 Nimzo-witsch used to say 'My king likes going for walks', this one is going on a very long journey. **16 . . . P–Q6+?** Black is so taken with the idea of driving the white king into the middle of the board that he overlooks the fact that it will be safer there than it was when nearer home. He should have played 16 . . . Q–B3! when after 17 P×B Q×N! the

threatened queen entry gives White severe problems. **17 K–K3! Q–B3** And now 17 . . . K×N is better, but Black has already missed his best chance. **18 K×B** (98)

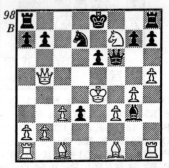

An heroic king. **18 . . . Q×N 19 R–R3** The idea of this is to cover the KBP while the king retires discreetly towards the Q-side. **19 . . . P–QR3 20 Q–N5 P–R3?** Kotov and Godes both question this and give Black a win with 20 . . . P–K4 21 R×B N–B4+ 22 K–K3 0–0 23 R–R3 (Black's threat was 23 . . . Q–KB5+) 23 . . . QR–Q1 24 B–Q2 N–K5! 25 K×N (25 P×N?? Q–B7 mate) 25 . . . Q–Q4+ 26 K–K3 Q–B4+ 27 K–K4 R–Q5+.

21 Q–K3! White must be careful. 21 Q–N6? loses to 21 . . . N–B4+ 22 K–K3 (Or 22 K–Q4 0–0–0+) 22 . . . B–B5+ 23 K–B2 Q×Q 24 P×Q P–Q7. **21 . . . P–K4** Black gets no win from 21 . . . N–B3+: 22 K×P N×NP 23 P×N Q×B+ 24 K–B2 Q×R as then 25 Q×KP+ leads to a draw by perpetual check. **22 K×QP** Not 22 R×B? Q–QB5+ and Black wins. Now White's king ends his stay in the centre by retiring, and picks up a golden handshake on the way. **22 . . . B–B5 23 Q–N1** Still keeping an eye on c5. **23 . . . 0–0–0 24 K–B2 B×B 25 R×B!** Much better than 25 K×B Q–KB5+ 26 K–B2 P–K5 27

P×P N–K4 when Black once again has a good attacking position. So Karpov returns the pawn to gain the initiative and 'his sort of position'. **25 ... Q×QRP 26 R–R2 KR–B1 27 R–Q2! Q–R5+** After 27 ... R×P 28 Q–R7 or 28 R1–Q1 followed by 29 B–N2 White obtains an overwhelming attack. Zaitsev decides it's time to go over to defence.

28 K–N1 ± Home at last! **28 ... Q–B3 29 B–Q3** Karpov plays with great energy; the threat of the pin by 30 B–B5 is sufficient to save his KBP. **29 ... K–B2 30 B–K4** Now that the bishop has reached this square there can no longer be any doubt about who is on top. **30 ... Q–QN3 31 Q–R2 R/Q1–K1 32 R1–Q1 N–B3 33 B–N6 R–K2 34 R–K1** Karpov systematically piles up the pressure on the unfortunate KP. **34 ... Q–N4 35 R2–K2 N–Q2 36 B–B5! ± R×B** In desperation Zaitsev gives up the exchange in a last-ditch attempt to hold his position together.

37 P×R Q–Q6+ 38 K–R1 Q×P/B4 39 Q–R4! The queen emerges from her burrow, and starts to make her presence felt. **39 ... N–B3 40 Q–QB4+ K–Q1** Or 40 ... K–N1 41 Q–B5. **41 Q–B5 N–Q2 42 Q–Q5 K–B1 43 R–K4 P–QN4** Otherwise 44 R–QB4+ or 44 R–QN4 will be crushing. **44 Q–B6+ K–Q1 45 Q×QRP Q×RP 46 P–KB4!** Finally he conquers the KP. **46 ... Q–B4 47 Q–R8+ K–B2 48 Q–R5+ K–B3 49 P–B4 P–N5 50 Q×NP R–K3 51 P×P 1–0**

1104 AK–Rashkovsky:

King's Indian

1 P–QB4 N–KB3 2 P–KN3 P–KN3 3 B–N2 B–N2 4 P–Q4 0–0 5 N–QB3 P–Q3 6 N–B3 N–B3 7 0–0 B–B4 8 P–Q5 N–QR4 9 N–Q4 B–Q2

10 P–N3 P–B4 11 P×Pep P×P 12 B–N2 P–B4 12 ... R–N1 is more normal. 13 N–B2 13 N4–N5 seems more testing. 13 ... R–N1 14 N–K3 N–B3 15 Q–Q2 N–QN5 16 P–KR3 B–B3 17 N/B3–Q5 N5×N 18 P×N B–N4 19 B–QB3 N–K1 20 B–R5 Q–Q2 21 QR–B1 B–QR3 22 KR–K1 R–N2 23 B–QB3 B×B 24 Q×B N–N2 25 N–B2 R–N3 26 P–K4 P–K4 27 P×Pep P×P 28 R/B1–Q1 Q–KB2 29 P–B4 N–R4 30 R–Q2 Q–KN2 31 Q–K3 P–K4 32 R–B2 P×P 33 P×P Q–R3 34 P–B5 Q×Q 35 N×Q N–B3 36 R–Q1 K–N2 37 R2–Q2 N–K1 38 P×P P×P 39 P–K5 P×P 40 R–Q7+ R–B2 41 R×R+ K×R 42 R–Q7+ K–K3 43 R×P N–B3 44 R–QB7 B–Q6 45 R×P R–R3 46 R–B6+ R×R 47 B×R K–Q3 48 B–N2 K–B4 49 P–R3 K–Q5 50 K–B2 P–K5 (99)

99
W

White sealed **51 P–QR4** One would think the position held no difficulties for Black: the active position of his king will compensate for the pawn minus.

When the adjournment session began, Rashkovsky made the strongest move **51 ... K–B6** saying that after 52 B–B1 N–Q2 53 P–R5 N–B4 the game would soon be drawn.

Since the threat 52 B–B1 is easily parried, White decided to try a different order of moves ... **52 P–R5**

N–Q2? The cunning is justified. Black proceeds to defend against the threat of 53 B–B1 and unexpectedly finds himself in a difficult situation. With 52 . . . K–N5 he could have forced the draw. **53 P–R4 K×P** And here 53 . . . K–N5 preserved drawing chances.

54 N–Q5 Suddenly it is clear that Black's king cannot approach the pawn on R5 or attack the knight because of N–N6+. **54 . . . N–B4 55 K–K3 K–R5** Naturally Black hastens to win back the RP, thinking that with one remaining pawn he can easily cope with the task in hand.

56 N–B4 K×P 57 N×P N–Q2 Forced. On 57 . . . K–N3 there follows 58 B–R3 B–B5 59 P–R5 B–N1 60 P–R6 K–B2 61 N–K7 B–R2 62 B–B5 and if 62 . . . K–Q3 63 N–B8+ or 62 . . . K–Q1 63 N–B6+ both win.

58 B×P B–B5 59 K–Q4 B–K7 60 B–B5 N–B3 61 K–K5 N–K1 61 . . . N–R4 is no use on account of 62 N–B4. If 61 . . . N–N5+ then 62 K–B4 N–R3 63 B–K6 and Black's knight is snared. Or 62 . . . N–B3 (instead of 62 . . . N–R3) 63 K–N5 N–R2+ 64 K–R6 N–B3 65 N–B4±±.

62 N–B4 B–Q8 63 B–N6 N–B2 64 B–R5 B×B 65 N×B K–N3 66 N–B4 N–K1 67 P–R5 K–B2 68 P–R6 N–Q3 69 P–R7 K–Q2 70 K–B6 1–0

1105 AK–Sergievsky:
Pirc

| 1 P–K4 | P–Q3 |
| 2 P–Q4 | |

The usual move. 2 P–KB4, 2 N–KB3 or 2 N–QB3 would give Black a chance to change his mind and go into a Sicilian with 2 . . . P–QB4.

| 2 . . . | N–KB3 |
| 3 N–QB3 | QN–Q2 |

A Sergievsky special which gives

the position a kind of Old Indian flavour. If 3 . . . P–B3 4 P–B4 B–N5 5 Q–Q3! leaves Black's bishop misplaced, and 3 . . . N–B3 4 N–B3 P–K4 5 P×P QN×P 6 N×N P×N 7 Q×Q+ K×Q 8 B–KN5 P–B3 9 B–QB4 K–K1 10 0–0–0 led to a clear advantage for White in Donner–Penrose, Amsterdam 1954.

The normal move is 3 . . . P–KN3. Spassky–Fischer continued 4 P–B4 B–N2 5 N–B3 P–B4 6 P×P Q–R4 7 B–Q3 Q×BP 8 Q–K2 0–0 9 B–K3 Q–QR4 10 0–0 B–N5 11 QR–Q1 N–B3 12 B–B4! N–R4 13 B–N3 B2×N 14 P×B Q×BP 15 P–B5! with a good attack for the pawn.

4 KN–K2

Pirc recommends 4 P–B4! as after 4 . . . P–B3 5 B–Q3, or 4 . . . P–K4 5 N–B3, or 4 . . . P–KN3 5 P–K5 Black stays cramped and White has plenty of opportunity to start attacking operations.

4 . . . P–QN4

An interesting move: we wonder if this position has ever occurred before in the history of chess! However, 4 . . . P–B4 was more natural, since if 5 P–Q5 P–QN4! or 5 B–K3 P×P going into a Sicilian.

5 P–K5!

Of course 5 N×P N×P is no good for White, but Karpov's move has a subtle result . . .

5 . . . P×P

Forced: 5 . . . N–KN1 6 P×P BP×P 7 N×P wins a pawn.

6 P×P N×P

If 6 . . . N–N5 7 P–K6! P×P 8 N–Q4 (threatening to 'smothermate' the black queen as well as to win the KN) 8 . . . N2–B3 9 B×P+ B–Q2 10 N×P wins.

| 7 Q×Q+ | K×Q |
| 8 N×P | |

This is the position that Karpov was after when he played 5 P–K5 and it is a fine example of his under-standing of the game. He now has:

(a) exposed the black king and disqualified it from castling;

(b) weakened Black's Q-side – because of the absence of the QP and QNP there exist several vulnerable squares which can serve as outposts for the white forces;

(c) achieved a Q-side pawn majority, which means a potential passed pawn.

These three factors are well exemplified in the subsequent play.

8 ...   **P–QR3**

Driving off the knight to relieve the pressure on c7. 8 . . . B–N2 9 B–B4 N3–Q2 10 0–0–0 (intending 11 B×N) 10 . . . K–B1 loses time for Black.

9 N5–Q4   **B–N2**

This piece has a nice diagonal here.

10 B–B4   **N–N3**
11 0–0–0!   **K–B1**

11 . . . N×B 12 N–K6++ K–K1 13 N×BP mate, or 12 . . . K–B1 13 R–Q8 mate.

12 B–Q2!

The idea of this back-step is to exploit some of the weak Q-side squares.

12 ...   **P–K3**

12 . . . P–QR4 to stop White's forthcoming manoeuvre is answered by 13 N–QN3! P–R5 14 N–B5 P–R6 15 P–QN4! P–K3 16 N×B K×N 17 P–N3 when White's bishops and Q-side pawns equal a winning position.

13 N–QN3!

Destination a5 to obliterate the dangerous bishop.

13 ...   **N–N5**
14 B–K1

A temporary inconvenience, but Black's pieces will later be pushed back as they have no support points.

14 ...   **B–Q3**

An attempt to preserve his beautiful QB fails after 14 . . . R–QN1 15 N–R5 B–R1 16 N–B3 R–N3 17 N–R4 and his QRP is lost.

15 P–KR3

Not 15 N–R5 at once because of 15 . . . B–B4 striking at f2.

15 ...   **N–B3**
16 N–R5

Progress at last! The elimination of Black's QB will not only give White the two bishops, but will also point up Black's Q-side weaknesses.

16 ...   **R–Q1**
17 P–QB4

Denying Black the use of d5, making more room for his own men, and beginning a general mobilization of his Q-side pawns.

17 ...   **N–B5**

Black could make a double bishop sacrifice if he is not careful – 17 . . . B–B4?? 18 R×R+ K×R 19 N×B+.

18 N×B

Now is the time for the exchange as g2 is attacked.

18 ...   **K×N**

18 . . . N×N+ is certainly no better: 19 B×N B–B5+ 20 K–B2 R×R 21 B×R K×N 22 B–KB3+ with a dream position.

19 K–B2

More preparation for the Q-side pawn advance, and also threatening 20 R×B!

19 ...   **B–K4**

Black is still averse to swapping knights and helping White's bishop to f3, so he stops the combination this way.

20 N–B3! (*100*)

Leaving the knight stranded on f4 and a target for a pawn attack.

20 ...   **R×R**

Black's best chance lay in 20 . . . B×N 21 B×B N–K5 since after 22 B–K1 (to keep the bishop pair) 22

100
B

... R×R 23 K×R R-Q1+ 24 K-B2 N-B4! Black's knights can deal with the bishops. White would play instead 22 R×R R×R 23 P-KN3! N×B 24 K×N N-N3 25 P-QN4! with a very favourable ending.

21 N×R

Though it seems that Karpov has got stuck in reverse gear the pieces will come bouncing back with a vengeance.

21 ...	**R-Q1**
22 P-KN3	**N-N3**
23 B-N2+	**K-N3**

The king is soon shown to be in a surprisingly ticklish position here.

24 N-B3!

Planning the manoeuvre N-K2, P-B4 and B-B2+.

24 ... **B-Q5**

Only helping White, but White's plans go through whatever Black does.

25 N-K2 **B-K4**

If 25 ... B-B4 26 P-QN4 B-K2 27 P-B4! K-R2 28 B-B2+ K-N1 29 N-B3! K-B1 30 R-QN1 and the creation of a deadly passed pawn will be decisive; White's method being P-QR4-R5 and then P-QN5.

26 P-B4 **B-Q3**

Or 26 ... B-Q5 when 27 N×B R×N 28 B-B2 wins.

27 N-B3!

For the third time this knight has played this move – making this

game an interesting twin of the game Karpov lost to Kavalek at Caracas 1970.

27 P-QN4 was also very strong e.g. 27 ... P-B4 28 B-B2 R-QB1 29 R-QN1. But as played White intends 28 B-B2+ P-B4 (28 ... K-R4 29 P-QB5 B-K2 30 P-R3! followed by P-QN4 mate) 29 N-R4+ K-R4 (29 ... K-R2 30 N×P) 30 B-K1+ K×N 31 B-B6 mate.

27 ... **P-B3** (*101*)

To answer 28 B-B2+ with 28 ... K-B2 but ...

101
W

28 P-QB5+!!

Conjuring tricks are an occasional habit with Karpov, but this one is a beauty.

28 ... **B×QBP**

If 28 ... K×P 29 B-B2+ K-B5 30 P-R3! and 31 B-B1 mate, or 29 ... K-N5 30 B-N6! Rany 31 P-R3+ K-B5 32 B-B1 mating again.

| **29 N-R4+** | **K-N4** |
| **30 K-N3!** | |

Not 30 P-N3 B-N5! and there is no mate. This king move rules out ... B-N5, covers the knight, and sets up B-B1 mate: Black has no choice.

| **30 ...** | **R-Q6+** |
| **31 B-B3** | **R×B+** |

Forced in view of the threat of B-B1.

32 N×R+ **K-R4**

32 ... K-N3 33 N-R4+ K-N4 34 B-B1+ wins the bishop.

33 N–R4	**B–B7**	
34 R–QB1!	**N–K2**	

34 ... B×P?? 35 R–B5 mate.

35 R–B2	**B–K6**	
36 B×P	**N–R4**	

Black is completely lost and this move enables Karpov to finish in elegant style.

37 B–K8!

Preserving the bishop to weave another mating web.

37 ...   **N×NP**

The condemned man . . .

38 K–B4

Threat 39 P–N4 mate.

38 ...	**N–Q4**	
39 P–R3	**N–N3+**	
40 K–Q3!!	**N×N**	

40 ... N–Q4 41 P–N4+ wins.

41 K×B	**N–KB4+**	
42 K–Q3	**1–0**	

Since if 42 ... N–N3 43 P–N4 is mate, and otherwise 43 P–N4+ K–N3 44 B×N leaves White with an extra rook.

A good illustration of Karpov's fusion of strategy and tactics, and what a lot of mates out of nowhere!

Presidente de la Republica

	1	2	3	4	5	6	7	8	9	0	1	2	3	4	5	6	7	8	
1 Kavalek	×	½	0	1	½	1	½	1	½	½	½	1	1	1	1	1	1	1	13
2 Panno	½	×	½	½	½	½	½	1	½	½	½	1	1	½	1	1	1	1	12
3 Stein	1	½	×	1	½	½	½	½	1	½	0	1	½	½	1	1	1	1	12
4 Benko	0	½	0	×	½	½	½	1	1	½	1	½	½	1	1	1	1	1	11½
5 Ivkov	½	½	½	½	×	1	½	½	½	½	½	½	1	1	1	1	½	1	11½
6 **Karpov**	0	½	½	½	0	×	1	½	1	½	½	1	½	1	1	1	1	1	11½
7 Parma	½	½	½	½	½	0	×	½	½	½	1	½	½	½	½	1	1	1	10
8 Sigurjonsson	0	0	½	0	½	½	½	×	1	½	1	½	1	½	½	1	1	1	10
9 Barcza	½	½	0	0	½	0	½	0	×	½	1	½	1	1	½	1	1	1	9½
10 Bisguier	½	½	½	½	½	½	½	½	½	×	½	½	½	0	½	1	1	1	9½
11 Addison	½	½	1	0	½	½	0	0	0	½	×	½	½	½	1	1	1	½	8½
12 O'Kelly	0	0	0	½	½	0	½	½	½	½	½	×	½	1	½	1	½	1	8
13 Ciocaltea	0	0	½	½	0	½	½	0	0	½	½	½	×	1	1	½	1	½	7½
14 Cuellar	0	½	½	0	0	0	½	½	0	1	½	0	0	×	½	½	½	1	6
15 Yepez	0	0	0	0	0	0	½	½	½	½	0	½	0	½	×	½	1	1	5½
16 Villaroel	0	0	0	0	0	0	0	0	0	0	0	0	½	½	½	×	½	1	3
17 Caro	0	0	0	0	½	0	0	0	0	0	0	½	0	½	0	½	×	1	3
18 Slujssar	0	0	0	0	0	0	0	0	0	0	½	0	½	0	0	0	0	×	1

In One Bound

A. Roshal

Anatoly Karpov obtained the grandmaster norm at the first attempt. This tournament in the capital of Venezuela was in itself interesting, but the most significant aspect of it was the success of the 19-year-old Soviet player.

Anatoly, quite tired after two hard events (prior to Caracas there was Kuibyshev, where Karpov won the title of RSFSR Champion), hurried home to Tula.

The Karpov's flat is still only beginning to resemble the home of a great sportsman. There is a silver cup for winning the World Junior Championship, and behind the glassware, amidst the crockery (a special place, for the time being, not having been devised), are medals. One of them, gold, for excellent work at school.

In almost every home there is a family album; old photographs, reminiscences and old tales . . . Nina Grigorievna proudly calls her collection her son's 'archives', but shows it seemingly with the fear that 'Tolik' will accuse his mother of immodesty.

It was in his native town in the Urals, Zlatoust, that Anatoly took his first steps in chess. To begin with, when he was seven, he won the third category title, and later on all his sporting ambitions, with the exception of the second category title, at the first attempt. All this time he always worked well at school. His achievements are by no means solely in the field of chess; there were photos of the ten-year-old Anatoly with the Red Banners of the All-Russian Young Pioneer camp 'Orlenok', and a document, presented to Karpov in the seventh class of Zlatoust School No. 3, on which it stated that he was awarded the title of 'honoured pupil', and so he went down in the annals of the school. All this, together with his success in the Tula technical and mathematical olympics, precisely characterize Anatoly Karpov – a talented youth, a conscientious person, whose name is noted in the roll of honour of the Central Committee of the Young Communist League. Although externally everything is at the summit it is easy to overlook the thoughtful and tense work that has gone into it.

He is no robot, it is his nature to be 'carried away'. He collects stamps – on the currently most popular themes of the cosmos and sport. Abroad (Anatoly has already been abroad seven times) he always acquires catalogues and more stamps, though at home he spends little time on them. This hobby is of some use for his future speciality – the political economy of foreign countries.

One of the reasons for his recent move from the Moscow State University to Leningrad University was the desire to live nearer his trainer, Semyon Furman, whom he holds in very high esteem and to whom is due no little part of the responsibility for Karpov's recent ascents.

'I have already played forty games this year, two of which I lost (in Caracas), which will suffice for the time being. Altogether in the last two years,' Karpov counts them up precisely, 'I have played 140 official games with the result $+75$ -9 $=56$. Now I have scored $11\frac{1}{2}$ points, but if these points had not amounted to the grandmaster title they would not have been satisfactory.'

Karpov is sober, rational, I might say has a practical outlook on life and on chess. The world's youngest grandmaster is a position player to the core.

Until the tournament in Caracas, Karpov had only played a total of five games against grandmasters: Gipslis, Krogius, A. Zaitsev and twice against Antoshin (+2 −1 =2). The young player confesses that from the very first he has exhausted his imagination in play against the bearers of the highest chess title.

1201 AK–Arthur Bisguier: R1:

Ruy Lopez

1 P–K4 P–K4 2 N–KB3 N–QB3 3 B–N5 N–B3 4 Q–K2 B–K2 5 P–B3 P–Q3 6 P–Q4 N–Q2 7 0–0 0–0 8 QN–Q2 8 P–Q5 should be played, but for the time being I was not concentrating in full and did not enter the struggle. 8 ... B–B3 9 P–Q5 N–K2 10 B–Q3 P–B3 11 P–B4 P–QR4 12 P–QN3 P–KN3 13 B–R3 P–B4 14 B–N2 B–N2 15 P–N3 K–R1 16 QR–K1 As long as Black cannot play ... P–B4 there is no sense White being in a hurry. 16 ... N–KB3 17 N–R4 N3–N1 18 N–N2 P–R5 19 P–B4 P–B3 20 N–K3 N–R3 21 B–B3 RP×P 22 RP×P B–R6 23 R–B2 B–Q2 24 Q–B1 Covering h3. 24 ... N–B2 25 P–B5 P–KN4 26 B–K2 N–N1 And here I began to bustle. Before opening the file it was necessary to put the king on h1 and to double rooks. 27 P–R4 P×P 28 P×P B–R3 29 B–KR5 Q–K2 30 K–R1 B–B5 31 Q–R3 P–N4 32 P×P B×NP 33 N2–B4 B/B5×N Necessary. Otherwise N–R5 and N3–B4±. 34 N×B R–R6 35 B–Q1 N1–R3 36 B–N2 R–R7 B–R5 R–KN1 38 N–Q1 R7–R1 39 N–B3 B–Q2 40 B–B1 QR–N1 41 B–Q1 R–R1 (*102*) 42 N–K2 R–R7 43 R–N1 R×R+ 44 K×R B–N4 45 N–B3 R×R 46 K×R B–R3 47 N–N1 I couldn't understand what to do next. It was only later, after the second adjournment, that we – L. Stein and I – established that in

102
W

order to realize the advantage it is necessary to exchange queens. 47 ... Q–N2 48 Q–QB3 N–N1 49 N–Q2 N–K2 50 B–R5 N–N1 51 K–K1 N1–R3 52 K–Q1 B–N4 Now if 53 K–B2 then 53 ... Q–R3 with the threat ... B–K7, after which it would be impossible to punch a hole through Black's position. 53 N–B3 Q–R3 54 N–N5 Still I could not see the right plan. It is interesting that three or four days later Bisguier told me that he could have drawn straight away with 54 ... P×N 55 P×P B–K1! 56 B–K2 B–N4 57 B–R5 and that afterwards he felt unhappy about thirty superfluous moves. When 54 N–N5 was played it was after one in the morning and, I can honestly say, I was totally unable to think anything out. 54 ... B–K1 55 B–K2 B–N4 56 B–R5 B–K1 Finally getting the chance to adjourn I sealed ... 57 N–B3 This position was to be continued at 10.00 a.m. the same morning. 57 ... B–N4 58 N–K1 Q–R7 59 Q–N2 Q–R4 60 B–Q2 Q–R1 61 Q–B3 Q–R7 62 N–B2 P–B5 63 P×P B×P

64 Q–QR3 After the game had finished my opponent told me that he was fully able to exchange queens here with an easy draw. But I don't think it's as simple as that. **64 . . . Q–N8+ 65 Q–B1** Now it's necessary to exchange queens all the same, or to sacrifice a piece. The grandmaster preferred . . . the second possibility. **65 . . . Q–N6 66 B/Q2×N Q–Q6+ 67 B–Q2 Q×KP 68 Q–R3** Much better was 68 N–K3 B–N6+ 69 K–K2 B×QP 70 Q–B7 and then B–QR3. **68 . . . B×P 69 N–K3 Q×RP 70 B×N B×B 71 Q×P Q–R5+ 72 K–K1 Q–R5+ 73 K–Q1 Q–R5+ 74 K–B1** Clearly one could escape the checks with 74 K–K2. **74 . . . Q–R8+ 75 K–B2 Q–R5+ 76 K–Q3 Q–N4+ 77 K–K4 Q–N2+ 78 N–Q5 Q–N8+ 79 K–K3 Q–N8+ 80 K–Q3 B×N 81 Q×BP+ Q–N2 82 Q–Q8+ Q–N1 83 Q–K7 Q–N6+ 84 B–K3 P–R4 ½–½** All this long and rather boring game demonstrates the persistence and the exhausting character of the struggle at the very start of an international tournament.

1202 Gedeon Barcza–AK: R2:

English

Karpov was not particularly put out by the draw (with Bisguier) because in between the sessions he had outplayed the experienced Hungarian grandmaster Barcza. In this game he cunningly exchanged the knights; Barcza's favourite pieces:

1 N–KB3 P–QB4 2 P–QB4 P–KN3 3 P–KN3 B–N2 4 B–N2 N–QB3 5 N–QB3 P–K4 6 P–Q3 KN–K2 7 0–0 0–0 8 N–K1 If 8 P–QR3 to initiate Q-side play then 8 . . . P–B4 is strong. **8 . . . R–N1** Also 8 . . . P–Q3 is worth a try. **9 N–B2 P–QR3 10 R–N1 P–Q3** If 10 . . . P–QN4 11 P×P P×P 12 P–QN4 P×P 13 N2×P

N×N 14 R×N Q–R4 15 P–QR3 is good for White. **11 P–QN4 B–K3 12 P×P P×P 13 N–K3± P–N3 14 N/K3–Q5 B–Q2 15 B–Q2 N×N 16 N×N N–K2 17 Q–B1?** Better 17 P–QR4 **17 . . . N×N 18 B×N? B–R6 19 R–K1?** (*103*) Now he should play 19 B–N2.

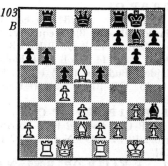

103
B

19 . . . P–QN4!∓ 20 P–R3 Q–Q3 21 B–KB3? And now 21 P–K4 would be preferable. **21 . . . B–K3 22 P×P? P×P 23 B–K3 KR–B1∓ 24 Q–Q2 P–N5! 25 P×P P×P 26 B–R7 R–N4 27 R/K1–QB1 R×R+ 28 Q×R P–N6 29 Q–B6??∓∓ Q×Q 30 B×Q R–R4 31 B–K3 R–R7 32 B–N5 P–N7 33 K–N2 P–K5 34 P–Q4 B–N6 0–1**

1203 AK–Bruno Parma: R3:

Nimzo–Indian

1 P–QB4 N–KB3 2 N–QB3 P–K3 3 P–Q4 B–N5 4 Q–B2

'When I came to the board I couldn't help thinking that in the next two rounds weaker opponents awaited me. I already had '+1' and there was no necessity to take risks right in the opening. In short, if I am to speak completely frankly, at the beginning I would not have been terribly worried only to draw.'

4 . . . P–QB4 5 P×P 0–0 6 N–KB3 N–R3! 7 B–Q2 N×P 8 P–K3

8 P–QR3 allows Black to equalize
with 8 . . . B×N 9 B×B N/B4–K5 as
in Kottnauer–Keres, Budapest 1952.

8 . . . P–QN3 9 B–K2 B–N2

9 . . . B–R3 is also possible e.g. 10
P–QR3 B×N 11 B×B R–B1 12 0–0
P–Q4 13 QR–Q1 N/B4–K5 14 B–
N4 B×P! Pirc–Bondarevsky, 1948.

10 0–0 P–Q3

Still 10 . . . N/B4–K5 can be
played, allowing Black equality: 11
N×N B×N 12 B–Q3 B/K5×B 13
Q×B B×B 14 Q×B (½–½ Flohr–
Najdorf, Budapest 1950) 14 . . . R–
B1 15 QR–B1 = Najdorf–Keres,
1952.

11 KR–Q1 P–QR3 12 P–QN3

12 P–QR3? would be a horrible
error: 12 . . . B5×N 13 B×B? B–
K5!

**12 . . . P–K4 13 P–QR3 B/N5×N 14
B×B Q–K2 15 N–K1!?**

15 P–QN4!? is suggested by
Milić: 15 . . . B–K5 16 Q–N2 N–R5
17 Q–N3 N×B 18 Q×N QR–B1 19
QR–B1 KR–Q1!

**15 . . . QR–B1 16 QR–B1 N3–
K5?!** (*104*)

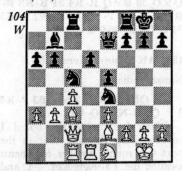

'Here I understood . . . to play passively for a draw was no longer
possible.'

Milić, in *Informator* 10, gives 16 . . .
P–Q4! 17 Q–N2 P×P 18 B×BP
KR–K1!?=.

17 P–QN4 N×B 18 Q×N N–K3?

'I daresay that it was because of
this mistake that Black lost the game,
because the knight on e6 did nothing.'

**19 Q–Q3 KR–Q1 20 B–B3 B×B 21
N×B± P–N3 22 N–Q2 N–B2?!**

22 . . . P–B4!? is probably preferable.

**23 N–K4 N–K1 24 Q–Q5 K–N2 25
P–R3 N–B3 26 N×N K×N**

Or 26 . . . Q×N 27 Q–N7

27 Q–K4 K–N2 28 R–Q5 Q–B2

'It is doubtful whether White
could succeed in winning by the
standard method Q–Q3, P–K4 etc.
Sensing this I found what was in my
opinion a very interesting solution
to the position.'

Milić points out that Black could
not avoid this position with 28 . . . P–
QN4 because of 29 P–B5 P–B4 30
Q–Q3!

29 P–B4! R–K1

Or 29 . . . P×P 30 Q–Q4+ K–N1
31 P×P with 32 P–KB5± to
follow.

**30 P×P P×P 31 P–B5 R–K3 32
Q–Q3!± P×P**

Not 32 . . . R–QB3? 33 R–Q7 R–
N1 34 R–B1 and wins.

33 P×P

If 33 R5×BP R–Q1!

**33 . . . Q–B3 34 R–N1 Q–B2 35 R–
KB1 R–B1 36 K–R1 Q–B3 37 R–
QN1 Q–B2 38 P–K4 R–QN1 39
R–KB1 R–N2 40 Q–QB3 R–N4 41
P–QR4 R–N1 42 R–B1 R–QB1 43
R–QN1 K–N1 44 R1–Q1 Q–K2 45
R–KB1 R–B2** (*105*)

If 45 . . . Q–B2 46 P–R5! with 47
R–QN1 to come.

46 P–R5 R3–QB3 47 R–B1 P–B3

'Aha, the enemy can't stand the
pressure!'

Or 47 . . . R–K3 48 R–QN1 R3–
QB3 49 R×P Q–B3 50 R–K8+ K–
N2 51 P–K5 and 52 P–K6!

48 Q–Q2 K–B2

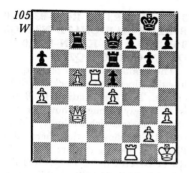

Not 48 . . . R×P? 49 R1×R
R×R 50 R–Q8+ with 51 R–
Q7±± to follow.
49 K–R2 K–K1 50 R–Q6!±±
With the idea 51 Q–Q5!
50 . . . R–Q2 51 R–Q1 R3×R
Not 51 . . . R2×R? because of 52
P×R Q–Q2 53 Q–Q5! K–B1 54
Q×R!±±.
**52 P×R Q–K3 53 Q–Q3 Q–R7 54
Q×P Q–QB7 55 Q–R8+ K–B2 56
Q–Q5+ K–N2**
'Deciding that my opponent was
making moves out of inertia and
that he was about to resign, I
played on at lightning speed. Meanwhile 57 P–R6 Q–R5 58 Q–Q3 Q–
B3 59 R–QR1 won immediately.'
57 R–Q2 Q–B6 58 R–R2(?) P–R4!
'Creating the threat of perpetual
check after . . . P–R5. It has become
clear that my rook is mistakenly
placed on the second rook, while its
right place is on the first or third
rank. It took me a long time – 40
minutes – to seal the most difficult
move . . .'
59 R–Q2
'Truly, for many players, to make
a "return" move is the most difficult
of all. The remainder was simple.'
**59 . . . P–R5 60 R–Q1 Q–B7 61 P–
R6 Q–R5 62 Q–Q3 P–N4 63 R–QN1
P–B4 64 R–N7 P–N5 65 RP×P
P×NP 66 Q–K2 1–0**

1204 Slujssar–AK: R4:

London System

1 P–Q4 N–KB3 2 N–KB3 P–B4 3
P–B3 P–QN3 4 B–B4 B–N2 5 QN–
Q2 P–N3 6 P–KR3 B–N2 7 P–K3
0–0 8 B–Q3 P–Q4 9 0–0 QN–Q2 10
R–K1 P–QR3 11 B–R2 P–QN4 12
P–K4 BP×P 13 BP×P P×P 14
N×P N–Q4 15 Q–N3 Q–N3 (*106*)

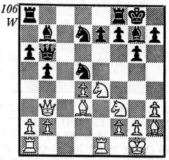

16 N–B3 N2–B3 17 QR–Q1 QR–B1
18 B–K5 N×N 19 P×N B–Q4 20
Q–N2 Q–B3 21 R–K3 Q×P 22
Q–K2 Q–N5 23 P–R3 Q–R5 24 B–
KB4 B–N6 0–1 25 R–R1 N–Q4

1205 AK–Miguel Cuellar: R5:

Sicilian

1 P–K4 P–QB4 2 N–QB3 N–
QB3 3 P–KN3 P–KN3 4 B–N2
B–N2 5 P–Q3 P–K3 6 P–B4 P–Q3
6 . . . P–K4!, Botvinnik's idea, may
well prove to be best here, provided
that Black follows normal praxis and
plays 5 . . . P–Q3. **7 N–B3 KN–K2 8
0–0 0–0 9 R–N1** 9 P–QR3 B–Q2 10
R–N1 R–B1 11 B–Q2 N–Q5 12 N–
K2 B–R5 was allright for Black in
Spassky–Geller, game 8 Candidates
1968; better still 12 . . . P–QN4 and if
13 P–B3 N×N/6+ 14 B×N P–QR4
with a strong initiative. **9 . . . R–N1
10 P–QR3 P–QN4 11 B–Q2 P–QR3
12 P–QN4 P×P 13 P×P B–N2 14**

Q–K1 N–Q5 15 N×N B×N+ 16 K–R1 B–N2 17 N–Q1 R–B1 18 R–B1 Q–Q2 19 B–QB3 B×B 20 N×B R–B2 21 N–Q1 P–B4 22 R–B2 P–Q4 (*107*)

23 R–K2 N–B3 24 P×QP P×P 25 Q–B3 Q–Q3 26 R–N1 P–Q5 27 Q–N3+ K–N2 28 N–B2 R1–B2 29 R–K6 Q–Q2 30 R1–K1 N–Q1 31 R6–K2 B×B+ 32 K×B Q–Q3 33 N–R3 R/KB2–K2 34 N–N1 R×R+ 35 R×R N–B2 36 N–B3 R–B6 37 Q–N1 Q–Q4 38 Q–N1 Q–B3 39 Q×P+ K–R3 40 Q–B2 P–N4 41 K–N1 R–R6 42 R–K1 P×P 43 N–Q4 Q–B2 44 P×P Q–Q1 45 N×BP+ K–N3 46 Q–B5 Q–B3 47 N–Q4 K–N2 48 K–R1 P–R3 49 R–KN1+ K–R2 50 Q–KB8 1–0

1206 Pal Benko–AK: R6:

Queen's Indian

1 P–Q4 N–KB3 2 P–QB4 P–K3 3 N–KB3 P–QN3 4 P–KN3 B–N2 5 B–N2 B–K2 6 N–B3 N–K5 7 B–Q2 P–Q4 8 N–K5 0–0 9 P×P N×N 10 B×N P×P 11 Q–R4 Q–Q3 12 0–0 R–Q1 13 KR–Q1 ½–½

1207 AK–Albéric O'Kelly: R7:

Ruy Lopez

1 P–K4 P–K4 2 N–KB3 N–QB3

3 B–N5 P–QR3 4 B–R4 N–B3 5 0–0 B–K2 6 R–K1 P–QN4 7 B–N3 P–Q3 8 P–B3 0–0 9 P–KR3 N–N1 10 P–Q4 QN–Q2 11 QN–Q2

The commencement of a quiet line that does not set Black any difficulties. The continuation 11 B–N5 is seemingly stronger, however the game Shamkovich–Holmov, Moscow 1970, showed that here also Black has nothing to fear: 11 ... P–R3 12 B–KR4 B–N2 13 QN–Q2 R–K1 14 B–B2 P–B4 15 P×KP P×P 16 N–B1 P–B5 17 N–K3 P–N3 18 P–R4 N–B4! 19 N×KP N3×P 20 B×B R×B 21 Q×Q+ R×Q.

'I refrained from the more committal 11 N–R4 and 11 P–B4 from purely practical considerations . . . opposite me sat a theoretical expert.'

11 ...	B–N2
12 B–B2	R–K1
13 N–B1	

I do not see the advisability of this manoeuvre. Korchnoi, against Portisch (USSR–World, Belgrade 1970), tried 13 P–QN3. After 13 ... B–KB1 14 B–N2 P–N3 15 P–QR4 B–N2 16 B–Q3 P–B3 17 Q–B2 R–QB1! Black had an excellent position.

13 ...	B–KB1
14 N–N3	P–N3
15 P–QR4	B–N2

This is often met with in tournament praxis. Only in place of the last move 15 ... P–B4 is usual. The Belgian grandmaster tries out a more original continuation.

| 16 B–Q3 | P–Q4 (*108*) |

Now the play takes on a forced character. Another, more reliable, possibility was 16 ... P–B3.

'Here I thought up a little trick. . . .'

17 B–N5!

'It turns out that this move practically forces the win of a pawn.'

The best reply. White gets nothing

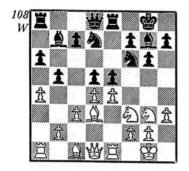

from 17 KP×P KP×P 18 N×P R×R+ 19 Q×R N–B4 20 B–B2 Q×P= or 18 R×R+ N×R! 19 N×P N–B4 20 P×P B×N! 21 P×B N×B 22 Q×N Q×P=.

17 ...	QP×P
18 B×KP	B×B
19 N×B	P×P
20 N×P	P–B4

'The threat was 21 N–B6.'

After 20 ... P–R3 21 N–B6 Q–B1 22 N×N+ N×N 23 R×R+? Q×R 24 B×N Q×N! Black holds on, however, after 23 B×N! R×R+ 24 Q×R B×B 25 Q–K4 K–N2 26 Q–Q5 Black's position leaves much to be desired!

21 B×N!

'O'Kelly, some way back, had not seen that here 21 ... B×B would be unplayable because of 22 N–B6 and 23 Q×N.'

| 21 ... | N×B |

Of course not 21 ... B×B? on account of 22 N–B6 Q–B1 23 Q×N! R×N 24 Q×Q+ etc.

| 22 N×BP | R×R+ |
| 23 Q×R | P–N5 (*109*) |

White has won a pawn, however, from being the attacker White is suddenly turned into the defender, which, undoubtedly, acts negatively upon the young player.

24 R–B1

'Right now I still don't know pre-cisely how I should have continued, but 24 R–B1 wasn't much use – that I do know.'

A. Karpov digs up this move which, however, does not fill the prescription of strengthening his position. This is increased by 24 R–Q1, so that on 24 ... P×P he can recapture with the queen. However, in that case, after 25 ... R–B1! it is not so easy for White to untie his position. For example: 26 P–QN4 N–K5 27 Q–B4 Q–R5! or 27 Q–B3 N×N 28 N–N3 Q–R5 29 P×N Q×QRP 30 Q–N7 R–B1 31 P–B6 B–K4 32 R–K1 B–Q3 or 28 ... N–Q2 29 N–B5 R×N 30 P×R Q–B2 31 Q–R8+ B–B1 32 P–B6 N–B4! 33 R–Q8 N–K3 34 R–B8 Q–K4 35 Q×P K–N2 and in both cases White gets nowhere.

The only solution is found in 27 Q–K1! N×N 28 N–B6! Q×R (28 ... N–Q6 29 N–K7+! K–B1 30 N×R etc.) 29 N–K7+! K–B1 30 Q×Q K×N 31 P×N R×P 32 Q–K2+ and Q×P.

26 ... N–Q4 is no good either: 27 Q–K1 N×P 28 N–B6! (28 Q×N? B–B1 29 R–QB1 P–QR4!) with advantage to White.

There was also a second possibility, namely: 24 N–K2, but in that case White would have had to consider the possibility of the sacrifice of a

second pawn: 24 . . . Q–K2!? 25
P×P R–K1 26 K–B1 Q–Q3 or 26 . . .
N–Q4 with an unclear position.

24 N–B6? was weak because of
24 . . . Q–Q3! 25 N–K7+ K–B1 and
White loses a piece.

24 . . .　　　　　P×P
25 P×P

This weakening of the Q-side com-
pensates Black for the missing pawn.
However, it is not so easy to decide
on 25 Q×P, the more so as after 25
. . . R–B1! 26 Q–Q2 (26 Q–Q3 N–
Q2!) Black would have had the
pleasant choice between 26 . . .
R×N! 27 R×R N–K5 28 N–K6!
Q–K1! (28 . . . Q–N1? 29 Q–B4 or
28 . . . Q–R1? 29 Q–Q5!) 29 N×B
Q–KB1 30 Q–Q4 N×R 31 P–R5 N–
N6 32 Q–B3 N×P 33 Q×N Q×N
with a draw, and 26 . . . N–K1 and
White is left with nothing but to give
back the pawn with 27 N4–N3.

25 . . .　　　　　Q–Q4!

Black centralizes his queen and
takes control of the important c4
square.

26 N4–N3

Also after 26 N5–N3 R–QB1
White will find it difficult to re-co-
ordinate his pieces.

26 . . .　　　　　B–B1
27 Q–Q1

The knight cannot leave QB5!
After 27 Q–K3 R–B1 28 P–QB4 Q–
B3 White must part with his QRP.

27 . . .　　　　　Q×Q+
28 R×Q　　　　　R–B1!

'After some unfortunate moves by
White O'Kelly has obtained the
moral right to offer a draw, but a
refusal followed.'

29 N×P　　　　　R×P
30 R–N1

30 N–R5!? would have been
interesting. Then on 30 . . . R–B1
there would follow 31 N–N7! R–B3
32 N–N8 R–N3 33 N–Q7! and the

chance appears for White to realize
his extra pawn. However, after 30
. . . N–K5! 31 P–B3 B–B4+! 32
N×B N×N 33 R–R1 K–B1 the
black king goes to Q2, while 34 N–
B6 is bad on account of 34 . . . N×P!

30 . . .　　　　　B–Q3!
31 R–Q1

The threat was 31 . . . R–B3.

31 . . .　　　　　B–B1
32 R–N1 (*110*)

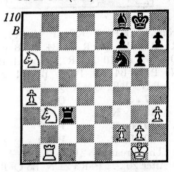

32 . . .　　　　　N–Q2?

'I was already prepared to agree a
draw, but the venerable grandmaster
wants, by taking advantage of the
time scramble, to trap my knight.
This was all that was necessary for
White.'

Black fancies that he is going to
trap the knight. He should play 32
. . . B–Q3! with a draw.

33 P–R5　　　　　R–B3
34 R–Q1!　　　　N–K4

Black placed his hopes on 34 . . .
B–Q3 to defend everything, but at
the last moment discovered that 35
N–N4! B×N 36 R×N R–B6 37 P–
R6! does not leave him any chance.

35 R–Q5　　　　　N–B5
36 N–N8　　　　　R–B1
37 N–Q7　　　　　B–K2
38 N–N6　　　　　R–B3
39 N×N　　　　　R×N
40 P–R6　　　　　R–QR5
41 R–QR5　　　　1–0

1208 Boris Ivkov–AK: R8:

Queen's Gambit Declined

1 N–KB3 N–KB3 2 P–QB4 P–
K3 3 N–QB3 P–Q4 4 P–Q4 B–K2 5
B–N5 0–0 6 P–K3 P–KR3 7 B–R4
P–QN3 8 B–Q3

A quiet and unusual line; White
has better prospects with 8 P × P as in
Fischer–Spassky, game 6 1972.

8 . . . B–N2 9 0–0 P–B4 10 Q–K2
BP × P 11 KP × P

11 KN × P is better according to
Taimanov.

11 . . . N–B3

11 . . . P × P 12 B × P N–B3 as in
Portisch–Filip, Budapest 1961, gives
rise to an unclear position with
chances for both sides.

12 QR–Q1?!

12 P × P should be an improvement.

12 . . . N–QN5! 13 B–N1 P × P 14
N–K5

Of course not 14 Q × BP B–R3.

14 . . . R–B1 ∓ 15 P–QR3 N5–Q4 16
B × N

'Here Ivkov offered a draw.

'In the street (the previous day,
Karpov and Stein had been taking a
stroll through the town and had met
Ivkov, who, upon seeing Karpov,
had called out 'already a grandmaster!'), in answer to the retort of
the Yugoslav grandmaster I had
observed that much could still
change, and this proved correct.

'The sporting result, the outcome
of my first games against grandmasters was very reassuring. Analysis
of the crosstable showed that if I
could avoid defeat against Ivkov,
Panno, Kavalek and Stein (far off –
in the penultimate round!) real
chances of first place could even
appear. And I had wanted to get a
draw, offered to me by a participant
in the USSR–World match, up until

the grandmaster lost a pawn, now I
somehow replied 'No', but I could
not play safely – my mind was
working hazily. Ivkov, on the other
hand, began to play with great
vigour and within a few moves the
game which brought me not only
my first zero, but also a lengthy de-
pression, was decided.'

16 . . . B × B

'A mistake. It was essential to
liquidate the dangerous knight.'

17 Q–B2 R–K1

The plausible 17 . . . P–N3 would
be a grave mistake: 18 N × NP
P × N 19 Q × P+ B–N2 20 Q–R7+
K–B2 21 B–N6+ K–B3 22 N–K4+
winning.

18 Q–R7+ K–B1 19 N–K4 R–B2 20
KR–K1!

White now has good compensation
for the pawn – Black's king is de-
cidedly unsafe.

'I didn't sense the danger, otherwise I would have played 20 . . . N–
B5.'

20 . . . P–B6 21 N–N3!

'The terrible combinational motif
N–B5 appears, but even here all is
not lost. It seems to me that 21 . . .
P–N3! gets a draw. Ivkov also, by the
way, thought this. In view of the
threats . . . B–N2 and . . . N–B3 it
seems that White is forced to take
perpetual check after 22 B × P B × N
23 R × B P × B.'

With the idea of 22 N–B5! winning, as the knight could not be
taken: 22 . . . P × N 23 N–Q7+ and
24 Q–R8 mate – Ivkov.

21 . . . N–K2!?

The best defence is 21 . . . P–N3!
e.g. 22 N–N4? B–N2! 23 N × P?? N–
B3 and Black wins! Or 22 B × P!
B × N! 23 P × B P × B 24 Q–R8+
K–B2 = – Ivkov.

22 Q–R8+ N–N1 23 B–R7 *(111)*
23 . . . B × N?

111
B

Black has much better here in 23 . . . K–K2! 24 N–B5+! P×N 25 N–B6++ K–Q2 26 N×Q P–N3!! (An easy move to overlook!) 27 Q×N! (27 R×R? B×Q 28 R×N and now 28 . . . P–B7 29 R–QB1 B×QP 30 N×B B×NP 31 R×BP R×R with an excellent position for Black was pointed out by Ivkov in the post mortem.) 27 . . . R×Q 28 B×R P–B7 29 N×B!! (not 29 R–QB1 K×N! 30 R–K2 B–K5∓) 29 . . . P×R=Q 30 R×Q K–K2 31 B×P!=. (analysis by Milić in *Informator 10*).

24 N–B5!±± P×N 25 Q×N+ K–K2 26 R×B+ K–B3 27 R×P+!

27 R×R? allows the tables to be turned dramatically by 27 . . . P–B7 28 R–KB1 Q–Q4!∓∓, or 28 R–QB1 Q×P and wins; while 27 Q×R is also an error: 27 . . . Q×Q 28 R×Q P×P! 29 R8–K1 B–K5!∓ **27 . . . K–K3 28 R–K1+ K–Q2 29 R×R 1–0** 29 . . . Q×R 30 R×P+ wins the queen and allows the bishop on KR7 to cover Black's QBP. A most important game.

1209 AK–Oscar Panno: R9:

Sicilian

1 P–K4 P–QB4 2 N–KB3 P–K3 3 P–Q4 P×P 4 N×P P–QR3 5 B–Q3 B–B4 6 P–QB3 A novelty in place of the usual 6 N–N3. **6 . . . P–Q3** Geller–Taimanov, 37 USSR Ch 1969, went 6 . . . N–K2 7 0–0 0–0 8 Q–R5 P–Q3 9 N–Q2 N–Q2 10 N2–N3 N–N3 11 Q–K2 B–R2 12 B–KN5 N–N3 13 QR–Q1 with some advantage to White. **7 0–0 N–KB3 8 Q–K2 QN–Q2 9 K–R1 N–K4 10 B–B2 B–Q2 11 P–QR4 R–QB1** Both sides now have roughly equal chances. **12 N–R3 0–0 13 P–KB4 B×N/Q5 14 P×B N–B3 15 Q–Q2 P–Q4 16 P–K5 N–KN5 17 B–Q1 Q–R5 18 P–R3 N–R3 19 N–B2 N–B4 20 R–B3 N–N6+ 21 K–R2 N–K5 22 Q–K2** (*112*)

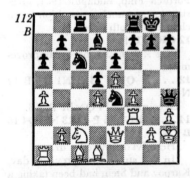

112
B

Black is now better; Karpov is still shaken up by his loss, and the circumstances surrounding it, against Ivkov. **22 . . . P–B4 23 B–Q2 B–K1 24 R–Q3 R–KB2 25 Q–K1 Q–Q1 26 N–R3 R2–B2 27 B–KB3 Q–K2 28 B–Q1 P–R3 29 R–B1 Q–Q1 30 Q–K3 P–KN4 31 R–B2 R–N2 32 P–KN3 N–K2 33 R×R Q×R 34 B–K1 N–N3 35 N–N1 Q–Q1 36 N–Q2 P×P 37 P×P N–R5 38 N×N BP×N 39 B×N Q×B 40 R–Q2 B–R4 41 B×B Q×B 42 R–N2 R×R+ 43 K×R K–B2 44 Q–KN3 Q–K7+ 45 Q–B2 Q–R4 46 Q–N3 P–R4 47 Q–N4 Q–Q3 48 K–N3 ½–½**

1210 Lubomir Kavalek–AK:
R10:

Ruy Lopez

1 P–K4 P–K4 2 N–KB3 N–QB3 3
B–N5 P–QR3 4 B–R4 N–B3 5 0–0
B–K2 6 R–K1 P–QN4 7 B–N3 P–
Q3 8 P–B3 0–0 9 P–KR3 N–QR4 10
B–B2 P–B4 11 P–Q4 Q–B2 12
QN–Q2 N–B3 I knew that Karpov
is a positional player. I studied
this variation before the game; I
had a feeling about it. **13 P×BP
P×P 14 N–B1 B–K3 15 N–K3
QR–Q1 16 Q–K2 P–B5 17 N–
B5 KR–K1** *The alternative is* 17 . . .
B×N 18 P×B KR–K1 or 18 . . . *P–
R3!?* *Igor Zaitsev's interesting idea
which can be found in game 0815.*
18 N3–R4! I think this is best.
Why should I not be able to go to the
wonderful KB5 square twice? And
why should I give my opponent good
drawing chances with Reshevsky's 18
B–N5 N–Q2 19 B×B N×B 20 N–N5
when Black has the wonderful move
20 . . . N–KB1! defending the K-
side? **18 . . . K–R1** The idea of this
move is 19 . . . N–KN1, 20 . . .
B2×N and . . . KN–K2. Then Black
will be in control of the important
squares d5 and f5. **19 N×B!** Just in
time! Otherwise Black's idea will be
successful. **19 . . . Q×N** If 19 . . .
N×N then 20 P–B4 is possible. Now
I have a free hand to go to KB5
again. **20 Q–B3 N–Q2 21 N–B5
Q–B1 22 B–K3** I was thinking that
Black should play 22 . . . P–B3 23
KR–Q1 N–B4 and then I have R–
Q6! as in the game. But let us see
what happened. **22 . . . N–B4? 23
KR–Q1?** I just picked up my rook
without looking at the position, and
when I had the rook in my hand I
saw the combination 23 N×P!
K×N (23 . . . Q×N 24 B×N) 24
B–R6+! K×B 25 Q–B6+ K–R4 26

P–KN4+ B×P 27 P×B+ K×P
28 R–K3 and mate.
Grandmaster David Bronstein
once told me he likes complicated
combinations better than the easy
ones. Let's follow him! **23 . . . P–B3
24 R–Q6** The only way to get into
Black's position. The next is forced.
**24 . . . R×R 25 B×N R–Q8+ 26
R×R Q×B 27 R–Q6!** (*113*)

Twice the same move! Now it is
with greater effect. White is already
threatening 28 Q–R5! P–N3 29 Q–
R4 P–N4 30 Q–R6 and wins. There
is no defence after 27 . . . P–N3 28
N–K7!! And after 27 . . . B×N 28
R–Q5! Q–K2 29 P×B the white
bishop gets on the h1–a8 diagonal
and White has a clear advantage.
Karpov makes the best move. **27 . . .
B–B2 28 Q–Q1 N–N1 29 R–Q8 Q–
B2** After the game Karpov told me
that he had the better move 29 . . .
Q–KB1 and after 30 N–Q6 the
choice between 30 . . . N–B3 which is
no good because of 31 N×R N×R
32 N–B7 winning a pawn, or 30 . . .
B–R4 after which I planned the
queen sacrifice 31 N×R!! B×Q 32
B×B N–B3 33 R–R8 and after
White wins the black knight he has a
clear advantage. **30 N–Q6!** Three
times on the same square! White
now gets a winning endgame. **30 . . .
R×R 31 N×B+ Q×N 32 Q×R+**

Q–N1 **33 Q–Q6** Also good was 33
Q–B7 followed by 34 P–QN3 and
Black is in zugzwang. **33 . . . Q–K1
34 B–Q1 P–KR4 35 B–K2 K–R2 36
P–QN3!** *More room for the bishop.
The black Q-side is weak, while the
bishop controls both sides of the
board.* **36 . . . P×P 37 P×P N–B3
38 P–QN4 K–R3 39 P–R4 Q–QB1
40 P–N3 K–N3 41 Q–Q1** *Black
should resign but he wanted to
'talk' some more before saying goodbye.* **41 . . . K–B2 42 B×RP+ K–
K2 43 B–N4 Q–B2 44 Q–Q5 N–Q1
45 B–B5 N–B2 46 Q–K6+ K–B1
47 Q×RP N–Q3 48 Q–R8+ K–K2
49 Q–KN8 N×B 50 P×N Q×P 51
Q×P+ K–Q3 52 Q×P+ K–Q4 53
Q–B7+ K–K5 54 Q–QN7+ K×P
55 Q×P Q–K8+ 56 K–N2 Q–
K5+ 57 K–R2 K–N5 58 Q–Q7+
K–B6 59 Q–Q2 1–0** (Notes by
Kavalek, except those in italics.)

1211 AK–Gudmundur Sigurjon-
sson: R11:

Pirc

**1 P–K4 P–KN3 2 P–Q4 P–Q3 3
N–QB3 B–N2 4 P–B3** It is more
forceful to play 4 B–K3 first.
**4 . . . P–QB3 5 KN–K2 P–QN4 6
B–K3 B–N2 7 P–KN4?!** 7 Q–Q2
N–Q2 8 Q–Q2 N–N3 N–N3! is also no
trouble for Black. **7 . . . P–KR4! 8
P–N5 P–K3 9 Q–Q2 N–K2 10 P–
QR4 P–N5 11 N–Q1 P–R4 12 P–
B3** Alternatively 12 P–R4!? B–QR3
13 N–N3!? **12 . . . P×P 13 P×P B–
QR3!∓** 14 N–N2 Not 14 N–N3?
P–R5! **14 . . . N–Q2 15 N–B1** 15 P–
R4 Q–B2! is good for Black, e.g. 16
N–N3?! P–Q4! 17 P–K5 (17 B–
KB4?! P–K4!∓) 17 . . . B×B with 18
. . . 0–0∓ to follow. **15 . . . B×B 16
R×B 0–0 17 B–KB4 P–K4 18 P×P
N×P 19 N1–Q3 N×N+ 20 N×N
Q–N3!∓** (*114*)

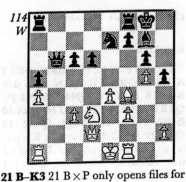

21 B–K3 21 B×P only opens files for
Black: 21 . . . KR–Q1 and 22 B×N
B×P! followed by 23 . . . Q–K6+
wins comfortably, or 22 B–B5?! Q–
R3! 23 R–Q1 Q–B5 and again the
illnesses of White's QBP and his Q3
are incurable. Also 22 P–K5 is no
good as it allows Black's knight to
jump on to f5. **21 . . . P–QB4 22 K–
B2 Q–N6 23 R/B1–B1 KR–Q1** 23
. . . KR–N1!? was worth considering. **24 N–B4 P–Q4 25 Q–B2 Q–N1
26 QR–N1 Q–Q3 27 K–N1 P–Q5**
If 27 . . . P×P 28 P×P! is a satisfactory antidote. **28 R–Q1 B–K4 29
N–R3 Q–K3 30 P×P Q×N?** Getting side-tracked, 30 . . . P×P! was
the consistent course. **31 P×B
Q×BP 32 B×P Q–N5+ 33 K–R1
R×R+ 34 R×R** White's pawns are
not a pretty sight, but he can survive. **34 . . . R–QB1** The KNP would
cause indigestion: 34 . . . Q×NP 35
P–K6! P×P 36 R–KN1 and
37 B×N±. **35 R–KB1! R×B!=**
Black could have gone wrong with
35 . . . Q–K3? 36 Q–B2!± **36 Q×R
Q×KP+ 37 K–N1 Q–KN5+ 38
K–R1 Q–K5+ ½–½**

1212 AK–G Villaroel: R12:

English

**1 P–QB4 N–KB3 2 P–KN3 P–Q3
3 B–N2 P–KN3 4 N–QB3 B–N2 5
P–K3 0–0 6 KN–K2 P–K4 7 0–0 P–**

B3 8 P–B4 R–K1 9 P–KR3 P–KR4
10 P–K4 P–Q4 (*115*)

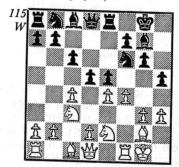

11 BP×QP BP×P 12 BP×P N×P
13 P–Q4 B–K3 14 K–R2 P–R5 15
P×P N–QB3 16 P–R5 Q–R5 17
N×N P×N 18 P×P P×P 19 R–
B4 Q–R4 20 R×P QR–Q1 21 B–
B4 R–KB1 22 B–N3 B–Q4 23 R–R4
Q–B4 24 B×B R×B 25 Q–N3 Q–
B2 26 R–B4 1–0

1213 Olavo Yepez–AK: R13:

Nimzo–Indian

1 P–Q4 N–KB3 2 P–QB4 P–K3 3
N–QB3 B–N5 4 P–K3 P–B4 5 B–Q3
0–0 6 N–B3 P–Q4 7 0–0 QP×P 8
B×BP QN–Q2 9 Q–K2 P×P 10
P×P P–QN3 11 R–Q1 B×N? 'It
was necessary to develop normally
with 11 . . . B–N2.' 12 P×B Q–B2 13
B–R3 R–K1 14 QR–B1 B–N2 15
N–K5! P–QR3 16 P–B4 'A dubious
move, giving up the opening advantage.' 16 . . . N–Q4 17 R–B1 (*116*)

'The dilemma arose: to retreat the
knight, risking going under to an
attack; or to allow the creation of
opposite coloured bishops with the
danger of a draw. I decided on the
second course, and if the worst had
come to the worst then I would have
had to try for a win against one of
the stronger players.' 17 . . . P–B3 18
N×N Q×N 19 B–N3 P–QN4 20

B–B5 B–B3 21 R–KB2 P–B4 22 Q–
K5 QR–B1 23 P–B4 P×P 24 B×P
B–N4 25 R–N2 'In vain, allowing
the exchange of bishops.' 25 . . .
B×B 26 R×B R–B2 27 R–B1
R–N2 28 R1–N1 R×R 29 R×R
K–B2 30 P–KR3 P–R3 31 P–KR4
R–Q1 32 P–N3 Q–B1 33 K–R2 Q–
R1 34 K–N1 Q–B3 35 P–R3 R–Q2
36 K–B2 N–B3 37 Q–K1 N–K5+ 38
K–N1 N×B 39 Q–B3 Q–K5 40
Q×N 'I was already starting to
make my move, in this winning position, when I noticed that my opponent's flag had fallen. So why go any
further? I asked to be given the full
point, but, unexpectedly, both the
controller and my opponent pro-
tested – only the immediate inter-
vention of several experienced players enabled this amusing conflict to
be resolved.' 0–1 time.

1214 AK–A Caro: R14:

English

1 P–QB4 P–K4 2 N–QB3 N–KB3
3 P–K4 B–B4 4 P–KN3 N–B3 5
B–N2 P–Q3 6 P–KR3 0–0 7 P–Q3
P–KR3 8 N–B3 P–QR4 9 0–0 N–Q5
10 N×N B×N 11 K–R2 B–K3 12
P–B4 K–R2 13 Q–B3 P–R5 14 N–
K2 Q–N3 15 R–QN1 B–QB4 16 R–
Q1 N–K1 17 P–KN4 P–B3 18 B–Q2
N–B2 19 P–B5 R–Q1 20 P–R4 R–
R1 21 K–N3 K–N1 (*117*)

117
W

22 P–N5 RP×P 23 P×P K–B2 24 R–KR1 B–Q2 25 Q–N4 QR–KN1 26 R×R R×R 27 P×P N–K1 28 Q–N6+ K–B1 29 P×P+ N×P 30 B–R6 B–B7+ 31 K–B3 1–0

1215 Victor Ciocaltea–AK: R15:

Petroff

1 P–K4 P–K4 2 N–KB3 N–KB3 3 N×P P–Q3 4 N–KB3 N×P 5 Q–K2 Q–K2 6 P–Q3 N–KB3 7 B–N5 Q×Q+ 8 B×Q B–K2 9 QN–Q2 N–Q4 10 B×B K×B 11 0–0–0 N–B5 12 B–B1 P–KR3 13 R–K1+ K–Q1 14 P–KR4 R–K1 15 R×R+ K×R 16 P–KN3 N–K3 17 P–Q4 N–Q2 18 B–Q3 N–KB3 ½–½ Another

two draws and Ivkov's comment 'already a grandmaster' would come true, so why should Karpov take any risks?

1216 AK–Leonid Stein: R16:

French

1 P–K4 P–K3 2 P–Q4 P–Q4 3 P×P P×P 4 B–KB4 B–KB4 5 B–Q3 B×B 6 Q×B P–QB3 7 N–Q2 B–Q3 8 B×B Q×B 9 KN–B3 N–K2 10 0–0 N–Q2 11 R–K1 0–0 12 R–K2 N–KN3 13 P–KN3 QR–K1 ½–½

1217 William Addison–AK: R 17

Petroff

1 P–K4 P–K4 2 N–KB3 N–KB3 3 N×P P–Q3 4 N–KB3 N×P 5 Q–K2 Q–K2 6 P–Q3 N–KB3 7 B–N5 Q×Q+ 8 B×Q B–K2 9 N–B3 P–B3 10 0–0–0 N–R3 11 N–K4 N×N 12 P×N N–B4 13 B×B K×B 14 N–Q2 ½–½ There is nothing wrong with quick draws in such circumstances – even Fischer was happy to draw games when it came to winning the World Championship.

Karpov's own view of the event appeared in *64*; 'This year I participated a great deal in competitions and already, after the first games of the Soviet Championship final, I felt overworked and very tired. Lack of confidence in my strength gave birth to caution – throughout the first half of the championship I tried not to take risks and made several quick draws. I cannot say that in the later stages I began to play better, it was simply that the other competitors were getting even more tired. In general it is difficult playing in the final. In international tournaments it is always possible to find some weaker opponents, but in our championships there are no outsiders. However, the advantage for me from playing in the tournament is unquestionable – I gained essential experience: you know a débutant is always a débutant!'

А. КАРПОВ.

	1	2	3	4	5	6	7	8	9	0	1	2	3	4	5	6	7	8	9	0	1	2	
1 Korchnoi	×	0	½	1	1	1	1	½	1	½	½	1	1	½	½	1	1	1	½	1	½	1	**16**
2 Tukmakov	1	×	½	½	½	½	½	½	0	½	½	1	1	1	½	1	½	1	½	1	1	1	**14½**
3 Stein	½	½	×	½	½	½	½	1	½	1	½	1	1	½	½	½	1	1	1	0	½	1	**14**
4 Balashov	0	½	½	×	0	½	½	½	½	0	½	½	1	1	½	1	1	1	1	1	1	0	**12½**
5 Gipslis	0	½	½	1	×	½	½	½	½	½	½	½	1	½	½	1	½	½	0	1	½	1	**12**
6 **Karpov**	0	½	½	½	½	×	½	½	½	1	0	½	1	½	½	1	1	1	½	½	½	½	**12**
7 Savon	0	½	½	½	½	½	×	½	½	½	1	½	½	0	½	½	½	1	1	1	1	½	**12**
8 Averbakh	½	½	0	½	½	½	½	×	½	½	0	½	1	0	½	½	1	½	½	1	1	½	**11**
9 Podgayets	0	1	½	½	½	½	½	½	×	½	½	0	1	1	½	½	½	½	½	½	0	1	**11**
10 Bagirov	½	½	0	1	½	0	½	½	½	×	1	½	0	1	½	1	0	0	0	1	1	½	**10½**
11 Dementiev	½	½	½	½	½	1	0	1	½	0	×	½	½	1	0	0	½	0	1	1	½	½	**10½**
12 Liberzon	0	0	0	½	½	½	½	½	1	½	½	×	0	½	1	0	1	½	1	½	1	½	**10½**
13 Doroshkevich	0	0	0	0	0	0	½	0	0	1	½	1	×	½	1	1	½	0	1	1	1	1	**10**
14 Holmov	½	0	½	0	½	½	1	1	0	0	0	½	½	×	½	½	½	½	½	½	1	1	**10**
15 Antoshin	½	½	½	½	½	½	½	½	½	½	1	0	0	½	×	0	0	½	1	½	½	½	**9½**
16 I. Zaitsev	0	0	½	0	0	0	½	½	½	0	1	1	0	½	1	×	½	0	1	1	½	1	**9½**
17 Vaganian	0	½	0	0	½	0	½	0	½	1	½	0	½	½	1	½	×	1	0	½	½	1	**9**
18 Mikenas	0	0	0	0	½	0	0	½	½	1	1	½	1	½	½	1	0	×	1	0	0	1	**9**
19 Karasev	½	½	0	0	1	½	0	½	½	1	0	0	0	½	0	0	1	0	×	½	1	1	**8½**
20 Platonov	0	0	1	0	0	½	0	0	½	0	0	½	0	½	½	0	½	1	½	×	1	1	**7½**
21 Tseitlin	½	0	½	0	½	½	0	0	1	0	½	0	0	0	½	½	½	1	0	0	×	0	**6**
22 Moiseyev	0	0	0	1	0	½	½	½	0	½	½	½	0	0	½	0	0	0	0	0	1	×	**5½**

1301 Leonid Stein–AK:
R1: 26 November:

Ruy Lopez

1 P–K4 P–K4 2 N–KB3 N–QB3 3
B–N5 P–QR3 4 B–R4 N–B3 5 0–0
B–K2 6 R–K1 P–QN4 7 B–N3 P–
Q3 8 P–B3 0–0 9 P–KR3 N–N1 10
P–Q3 P–B4 Introducing a novel
system in this line. 11 QN–Q2 P–R3
12 N–B1 N–B3 13 N–N3 R–K1 14
P–QR4 B–Q2 15 B–K3 B–KB1 16
N–Q2 N–QR4 17 B–B2 P–Q4!∓
18 P–Q4! BP×P 19 BP×P KP×P
20 B×QP N–B3 21 B×N Q×B 22
RP×P N–N5 23 NP×P R×RP 24
R×R Q×R 25 B–N1 P–Q5 26 N–
K2 P–Q6 Black has good play for his
pawn. 27 N–KB4 B–Q3 28 N×P!
N×N 29 B×N Q×B 30 N–B3 B–
N4 31 Q×Q B×Q 32 R–Q1 (*118*)

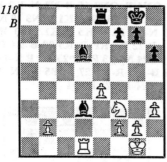

118
B

32 ... B×P?! 32 ... R–Q1 33 R×B
B–R7+ leads to an unclear position
with Black having some winning
chances. The rook ending is a safe
draw. 33 R×B B×N 34 P×B R–
N1 35 R–Q2 K–R2 36 K–N2 K–N3
37 K–N3 K–B4 38 P–R4 P–N3 ½–½

1302 AK–Vladimir Savon:
R2: 27 November:

Sicilian

1 P–K4 P–QB4 2 N–KB3 P–Q3 3
P–Q4 P×P 4 N×P N–KB3 5 N–

QB3 P–QR3 6 B–K2 P–KN3 7 0–0
B–N2 8 K–R1 0–0 9 P–B4 N–B3 10
B–K3 B–Q2 11 N–N3 P–QN4 A
little-known hybrid variation. 11 . . .
R–B1 12 B–B3 Q–B2 13 N–Q5± was
Euwe–Landau, Delft 1940. **12 B–B3**
R–N1 13 P–QR3 Q–B2 14 R–K1
P–K4 15 Q–Q2 P×P 16 B×P N–
K4 17 QR–Q1 R–N3 18 B–K2 B–
K3 19 N–Q4 R–K1 (*119*) ½–½

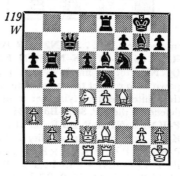

119
W

1303 Vladimir Karasev–AK:
R3: 28+29 November:

Queen's Indian

1 N–KB3 N–KB3 2 P–KN3 P–
QN3 3 B–N2 B–N2 4 0–0 P–K3 5 P–
B4 B–K2 6 N–B3 0–0 7 P–Q4 N–K5
8 B–Q2 This gives White some sur-
prisingly dynamic possibilities. 8 . . .
N×N 9 B×N P–Q4 10 N–K5 N–Q2
11 N–Q3 N–B3 12 Q–B2 N–K5 13
P×P P×P 14 QR–B1 P–QR4 15
KR–Q1 B–Q3 16 B–K1 Q–K2 17
P–B3 N–N4 18 B–B2 P–KB4 19
N–K5 K–R1 20 P–KR4 N–B2 21
P–B4 N–R3 22 B–B3 Q–K3 23 P–
R4 N–N5 24 Q–N3 N–B3 25 K–N2
QR–B1 26 B–K1 B–R1 27 R–B2
N–K5 28 R1–B1 R–QN1 29 B×N
BP×B (*120*)
30 R×P!? B×R 31 R×B R/B1–B1
32 R–B7 P–QN4 33 P×P Q–QN3
34 Q–K3 With the idea of P–B5 and
Q–N5. Tal suggested 34 P–B5!?

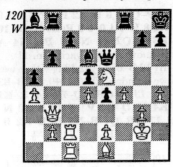

immediately. **34 ... R–N2 35 P–B5 R×R 36 N×R+ K–N1 37 N–K5 Q×NP** Not so much to win the pawn as to restrict the movements of the white queen by tying her to the defence of the KP. **38 B–B3 R–B1 39 P–KN4 B–N2 40 P–R5 R–B3 41 B–K1**(s) An amusing possibility is 41 P–R6 P×P 42 P–N5 R×P (42 ... P×P 43 Q×NP+) 43 P×P K–B1 44 N–N6+ P×N 45 P–R7 K–N2? (45 ... R–R4 busts White's idea) 46 Q–R6+! K×Q 47 P–R8=Q+ K–N4 48 B–Q2+ and wins. **41 ... B–R3 42 B–R4 R–QN3 43 P–N4** White hasn't really got enough for his sacrifice, but he hangs on well. 43 ... **Q×KP+ 44 Q×Q B×Q 45 P×P R–N7 46 K–N3 P–R3 47 K–B4 R–B7 48 B–K1 B–N4 49 B–N4 R–QN7 50 B–B3 R–N6 51 B–Q2 K–R2 52 B–K3 R–N7 53 N–N6 R–QR7 54 N–K7 B–B5 55 N–B6 R–R6 56 N–K5 B–R3 57 B–Q2 B–N4 58 B–N4 R–QN6 59 B–Q2 B–R3 60 B–B1 R–QB6 61 B–Q2 R–B7 62 B–N4 R–B7+ 63 K–K3 R–QN7 64 B–Q2 K–N1 65 B–B1 R–K7+ 66 K–B4 R–QB7 67 B–K3 R–QR7 68 P–N5 P×P+ 69 K×P K–R2 70 N–N4 B–K7 71 P–B6 K–N1 72 P–KR6 P×BP+ 73 N×P+ K–B2 74 N–K8 B–Q6 75 N–Q6+ K–N1 76 K–N6 R–KN7+ 77 K–B6 K–R2 78 K–K5 R–K7 79 N–B5 B–B5 80 B–B4 R–**

QR7 **81 N–K3 B–N6 82 N–N4 R×P 83 K–B5 K–N1 84 K–N6 R–R3+ 85 N–B6+ K–R1 86 K–N5 R–K3 87 K–B5 R–K2 88 B–Q6** ½–½

1304 AK–Vladimir Antoshin:
R4: 30 November:

Ruy Lopez

1 P–K4 P–K4 2 N–KB3 N–QB3 3 B–N5 P–QR3 4 B–R4 N–B3 5 0–0 N×P 6 P–Q4 P–QN4 7 B–N3 P–Q4 8 P×P B–K3 9 P–B3 B–QB4 10 QN–Q2 0–0 11 B–B2 N×N 11 ... P–B4, though more usual, had been obtaining some poor results. **12 Q×N P–B3 13 P×P R×P 14 N–N5** Or 14 N–Q4 N×N 15 P×N B–N3 16 P–QR4± Lasker–Rubinstein, St Petersburg 1914. **14 ... B–B4 15 P–QN4 B–QN3 16 B–N3 N–K2 17 P–QR4 P–B3 18 R–K1 B–N3 19 N–B3 N–B4 20 N–K5 B–K1 21 Q–R2 P×P 22 B×RP P–R3 23 B–B4 P–QR4 24 N–Q3 P×P 25 P×P N–Q3 26 B–K5 R–B2 27 N–B5 B×N 28 P×B N–K5 29 B–Q4** *(121)*

29 ... **R2–R2 30 Q–B2 B–Q2 31 P–B3 N–N4 32 R–R2 N–K3 33 B–B2 Q–B3 34 B–QN3 N–Q5 35 R×R R×R 36 Q–Q3 N×B 37 Q×N R–R8 38 Q–N4 B–B4 39 P–R3 R×R+ 40 Q×R P–Q5** ½–½

1305 Mark Tseitlin–AK:
R5: 1+3 December:

English

1 P–KN3 P–QB4 2 B–N2 P–KN3
3 N–KB3 B–N2 4 0–0 N–QB3 5 P–
B4 P–K3 6 N–B3 KN–K2 7 R–N1
0–0 8 P–QR3 P–Q4 9 P–N3 P–N3 10
B–N2 R–N1 11 N–QR4 P–Q5 12 P–
Q3 P–K4 13 B–B1 B–N5 14 B–Q2
Q–B1 15 P–N4 P×P 16 P×P B–R6
17 P–N5 B×B 18 K×B N–Q1 19
B–N4 Q–Q2 20 Q–B1 R–K1 21 Q–
R3 N–N2 22 KR–B1 N–B1 23 P–B5
P×P 24 B×P N×B 25 N×N Q–
K2 26 Q–R5 N–Q3 27 N–R6 R–N2
28 N–B5 R–N3 29 N–Q2 R1–N1
(*122*)

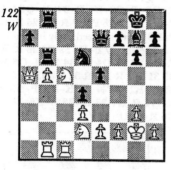

122
W

30 N5–K4 N×P 31 N–B4 R3–N2
32 Q–R2 N–B6 33 N×N P×N 34
R×R Q×R+ 35 P–K4 P–KR4 36
R×P Q–Q2 37 N–K3 P–R5 38 N–
Q5 R–N2 39 Q–B4 K–R2 40 Q–B8
Q×Q 41 R×Q P×P 42 RP×P P–
R4 43 R–QR8 R–N6 44 R–R7 K–
N1(s) 45 N–K7+ K–R1 46 N–B6
P–R5 47 R–R8+ K–R2 48 N–Q8
P–B3 49 N–K6 B–R3 50 N–B5 R–
B6 51 N–Q7 B–N2 52 R–R7 K–N1
53 R–R8+ K–R2 54 R×P R×P 55
R–R7 K–N1 56 N–B5 R–Q7 57
K–B3 B–R3 58 N–Q7 B–N2 59 K–
K3 R–Q5 60 P–B4 P–B4 61 KP×P
KP×P+ 62 NP×P P×P 63 R–
R8+ K–B2 ½–½

1306 AK–Oleg Moiseyev:
R6: 2 December:

QGD – Semi-Tarrasch

1 N–KB3 P–Q4 2 P–Q4 N–KB3
3 P–B4 P–K3 4 N–B3 P–B4 5
BP×P N×P 6 P–K3 N–QB3 7 B–
Q3 B–K2 8 0–0 0–0 9 P–QR3
Preparing to play Fischer already?
9...N×N... but Black varies from
the 9 ... P×P 10 P×P N–B3 11
B–B2 P–QN3 12 Q–Q3 B–N2 13
B–N5 P–N3 14 KR–K1 R–K1 15 P–
KR4 with an unclear position (can
White make any headway on the K-
side before Black's pressure forces his
QP to desert?), Reshevsky–Fischer,
5th match game 1961. 10 P×NP
Q–N3 11 P–B4 B–B3 12 B–N2 P×P
13 P×P B–N2 14 R–N1 Q–Q3 15
B–K4 N–R4 16 B×B N×B 17 N–
Q2 Q–B5 18 P–N3 Q–B4 19 Q–B2
Q×Q 20 R×Q KR–Q1 (*123*)

123
W

21 N–N3 QR–B1 22 R1–B1 R–Q3 23
K–B1 R3–B3 ½–½

1307 Vladimir Liberzon–AK:
R7: 5 December:

English

1 P–QB4 P–QB4 2 N–KB3 N–
QB3 3 N–B3 P–KN3 4 P–K3 N–B3 5
P–Q4 B–N2 6 P–Q5 N–QR4 7 B–K2
P–Q3 ½–½ 'The competitors were
given three rest days and the pre-
vious day had been one of these. But

there was a football match and Liberzon is the greatest enthusiast amongst the competitors' – Tal.

1308 AK–Yuri Balashov:
R8: 6+8 December:

Sicilian

1 P–K4 P–QB4 2 N–KB3 P–Q3 3 P–Q4 P×P 4 N×P N–KB3 5 N–QB3 P–QR3 6 B–K2 P–K4 7 N–N3 B–K2 8 B–N5 QN–Q2 9 P–QR4 P–QN3 10 B–QB4 B–N2 11 Q–K2 0–0 12 0–0 Q–B2 13 KR–Q1 KR–B1 14 N–Q2 P–R3 15 B×N N×B 16 B–N3 B–B1 Larsen–Gligorić, Moscow Olympiad 1956, went 16 . . . B–B3 17 N–B4!± 17 N–B1 B–B3 18 P–B3 P–QN4 19 N–K3 Q–N3 20 K–R1 P×P 21 N×P Q–N2 22 Q–Q2 R–Q1 23 Q–R5 R/Q1–N1 24 N–B3 R–R2 25 N–B4 N–K1 26 B–R4 B–K2 27 B×B Q×B 28 P–QN3 N–B2 29 N–Q5 (*124*)

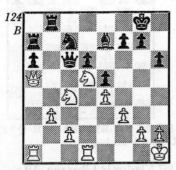

29 . . . B–Q1 30 N×N B×N 31 Q–Q5 Q×Q 32 R×Q R–Q1 33 R–R2 K–B1 34 P–QN4 K–K2 35 P–N4 R2–R1 36 R–Q1 P–QR4 37 R1–R1 P–Q4 38 N–K3 QP×P 39 BP×P R–Q7 40 P–B3 R×R 41 R×R K–Q3(s) 42 K–N2 K–B3 43 K–B3 K–N4 44 N–Q5 B–Q1 45 K–K2 K–B5 46 R–R3 R–R2 47 P–

R3 P–N3 48 N–K3+ K–N4 49 K–Q3 R–Q2+ 50 N–Q5 P×P 51 P×P P–B4 52 NP×P P P×P 53 R–R8 ½–½

1309 Viktor Korchnoi–AK:
R9: 7+8 December:

English

1 P–QB4 P–QB4 2 N–KB3 N–KB3 3 N–B3 P–Q4 4 P×P N×P 5 P–Q4 P×P 6 Q×P N×N 7 Q×N N–B3 8 P–K4 P–QR3 9 B–QB4 Q–R4 10 B–Q2 Q×Q 11 B×Q P–K3 12 0–0 R–KN1 13 KR–Q1 R–QN4 14 B–Q3 P–B3 15 P–QR4 P–N5 16 B–Q4 N×B 17 N×N B–B4 18 B–B4 B×N 19 R×B K–K2 20 R1–Q1 R–R2 21 P–QN3 P–QR4 22 R–Q6 B–Q2 23 P–B4 R–QB1 24 P–K5 P×P 25 P×P R–B4 26 R–K1 P–R3? This succeeds only in creating weaknesses. 27 P–R4 R–R1 28 R–K3 R–B3 29 R–Q4 R–B4 30 R–Q6 R–B3 31 R×R B×R 32 R–N3 R–KN1 33 K–B2 P–N4 34 K–K3 P–N5 35 K–Q4 P–R4 36 K–B5 B–K5 37 K–N6 R–QR1 (*125*)

38 B–Q3 B–B4 39 R–K3 R–QB1 40 B–B4 B–B7 41 K–N5 R–QR1(s) 42 R–K2 B–N3 43 P–N3 B–B4 44 R–Q2 B–K5 45 R–Q6 B–Q4 46 B×B P×B 47 R×P K–K3 48 R–B5 R–R2 49 K–N6 R–Q2 50 K×P R–Q6 51 K×P R×KNP 52 P–R5 R–N8 53 R–B2 P–N6 54 R–

QR2 R–KR8 55 P–R6 R×P+ 56
K–B3 R–R6 57 R–KN2 1–0

1310 AK–Mikhail Podgayets:
  R10: 9 December:

Ruy Lopez

1 P–K4 P–K4 2 N–KB3 N–QB3 3
B–N5 P–QR3 4 B–R4 N–B3 5 0–0 B–
K2 6 R–K1 P–QN4 7 B–N3 P–Q3 8
P–B3 0–0 9 P–KR3 N–N1 10 P–Q4
QN–Q2 11 QN–Q2 B–N2 12 B–B2
R–K1 13 N–B1 B–KB1 14 N–N3 P–
N3 15 P–QR4 P–B4 16 P×KP QP
×P 17 P–N3 Q–B2 18 B–N5 B–N2
19 Q–K2 B–B3 20 P×P P×P ½–½

1311 Yuri Averbakh–AK:
  R11: 10+11 December:

Semi–Tarrasch

1 P–QB4 P–QB4 2 N–KB3 N–
KB3 3 N–B3 P–Q4 4 P×P N×P
5 P–K3 P–K3 6 P–Q4 N–QB3
Reaching the semi-Tarrasch. 7 B–Q3
B–K2 8 0–0 0–0 9 P–QR3 N–B3 Or
9 . . . P×P 10 P×P B–B3 11 B–K4
Q–Q3 12 R–K1 R–Q1 13 B×N
P×B 14 N–QN5 Q–B1 15 P–R3 P–
QR3 16 N–B3 Q–Q3= Averbakh–
Furman, 26 USSR Ch 1959. 10 P×P
B×P 11 P–QN4 Obtaining a
slightly different position from 11
Q–B2 P–KR3 12 P–QN4 B–Q3 13
B–N2 Q–K2 14 N–K4! Flohr–
Levenfish, Moscow 1936. 11 . . . B–
Q3 12 N–K4 N×N 13 B×N Q–K2
14 B–N2 P–B4 15 B×N P×B 16
B–K5 B×B 17 N×B
After a rather shaky start Karpov
is saddled with this compromised
position, with its weakened pawns
and largely unprotected dark squares.
There is also the danger that Black
might be forced into a good knight *v*
bad bishop ending, especially so if
his e+c pawns are effectively blockaded. With these factors in mind

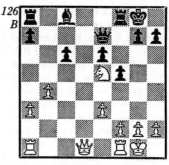

126
B

Anatoly continued 17 . . . P–B4 and
White replied with 18 R–B1! Preparing to launch an invasion into the
depths of enemy territory before
Black has time to mobilize. 18 . . .
P×P 19 N–B6 Q–B3 20 P×P B–R3
21 R–K1 B–N4! By placing the
bishop here, in preference to b7,
Black denies White the opportunity
of playing P–QN5 when 22 . . .
B×N 23 P×B! or 22 . . . P–QR3 23
P–N6! both allow White a dangerous
passed pawn. 22 Q–Q6 Threatening
23 N–Q4 winning the KP. 22 . . .
B×N 23 R×B Now Karpov must
hold on for his life. 23 . . . QR–K1 24
P–N3 Ruling out all possibilities of
. . . . P–B5 or back rank mates. If 24
R–R6 R–B2 25 R1–R1 Q–B6! 26
P–N3 R–N2! gives Black adequate
counterplay. 24 . . . Q–K2 So that if
25 Q×Q R×Q 26 R–R1 R–N1 etc.
25 R–Q1 R–B2 If 25 . . . Q×Q 26
R1×Q P–K4 27 P–N5 R–N1 28 R–
Q5 keeps the pressure on. 26 Q–B5!
Aiming for 27 R1–Q6 and since 27
. . . R–Q1 28 R×R+ Q×R 29
R×P loses a pawn, Black is obliged
to exchange queens thereby giving
White a passed pawn. 26 . . . Q×Q
27 P×Q R–N2 To answer 28 R1–
Q6 with 28 . . . K–B2. 28 R–R6 To
free the way for the QBP. 28 . . . R–
QB1 29 P–B6 R2–QB2 Now if
White tries 30 R–Q6 K–B2! 31 R–
Q7+ R×R 32 P×R R–Q1 33

R×RP K–K2 equalizes. **30 R–Q7!** The best way to preserve his initiative, since it would be very bad for Black to play 30 ... R×P 31 R6×P! **30 ... R×R!** Karpov has seen the full ramifications of this move, realizing that he can hold the inferior endgame which results. Since Averbakh is one of the world's greatest experts in the realm of endgame theory, Karpov's conduct of this position is all the more commendable. **31** P×R **R–Q1 32** R×RP 32 R×KP R×P 33 R–QR6 is also insufficient to win. **32 ... K–B2 33 K–N2 K–K2 34 K–B3** R×P Now material is level, but White places great hopes on his more aggressive king. **35 R×R+ K×R** (*127*)

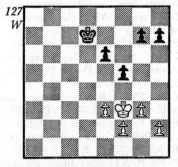

127
W

36 K–B4 K–Q3! Not 36 ... P–N3 37 K–N5. **37 P–K4!** Averbakh is doing his best to win this ending: the text stops 37 ... K–Q4 and threatens to win the KBP. **37 ...** P×P If 37 ... P–N3 then 38 P×P followed by 39 K–N5. **38 K×P K–Q2 39 K–K5 K–K2 40 P–R3 K–Q2 41 P–R4 K–K2** (s) **42 P–B3 K–Q2** Now White switches around the K-side to try and create a point of entry. **43 K–B4! K–K2 44 K–N5 K–B2** A big mistake would be the sequence 44 ... K–Q3 45 P–R5 K–K4 46 P–R6 P–N3 (46 ... P×P+ 47 K×P K–Q5 48 K×P K–K6 49 P–N4 wins) 47

P–B4+ K–K5 48 K–B6 and capture of the RP wins. **45 P–N4 K–K2 46 P–R5 K–B2!** If 46 ... P–R3+ 47 K–N6 K–B1 48 K–R7! K–B2 (48 ... P–K4 49 K–N6 K–N1 50 K–B5) 49 P–B4 K–B1 (49 ... K–B3 50 K–N8!) 50 P–N5 P×P (50 ... K–B2 51 P×P P×P 52 K×P K–B3 53 K–R7) 51 P×P P–K4 52 P–R6 P×P 53 P–N6! and again White wins. **47 P–R6 P–N3!** Not 47 ... P×P+ 48 K×P K–N1 49 P–B4 K–R1 50 K–N5 K–N1 51 K–B6. **48 K–B4 K–B3 49 P–N5+ K–B2 50 K–K5** The situation Averbakh envisaged when playing his 43rd move – White now penetrates ... **50 ... K–K2 51 P–B4 K–B2 52 K–Q6 K–B1! ...** but Black still draws a pawn down! ½–½ If now 53 K×P K–N1! (but not 53 ... K–K1? 54 P–B5 P×P–*54 ... K–B1 55 P×P P×P 56 K–B6–*55 P–N6! P×P 56 P–R7 and queens) 54 K–K7 K–R1 55 K–B7 stalemate, or 55 K–B6 K–N1 56 P–B5 P×P 57 K×P K–R1 and White cannot get through.

1312 AK–Vladimir Bagirov: R12: 12+14 December:

Alekhine

1 P–K4 N–KB3 2 P–K5 N–Q4 3 P–Q4 P–Q3 4 N–KB3 B–N5 5 B–K2 P–K3 6 0–0 B–K2 7 P–B4 N–N3 8 P×P P×P **9 N–B3 0–0 10 B–K3 P–Q4 11 P–B5 B×N 12 B×B** Also possible is 12 P×B: if 12 ... N–B5 13 B×N P×B 14 Q–K2 wins a pawn, and 12 ... N–B1 13 P–B4 gives White good chances. **12 ... N–B5 13 B–B1!?** 13 P–QN3!?, without the pawn exchange on move eight was tried in Spassky–Fischer: 13 ... N×B 14 P×N P–QN3!? (Safer would be 14 ... P–KB3!?= or 14 ... N–B3 15 R–N1 P–QR4 16 P–R3 P–QN3 17 P–QN4 RP×P 18 RP×P

P×P 19 NP×P R–R6=) 15 P–K4!
P–QB3! 16 P–QN4 NP×P 17
NP×P Q–R4 when 18 N×P!! was
both necessary and strong. **13 . . .
N–B3** (*128*)

128
W

In this position Anatoly is in pos-
session of a Q-side pawn majority –
how this can be turned to advantage
is clearly demonstrated by his subse-
quent play: **14 P–QN3 N5–R4 15
B–K3 P–QN3 16 N–R4! R–N1 17 R–
B1 P×P 18 N×P B–B3 19 P–QR3
N–K2 20 B–K2 N–B4 21 P–QN4**
Watch these pawns grow. **21 . . . N–
N2 22 B–KB4 N2–Q3 23 B–K5!
B×B 24 P×B N–N2 25 N–N3 Q–
N3 26 B–Q3 N–K2 27 Q–N4! P–B4
28 Q–Q4** (*129*)

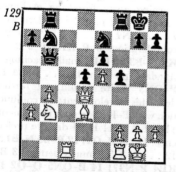

129
B

Now the centre is well under control full attention can be given to
creating that passed pawn. **28 . . .
N–Q1 29 P–N5 P–N4 30 P–QR4 N–**

N3 31 Q–R1! Q–N2 32 KR–K1 Q–
N2 33 N–B5 R–B2 34 P–R5 R–K2
35 N–R6! R–R1 36 B–B1 N–B2 37
N–B7 R–Q1 38 R–B6 N–B1** Karpov
has outplayed his opponent right
from the opening (and Bagirov has
written a book on Alekhine's defence!), having combined the
advance of the a+b pawns with an
ideal posting of his pieces in readiness for the final push. **39 P–N6 P×P
40 P–R6! N–R3 41 R1–B1 N–N5 42
P–R7 N×KP 43 R6–B2 N–B5 44
P–R8=Q** The single-mindedness
with which Karpov has cashed in on
his pawn majority illustrates how
dangerous this weapon is in his
hands. **44 . . . R×Q 45 N×R P–N4
46 R–R2 R–N2 1–0**

1313 Igor Platonov–AK:
R13: 13 December:

English

**1 P–QB4 P–QB4 2 N–QB3 P–
KN3 3 P–KN3 B–N2 4 B–N2 N–
QB3 5 P–QR3 P–K3 6 P–QN4 P–
Q3 7 R–N1 KN–K2 8 N–R3 0–0 9
N–B4 R–N1 10 P×P P×P 11 B–N2
P–N3 12 0–0 B–N2 13 N–N5 N–
K4?!** Better **13 . . . Q–Q2 14 B×N
B×B/4 15 N–Q3 B×B 16 K×B B–
N2 17 N×RP Q–Q5 18 R–B1 KR–
Q1 19 N–N5 Q–Q2 20 Q–N3 N–B3
21 R–B2 R–R1 22 N–K1 R–R3**
(*130*)

130
W

The pressure on the QRP will keep the draw in hand. **23 N–KB3 R1–R1 24 P–Q3 P–R3 25 K–N1 N–R4 26 Q–N1 N–B3 27 Q–N3 N–R4 28 Q–N1 N–B3 29 N–Q2 ½–½**

1314 AK–Igor Zaitsev:
R14: 16+18 December:

Ruy Lopez

1 P–K4 P–K4 2 N–KB3 N–QB3 3 B–N5 P–QR3 4 B–R4 N–B3 5 0–0 B–K2 6 R–K1 P–QN4 7 B–N3 P–Q3 8 P–B3 0–0 9 P–KR3 Q–Q2 10 P–Q4 B–N2 Not wanting a repeat performance of Fischer–Wade, Buenos Aires 1960, with 10 . . . R–K1 11 QN–Q2 B–B1 12 P–Q5!±, as Karpov would be almost certain to improve upon 12 B–B2 B–N2 13 P–Q5 N–K2 14 P–B4 P–B3 15 P–QN3 P–N3 16 N–B1 B–N2 17 N–K3 BP×P 18 BP×QP N–R4 19 R–N1 N–B5 20 B–Q3 P–B4∓ Neikirch–I. Zaitsev, Riga 1968. **11 QN–Q2 QR–K1** Aleksandr Geller queries this and suggests the plan 11 . . . KR–K1 followed by . . . B–KB1 and . . . QR–Q1. **12 N–B1** Better than 12 P–QR4 B–Q1 13 RP×P P×P 14 P–Q5 N–K2 15 B–B2 P–B3 16 P×P B×P 17 N–N3 N–N3 18 B–K3 P–R3 and Black does not stand badly, Shamkovich–Borisenko, ½–final RSFSR Ch 1959. **12 . . . B–Q1 13 N–N3 P–R3 14 B–B2 K–R1 15 P–N3 N–KN1 16 P–Q5 N3–K2 17 P–B4 P–QB3 18 QP×P Q×BP 19 P×P P P×P 20 P–N4 B–N3 21 B–Q3 P–Q4 22 B–N2 N–N3 23 P×P Q×P 24 B–K4 Q×Q 25 QR×Q B×B 26 N×B R–R1 27 P–R3 P–B4 28 N–Q6 P–K5 29 N–Q4 B×N 30 R×B N–B5 31 N×NP N–Q6 32 R–N1 KR–N1 33 N–Q6 N×B 34 R×N R×RP 35 N×BP N–B3 36 P–N5 R–R8+ 37 K–R2 R–R4 38 N–Q6 R–N3 39 R–**

B2 R–R1 40 R–B6 R1–QN1 41 R4–B4 (*131*)

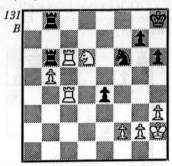

131
B

41 . . . R×P 42 N×R(s) R×N 43 R–B2 K–R2 44 R–B7 R–Q4 45 R–K7 R–KN4 46 R–R2 N–Q4 47 R–K8 N–B3 48 R–QN8 P–R4 49 P–N3 R–KB4 50 K–N2 P–N4 51 P–N6 P–N5 52 P–R4 K–N3 53 R–R7 R–B6 54 R–K7 K–B4 55 R–N5+ K–N3 56 R–N5+ 1–0

1315 Oleg Dementiev–AK:
R15: 17 December:

Alekhine

1 P–K4 N–KB3 2 P–K5 N–Q4 3 P–Q4 P–Q3 4 P–QB4 N–N3 5 P×P BP×P 6 N–QB3 P–N3 7 N–B3 Turning away from the exchange variation and into the modern line. **7 . . . B–N2** 7 . . . B–N5!? deserves consideration. **8 P–KR3 0–0 9 B–K2 N–B3 10 0–0** Finally reaching a standard position. **10 . . . B–B4 11 P–QN3** White should not further delay his development; in conjunction with P–KR3, a poor investment. 11 B–K3 or 11 B–B4 deserve preference. **11 . . . P–Q4! 12 P–B5 N–B1?!** 12 . . . N–Q2 is much better. **13 B–KB4 P–N3?! 14 B–QN5 Q–Q2 15 R–B1!± P- . QR3 16 B×N Q×B 17 BP×P N×P 18 N–QR4 Q–N2 19 N–B5** Stronger than 19 R–B7 Q–N1 20 N×N Q×N 21 R×P B–K5 which leaves Black chances of survival. **19 . . . Q–R2 20 R–K1 B–B1 21 Q–Q2** 21 N–Q3!? is also possible, with the idea of R–B7. **21 . . . R–K1 22 N–K5 B–N2 23 P–QR4 QR–Q1 24 Q–N4 B×N 25 B×B B–B1 26 N–Q3** 26 N×P! is also possible: 26 . . . Q×N 27 R–B6, or 26 . . . B×N 27 R–B7 B–N2 28 P–R5. **26 . . . N–R1 27 N–B5 N–N3** There is no real improvement available. **28 N×P! B×N 29 R–B7 Q–R1 30 Q×N R–N1 31 Q–B5 R×P 32 R×P B–Q6** (*132*)

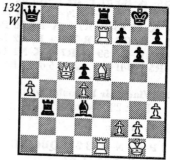

132
W

33 Q×P! 1–0

1316 AK–Rafael Vaganian:
R16: 19+22 December:

English

1 P–QB4 N–KB3 Trying to continue their theoretical argument in the Alekhine?! **2 N–QB3 P–Q4 3 P×P N×P 4 N–B3 P–KN3 5 Q–N3 N–N3 6 P–Q4 B–N2 7 B–N5 B–K3 8 Q–B2 N–B3 9 R–Q1 0–0 10 P–K3 N–N5 11 Q–N1 P–QR4 12 B–K2 P–R5 13 0–0 P–R3 14 B–R4 P–QB3 15 P–KR3 N5–Q4 16 R–B1 P–R6 17 N×N B×N 18 P–QN3 P–KB4 19 B–N3 N–Q2 20 B–QB4 N–B3 21 B–K5 K–B2 22 B×B+ Q×B 23 KR–Q1 KR–Q1 24 N–K1 N–Q2 25 B×B K×B 26 R–B3 Q–Q3 27 P–QN4 N–N3 28 N–B2 N–Q4** (*133*)

133
W

29 R–N3 R–R5 30 N×P R1–R1 31 N–B4 Q–K3 32 R–Q2 R1–R3 33 N–K5 Q–Q3 34 N–Q3 P–N3 35 R–B2 White will have a won position if he can open some Q-side files. **35 . . . P–K3 36 P–N5 P×P 37 R×P R–R2 38 R5–N2 R–R6 39 N–K5 R–B6 40 R×R N×R 41 R×P Q–Q4 (s) 42 Q–N3 1–0**

1317 Aivar Gipslis–AK:
R17: 20 December:

Ruy Lopez

1 P–K4 P–K4 2 N–KB3 N–QB3 3 B–N5 P–QR3 4 B×N QP×B 5 0–0 P–B3 6 P–Q4 P×P 7 N×P P–QB4 8 N–N3 Q×Q 9 R×Q B–Q2 Or 9 . . . B–Q3 10 N–R5 and not 10 . . . P–QN4 11 P–QB4 N–K2 12 B–K3± Fischer–Portisch, Havana 1966, but 10 . . . N–R3 11 B×N P×B 12 N–B4 B–K2 13 N–B3 K–B2 14 N–Q5 B–K3= Bagirov–Keres, Moscow 1967. **10 P–QR4! P–QN3** Varying from 10 . . . 0–0–0 11 B–K3 P–QN3 Fischer–Anastasopoulos, Athens, 1968, when Fischer could have continued with 12 P–R5! e.g. 12 . . . P–B5 13 P×P! P×N 14 BP×P±. **11 N–B3 0–0–0** (*134*) **12 B–B4** Also possible are 12 P–R5 and 12 B–K3 transposing back to the Fischer game. **12 . . . P–B5! 13 N–Q2 B–K3 14 N–B3 R×R+ 15 R×R**

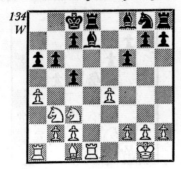

134
W

B–QB4 16 N–Q4 B×N 17 R×B±
½–½

1318 AK–Vladas Mikenas:
R18: 21+22 December:

Alekhine

1 P–K4 N–KB3 2 P–K5 N–Q4 3
P–Q4 P–Q3 4 N–KB3 B–N5 5 B–K2
N–QB3 6 P×P KP×P 6 . . .
Q×P!? – Reti. 7 P–B4 N–B3 8
0–0 B–K2 9 P–KR3 B–R4 10 P–Q5
B×N 11 B×B N–K4 12 B–K2
0–0 13 N–B3 N4–Q2 14 B–K3 P–
QR4 15 Q–B2 N–B4 16 P–QR3
N3–Q2 17 P–QN4 P×P 18 P×P
R×R 19 R×R N–R3 20 Q–Q2
N×P 21 R–N1 N–R3 22 R×P N3–
B4 23 R–R7 Q–N1 24 N–N5 B–Q1
25 Q–R2 White has very strong
pressure against Black's cramped
position. 25 . . . Q–N3 26 R–R8 P–
QB3 (135)

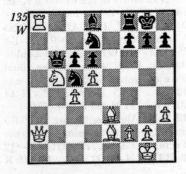

135
W

27 N×P P P×P 28 N–B8 Q–N2 29
B–B3 N–K5 30 P×P N–B6 31 Q–
R6 Q×Q 32 R×Q B–B3 33 R–R8
N–K4 34 B–B5 R–Q1 35 B–N6
N×B+ 36 P×N R–B1 36 . . .
R×P 37 N–K7+ R–Q1 38 R×R
mate would not be very amusing for
Black. 37 B–B5 R–Q1 38 B–K7 R–
K1 39 P–Q6 B×B 40 P–Q7! K–
B1 41 P×R=Q+ (s) K×Q 42 N–
Q6+ K–Q2 43 N×P K–K3 44 N–
Q8+ K–Q2 45 N–N7 N–K7+ 46
K–R2 K K3 47 R–R4 B–B3 48 N–
B5+ K–B4 49 N–Q3 K–N4 50 R–
R5+ K–R3 51 P–B4 K–N3 52 K–
N2 P–R3 53 K–B3 N–Q5+ 54 K–
N4 K–B2 55 R–R7+ K–K3 56 P–
B5+ K–Q3 57 R–R6+ K–K2 58
N–B4 K–B2 59 R–R7+ K–N1 60
N–R5 1–0 If 60 . . . B–K5 61 P–B4.

1319 Vladimir Doroshkevich–AK
R19: 23 December:

Nimzo–Indian

1 P–Q4 N–KB3 2 P–QB4 P–K3 3
N–QB3 B–N5 4 Q–B2
A move which used to be played
frequently in years gone by, though
nowadays 4 P–K3 is usual. The idea
is to recapture on QB3 with the
queen if Black exchanges, thereby
avoiding doubled pawns. Though
from QB2 the queen observes K4 it
leaves the QP unprotected and also
can itself become an object of attack
by Black's minor pieces or rooks
should the QB-file become opened.
4 . . . 0–0
A solid system; the alternatives
are 4 . . . N–B3, 4 . . . P–Q4 and 4
. . . P–B4.
5 P–QR3
The best; 5 P–K4 is answered by 5
. . . P–Q4 6 P–K5 N–K5. Doroshkevich has also tried 5 B–N5 here,
e.g. against Giterman, Riga 1968,
when he got a good game after 5 . . .

P–KR3 6 B–R4 P–Q3 7 P–K3 QN–
Q2 8 B–Q3 P–K4 9 KN–K2 B×N+
10 N×B P×P 11 P×P R–K1+ 12
N–K2 P–Q4 13 P–B5. Black does
better to strike with . . . P–QB4 as
Karpov plays in this game.

5 . . . B×N+ 6 Q×B P–Q3

6 . . . N–K5 7 Q–B2 P–Q4 is
another, more complex, line.

7 B–N5 QN–Q2 8 P–K3

8 N–B3 would transpose into
Doroshkevich–Smyslov, Riga 1968,
when the ex-world champion equalized without too much trouble after
8 . . . P–QN3 9 P–KN3 B–N2 10 B–
N2 Q–B1 11 B×N N×B 12 0–0 P–
B4 13 KR–Q1 R–Q1 and a draw
was soon agreed. Here Doroshkevich
plans a different development.

**8 . . . P–QN3 9 B–Q3 B–N2 10 P–
B3**

Stopping the attack on KN2 and
getting control of the important K4
square.

10 . . . P–B4!

10 . . . P–KR3 11 B–R4 P–K4? 12
B–B5! P×P 13 Q×P! gave White a
nice game in Forintos–Filip, Reggio
Emilia 1962/3, when the bishop pair
sprang to life.

11 N–K2 R–B1

Shadowing the white queen.

**12 R–QB1 P–KR3 13 B–R4 P×P!
14 P×P**

14 Q×P N–K4 15 B–N1 B×P! is
good for Black.

14 . . . P–QN4!

Taking full advantage of the pin to
fix White with weak pawns.

15 P–QN3

If 15 Q–N3 P×P 16 B×P Q–
R4+ 17 N–B3 N–N3 18 B–Q3 N/B3–
Q4 exploiting the weaknesses in
White's camp.

15 . . . P×P 16 P×P *(136)*

Now White has the celebrated
'hanging pawns' – the QB and QPs
in their present state can only be pro-

136
B

tected with pieces and Black should
try to cash in on this. He will try to
exchange pieces whenever possible
so as to weaken the support for the
hanging centre; he will also use his
pieces to put pressure on the pawns
– possibly forcing an advance which
would further weaken them. As for
White, he must try to use the space
advantage conferred by his centre
pawns to create attacking chances,
having the possibility of a breakthrough with P–Q5 or P–KB4–B5.

However, the present position is
clearly in Black's favour and rather
unusual in that Black still has his
QP, having used the QNP to set up
the hanging pawns: usually in these
Nimzo–Indian type positions it is the
other way around. This means that
Black has:

(a) more control of the central
squares;

(b) more room on the Q-side in
which to manoeuvre, since a pawn on
QN3 would only have a restricting
effect on Black's mobility.

16 . . . B–R3!

The pressure begins.

17 B×N

A rather surprising exchange but
after 17 0–0 B×P! 18 B×B P–Q4 19
Q–N4 P×B 20 R×P R×R 21 Q×R
Q–R4 Black has a clear advantage
because of the isolated pawns on d4
and a3 and the consequent weak

squares which will serve as beautiful outposts for Black's marauding knights. So White realizes that his QB is inferior to the opponent's knight and therefore takes the opportunity to exchange.

After 17 0–0 N–Q4? 18 B×Q N×Q 19 B–K7! is good only for White.

17 . . . Q×B

17 . . . N×B intending 18 . . . N–Q4 was also good, White would play 18 Q–Q2 Q–Q2 (to go to QR5) 19 Q–R5 R–B3 which is still better for Black.

18 Q–R5

Getting away from the hypnotic gaze of the black rook, and hitting the bishop.

18 . . . N–N1!

Not only protecting the bishop, but preparing a great future for this black stallion. 18 . . . R–B3 allows 19 B–K4.

19 R–B3

Black's threat of 19 . . . P–Q4 is met by protection of the KB so as to break the pin on the QBP.

19 Q–Q2 with the same idea is met by 19 . . . N–B3! 20 B–N1 (20 0–0 N×P!) 20 . . . P–Q4! 21 P×P (21 P–B5 B×N wins the QP) 21 . . . P×P 22 R–Q1 KR–K1 23 B–Q3 N×P! 24 B×B Q×B wins.

19 . . . P–Q4! (*137*)

The most forceful, although 19 . . .

P–K4 came into consideration e.g. 20 P×P Q×KP or 20 P–Q5 R–B4 and the QBP remains under fire.

20 P–B5

If 20 P×P B×B 21 R×B Q–N4 22 0–0 (22 Q–Q2 Q×NP 23 R–N1 Q×RP or 22 P–B4 Q×NP 23 R–N1 Q×QP) 22 . . . R–B7! keeps a sharp initiative. As played White gets positionally crushed by simple, strong, Capablanca–like moves.

20 . . . B×B 21 R×B N–B3

From now on Black goes like clockwork.

22 Q–Q2

22 Q–R4 allows 22 . . . P–K4! 23 P×P N×P 24 R×P N×P+! 25 P×N Q×P or 24 R–B3 KR–K1! is very strong e.g. 25 Q×P N–B3! winning a piece.

22 . . . R–N1 23 0–0 R–N2 24 P–B4

If White tries to combat the coming rook invasion he runs into trouble e.g. 24 R–B1 R1–N1 25 R3–B3 R–N7 26 R3–B2 R×R 27 R×R (27 Q×R N×P) 27 . . . R–N8+ 28 K–B2 (28 R–B1 R×R+) 28 . . . Q–R5+ wins. So White tries a desperate demonstration on the K-side.

24 . . . R1–N1 25 P–R3

Making a flight square for the king.

25 . . . R–N7 26 Q–K3

26 Q–Q1 R–R7 intending to double rooks on the seventh rank is tremendous for Black.

26 . . . N–R4

It's getting to be a jig-saw puzzle and Karpov is having no problems making the pieces fit!

27 N–N3 N–B5 28 Q–K1

Not 28 Q–B3 N–Q7.

28 . . . R1–N6

This is the climax of the black offensive; now pawns start disappearing fast.

29 R×R

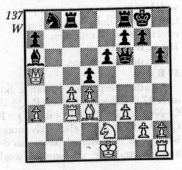

Or 29 R1–B3 R–N8.

29 . . . Q × QP+ 30 K–R2 R × R
White could resign – the rest is just cleaning up.
31 P–B5 N–K6 32 R–B3 Q × P 33 P × P P × P 34 N–R5 Q–Q3+ 35 K–N1

35 R–N3 N–B4∓∓ **35 . . . P–Q5**
Covering the knight **36 R–N3 R–N2 37 Q–Q2 R–N8+ 38 K–B2** Or 38 K–R2 N–B8+ winning the queen also.
38 . . . R–KB8+ 39 K–K2 Q–R3+ 40 Q–Q3 R–K8+! 0–1 A fine exhibition by Karpov, who carried out the anti-hanging pawns plan, outlined in the note to White's sixteenth move, in text-book fashion.

1320 AK–Vladimir Tukmakov:
R20: 24 December:

Ruy Lopez

1 P–K4 P–K4 2 N–KB3 N–QB3 3 B–N5 P–QR3 4 B–R4 N–B3 5 0–0 B–K2 6 R–K1 P–QN4 7 B–N3 P–Q3 8 P–B3 0–0 9 P–KR3 N–N1 10 P–Q4 QN–Q2 11 QN–Q2 B–N2 12 B–B2 R–K1 13 N–B1 B–KB1 14 N–N3 P–N3 15 P–QR4 P–B4 16 P–QN4 TN Varying from Karpov–Podgayets (1310). **16 . . . BP × QP 17 BP × P P–Q4 18 QP × P QP × P 19 N × P N × N 20 B × N B × B 21 R × B** (*138*)

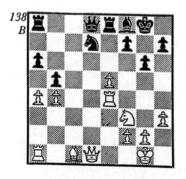

138
B

21 . . . N × P 22 Q × Q N × N+ 23 P × N QR × Q 24 B–K3 R × R 25 P × R R R–K1 26 P × P P × P 27 P–B3 P–B4 28 R–R5 ½–½

1321 Ratmir Holmov–AK:
R21: 27 December:

Sicilian

1 P–K4 P–QB4 2 N–KB3 N–QB3 3 P–Q4 P × P 4 N × P P–K3 5 N–QB3 P–QR3 6 P–KN3 N × N 7 Q × N N–K2 8 B–KB4 N–N3 9 B–Q6 B × B 10 Q × B Q–K2 11 Q–N6!± Black's opening innovation has not been a success, but it was soon to be honed into a fearsome weapon – see game 1501, p. 140.
11 . . . Q–Q1 12 N–R4 Q × Q 13 N × Q R–QN1 14 0–0–0 K–K2 15 P–KB4 P–Q3 16 B–N2 R–Q1 17 R–Q2 P–B3 18 R1–Q1 P–K4 19 P–B5 N–R1 20 B–B1 N–B2 21 B–B4 N–N4 22 R–K2 B–Q2 23 P–KR4 N–B2 24 N × B The bishop was threatening to return from the dead on c6. **24 . . . R × N 25 B–K6 R2–Q1 26 R–K3 P–QN3 27 R–QB3 R–N2 28 B–Q5 R–R2 29 R–B6 P–QN4** (*139*)

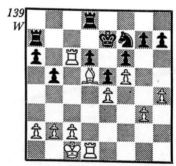

139
W

30 B × N?! White is still winning, but there is no good reason for this exchange. **30 . . . K × B 31 R6 × QP R × R 32 R × R P–N3 33 P–KN4** Karpov now begins a long struggle –

ultimately successful – to hold the ending. **33 . . . P×P 34 NP×P P–KR4** Taking away possible entry points from the white king. **35 K–Q2 K–K2 36 R–N6 R–Q2+ 37 K–K3 R–Q8 38 R–K6+ K–B2 39 R×RP R–KR8** Another point to Black's

32nd–34th moves becomes apparent. **40 P–R4 R–R6+ 41 K–Q2 P×P 42 R×RP R×P 43 R–B4 K–N2 44 P–N4 R–R8 45 R–B7+ K–R3 46 R–B8 P–R5 47 R–KR8+ K–N4 48 P–B4 R–R7+ 49 K–Q3 R–R6+ ½–½**

14 DAUGAVPILS

30.5–26.6.1971

39 *USSR Championship semi-final*

	1	2	3	4	5	6	7	8	9	0	1	2	3	4	5	6	7	8	
1 **Karpov**	×	½	½	1	1	½	½	1	½	½	1	1	1	1	½	½	1	1	**13**
2 Vaganian	½	×	½	0	½	½	1	1	1	0	½	1	1	½	1	1	1	1	**12**
3 Dzhindzhikhashvili	½	½	×	0	½	½	½	1	1	½	1	½	½	1	½	1	1	1	**11½**
4 Karasev	0	1	1	×	½	½	½	½	1	½	1	½	0	1	1	½	1	1	**11½**
5 Alburt	0	½	½	½	×	½	1	0	1	½	0	1	1	½	1	1	½	0	**9½**
6 Gipslis	½	½	½	½	½	×	½	1	0	½	½	½	½	1	½	½	½	½	**9**
7 Furman	½	0	½	½	0	½	×	1	½	1	1	0	1	0	0	0	1	1	**8½**
8 Shabanov	0	0	0	½	1	0	0	×	½	1	½	1	½	1	½	½	1	½	**8½**
9 V. Zhuravlev	½	0	0	0	0	1	½	½	×	½	0	1	1	½	1	1	0	½	**8**
10 Ignatiev	½	1	½	½	½	½	0	0	½	×	½	½	0	½	1	½	½	½	**8**
11 Klovan	0	½	0	0	1	½	0	½	1	½	×	0	½	1	1	1	½	0	**8**
12 Mnatsakanian	0	0	½	½	0	½	1	0	0	½	1	×	½	½	½	½	1	1	**8**
13 Lerner	0	0	½	1	0	½	0	½	0	1	½	½	×	½	½	0	½	1	**7**
14 Ruderfer	0	½	0	0	½	0	1	0	½	½	0	½	½	×	½	1	½	1	**7**
15 Ubilava	½	0	½	0	0	½	1	½	0	½	0	½	½	½	×	0	1	1	**7**
16 Petukhov	½	0	0	½	0	½	1	½	0	0	0	½	1	0	1	×	½	0	**6**
17 Kirillov	0	0	0	0	½	½	0	0	1	½	½	0	½	½	0	½	×	1	**5½**
18 Katalimov	0	0	0	0	1	½	0	½	½	½	1	0	0	0	0	1	0	×	**5**

Five games are available from this event:

1401 AK–Yanis Klovan:

Ruy Lopez

1 P–K4 P–K4 2 N–KB3 N–QB3 3 B–N5 P–QR3 4 B×N QP×B 5 0–0 P–B3 6 P–Q4 P×P 7 N×P N–K2!? 8 B–K3 N–N3 9 N–Q2 For 9 Q–R5 see game 1602. Another idea is 9 N–QB3 B–Q3 10 N–B5 0–0 (10 . . . B×N? 11 P×B N–K4 12 Q–R5+ N–B2 13 KR–K1 0–0 14 QR–Q1 Q–Q2 15 N–K4!± Adorjan–Lukacs, Hungary 1970) 11 Q–N4 (also possible is 11 N×B P×N 12 Q–Q2 P–KB4 13 P×P B×P 14 QR–Q1±) 11 . . . B–K4 12 P–KR4 B×N 13 P×B B×N 14 P×B N–K4 15 Q–B4 with an unclear position, and probably rather better chances for White. **9 . . . B–Q3 10 P–QB3** Varying from, and not improving upon 10 N–B4 0–0 11 Q–Q3 N–K4 12 N×N B×N 13 P–KB4 B–Q3 14 P–B5!± Fischer–Unzicker, Siegen 1970. **10 . . . 0–0 11 Q–N3+ K–R1 12 N–B5 B×N 13 P×B N–R5 14 Q×P Q–Q2** Threat 15 . . . KR–QN1 **15 Q–N3 N×BP 16 N–B4**± **KR–K1 17 QR–Q1 QR–N1 18 Q–B2 Q–K3 19 P–QN3 N×B 20 N×N R–N4 21 KR–K1 R–K4 22 P–N3 K–N1 23 N–N2 R–K7 24 R×R**

Q×R 25 R–Q2 Q–B6 26 K–B1 R–
K4 27 Q–Q3 Q×Q+ 28 R×Q K–
B2 29 N–K3 K–K2 30 N–B4 R–
KR4 31 P–KR4 B–B4 32 N–N2 R–
B4 33 R–Q2 K–K3 34 N–Q3 B–Q3
35 R K2+ K–Q2 36 R–K3 (*140*)

140
B

36 . . . P–N4? Black had to play 36
. . . R–QN4. Now his rook is in
trouble. **37 P–QB4 P–B4** And
now 37 . . . P×P would prevent
matters getting too much worse.
**38 K–N2 P–B3 39 P–B3 P×P 40
P×P B–B5 41 R–K4 1–0**

1402 Ubilava–AK:

Sicilian

1 P–K4 P–QB4 2 N–KB3 P–K3 3
N–B3 P–QR3 4 P–KN3 N–QB3 5
B–N2 P–Q3 6 0–0 N–B3 7 P–Q4
P×P 8 N×P B–Q2 9 B–K3 B–K2
10 N–N3?! The knight is ineffective
here, better 10 N4–K2. **10 . . . P–
QN4** Also 10 . . . N–R4 is good. **11
P–B4 0–0 12 P–K5 P×P 12** . . . N–
K1!? **13 P×P N×P 14 B×R Q×B
15 B–Q4** (*141*)
**15 . . . N4–N5 16 B×N N×B 17
R×N B×R 18 Q×B R–Q1 19 Q–
B7 P–N5 20 N–K2 R–QB1 21 Q–Q7
B×P 22 R–KB1 B–B3 23 Q–Q3**
½–½

141
B

1403 V. Zhuravlev–AK:

Sicilian

1 P–K4 P–QB4 2 N–KB3 N–QB3
3 P–B3 P–Q4 4 P×P Q×P 5 P–Q4
P–K3 6 B–Q3 N–B3 7 0–0 P×P 8
P×P B–K2 9 N–B3 Q–Q3 10 Q–K2
0–0 11 R–Q1 N–Q4 12 Q–K4 P–B4
13 Q–K1 B–B3 14 B–QB4 K–R1 15
B×N P×B 16 N–QN5 Q–Q2 17
B–B4 P–QR3 18 N–Q6 B–K2 19 N–
K5 Q×N (*142*)

142
W

20 N×N 20 N–B7+ R×N 21 B×Q
B×B is unclear, but probably Black's
three pieces would be better than the
queen. **20 . . . Q×N 21 Q×B R–K1
22 Q–R3 B–Q2 23 QR–B1 Q–K3 24
B–K5 QR–B1 25 P–B4 R×R 26
R×R B–B3 27 R–B3 R–K2 28 R–
KN3 K–N1 29 Q–R5 Q–Q2 30 P–
N3 P–R3 31 Q–N6 K–R2 32 P–QR4
Q–K1 33 P–R3 R–Q2 34 Q–B5 Q–**

Q1 35 Q–B2 R–KB2 36 K–R2 Q–
K2 37 R–K3 Q–K3 38 Q–K2 R–K2
39 Q–R5 Q–B2 40 Q–R4 R–K3 41
P–KN4 B–K1 42 Q–B2 B–Q2 43
Q–K2 K–N1 44 R–N3 R–KN3 45
Q–KN2 K–R2 46 Q–QB2 P–KR4
47 P–N5 R–QB3 48 R–QB3 Q–K3
49 R–B5 P–QN3 ½–½

1404 AK–Vladimir Kirillov:

Pirc

1 P–K4 P–KN3 2 P–Q4 B–N2 3
N–KB3 P–Q3 4 P–B3 N–KB3 5 B–
Q3 0–0 6 0–0 QN–Q2 7 QN–Q2 P–
K4 8 R–K1 P–B3 9 P–QR4 P–QR4
10 Q–B2 Q–B2 11 P–QN3 R–K1
12 B–R3 P–N3 13 B–KB1 B–N2 14
P×P P×P 15 N–B4!± B–KB1 16
B×B K×B 17 P–QN4 B–R3 18
QR–Q1 B×N 19 B×B P–R3 20 R–
Q2 K–N2 21 R1–Q1 R–K2 22 R–
Q6 N–K1 23 R6–Q2 (*143*)

143
B

23 . . . N1–B3 24 P–R3 N–B1 25 N–
R2 N–K3 26 B×N R×B 27 N–
N4 N×N 28 P×N R3–K1 29
R–Q7 Q–N1 30 Q–N3 R–KB1 31
Q–K6 P×P 32 R1–Q6 Threat 33
Q×NP+ K–R1 34 Q×RP+ K–N1
35 R–N6+ P×R 36 Q–N7/R7
mate. 32 . . . K–N1 33 Q×KP
Threat 34 R×NP+ 33...K–R2 34
Q–B6 A pleasing repetition of
theme: it is 35 Q×NP+ this time.
34...K–N1 35 P×P R×P 36 P–

K5 1–0 The threats involved with 37
P–K6 cannot be met.

1405 AK–Shabanov:

Bogoljubow

1 P–Q4 N–KB3 2 P–QB4 P–K3 3
P–KN3 B–N5+ 4 N–Q2 0–0 5 B–
N2 P–Q4 6 Q–B2 QN–Q2 7 KN–B3
P–B3 8 0–0 R–K1 9 R–Q1 P–QN4
10 P–B5 B–R4 11 P–K4 P×P 12
N×P N×N 13 Q×N B–N2 (*144*)

144
W

Black has a constricted position
with a weakness at d6 which, as the
game shows, is of more consequence
than White's at d5. 14 B–B4 N–B3 15
Q–B2 N–Q4 16 B–Q6! Now if Black
elects to trade his dark square bishop
for this unwelcome guest, a white
knight will soon take up residence
with even more unpleasant consequences. 16 . . . P–B3 17 P–QR3 Q–
Q2 18 N–Q2! Going ahead with his
knight manoeuvre, for if 18 . . .
B×N White is left master of the dark
squares. 18 . . . B–Q1 19 R–K1 P–
QR4 20 B–R3! Q–KB2 21 Q–K4 B–
B1 22 P–B4 Black is now getting
slowly strangled – a little more preliminary work and there comes a
breakthrough. 22 . . . B–Q2 23 R–
K2 P–R5 24 Q–B3 B–R4 25 N–K4
P–R3 26 N–B2 R–R2 27 N–Q3
R2–R1 28 K–R1 K–R1 29 B–N4!
P–N3 (*145*)

145
W

**30 B–R3 R–KN1 31 B–N2 QR–K1
32 R–KB1 K–R2 33 P–KN4!** This
pawn advance, in conjunction with
the further weakness created on
move 29 is sufficient to give Karpov
decisive threats. **33 . . . B–Q1 34 Q–**

N3 B–K2 35 P–N5! **B–Q1** If 35 . . .
B×B 36 P×B Q–B1 37 Q–R4 P–R4
38 P×P followed by a knight entry
at e5 leaves Black's position in a
state of disarray. **36 P×BP B×P 37
N–K5 Q–N2 38 R2–KB2!** Doubling
rooks on a closed file which will later
be opened. **38 . . . B–B1 39 Q–R3
B×N** Though this exchange allows
the white rooks to penetrate, it was
forced sooner or later owing to the
threat of piling up on g6 with B–K4
and R–KN1. **40 BP×B Q–R1** To
save the lady. **41 R–B7+ R–N2 42
B–B8!** **1–0** A picturesque finale:
after 42 . . . R×R 43 Q×RP+ K–
N1 44 Q×P+ R–KN2 45 B×R
Q×B 46 Q×R+ K–R2 47 R–B7
and Black loses all his pieces.

15 STUDENT OLYMPIAD

Mayaguez, Puerto Rico, 1–17.7.1971

	1	2	3	4	5	6	7	8	9	
1 USSR	×	3½	4	2½	4	4	4	4	3½	29½
2 USA	½	×	1½	2½	2½	3½	4	3	4	21½
3 Canada	0	2½	×	2	3	3½	2	4	4	21
4 Israel	1½	1½	2	×	2½	3½	2½	3	4	20½
5 Iceland	0	1½	1	1½	×	2	2½	2½	3½	14½
6 Brazil	0	½	½	½	2	×	2	3	2½	11
7 Austria	0	0	2	1½	1½	2	×	2	2	11
8 Puerto Rico	0	1	0	1	1½	1	2	×	2½	9
9 Colombia	½	0	0	0	½	1½	2	1½	×	6

The Soviet Union won with their accustomed ease – this was their thirteenth victory in seventeen attempts (they have been second on three occasions. There was also their 1963 'disaster' when they finished fourth). Karpov participated as the third board (four boards and two reserves), the full team being Tukmakov, Balashov, Karpov, Podgayets, Kuzmin and Razuvayev. Round by round results were as follows:

Preliminaries

1	board 3 v. Silva	1	USSR 3	Peru	1
2	board 2 v. Torres	1	USSR 3	Puerto Rico	1
3	Karpov free		USSR 3	Ecuador	1
4	board 3 v. Markula	1	USSR 4	Austria	0
5	USSR free				

Finals

1	USSR free				
2	Karpov free		USSR 4	Brazil	0
3	board 2 v. Camacho	1	USSR 4	Puerto Rico	0
4	board 2 v. Amos	1	USSR 4	Canada	0
5	Karpov free		USSR 4	Iceland	0
6	board 3 v. Rogoff	1	USSR 3½	USA	½
7	Karpov free		USSR 2½	Israel	1½
8	board 1 v. Wittmann	1	USSR 4	Austria	0
9	board 3 v. Ruiz	½	USSR 3½	Colombia	½

It was only in the last round that Karpov missed sharing the absolute best result of the event (Razuvayev had already scored 7/7), but his score of 7½/8 (93·8%) was the best score by a board three and was equalled only by Kuzmin (with an identical score).

'Karpov played . . . very effortlessly and with elegance. Normally he was the first to finish his game, not using up more than an hour on the clock. It seemed that his opponents did not understand the thinking of the young grandmaster. In my opinion Karpov possesses a very original and subtle chess style, and it would be difficult to name his chess predecessor. That is always the sign of a great talent.' Grandmaster Aivar Gipslis in his report on Mayaguez in *64*.

1501 Amos–Karpov:
FR4:

Sicilian

1 P–K4   P–QB4
Karpov added the Sicilian to his bag of openings in late 1970, before that 1 . . . P–K4 was his habitual answer to the king pawn opening.

2 N–KB3   P–K3
3 P–Q4   P×P
4 N×P   N–QB3
This variation is named after Soviet grandmaster Mark Taimanov who unearthed it from the distant past and revitalized it; in the 1962 USSR Championship he scored an amazing 7/9 with his system – no wonder it became popular!

5 N–QB3
In the first and sixth games of the Fischer–Taimanov Candidates match Fischer had played 5 N–N5 P–Q3 6 B–KB4 P–K4 7 B–K3 N–B3 8 B–N5.

5 . . .   P–QR3
6 P–KN3
Fischer also tried this against Taimanov, their fourth game going 6 . . . Q–B2 7 B–N2 N–B3 8 0–0 N×N 9 Q×N B–B4 10 B–B4 P–Q3 11 Q–Q2 P–R3 12 QR–Q1 P–K4 13 B–K3 B–KN5 14 B×B P×B 15 P–B3 B–K3 16 P–B4 R–Q1 17 N–Q5! with advantage. Black can also avoid 8 . . . N×N and play 8 . . . B–K2 9 R–K1 P–Q3 but 10 N×N P×N 11 P–K5 P×P 12 R×P gives White good chances, e.g. 12 . . . B–N2

13 B–B4!? B–Q3 14 R×P+ P×R 15 B×B as in Browne–Langeweg, Amsterdam 1972.

6 . . .   KN–K2!
It was because of White's possibility of advancing his KP, both striking at KB6 and opening the diagonal for the KB, that Taimanov realized that the KN was better developed here.

This innovation moreover introduces the idea of playing 7 . . . N×N to be followed by 8 . . . N–B3 and . . . P–QN4 and Q-side mobilization. Against Holmov in the 1970 USSR Championship, Karpov played an immediate 6 . . . N×N 7 Q×N N–K2 8 B–KB4 N–N3 9 B–Q6 B×B 10 Q×B Q–K2 11 Q–N6 when White had a clear initiative. In the 1972 Student Olympiad at Graz, against Albano, Karpov played a slightly different manoeuvre in a similar position and got the better game. In that position the white KB was already on N2, while the white QN was unmoved and play continued 6 . . . N×N 7 Q×N N–K2 8 0–0 N–B3! 9 Q–B3 P–Q3 10 B–K3 B–Q2 11 N–Q2 R–QB1 12 P–QR4 P–QN4 with active Q-side counter-play. More critical, however, would have been 8 B–B4 N–B3 9 Q–Q2.

7 N–N3
7 N4–K2, with the same motive of preventing Black's freeing knight exchange, came unstuck in Veselovsky–Karpov, USSR Team Ch 1971, when after 7 . . . P–QN4 8 P–QR3 B–N2 9 B–N2 N–B1 10 0–0 B–K2 11

P–B4 0–0 12 K–R1 N–Q3! Black soon got a grip on the position.

After 7 B–N2 N×N 8 Q×N N–B3 9 Q–Q1 (9 Q–K3 is better) 9 . . . B–K2 10 0–0 0–0 11 B–K3 Q–B2 12 N–K2 P–QN4 13 Q–Q2 B–N2 14 P–QB3 N–K4 15 B–B4 P–Q3 16 P–N3 KR–Q1 17 QR–B1 QR–B1 Black had achieved a total development with no problems, Cortlever–Taimanov, Wijk aan Zee 1970.

7 B–K3 is an interesting suggestion from Keres: 7 . . . N×N 8 Q×N N–B3 9 Q–N6! Clearly the theory of this line is still being created (largely by Karpov) and we must wait and see what the future holds . . .

7 . . .　　　　N–R4!

Another original contribution by Karpov for the next editions of Euwe, Pachman, Boleslavsky etc. Black clears QB3 for his KN whilst easing his defensive task should White exchange knights.

8 B–N2

8 Q–R5 is best met by 8 . . . P–QN4!

8 . . .　　　　N2–B3
9 0–0　　　　P–Q3

9 . . . N×N 10 RP×N allows White the open a-file as compensation for the doubled pawns, which makes any . . . P–QN4 rather more awkward.

10 N–Q2

A serious attempt to exploit the rather off-side position of the black QN – by leaving it dangling in midair. Keene, against Karpov at Hastings 1971–2, played more orthodoxly with 10 N×N Q×N 11 N–K2 B–K2 12 P–N3 0–0 13 B–N2 B–Q2 14 P–QB4 KR–Q1 15 P–QR4 QR–B1 16 B–QB3 Q–B2 with a balanced game: Black is not so congested as he would have been if the pair of knights had not been swapped.

10 . . .　　　　B–Q2

Q-side development takes priority in this situation, since if now 11 P–QR3 (to win the knight with 12 P–QN4) then 11 . . . R–B1! 12 P–QN4 N–K4!

11 P–N3

The best way of activating the QB.

11 . . .　　　　B–K2
12 B–N2　　　　R–QB1!

12 . . . 0–0? 13 P–QR3 P–QN4 14 P–QN4 N–B5 15 N×N favours White.

13 N–K2

Now if 13 P–QR3 N–K4 14 P–B4 N/K4–B5! 15 P×N Q–N3+ or 14 K–R1 Q–N3! 15 R–QN1 P–KR4! with excellent piece-play for Black in both cases.

13 . . .　　　　0–0 (146)

Protecting the KNP!

14 P–QB4?

14 P–QR3 still doesn't click – 14 . . . N–K4! 15 P–KB4 N–N5 16 R–B3 B–KB3! 17 B×B P×B! (threatening to win the exchange with 18 . . . Q–N3+ followed by the knight check at KB7) 18 N–KB1 Q–N3+ 19 Q–Q4 (19 N–Q4? P–K4!) 19 . . . Q×Q+ 20 N×Q P–K4! and Black is winning, e.g.:

(a) 21 N–B5 B×N 22 P×B P–K5 winning the rook.

(b) 21 P–QN4 P×N 22 P×N R×P.

So 14 P–QR3 is bad, but the text is worse: the Q-side pawns soon come under fire from their black counterparts, and the weak squares in White's camp will also be ravaged by enemy artillery.

14 . . .   P–QN4!

Goodbye 'Maroczy Bind'.

15 P×P

The threat to give White a lousy pawn structure by 15 . . . P×P could not be met by 15 R–B1 because of 15 . . . N–N5! e.g. 16 B–QB3 N×RP 17 B×N Q×B 18 R–R1 B–KB3 19 P–QN4 Q–R6 or 19 N–KB3 B×R 20 Q×B P×P.

15 . . .   P×P

16 N–KB3

Or 16 P–QR3 P–N5! as in the game.

16 . . .   P–N5!

Putting a block on any ideas of Q-side expansion by White – it is Black who is the invader.

17 P–QR3?

Further weakening his pawns – Karpov soon shows his opponent why this attempt to gain Q-side play is all wrong.

17 . . .   R–N1!

18 P–QR4

18 P×P N3×P with forthcoming pressurization of b3 as well as some mighty activity with his knights and bishops leaves Black dictating the proceedings – so Amos makes the best of a bad job and seals the Q-wing.

18 . . .   P–K4!

Preparing 19 . . . B–K3 hitting the invalid white QNP.

19 N–Q2

Anticipating the bishop move, which could now be countered with 20 P–B4 P×P 21 N×P B–B3 22 N×B P×N 23 B×B with some hope for White.

19 . . .   B–B3!

Directed against White's potentially freeing P–B4 – the point is seen later.

20 R–B1

20 N–QB4 N×N 21 P×N B–K3 22 R–B1 N–R4 is winning for Black.

20 . . .   B–K3

21 P–B4

If White tries to take it lying down with non-committal moves his opponent will trample all over him with . . . P–Q4.

21 . . .   P×P!

Now the point of Black's 19th is seen – his queen reaches the battlefront.

22 B×B   Q×B

23 N×P

If 23 P×P N–Q5! (also 23 . . . B–N5 ∓ – Karpov) 24 N×N Q×N+ 25 K–R1 N×P! 26 N×N Q×Q 27 KR×Q B×N 28 R×P B×P. Or 23 R×P Q–K4! 24 N–KB3 Q–N7 25 R–N1 B×P! White's achilles heel is his QNP – so unnecessarily weakened by his 17th move.

23 . . .   KR–B1

Contesting the open QB-file and protecting his knight on QB3, which would be lost in a variation such as 23 . . . Q–Q5+ 24 K–R1 B×P 25 N×B Q×Q 26 KR×Q N×N 27 R×N – but now this variation is on.

24 N–Q5

Shielding the QNP from the glare of Black's QB. After 24 N×B Q×N the poor pawn would be in real trouble e.g. 25 N–B4 N×N 26 R×N N–R4 and Black will soon have a deadly passed pawn.

24 . . .   Q–Q5+

25 K–R1

If 25 R–KB2 N–K4 and the threat of . . . N–Q6 is decisive.

25 . . .   K–R1!

Stopping all possibilities of a knight fork at his K2.

26 Q–K2

Trying to get himself organized. If 26 N–KB3 Q×Q 27 KR×Q N×P and White doesn't have 28 R×N R×R because 29 N–K7 isn't check anymore.

26 . . .   N–K4

Black is now ready to open up with all guns into White's defenceless territory.

27 P–R3

After 27 N–KB3 N×N 28 R×R+ R×R 29 Q×N R–B7! or 28 Q×N Q–Q7! is overwhelming.

27 . . .   P–R3!

Surprisingly enough Black has to watch out against back rank mates. 27 . . . Q–N7 28 R–QN1 Q–B7 was not so clear, but Karpov gives 28 . . . Q–R7 29 R–R1 Q–B7∓.

28 KR–Q1

Hoping to get away with 29 N–QB4 but . . .

28 . . .   N–Q6! (*147*)
0–1

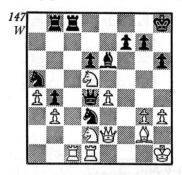

147
W

White is helpless. After 29 R×R+ R×R (with the idea of 30 . . . N–B7+) and:

(a) 30 K–R2 R–B7 31 N–KB3 (else 31 . . . N–N7) 31 . . . Q–N7! 32 Q×N R×B+ 33 K–R1 R×P wins e.g. 34 Q–Q2 (or 34 R–Q2 R×N!) 34 . . . Q×Q 35 N×Q B×N 36 P×B R–Q6! 37 K–N1 N×P.

(b) 30 R–QN1 R–B8+! 31 R×R (31 B–B1 R×R 32 N×R N–B7+

33 K–R2 N×KP) 31 . . . N×R 32 Q–N5 (32 Q–Q1 N8×P) 32 . . . Q×N7 33 Q×N Q–K8+ 34 K–R2 N–K7 35 Q–N6 Q×P+ 36 K–R1 B×P 37 N–K3 B×B+ 38 N×B Q–R6 mate.

(c) 30 R–KB1 R–B7! 31 N–KB3 Q–N7 32 Q×N R×B wins: 33 P–N4 R–N6 or 33 N×P B×RP and it's all over bar the mating.

1502 AK–Kenneth Rogoff:
FR6:

English

1 P–QB4 P–K4 2 N–QB3 N–KB3 3 P–KN3 B–N5 4 B–N2 0–0 5 P–Q3 P–B3 6 Q–N3 B–R4 7 N–B3 P–Q4 8 0–0 P–Q5 9 N–QR4 QN–Q2 10 P–K3 P×P 11 B×P R–K1 12 P–QR3 B–B2 13 QR–Q1 B–Q3 14 P–Q4 P×P 15 N×P B–B1 16 Q–B3 Q–K2 (*148*)

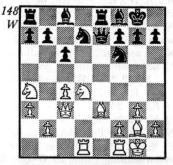

148
W

Having played the opening inaccurately Rogoff found himself in this very awkward predicament, being very much pinned down. Play continued **17 KR–K1** which threatens to crush Black after 18 B–B4 Q–Q1 19 B×P! P×B 20 N×P R×R+ 21 R×R B–N5 22 P×B Q–B1. So Rogoff decided that he had better run with the queen to the K-side. **17 . . . Q–K4 18 P–QN4!** Taking a few more squares away from Black.

18 . . . Q–KR4 19 P–R3! A web is being woven to catch the displaced person on h5. **19 . . . N–N3 20 N×N P×N 21 P–N4 Q–N3** (*149*) If 21 . . . Q–R5 22 N–B3 does the necessary, while if 21 . . . B×KNP 22 P×B N×P 23 B–B4 stops any non-sense.

22 B–B4! Subtly played, for if now 22 . . . N–K5 23 Q–B2 N–Q3 24 R×R N×R 25 B–K4, or 22 . . . P–R4 23 P–KN5 R×R+ 24 R×R N–R2 25 B–K4 P–KB4 26 B–N2! when 26 . . . N×P loses to 27 Q–KN3! and 26 . . . B–Q2 allows 27 N–B3! with a winning position. **22 . . . B–Q2 23 N–B3! R×R+** If 23 . . . P–R3 24 N–K5 wins. **24 R×R N–K1** If 24 . . . P–R3 25 N–K5 Q–R2 26 N×B N×N 27 B–K4 P–N3 28 Q–Q4 P–KB4 (28 . . . R–Q1 29 B–B7) 29 R–Q1 gives White an overwhelming game. **25 Q–Q2! R–Q1** Black loses a piece after 25 . . . B–Q3 26 B×B Q×B 27 Q×Q

N×Q 28 R–Q1. **26 N–R4 1–0** After 26 . . . Q–B3 27 P–KN5.

1503 AK–Wittmann:
  FR8:

King's Indian

1 P–QB4 N–KB3 2 N–QB3 P–KN3 3 P–KN3 B–N2 4 B–N2 0–0 5 N–B3 P–B3 6 0–0 P–Q3 6 . . . P–Q4!? 7 P–Q4 Q–R4 8 P–KR3 P–K4 9 P–K4 KN–Q2? 9 . . . QN–Q2 is safest and best, though 9 . . . P×P 10 N×P Q–QB4!? may also be possible. **10 P–Q5 P–QB4 11 P–R3± N–R3 12 B–K3 Q–Q1 13 N–K1 P–B4 14 P×P P×P 15 P–B4 P–K5 16 P–KN4!** Now, according to Karpov, White is winning. **16 . . . P×P 17 P×P N–B3 18 P–B5 P–R4 19 P×P N–R2 20 P–R6! B–K4 21 Q–R5 K–R1 22 N×P B×NP 23 R–R2 N–B3 24 Q–N6! R–KN1 25 R×B!** (*150*)

1–0 After 25 . . . R×Q 26 P×R is clearly decisive.

16 USSR ARMED FORCES TEAM CHAMPIONSHIP

Leningrad, 16–26.8.1971

	1	2	3	4	5	6	7	8	
1 Zakavkaz VO	×	4	7	4	3	3	6½	5	**32½**
2 Leningrad VO	3	×	4½	4½	5	4½	4	5½	**31**
3 Odessa VO	0	2½	×	3½	4	4½	6	6	**26½**
4 Moscow VO	3	2½	3½	×	4	3½	5	5	**26½**
5 Baltic VO	4	2	3	3	×	3½	5½	4½	**25½**
6 Baltic Fleet	4	2½	2½	3½	3½	×	4½	4	**24½**
7 GSVG	½	3	1	2	1½	2½	×	4½	**15**
8 Siberia VO	2	1½	1	2	2½	3	2½	×	**14½**

VO = military district   GSVG = Soviet Armed Forces in Germany.

Karpov played board one for the Leningrad team, taking over from his trainer, Semyon Furman, who played at board two.

Scores by the first board players were: Vasyukov, Tukmakov and Tseshkovsky 4½/7, Gufeld and Karpov 4/7, Klovan 3/7, Dementiev 2½/7 and Zhelyandinov 1/7.

1601 AK–Vladimir Tukmakov:

Sicilian

1 P–K4 P–QB4 2 N–KB3 P–Q3 3 P–Q4 P×P 4 N×P N–KB3 5 N–QB3 P–QR3 6 B–K2 P–K3 7 0–0 B–K2 8 P–B4 0–0 9 B–K3 Stronger than 9 Q–K1?! Q–N3 10 B–K3 Q×P!∓ **9 . . . N–B3 10 P–QR4 Q–B2** Also possible is 10 . . . B–Q2 11 Q–K1 N×N 12 B×N B–B3 – Gufeld in *Informator*. **11 K–R1± N–QR4?!** 11 . . . B–Q2 is better, giving White the chance to go wrong with 12 P–KN4 N×N 13 B×N B–QB3 and Black stands well, but White has simply 12 N–N3±. **12 Q–K1** Not following 12 Q–Q3 B–Q2 (Or 12 . . . P–Q4 13 P–K5 N–Q2 14 QR–K1 N–QB3 with complicated play – Tukmakov) 13 P–KN4 K–R1? (Still 13 . . . P–Q4 although now 14 P–K5

N–K1 15 QR–K1 B–QB3 16 B–B3 allows White to maintain a positional advantage) 14 P–N5 N–N1 15 R–B3! N–QB3 16 R–KN1 N×N 17 B×N P–B4? 18 R–R3 P–K4 19 N–Q5 Q–Q1 20 BP×P BP×P (151)

151
W

21 P–K6!! P–R3 (21 . . . P×Q 22 B×QP and mates) 22 P×P 1–0 Tukmakov–Panno, Buenos Aires

1970. **12 ... N–B5 13 B–B1 B–Q2 14 P–QN3 N–QR4 15 B–Q3 N–B3 16 N×N B×N! 17 B–N2 P–K4 18 Q–K2** Aleksandr Geller and A. Deuel, in *64*, point out that 18 Q–N3 is also not bad, e.g. 18 ... N–R4 19 Q–N4 and not 19 ... N×P on account of 20 R×N P×R 21 N–Q5. **18 ... QR–Q1 19 P–QN4!**± P–QR4 Or 19 ... P×P 20 P–N5 P×P 21 P×P B–Q2 22 N–Q5 and White wins. **20 P–N5 B–Q2 21 P–B5** 21 N–Q5!? is also possible, for example 21 ... N×N 22 P×N±. **21 ... B–B1 22 N–Q1** (*152*) Gufeld again suggests 22 N–Q5!?

152
B

22 ... P–Q4!? 23 P×P N×P 24 Q×P Q×Q 25 B×Q KR–K1 26 N–N2 Gufeld suggests 26 ... B–N5!? as a last try. **27 N–B4**±± **P–QN3 28 B–N3 B–N2 29 QR–K1 B–N5 30 R×R+ R×R 31 P–R4 P–N3 32 K–R2 B–B4 33 B–B2 B×B 34 R×B R–K8 35 K–N3 N–N5 36 K–B4 N–Q4+ 37 K–N3 N–N5 38 R–Q2 N–Q4 39 N–Q6 B–R1 40 B–K4 N–B2 41 B×B N×B 42 P–B6 P–R3 43 N–B4 R–K1 44 R–Q6 1–0**

1602 AK–Yanis Klovan:

Ruy Lopez

1 P–K4 P–K4 2 N–KB3 N–QB3 3 B–N5 P–QR3 4 B×N QP×B 5 0–0 P–B3 6 P–Q4 P×P 7 N×P N–K2 8 B–K3 N–N3 9 Q–R5

In their game at Daugavpils, Karpov gained the initiative after 9 N–Q2 B–Q3 10 P–QB3 0–0 11 Q–N3+ K–R1 12 N–B5 B×N 13 P×B N–R5 14 Q×P Q–Q2 15 Q–N3 N×BP 16 N–B4. This time White tries another plan.

9 ... B–Q3 10 N–B5 0–0 11 P–KB4 Q–K1

In the game Gipslis–Savon, 37 USSR Ch 1970, Black played 11 ... B×N 12 Q×B Q–K2 13 N–Q2 QR–Q1, however after 14 QR–K1 White obtained a not inconsiderable advantage. Klovan's move also fails to save Black from difficulties.

12 N–Q2 N–K2 (*153*)

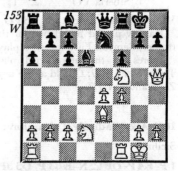

153
W

13 N×N+?

An incorrect decision. Now everything in Black's position is in order; the bishop pair fully compensate for the presence of his doubled pawns.

After 13 Q×Q R×Q 14 N×B P×N 15 N–B4 Black's position would have been critical; 15 ... P–Q4 is weak: 16 N–N6 R–N1 17 P–B5 with the threat of 18 B–B4, while after 15 ... R–Q1 both 16 B–N6 R–Q2 17 B–R5 and 16 KR–Q1 are possible.

13 ... B×N 14 Q–B3 B–K3 15 QR–K1 R–Q1 16 P–QR3 P–QB4 17 P–B5 B–B2 18 B–B4 B–Q3 19 Q–K3 Q–B3 20 N–B3 Q–N3 21 B×B P×B 22 P–QN4 KR–K1 (*154*)

154
W

Black already has the initiative. With his next move White intends to start an attack on the black king, but at the same time weakens the position of his own king.

23 P–N4?! B–Q4 24 P×P P×P 25 Q–B4 B–B3 26 P–N5 R–Q2 27 P×P P×P 28 K–R1 Q–Q1 29 R–KN1+ K–R1 30 P–KR4 R–N1 31 P–R5 R×R+ 32 R×R R–Q8!

White's position is critical; Karpov's tactics have not demonstrated their value.

33 Q–R4 R×R+ 34 K×R Q–Q8+ 35 K–B2 Q×P+ 36 K–N3 K–N2 37 P–R6+ K–B2 38 Q–N4 Q×P 39 Q–N7+ K–K1 40 Q–N8+ K–K2 41 Q×P+ K–Q3 42 N–R4

Here the game was adjourned. On home analysis it became clear that Black's win is simply a question of time, since, after a series of checks, he captures the QRP and forces White to play an utterly hopeless queen ending.

42 ... Q–K8+ 43 K–R3 Q–B6+ 44 K–N4 Q–B5+ 45 K–R3

On 45 K–R5 follows 45 ... Q–B5 and White, in order to save himself from the mate, must part with his knight.

45 ... Q–N6+ 46 K–R2 Q–N7+ 47 K–N3 Q×P+ 48 K–N4 Q–R5+ 49 K–N3 Q–N6+ 50 K–R2 Q–N7+ 51 K–N3 Q–B6 + 52 K–R2 Q–B7+ 53

K–N3 Q–Q6+ 54 K–R2 Q–Q7+ 55 K–N3 Q–K6+ 56 K–R2 Q–B5+ 57 K–R3 Q–KB8+ 58 K–N3 Q–KN8+ 59 K–R3 B–N4

The last move of 'homework'.

60 N–B3

This loses quickly, but it is clear that White had not the slightest desire to play the queen ending after 60 Q×P B–B8+ 61 N–N2 Q–K6+! 62 K–R2 Q×P+ 63 K–N1 B×N.

60 ... B–B8+ 61 K–R4 Q–N7 0–1

1603 Evgeny Vasyukov–AK:

Ruy Lopez

1 P–K4 P–K4 2 N–KB3 N–QB3 3 B–N5 P–QR3 4 B–R4 N–B3 5 0–0 B–K2 6 R–K1 P–QN4 7 B–N3 P–Q3 8 P–B3 0–0 9 P–KR3 N–N1 10 P–Q3 QN–Q2 11 QN–Q2 B–N2 12 N–B1 N–B4 13 B–B2 R–K1 14 N–N3 B–KB1 15 N–R2 P–Q4 15 ... N–K3! is a good equaliser. **16 Q–B3 P–R3** This seems to be new. 16 ... N–K3, 16 ... P–N3 and 16 ... N4–Q2 are all adequate for Black. 16 ... Q–B1!? is bad though: 17 B–N5 P×P 18 P×P N3–Q2 19 QR–Q1 N–N3 20 N–N4± Browne–Spassky, San Juan 1969. **17 N–B5 P–QR4 18 N–N4 N×N 19 P×N P–R5 20 B–K3 N–K3 21 Q–N3 P×P 22 P×P Q–B3 23 QR–Q1 QR–Q1** (155)

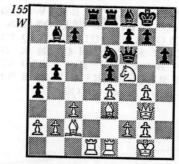

155
W

24 Q–B3 N–N4 25 Q–K2 B–B3 26

B–Q3 R–N1 27 P–B3 P–N3 28 N–
N3 N–K3 29 Q–KB2 R/K1–Q1 30
P–R3 R–Q3 31 R–Q2 R1–Q1 32
R1–Q1 B–K1 33 B–B2 ½–½

1604 AK–Oleg Dementiev:

Slav

1 P–Q4 P–Q4 2 N–KB3 N–KB3 3
P–B4 P–B3 4 P–K3 B–B4 5 N–B3
P–K3 6 B–K2 N–K5 7 0–0 B–K2 8
Q–N3 Q–N3 9 P–B5 Q–B2 10 N×N
B×N 11 Q–B3 P–QN3 12 P×P P×P
13 P–QN4 B–Q3 14 P–KR3 0–0 15
B–N2 Q–K2 16 P–R3 P–B3 17 KR–
B1 R–R2 18 Q–N3 B–B2 19 P–QR4
P–KN4 20 B–R3 B–Q3 21 N–Q2
B–N3 22 P–N5 P×P 23 B×P K–N2
24 N–B1 P–R4 25 B×B Q×B 26
Q–Q1 Q–K2 27 R–B3 N–R3 28
Q–N3 R–QN1 29 R–K1 N–B2 30
B–B6 N–K1 (*156*)

156
W

31 P–K4 P×P 32 B×P B–B2 33
B–Q5 N–B2 34 B–B6 Q–Q3 35 N–
K3 Q–Q1 36 R–Q1 K–R1 37 Q–N4
K–N2 38 P–R4 N–Q4 39 B×N
P×B 40 P×P P×P 41 R–B6 B–N3
42 R1–QB1 B–K5 43 P–B3 B–R2
1–0 In view of 44 R–Q6.

1605 Eduard Gufeld–AK:

Ruy Lopez

1 P–K4 P–K4 2 N–KB3 N–QB3
3 B–N5 P–QR3 4 B–R4 N–B3 5 0–0
B–K2 6 R–K1 P–QN4 7 B–N3 P–
Q3 8 P–B3 0–0 9 P–KR3 N–QR4 10
B–B2 P–B4 11 P–Q4 Q–B2 12 QN–
Q2 N–B3 13 P–QR3 B–Q2 14 P–QN4
BP×QP 15 P×P KR–B1 16 B–N3
P–QR4 17 B–N2 RP×P Varying
from Gufeld–Smyslov, 37 USSR Ch
1969, which went 17 . . . KP×P 18
N×P N×N 19 B×N P×P 20 P×P
R×R 21 Q×R B–K3 22 B×B ½–½.
18 RP×P R×R 19 B×R P×P 20
N×P N×N 21 B×N B–K3 22 B×B
P×B (*157*)

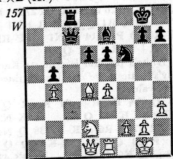

157
W

23 Q–N3 K–B2 24 P–K5 P×P 25
R×P Q–Q3 26 R–K1 Q–Q4 27 Q–
N2 K–N1 28 R–K5 Q–B3 29 Q–N3
N–Q4 30 B–B5 B×B 31 P×B Q×P
32 R×P Q–B8+ 33 N–B1 Q–QB5
34 Q–N2 N–B6 35 R–K7 Q–R7 36
Q×Q N×Q 37 R–N7 R–B4 38 N–
K3 N–B6 ½–½.

Karpov's games against Tseshkovsky and Zhelyandinov are unavailable.

Rostov on Don, 1–10.8.1971

Final A	1	2	3	4	5	6	
1 Burevestnik	×	5	5	4	5½	7	26½
2 Armed Forces	4	×	7½	5½	4½	5	26½
3 Avangard	4	1½	×	6	5½	7	24
4 Spartak	5	3½	3	×	4	5	20½
5 Lokomotiv	3½	4½	3½	5	×	3½	20
6 Trud	2	4	2	4	5½	×	17½

Karpov played on board six for the Armed Forces team, his 6½/7 earned him a board prize and was also the absolute best result. Karpov's round-by-round results;

PR1 1 v. Lisenko
PR2 1 v. Gofstein
PR3 1 v. Markevsky
FR1 1 v. Steinberg

FR2 1 v. Peresipkin
FR3 ½ v. A. Petrosian
(FR4 = PR1)
FR5 1 v. Veselovsky

1701 AK–Mikhail Steinberg:
FR1:

Sicilian

1 P–K4 P–QB4 2 N–KB3 P–Q3 3 P–Q4 P×P 4 N×P N–KB3 5 N–QB3 P–K3 6 P–KN4 P–KR3 7 P–N5 P×P 8 B×P P–R3 9 Q–Q2 B–Q2 10 0–0–0 N–B3 11 P–KR4 Q–B2 12 B–K2 0–0–0 13 P–B4 B–K2 14 P–R5 ± K–N1 15 K–N1 P–Q4 16 P–K5 N–K5 17 N3×N P×N 18 B×B N×B 19 Q–K3 N–B4 20 N×N P×N 21 KR–N1 KR–N1 22 P–N3?! 22 R–Q6 B–K3 23 Q–Q4 R–QB1 24 P–B3 ± 22 ... B–K3 23 R×R+ Q×R 24 R–Q1 Q–B2 25 R–Q6 P–KN3 26 P×P R×P 27 Q–Q4 R–N1 = 28 K–N2 R–QB1 29 P–B3 R–R1 30 P–R4 R–R7 31 Q–K3 Q–K2 32 R–Q2 B–B1 33 Q–N6

Q–B2 34 Q–Q4 B–K3 35 Q–K3 R–N7 36 Q–Q4 R–R7 37 P–B4 R–R6 38 B–Q1 (158)

158
B

38 ... Q–R4? better 38 ... P–R4 39 P–B5 ± R–R5 40 P–N4 Q–B2 41 Q–K3 R–R1 42 Q–QB3 R–QB1 43 R–Q6 Q–K2 43 ... P–R4! 44 K–R3 P×P+ 45 K×P Q–K2 46

K–R5!± 44 Q–K3± R–N1 45 B–
B2 Q–B2 46 Q–QB3 R–QB1 47 B–
N3 B×B 48 K×B P–R4 49 Q–Q4
P×P 50 K×P Q–K2 51 Q–K3 R–
B3 52 Q–Q2 K–R2 53 Q–Q4 Q–
R5? 54 R×R Q–K8+ 55 K–B4 Q–
K7+ 56 K–N3!±± P×R 57 Q–
Q7+ K–N1 58 Q–K8+ K–N2 59
Q×KBP+ K–N1 60 Q–K8+ K–
N2 61 Q–Q7+ K–N1 62 Q–Q8+
K–N2 63 Q–N6+ K–B1 64 Q×P+
K–Q1 65 Q–Q6+ K–B1 66 P–B6
Q–B6+ 67 K–B4 Q–K7+ 68 K–Q5
1–0

1702 Peresipkin–AK:
FR2:

Sicilian

1 P–K4 P–QB4 2 N–KB3 P–K3 3
P–Q4 P×P 4 N×P N–QB3 5 N–N5
P–Q3 6 B–KB4 P–K4 7 B–K3 P–
QR3 8 N5–B3 N–B3 9 B–KN5
Gufeld, in his notes to this game, in
Informator 12 gives 9 B–QB4!?
Against this Black should not play
9 . . . B–K2 10 N–Q5! N×N 11
B×N 0–0 12 N–B3± Fischer–
Badilles, Manila 1967, but 9 . . . N–
QR4 10 B–Q5 B–K3 11 Q–Q3 R–
B1 12 N–Q2 N–N5 and Black gains
control of . . . QB5. 9 . . . B–K2 10
B×N B×B 11 B–B4± 11 N–Q5 is
not so good: 11 . . . B–N4! 12 B–B4
0–0 13 0–0 B–K3 14 B–N3 B–R3 15
N1–B3 K–R1 16 Q–Q3 R–B1 17
QR–Q1 Q–R5 18 P–B3 N–Q5 and
Black's counterplay was more than
adequate compensation for the weak-
ness of his Q4, Kapengut–Tal, 1965,
or, in this, 13 N1–B3 B–K3 14 0–0
P–N4 15 B–N3 N–Q5 16 N–K2
N×B 17 RP×N Q–N1= Kapen-
gut–Furman, USSR Ch 1967. 11 . . .
N–R4 Or 11 . . . 0–0 12 0–0 B–K3 13
B–N3 R–B1± – Gufeld 12 B–N3 0–0
12 . . . N×B 13 RP×B B–K3= is
Fischer's opinion. 13 0–0 B–K3 14

N–Q5 B–N4 15 N1–B3 R–B1 16 Q–
K2 B–R3 17 KR–Q1 K–R1 18 R–
Q3 N–B3 Gufeld assesses this posi-
tion as equal. 19 Q–Q1 N–Q5 20 N–
K3 P–QN4 Kapengut–Furman
would, almost certainly, have been
discussed by Karpov with his trainer.
Here 20 . . . Q–R5!? is Gufeld's sug-
gestion. 21 N/B3–Q5 Q–R5 22 P–
KB3 P–B4 23 P×P N×P/f5 24
N–KN4 R–B4 25 N–N6 25 P–B3!?–
Gufeld 25 . . . Q–K2 26 N×B If 26
B×B Q×B 27 N–Q5 P–K5 28
P×P Q×KP 29 N×B N×N 30
N–B3 Q–KR5 and White's K-side is
probably untenable. 26 . . . P×N∓
(*159*)

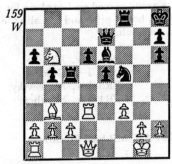

159
W

27 B×B Q×B 28 N–Q5 R–KN1 29
K–R1 P–KR4 30 Q–Q2 P–R5∓
31 N–K3 P–R6 32 P×P No better
is 32 P–KN3 P–K5 33 R–B3 P×P 34
N×N R×N 35 Q–Q4+ Q–K4∓.
32 . . . N–Q5 33 R–KB1 Q×KRP
34 R×N P×R 35 Q×P+ R–K4 36
Q×P? 36 R–B2 R–N2 37 Q×P Q–
K3∓ would have prolonged the
game. 36 . . . Q×RP+ 0–1

1703 AK–Arshak Petrosian:
FR3:

Alekhine

1 P–K4 N–KB3 2 P–K5 N–Q4 3
P–Q4 P–Q3 4 P×P BP×P 5 P–
QB4 N–N3 6 P–KR3 P–KN3 7 B–

K2 B–N2 8 N–KB3 0–0 9 0–0 N–B3
10 N–B3 B–B4 11 B–B4 P–KR3!
12 B–K3 P–Q4 13 P–QN3 P×P 14
P×P R–B1! Stronger than 14 . . .
N–R4 of Karpov–Neckar. Now
Black has fully sufficient counter-
play – Suetin. **15 R–B1 N–R4 16
P–B5 N3–B5 17 B–B4 P–KN4 18
B–N3** Krogius, in an openings survey
of the Team Championship in
Shakhmatny Bulletin No. 10 1971, gives
the continuation of the game as: 18
B–K3? Q–Q2 19 R–K1 P–N3 20
B×N N×B 21 Q–K2? P×P 22 P–
Q5 B×N and Black has an extra
pawn. **18 . . . P–N3! 19 B×N N×B
20 Q–K2? P×P!** (*160*)

P–Q4 P×P 4 N×P N–QB3 5 N–
QB3 P–QR3 6 P–KN3 KN–K2 7
N4–K2 P–QN4 7 . . . N–N3 of
Kapengut–Taimanov, 39 USSR Ch
1971, also works well. **8 P–QR3** This
attempt to prevent further Q-side
expansion fails miserably. Better 8
B–N2 e.g. 8 . . . B–N2 9 0–0 N–B1 10
P–B4 P–N5 Ozanić–Taimanov, Vin-
kovci 1970, though even then Black
has at least equal chances. **8 . . .
B–N2 9 B–N2 N–B1 10 0–0 B–K2 11
P–B4 0–0 12 K–R1 N–Q3 13 P–KN4
P–N5 14 P×P N×NP 15 P–N5 R–
B1 16 N–N3 N–B5 17 P–N3 N–R6 18
B×N R×N 19 N–R5 P–K4** (*161*)

21 **P–Q5** or 21 Q×N P×P!∓
21 . . . B×N∓ 22 R×B N–N3 ½–½

1704 Veselovsky–AK:
FR5:

Sicilian

1 P–K4 P–QB4 2 N–KB3 P–K3 3

Black has a very solid grasp on the
initiative. **20 R–B1 N–R7 21 B–N2
R–B4 22 R–R1 N–B6 23 Q–K1 Q–
B2 24 P×P B×NP 25 N×P**
Despair! **25 . . . K×N 26 R–B5 B–
K2 27 Q–K3 K–R1 28 Q–R6 R×P**
0–1

1801 AK–Mark Taimanov:
R1: 15 September:

Sicilian

1 P–K4	**P–QB4**
2 N–KB3	**P–K3**
3 P–Q4	**P×P**
4 N×P	**N–QB3**

Taimanov's system has gained a great deal of popularity as a result of Taimanov's own experimentation with it. The fact that he plays it almost invariably when facing 1 P–K4 does, however, make preparation a lot easier for his opponents. Taimanov puts his faith in the fundamental soundness of his system, and on the whole this faith has been justified.

5 N–N5	**P–Q3**
6 B–KB4	**P–K4**
7 B–K3	**N–B3**
8 B–N5	

With some loss of tempo, White aims to establish control over Q5. This variation also occurred in the second and sixth games of Taimanov's Candidates match with Fischer earlier in 1971. In the second game Taimanov tried 8 ... Q–R4+, in the sixth he continued as he does here.

8 ...	**B–K3**
9 N1–B3	**P–QR3**
10 B×N	**P×B**
11 N–R3	**N–K2**

A new move. Taimanov had previously tried 11 ... N–Q5 12 N–B4

P–B4 13 P×P N×KBP 14 B–Q3 R–B1 15 B×N R×N 16 B×B P×B 17 Q–K2± with little success for Black, Fischer–Taimanov, game 6.

In the first Fischer–Petrosian match game, Buenos Aires 1971, Black played 11 . . . P–Q4! and obtained an excellent position after 12 P×P B×N 13 P×B Q–R4 14 Q–Q2 0–0–0 15 B–B4 KR–N1. Unfortunately for Taimanov, however, Petrosian's innovation, dreamed up by Suetin, was not unveiled in Buenos Aires for another fifteen days!

12 N–B4!

The knight is recentralized with the immediate threat of establishing a bind on Q5 by 13 N–K3, so Black must free himself at once.

12 ...	**P–Q4**
13 P×P	**N×P**
14 N×N	**B×N**
15 N–K3	

White is heading for an ending in which his Q-side majority will be superior to Black's on the K-side because of the doubled KBPs. White's first aim is to eliminate the dangerous black bishop-pair.

15 ...	**B–B3**
16 B–B4	

After the sharp 16 Q–R5 Q–R4+ 17 P–QB3 0–0–0 Black gets strong counterplay.

16 ...	**Q×Q+**
17 R×Q	**R–B1**

		1	2	3	4	5	6	7	8	9	0	1	2	3	4	5	6	7	8	9	0	1	2	
1	Savon	×	½	½	½	1	1	½	1	½	½	1	1	1	½	½	1	½	½	½	½	1	1	**15**
2	Smyslov	½	×	½	1	½	½	½	½	½	½	½	½	½	½	1	½	½	1	1	1	½	1	**13½**
3	Tal	½	½	×	½	1	0	1	0	½	½	1	1	½	1	½	0	1	1	1	½	½	1	**13½**
4	**Karpov**	½	0	½	×	½	1	½	½	1	½	½	½	½	½	½	1	0	1	1	1	½	1	**13**
5	Balashov	0	½	0	½	×	1	1	½	½	0	0	0	½	½	1	½	1	1	½	1	1	1	**12**
6	Stein	0	½	1	0	0	×	½	1	1	0	1	½	½	½	½	1	½	1	½	0	1	1	**12**
7	Bronstein	½	½	0	½	0	½	×	1	½	1	½	1	½	1	0	1	1	½	0	0	½	1	**11½**
8	Polugayevsky	0	½	1	½	½	0	0	×	1	1	½	1	½	½	½	½	½	½	1	1	½	0	**11½**
9	Taimanov	½	½	½	0	½	0	½	0	×	1	1	0	½	1	½	½	1	0	½	1	½	1	**11**
10	Kapengut	½	½	½	½	1	1	0	0	0	×	½	0	½	0	½	½	½	0	1	1	1	1	**10½**
11	Krogius	0	½	0	½	1	0	½	½	0	½	×	½	0	1	1	½	1	1	½	½	½	½	**10½**
12	Lein	0	½	0	½	1	½	0	0	1	1	½	×	½	0	1	0	½	1	0	½	½	1	**10**
13	Platonov	0	½	½	½	½	½	½	½	½	½	1	½	×	½	0	0	0	½	1	1	1	0	**10**
14	Geller	½	½	0	½	½	½	0	½	0	1	0	1	½	×	1	0	½	½	0	½	½	1	**9½**
15	Karasev	½	0	½	½	0	½	1	½	½	½	0	0	1	0	×	1	½	½	½	0	1	0	**9**
16	Shamkovich	0	½	1	0	½	0	0	½	½	½	½	1	1	1	0	×	0	0	½	1	½	0	**9**
17	Vaganian	½	½	0	1	0	½	0	½	0	½	0	½	1	½	½	1	×	0	0	½	1	0	**8½**
18	Nikolayevsky	½	0	0	0	0	0	½	½	1	1	0	0	½	½	½	1	1	×	1	0	½	0	**8½**
19	Tukmakov	½	0	0	0	½	½	1	0	½	0	½	1	0	1	½	½	1	0	×	½	0	½	**8½**
20	Grigorian	½	0	½	0	0	1	1	0	0	0	½	½	0	½	1	0	½	1	½	×	0	½	**8**
21	Dzhindzhikhashvili	0	½	½	½	0	0	½	½	½	0	½	½	0	½	0	½	0	½	1	1	×	½	**8**
22	Tseitlin	0	0	0	0	0	0	0	1	0	0	½	0	1	0	1	1	1	1	½	½	½	×	**8**

| 18 B–Q5! | B×B |
| 19 R×B | K–K2 |

White now has a small but clear endgame edge, based mainly on the fact that Black cannot exchange all the rooks on the Q-file without allowing White a won knight *v.* bishop ending in which Black's majority could be permanently blockaded on dark squares. It is strategically essential for Black to get his pawn to KB4 if he is to survive at all, so he brings his king up to help it to advance.

20 K–K2

If 20 P–KN4 then 20 . . . P–KR4.

| 20 . . . | K–K3 |
| 21 R1–Q1 | P–B4 (*162*) |

162
W

With the threat 22 . . . P–B5 to win the QBP, and if 22 P–QB3 then still 22 . . . P–B5 and the knight has no good square.

| **22 P–KN3!** | **P–B5** |

22 . . . P–B3 allows 23 P–QB3 with a clear advantage.

| **23 P×P** | **P×P** |
| **24 N–N2** | |

24 N–N4? allows 24 . . . P–B3 with the threat of 25 . . . P–KR4.

| **24 . . .** | **R×P+** |
| **25 K–B3** | |

Now White's static advantage of the better pawn structure is converted into the dynamic one of attacking chances against the exposed black king.

| 25 . . . | B–B4 |

Not 25 . . . B–R3? 26 R–Q6+, nor has he time for 25 . . . R×NP? 26 N×P+ K–B3 27 R–K1 and Black must surrender material to avoid mate.

| **26 N×P+** | **K–B3** |
| **27 N–Q3** | **R–QB1!** |

Black is making strenuous efforts to make his pieces co-operate, and should be able to hold the position in spite of the superior tactical agility of White's minor piece.

| **28 R–Q7** | **P–N4?** |

This move weakens the QRP. A more solid defence was 28 . . . P–N3 to support the QRP on QR4 if necessary.

| **29 R–K1** | **K–N2** |
| **30 R–K4** | |

30 R–K6 allows Black counterplay by 30 . . . R–Q7! Since 30 . . . R–Q7 now loses to 31 N×B, Black must look for some other way of handling the threats to his loose pawns on KB2 and QR3.

| **30 . . .** | **R–B5** |

This loses a pawn, but he has nothing better, thus 30 . . . R–B3 31 R–KB4 R–B3 32 R×R K×R 33 R–B7 wins.

31 N–K5!

Much stronger than 31 R×R P×R 32 N–K5 K–B3.

31 . . .	**R×R**
32 K×R	**K–N1**
33 P–B4!	

White could throw away his winning chances here by 33 R×P? B–Q3! when Black forces the transition to a rook ending in which there will be terrible slaughter along White's second rank.

| **33 . . .** | **B–B1** |

33 . . . R–B1?! is probably too passive to hold any hopes for Black, and 33 . . . P–B3? 34 N–N4 R–B3 35 K–B5 only makes matters worse. Beilin

felt that 33 ... R–K1 was essential, though not very promising.

By keeping his rook active, Black hopes to mop up some pawns, but his king is about to get into trouble again. With the minor pieces on the board White always maintains attacking chances.

34 N×P   R–B7
35 N–N5

With the idea of 36 R–Q8 and 37 N–K6 to follow.

35 ...   B–R3
36 N–K6!   R×RP

Furman points out that 36 ... R×NP with the idea of sacrificing the bishop as in the game, and then capturing the QRP to obtain two united passed pawns, fails to 37 K–B5 B×P 38 K×B R×QRP 39 R–KN7+ K–R1 40 R–R7.

37 K–B5

The threat of 38 K–B6 now forces Black to give up his bishop, since 37 ... R–N7 loses to 38 R–Q8+ (also 38 K–B6 R–N3+ 39 K–K7 K–R1 40 P–B5) 38 ... K–B2 39 R–KR8.

37 ...   B×P (*163*)

163
W

38 K×B?

Here Karpov misses an easy win with 38 N×B R×P 39 K–B6 P–R3 40 R–KN7+ K–B1 (40 ... K–R1 41 N–N6 mate) 41 N–K6+ K–K1 42 R–K7 mate.

38 ...   R×P

39 R–KN7+   K–R1
40 R–R7

Unfortunately for Black, White can preserve his last pawn.

40 ...   P–KR4
41 R×P   P–N5
42 N–Q4

Just in time to stop 42 ... P–N6.

42 ...   R–N7
43 K–B3

Here it would be simpler to play 43 N–B5, aiming for the same position as in the game.

43 ...   R–Q7
44 K–K3   R–QN7

44 ... R–R7 might be slightly better.

45 K–B4   R–Q7
46 N–B5   R–QN7

Black could prolong the game somewhat by 46 ... K–N1.

47 K–N5   P–N6

Or 47 ... K–N1 48 K–N6 R–N7+ 49 K×P.

48 R–R6+   K–N1
49 K–B6   1–0

1802 Rafael Vaganian–AK:
R2: 16 September:

Reti

1 N–KB3 N–KB3 2 P–QB4 P–QN3 3 P–KN3 B–N2 4 B–N2 P–K3 5 O–O B–K2 6 P–N3 O–O 7 B–N2 P–B4 8 P–K3 P–Q4 9 Q–K2 N–B3 10 R–Q1 Q–B2 10 ... R–B1 **11 P–Q3 Q–B2 12 N–B3 KR–Q1 13 N–KR4** (threat 14 P×P P×P 15 N–B5) 13 ... P×P 14 NP×P P–QR3 15 P–B4± but not 15 QR–N1 allowing 15 ... N–R2! Korchnoi–Spassky, game 8, Candidates 1968. **11 N–B3 QR–Q1 12 P×P N×P** If 12 ... P×P Radashkovich suggests 13 P–QN4±. **13 N×N R×N 14 P–Q4 P×P 15 N×P N×N 16 B×N R–Q3?** (*164*) 16 ... R–Q2 is better e.g. 17 QR–B1 Q–N1 18 Q–N4 P–N3 19 B–QB6 and now 19 . . . R–Q3 and Black survives.

164
W

17 R/Q1–QB1!± Q–Q2 18 B–K5
R–Q4 18 . . . R–Q7 is no remedy
because of 19 Q–N4 P–N3 20 R–B7
Q–N4 21 B–QB3 obviating Black's
threat, rendering effective his own
20th move threat and introducing a
new one. 19 R–B7 Q–Q1 20 R×B/
N7 R×B 21 R–Q1! Q–K1 22
R×RP R–QR4 23 R–N7 B–B4 24
P–QR4 R–R1 25 R7–Q7 R–N1 26
Q–N5 introducing the threat of P–
QN4, driving the bishop away from
the defence of the QNP, and the
follow-up B–B6 or B–N7 26 . . . B–
R6 27 B–N7! 1–0 Two connected
passed pawns are enough.

'The game finished in 2½ hours. It
seems that here ease of play bordered on the frivolous' – Korchnoi.

1803 AK–Anatoly Lein:
R3: 17 September:

Queen's Gambit Declined

1 N–KB3 P–Q4 2 P–QB4 P–K3 3
P–Q4 B–K2 4 N–QB3 N–KB3 5 B–
N5 P–KR3 6 B–R4 N–K5 7 B×B
Q×B 8 Q–B2 0–0 9 P–K3 N×N 10
Q×N P–QB3 11 B–K2 P×P 12
B×P P–QN3 13 B–K2 B–N2 14 N–
K5 R–B1 15 B–R5 P–N3 16 B–B3
P–QB4 17 B×B Q×B 18 0–0 N–
Q2 ½–½

1804 Igor Platonov–AK:
R4: 19 September:

Queen Pawn

1 P–Q4 N–KB3 2 N–KB3 P–K3
3 P–K3 P–QN3 4 B–Q3 B–N2 5
QN–Q2 P–B4 6 0–0 P×P Varying
from 6 . . . N–B3 7 P–B3 B–K2 8 P–
K4 P×P 9 N×P 0–0 10 Q–K2 N–
K4 11 B–B2 Q–B1 12 P–KB4 B–R3
13 Q–Q1 N–B3 14 R–B3 P–N3=
Colle–Capablanca, Carlsbad 1929.
7 P×P B–K2 8 P–QN3 0–0 9
B–N2 N–B3 10 P–QR3 Q–B2 11 R–
K1 QR–B1 12 P–B4 P–Q4 13 R–
QB1 KR–Q1 14 Q–K2 P×P 15
P×P Q–B5 16 P–N3 Q–R3 17 R–
B2 Q–R4 18 Q–B1 R–B2 19 B–K2
Q–KB4 20 B–Q3 Q–KR4 21 B–K2
½–½ Karpov is still happy to take
things quietly after the disaster
against Vaganian.

1805 AK–Karen Grigorian:
R5: 20 September:

Alekhine

1 P–K4	N–KB3
2 P–K5	N–Q4
3 P–Q4	P–Q3
4 N–KB3	P–KN3

At one time this was thought to be
unplayable because of 5 N–N5, but
analysis by the ex-world correspondence champion Hans Berliner
and others has shown that Black can
safely play either 5 . . . P–KB3 or 5
. . . P×P 6 P×P B–N2 and if 7 P–
QB4 N–N5!

5 B–QB4

A Karpov favourite.

5 . . .   N–N3

5 . . . P–QB3 6 P×P is good for
White.

6 B–N3   B–N2

Furman prefers 6 . . . P–Q4.

7 N–N5

A promising alternative is to keep his pawn-structure flexible with a build-up involving 0–0, P–KR3 and Q–K2.

7 ...   **P–Q4**

Since 7 ... P–K3 weakens the dark squares too much, and 7 . . . 0–0 allows 8 P–K6!, Black must release his pressure on White's centre.

8 0–0

Furman suggests 8 P–KB4!?

8 ...   **0–0?!**

And here Furman prefers 8 . . . P–KR3.

9 P–KB4 ± (*165*)

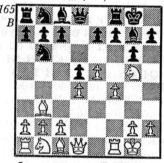

9 ...   **P–KB3**
10 N–KB3   **B–N5?!**

This loses time. A logical equalizing plan is 10 . . . N–B3 11 P–B3 P×P 12 BP×P B–B4 preparing to exchange the white KB with . . . N–QR4 and then to manoeuvre a knight to K3. The coming exchanges on the KB-file would then make the game rather drawish.

11 QN–Q2   **N–B3**
12 P–KR3   **B–B4**

If this bishop exchanges itself for a knight, Black will have difficulties over the weakness of K3. But now he must always reckon with P–KN4 by White.

13 R–B2

Karpov is preparing to bring his QN to the K-side to harass the bishop.

13 ...   **K–R1**

Better was 13 . . . P×P 14 BP×P N–R4 to exchange the bishop. Black is about to embark on a positionally unsound plan.

14 P–B3   **P–N4?**

This move is based on 15 BP×P? P×P which is favourable for Black. But Karpov can maintain his central control and prepare to infiltrate by using the weakness Black has created at his KB4.

Better was 14 ... N–R4 – Furman.

15 KP×P   **KP×P**
16 N–B1!   **P–KR3**
17 N–N3   **B–N3**
18 B–B2

The exchange of these bishops accentuates the weakness of the light squares in Black's K-side.

18 ...   **Q–K1**

Grigorian is hoping to get his queen to KN3 but Karpov isn't having any.

19 P–N3! ±

A fine multi-purpose move which restricts the knight on QN6 and prepares to make life awkward for Black's K-side pieces by 20 B–R3.

19 ...   **N–B1**
20 B–R3   **N–Q3**

20 ... N1–K2 is no better. At least this way he gets a little counterplay on the QB-file.

21 B×N

Karpov will not allow the knight to establish itself on e4, even at the cost of the exchange.

21 ...   **P×B**
22 R–K2   **Q–B2**
23 Q–N1! (*166*)
23 ...   **B×B**
24 Q×B   **KR–K1**
25 R1–K1   **N–K2**

25 ... P×P 26 N–B5 only makes Black's position worse.

26 P–B5

Transferring his attentions to the

166
B

K6 square. Black's bishop is now quite helpless.

26 ...	**B–B1**
27 R–K6	**N–N1**
28 N–R2	

To come in on KN4. If now 28 ... P–KR4? 29 Q–K2 wins a pawn.

28 ...   **R/K1–B1**

Black decides to abandon the K-file as he cannot afford to capture on e6 and give White a passed pawn and the f5 square.

29 R1–K3	**R–B3**
30 Q–K2	**R1–B1**
31 Q–B3	**Q–B2** (*167*)

167
W

32 N–K2

Now QB3 is covered and White is ready to proceed to the K-side.

32 ...	**Q–R4**
33 P–QR4	

But there is no point in giving anything away!

33 ...   **R3–B2**

34 R–K8	**B–N2**
35 Q–R5	**Q–N3**
36 N–N4	

Karpov overcomes his natural reluctance to leave pawns en prise in view of the threat of 37 N×RP. Grigorian finds another way to lose.

36 ...	**R×R**
37 R×R	**R–K2**
38 N×RP	**R×R**
39 N–B7 *mate*	

1806 Efim Geller–AK:
R6: 23 September:

Ruy Lopez

1 P–K4 P–K4 2 N–KB3 N–QB3 3 B–N5 P–QR3 4 B–R4 N–B3 5 0–0 B–K2 6 R–K1 P–QN4 7 B–N3 P–Q3 8 P–B3 0–0 9 P–KR3 N–N1 10 P–Q4 QN–Q2 11 P–B4 P–B3! 12 BP×P Or 12 P–B5 Q–B2 13 BP×P B×P 14 B–N5 P×P! 15 B×N P×B and 16 N×P N–B4= or 16 Q×P N–K4 17 QN–Q2 R–Q1 18 Q–K3 N–Q6 19 Q–R6!= Fischer-Portisch, Santa Monica 1966. **12 ... RP×P 13 N–B3 B–R3** An interesting idea in place of the usual 13 ... B–N2 14 B–N5 and either 14 ... P–R3 15 B×N B×B 16 P–Q5± Gufeld–Tukmakov, Leningrad 1971, or 14 ... P–N5 15 N–N1 N–K1 16 B×B Q×B 17 QN–Q2 N–B2 18 N–B4± Geller–Portisch, Palma 1970. In his notes in *The Chess Player,* Furman gives the text a TN; it is surprising that he was not aware of Gipslis–Portisch, Sousse 1967, which went 14 P–R3 P–B4 15 P×KP P×P 16 N–Q5 N×N 17 B×N ½–½. **14 B–N5 P–R3 15 P×P N2×P!?** (*168*) Better than 15 ... P×P?! 16 B×N B×B 17 Q–Q6. **16 N×P P×N= 17 B×N B×B 18 Q–R5 Q–K2 19 QR–Q1 QR–Q1 20 N–K2 B–N4 21 N–N3 Q–B3 22 R×R R×R 23 R–Q1 R×R+ 24**

168
W

Q×R B–B1 25 P–QR4 P×P 26 B×RP P–N3 27 N–B1 Q–K3 28 Q–B2 B–Q2 29 N–R2 Q–Q3 30 N–B3 B–Q1 31 Q–B3 B–B2 32 P–R4 K–N2 33 P–KN3 K–B3 34 K–N2 ½–½

1807 AK–Roman Dzhindzhik-hashvili:

R7: 24 September:

Centre Counter

1 P–K4 P–Q4!? 2 P×P N–KB3 3 B–N5+ This is favoured by Fischer and more aggressive than 3 P–Q4 or 3 P–QB4 when 3 . . . P–B3!? gives Black some interesting possibilities. **3 . . . B–Q2 4 B–K2!?** 4 B–B4 is the Fischer treatment e.g. 4 . . . B–N5 5 P–KB3 B–B4 6 P–KN4 B–B1 7 N–B3 QN–Q2 8 P–N5 N–N3 9 B–N5+± Fischer–Bergraser, Monaco 1967. Perhaps Karpov was worried by the possibility of 5 . . . B–B1 6 N–QB3 QN–Q2 7 Q–K2 N–N3 8 Q–Q3 P–N3 9 KN–K2 B–N2 10 N–N3 0–0 11 P–N3 P–QR3 with the idea of . . . P–QN4 which gave Black a good game in Belov–Shilin, USSR 1961. **4 . . . N×P 5 P–Q4 B–B4** Stronger than 5 . . . P–KN3 6 P–QB4 N–N3 7 N–QB3 B–N2 8 P–B5 N–B1 9 P–Q5± Bronstein–Lutikov, 27 USSR Ch 1960. **6 N–KB3 P–K3 7 0–0± N–QB3** Boleslavsky in *Skandinavisch bis Sizilianisch* quotes 7 . . . B–K2 8 P–QR3 0–0 9

P–B4 N–KB3 10 N–B3 N–K5 with good play for Black, Gurgenidze–Kuznetsov, ½-final 28 USSR Ch 1960, but White's play was not very convincing. **8 R–K1 B–K2 9 B–B1 0–0 10 P–B3 B–KN5 11 QN–Q2 P–QR3 12 Q–N3 B–R4?!** 12 . . . R–N1!? keeps White's advantage to a minimum. **13 N–K5!± B–N3** 13 . . . N×N 14 R×N leaves White winning thanks to the double attack on the bishop and QNP. **14 N×B RP×N 15 N–B3 N–N3 16 Q–B2 Q–Q4 17 P–QN3 KR–K1 18 B–Q3 QR–Q1 19 B–KB4 Q–Q2 20 P–QR4** 20 QR–Q1, continuing to build up pressure in the centre, is probably better. **20 . . . N–Q4 21 B–Q2?** (*169*)

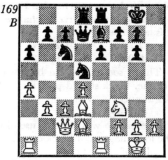

169
B

overlooking . . . **21 . . . N4–N5! 22 Q–N1** If 22 P×N N×QP 23 N×N Q×N∓ **22 . . . N×B 23 Q×N B–B3 24 P–QN4 P–K4 ½–½** Or 24 . . . P–QN4 25 P×P P×P 26 Q×QNP N×QP 27 N×N Q×Q 28 N×Q R×B 29 N×P R–QB1 30 N–N5 R–Q4 when Black has something to play for – Gufeld.

1808 AK–Leonid Stein:

R8: 25 September:

Sicilian

1 P–K4	**P–QB4**
2 N–KB3	**N–QB3**
3 P–Q4	**P×P**

4 N×P	N–B3
5 N–QB3	P–Q3
6 B–QB4	Q–N3

Stein is well-known for his experiments in the Sicilian. This one has achieved a degree of respectability and has been tried by Hort and Polugayevsky among others.

7 N×N

Various moves which have been tried here have failed to produce any convincing refutation of Black's queen move. The attacked knight can go to K2, QN3 or QN5, or it can even be protected by 7 B–K3?!

The exchange played in this game is generally regarded as positionally inferior for White and of value only as the quickest possible way to complete development. The plan Karpov now adopts may force a change in this assessment.

7 ...	P×N
8 0–0	P–K3?

This is soon shown to be a waste of time. Black should play 8 . . . P–K4 at once.

9 P–QN3!

The bishop will be very useful on the long diagonal if Black carries out his plan of . . . P–Q4.

9 ...	B–K2
10 B–N2	0–0
11 Q–K2!	

White is threatening to spoil Black's pawn-structure with 12 P–K5, so Black must admit the error of his eighth move.

11 ...	P–K4

Now 11 . . . P–Q4 would lose a pawn after 12 P×P BP×P 13 B×P.

12 K–R1

To be able to answer . . . B–KN5 with P–KB3; White is also keeping open the possibility of P–KB4 with a K-side attack.

12 ...	Q–B2
13 QR–K1	

White is ready to meet 13 . . . B–K3 with 14 B×B P×B 15 P–B4 and if 15 . . . P×P 16 P–K5! Stein, therefore, prepares to meet P–KB4 by playing the knight to a square from which it can help control his K4.

13 ...	N–Q2

Now 14 P–B4 is no longer good, so Karpov sets about increasing his control of the centre. Meanwhile Stein is having great difficulty in finding a plan.

14 N–R4	B–N2

14 . . . N–N3 is answered by 15 N×N P×N 16 P–QR4 still with advantage, e.g. 16 . . . B–K3 17 B×B P×B 18 P–KB4 or 16 . . . B–N2 17 P–KB4! and if 17 . . . P×P? 18 Q–N4 P–N3 19 Q×BP±±.

Black should play 14 . . . B–B3, covering the KP, so as to answer 15 B–Q3 with 15 . . . P–Q4. He should then be able to hold the balance, whereas White can now carry out his plan.

15 B–Q3	KR–K1
16 P–QB4	

Now White has a small but definite plus.

16 ...	B–N4
17 Q–B2!	

Placing more difficulties in the way of . . . P–Q4.

17 ...	P–KR3
18 P–QN4	

Intending to continue with 19 P–N5, weakening the Q5 square and establishing a Q-side pawn majority.

18 ...	P–R3
19 Q–N3	QR–N1
20 P–QR3	B–B1
21 Q–B3	B–B3

Forestalling White's P–KB4–B5.

22 Q–B2 (*170*)

22 ...	P–QR4

Stein decides that he must do something active or perish; but this means that Karpov's waiting tactics

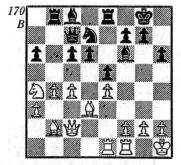

170
B

have paid off, as P–N5 will soon become possible.

22 ... N–N3!? would probably have put up greater resistance.

23 B–B3	**P×P**
24 P×P	**N–B1**
25 P–N5	**P×P?!**

25 ... B–Q2! would minimize Black's disadvantage. White would then probably play 26 R–QN1 before committing himself on the Q-side. As Stein plays, White has too many open lines to help him in his advance of the QNP.

26 P×P±	**B–Q2**
27 R–QN1	**R/K1–B1**
	(171)

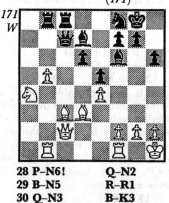

171
W

28 P–N6!	**Q–N2**
29 B–N5	**R–R1**
30 Q–N3	**B–K3**

Not 30 ... B×B? 31 Q×B R×N 32 Q×R R×B 33 Q–R7!±±.

Stein is making it as difficult as possible for Karpov to get his pieces

organized, but Anatoly hangs on grimly to his advantage.

31 Q–N4	**B–K2**
32 KR–B1	

He must allow ... P–Q4 as he has too many pieces 'hanging', but everything is still under control.

32 ...	**P–Q4**
33 Q–N2	**P–Q5**
34 B–N4!	**B–N4**

He does no better with 34 ... B×B 35 Q×B when 35 ... Q×KP? 36 N–B5 with P–QN7 to follow loses material for Black, and 35 ... R×R+ 36 R×R Q×KP gives White a clear win after 37 B–B6 Q–B5 38 R–QN1.

35 R×R	**R×R**
36 Q–K2!	

The black queen is a poor blockader: White now threatens 37 B–R6.

36 ...	**R–R1**
37 B–Q6±±	

Covering the queening square as well as attacking the KP.

37 ...	**B–B3**
38 Q–B2	**R–B1**
39 B–B7	

With the crushing threats of 40 Q–B6, 40 B–B6 and 40 N–B5. Stein has one last try.

39 ...	**B–Q1**
40 N–B5	**R×B**
41 N×Q!	**R×Q**
42 N×B	**B–B1**

If 42 ... B–R7 43 P–N7! B×R 44 P–R4 wins.

43 P–N3	**R×P**
44 R–QB1	**R–B3**
45 R×B	**R×P**
46 B–B4	**K–R2**
47 N×P	**1–0**

1809 Vasily Smyslov–AK:
R9: 27 September:

Semi–Tarrasch

1 P–QB4	**P–QB4**

2 N–KB3	N–KB3
3 N–B3	P–Q4

Karpov likes this method of dealing with the English. One line for White now continues 4 P × P N × P 5 P–KN3, but Smyslov decides on a Queen's Gambit Declined type of position with an isolated QP.

4 P × P	N × P
5 P–K3	P–K3
6 P–Q4	P × P
7 P × P	B–K2
8 B–Q3	0–0
9 0–0	N–QB3
10 R–K1	N–B3

Smyslov suggests 10 . . . B–B3 as an alternative in his notes to this game in *Informator*.

The text move is played to avoid the difficulties arising after 10 . . . P–QN3 11 B–K4!, but it involves a clear loss of time for Black and White's next move gives him the edge.

10 . . . N × N, as pointed out by Yudovich, is also possible.

11 P–QR3!

This prevents the manoeuvre . . . N–QN5–Q4 and prepares to line up the queen and bishop against the black king. Now Black will have trouble blockading the QP.

11 . . .	P–QN3
12 B–B2	B–N2
13 Q–Q3	R–B1?

He should have played 13 . . . P–N3. Now the isolated pawn gets its chance for a glorious death. . . .

14 B–N5?

But Smyslov misses it! He should have played 14 P–Q5!:
(a) 14 . . . P × P 15 B–N5 P–N3 16 R × B Q × R 17 N × P N × N 18 B × Q N3 × B with a substantial material plus for White;
(b) 14 . . . N–QR4 15 B–N5 R × N (15 . . . P–N3 16 P–Q6!±±) 16 P × R Q × P±.

14 . . .	P–N3
15 QR–Q1	

White still has much the better game, and it is hard for Black to find a move which does not allow his opponent to improve his position.

15 . . .	N–Q4
16 B–R6	R–K1 (172)

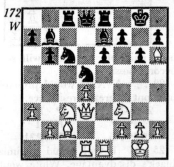

172
W

17 B–R4!　　P–R3

Preparing to drive away the bishop with . . . P–QN4, but this move falls in with White's idea.

'On 17 . . . N × N White had the choice between the solid 18 Q × N or a promising pawn sacrifice with 18 P × N B × P 19 P–B4, having in mind a later P–Q5. The text leads to difficulties of another kind.' – Keres.

Korchnoi gives 17 . . . N × N 18 P × N B × P 19 P–B4 B–B1 20 Q–K3± or 20 B–KN5±.

18 N × N!　　Q × N

'It is understandable that Black does not want to remain in a slightly inferior position after 18 . . . P × N, but that may have been the lesser evil. Now he has to be alert to the possibility of a breakthrough with P–Q5, which finally brings the decision.' – Keres.

19 Q–K3!

Now the point of White's seventeenth move is shown; without the interposition of 17 B–R4 P–R3, Black could meet the threat of 20

B–N3 with 19 . . . N–R4! White's last move covers the QB so that 20 B–N3 Q–KR4 21 P–Q5! is possible.

19 . . .   B–B3?

'This leads by force to material loss, but Black's position is already difficult. After 19 . . . Q–KR4 the continuation 20 P–Q5! P×P 21 Q×P is very strong, but 19 . . . R/K1–Q1 was probably his best practical chance. Now Smyslov finishes the game with a few strong blows.' – Keres.

20 B–N3   Q–KR4
21 P–Q5!±

'This Sword of Damocles has been hanging over Black's head for some time, and now it falls with decisive effect. Even Tarrasch mentioned that isolated central pawns can sometimes change from weaknesses into formidable striking forces!' – Keres.

21 . . .   N–Q1
22 P–Q6   R–B4

'Black has no time for 22 . . . B×N, as 23 P–Q7! would then cost him a whole rook. But with 22 . . . R–R1, Black could probably put up tougher resistance, protecting his first rank.' – Keres.

23 P–Q7   R–K2?

The decisive mistake. He can hold out a little longer by 23 . . . R–KB1 24 B×R K×B, but it hardly matters any more. Korchnoi recommended 23 . . . R–KB1 (23 . . . R68 sic) as better.

24 Q–B4!±±

'A move of terrible strength. The double threat 25 Q×B and 25 Q–N8 cannot be stopped simultaneously!' – Keres.

24 . . .   B–N2
25 Q–N8   Q×B
26 Q×N+   B–KB1
27 R–K3!

A rather cruel touch; Smyslov sees no reason to allow his pawns to be

broken up (as they would be after the immediate 27 Q×B+, which also wins), since his next move cannot be prevented.

27 . . .   B–B3
28 Q×B+   Q×Q
29 P–Q8=Q   1–0

1810 AK–Vladimir Savon:
R10: 28 September:

Sicilian

1 P–K4 P–QB4 2 N–KB3 P–Q3 3 P–Q4 P×P 4 N×P N–KB3 5 N–QB3 P–QR3 6 B–K2 P–K3 7 P–B4 B–K2 8 0–0 Q–B2 9 B–B3 N–B3 10 B–K3 Q–B2 11 P–QR4 N–QR4 12 K–R1 R–QB1 13 Q–Q3 N–B5 14 B–B1 0–0 15 P–QN3 N–R4 16 B–N2 N–B3 17 QR–B1 N×N 18 Q×N B–B3 19 Q–Q3 KR–Q1 20 N–K2 P–Q4 21 P–K5 N–K5 22 N–Q4 B–B4 23 R/QB1–Q1 B×N 24 B×B P–QN4 25 Q–K3 Q–N2 Sidestepping 26 B–N6 26 P–R5!? P–N5 27 B–N6 R–Q2 28 R–B1 B–N4 29 KR–Q1 Q–B3 30 R–Q4 N–B6 31 R–R1 N–K5 32 R1–Q1 N–B6 Not 32 . . . Q×P? 33 B×N Q×B 34 Q×Q P×Q 35 R×R B×R 36 R×R R–B8+ 37 B–N1!±±. **33 R–R1 N–K5 34 R–QB1 Q–B6 35 Q×Q P×Q 36 K–N1 P–B4 37 P×Pep P×P 38 B×N P×B 39 R×R B×R 40 K–B2 K–B2** (*173*)

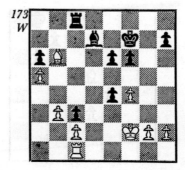

173
W

41 K–K3 41 R–Q1 is more promising. **41 . . . P–K4 42 P×P P×P 43 R–B1+ K–K3 44 R–B2 P–R4 45 P–N3 B–N4 46 K×P ½–½** Or 46 P–R3 R–KN1 47 R–N2 B–B8 – Vasiliev.

1811 Kapengut–AK:
R11: 1 October:

Sicilian

1 P–K4 P–QB4 2 N–KB3 P–K3 3 P–Q4 P×P 4 N×P N–KB3 5 N–QB3 P–Q3 6 B–K2 B–K2 7 0–0 P–QR3 8 P–B4 Q–B2 9 B–B3 0–0 10 P–QR4 N–B3 11 N–N3 P–QN3 12 B–K3 R–N1 13 Q–K1 N–QR4 14 N×N P×N 15 P–QN3 B–N2 16 R–Q1 KR–B1 17 R–Q3 B–R1 18 B–Q2 R–N5 19 P–B5 B–B1 20 P×P ½–½

1812 AK–Karasev:
R12: 2 October:

English

1 P–QB4 P–K4 2 N–QB3 N–KB3 3 P–KN3 B–N5 4 B–N2 0–0 5 P–K4 R–K1 6 KN–K2 N–B3 7 P–QR3 B–B1 8 0–0 N–Q5 9 P–Q3 N×N+ 10 Q×N P–B3 11 B–K3 P–Q3 12 P–R3 P–Q4 13 KP×P P P×P 14 B–N5 P–Q5 15 N–Q5 B–K3 16 KR–K1 B×N 17 B×B R–N1 18 P–QN4 P–KR3 19 B×N Q×B 20 P–KR4 P–KN3 (*174*)

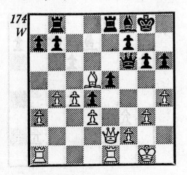

174
W

21 P–R5 K–N2 22 P–B5 P–N3 23 BP×P RP×P 24 P–N5 B–B4 25 KR–QB1 K–K2 26 P–R4 Q–Q3 27 B–N2 R–R2 28 R–B4 R–K1 29 P×P P P×P 30 Q–K1 R–R4 31 R–R2 R–K2 32 B–B6 P–R4 33 K–N2 R2–R2 34 R–K2 R×RP 35 R×R R×R 36 R×P R–R2 37 R–Q5 R–K2 38 Q–Q2 Q–B3 39 R–Q8 R–K7 40 R–Q7+ R–K2 41 R–Q5 R–K4 ½–½

1813 David Bronstein–AK:
R13: 3 October:

King's Indian Attack

1 P–K4 P–QB4 2 N–KB3 P–K3 3 P–Q3 N–QB3 4 P–KN3 KN–K2 5 B–N2 P–KN3 6 B–K3 B–N2 7 P–B3 P–N3 8 0–0 P–Q4 9 Q–B1 0–0 (*175*)

175
W

10 B–R6 Q–B2 11 B×B K×B 12 QN–Q2 B–R3 13 P×P N×P 14 N–B4 QR–Q1 15 R–K1 P–R3 16 Q–B2 N–B3 17 P–QR4 R–Q2 18 P–N3 ½–½

1814 AK–Nikolayevsky:
R14: 5 October:

Pirc

1 P–K4 P–KN3 2 P–Q4 B–N2 3 N–QB3 P–Q3 4 P–B4 N–KB3 5 N–B3 0–0 6 B–Q3 A favourite of Fischer **6 . . . N–B3 7 P–K5 P×P 8**

BP×**P** 8 QP×P leads only to early equality. **8 . . . N–KR4!** Suggested by Fischer and popularized by Keene. **9 B–K3 B–N5 10 B–QB4!?** TN 10 B–K4 is probably the best available. **10 . . . K–R1** Keene and Botterill suggest 10 . . . N–R4! e.g. 11 B–Q5 P–QB3 12 B–K4 P–KB4 13 B–Q3 P–B4 with good play against White's centre. **11 Q–Q2 P–B3 12 P×P B×P?**± 12 . . . P×P is the appropriate response, with the idea of . . . N–K2–B4. **13 0–0 B×N?!** Gufeld suggests 13 . . . Q–Q2. **14 R×B P–K4 15 P–Q5 N–Q5 16 R3–B1 N–B4 17 B–B2** Korchnoi, in *Informator*, suggests 17 N–K4±. **17 . . . N–Q3** a blockade, but how effective will it prove? . . . **18 B–QN3 B–N4** Or 18 . . . N–N2 with the idea of N2–B4 is still good for White. **19 Q–K1 Q–K2 20 N–K4 N×N 21 Q×N** The blockade is gone and Black's position is creaking with weaknesses. **21 . . . R–B5 22 Q–K2± R1–KB1 23 QR–K1 P–R4 24 P–B3** But not 24 Q×P? Q×Q 25 R×Q B–B3 with . . . P–R5 to follow – Korchnoi. **24 . . . N–B3** *(176)* Or 24 . . . B–B3 25 P–N3 R–B4 26 B–B2 R–N4 27 B–K3 – Korchnoi.

25 Q×P! Q×Q 26 R×Q N–N5 Or 26 . . . N–K5 27 R×B N×R? 28 B–Q4+ K–N1 29 P–Q6+ and White wins. **27 R×B N×B 28 B–B4!**±

taking all the sting out of the threatened . . . N–R6+ **28 . . . P–R5 29 R–N3 P–R6 30 P–N3 N–K5 31 R×R R×R 32 R–K3 N–Q3 33 B–Q3 R–B2 34 P–B4±± P–N3 35 P–N3 K–N2 36 P–QN4 K–B3 37 K–B2 R–Q2 38 B–K2 N–B4 39 R×P K–K4 40 P–N4 N–R5 41 R–K3+ 1–0**

1815 Nikolai Krogius–AK:
R15: 6 October:

Queen's Indian

1 P–Q4 N–KB3 2 P–QB4 P–K3 3 N–KB3 P–QN3 4 P–KN3 B–N2 5 B–N2 B–K2 6 0–0 0–0 7 N–B3 N–K5 8 N×N B×N 9 N–K1 B×B 10 N×B P–Q3 11 P–N3 B–B3 12 B–N2 P–B4 ½–½

1816 AK–Mark Tseitlin:
R16: 9 October:

Ruy Lopez

1 P–K4	**P–K4**
2 N–KB3	**N–QB3**
3 B–N5	**P–B4!?**

Tseitlin may have been tempted to play this risky line because of his opponent's well-known preference for quiet positions; and if he was hoping for a short brilliancy he was not to be disappointed!

4 N–B3

The most popular move.

4 . . .   N–Q5?!

The most usual line continues 4 . . . P×P 5 QN×P P–Q4 when White can choose between 6 N×P and 6 N–N3. Tseitlin's move is rarely played and not particularly good, though it could have surprise value.

5 B–R4

Karpov is duly surprised. Theory recommends 5 N×P! as giving White the advantage. But the text move is not bad and Black does not

succeed in justifying his opening here
either.

Karpov gives as alternatives 5 B–
B4 and 5 N × P!

5 . . .   N–KB3

Not 5 . . . P × P? 6 N × N P × N 7
Q–R5+ and wins.

6 N × P   P × P

Karpov, in his notes in *The Chess
Player*, points out 6 . . . B–B4 7 N–
Q3 B–N3 8 P–K5± and 6 . . . Q–
K2!? 7 N–B3 N × N+ 8 Q × N P × P
9 Q–N3 P–B3 10 0–0 P–QN4 11
B–N3 P–Q4 12 R–K1 and then P–
Q3±.

After the game Tseitlin condemned
this move and suggested instead 6 . . .
Q–K2 7 P–B4 P–QN4!? 8 N × NP
N × N 9 B × N P × P with some initiative for the pawn – Korchnoi.

7 0–0   B–B4

On 7 . . . B–K2 White can
simply win a pawn with 8 R–K1;
and after 7 . . . B–Q3 Karpov gives
8 N–B4 B–K2 9 P–Q3 P × P 10
Q × P N–K3 11 N–K5 with a small
edge for White.

Safer was 7 . . . B–Q3 8 N–B4 B–
K2 or 8 N–N4 0–0 – Korchnoi.

8 N × KP!?

The move one would expect from
Karpov is 8 P–Q3 (also suggested by
Korchnoi and by Yudovich), which
is good for White e.g. 8 . . . P × P 9
N × P/3 B–K2 10 N–B4! Instead he
tries a tricky combinative line which
is sound enough, but is possibly not
objectively the strongest.

8 . . .   N × N
9 Q–R5+   P–KN3

Not 9 . . . K–K2? 10 Q–B7+ K–
Q3 11 N–B4 mate!

10 N × NP (*177*)

The critical position. Black should
now play 10 . . . Q–N4!? when
Karpov gives 11 Q × Q N × Q 12
N × R (12 R–K1+ N/4–K3 13 N × R
P–N4 – Yudovich) 12 . . . P–N4 (12

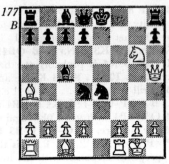

. . . N–K7+ 13 K–R1 N–K5 14 P–
Q3 N × P+ 15 R × N B × R 16 B–
R6±±) 13 B–N3 N × B 14 RP × N
B–Q5 15 P–QB3 B × N 16 P–Q4± –
White has the better ending, but
Black is not devoid of counter-
chances.

10 . . .   N–KB3?

Also bad for Black is 10 . . . P × N
11 Q × R+ K–K2 12 Q–K5+ etc.

Correct was 10 . . . Q–N4 11 Q × Q
N × Q 12 N × R P–N4 13 N–B3
N × N 14 RP × N B–Q5 – Korchnoi.

11 Q–K5+!

This is stronger than either 11 R–
K1+ B–K2! or 11 Q × B N–K3 12
R–K1 P × N 13 R × N+ K–B2.

11 . . .   B–K2
12 N × R±

Less clear is 12 R–K1 N–B6+! 13
P × N R–KN1 14 Q × B+ Q × Q 15
R × Q+ K–Q1 as pointed out by
Karpov.

12 . . .   P–N4

And not 12 . . . N–K3 13 Q × N/
K6. After 12 . . . N–B3 13 Q–KN5
wins quickly.

13 Q × N/4   P × B
14 R–K1   K–B1
15 P–Q3   R–N1

Hoping to air-lift this rook to the
K-side disaster area. If he tries 15 . . .
K–N1 16 B–N5 K × N 17 R × B wins.

16 Q–K5!

With the very nasty threat of 17
B–R6+.

16 ...	N–N1
17 Q–KR5	K–N2

17 ... Q–K1 18 Q×P R–N3 19 R–K4 is altogether too much.

18 N–B7	Q–K1
19 B–R6+	N×B
20 Q×N+	K×N
21 Q×P+	K–B1

21 ... K–B3 22 R–K4 is no fun for Black either.

22 R–K3	R–N3
23 R–N3	1–0

1817 Leonid Shamkovich–AK:
R17: 10 October:

English

1 P–QB4 P–QB4 2 N–KB3 N–KB3 3 N–QB3 P–Q4 4 P×P N×P 5 P–K3 5 P–K4 and 5 P–KN3 are the alternatives. 5 ... N×N 6 NP×N P–KN3 The position is equal – Gufeld. 7 B–R3 TN – theory gives 7 P–KR4!? P–KR4!? 8 B–B4 B–N2 9 N–N5 0–0 10 Q–B2± or 7 Q–R4+ N–Q2 8 Q–R4 B–N2 9 B–B4∓. 7 ... Q–B2 8 B–B4 B–N2 9 0–0 0–0 10 R–B1 N–Q2 11 P–Q4 The position now closely resembles a standard Grünfeld situation, except that White has played R–QB1 instead of Q–K2 and Black would normally have played ... N–QB3 or ... B–KN5. 11 ... R–N1 12 B–N5 P–N3 13 N–Q4 Q–B3 P–QR3 15 B–K2 N–N3 Q–B3 17 B–N2 (*178*)

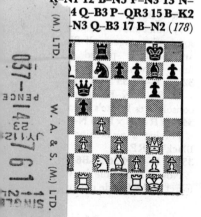

17 ... P–K4! Black's position was already clearly better; now he starts to put real pressure on White's centre. 18 P–K4 KP×P 19 P×P Q–R5∓ 20 B–B4!? P×P 21 B–N3 Q–N4 22 Q–B4 R–KB1 23 N–B3 N–B4 24 B×QP B×B Not 24 ... N–Q6?? 25 B×BP+ K–R1 26 Q–B6!! and wins. 25 N×B Q–K1 26 B–Q5 N–Q6 27 Q–B6 Q–Q1!∓ 27 ... N×R would allow White to draw with 28 N–B5! P×N 29 Q–N5+. 28 Q×Q KR×Q 29 QR–Q1 N–B5 30 N–B6 Or 30 B×B R×B 31 N–N3 N–K7+ 32 K–R1 R×R 33 R×R N–B6∓ 30 ... B×N 31 B×B N–K7+ 32 K–R1 N–B6 33 R×R+ R×R 34 B–Q5 K–B1 35 P–N3 N×B 36 R–Q1 K–K2 37 P×N R–QB1 The ending is not difficult to win. 38 R–Q2 K–Q3 39 P–QR4 R–B4 40 R–N2 P–QN4 41 P×P P×P 42 K–N2 K×P White could safely resign. 43 R–N4 K–B3 44 K–B3 R–B5 45 R–N1 P–N5 46 K–K3 K–N4 47 P–B4 P–B4 48 K–Q2 R–B3 49 K–Q3 K–R5 50 R–QR1+ K–N6 0–1

1818 AK–Vladimir Tukmakov:
R18: 11 October:

Sicilian

1 P–K4 P–QB4 2 N–KB3 P–K3 3 P–Q4 P×P 4 N×P N–QB3 5 N–N5 P–Q3 6 P–QB4 N–B3 7 N1–B3 P–QR3 8 N–R3 B–K2 9 B–K2 0–0 10 0–0 P–QN3 11 B–K3 B–N2

For 11 ... B–Q2!? see Karpov-Hartston.

12 R–B1!

The most promising of White's choices in this position. Much worse is 12 P–B3 R–K1! – Black exploits White's undefended QB to threaten ... P–Q4 in earnest and so forces White's reply: 13 Q–N3 N–Q2 14 KR–Q1 N–B4! 15 Q–B2 B–B3 16

B–B1 B–K4 17 Q–B2 Q–B2 18 K–R1 R–KB1! 19 N–B2 P–B4! Gufeld–Furman, 31 USSR Ch 1963.

12 . . . N–K4 13 Q–Q4 N4–Q2

13 . . . N3–Q2 leaves White with some advantage after 14 P–B3 e.g. 14 . . . B–QB3 15 KR–Q1 Q–N1 16 Q–Q2 R–Q1 17 N–B2 N–KB3 18 N–Q4 Gipslis–Averkin, 37 USSR Ch 1969.

14 P–B3?! (*179*)

14 KR–Q1 is required first to maintain restraint on the black QP. Thus 14 KR–Q1 and now:
(a) 14 . . . R–K1 15 N–B2 – Karpov.
(b) 14 . . . R–B1 15 P–B3 with the idea of Q–Q2 (Karpov in *The Chess Player*), but not 15 . . . R–K1 16 Q–Q2?! P–Q4! Instead 16 N–B2! is much stronger as 16 . . . P–Q4 now fails to 17 BP×P P×P 18 P×P B–B4 19 Q–Q2 P–QN4 20 B×B R×B 21 P–Q6.

179
B

14 . . . P–Q4!

14 . . . R–K1 15 B–B2 P–Q4 16 BP×P P×P 17 P×P B–B4 Reshevsky–Matulović, Sousse 1967, was also in Black's favour.

15 KP×P B–B4?!

More exact is 15 . . . P×P 16 P×P B–B4 17 Q–Q2 B×B+ 18 Q×B N×P 19 N×N B×N= – Karpov.

16 Q–Q2 B×B+? 17 Q×B P×P 18 KR–Q1 R–K1 19 Q–B2 R–QB1 20 R–B2 Q–K2 21 B–B1?

White could secure a real plus with 21 R2–Q2! e.g. 21 . . . P–QN4 22 N×QP N×N 23 P×N Q–Q3 24 N–B2± as pointed out by Karpov. The text is too slow and gives Black time to regroup.

21 . . . Q–Q3 22 R2–Q2 P–QN4 23 N×QP

Not 23 P×NP? R×N and the white knight on QR3 loses its protection.

23 . . . N×N 24 P×N N–B3 25 B–Q3 B×P 26 B–K4 R–K4 27 B×B R×B 28 R×R N×R?!

Black misses a chance of dead equality with the surprising 28 . . . Q×R!, for if 29 R×Q R–B8+ 30 Q–B1 R×Q+ 31 K×R N×Q (Karpov) with a dead draw.

29 Q–Q4 Q–QN3 30 Q×Q N×Q 31 R–Q6 R–N1 (*180*)

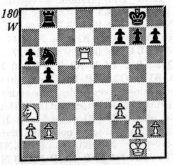

180
W

32 R–QB6!±

A quiet move which gives White some advantage – all Black's pieces are passively placed and cannot move without shedding material.

32 . . . K–B1 33 N–B2 R–B1

If 33 . . . K–K2 simply 34 N–Q4 consolidates White's advantage.

34 R×R+ N×R 35 N–N4!

Forcing a weakening advance of Black's QRP.

35 . . . P–QR4 36 N–B6 P–R5

Now it is possible for White's king to get at the Q-side pawns.

37 K–B2 K–K1 38 K–K3 K–Q2 39 N–K5+?

The right way to increase White's advantage was 39 N–Q4! N–Q3 40 K–Q3 K–B2 41 K–B3 K–N3 42 K–N4± (Karpov) and Black's pieces are restricted to running on the spot. **39 . . . K–K3 40 K–Q4 P–B3?**

40 . . . N–K2 was correct.

41 N–Q3 K–Q3 42 N–B4 P–N3 43 N–Q5 P–B4 44 P–KN4 N–R2 45 N–N4 P×P 46 P×P N–B1 47 N–Q3

If 47 N–Q5 N–R2 48 P–N5 N–B3+ 49 K–K4 N–R4= – Karpov. **47 . . . N–K2 48 N–K5 K–K3 49 P–QR3 N–Q4 50 N–Q7! K–Q3 51 P–N5**

51 N–B5 N–N3 and White can make no progress.

51 . . . N–K2 52 N–B8 N–B3+ 53 K–B3 N–K4?

The decisive error. 53 . . . K–K4 54 N×RP K–B4 55 K–Q3± and White's advantage is kept to a minimum.

54 N×RP N–B6 55 K–N4 1–0

If 55 . . . K–B3 then the KNP wreaks havoc: 56 N–B8 N×RP 57 N×P N–B6 58 N–K7+.

1819 Mikhail Tal–AK:
R19: 13 October:
Queen's Indian

1 N–KB3 N–KB3 2 P–KN3 P–QN3 3 B–N2 B–N2 4 P–B4 P–K3 5 0–0 B–K2 6 P–Q4 0–0 7 N–B3 N–K5 8 Q–B2 N×N 9 Q×N P–QB4 10 B–K3 Q–B2 Or 10 . . . B–KB3 11 KR–Q1 B×N 12 B×B N–B3 13 B×N P×B 14 Q–Q3 (Karpov stops here – is this significant?) 14 . . . P×P 15 B×P P–B4! Tal–Korchnoi, game 1 Candidates 1968 has been regarded as equalizing, but obviously Tal would be prepared for that line. **11 KR–Q1 P–Q3 12 QR–B1 N–Q2 13 P–QR3 P–QR4!** (*181*)

181
W

14 P–QN4 14 P–N3!? (Karpov) might be better. **14 . . . RP×P 15 RP×P R–R7 16 R–Q2** Karpov, in *The Chess Player*, suggests 16 R–R1. **16 . . . R×R 17 Q×R R–R1 18 N–K1 B×B 19 K×B** If 19 N×B R–R5 is still more embarrassing. **19 . . . R–R5 20 NP×P NP×P 21 P×P N×P 22 Q–B2** Now if 22 . . . Q–B3+ 23 K–N1 R–R1 24 N–Q3 is equal, so **. . . . ½–½**

1820 AK–Yuri Balashov:
R20: 14 October:

Sicilian

1 P–K4 P–QB4 2 N–KB3 P–Q3 3 P–Q4 P×P 4 N×P N–KB3 5 N–QB3 N–QB3 6 B–KN5 Karpov has had many successes with this. **6 . . . B–Q2 7 Q–Q2 R–B1 8 0–0–0 N×N 9 Q×N Q–R4** The speculative 9 . . . R×N!? is not good enough; e.g. 10 Q×R N×P 11 Q–K3 N×B 12 Q×N Q–N3 13 B–B4 P–K3 14 Q–N3 P–KN3 15 B–N3 B–K2 16 P–KR4 P–KR4 17 KR–K1 Q–N5 18 Q–K3 P–R4 Bednarski–Simagin, Polanica Zdroj 1968, and now 19 Q–Q4±. **10 P–B4** Karpov has since switched his allegiance to 10 B–Q2. **10 . . . P–K3** An early game with this line went 10 . . . Q–QB4 11 P–K5 Q×Q 12 R×Q P×P 13 P×P R–B4 14 B–N5 B×B 15 KR–Q1 N–Q4 16 N×N P–B3 17 P–K6 K–Q1 18 B–

B4 1–0 Bikov–Klaman, Leningrad 1963. **11 P–K5** Theory, and good at that, at the time was 11 K–N1 B–B3 12 B×N P×B 13 B–B4 R–KN1 14 P–B5! Jansa–Simagin, Polanica Zdroj 1968. **11 . . . P×P 12 P×P B–B3?!** 12 . . . R×N!? is a much better chance for Black now, though the complications are unclear to say the least. **13 B–N5** A strong alternative is 13 B×N P×B 14 N–K4 P×P 15 N–B6+ K–K2 16 Q–KR4. **13 . . . N–Q4** (*182*)

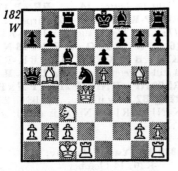

182
W

14 B×B+ In *The Chess Player* 1, Shamkovich and Fedorov now give 14 N×N! with:

(a) 14 . . . Q×B 15 N–B7+! and mate at Q8;

(b) 14 . . . P×N 15 Q×QP B×B 16 P–K6! P–B3 17 Q×P;

(c) 14 . . . B×B 15 Q×P! B–R3 16 Q–N6.

However, in the last variation they appear to have overlooked 15 . . . B–N5! (better than 15 . . . B–R3 and immensely superior to 15 . . . Q×Q? 16 N–B7+ R×N 17 R–Q8 mate) 16 Q×Q (or 16 Q×P 0–0 17 N×B Q×N gives Black a strong attack) 16 . . . B×Q with a level ending: 17

N–B4? P–R3 and 17 N–K3 B–K7 are both difficult for White, while 17 P–QN4 P×N 18 P×B B–B5 led to a drawish ending in Hort–Panno, Palma 1970. Perhaps Soviet analysts have discovered something new in this line . . .

14 . . . P×B 15 P–QR3 P–KR3 16 B–Q2 Q–N3 17 Q×Q P×Q 18 N–K4 P–QN4 19 K–N1 P–KB4 20 P×Pep P×P 21 P–KN4 P–R4 22 P–R3 B–K2 23 KR–N1 P×P 24 P×P R–KN1 ½–½

1821 Lev Polugayevsky–AK:
R21: 16 October:

English

1 P–QB4 P–QB4 2 N–KB3 N–KB3 3 N–B3 P–Q4 4 P×P N×P 5 P–KN3 P–KN3 6 B–N2 B–N2 7 0–0 0–0 8 N×N Q×N 9 P–Q3 N–R3 10 P–QR3 Q–R4 11 R–N1 B–R6 12 Q–N3 P–N3 13 Q–B4 N–B2 14 B×B Q×B 15 P–QN4 N–K3 16 B–K3 QR–B1 17 Q–R6 (*183*)

183
B

17 . . . N–Q5 18 B×N P×B 19 Q×RP Q–K3 20 KR–K1 R–R1 21 Q–N7 R×P 22 N–N5 Q–K4 23 N–B3 ½–½

19 ALEKHINE MEMORIAL Moscow, 23.11–19.12.1971

		1	2	3	4	5	6	7	8	9	0	1	2	3	4	5	6	7	8	
1	**Karpov**	×	½	½	½	½	½	½	1	½	1	1	½	½	1	½	½	½	1	**11**
2	Stein	½	×	½	½	½	½	½	1	½	½	½	1	½	½	½	1	1	1	**11**
3	Smyslov	½	½	×	1	½	½	½	½	½	½	½	½	1	½	½	1	1	½	**10½**
4	Petrosian	½	½	0	×	½	1	½	½	½	½	1	½	½	½	1	½	1	½	**10**
5	Tukmakov	½	½	½	½	×	½	½	½	½	½	1	½	½	½	1	½	1	½	**10**
6	Spassky	½	½	½	0	½	×	½	½	½	½	0	1	1	1	½	½	½	1	**9½**
7	Tal	½	½	½	½	½	½	×	½	1	½	0	½	0	½	½	1	1	1	**9½**
8	Bronstein	0	0	½	½	½	½	½	×	½	½	0	½	½	½	1	1	1	1	**9**
9	R. Byrne	½	½	½	½	½	½	0	½	×	1	0	½	½	1	1	½	½	½	**9**
10	Hort	0	½	½	½	½	½	½	½	0	×	1	½	1	½	½	½	½	1	**9**
11	Korchnoi	0	½	½	0	0	1	1	1	1	0	×	1	½	0	1	5	½	½	**8½**
12	Gheorghiu	½	0	½	½	½	0	½	½	½	½	0	×	1	½	½	½	½	½	**7½**
13	Olafsson	½	½	0	½	½	0	1	½	½	0	½	0	×	1	0	½	½	1	**7½**
14	Savon	0	½	½	½	½	0	½	½	0	½	1	½	0	×	½	½	½	1	**7½**
15	Balashov	½	½	½	0	0	½	½	0	0	½	0	½	1	½	×	½	0	½	**6½**
16	Uhlmann	½	0	0	½	½	½	0	0	½	½	1	½	½	½	0	×	½	½	**6½**
17	Parma	½	0	0	0	0	½	0	0	½	½	½	½	½	½	1	½	×	½	**6**
18	Lengyel	0	0	½	½	½	0	0	0	½	0	½	½	0	0	½	½	½	×	**4½**

Karpov's success in this event signalled the arrival of 'Anatoly Grozny' – since this event Karpov has had only two 'failures' (2nd at Budapest and 2nd in the 1973 Soviet Championship), in every other event in which he has competed he has taken first prize (in tournaments) or has won the board prize (in team events). This phenomenal run of success can only be compared (in modern times) with Fischer's very similar record in the period 1963–1972.

Interview with Karpov and Furman

The discussion with Anatoly Karpov (conducted by A. Roshal and published in *64* No. 52 1971) took place in the presence of Semyon Abramovich Furman and, understandably, the trainer took part in the conversation.

AR: It is difficult to suppose that your sporting goal in this tournament was to share first place.

AK: Even some people very favourably disposed towards me hoped for a place in the top ten for me. I myself was prepared to get one of the first five places.

SF: For me personally today's success is not so unexpected, partly because during recent years his results have been stable and with every tournament they have improved. Certainly I could not have foreseen that he would share first place, but I did estimate that he could get about the same number of points as he did get. I calculated that he would get plus 4 or plus 5. One's placing in a tournament is not always decided by the total of points, everything depends on how the struggle takes shape. But the even standard of the participants suggested in advance that such a showing would achieve a very high placing.

AR: Well, how did things take shape?

AK: I was not satisfied with the way the draw worked out for me. It dictated a stormy start, and I did not feel any special wish to play. Nothing much happened. All the time I wanted a great deal, but nothing worthwhile came up, the games took shape in a difficult way. The turning point was the meeting with Vlastimil Hort, it stood out not only in a sporting but also in an artistic connection. My spirits immediately rose. In the outcome I even got the prize for the best finish. Here I emerged victor over David Bronstein and Viktor Korchnoi. True, in the game with Viktor Lvovich we both unfortunately made several mistakes. Well, and against Vladimir Savon in the last round it somehow happened that he walked into an ambush. We expected that he would adopt the Open defence in the Ruy Lopez, although to guess exactly which system was difficult. When already at the board, I recalled one of his games in which he developed in a similar fashion. I found a strong manoeuvre with the queen (18 Q–B1! – eds), which turned out to be fatal for my opponent.

SF: We had been looking at a similar idea beforehand. It should be added that Karpov embarked on this encounter with the express wish of winning. In addition he was White.

AR: Does which colour you have and fighting spirit mean much?

AK: It is undoubtedly more difficult to play Black. But it is also not bad, especially when the opponent starts to play sharply for a win. I am always disposed for a fight, but nevertheless for some reason colourless games sometimes arise.

AR: To amateurs the style of the 20-year-old Karpov seems somewhat dry, rather academic. Frequent draws . . . At your age doesn't the wish arise to sacrifice a bit, to burn your bridges, and – charge!?

AK: So far I have a somewhat narrow opening repertoire – in consequence of having little spare time to work on broadening it. Of course I would like to play sharper and more modern systems, but in my opinion this is not in keeping with my style. At least I am satisfied with my style and I have not yet thought of changing it. Certainly it is possible to sacrifice pieces. Why not sacrifice? – if it is correct. But bridges I don't burn, it's not my speciality.

Draws are a separate matter. With a tournament schedule like the Memorial's they are unavoidable. It is true that they say that there is now a difficult tournament schedule everywhere, but you know you don't get such a first-class field everywhere. As regards me personally, I normally go out simply to play chess, I do not agree to draws beforehand. I settle for draws if the game which develops is not the type which I like, or if the half-points enable me to achieve the desired sporting result in the tournament. But in general it is necessary to learn not to lose, and wins will come afterwards.

SF: Prudence, or discretion – that is his characteristic feature. This particularly pleased me, even on first acquaintance; such a valuable quality is rarely met with in such young players. But for further achievements of the highest order a healthy risk is necessary; great aggressiveness. There arises a danger of changing a good quality into its opposite. Fortunately Tolya has proved, to some extent against expectation, a most dutiful student in the chess sense.

AK: Of the players in the tournament, Petrosian and Smyslov made the greatest impression on me.

SF: Clearly this is because both ex-champions are close to Karpov in their style of play, although there is not a complete resemblance. Therefore they are the most interesting for him.

AK: I don't know why. I just feel that here are chessplayers who understand everything, for whom there are no secrets.

AR: Do you ever experience time-trouble agonies these days?

AK: In all, two or three times in my life. This is not at all because while others think everything is clear to me. It is simply that I don't want to make stupid mistakes, and then lose, because of time shortage. Therefore I feel compelled to content myself with normal moves (they seem good to me) instead of searching for the best ones.

AR: The burden of first place – now many people will expect a repeat of your success. Someone even laid a bet . . .

AK: . . . But I, as a rule, never bet on anything. And so far no burden of compulsion to demonstrate anything has been laid on me. One must learn to play. You know in the last count absolutely all chessplayers are only occupied in learning to play better.

SF: In order to achieve further goals it's probably necessary to experiment somewhere. One just cannot do this in invitation tournaments. There, as grandmaster Uhlmann puts it, 'keine fokus!'

AR: What tournaments lie ahead?

AK: Next the international tournament at Hastings. Apparently in February, a match with the World Junior Champion, Hug, for the right of taking part in the Interzonal tournament (the match didn't take place, both players were given places in the Interzonal – eds), at the beginning of March the final of the All-Union Olympiad.

AR: Isn't that rather a lot?

AK: In the first half of 1971 I hardly played at all, but beginning with June I scarcely left the board – June, semi-final of the Soviet Championship; July, Student Olympiad; August, two team championships (national and Armed Forces); September–October, final of the national championship. If the Alekhine tournament hadn't been so outstanding and so tempting, I would have had to decline.

AR: Isn't it possible to give the All-Union Federation the individual plan of grandmaster Karpov, to have it ratified there, and afterwards to play and to occupy yourself in accordance with this plan?

SF: Unfortunately alterations, for reasons unknown to us, are quite often made. We expected that Karpov would take part in another foreign international tournament next spring. Now we again have to change all our plans.

AR: Is Anatoly really, at the same time, counted as a student of Leningrad University?

AK: I'm not just counted as one – I study the third year course in the Economics faculty. So far in my examination successes there has not yet been a 'four' and in the forthcoming session I'm desperate for an 'excellent'.

AR: Good Luck!

1901 Bruno Parma–AK:

R1: 24 November:

Sicilian

1 P–K4 P–QB4 2 N–KB3 P–K3
3 P–Q4 P×P 4 N×P N–QB3 5 N–
QB3 P–QR3 6 P–B4 Q–B2 7 B–
K3 P–QN4 8 N–N3 '!±' – Gheorghiu. 8 ... N–B3 9 B–Q3 Or 9 P–
K5 P–N5! 9 ... P–Q3 10 0–0 B–K2
11 Q–B3 0–0 11 ... B–N2 is widely
regarded as being more accurate.
12 P–QR4! 12 P–K5 P×P 13 P×P
N×P 14 Q×R N4–N5! is very
risky, but Moiseyev gives 12 P–
KN4!± e.g. 12 ... P–N5 13 N–K2
P–Q4 14 P–K5 N–K5 15 N–N3.
12 ... P–N5 13 N–N1 P–QR4!?
Gheorghiu suggested 13 ... P–K4.
14 N1–Q2 B–R3 Parma–Petrosian,
later in the tournament, reached a
very similar position – Black's QB
had gone to b7 on the eleventh move,
and after 15 K–R1 N–N1 16 N–Q4
N1–Q2 17 Q–R3 would have been
very strong, but the bishop is
probably better there than on a6.
15 B–B2! KR–B1 16 QR–K1 P–Q4
17 P–K5 N–Q2 18 Q–R3 P–N3 19
K–R1 N–Q1 20 N–B3 Q–N2 21 B–
R4!± B2×B 22 Q×B N–B1 23 N/
N3–Q4! B×B 24 P×B Q–Q2 (*184*)

184
W

25 Q–N5? 25 P–N4! with the idea of
P–B5 gives White a strong attack.
25 ... P–R4! 26 Q–R6? Throwing

away what remained of White's
advantage. 26 N–R4± was better.
26 ... N–B3! 27 N–QN5 N–K2 28
N3–Q4 N–B4!∓ 29 N×N KP×N
30 Q–N5 R–B7 31 P–N3 R1–B1 32
Q–N3 P–Q5! Creating problems of
communication for the white army.
33 Q–B3 R–N7 34 R–QN1 R×R 35
R×R N–K3 36 N–Q6 R–B6 37 P–
R3 Q–B3 38 Q–N3 R–B8+?! 39
R×R Q×R+ 40 K–R2 Q×P
41 N–B4!∓ Q–QB8! If 41 ... P–R5
42 Q×Q N×Q 43 N×P N×QP
44 N–B6! holds. 42 Q–B3 Q–K8 43
Q–N3 Q–B6 44 N×P K–N2 45
Q–B3 P–R5 46 N–B4! Q×NP 47
P–R5 Q–R7 48 Q–N7! N–N4 49 P–
K6! The equalizer. 49 ... Q–KB7
50 P×P 50 P–K7? would allow 50
... N×P! winning for Black thanks
to the threat of 51 ... Q–N8+ 52
K×N Q–KR8 mate. 50 ... Q–
N6+ 51 K–R1 Q–K8+ 52 K–R2
Q–N6+ ½–½

1902 AK–Fridrik Olafsson:

R2: 25 November:

Sicilian

1 P–K4 P–QB4 2 N–KB3 N–QB3
3 P–Q4 P×P 4 N×P P–K3 5 N–N5
P–Q3 6 P–QB4 N–B3 7 N1–B3 P–
QR3 8 N–R3 B–K2 9 B–K2 0–0 10
0–0 P–QN3 11 B–K3 B–N2 12 R–
B1 R–N1 For 12 ... N–K4 see game
1818. 13 Q–Q2 Furman suggests
13 P–B3 so that on 13 ... N–K4
White can play 14 Q–Q4 followed by
15 KR–Q1 with a very firm hold on
d5. 13 ... N–K4 14 P–B3 (*185*)
14 ... P–Q4 15 BP×P P×P 16 N×P
16 B–KB4 is apparently the right answer, but then 16 ... N–N3 17 B×R
Q×B 18 N×P B×N/4 19 P×B B–Q3
20 P–KN3 B×P 21 P×B Q×P+ 22
K–R1 Q–R5+= 23 K–N1 N–B5 24
B×P N–R6+ 25 K–N2 ½–½ Kavalek–Olafsson, Lugano 1970. 16 ...

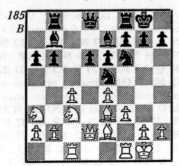

B×N/4 17 P×B N×QP 18 KR–
Q1 N×B 19 Q×N Q–K1 20 Q×N
½–½ Nothing is left after 20 . . . B×N.

1903 Levente Lengyel–AK:
R3: 26 November:

Catalan

1 P–Q4 N–KB3 2 P–QB4 P–K3 3
P–KN3 P–Q4 4 B–N2 P×P 5 N–
KB3 For 5 Q–R4+ see Smyslov–
Karpov (1916). 5 . . . P–QN4
6 N–K5 6 P–QR4 P–B3 7 0–0 B–N2
8 N–K5 Q–B1 Krogius–Furman,
Moscow 1967, is all right for Black.
6 . . . N–Q4 7 0–0 Kotov, in *Infor-
mator 13*, queries this and suggests 7
P–QR4! P–B3 8 0–0 with 9 P–K4, 10
RP×P and 11 P–N3 to follow.
7 . . . B–N2 8 P–K4 Now if 8 P–QR4
P–QR3. 8 . . . N–KB3 9 R–K1 QN–
Q2 10 Q–K2 P–QR3∓ 11 N–QB3
N×N Furman considers this ques-
tionable and suggests instead 11 . . .
P–B4. 12 P×N N–Q2 13 R–Q1 Q–
B1 14 P–B4 B–B4+ 15 B–K3 0–0 16
R–Q2 B×B+ 17 Q×B P–QB4 18
R1–Q1 equal according to Gheor-
ghiu. 18 . . . B–B3 19 R–Q6 White's
control of the Q-file is probably
sufficient compensation for the pawn.
19 . . . R–K1 20 R1–Q2 Q–B2 21 N–
Q1 (*186*)
21 . . . P–N5 Black begins to take the
initiative on the Q-side. 22 B–B1 B–
N4 23 B×P N–N3! 24 B×B P×B

25 P–N3 N–B1 26 R–Q7 Q–N3 27
R–QB2 P–B5! 28 R–Q4 28 Q×Q
is no better. 28 . . . R–R6∓ 29 N–
B2 N–K2 30 Q–Q2 P–B6 31 Q–
Q3 N–B3 32 R–Q6 R6–R1 33 K–
N2 KR–Q1 34 P–QR3?! R×R 35
P×R Not 35 Q×R? R–Q1 and it's
all over. 35 . . . N–Q5! 36 P×P
N×R 37 Q×N Q–Q5 38 K–B3 P–
K4 39 N–Q3 P×P 40 P×P P–B3 41
P–K5 (s) 0–1

1904 AK–Florin Gheorghiu:
R4: 28 November:

Sicilian

1 P–K4 P–QB4 2 N–KB3 P–Q3 3
P–Q4 P×P 4 N×P N–KB3 5 N–
QB3 P–QR3 6 B–K2 P–K4 7 N–N3
B–K3 8 0–0 QN–Q2 Gheorghiu also
mentions 8 . . . B–K2 9 P–B4 P×P 10
B×BP N–B3=. 9 P–B4 Q–B2 10
P–B5 B–B5 11 P–QR4 B–K2 12 B–
KN5 TN – Karpov, in *Informator 12*,
this is also the move-order given in
64. In *The Chess Player 1* Gheorghiu
gives the move order as 12 P–R5 0–0
13 B–N5! 12 . . . 0–0 13 P–R5 KR–
B1 ± – Gheorghiu 14 B×N Q×B 15
R–B2 P–R3 (*187*)
Gheorghiu gives this move an
exclamation mark. 16 B×N? Gheor-
ghiu gives 16 B–R4 as an alternative.
Karpov elucidates on this with 16
B–R4!? ± P–QN4 17 P×Pep N×NP
18 B×N winning. 16 . . . N×B 17

R–R4 Q–B2 18 R–Q2 If 18 N–Q5 N×N 19 P×N P–QN4= – AK. **18 ... P–QN4!** ∓ – FG ½–½ AK: 19 P×Pep Q×P+ 20 K–R1 R×N 21 P×R R–QB1 is unclear. FG: 19 P×Pep Q×P+ 20 K–R1 R×N! 21 P×R Q–B3 (If 21 ... R–QB1 22 Q–K2 R×P 23 R×RP Q–N5 24 R–R7 P–Q4?! 25 R×B Q×R 26 P×P±) 22 Q–R1 N×P 23 N–R5 Q×P∓.

1905 Robert Byrne–AK:
R5: 29 November:

Sicilian

1 P–K4 P–QB4 2 N–KB3 N–QB3 3 P–Q4 P×P 4 N×P P–K3 5 B–K3 Q–B2 6 N–QB3 P–QR3 7 B–Q3 P–QN4 8 0–0 B–N2 9 Q–K2 N–B3 10 P–B4 N×N 11 B×N B–B4 12 B×B Q×B+ 13 K–R1 P–N5 14 N–Q1 P–Q3 15 N–B2 P–K4 16 N–N4 N×N 17 Q×N 0–0 (*188*)

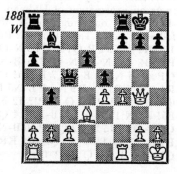

18 P–QR3 B–B3 19 Q–B5 NP×P 20 R×P B–N4 21 R–QB3 Q–N5 22 R–N3 Q–B4 23 R–QB3 ½–½

1906 AK–Yuri Balashov:
R6: 30 November:

Ruy Lopez

1 P–K4 P–K4 2 N–KB3 N–QB3 3 B–N5 P–QR3 4 B–R4 N–B3 5 0–0 B–K2 6 R–K1 P–QN4 7 B–N3 P–Q3 8 P–B3 0–0 9 P–KR3 P–R3 10 P–Q4 R–K1 11 QN–Q2 B–B1 12 N–B1 B–N2 13 N–N3 N–QR4 14 B–B2 N–B5 15 P–N3 This does not give Black severe problems, but Balashov probably expected 15 B–Q3! – the Korchnoi–*Furman* line. **15 ... N–N3** Black's knight is well placed here. **16 N–R2** (*189*) A novelty, played with the idea of 17 P–KB4. 16 B–N2 is better.

16 ... P–Q4!= **17 QP×P** Weaker would be 17 KP×P KP×P∓. **17 ... N×P** Not 17 ... R×P? allowing 18 N–B3 R–K1 19 P–K5 N–K5 20 N×N P×N 21 Q×Q QR×Q 22 B×KP B×B 23 R×B R–Q8+ 24 K–R2±. **18 Q–Q3** Not 18 N–B5? R×P 19 Q–N4 Q–B3∓, but 18 N×N is also possible, e.g. 18 ... P×N 19 Q×Q QR×Q 20 B×KP B×B 21 R×B R–Q8+ 22 N–B1 N–Q2 23 B–N2 R×R 24 B×R R×P=.

**18 . . . N–Q2 19 P–KB4 Q–R5 20
N2–B1 N2–B4** 20 . . . B–B4+? 21
K–R2± is bad. **21 Q–B3 N×N** Not
possible before because of the mate at
h7. **22 Q×N** If 22 N×N P–Q5∓ is
very strong. **22 . . . B–K2 23 B–K3
Q×Q** 23 . . . N–K5 may seem
tempting, but is proven bad by 24
B×N   Q×Q   25   N×Q   P×B   26
B–B2±. **24 N×Q B–R5 25 K–R2
B×N+ 26 K×B N–K5+ 27 B×N
P×B ½–½**

1907 Wolfgang Uhlmann–AK:
    R7: 3 December:

English

**1 P–QB4 P–QB4 2 N–KB3 N–
KB3 3 N–QB3 P–Q4 4 P×P N×P 5
P–KN3 P–KN3 6 P–Q3 B–N2 7 B–
Q2 P–N3?** Better 7 . . . 0–0 8 B–N2
with some initiative for White.
8 Q–R4+ B–Q2 9 Q–KR4! P–K3
Kotov queries this and gives 9 . . .
B–QB3! 10 B–N2 N–KB3 which is,
undoubtedly, better. **10 Q×Q+?!**
There is nothing wrong with this,
except for the fact that the stronger
10 B–N5!± was available. **10 . . .
K×Q 11 B–N2 P–KR3 12 0–0 N–
QB3 13 N–K1 N–B2 14 P–QR3 P–
QR4 15 N–B2 R–QN1 16 P–K3**
Kotov gives this an exclamation
mark. **16 . . . N–K4 17 P–Q4 N–B5
18 B–B1** A case of 'reculer pour
mieux sauter'. **18 . . . P–R5 19 R–
Q1 K–K2 20 R–N1 N–R4 21 P–K4
P×P 22 N×P** (*190*)
22 . . . P–K4? Better would have
been 22 . . . KR–Q1 23 B–B1±,
while Kotov suggests 22 . . . KR–
QB1! **23 N–B2! B–N5 24 R–Q3
B–K3 25 B–K3 B–N6 26 N–N4 KR–
Q1 27 R×R K×R 28 B–B3 K–K1
29 B–K2 P–QN4 30 R–QB1! K–Q2**
Not 30 . . . B–B5? 31 B×B N×B 32

N×RP   N×B   33   R×N   P×N   34
P×N B–B1 35 N–Q5±. **31 B–N4+
B–K3 32 R–Q1+ K–K1 33 B×B
P×B 34 R–Q6** Uhlmann doesn't
comment on this. Kotov, in *Infor-
mator 13*, queries it and prefers 34
B–R7! R–N2 35 B–B5!±. **34 . . . B–
B1!** by Kotov **35 R–N6 !** by Uhl-
mann.

35 . . . R–N2 36 R×R Uhlmann
queries this and gives instead 36 N–
R6! N×N 37 R×KP+ K–B2 38
R×N N–B5 39 B–B1 when White
stands much better. **36 . . . N×R 37
N–B6 B–N2! 38 N–R7** According to
Kotov, White can retain some
advantage with 38 B–N6! N–R1 39
B–R7 N–B2 40 B–N8±. **38 . . . N–
Q3 39 B–N6 N–R1** Now the bishop
manoeuvre is no longer available.
40 B–B5 N–B5 41 N7×P N×NP
Informator gives the game as drawn
here. **42 K–B1 ½–½**

As an explanation of Uhlmann's
shaky play one might offer the
following game: Tal–Uhlmann: R6:
1 P–K4 P–K3 2 P–Q4 P–Q4 3 N–Q2
P–QB4 4 KN–B3 N–QB3 5 B–N5
QP×P 6 N×P B–Q2 7 B–N5! Q–
R4+ 8 N–B3 P×P 9 N×P B–N5 10
0–0 B×N 11 P×B Q×BP!? 12 N–
B5! P×N 13 R–K1+ B–K3 14 Q–
Q6 P–QR3 15 B–Q2 Q×P 16 B–N4
P×B   17   Q–B8+   K–Q2   18   KR–
Q1+! K–B2 19 Q×R 1–0

1908 AK–Boris Spassky:
R8: 4 December:

Ruy Lopez

**1 P–K4 P–K4 2 N–KB3 N–QB3 3
B–N5 P–QR3 4 B–R4 N–B3 5 0–0
P–Q3 6 R–K1 P–QN4 7 B–N3 B–
N5 8 P–B3 B–K2 9 P–Q3 0–0 10
P–KR3 B–R4 11 QN–Q2 N–R4** 11
... P–Q4 12 P–N4 P×P 13 P×P
B–N3 14 Q–K2 Q–Q2 15 N–R4±
Ivkov–Hort, Varna Olympiad 1962.
12 B–B2 P–B4 13 N–B1 B×N 13 ...
N–K1 14 N–K3 R–N1 15 P–Q4 N–
QB3? 16 P–Q5± Schmid–Aguirre,
Leipzig Olympiad 1960. **14 Q×B
N–Q2 15 Q–N4 B–B3 16 N–N3 P–
N3 17 B–R6 B–N2 18 B×B K×B
19 P–KB4 N–KB3 20 Q–B3 P–R4
21 QR–Q1 R–B1 22 B–N1 P–R5 23
N–K2 N–R4 24 P–R3 P–B5 25 P–
Q4 Q–K2** *(191)*

**26 Q–N4 QR–Q1 27 B–B2 N–QB3
28 K–R2 R–KR1 29 R–Q2 N–B3 30
Q–B3 N–KR4 31 Q–N4 N–B3 32
Q–B3 N–KR4** ½–½ 'I had the better
position at the moment I agreed to a
draw. But I couldn't help doing that,
for I did not see any clear-cut plan of
action' – Karpov.

1909 Mikhail Tal–AK:
R9: 5+6 December:

Queen's Indian

**1 P–Q4 N–KB3 2 N–KB3 P–K3 3
P–B4 P–QN3 4 P–KN3 B–K2 5 B–
N2 B–N2 6 0–0 0–0 7 N–B3 N–K5 8
B–Q2 P–Q4 9 P×P** 9 Q–B2 N×N
10 B×N N–Q2 11 KR–Q1 Q–B1 12
P–N3 N–B3 13 QR–B1± Krogius–
Wade, Hastings 1970–71. **9 . . .
KP×P 10 N–K5** By delaying
castling, on both sides, Savon–
Furman, Dniepropetrovsk 1970, had
gone 9 Q–R4+ Q–Q2 10 Q–B2
N×B 11 Q×N 0–0 12 N–K5 Q–K3
13 N–Q3 P–QB3 14 0–0 N–Q2 with
a reasonable game for Black. **10 . . .
N–Q2 11 N–Q3 P–QR4** Black uses a
tempo to prevent 12 P–QN4. Fur-
man prefers 11 ... N2–B3 12 P–QN4
P–B3 13 R–B1 R–K1 14 B–B4 B–
KB1 15 N×N N×N= Peev–
Balashov, Kapfenberg 1970. **12 R–
B1 N2–B3 13 B–B4 P–B3 14 N–K5
P–B4 15 P×P N×N 16 P×N B×P
17 B–N5 R–K1 18 N–N4 B–K2 19
B×N B×B 20 P–QB4± B–K2 21
N–K3 B–N4 22 Q–Q3 P–Q5 23
B×B P×N 24 B×R P×P+ 25
K×P B–K6+ 26 Q×B R×Q 27
K×R Q×B 28 KR–Q1 Q–QB1 29
R–Q5 P–R3** *(192)*

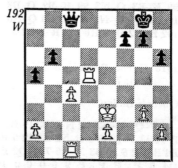

**30 P–KR4 Q–N5 31 K–B2 Q–K3 32
R–B3 Q–R6 33 K–N1 Q–N5 34 K–
B2 Q–R6 35 P–R3 Q–R7+ 36 K–
K1 Q–R8+ 37 K–Q2 Q–K5 38 K–
K1 P–N3 39 K–B2 K–N2 40 K–K1
Q–N8+ 41 K–B2** (s) **Q–K5 42 K–
K1 Q–N8+ 43 R–Q1 Q–K5 44
R1–Q3 Q–B3 45 K–Q2 P–KN4**

46 P×P P×P 47 R–N3 K–N3 48
R–N5 P–B3 49 R–Q4 K–R4 50 R–
R4+ K–N3 51 R–Q4 K–R4 52 R–
N3 Q–B4 53 R3–Q3 P–N4 54 P×P
Q×NP 55 R–Q5 Q–N3 56 R–Q6
Q–QN8 57 R6–Q5 57 R×P??
Q–N7+ 57 . . . Q–N3 58 R5–Q4
Q–N8 59 R–Q6 K–N5 60 R–KB3
Q–N7+ 61 K–K1 Q–B8+ 62 R–Q1
Q–B4 63 K–B1 Q–K4 64 R–Q8 Q–
R8+ 65 K–B2 Q–K4 66 R3–Q3 Q–
KB4+ 67 K–N1 Q–K4 68 R8–Q4+
K–R6 69 K–B1 Q–KB4+ 70 K–N1
Q–K4 71 K–B2 Q–KB4+ 72 R–
KB3 Q–K4 73 R–QB4 Q–Q4 74
R3–B3 Q–KB4+ 75 R–B3 Q–Q4 76
P–N4+ K–R5 77 R3–B3 Q–K4 78
R–Q3 Q–R7+ 79 K–B1 Q–R8+ 80
K–B2 Q–R7+ 81 K–K1 Q–K4 82
R–KB3 Q–Q4 83 R3–B3 Q–K4 84
R–Q3 Q–K3 85 R–R4 Q–K4 86
R4–Q4 Q–K2 87 K–B2 Q–K4 88
K–B1 Q–R7 89 R–K3 Q–R8+ 90
K–B2 Q–R8 91 R4–K4 Q–QN8 92
R–Q3 Q–N7 93 K–K1 Q–B8+ 94
K–B2 Q–KR8 95 R3–K3 Q–R7+
96 K–K1 Q–R8+ 97 K–Q2 Q–QN8
98 K–B3 Q–N3 99 K–B2 Q–B3+
100 K–Q1 Q–N2 101 K–K1 Q–N8+
102 K–B2 Q–KR8 103 R–QB4 ½–½

1910 Tigran Petrosian–AK:
R10: 7 December:

Queen's Indian

1 P–Q4 N–KB3 2 N–KB3 P–K3 3
P–KN3 P–QN3 4 B–N2 B–N2 5 P–
B4 B–K2 6 N–B3 N–K5 7 B–Q2 P–
Q4 8 P×P P×P 9 0–0 0–0 10
R–B1 N–Q2 11 B–B4 P–QB4 12 N–
Q2 N×N/6 13 P×N N–B3 14 P×P
B×P 15 N–N3 B–R6 16 R–B2 R–
B1 ½–½

1911 AK–Vlastimil Hort:
R11: 8 December:

Sicilian

1 P–K4	P–QB4
2 N–KB3	P–Q3
3 P–Q4	P×P
4 N×P	N–KB3
5 N–QB3	P–K3
6 P–KN4	N–QB3

The alternatives are:

(a) 6 . . . P–QR3?! 7 P–N5 KN–Q2
8 B–N2 P–QN4 9 P–B4 B–N2 10 P–
B5 P–K4 11 N4–K2 B–K2 12 P–B6!
– Nikitin.
(b) 6 . . . P–Q4 7 P×P N×QP 8
B–QN5+! B–Q2 9 N×N P×N 10
Q–K2+ ± – Furman.
(c) 6 . . . P–KR3!? and 7 B–N2 N–
B3 8 P–KR3 B–K2 9 B–K3 B–Q2 10
N4–K2 P–KN4!? with unclear com-
plications, Westerinen–Polugayev-
sky, 1967, or 7 P–N5 P×P 8 B×P
N–B3 9 Q–Q2 Q–N3! with counter-
chances, Stein–Krogius, 1966.

7 P–N5   N–Q2
8 B–K3

Informator, with notes by Karpov,
gives the move-order as 8 P–B4 P–
QR3 (If 8 . . . P–KR3 9 N×P P×N
10 Q–R5+ is unclear) 9 B–K3. However the majority of sources, includ-
ing *64* in which the game was
annotated by Furman, give the
move-order employed in the text.

8 . . .   P–QR3
9 P–B4

Furman prefers the immediate 9
R–KN1, criticizing the text as
premature.

9 . . .   B–K2

9 . . . P–R3 can lead to interesting
play, e.g. 10 P–N6 Q–R5+, or 10
P×P Q–R5+, but White can play
simply 10 N–B3.

10 R–KN1   N×N

Perhaps this leads to a premature
fixing of the central pawn structure.

11 Q×N	P–K4
12 Q–Q2	P×P
13 B×BP	N–K4

It is true that Black has obtained the e5 square, but White has control of d5 and also the position of the black king is rather unsafe.

14 B–K2	B–K3
15 N–Q5	B×N
16 P×B	N–N3

16 . . . Q–B2 with the idea of 17 . . . 0–0–0, though more passive, would have been more prudent, e.g. 17 R–N3 0–0 18 0–0–0 QR–Q1 and with 19 . . . KR–K1 to follow Black would not be so badly off.

17 B–K3

17 0–0–0 would also have been good, for example 17 . . . N×B 18 Q×N±.

17 . . .	P–KR3
18 P×P	B–R5+
19 K–Q1	P×P
20 B×KRP	B–B3

This is Black's best. The unhappy alternatives are 20 . . . Q–B3 21 B–K3 and 20 . . . Q–Q2 21 B–N7.

21 P–B3 B–K4 (193)

Creating an outlet for the queen to KR5.

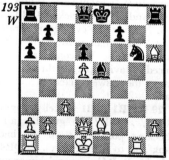

22 R–N4!

The rook has great scope here; both for attack and defence; for example it prevents . . . Q–R5 and is ready to go to K4 or QB4.

The text is immeasurably stronger than the paltry 22 B–KN5 Q–N3 23 B–K3 Q–B2 when Black begins to emerge from his straitjacket.

22 . . . Q–B3

22 . . . B×RP!? would not improve Black's position – he would have to reckon with 23 B–Q3 or, probably stronger, 23 K–B2 N–K4 24 R–N4 Q–B3 – but at least he would have the same number of pawns!

23 P–KR4!	Q–B4
24 R–N4!	

Black's king cannot run away; if 24 . . . 0–0–0 25 B–N4 is a bone-crusher.

24 . . . B–B3

Or 24 . . . R–KN1 25 B–Q3 Q–B6 26 K–B2 with 27 B–K4+ to follow.

25 P–R5 N–K2

25 . . . N–K4? loses the bishop to 26 R–KB4!

26 R–KB4! Q–K4 (194)

27 R–B3!

With the terrible threat of 28 B–KB4.

27 . . .	N×P
28 R–Q3	R×B

There is nothing better to be seen. If 28 . . . N–K2 then 29 B–KB4 with unpleasant consequences for Black.

29 R×N

29 Q×R allows 29 . . . B–N4 with . . . N–K6+ to follow.

| 29 ... | Q–K5 |

Or 29 ... Q–K3!? 30 R×P Q×R 31 Q×Q R–Q1 32 Q×R+ with a very advantageous ending despite the bishops of opposite colour.

30 R–Q3!

Out of his last nine moves, White has shifted the rook seven times ... and has a won position to show for it – not an everyday occurrence.

30 ...	Q–R8+
31 K–B2	Q×R
32 Q×R	B–K4
33 Q–N5	1–0 time

Is there one particular game ... which you like most of all? AK: 'It was in the Alekhine Memorial tournament . . . the game with Hort.'

1912 Vladimir Tukmakov–AK:
R12: 9 December:

Ruy Lopez

1 P–K4 P–K4 2 N–KB3 N–QB3 3 B–N5 P–QR3 4 B–R4 N–B3 5 0–0 B–K2 6 R–K1 P–QN4 7 B–N3 P–Q3 8 P–B3 0–0 9 P–KR3 N–N1 10 P–Q4 QN–Q2 11 P–B4 P–B3 12 BP×P RP×P 13 N–B3 B–R3 Gheorghiu gives this an exclamation mark; it does seem to be an improvement over the older 13 ... B–N2. **14 P–R3** For 14 B–N5 see Geller–Karpov. **14 ... P–B4= 15 P×BP P×P 16 B–N5 P–B5 17 B–B2 Q–B2** (195)

18 N–KR2 Q–N3 19 N–N4 KR–K1 20 Q–B3 B–N2 21 B×N ½–½

1913 AK–David Bronstein:
R13: 12+14 December:

Sicilian

1 P–K4 P–QB4 2 N–KB3 P–Q3 3 P–Q4 P×P 4 N×P N–KB3 5 N–QB3 P–QR3 6 B–K2 P–K4 7 N–N3 B–K3 8 P–B4 Q–B2 9 0–0 QN–Q2 For 9 ... N–B3?! see Karpov–Mecking. **10 P–B5 B–B5 11 P–QR4 B–K2 12 B–K3 0–0 13 P–R5 P–QN4 14 P×Pep N×NP 15 K–R1!** Better than 15 B×N Q×B+ 16 K–R1 B–N4!∓ Tal–Fischer, Curaçao 1962. **15 ... KR–B1 16 B×N Q×B 17 B×B R×B 18 Q–K2 R–N5** 18 ... R1–QB1 has since become more popular. **19 R–R2 P–R3**

Geller–Fischer, Curaçao 1962, continued 19 ... Q–N2?! 20 N–R5! Q–B2 21 N–Q5 N×N 22 P×N R–N4 23 Q–Q2 (Karpov gives 23 Q–B4±) 23 ... Q–B4 24 P–B4±. O'Kelly, in *The Sicilian Flank Game*, says 'if we consider the position after 19 R–R2 we find that both sides have two weaknesses; White on QN2 and K4 and Black on QR3 and Q3. Nobody has ever demonstrated that 2+2 equals more than 4; the position must be considered balanced'. Having played through this game, the answer is clear ... in this case 2+2=5!

20 R1–R1 B–B1 O'Kelly suggests 20 ... K–R2; to guard against checking possibilities on the back rank and to threaten ... P–QR4–R5. **21 R–R4!** Karpov's improvement. Previously theory knew only of 21 R×P R×R 22 R×R Q–N2 23 N–R5 Q–B2 24 N–N3 Q–N2=. **21 ... R–B1 22 R×R** If now 22 R×P then 22 ... Q–Q1 with ...

R1×N and . . . R×P to follow. **22 . . . Q×R 23 Q×P** *(196)*

196
B

23 . . . R×N Black cannot get equality, so he sacs the exchange to activate his game. Another possibility was 23 . . . R–B5 24 R–R4 R×P 25 Q–B1 and:

(a) 25 . . . R–KB5? 26 Q×R Q×Q 27 R×Q P×R with much the better ending for White.

(b) 25 . . . Q×N/B6 26 P×Q R×R and White won't find it so easy to turn his material advantage to account.

(c) 25 . . . Q×R 26 N×Q R×N 27 P–N3±.

24 P×R Q×KP 25 Q–Q3 Black doesn't have sufficient compensation for the exchange. **25 . . . Q–KB5 26 R–KB1 Q–KR5 27 N–Q2** 27 P–B4?! looks good but is dubious: 27 . . . N–N5 28 Q–KN3 Q×Q 29 P×Q N–K6=. **27 . . . P–K5 28 Q–N3 Q×Q 29 P×Q P–Q4 30 R–QN1!** Activating the rook. **30 . . . B–Q3 31 K–N1 B×P** Or 31 . . . N–N5 32 R–N5±. **32 K–B1** The king commences a victory march. **32 . . . B–B5 33 K–K2 N–R4 34 N–B1 B–K4 35 N–K3 B×P 36 R–N8+?** Pointless. 36 N×P is more logical. **36 . . . K–R2 37 N×P N–N6+ 38 K–B2?** The king should march forwards, not sideways. Now he is forced back. 38 . . . B–Q5+! 39 K–K1 N×P 40 R–N4 N–K6 41 K–K2

If 41 R×B?? then 41 . . . N×BP+ wins. **41 . . . B–B4 42 R–N5 N×N 43 R×B N–B5+ 44 K–B2** the sealed move 44 . . . K–N3 **45 P–N3 N–K3 46 R–Q5! P–B4 47 P–B4 P–B5 48 P–B5 P–K6+ 49 K–B3 P×P 50 K×NP P–R4 51 P–B6 P–K7** Against 51 . . . P–R5+ White wins by 52 K×P P–K7 53 R–K5 N–Q5 54 R×P! and the knight is absolutely helpless – attacking White's remaining pieces but unable to capture either: 54 . . . N×R allows the pawn to queen, while 54 . . . N×P 55 R–K6+ and it's all over. **52 K–B2 K–B3 53 R–Q7 1–0**

1914 Viktor Korchnoi–AK:
R14: 13 December:

English

1 P–QB4	**P–QB4**
2 N–KB3	**N–KB3**
3 P–KN3	**P–Q4**
4 P×P	**N×P**
5 B–N2	**P–KN3?!**

5 . . . N–B3 first was more accurate
6 P–Q4! **B–N2**

If 6 . . . P×P White recaptures with the queen.
7 P–K4 **N–B2!?**

After 7 . . . N–B3 White still plays 8 P–Q5, since the KP is immune because of the check on QR4. 7 . . . N–N3 would be more usual in this type of position.
8 P–Q5 **N–N4**

The knight gets ready to jump in on d4 at an appropriate moment.
9 0–0 **0–0**

9 . . . B–N5!? – Karpov.
10 Q–B2 **N–R3**
11 B–B4 **B–N5**
12 QN–Q2± *(197)*

White maintains control over Q4 and his strong centre gives him a good game.

197
B

12 ...   **N–Q5**

If 12 . . . R–B1 then 13 Q–N3 is unpleasant.

13 N×N   **P×N**
14 N–B3!   **Q–N3**
15 N–K5?!

This is premature. Korchnoi should have prepared it with 15 Q–Q2 so as to keep watch on the QP and thus avoid Karpov's continuation in the game.

15 ...   **B×N!**
16 B×B   **P–B3**
17 B–B4   **QR–B1**

With some advantage for Black – Karpov.

All of a sudden Korchnoi faces problems, which are not so simple to solve:

(a) To find a suitable place for his queen. She can't go to Q2 – that loses a bishop after . . . P–KN4, on QN1 the queen is extremely passive and, at the same time, 18 . . . B–K7 with . . . P–Q6 to follow would be very strong.

(b) To defend himself from the tip-and-run attack . . . N–QN5 followed by . . . R–B7.

(c) To defend the QNP.

18 Q–R4   **P–N4**
19 B–B1   **B–K7**

19 . . . N–N5!? was also possible e.g. 20 P–B3 B–R4∓.

20 R–K1   **P–Q6**
21 B–B1

Offering the exchange after 21 . . . Q–N5 22 Q×Q N×Q 23 B×B N–B7 24 B×QP, but Karpov is not interested in such insignificant gains.

21 ...   **B×B**

21 . . . N–N5 is not possible now because of 22 B×B N–B7 23 B×QP N×R/K8 24 B–K2 (coveting KN4) 24 . . . R–B7 25 B–K3 Q×P 26 B–Q4.

22 R×B   **R–B7**
23 B–K3   **N–B4**

This is much stronger than 23 . . . Q×NP 24 QR–N1 with counterplay for White.

24 Q–Q4

24 Q–R3 is better. Gheorghiu gives the move an exclamation mark and assesses the position as ±. Karpov gives 24 . . . R–B1∓.

24 ...   **P–K4**
25 P×Pep   **Q×KP**
26 QR–B1?

This soon allows Black a neat tactical blow. Better was 26 P–QN4 immediately – before the rooks can be doubled on the QB-file – e.g. 26 . . . N×P 27 Q×QP R–B6∓.

26 ...   **R–B1**
27 P–QN4   **N×P!** (*198*)

Now this move is very good as 28 Q×QP is no longer an answer for White because of 28 . . . N×BP! winning.

198
W

28 R×R   **P×R**
29 R–B1   **P–N3**

| 30 P–B3 | N–Q3 |
| 31 Q–Q3 | R–B3! |

Preparing to improve his position by offering the exchange of queens. There is nothing left for White to do.

32 P–QR4	Q–B5
33 Q–Q2	N–B2
34 P–B4	

To prevent . . . N–K4.

| 34 . . . | P–N5 |
| 35 P–N5 | R–B1 |

Gheorghiu prefers 35 . . . R–B2 which is slightly more accurate.

36 Q–Q7	P–KR4
37 K–B2	Q–B6
38 Q–B5	R–K1
0–1	

After 39 R–K1 Q×R+ 40 K×Q P–B8=Q+ leaves Black with a lot of extra material and a mating attack.

Karpov's third great game in the space of four rounds.

1915 AK–Leonid Stein:
R15: 15 December:

Ruy Lopez

1 P–K4 P–K4 2 N–KB3 N–QB3 3 B–N5 P–QR3 4 B–R4 N–B3 5 0–0 B–K2 6 R–K1 P–QN4 7 B–N3 P–Q3 8 P–B3 0–0 9 P–KR3 N–N1 10 P–Q4 QN–Q2 11 B–N5 B–N2 12 QN–Q2 P–R3 13 B–R4 R–K1 (*199*)

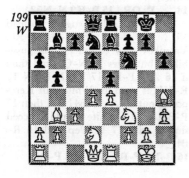

1916 Vasily Smyslov–AK:
R16: 16 December:

Catalan

1 P–Q4 N–KB3 2 P–QB4 P–K3 3 P–KN3 P–Q4 4 B–N2 P×P 5 Q–R4+ QN–Q2 6 Q×BP P–QR3 7 N–Q2 Usual here are 7 Q–B2 or 7 N–KB3. 7 . . . P–B4 8 P×P B×P 9 N–N3 B–K2 10 N–B3 Also 10 B–Q2!? with the idea of B–R5. 10 . . . P–QN4 11 Q–Q4 If 11 Q–B3 P–N5 12 Q–Q4 B–N2 = 11 . . . B–N2 12 0–0 0–0 13 R–Q1 P–QR4! 14 B–N5 Not 14 P–QR4 B–Q4∓ when White suddenly finds his Q-side very weak and his queen rather short of squares. 14 . . . P–R5 15 N–B1 P–R3 16 B×N N×B 17 N–Q3 Q–N1 (*200*)

14 Q–N1 Surprisingly, a new move. More usual are 14 B–N3 B–KB1 15 Q–N1 (15 B–B2=) 15 . . . P–B4 16 P–QR4 N–R4 17 B–KR2 Q–B3∓ Korchnoi–Tukmakov, Sochi 1970, or 14 P–QR4 P–B4 15 P×KP QP×P 16 B×N N×B! 17 P×P P×P 18 R×R B×R 19 N×P P–B5 20 B–B2 B–B4 21 N5–B3 Q–N3= Smejkal–Parma, Siegen Olympiad 1970. Other moves seen here are 14 Q–K2 and 14 B–B2. 14 . . . P–B4 15 P–QR4 Q–N3 16 P×KP N2×P 17 P×P P×P 18 R×R ½–½

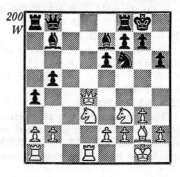

Furman states 'Black has a satisfactory game'. Karpov suggests, instead of the text, 17 . . . R–B1!? **18 Q–K5! N–Q4 19 Q×Q QR×Q 20 P–QR3** If 20 N–Q4 P–N5 and the pawns, though far advanced, do not seem to be weak. **20 . . . N–N3∓ 21 N/B3–K5** 21 N–Q4 B×B 22 K×B B–B3 gives Black pressure against White's Q-side. **21 . . . B×B 22 K×B KR–B1 23 QR–B1 N–B5 24 P–K3 ½–½**

1917 AK–Vladimir Savon:
R17: 18 December:

Ruy Lopez

1 P–K4 P–K4 2 N–KB3 N–QB3 3 B–N5 P–QR3 4 B–R4 N–B3 5 0–0 N×P

'This game was played in the last round, when Stein was leading the tournament a half point ahead of Karpov. Logically therefore, Karpov was playing for a win and Savon must have known this.

'Under the present circumstances, I do not like Savon's choice in this game. The Open Ruy Lopez is a variation in which Black gets active pieces at the price of positional weaknesses; thus it is a type of play with no way back. As we will further see, Savon goes for a dubious variation without having prepared any improvements.' *Keres.*

6 P–Q4 P–QN4 7 B–N3 P–Q4 8 P×P B–K3 9 P–B3 B–QB4 10 QN–Q2 0–0 11 B–B2 B–B4

Less well known than the main alternatives 11 . . . P–B4, 11 . . . N×N and 11 . . . N×KBP!? 12 R×N P–B3.

12 N–N3 B–KN3

'This leads by force to an inferior position for Black. If he wanted to play this variation, 12 . . . B–KN5 was better here. The theoreticians

recommend then 13 N×B N×N 14 R–K1 R–K1 (but not 14 . . . B–R4? 15 B–N5! . . .) 15 B–B4, but Larsen thinks 15 . . . P–Q5 16 P–N4 N–K3 17 B–K4 Q–Q2! is then quite playable for Black.' *Keres.*

The text move is Savon's patent.
13 N/B3–Q4 (*201*)

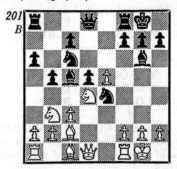

Much better than 13 P–QR4? B–N3 14 P×P P×P 15 R×R Q×R 16 Q×P? N×QBP! 17 P×N B×B∓ Tukmakov–Savon, 37 USSR Ch 1967. Karpov must have wondered why his opponent entered this inferior variation for the second time.
13 . . . B×N 14 P×B!

Maybe Savon expected 14 N×N N×N 15 P×N P–QB4 16 P–B3 P×P when 17 P×N P×P is good for Black, while 17 Q×P (Karpov simply gives this an!) 17 . . . N–N6! 18 P×N B×B isn't bad for Black either.
14 . . . P–QR4 15 B–K3 N–N5?

Tal and Kirillov suggest instead 15 . . . P–R5 16 N–B1 P–R6. Vatnikov also considers this possibility, but gives 16 N–Q2 and then if 16 . . . P–R6 17 N×N B×N 18 R–N1! is good for White, but Keres points out 16 . . . P–B4! and then 17 P–B3 P–B5!; White should proceed simply with 17 P×Pep and 18 R–B1 ±.

16 B–N1 P–R5 17 N–Q2 P–R6

Or 17 . . . P–QB4 18 QP×P P–
Q5 19 N×N P×B 20 N–Q6±, but
Petrosian's idea of 17 . . . N×N 18
Q×N N–B3 with . . . Q–Q2 and . . .
N–Q1–K3 to follow was better.

18 Q–B1!

'Even better than 18 Q–N3 N×N
19 B×N N–B3. Now Black's activity
has come to an end and he must
already meet the threat of 19 P×P.'
Keres.

18 . . . R–R3?

Karpov mentions the alternatives
18 . . . N×N 19 Q×N N–B3 20
R–B1 and Petrosian's idea is still
almost workable for Black, and 18 . . .
P–QB4!? 19 QP×P P–Q5 20 N×N
P×B 21 NP×P P P×P+ 22 N×P±.

Keres' recipe for avoiding the
worst is to offer a pawn by 18 . . .
Q–Q2 19 P×P N×N 20 Q×N N–
B3.

19 P×P R–QB3

Now if 19 . . . N×N 20 B×N N–
B3 21 B×B BP×B 22 Q–B5 is winning. Savon is playing for a combination, but Anatoly refutes this
nicely.

20 Q–N2 N–B7

20 . . . N×N is again no better:
21 B×N! and White is clearly winning after either 21 . . . N–B7 22 R–
B1, or 21 . . . N–Q6 22 Q–N3. The
text move gives White the chance to
play 21 B×N N×N 22 B×B N×R,
or 22 B×N R×B with a trouble-
free game for Black.

21 R–B1! *(202)*

21 . . . N×B 22 R×R N×BP

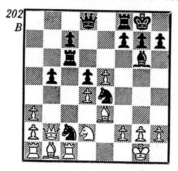

202
B

A final fling. Equally hopeless is
22 . . . Q–N4 and both 23 B×N
B×B 24 P–N3 (Karpov), and 23
R×B! BP×R (Furman gives 23 . . .
RP×R 24 B×N) 24 B×N P×B 25
Q–N3+ (Vatnikov) put an end to
further resistance.

23 N–B1!

'This eliminates all of Black's
possible attacking chances. Further
simplification is unavoidable, after
which White's exchange plus must
tell.' *Keres.*

23 . . . Q–Q2?

'A grave mistake in great time
trouble, but the position was already
lost. Black could not play 23 . . .
N×N because of 24 Q×N, and
after 23 . . . N7–N5 24 N×N N×N
25 Q–K2 White would not have
much work to do to make his
exchange tell.' *Keres.*

24 N×N 1–0

'A good game by Karpov, showing
that his play deserved the points he
gathered in the tournament.' *Keres.*

20 HASTINGS 29.12.1971–15.1.1972

	1	2	3	4	5	6	7	8	9	0	1	2	3	4	5	6	
1 **Karpov**	×	0	1	1	½	½	½	½	½	1	½	1	1	1	1	1	**11**
2 Korchnoi	1	×	½	½	½	½	0	1	1	1	½	1	1	½	1	1	**11**
3 R. Byrne	0	½	×	½	½	1	1	½	½	½	1	0	½	1	1	1	**9½**
4 Mecking	0	½	½	×	½	1	½	½	1	½	½	1	½	1	1	½	**9½**
5 Gligorić	½	½	½	½	×	½	½	½	½	½	½	½	½	½	1	1	**8½**
6 Najdorf	½	½	0	0	½	×	1	½	½	1	½	½	1	½	½	1	**8½**
7 Andersson	½	1	0	½	½	0	×	½	½	1	½	½	½	½	½	1	**8**
8 Unzicker	½	0	½	½	½	½	½	×	½	½	1	1	½	½	½	½	**8**
9 Pfleger	½	0	½	0	½	½	½	½	×	½	½	½	½	½	1	1	**7½**
10 Kurajica	0	0	½	½	½	0	0	½	½	×	½	½	1	½	1	1	**7**
11 Ciocaltea	½	½	0	½	½	½	½	0	½	½	×	½	½	½	½	½	**6½**
12 Botterill	0	0	1	0	½	½	½	0	½	½	½	×	½	½	0	1	**6**
13 Hartston	0	0	½	½	½	0	½	½	½	0	½	½	×	½	1	½	**6**
14 Keene	0	½	0	0	½	½	½	½	½	½	½	½	½	×	½	0	**5½**
15 Markland	0	0	0	0	0	½	½	½	0	0	½	1	0	½	×	1	**4½**
16 Franklin	0	0	0	½	0	0	0	½	0	0	½	0	½	1	0	×	**3**

On February 24 1972, Anatoly Karpov discussed the Hastings tournament at the Moscow Central Chess Club.

The international tournament at Hastings, over a period of many years, took place as a rule with ten participants. In recent years this formula has begun to be outmoded. Over such a short distance the players avoided risks because even one defeat could have a fatal significance on the result. The tournament table was decorated with frequent draws. The element of fight was kept to a minimum. Such a situation did not suit either the participants or the organizers. Therefore the Englishmen came to the conclusion that it was essential to break with tradition and increase the number of participants.

This year eight grandmasters and eight masters were invited to the main tournament. At the last moment Szabo could not come and he was replaced by the 1965 World Junior Champion, Kurajica, who had been down to participate in the first subsidiary tournament (Challengers – eds). Although as a result of this change the main tournament did not forfeit its rating status the grandmaster norm turned out to be very high.

Korchnoi and I came to Hastings immediately after the Alekhine Memorial, and we felt tired. The 'echo' of the Moscow tournament was unexpectedly heard at the time of the draw.

'Of course I will draw "my" number one, that unlucky one, just as in the

Alekhine Memorial', said Viktor Korchnoi as he approached the judges' dais.

Amid general laughter Viktor Korchnoi duly drew this number. But the strangest occurrence was still to come – I also got 'my' number fourteen, under which I played in Moscow! However I managed it I don't know, only unlike Viktor Korchnoi, I was not put out. It is true that I had Black against practically all my rivals, but every cloud has a silver lining: against the weakest participants I had White, and that made beating them that much easier.

Conditions in the tournament hall, although it was large enough, turned out to be very difficult. Our tournament took place parallel to the master tournament, the distance between the players and spectators was insufficient – the public were 2–3 metres away from the participants – we heard every conversation and remark. Viktor Korchnoi suffered especially – it was agonizingly painful for him to play.

The tournament began successfully for me. After drawing with Pfleger in the first round I won three successive games, and after another draw I again scored three victories. Here I felt that my strength was giving out. In the previous eight months I had played about a hundred games, and, speaking frankly, I had simply become played out. In my game against Korchnoi, who had proved to be my only rival, I could no longer fight as before – Viktor Korchnoi easily beat me

Before the last round Viktor Korchnoi led me by half a point, and on the final day of the tournament took no risks; agreeing a quick draw with Najdorf. The question of first place was decided by my game with the Englishman Markland. At the cost of an incredible amount of effort I succeeded in overcoming this opponent and catching up with Viktor Korchnoi.

The fight for third place was between Byrne and Mecking. Success accompanied the Brazilian player, or, more accurately, not success but good luck. Thus Pfleger, in an advantageous position, forgot to make the last move before the time control. A very ugly incident took place in the meeting Mecking-Botterill; the players were in time-trouble with two or three minutes for eight moves – Mecking put his hand on the clock and would not allow the Englishman to press it – the judge did not notice and Botterill lost his calm and, in two moves, the game. Everybody was extremely indignant and Najdorf called Mecking 'the bandit of the chessboard'.

Although Mecking succeeded in fulfilling the grandmaster norm, I don't have too high an opinion of his play. I was ever so much more pleased with the play of the Swede, Andersson – a very talented and promising player.

As for Kurajica, who in his time raised high hopes, in my opinion he has not advanced. At any rate, there is no sign that the Yugoslav works at his chess. It is possible that he was unprepared for playing in such a strong tournament. At first Kurajica was rejoicing in his unexpected 'promotion', but later he lamented that he had accepted the invitation and moved from the master to the grandmaster tournament. . . .

I will show you two of my games, to some extent similar to each other. In both of them the Sicilian was played, an early exchange of queens took place, and an ending with opposite coloured bishops arose. In both games White succeeded in realizing a positional advantage and in getting up an attack on the black king despite the meagre quantity of material left on the board. (The games referred to are those against Byrne and Mecking – eds.).

The above article was translated from the *Central Chess Club Bulletin*.

2001 Helmut Pfleger–AK:
R1: 29 December:

Queen's Indian

1 P–Q4 N–KB3 2 P–QB4 P–K3
3 N–KB3 P–QN3 4 P–KN3 B–N2
5 B–N2 B–K2 6 N–B3 N–K5 7
Q–B2 N×N 8 Q×N 0–0 9 0–0
P–Q3 10 P–N3 P–QB4 11 B–N2
B–KB3 12 Q–B2 N–B3 13 R/R1–Q1
Q–K2 14 P–K4 P–N3 15 P–Q5
N–N5 16 Q–Q2 B×B 17 Q×B
P×P 18 KP×P R/R1–K1 19
P–QR3 N–R3 20 R/B1–K1 Q–Q1
21 N–Q2 P–B4 22 P–B4 N–B2 (*203*)

203
W

23 P–QN4 B–R3 24 Q–B3 R×R+
25 R×R R–K1 26 R×R+ Q×R
27 K–B2 Q–K2 28 B–B1 N–K1 29
B–K2 N–N3 30 B–B3 K–B2 31
P–R3 B–B1 32 N–B1 P×P 33 P×P
Q–B2 34 N–K3 P–KR4 35 P–N5
P–R3 36 P×P B×P 37 P–N4 RP×P
½–½ A quiet start to the tournament.

2002 AK–Robert Byrne:
R2: 30 December:

Sicilian

The notes to this game are

Karpov's from the Soviet Central Chess Club Bulletin No. 2 1972.

1 P–K4	P–QB4
2 N–KB3	N–QB3
3 P–Q4	P×P
4 N×P	N–B3
5 N–QB3	P–Q3
6 B–KN5	B–Q2
7 Q–Q2	R–B1
8 0–0–0	N×N
9 Q×N	Q–R4

A well-known theoretical position has arisen.

10 P–B4

Another possibility is 10 Q–Q2.

10 . . .   P–KR3

Formerly 10 . . . P–K3 11 P–K5
P×P 12 P×P B–B3 was played here.

11 B–R4   P–KN4
12 P–K5 (*204*)

204
B

This position also is not new. In one Yugoslav tournament a game went 12 . . . B–N2 which led to great complications. The variation 13 B–K1 N–R4 14 N–Q5 Q×P 15 N×P is obviously good for White. But I think that Black's idea is worth considering and is interesting to analyse.

12 ...	P×B
13 P×N	P–K3
14 B–K2	

A good move. The white bishop, depending on circumstances, can be transferred to f3 or h5, where it will control important squares.

14 ...	B–B3
15 KR–K1	R–KN1
16 B–B3	

It's far from simple for Black to find a move, and it's no coincidence that Byrne thought for 20 minutes

16 ...	K–Q2

Black decides on evacuating the king to the Q-side. I succeeded in finding a line which led to a clear positional advantage.

17 R–K5	Q–N3
18 Q×Q	P×Q
19 B–R5	

Now the KBP cannot be defended. A series of forced moves begins – each side strives to gobble up as many pawns as possible

19 ...	R×P
20 B×P	R×RP
21 B×P+	K–B2
22 R–K3	

White's position is better because his pawns on the KB-file are more dangerous than the black pawns on the KR-file. In addition to which Black's KB is, for the time-being, out of play.

Now Black faces the problem – where to put the R/B1?. It's possible he should have moved it to R1, but this was a difficult decision to make; it took the b8 square away from the king.

22 ...	R–Q1
23 N–Q5+	B×N
24 R×B	

In spite of the opposite coloured bishops White's position is very much better because Black has very weak pawns.

24 ...	R–B7

Provoking an advance of the KBP (KB4), Black prepares to bring out his bishop on h6.

25 P–B5	P–R4
26 R–QB3+	K–N1 (205)
27 P–R4	

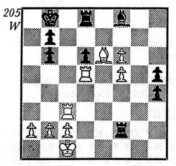

205
W

I'm not convinced with the correctness of the plan of attack on the king – it's possible that the correct procedure was to concern myself with the opponent's passed pawns, but this course seemed to me too slow.

27 ...	R–B5
28 R–QR3	R–KN5
29 P–R5	B–R3+
30 K–N1	P×P
31 R5×RP	

The pawn on b7 is in danger and there is no way to defend it. Black's only counterplay consisted of the line 31 . . . R–N8+ 32 K–Q2 B–R3+. Byrne, however, began immediately with the second move and allowed the white king to hide itself away on a2.

31 ...	K–B2
32 R–N5	R–N6
33 R–R7	R–QN1
34 B–Q5	R–N8+
35 K–R2	R–KB8
36 R7×P+	R×R
37 R×R+	K–Q1
38 B–K6	P–R6

The last chance. . . .

   39 R–Q7+

In time-trouble Byrne noticed that if 39 . . . K–B1 40 R–KR7+ K–Q1 41 R×B P–R7, White succeeds in holding the pawn by 42 B–Q5, and played . . .

   39 . . .   K–K1

but after . . .

   40 R–QB7   1–0

resigned because of the unavoidable mate.

2003 George Botterill AK:
   R3: 31 December:

QGD

   1 P–Q4 N–KB3 2 P–QB4 P–K3 3 N–KB3 P–Q4 4 N–B3 B–K2 5 B–N5 0–0 6 P–K3 P–KR3 7 B–R4 P–QN3 8 B×N B×N 9 P×P P×P 10 B–K2 B–N2 11 0–0 R–K1!? 11 . . . Q–K2 12 Q–N3! R–Q1 13 QR–Q1± Korchnoi-Geller, game 5, Candidates 1971. **12 P–QN4 P–R3 13 Q–N3 Q–Q3 14 N–Q2?!** 14 N–K1 allowing the redeployment B–B3 and N–Q3 is better. **14 . . . N–B3 15 P–QR3** Better 15 B–B3. **15 . . . N–K2 16 B–B3 QR–Q1 17 P–N3 N–B4 18 Q–B2 P–N3 19 N–N3 R–K2 20 QR–Q1 Q–K3 21 N–B1 N–Q3 22 N–Q3 Q–B4 23 B–N2 P–KN4 24 Q–N3 N–K5 25 P–QR4 P–KR4 26 P–R3 B–N2 27 P–R5 Q–K3 28 N–R4 Q–Q3 29 R/B1–K1 R1–K1?!** A better idea is 29 . . . K–R1 to get the K-side pawns moving. **30 N–B3! K–R1 31 P–N5!** (*206*) **31 . . . RP×P** If 31 . . . NP×P then 32 N–B5! N×N 33 P×N Q×BP 34 N×P is good for White. **32 N×NP Q–R3 33 N–B3 N×N 34 Q×N P×P 35 Q×RP P–QB3 36 R–N1 P–R5 37 P–N4 P–KB4! 38 P×P B–QB1 39 R–N8 B×BP 40 Q–R8 Q–N3 41 N–N4 B–Q2 42 R×R+ R×R 43 Q–N7 R–K2 44 R–QB1?**

44 P–B3, to avoid Black's next, would be better. **44 . . . P–N5! 45 R×P Q–N8+ 46 B–B1** 46 K–R2 P–N6+ 47 P×P P×P+ 48 K×P R×P+ is no improvement. **46 . . . P×P 47 Q–N5** The only way to parry the threat of 47 . . . P–R7+. **47 . . . R–K3 48 Q–N8+ R–K1 49 Q–Q6 R–KN1! 0–1**

2004 AK–William Hartston
   R4: 1 January:

Sicilian

   1 P–K4 P–QB4 2 N–KB3 P–K3 3 P–Q4 P×P 4 N×P N–QB3 5 N–N5 P–Q3 6 P–QB4 N–B3 7 N1–B3 P–QR3 8 N–R3 B–K2 9 B–K2 0–0 10 0–0 P–QN3 11 B–K3 B–Q2!? An interesting innovation. This move is sometimes played on move ten, but after 11 B–K3 the theoretical continuations are 11 . . . Q–R4, 11 . . . R–N1, 11 . . . N–R2 and 11 . . . N–K4 with the aim of making possible the advance . . . P–QN4.

   12 R–B1 12 P–B3 Q–N1 13 Q–K1 R–R2 14 Q–B2 R–N2 15 KR–Q1 N–QN5 16 R–Q2 R–Q1 17 R1–Q1 B–K1   18   P–B4± Kapengut-Balashov, 39 USSR Ch 1971.

   12 . . . Q–N1 13 P–KN4!? (*207*) Fischer, against Taimanov at Palma 1970, played 13 P–B3 but had no more than equality after 13 . . .

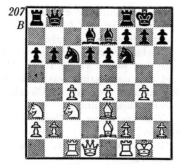

R–R2 14 N–B2 R–Q1 15 Q–K1 B–K1 16 Q–B2 R–N2 17 P–QR4 P–QR4 establishing QB4 for the N/KB3.

13 ... R–B1 If 13 ... P–QN4 then 14 P×P P×P 15 N/R3×P N–N5 16 P–QR3 N–R7 17 N×N B×N 18 P–B3 and the weaknesses in White's K-side do not sufficiently compensate Black for the connected passed pawns.

14 P–N5 N–K1 15 P–B4 R–R2 16 Q–K1 R–N2 17 Q–R4 P–N3! 18 R–B3 N–N2 19 R1–B1 19 R–R3 only wastes time as then 19 . . . P–KR4 leaves the K-side blocked.

19 ... R–K1 20 B–Q3 20 N–B2!? is an interesting alternative e.g. 20 . . . P–N4 21 N–Q5 P×N 22 BP×N is unclear. But 20 R3–B2, with the idea of N–Q5 is not so good on account of 20 . . . B–KB1 – removing the bishop from attack and strengthening the K-side.

20 ... P–KR4 21 Q–B2 N–N5! 22 B–N1 B–QB3 23 R–R3 White wants to play P–B5. Minić and Marić in *Informator 13* point out the interesting line 23 B–Q4 P–K4 24 P×P P×P 25 R×P P P×B! 26 R×N+ K×R 27 Q–B7+ K–R1 28 Q×NP B–B4!∓∓ **23 . . . B–Q2 24 Q–R4 Q–B1 25 R–B1** N–Q5 is now a threat.

25 ... Q–N1 26 R–B1 Q–B1 27 R3–B3 P–Q4!= 28 BP×P P×P 29 P–B5!? B–B4 30 B×B Q×B+

31 Q–B2 Q×Q+ 32 R3×Q P–Q5 33 N–K2 P–Q6 34 P×P P×P Not 34 . . . P×N? 35 P×P+ K–R2 36 P–K5+! and White wins. **35 N–KB4 R×P 36 N×QP** (*208*)

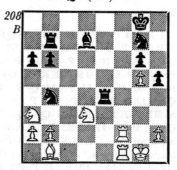

36 ... R–N5+?! 36 . . . B–R6 was better. **37 R–N2 R×R+ 38 K×R N×N?!** And now 38 . . . N–Q4! was the right course, though even then White would have some advantage – Black's K-side pawns are probably weaker than White's, and White's pieces are more actively placed. Now Black loses a pawn.

39 B×N N–B4 40 B×P B–B3+? Here 40 . . . N–K6+ was essential. After 41 K–N1 R–R2 42 B–B4+ N×B 43 N×N B–N4 posing White some problems. **41 K–B2 R–Q2 42 R–B1! B–K5 43 B–K2 N–Q3?** 43 . . . N–Q5!? was the last chance of fighting White's growing advantage.

44 N–B4 N×N If 44 . . . R–QB2 then 45 N×N R×R 46 N×B and White should have no real problems converting his material advantage. **45 R×N B–Q4 46 R–QN4 B×P 47 R×P K–N2 48 R–N4 B–N8 49 P–R4 K–B2 50 K–K3 R–K2+ 51 K–Q2 K–K3 52 R–N5 B–K5 53 P–N4 R–QB2 54 K–K3 B–N8 55 R–QB5 R–K2** Black cannot exchange rooks – White simply marches to the K-side and gobbles up the pawns. **56 B–B3 K–Q3+ 57 K–Q4**

R–KB2 58 R–B6+ K–Q2 59 R–B6 R–K2 60 P–N5 1–0

2005: Victor Ciocaltea–AK:
R5: 2 January:

Ruy Lopez

1 P–K4 P–K4 2 N–KB3 N–QB3 3 B–N5 P–QR3 4 B–R4 N–B3 5 0–0 B–K2 6 R–K1 P–QN4 7 B–N3 P–Q3 8 P–B3 0–0 9 P–KR3 N–QR4 10 B–B2 P–B4 11 P–Q4 Q–B2 12 QN–Q2 N–B3 13 P×BP P×P 14 N–B1 B–K3 15 N–K3 QR–Q1 16 Q–K2 P–B5 17 N–B5 B×N Varying from 17 ... KR–K1 18 N3–R4! Kavalek–Karpov, Caracas 1970 (1210, p. 115). 18 P×B P–R3 19 N–Q2 If 19 N×P N×N 20 Q×N B–Q3 21 Q–K2 KR–K1 with equality. 19 ... KR–K1 20 N–K4 N–N1 21 P–QR4 N1–Q2! Much better than 21 ... N×N?! 22 B×N N–Q2 23 P×P P×P 24 R–R6± – Ciocaltea. 22 P×P P×P 23 B–K3 N×N 24 B×N N–B4! (209)

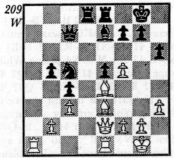

25 B×N B×B 26 KR–Q1 B–N3 27 P–KN3 Q–B4= ½–½

2006: AK–Henrique Mecking:
R6: 4 January:

Sicilian

The notes to this game are Karpov's from the Soviet Central Chess Club Bulletin No. 2 1972.

Mecking introduced a new move in the opening, but I think that he had not foreseen the reply.

Mecking very much wanted to take first place. When I had 3½/4 and my next game was with the Romanian master Ciocaltea, Mecking asked him,

'You are going to "get rid" of Karpov?',

'I am going to play,' answered Ciocaltea.

'Make sure you don't lose, otherwise I can't be first.'

Understandably my game with Mecking took on the character of a needle-match.

1 P–K4	P–QB4
2 N–KB3	P–Q3
3 P–Q4	P×P
4 N×P	N–KB3
5 N–QB3	P–QR3
6 B–K2	

I frequently use this system and I know it quite well. In games against many foreign chessplayers the winner is often not he who plays best, but he who has analysed the opening variation the furthest.

6 ...	P–K4
7 N–N3	B–K3
8 P–B4	Q–B2
9 P–QR4 (210)	

Here the usual replies are 9 ... B–K2 or 9 ... QN–Q2, but Mecking

In play, Leningrad Interzonal 1973

Karpov analysing his game against Hecht, Bath 1973

Karpov analysing his game against Hecht, Bath 1973

Leningrad Interzonal 1973

Working hard against Kuzmin, Leningrad 1973

Karpov – Gligoric

1. e4 e5 2. Kf3 Kc6 3. Cb5 a6 4. Ca4 Kf6 5. 0-0 Ce7
6. Лe1 b5 7. Cb3 d6 8. c3 0-0 9. h3 Kb8 10. d4 Kbd7 11. Kbd2
Cb7 12. Cc2 c5 13. d5 [13. Kf1!?] 13... Ke8 14. Kf1 g6 15. Ch6
Kg7 16. Ke3 Kf6 17. a4 Kph8 18. b3 [18. Фe2 c4=] 18... Лb8
19. Фe2 Cc8 [19... Фb6] 20. ab ab 21. Лa7 Kg8 22. Cxg7+ Kpxg7
23. Лea1 Kf6 24. Cd3 Cd7 25. Фa2 Ke8?! [25... Фb6!?] 26. Фa6
[26. Фa5 Фc8 27. Фa6 cd8=] 26... Лb6 [26... Kc7 27. Фa5 Лa8
(27... Лc8 28. Фb6, 29. Лb7 ±) 28. Лxa8 Фxa8 29. Фxc7! Фa1+
30. Kph2 Лd8 31. c×b5 c×b5 32. Фxe7 Лd7 33. Фh4 ∆34. c4, 34. Kg4±]
27. Фa5 Kf6 28. Kg4! Лb8 29. Kxf6 [29. Фc7?! Cxg4 30. hg Фxc7
31. Лxc7 cd8 32. Лc6 c4 33. bc bc 34. Лxc4 Kxg4=] 29... c×b6
30. Фc7 Фxc7 31. Лxc7 Лfd8 32. Лaa7 Ce8 33. Лb7 [34. c×b5
c×b5 35. Л×b7+ Kpg8 36. Л×b8] 33... Kpg8 34. g4 h6 35. h4 Лxb7
36. Л×b7 c4 37. bc bc 38. Ce2 [38. C×c4 Cd7 39. g5 cg4!
(39... hy 40. Kxg5±) 40. gf Cxf3 41. Cd3 g5] 38... Лa8 39. c×c4
39... Ca4 [39... Лc8 40. Ce2 Ca4 41. g5 hg 42. Kxg5 C×g5 43. hg
Лxc3 44. Лb6 ±] 40. Cb3! C×b3 41. Л×b3 Лc8 [41... Лa4 42. Лb4+-]
42. Kpg2 h5 43. gh gh 44. Лb6 Лxc3 45. Лxd6 Kpg7 46. Лc6 Лd3
[46... Лa3] 47. Лc7 Kpg6 48. Лc8 [∆ 48. Лa3 49. Лe8 Лa4 50. Kxe5+]
48... Cg7 49. Лc6+ Kph7 50. Kg5+ Kpg8 51. Лc8+ Cf8 52. Лc7 f6
53. Ke6 Ch6 54. Лd7 +- Лd2 55. Kpf1 Лd1+ 56. Kpe2 Лd2+ 57. Kpe1
Лc2 58. d6 Лc1+ 59. Kpe2 Лc2+ 60. Kpf1 Лc6 61. Kpg2 Лb6
[61... Cd2 62. Лg7+ Kph8 63. d7 Лd6 64. Лe7 Ca5 65. d8Ф+ Cxd8
66. Лe8+ +-] 62. Kc7 Лb7 [62... Cf8 63. Ke8] 63. Kd5

1:0

The game Karpov-Gligoric, Leningrad 1973, in Karpov's own hand

Before a game at Bath 1973

Karpov as seen by a
Russian cartoonist

А. КАРПОВ.

'Sweet dreams the Karpov way'. *British Chess Magazine*

didn't fancy either of them. He thought for a long time and chose a new, but far from the strongest continuation.

9 . . .	N–B3
10 P–B5	B×N
11 P×B	Q–N3

If White succeeds in castling K-side and putting his bishop on QB4, his advantage will be overwhelming. Mecking hinders the achievement of this plan.

12 B–KN5	B–K2
13 B×N	B×B
14 N–Q5	Q–R4+
15 Q–Q2	Q×Q+
16 K×Q	B–N4+
17 K–Q3	0–0
18 P–R4	B–Q1

On . . . KR3 the bishop might be dangerously placed (after P–KN4).

19 QR–QB1

It's not yet possible to smoke out the knight from d5 because on 19 . . . N–K2 follows 20 N×N+ B×N 21 R–B7. And if 19 . . . N–Q5 then 20 P–QN4.

19 . . .	P–QR4
20 K–Q2	R–N1
21 P–KN4	

White's plan is clear – a pawn storm on the K-side; after B–B4 it will be very dangerous. Appreciating this, Mecking seeks succour in the opposite coloured bishops.

21 . . .	N–N5
22 B–B4	N×N
23 B×N	

The position has stabilized. White has a big advantage in the complete absence of counterplay for the opponent. Mecking had placed great hopes on his next move, thinking that he would be able to blockade the K-side pawns and halt their advance.

| 23 . . . | P–KN4 |
| 24 BP×Pep | RP×P |

| 25 K–Q3 | K–N2 |
| 26 P–R5 | B–N3 |

No better is 26 . . . B–N4 27 R–B7.

27 R–R3

In order to seize the KR-file after the exchange on KN6.

| 27 . . . | B–B4 |
| 28 R–KB1 | P–B3 |

Forced. 29 P–R6+ was threatened.

29 P×P	K×P
30 R1–KR1	R/N1–K1
31 R–R7	K–N4

Mecking was in time-trouble and was afraid of mating threats after R1–R5.

32 K–K2   **K–B5**

Here a devastating idea came into my head and I played . . .

33 R1–R3 *(211)*

Mecking didn't appreciate the threat and replied . . .

33 . . .   **B–Q5**

and after . . .

34 R–N7   **1–0** (time)

he exceeded the time limit, although he could have resigned in view of the unavoidable mate.

But even after the best defence – 33 . . . K×NP 34 R–R1 R–KN1 35 B×R R×B 36 R–KB1 White wins easily.

2007: Raymond-Keene–AK:
    R7: 5 January:

Sicilian

1 N–KB3 P–QB4 2 P–K4!? Very unusual for Keene. **2 . . . P–K3 3 P–Q4 P×P 4 N×P N–QB3 5 N–QB3 5 P–QR3 6 P–KN3 KN–K2 7 N–N3 N–R4 8 B–N2 N2–B3 9 0–0 P–Q3 10 N×N Q×N= 11 N–K2 B–K2 12 P–N3 0–0** If 12 . . . B–B3 simply 13 B–Q2±. **13 B–N2 B–Q2** 13 . . . R–Q1!? with . . . P–QN4 to follow is another idea. **14 P–QB4 KR–Q1** Now if 14 . . . P–QN4 15 P–B5!±. **15 P–QR4± QR–B1 16 B–QB3! Q–B2 17 Q–Q2** 17 R–R2!? with the idea of Q–R1 and R–Q1 is an interesting idea which one might have expected Keene to find very attractive. **17 . . . P–QN3 18 Q–N2 B–B1 19 P–B4?** (*212*)

This is wrong. It allows Black to effect, in advantageous circumstances, the freeing . . .P–QN4. White should have continued with 19 QR–B1 Q–N1 20 N–Q4 N–K4 21 KR–Q1 P–QN4 22 RP×P P×P 23 P×P B×P 24 N×B Q×N 25 B×N=. **19 . . . P–QN4!∓ 20 RP×P** 20 BP×P is no better: 20 . . . P×P 21 N–Q4 P×P 22 P×P N–R4 and White is in bad trouble. **20 . . . P×P 21 P×P Q–N3+** The point –

White's 19th seriously weakened this diagonal. **22 K–R1** White does no better with 22 N–Q4 N×N 23 B×N (23 B–R5?! Q–B4 24 P–QN4 Q–B5∓) 23 . . .Q×P∓. **22 . . . Q×P 23 P–QN4 P–Q4 24 QR–N1 R–N1 25 P×P P P×P 26 P–B5 N×P 27 Q–Q2 R–K1 28 N–Q4 Q–B5 29 R/N1–Q1** Better is 29 KR–B1!? and then not 29 . . . N–Q6?? 30 R×R R×R 31 B–B1 B×P 32 N×B Q–K5+ 33 B–KN2 and White wins, but 29 . . .N–R7 30 R×R R×R 31 B–B1 Q–R5 32 R–R1 and White is a little less badly off. **29 . . .R/N1–B1 30 B–R1 R–R1 31 R–B1 R–R7 32 Q–N5** 32 R×Q R×Q 33 R–B7 B–R5 only increases Black's advantage. **32 . . . Q–R3 33 N–K6 P–R3 34 Q–N4** (*213*)

34 . . .B×N The last hope for White was 34 . . .P×N?? 35 P×P with 36 R×B+ to follow and White wins. Now it's all over. **35 B×NP Q–K7! 36 Q×Q R×Q∓∓** The simplest **37 B×B R1×B 38 P×B P×P 39 KR–K1 R1–B7 40 R×R R×R 0–1** The pawns are too strong.

2008 AK–Michael Franklin:
    R8: 6 January:

Sicilian

1   P–K4   P–QB4   2   N–KB3 P–QR3!?   3   P–B3   P–Q4   4   P×P

Q×P **5 P–Q4 P–K3** 5 . . . N–KB3
6 B–K2 P–K3 7 0–0 P×**P 8 P**×**P
N–B3 9 N–B3 Q–Q3 10 B–K3 B–K2
11 N–Q2!** N–QN5 **12 N2–K4 N**×**N
13 N**×**N Q–Q1 14 N–B3 0–0 15
B–B3**± Ćirić-Taimanov, Rostov-
on-Don 1961, is regarded as the
main line! **6 B–K3 P**×**P 7 P**×**P
N–KB3 8 N–B3 Q–QR4 9 B–Q3
N–B3 10 P–QR3 B–K2 11 0–0 0–0
12 Q–B2 B–Q2** *(214)*

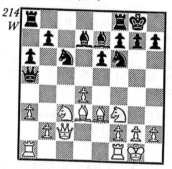

214
W

13 P–QN4 It's the Q-side for
starters. **13 . . . Q–R4 14 N–K2**
Threatening to trap the queen with
15 N–B4 Q–N5 16 P–R3, or else win
material after 15 . . . Q–R3. **14 . . .
N–Q4 15 B–Q2 B–Q3 16 N–N3
B**×**N 17 BP**×**B!** Karpov intends
to continue to molest the queen with
a K-side pawn advance. **17 . . .
QR–B1 18 Q–N2 P–B3 19 P–R3
P–KN4** Black had no desire to allow
White to continue 20 P–N4 Q–K1
21 Q–N1 with uncomfortable pres-
sure. **20 P–N4 Q–R3 21 P–QR4!**
Meanwhile back on the Q-side
White plans 22 P–N5 followed by a
rook entry. **21 . . . P–N4 22 P**×**P
P**×**P 23 KR–B1 R–N1 24 R–B5
N–Q1 25 P–R4!** The K-side has not
been forgotten. **25 . . . Q–N2** If 25
. . . N–KB2 26 R–R5 wins the QNP.
26 P×**P P**×**P 27 N**×**P N–N2 28
R5–B1 N–B5 29 B**×**N R**×**B 30
N–B3 Q**×**NP** If 30 . . . R×NP 31

R–B7. **31 B–K2 N–Q1 32 R–B5**
Using the fifth rank to liaise between
K- and Q-side – the threat is 33
R–N5+. **32 . . . N–B2 33 R–R3!**
Intending 34 N–K5 without allow-
ing 34 . . . Q–N6! **33 . . . Q–N2 34
R–R7 B–K1 35 R–N5 Q**×**R 36
N**×**Q N**×**N 37 P–Q5!** 1–0 After
37 . . . R–B2 38 R×R N×R (38 . . .
B×R 39 Q–K5) 39 P×P wins easily.

2009 Svetozar Gligorić–AK:
R9: 7 January:

Nimzo–Indian

**1 P–Q4 N–KB3 2 P–QB4 P–K3 3
N–QB3 B–N5 4 P–K3 0–0 5 B–Q3
P–B4 6 N–B3 P–Q4 7 0–0 QP**×**P 8
B**×**BP N–B3 9 P–QR3 B–R4 10
B–Q3 P**×**P 11 P**×**P B–N3 12
B–K3 N–Q4 13 N**×**N P**×**N 14
P–R3 N–K2 TN** *(215)*

215
B

14 . . .Q–Q3 15 R–K1 B–B2 16
R–QB1 B–K3 was played in
Gligorić–Polugayevsky, Palma 1970,
and now Gligorić gives 17 Q–B2 ±.
15 B–KN5!? Also 15 B–Q2 **15 . . .
P–B3! 16 B–Q2 B–KB4 17 B–N4
B**×**B 18 Q**×**B R–K1 19 KR–K1
Q–Q2 20 B–B5 B–B2** If 20 . . . B×B
21 P×B with N–Q4± to follow. **21
B**×**N R**×**B 22 R**×**R Q**×**R 23
Q–N5 Q–B2 24 K–B1 B–Q3**=
½–½

2010 AK–Bojan Kurajica:
R10: 8 January:

Sicilian

**1 P–K4 P–QB4 2 N–KB3 N–QB3
3 P–Q4 P×P 4 N×P Q–B2 5
N–N5!?** Probably Karpov regarded
this as more reliable than 5 P–QB4
N–B3 6 N–QB3 N×P 7 N×N
Q–K4 8 N–QN5 Q×N+ 9 B–K2
Q–K4 10 P–B4 Q–N1 with an
unclear position, Nikitin–Furman,
27 USSR Ch 1960. **5 . . . Q–N1 6
P–QB4 N–B3 7 N5–B3 P–K3 8
B–K3** Also White can try 8 P–B4
P–Q3 9 B–Q3 B–K2 10 N–Q2 0–0
11 N–B3± Bronstein–Taimanov, 39
USSR Ch 1971. **8 . . . B–K2** 8 . . .
P–QN3!? with . . . B–B4 to follow
might be tried. **9 B–K2 P–Q3 10
P–QR3 P–QN3 11 N–Q2 B–N2 12
P–B4 0–0 13 0–0± R–Q1 14 B–B3
B–KB1 15 B–B2?!** 15 P–QN4! is
stronger. **15 . . . N–Q2 16 P–QN4
P–N3 17 R–N1 B–N2** Now Black
can play . . . N–Q5. **18 N–N3
P–QR4** If 18 . . . B–KR3 19 P–N3
(Stronger than 19 Q–Q2 N3–K4 20
B–K2 N–KB3) 19 . . . P–KN4 20
B–K3 P×P 21 B×BP± **19 P–N5
N–R2 20 N–R4! N–QB1 21 R–B2**
Black hangs on after 21 P–KB5
R–K1 22 P×KP P×P 23 N–Q4
N–K4 24 B–N4 N×B 25 Q×N
Q–B2 **21 . . . R–K1** 21 . . . Q–B2
meets with 22 Q–K2 N–B3 23
N3×N NP×N 24 P–K5!± **22
Q–K2 Q–B2 23 R–Q1 P–K4 24 P–
B5** (*216*)
24 . . . P×P **25 P×P P–K5 26
B–N4** 26 B–Q4 allows 26 . . . N–B4!
and the QP will be able to recap-
ture, allowing the N/c8 to hop on to
d6 – there being no nasty B–N3 to
interfere. **26 . . . N–K4** Now if 26 . . .
N–B4!? **27 N3×N NP×N±** is
forced as 27 . . . QP×N? loses to 28
B–N3! Also 27 P–B6!? might be tried.

216
B

**27 B–R3 R–N1 28 B–Q4 R–R1 29
R–KB1±±** Q–K2 If 29 . . . B–KB3
30 N–B3 **30 N–B3 P–Q4 31 N×QP
B×N 32 P×B P–R5 33 N–Q2
N–B6+ 34 N×N P×N 35 Q–Q3
1–0**

2011 Wolfgang Unzicker–AK:
R11: 9 January:

Ruy Lopez

**1 P–K4 P–K4 2 N–KB3 N–QB3
3 B–N5 P–QR3 4 B–R4 N–B3 5 0–0
B–K2 6 R–K1 P–QN4 7 B–N3
P–Q3 8 P–B3 0–0 9 P–KR3 N–N1
10 P–Q4 QN–Q2 11 QN–Q2 B–N2
12 B–B2 R–K1 13 N–B1 B–KB1 14
N–N3 P–N3 15 B–Q2** White can
expect some advantage from 15
B–N5 e.g. 15 . . . P–R3 16 B–Q2
B–N2 17 Q–B1 K–R2 18 P–KR4±,
an idea of Tal's. Karpov gives 18 . . .
P–KR4, another idea is 18 . . .
P–B4, but White retains the initia-
tive in each case. **15 . . . B–N2 16
Q–B1 P–B4** (*217*)
Black can achieve equality with 16
. . . P–Q4 17 B–N5 Q–B1 18 QP×P
(18 KP×P P×P=) 18 . . . N/B3×P
19 N×N P×N 20 B×P N×P= 21
B×B Q×B ½–½ Unzicker–Portisch,
Santa Monica 1966. **17 B–R6** With
the idea of 18 N–B5. **17 . . . Q–K2**
So that if 18 N–B5 P×N 19 Q–N5
Q–B1 will be possible. **18 B×B** 18
Q–Q2 turned out well for Black

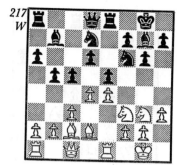

217
W

after 18 . . . B×B 19 Q×B QR–B1
20 B–N3 N–R4 21 N–N5 P–B5∓
in Zhukhovitsky–Lein, Sochi 1967.
18 . . . K×B 19 Q–Q2 If 19 Q–N5
(threat 20 N–B5+) 19 . . . K–R1=.
19 . . . N–N3 20 QR–Q1 QR–B1
But not 20 . . . QR–Q1? 21 P×KP
P×P 22 Q–N5 and White wins – the
black rook on e8 is overloaded: 22
. . . K–R1 (to take care of the
threatened 23 N–B5+) 23 R×R and
24 Q×KP or 24 N×KP. **21 B–N1**
Not 21 P–N3 P–N5! and suddenly
Black has the initiative. **21 . . .
N–B5 22 Q–B1** Or 22 Q–K2
Q–B2=. **22 . . . N–Q2! 23 P–N3 ½–½**

2012 Ulf Andersson–AK:

R12: 11 January:

Grünfeld

**1 N–KB3 N–KB3 2 P–KN3 P–B4
3 B–N2 P–KN3 4 0–0 B–N2 5
P–B4 P–Q4 6 P–Q4 BP×P 7 N×P
0–0 8 P×P N×P 9 N–N5 P–QR3
10 N1–B3 P×N 11 N×N N–B3 12
B–N5 B×P 13 R–N1 B–N2 14
N×P+ N×N ½–½ 15 Q×Q R×Q
16 B×N=**

2013 AK–Miguel Najdorf:

R13: 12 January:

Sicilian

**1 P–K4 P–QB4 2 N–KB3 P–Q3
3 P–Q4 P×P 4 N×P N–KB3 5
N–QB3 P–QR3 6 B–K2 P–K4 7
N–N3 B–K2 8 0–0 0–0 9 B–KN5
B–K3 10 P–B4 P×P 11 B×BP
N–B3 12 K–R1 P–Q4 13 P–K5
N–K5 14 N×N P×N 15 N–Q2
B–N4 16 N×P ½–½**

2014 Viktor Korchnoi–AK:

R14: 13 January:

QP – Torre

1 P–Q4	**N–KB3**
2 N–KB3	**P–K3**
3 B–N5	**P–QN3**

Somewhat unusual; 3 . . . P–B4 is
normal. I adopted this opening
against Paul Keres in the tournament at Tallinn in 1965 – my only
previous trial of it. Black gets the
advantage of the two bishops; White
secures a lead in development and a
strong centre.

4 P–K4	**P–KR3**
5 B×N	**Q×B**
6 B–Q3	

I played an early N–QB3, castling
Q-side, in the game against Keres,
encountering slight difficulties because he was able to set up an attack
on my king along the QN-file. So I
switch to QN–Q2 here. The choice,
however, is really only a matter of
taste.

6 . . .	**B–N2**
7 QN–Q2	**P–Q3**
8 Q–K2	**P–QR3**

Or 8 . . . N–B3 9 P–B3 0–0–0
followed by . . . B–R6.

I was rather expecting 8 . . . Q–Q1
followed by . . . B–K2 and . . . 0–0.
It is natural for such an undevelop-
ing move as . . . Q–Q1 to go against
the grain but I felt that the queen
was misplaced on f6 and expected
Karpov to retreat it at more than
one stage. The course of the game
repeatedly reinforced my opinion.

Najdorf and I, analysing together

after the game, found it surprisingly difficult to establish any definite advantage for White if Black goes 8 . . . Q–Q1.

I had planned to answer 8 . . . P–B4 by 9 P–K5 but, on subsequent consideration it seems to me that quietly maintaining the pawn centre by 9 P–B3 might be best.

My last move or my next could well have been P–K5, but I did not feel inclined to start an attack before completing the development of my pieces.

9 0–0–0   N–Q2
10 K–N1

A move which, as so often after 0–0–0, proves to have been a useful safety measure in the sequel.

10 . . .   P–K4

10 . . . B–K2? would have shown up the bad positioning of Black's queen in a drastic way; after 11 P–K5 P×P 12 P×P Q–B5 13 P–KN3 the queen would have been driven all around the board, with White continuously improving his position.

To 10 . . . Q–Q1, just as to the move played, 11 N–B4 would have been the answer: any attempt to dislodge this well-placed knight by pawn attack would seriously weaken Black's position.

11 P–B3   B–K2

I had still been expecting 11 . . . Q–Q1!

12 N–B4   0–0
13 B–B2   KR–K1 (*218*)

Perhaps 13 . . . P×P should have been played first, even though it appears to strengthen White's centre dangerously; the point being that after 14 P×P, 14 . . . R–K1 would have some counter-attacking effect. 15 P–K5, however, would still leave White on top.

14 P–Q5   P–B4

After long thought, but a bad move. 14 . . . P–B3 seems indicated, followed, if 15 P–KN4, by 15 . . . P–QN4 16 N–K3 P×P and 17 . . . N–N3, or by 16 . . . N–N3 at once, securing some play on the Q-side for Black.

15 N–K3

Now White is all set to start a direct attack by 16 P–KN4.

15 . . .   B–KB1

Both the next move and Black's reply came on the instant.

16 P–KN4   Q–Q1
17 P–N5   P–KR4

If 17 . . . P×P 18 QR–KN1 followed by P–KR4 would expose Black's king to a terrific attack.

18 P–N6   P×P
19 KR–N1   Q–B3
20 N–N5   B–K2
21 N–K6   N–B1

After the game I asked Karpov had he overlooked the loss of the exchange. 'No' he replied, 'I invited it feeling that, in view of the strength of your advanced knight, it was my best chance'. Of course he already has a pawn . . .

But 21 . . . QR–QB1 seemed a natural measure to me, e.g. 22 R–N2 N–B1 23 QR–N1 K–R2 24 N×N R×N 25 R×P Q×R 26 R×Q K×R 27 N–B5; White has B–Q1, P–KB4 etc to follow with, probably, a winning attack, but the game is not over by any means. Whereas from now on, Black really has little or no prospect of salvation.

Note that in answer to 21 . . . QR–QB1 22 N–KB5? would get nowhere because of 22 . . . B–B1!

22 N–B7   Q–B2
23 QR–KB1?

With victory in sight, I begin to relax. I have the K-side under control and should now have killed Black's prospects on the Q-side as well.

I am convinced that the one correct move here was 23 P–QR4 followed by P–QN3, B–Q3, K–B2 etc.

23 . . .   P–QN4?

Inaccurate play on both sides. 23 . . . QR–B1 24 N×R Q×N would have cost me a clear tempo compared with the game.

24 N×R/R8?!   B×N?

It would have been easier to bring the rook back into the game after 24 . . . R×N, than to activate this very poor bishop anew.

25 P–QB4

To block the Q-side, at least partially.

25 . . .   R–N1
26 B–Q3

Black should now have reconciled himself to 26 . . . P–N5. It slows down his counter-attack, but it does ease a little the urgent task of bringing back his QB into play.

26 . . .   Q–K1?

In answer to 26 . . . P–N5, I planned B–B2–QR4 (if 27 . . . Q–K1 then 28 Q–Q1 conquering the diagonal from White's QR4) followed by manoeuvring my knight to Q3 and K–R1, P–QR3 and either R–QN1 or P–KB4.

27 R–B1   B–KB3
28 R–N2

I thought of playing 28 P×P P×P

29 P–N4 followed by N–Q1–B3, but realised that both the opportunity and the necessity of activity on the Q-side had passed by.

28 . . .   R–N3

So as to play 29 . . . B–N2 and 30 . . . B–B1 but I am able to ensure that he never gets the time. The text is an ugly move and if any move can be said to lose the game, this is it.

29 R/B1–N1   R–N1

Forced, because White threatened 30 R×P N×R 31 Q×P.

30 Q–B1   P–N5

He might well have tried 30 . . . B–N2 31 P×P B–B1 and if 32 P×P? B–R6 followed by 33 . . . B×R 34 Q×B. This could only be regarded as a desperate measure for White's QRP remains strong, and QB4 will be a fine square for his knight.

31 B–K2

This is the winning move, if there is one. Now Black has no answer to the threat of 32 R×P.

31 . . .   P–R5
32 R×P   Q×R

or 32 . . . N×R 33 B–R5 Q–K2 34 N–B5 etc.

33 R×Q   N×R

A queen doesn't always win against a rook and bishop, but here White has a big positional advantage as well; Black's pieces are poorly co-ordinated.

34 B–N4   N–B5
35 Q–Q1

Heading for QR4.

35 . . .   P–N6

Agony!

36 P×P   B–N2 *(219)*

Coming back into play at last.

37 N–N2!

A move which drew applause from the spectators – B. H. Wood.

37 . . .   B–B1

If 37 . . . N×N White would win by 38 B–K6+ followed by 39 Q–R5.

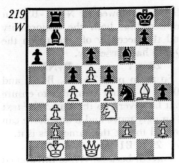

219
W

37 . . . K–B1 would be a little better than the move played.

38 B×B	R×B
39 Q–N4	R–K1
40 N×N	P×N
41 Q×BP	B–K4
42 Q×P	R–KB1
43 P–N4	B–Q5

Queen and *seven* pawns against rook, bishop and three – it is too much!

44 P×P	1–0

If 44 . . . B×QBP 45 Q–K7 R×P 46 P–K5 wins.

The notes (by Korchnoi) to this game originally appeared in the February 1972 issue of *Chess* and are reproduced here by special permission.

2015 AK–Peter Markland:

R15: 15 January:

French

1 P–K4 P–K3 2 P–Q4 P–Q4 3 N–QB3 B–N5 4 P–K5 P–QB4 5 P–QR3 B×N+ 6 P×B Q–B2 7 N–B3 N–K2 8 P–QR4 P–QN3 9 B–QN5+ B–Q2 10 B–Q3

White also gets an advantage from 10 0–0 B×B 11 P×B P–QR4 12 N–N5 P–R3 13 N–R3± with a positional bind and the possibility of advancing P–KB4–B5.

10 . . . N1–B3 11 0–0 P–KR3 12 R–K1 N–R4 13 Q–Q2?!

13 B–K3 to be followed by N–Q2, as Byrne had played against Markland in the 5th round, is better.

13 . . . R–QB1!

Much better than 13 . . .0–0?! 14 Q–B4 P–B4 15 KP×Pep Q×Q 16 B×Q± Mecking-Markland, 9th round.

14 P–R4

14 Q–B4 doesn't promise much: 14 . . . P–B4 15 Q–N3 (15 KP×Pep Q×Q 16 B×Q P×P∓ when Black has good attacking chances) 15 . . . K–B2 to be followed by . . . QR–KN1=.

14 . . . 0–0 15 Q–B4 P–B4 16 KP× Pep R×P 17 Q×Q R×Q (*220*)

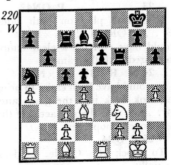

220
W

18 P×P!±

This guarantees White some advantage: Black's central pawns are only strong optically. 18 N–K5 would have been wrong because of 18 . . . P×P! 19 P×P N2–B3∓. **18 . . . P×P 18 . . . R×P? 19 B–R3±±** **19 N–K5 B–B1 20 P–QB4?!**

20 P–N3!? with 21 B–KB4 to follow is a more suitable treatment. **20 . . .N4–B3 21 B–N2 N–N5 22 P–R5 R–B1 23 B–R3 P×P 24 N×P R–B5 25 N–Q6!**

The only way to make progress. 25 P–N3? R×N 26 B×R N×P is good for Black, while 25 R–K4 N×B 26 P×N R×R 27 P×R

N–B3 and White can do little for fear of the QBP.

25 ... N×B 26 P×N R×RP 27 N–K4

If 27 QR–B1 R–R5 28 B×P then not 28 ... R×P? 29 B–N4 and wins, but simply 28 ... B–Q2!

27 ... R–R4 28 KR–QB1 B–N2

28 ... P–B5 allows 29 B–Q6 R–Q2 30 P–R6!±

29 N×P B–Q4 30 P–B3 R–B4 31 P–R6 (*221*)

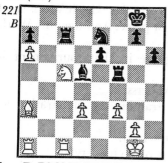

221
B

31 ... R–B2 32 N–K4 N–B4

With the idea of ... N–Q5.

33 B–B5 R–QB1 34 B–B2 R2–B2 35 R×R R×R 36 R–N1 N–K2 37 R–N8+ K–R2 38 K–R2 N–N3

Or 38 ... N–B1 39 N–B5 with R–N7 to follow.

39 N–B5 Again angling for R–N7.

39 ... R–B3 Or 39 ... N–K4 40 R–N7 B×R 41 P×B N–B3 (41 ... N–Q2 42 P–Q4 wins) 42 B–N3±.

40 R–Q8 Not now 40 R–N7? R×P!=.

40 ... R–B2 41 R–Q7±± R×R 42 N×R B–B3 43 N–N8 B–N4 44 B×P N–K2 45 B–N6 Not 45 B–B5? allowing 45 ... N–Q4–B2–R1. **45 ... N–B1 46 B–B5 K–N3?** 46 ... B×QP 47 P–R7 N×P 48 B×N B–N4 49 P–B4 allows Black to hold out longer. **47 P–R7 N×P 48 B×N P–K4 49 P–Q4 P×P 50 B×P K–B2 51 P–B4 P–N4 52 P×P P×P 53 K–N3 K–N3 54 K–B3 K–B4 55 P–N3 1–0** Only not 55 P–N4+?? K–N3=.

Interview–London 1972

Q: Grandmaster Anatoly Karpov, can you say something about the British players who played at Hastings?

AK: Best of all played Keene; at Hastings he played less well than he can do, it seemed to me that he was afraid to lose.

Q: Is there one particular game or two games which you played at some time which you like most of all?

AK: It was in the Alekhine Memorial tournament in Moscow recently; the game with Hort, and here the game with Byrne.

Q: Would you like to say who will win the forthcoming match, Spassky or Fischer?

A: I don't know!

Q: Which games in the history of chess do you admire most of all?

AK: There are very many games which are very good. All the good games I like.

Q: Who are your chess heroes?

AK: Capablanca and Botvinnik.

Q: As well as chess what do you like to do? What are your main interests?

AK: I am a student studying economics in the faculty in Leningrad.

Q: What can you say about London?

AK: Interesting city!

Q: When did you have your first significant chess achievement?

AK: At what particular level?

Q: At international level.

AK: The first time I played in Czechoslovakia, it was a small international tournament – I took first place. And then the World Junior Championship in Sweden.

Q: Was there one particular game in that tournament in Sweden which left a big impression?

AK: Most of all the game with Andersson.

Q: Do you do some physical training as preparation for chess?

AK: Yes I swim, and in the winter I ski.

Q: What do you think about your own chess style?

AK: I haven't got any particular opinion of my own style – I just play chess.

Q: What do you think of Walter Browne, the Australian grandmaster?

AK: I haven't met him yet!

Q: Have you seen Browne's games?

AK: Not a great deal, I don't feel able to say anything about him.

Q: Is this the first time that you have visited London?

AK: Yes it is.

Q: Can you advise us what we must do if we want to improve?

AK: I don't know what you do at the moment.

Q: We study openings a lot, we play a lot I suppose.

AK: But endgames not very much – do the opposite study endgames!

Q: When you were a child did you play in simultaneous displays against Soviet grandmasters?

AK: Yes I did play against Botvinnik, Korchnoi, Spassky – almost all the Russian grandmasters.

Q: Did you win against some of them?

AK: I don't remember, I think I drew with Botvinnik, Spassky and Korchnoi, the others I don't really remember.

Q: What is your opinion of Vaganian?

AK: Some months ago he had a very good result (first at Vrnjacka Banja 1971 – eds), was it just one result or will he in future get equally good results? We shall see.

Q: Do you play blindfold chess?

AK: No.

Q: Have you tried?

AK: It's very tiring, bad for the head, and there's not a great deal of point to it.

Q: What particular branch of economics do you study?

AK: I study the economics of foreign countries.

Q: Do simultaneous displays help you?

AK: No they do not help me, but they are necessary for popular results at chess.

This interview took place at the London Central YMCA Club on Saturday evening 22 January 1972 on the occasion of a simultaneous display. The questions were put and the answers translated by Mike Wills.

Final A	1	2	3	4	5	6	
1 Moscow	×	5	8	5½	10	9	**37½**
2 RSFSR	7	×	6	7	6½	8	**34½**
3 Ukraine	4	6	×	5½	9	8½	**33**
4 Leningrad	6½	5	6½	×	4½	7½	**30**
5 Georgia	2	5½	3	7½	×	6	**24**
6 Latvia	3	4	3½	4½	6	×	**21**

Board 2	1	2	3	4	5	6	
1 **Karpov**	×	0	1	1	½	1	**3½**
2 Gipslis	1	×	½	½	½	½	**3**
3 Stein	0	½	×	1	1	½	**3**
4 Smyslov	0	½	0	×	1	½	**2**
5 Dzhindzhikhashvili	½	½	0	0	×	1	**2**
6 Taimanov	0	½	½	½	0	×	**1½**

Karpov played on board two (below Polugayevsky) for the RSFSR team. All but one of the games from this event are available:

2101 AK–Anatoly Kudriashov:
    PR1 v. Turkmen SSR:

Sicilian

1 P–K4 P–QB4 2 N–KB3 P–K3 3 P–Q4 P×P 4 N×P N–KB3 5 N–QB3 P–Q3 6 P–KN4 P–QR3?! 7 P–N5 KN–Q2 8 B–K3 P–QN4 9 P–QR3
9 P–B4!? has now been unearthed: 9 . . . B–N2 10 P–B5! P–N5 11 P×P! P×N 12 KP×P+! K×P 13 B–QB4+ K–K1 Belyavsky–Tal, Sukhumi 1972, and now 14 P×P! – Tal.

9 . . . N–N3 Or 9 . . . B–N2 10 Q–Q2 Q–B2 (10 . . . N–B4 11 P–B3 N–B3 12 N×N B×N 13 0–0–0 Q–B2 14 B–KB4 R–Q1 15 P–N4 N–N2 16 P–KR4± Adorjan–Ostojić,

Polanica Zdroj 1970) 11 B–K2 N–B4 12 P–B3 N–B3 with a complicated double-edged position.

10 Q–Q2 10 P–B4 may be better e.g. 10 . . . N1–Q2 11 B–N2 P–K4 12 N–B6! Q–B2 13 N–N4 B–N2 14 P–B5!± Padevsky–Malich, Amsterdam 1972.

10 . . . Q–B2 11 0–0–0 N1–Q2 12 P–B4 N–R5!? 13 N×N P×N 14 N–K2 N–B4 15 B–N2 N–B4 16 N–B3 B–B3 17 B×N! Liquidating the hub of Black's position. **17 . . . P×B 18 P–K5 B–K2 19 B×B+ Q×B 20 Q–K2 P–B5 21 Q–K4 R–QB1** (*222*)
Now Black is left with a lost ending, but 21 . . . Q–B1 22 R–Q4 was not really an alternative. **22 Q×Q+ R×Q 23 N×P P–R3 24 P–R4**

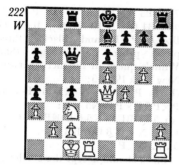

222
W

P–B6 Ridding himself of one weak pawn, but it also brings the white knight back towards the centre.

25 N×P B×RP 26 N–K4 B–K2 27 P–N3 P–QR4 28 P–B3 P–R5 This sacrifice is Black's last chance – its effect is to weaken the white Q-side pawns and create some open files to White's king.

29 P×P R–R3 30 R–Q4 P×P 31 N×P P–B3 32 N–B3 K–B2 33 K–B2 R1–R1 So Black has finally activated his position, but at a very high price. **34 R–R1 K–N3 35 R–Q7 B–B4 36 P–KR5+ K–B4 37 R×P K×BP 38 R–KB1 R×P 39 P×P K–K6 40 N–K5 K–K7 41 R–QN1 R–Q1 42 R–Q7 R–R7+ 43 R–N2 R×R+ 44 K×R R–QN1+ 45 K–B2 K–K6 46 P–R6 K–K5 47 N–B7 B–R6 48 P–R7 R–N7+ 49 K–Q1 K–K6** So that 50 P–R8=Q R–N8+ 51 K–B2 R–N7+ draws! but . . . **50 P–B4! 1–0**

2102 AK–Mark Taimanov:
PR2 v. Leningrad:

Sicilian

1 P–K4 P–QB4 2 N–KB3 P–K3 3 P–Q4 P×P 4 N×P P–QR3 5 B–Q3 B–B4 6 N–N3 B–N3 For 6 . . . B–R2 see Karpov–Hübner (No. 2208). **7 0–0 N–K2 8 Q–K2 QN–B3 9 B–K3 N–K4** 9 . . . B×B 10 Q×B P–Q3 11 P–QB4± with a bind **10 P–**

QB4! After 10 P–KB4 Black has the aggressive 10 . . . N–N5 11 B×B Q×B+ 12 K–R1 P–KR4 with a good game, or a simple path to equality with 10 . . . N×B 11 P×N P–Q4. **10 . . . B×B 11 Q×B Q–B2** If 11 . . . N×B then 12 Q×N±, but 11 . . . P–Q3 is an alternative though White still has the edge and two good plans in 12 B–K2 to be followed by P–B4, and 12 R–Q1 Q–B2 13 N–R3±. **12 P–B5! N×B 13 Q×N P–QN3 14 P×P Q×NP 15 N1–Q2! P–Q4 16 P–K5!** Much better than 16 P×P which lets Black off with equality after both 16 . . . P×P 17 KR–K1 B–K3 18 N–Q4 0–0 and 16 . . . N×P 17 N–B4 Q–N5 18 P–QR3 Q–K2. **16 . . . B–Q2 17 KR–B1 0–0 18 Q–Q4! Q–N1** Or 18 . . . Q×Q 19 N×Q KR–B1 20 N2–N3 N–B3 21 N×N B×N and White has 22 R–B3± or 22 N–Q4±. **19 N–B3 N–B3** 19 . . . N–B4 20 Q–KB4± **20 Q–K3 R–B1** If 20 . . . P–B3? 21 N–B5 wins. **21 R–B5 P–QR4 22 R1–QB1 P–R5 23 N/N3–Q4 N–R4** 23 . . . N×N 24 Q×N± **24 R×R+ B×R 25 P–QN3 B–Q2** (*223*) Or 25 . . . P×P 26 P×P B–Q2 27 P–R4±

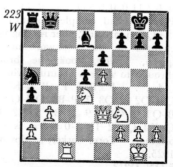

223
W

White now commences a K-side pawn storm. **26 P–R4 P–R3 27 P–KN4! Q–N2** 27 . . . Q–Q1, to control some of the dark squares on the K-side, followed by . . . R–QB1, would have been better. **28 P–R5 N–B3** 28 . . . R–QB1 brings no relief: 29 R×R+ Q×R 30 P–N5±. **29 P–N5 N×N 30 N×N KRP×P 31 Q×P K–R2** 32 P–R6 P–N3 33 Q–B6 K–B1 34 P–R7 was a terrible way to go. **32 R–B3!±± Q–N5 33 R–N3 R–KN1 34 N–B3 P×P 35 P×P Q×P** This loses, but 35 . . . Q–B1 36 Q–B4 was hardly any better. **36 Q–B1! Q–R7 37 N–N5+ K–R1 38 N×BP+ K–R2 39 Q–N5 Q–N8+ 40 K–R2 1–0** There is no defence against 41 Q–N6+ Q×Q 42 P×Q mate.

2103 Hillar Kärner–AK:
PR3 v. Estonian SSR:

QP – Torre

1 P–Q4 N–KB3 2 N–KB3 P–K3 3 B–N5 P–B4 4 P–K3 Q–N3

Petrosian annotated this game for *Informator*. He must have some fond memories of this system; at the Munich Olympiad 1958, he played it against Kozma, to be greeted by 4 . . . P–QN3? 5 P–Q5 P×P 6 N–B3 B–N2 7 N×P B×N?! 8 B×N Q×B 9 Q×B N–B3 10 B–B4 B–K2 11 0–0–0 R–Q1 12 R–Q2 and Petrosian had complete control of the Q5 square and, after ringing the changes on d5 – pawn, knight, queen, bishop, rook, he broke through to score a beautiful win.

4 . . . P×P 5 P×P B–K2 6 QN–Q2 P–Q3 7 P–B3 QN–Q2 8 B–Q3 P–QN3 9 N–B4 B–N2 10 Q–K2 Q–B2 11 0–0 0–0–0= is the original, Torre–Lasker, Moscow 1925.

5 QN–Q2!?
Probably strongest. Alternatives are:
(a) 5 N–B3!? Q×P 6 N–N5 Q–N5+

7 P–B3 Q–R4 8 N–Q2 P–QR3! 9 N–B4 Q×N 10 N–Q6+ B×N 11 B×Q P×B and Black's three pieces proved far stronger than White's queen in Bisguier–Sherwin, New York 1954–5;
(b) 5 P–QN3? N–K5 6 B–KB4 P×P 7 P×P B–N5+∓;
(c) 5 Q–B1 N–K5 6 B–KB4 P–Q4 7 B–Q3 N–Q2 8 0–0 B–Q3=.

5 . . . Q×P
Black should accept the challenge as 5 . . . P–Q4 6 B×N! P×B 7 P–B4! Spassky–A. Zaitsev, 30 USSR Ch 1962, is already clearly better for White.

6 B–Q3
Black also comes out on top after 6 B–QB4 P–Q4 7 R–QN1 Q–B6 8 B–N5+ N–B3 9 N–K5 N–K5 10 N5× N P–QR3!∓ – Petrosian.

6 . . . P–Q4 7 P–B4
Or 7 P×P QN–Q2 8 0–0 N×P∓ Kan–Goldenov, 15 USSR Ch 1947.

7 . . . Q–B6 8 N–K5 N3–Q2 9 R–QB1 Q–R6 10 N×N B×N 11 B–N1 P–KR3 12 B–B4
A rather strange position – Black only has his queen in play, yet almost all White's pieces have been forced to occupy awkward positions.

12 . . . BP×P 13 0–0 B–Q3 14 B×B Q×B 15 BP×P KP×P 16 P–K4!?
White tries to conjure up some play to compensate for his dwindling army of pawns.

16 . . . N–B3 17 Q–N3 N–R4 18 Q–Q3 N–B3 19 KR–K1 B–K3 20 P–B4 0–0–0
Since castling K-side is out of the question in view of 21 P–K5.

21 P–K5 Q–N5 22 P–B5 B–Q2 23 P–K6 P×P 24 P×P B–K1 25 N–N3 Q–N3 26 P–QR4
If 26 N×P K–N1 allows Black to exchange off into a very favourable ending.

26 . . . K–N1 27 R–B5 Q–N5 28

Q–N3+ K–R1 29 R–N5 Q–K2

Black has enough booty for now, besides 29 . . . Q×P 30 R×NP is rather embarrassing e.g. 30 . . . K×R 31 N–B5+.

30 N–B5 P–R3 31 Q–QR3

Trying to keep some threats going.

31 . . . R–QN1 32 B–Q3 P–QN3 33 P–R5 P×N

Black now has an easy win – too easy perhaps!?

34 R–N6 R×R 35 P×R P–B5 36 Q×P+ K–N1 37 R–R1 Q–N2! 38 Q–R3 P×B

Black has no objection to his 'ugly' QPs – bearing in mind how they got there!

39 Q–Q6+ K–B1 40 R–R8+

White keeps trying . . . 40 . . . Q×R?? 41 Q–B7 mate.

40 . . . N–N1 41 Q–B5+ B–B3 42 Q–Q6 (*224*)

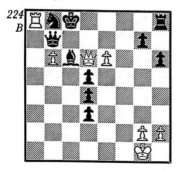

224
B

Why doesn't White resign? Obviously Black isn't going to fall for 42 . . . Q×R?? – he's already avoided that. Karpov perhaps felt insulted here: a top-flight grandmaster two pieces up against a mere master who nevertheless continues playing . . . Well he *couldn't* carry on two pieces *and* a queen down, so . . .

42 . . . P–Q7??

THE CATASTROPHE

In tournament or friendly game,

A hasty slip may mean the same:

Your hopes are changed to dark despair;

Do see each move is made with care.

S. G. Tartakower

Black had a simple win with 42 . . . B–N4 (But not 42 . . . Q×P? 43 R×N+ Q×R 44 Q×B+ and White draws by perpetual) 43 R–R7 P–Q7 44 R×Q P–Q8=Q+ 45 K–B2 R–B1+ (45 . . . Q–Q7+ is not so clear) 46 Q×R+ (46 K–N3 Q–K8+; 47 K–R3 Q–K6+; 46 R–KB7 R×R+ 47 P×R Q–KB8+ 48 K–N3 Q×BP and White *does* resign) 46 . . . K×R and wins. But now . . .

43 R×N+! 1–0!

43 . . . Q×R 44 Q×B+ K–Q1 45 Q–Q7 mate and Black's queue of potential queens is of no avail.

2104 AK–Gennady Kuzmin:
PR4 v. Azerbaizhan SSR:

Sicilian

1 P–K4 P–QB4 2 N–KB3 P–K3 3 P–Q4 P×P 4 N×P N–QB3 5 N–N5 P–Q3 6 P–QB4 N–B3 7 N1–B3 P–QR3 8 N–R3 B–K2 9 B–K2 0–0 10 0–0 B–Q2 11 B–K3 Q–R4!? 12 Q–K1!? Taimanov prefers 12 Q–N3 **12 . . . KR–K1 13 R–Q1 QR–Q1 14 P–B3 B–QB1** and Black has a satisfactory and harmonious development. **15 N–B2 Q–B2 16 Q–B2 N–Q2 17 R–B1 B–B3 18 N–R3**

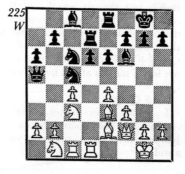

225
W

Q–R4 19 KR–Q1 N–B4 20 N/R3–N1 R–Q2 (225)

21 B–B1 Q–Q1 22 N–Q2 K–R1 23 N–N3 P–QN3 24 R–Q2 Q–K2 25 N–Q4 B×N 26 B×B N×B 27 R×N P–QR4 28 R1–Q1 B–N2 29 Q–N3 R1–Q1 30 N–N5 P–K4 ½–½

2105 AK–Donatas–Piatras Lapenis:

PR5 v. Lithuanian SSR: ½–½, X moves.

This game, is unfortunately, un-available – it is the only one of Karpov's games which did not appear in the Russian bulletins of this event.

2106 AK–Aivar Gipslis:

FR2 v. Latvian SSR:

Pirc

1 P–K4	P–Q3
2 P–Q4	N–KB3
3 N–QB3	P–KN3
4 B–KN5	

Until the sharp variation, begin-ning with 4 P–B4 was worked out-the continuation 4 B–KN5 was reckoned to be the most active. There is a straightforward plan: White castles long and inaugurates a K-side pawn storm.

4 ...   **P–B3**

Ten to fifteen years ago the auto-matic reply to 4 B–KN5 was 4 ... B–N2, but then it was found that it is most important to secure the defence of the d5 square at once, so that after 5 P–K5 P×P 6 P×P Q×Q+ 7 R×Q N–N5 one need not fear a sudden attack by the white QN.

5 Q–Q2

5 P–B4 gives better chances. Against the old plan chosen by Karpov there is a perfectly good antidote.

5 ...   **QN–Q2**

6 P–B3

White sets up a consistent pawn formation, neglecting the possibility of adding a new direction to play by means of 6 P–B4.

6 ...   **P–QN4**

7 N–R3

On 7 KN–K2 the QN loses the use of K2 and the QB4 square is cut off from the KB. Now White pre-pares the transfer of the knight to KB2, whence it defends both K4 and KN4 at the same time. The defect of putting the knight on KB2 reveals itself as being that (as in the game) the Q4 square may find itself in trouble.

Another move order comes into consideration: first to castle long and then develop the knight on K2 or R3 depending upon Black's choice of plan.

7 ...   **B–KN2**

8 B–R6

Now 8 ... B×B 9 Q×B Q–R4, forcing the white queen to return to Q2, doesn't seem bad. But Gipslis boldly castles K-side.

8 ...	**0–0**
9 N–B2	**P–K4**

With this central counter-action, Black makes it more difficult for his opponent to develop a K-side initi-ative.

10 B×B	**K×B**
11 0–0–0	**Q–R4**
12 K–N1	**R–K1**

In order to move the knight away from Q2, Black strengthens his K4 square.

13 P–KR4	**P–R4**
14 P–KN4	**N–N3**
15 P–N5	

Since it is not possible to open the KN– and KR– files, Karpov puts his hopes on opening the KB-file.

15 ...   **N/B3–Q2**

16 P-R3   R-QN1
17 P-B4? (226)

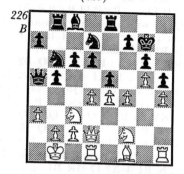

White under-estimates his opponent's threats and immediately finds
himself in a difficult position. It
follows that he should have offered
the exchange of queens with 17
N-R2. Black can scarcely avoid the
exchange without weakening his
position. After 17 . . . Q×Q 18
R×Q White's game is preferable,
since he will have time to double
rooks on the Q-file. It is true that
18 . . . P-R4 19 B-K2 K-B1 20
R1-Q1 K-K2 does not grant White
any clear way to strengthen his
position, but, in any case, he would
have the initiative.

17 . . .   N-B5!
18 Q-K1

An unfortunate necessity! After 18
B×N P×B the threat is 19 . . . Q×P
and if 19 K-R2 then 19 . . . Q-N3
and White stands badly. 19 R/Q1-
KB1 is also dubious on account of
19 . . . Q×P 20 N2-Q1 P×QP 21
Q×P+ K-N1 22 K-B1 Q-B4.

18 . . .   P×BP
19 N-Q3   N-K6
20 R-Q2   P-QB4!

Not giving his opponent a breath-
ing space. Now 21. . . P-N5 is a very
strong threat.

21 R-B2

21 P×P is no better: 21 . . . N2×P

22 N×N (22 N×BP P-N5! with
decisive threats) 22 . . . P×N 23
R-B2 P-N5 24 N-R2 R×P and
Black has an overwhelming advantage.

21 . . .   P-N5?

This unjustified attempt to sharpen
the struggle puts the game's outcome
in doubt. 21 . . . P×P 22 N-K2
Q×Q+ 23 N×Q R×P gave
Black a winning advantage. 22 R×P
is better instead of 22 N-K2. In that
case Black should not continue 22
. . . N×B 23 R1×N P×N on account
of 24 R×P+ K-N1 25 Q-B2 with
strong threats, but 22 . . . N-B5! 23
N-Q5 (23 Q-B2 is weaker: 23 . . .
P×N 24 R×P+ K-N1) 23 . . .
Q×Q+ 24 N×Q R×P and Black's
win is merely a question of time.

22 N-R2   R×P (227)

23 R×P?

Now White perishes without a
fight. Meanwhile after 23 QP×P!
QP×P 24 R×P he could get
strong counterplay and Black would
have bitterly regretted his twenty-
first move. If 24 . . . R×R 25 N×R
N×P then 26 Q-K7 Q-N3 27 P-R4
with unclear play.

23 . . .   R×R
24 N×R   BP×P!
25 P×P   Q-KB4

Now comes the concluding stage
of Black's strategy – the attack
against QB7.

26 N–Q3	N–K4
27 B–K2	B–K3
28 N2–B1	R–QB1
29 B–Q1	N4–N5
30 Q–Q2	K–N1

Sheltering the king from any checks. Black is not rushing anywhere.

31 B×N	P×B
32 N–K1	Q–K5
33 R–N1	B–B4
34 Q–Q3	

Despair! If 34 N/B1–Q3 then 34 ... N×P wins.

34 ...	Q–K4
35 Q–R6	Q–R7
0–1	

Notes by Boleslavsky translated from *Shakhmaty v SSSR* No. 5 1972.

2107 Roman Dzhindzhikhashvili–AK:

FR3 v. Georgian SSR:

Queen's Indian

1 P–Q4 N–KB3 2 P–QB4 P–K3 3 N–KB3 P–QN3 4 P–KN3 B–N2 5 B–N2 B–K2 6 N–B3 N–K5 7 B–Q2 P–Q4 8 P×P P×P 9 0–0

This system was given a good work-out in the Olympiad. Other moves tried here were:
(a) 9 B–B4 0–0 10 Q–B2 N×N! 11 Q×N P–QB4 12 0–0 N–Q2 13 KR–Q1 P–B5 14 N–K5? (14 P–N3 is more exact – Taimanov) 14 ... P–QN4∓ Pavlenko–Furman;
(b) 9 R–QB1 0–0 10 0–0 N–Q2 11 B–B4 P–QB4 12 N×N P×N 13 N–Q2 P–B4 Korchnoi–Polugayevsky (13 ... N–B3 14 P×P B×P 15 N–N3± Dzhindzhikhashvili–Furman, Gori 1971) and now 14 N–B4± –Taimanov.

9 ... 0–0 10 B–B4 N–Q2 11 Q–B2

New. 11 R–B1 P–QB4 12 N×N P×N 13 N–Q2 would transpose into (b) above.

11 ... P–QB4 12 N×N P×N 13 N–K5 N–B3

If 13 ... P×P 14 B×P R–B1 15 Q–N1 with an unclear position, but not 15 B×P+?? K–R1 16 Q–KB5 N–B3 and Black wins easily.

14 P×P± B×P 15 B–N5 Q–B2

15 ... R–K1 is no better: 16 B×N! (the 'clever' 16 N–N4? fails to 16 ... Q–B1! 17 N×N+ P×N 18 B–K3 B×B 19 Q×Q QR×Q 20 P×B R–B7∓) 16 ... Q×B 17 N–Q7± and Black's bishop battery will soon be firing on only one barrel.

16 N–B4 B–K2 17 QR–B1 (*228*)

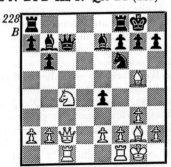

White stands very well out of the opening.

17 ... KR–K1 18 N–K3 Q–K4

Exchanging queens by 18 ... Q×Q allows 19 R×Q P–KR3 20 B×N B×B 21 R1–B1 and White has succeeded in doubling his rooks, with much the better game, e.g. 21 ... QR–B1 22 R×R R×R 23 R×R+ B×R 24 N–Q5 ruining Black's K-side pawn formation or picking up the KP free as 24 ... B×P?? allows 25 N–K7+.

19 B–B4 Q–KR4 20 P–KR3 KR–QB1 21 Q–R4 Q×KP 22 R×R+ R×R

22 ... B×R?? would be terrible: 23 Q–B6! and Black has to play 23 ... Q–R3 when White has many threats.

23 Q×RP Q-R3 24 Q×Q B×Q 25
N-B5 B-B4 26 R-Q1 P-N3 27
B-N5 27 N-K3! is much stronger.
**27 . . . P×N 28 B×N B-B5 29
P-N3 B-K3 30 B-B1 K-B1 31
B-R6 R-R1 32 B-QN7!?** If 32
R-Q8+ R×R 33 B×R P-B5!
**32 . . .R-N1 33 R-Q8+ R×R 34
B×R K-K1 35 B-N5 K-Q2 36
B-B4 B-Q3 37 B-K3 K-B2 38
B-QR6 P-B5 39 B×BP B×RP 40
B-B4 B×B 41 P×B ½-½**

2108 AK-Vasily Smyslov:
FR4 v. RSFSR Moscow:

Petroff

**1 P-K4 P-K4 2 N-KB3 N-KB3 3
N×P P-Q3 4 N-KB3 N×P 5
P-Q4 B-K2 6 B-Q3 N-KB3 7
P-KR3**
White gets nowhere with 7 0-0
0-0 8 B-KN5 B-N5 9 QN-Q2
N-B3 10 P-B3 P-KR3 11 B-R4
N-KR4 12 B×B N×B 13 P-KN3
N-KB3 14 R-K1 Q-Q2 15 Q-N3
P-B3= Keres-Bronstein, USSR Ch
1961.
7 . . . 0-0 8 0-0 P-B4?
Or 8 . . . R-K1 9 P-B4 QN-Q2
(9 . . . N-B3 Fischer-Gheorghiu,
Buenos Aires 1970) 10 N-B3 N-B1
11 P-Q5 N-N3 12 R-K1 B-Q2 13
B-KN5 N-R4 14 B-Q2 N4-B5 15
B-KB1 B-KB3= Tal-Smyslov, 39
USSR Ch 1971. Also 8 . . . P-B3 9
R-K1 QN-Q2 10 B-KB4 R-K1 11
P-B4 N-B1 12 N-B3 P-QR3 13
Q-N3 N-K3= Fischer-Petrosian,
game 5 Candidates 1971.
**9 N-B3 N-B3 10 R-K1 P-QR3 11
P-Q5 N-R2 12 P-QR4 B-Q2 13
P-R5 R-K1 14 B-B1 P-R3 15
B-KB4 B-KB1 16 R×R Q×R 17
B-R2 Q-Q1 18 N-Q2 Q-B2 19
N2-K4 N×N 20 N×N B-B4 21
N-Q2 R-K1 22 P-QB3 Q-Q1 23
Q-N3 Q-Q2 24 P-QB4 N-B1 25**

**P-N4 B-R2 26 B-Q3 B×B 27
Q×B P-KN3 28 R-N1 B-N2** (229)

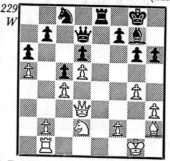

29 P-N4! A similar manoeuvre to
that which occurs in a very similar
position from the Averbakh variation
of the King's Indian. **29 . . . P×P 30
R×P Q-B2 31 N-N3 B-K4 32
B×B R×B 33 N-K2 P-KN4 34
Q-Q4 Q-K2 35 N-Q2 R-K8 36
R-N3 R-K7 37 K-B3 R-K4 38
R-K3 P-B3 39 N-K4 K-N2 40
K-N2 Q-QB2 41 R-KB3 P-N4 42
RP×Pep 1-0** If 42 . . . N×P 43
N×BP (with the idea of 44 N-K8+)
43 . . . Q-Q1 44 N-R5+ K-N1 45
Q-Q3! and the white queen pene-
trates.

2109 Leonid Stein-AK:
FR5 v. Ukraine:

Grünfeld

**1 P-QB4 P-QB4 2 N-KB3
N-KB3 3 N-QB3 P-Q4 4 P×P
N×P 5 P-Q4 N×N 6 P×N
P-KN3 7 P-K4 B-N2 8 B-N5+
N-Q2** Normal here has been 8 . . .
B-Q2. Karpov's move seems to be
new. **9 0-0 0-0 10 P-QR4 P-QR3 11
B-QB4 Q-B2 12 Q-K2 P-N3 13
P-K5 P-K3 14 N-N5 B-N2 15
P-B4 P-R3** (230)
Here the Kiev grandmaster de-
cided to smash open the defences
around the black king with a piece
sacrifice.

16 N×KP!?

Another tempting possibility was 16 P-B5!? P×N (16 . . .KP×P? 17 N×P or 16 . . .NP×P 17 N-R3 obviously suits White) 17 P-B6 B-R1 (after 17 . . . B-R3 18 Q-N4 KR-Q1 19 Q-R3 B-KB1 20 B×KP P×B 21 P-B7+ K-N2 22 B×P Black is doomed) 18 B×NP and White, after the rook manoeuvre R-B4-KR4, would have developed a strong attack.

16 . . . P×N 17 B×KP+ K-R1

17 . . . K-R2 is more exact.

18 Q-N4 KR-Q1 19 P-B5

Nothing good comes from 19 P-Q5 N-B1 20 P-Q6 Q-B3!

19 . . . N-B1 20 P-B6 N×B 21 Q×N

A line in which White risks nothing is 21 P×B+ N×NP 22 Q×P Q-B3 23 R-B6 Q-K5 24 Q×Q B×Q 25 R×RP+, but he wanted more . . .

21 . . . B-KB1 22 Q-R3

22 B-K3, to protect Q4, is also possible. Stein's move seems to be more energetic.

22 . . . P×P 23 P×P

White overestimates his position, otherwise he would have played 23 P-K6 Q×BP 24 Q×Q (24 R-R3?

Q×Q 25 R×Q B-B1) 24 . . . P×Q 25 P-K7 reaching a drawn ending.

23 . . . R×P 24 P-K6 B-B4 (*231*)

Black's pieces are now very active and he already has the initiative.

25 K-R1

25 Q×P+ Q-R2 26 Q×Q+ K×Q 27 K-R1 (27 B-K3 R-KN5) 27 . . . R-K5 28 P-K7 R-K7 does not make White's defensive task any easier.

25 B-K3 is slightly better, though after 25 . . . R-Q7 26 Q×P+ Q-R2 27 Q×Q+ K×Q 28 B-B2 R-KB1 29 P-B7 R-K7 and Black will still win.

25 . . . P-KR4 26 R-R2 B-Q4 27 R-Q2 R×R 28 B×R Q-K4 29 Q-Q3 Q×KP 30 Q×NP Q-N5 31 Q-R6+ K-N1 32 P-B7+ B×BP 33 B-B3 B-Q5 34 P-R3 Q-N2 35 Q-QB6

White continues to the time control, besides he could not have been unaware of Karpov's game against Kiarner. This time Karpov is careful . . .

35 . . . R-Q1 36 B×B Q×B 37 Q-N7 R-Q2 38 Q-B6 K-N2 39 Q-B1 Q-K4 40 R-K1 Q-B3 41 R-B1 Q-Q5 0-1

Final A	1	2	3	4	5	6	7	8	9	10	
1 USSR	×	2	3½	2	3½	3½	3½	3½	3½	3½	**28½**
2 Hungary	2	×	1½	2	2½	2	2½	2½	2	2½	**19½**
3 W. Germany	½	2½	×	1½	2	2½	1½	3	3½	2½	**19½**
4 USA	2	2	2½	×	2	1½	2	1½	2½	2	**18**
5 Bulgaria	½	1½	2	2	×	2½	2	2	3	2	**17½**
6 Israel	½	2	1½	2½	1½	×	1½	3	3	2	**17½**
7 Romania	½	1½	2½	2	2	2½	×	1½	2	2½	**17**
8 Cuba	½	1½	1	2½	2	1	2½	×	1	2½	**14½**
9 Denmark	½	2	½	1½	1	1	2	3	×	2½	**14**
10 England	½	1½	1½	2	2	2	1½	1½	1½	×	**14**

Board 1: Karpov 7/9 (77·8%), Hübner 9½/13 (73·1%), Rogoff 7/10 (70·0%).

The USSR team of Karpov, Balashov, Tukmakov, Vaganian, Podgayets and Anikayev was quite probably the strongest team ever seen at a student Olympiad.

Alan Perkins (of the English team) mentioned some interesting points in the *British Chess Magazine, Sept.* 1972: 'Balashov has obviously benefited from Russian training methods in one respect at least; he is noticeably physically more substantial than formerly. One feels that Karpov has scope for similar improvement (he plays well enough already). Someone asked him when he thought he would be playing Fischer – "not just yet" he said. I doubt if even Fischer had ever been photographed as much as Karpov here, but the Russian did not seem to mind.'

2201 AK–Werner Hug:
PR1: 16 July:

Sicilian

1 P–K4 P–QB4 2 N–KB3 N–QB3 3 P–Q4 P×P 4 N×P N–B3 5 N–QB3 P–K4 6 N4–N5 P–KR3 7 B–QB4 P–R3 8 N–Q6+ B×N 9 Q×B Q–K2 10 Q×Q+ K×Q 11 B–K3 Not 11 P–QN3? P–QN4 **11 . . . P–Q3 12 0–0–0 B–K3** The position is approximately equal. **13 N–Q5+ B×N 14 P×B** Or 14 B×B!? N×B 15 P×N N–N1 16 P–KB4 N–Q2 **14 . . . P–QN4 15 B–N3 N–QR4 16 P–KB3 KR–QB1 17 P–N4** Planning P–KR4 and P–N5 **17 . . . N–Q2 18 P–KR4 N×B+ 19 RP×N P–QR4 20 K–N1 R–R3 21 KR–K1 N–N3 22 P–KB4 N–Q2** (*232*) 22 . . . P–B3 is dubious on account of 23 P–N5! **23 P–N5 P–R4 24 P×P P×P 25 R–KB1 P–R5 26 B–Q2 P×P 27 B–N4+ K–K1 28 P×P P–B3 29 P–N6 N–B1 30 R–N1** Not 30 B×N?!

232
W

K×B 31 R–B5? R–Q3 32 R×RP
K–N1∓ 30 . . . R1–R1 31 K–B2
R–Q1 32 K–N1 R1–R1 33 K–B2
R–Q1 ½–½

2202 AK–Amikan Balshan:
PR2: 17 July:

Ruy Lopez

1 P–K4 P–K4 2 N–KB3 N–QB3
B–N5 P–QR3 4 B×N QP×B 5 0–0
P–B3 6 P–Q4 B–KN5 7 P×P Q×Q
8 R×Q P×P 9 R–Q3 B×N 10
P×B R–Q1 11 P–KB4 N–B3 12
N–B3 B–Q3 13 P–B5 B–B4 14
R×R+ K×R 15 B–N5 K–B1 16
R–Q1 R–B1 17 K–B1 P–KN3 18
P×P P×P 19 K–N2 B–Q5 20
P–B3 N–R4 21 B–B1 B×N 22
P×B P–QN4 23 B–K3 (*233*)

233
B

23 . . . R–B3 24 K–B2 R–Q3 25
R–KN1 K–Q2 26 K–K2 R–K3 27
R–Q1+ K–K1 28 B–N5 R–Q3 29

R–KN1 P–B4 30 B–K3 P–B5 31
B–N5 R–K3 32 B–K3 K–B2 33
R–N1 R–Q3 34 R–N1 N–B3 35
B–B5 R–Q1 36 B–B2 R–KR1 37
B–N3 K–K3 38 R–Q1 N–R4 39
K–B2 P–B3 40 R–Q2 P–R4 41
P–QR3 N–B3 42 K–K3 P–N4 43
R–Q1 N–Q2 44 R–KR1 N–B1 45
R–QN1 N–N3 46 R–N1 N–B5 47
K–Q2 N–R6 48 R–N1 R–QN1 49
K–K3 N–B5 50 R–Q1 P–B4 51
B×N NP×B+ 52 K–B2 P–N5 53
BP×P BP×P 54 P×P P×P 55
R–QN1 P–N6 56 P×P P×P 57
K–K2 P–N7 58 K–Q3 R–N6+
59 K–B4 R×P 60 R×P K–B3 61
R–N6+ K–N4 62 K–Q5 R–QR6 63
K×P P–B6 64 R–N8 K–N5 65
R–KB8 K–R6 66 K–Q6 R–Q6+ 67
K–B6 ½–½

2203 Marco Albano–AK:
PR4: 19 July:

Sicilian

1 P–K4 P–QB4 2 N–KB3 P–K3 3
P–Q4 P×P 4 N×P N–QB3 5
P–KN3 P–QR3 6 B–N2 N×N See
game 1501 for a discussion of this
line. 7 Q×N N–K2 8 0–0 White
did even better with 8 B–KB4 N–N3
9 B–Q6 B×B 10 Q×B Q–K2 11
Q–N6!± in Holmov–AK. Presum-
ably Karpov had an improvement
prepared. 8 . . . N–B3 9 Q–B3
P–Q3 10 B–K3 B–Q2 11 N–Q2
R–B1 12 P–QR4 P–QN4 13 P×P
P×P 14 KR–B1 B–K2 15 B–B1
N–K4 16 Q–R5 Q×Q 17 R×Q 0–0
18 B×P B×B 19 R×B N–Q6 (*234*)
20 R–R1 R×P 21 R–R7 B–B3 22
R–Q7 N×NP 23 R×QP N–Q8 24
R–N3 P–N4 25 N–B1 N–B6 26
R–Q2 R×R 27 N×R P–N5 28
N–N1 N–K7+ 29 K–B1 N–Q5 30
B×N B×B 31 R–Q3 P–K4 32
N–B3 R–R1 33 N–Q5 R–R8+ 34
K–N2 P–R4 35 R–Q2 R–R2 36

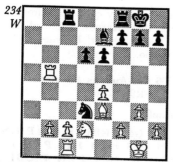

234 W

P–R3 K–N2 37 P×P P×P 38
P–B3 K–N3 39 P×P K–N4 40
K–R3 R–R8 41 R–K2 R–R8+ 42
K–N2 R–R1 43 R–K1 K×P 44
R–KB1 R–R1 45 R×P R–R7+
46 K–B1 K×P 47 R–B5 B–R8 48
N–B6 R–Q7 49 N–R5+ K–R5 50
N–B6 ½–½

2204 AK–Carlos Gouveia:
PR5: 20 July:

Sicilian

1 P–K4 P–QB4 2 N–KB3 P–K3 3
P–Q4 P×P 4 N×P P–QR3 5
N–QB3 Q–B2 6 P–KN3 P–QN4 7
B–N2 B–N2 8 0–0 N–KB3 9
P–QR3?! 9 R–K1 9 . . . P–Q3 10
P–R3 QN–Q2 11 P–KN4 P–R3 12
N4–K2 B–K2 13 P–B4 N–N3 14
Q–Q3 R–Q1 15 N–N3 P–Q4 16
P–K5 N–K5 17 N/B3–K2 N–R5 18
N–Q4 N/R5–B4 19 Q–K3 N×N 20
Q×N N–K5 21 Q–KB3 B–B4 22
P–B3 0–0 (235)

235 W

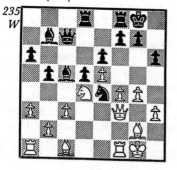

23 B–K3 R/Q1–K1 24 N–N3 P–B3
25 N×B N×N 26 B–Q4 P–B4 27
Q–K3 N–N6 28 QR–Q1 P–N3 29
B–B3 K–R2 30 K–R2 Q–Q2 31
R–B2 R–B1 32 R–KN1 N×B 33
P×N R–KN1 34 R2–N2 Q–K2 35
Q–B2 R/B1–B1 36 B–K2 R–B1 37
B–Q3 B–B3 38 P–KR4 B–Q2 39
K–R3 Q–B2 40 Q–B3 R/B1–B1 41
Q–Q1 K–R1 42 R–N3 P–N4 43
NP×P P–KN5+ 44 R×P P×P 45
R×R+ R×R 46 R×R+ K×R 47
B–K2 Q–N2 48 Q–QB1 P–QR4 49
K–R2 Q–K2 50 K–R3 Q–N2 51
Q–B7 P–N5 52 Q×P 1–0

2205 AK–Valentin Stoica:
FR1: 21 July:

Sicilian

1 P–K4 P–QB4 2 N–KB3 P–Q3 3
P–Q4 P×P 4 N×P N–KB3 5
N–QB3 P–QR3 6 B–K2 Karpov's
favourite 6 . . . P–K4 7 N–N3
B–K3 8 P–B4 Q–B2 9 0–0 Varying
from 9 P–QR4 with which Karpov
was very successful against Mecking.
9 . . . QN–Q2 10 P–B5 B–B5 11
P–QR4 B–K2 12 P–R5 0–0 13
B–K3 13 B–N5 KR–B1! is Karpov-
Gheorghiu, Moscow 1971 (game
1904). 13 . . . P–QN4 14 P×Pep
N×NP 15 K–R1 15 B×N? Q×B+
16 K–R1 B–N4!∓ Tal-Fischer,
Curaçao 1962 15 . . . KR–B1 16
B×N Q×B 17 B×B R×B 18
Q–K2 R1–QB1! After Karpov-
Bronstein, Moscow 1971, which went
18 . . . R–N5 19 R–R2 P–R3 20
R1–R1 B–B1 21 R–R4±, the search
began for an improvement. The text
is the said improvement which had
been successful a few months earlier
in Kostro-Pytel, Poland 1972. 19
R–R2 B–Q1! 20 R1–R1 Q–N2 21
R–R4 R×R 22 R×R R–B3 Per-
haps 22 . . . P–QR4!? 23 N–N5
P–Q4 and if 24 N–Q6? Q×N! –

Marić. **23 Q–Q3** Not 23 N–Q5?
Q×N!∓±. 23 P–R3?! P–KR4∓
24 Q–Q3 P–R5 25 N–Q5 Q–B1!
26 N–B3 N–R4 27 N–B1 N–N6+ 28
K–R2 Q–N2! 29 P–N3 Q–B1 left
Black with a winning position in
Campos–Lopez—Browne, San An-
tonio 1972. **23 . . . P–N3!?** (*236*)

236
W

24 P–R3 Browne considers only 24
P×P RP×P∓. **24 . . . N–R4 25
R–R1 N–B5 26 Q–B3 R–B5 27
R–Q1 Q–B3 28 P×P RP×P 29
Q–B1!** With the dual idea of 30
R×P and 30 P–N3 **29 . . . R–N5 30
P–N3 N–R4 31 Q–Q3 R–B5?** 31 . . .
P–R4! 32 Q×P N×P+ 33 K–N2
Q×Q 34 R×Q B–R5∓ or 32 N–Q5
R×P! 33 Q–KB3! K–B1!! 34
P–N4 N–B3 35 N×N R–K8+∓
was pointed out by Ghizdavu. **32
K–R2± B–B2 33 R–KB1 P–R4 34
R–B2! P–R5?** He could keep the
game going with 34 . . . B–N3! 35
N–Q5 K–N2 36 N×B Q×N 37
R×P+ K×R 38 Q×R+ K–N2
39 K–N2 Q–K6 40 Q–Q3±, a line
pointed out by Ghizdavu and con-
tinued by Marić: 40 . . . Q–K8 41
N–Q2!± N×P 42 N–B3±±. **35
N–Q2! R–Q5 36 Q–B3 Q–Q2 37
N–Q5 P–R6 38 Q×RP B–Q1 39
Q–KB3 R–N5? 40 N×R 1–0** The
last word on this variation will have
to await the next meeting between
Karpov and Browne, unless one

can draw any conclusions from the
fact that Karpov refrained from
1 P–K4 against Browne at San
Antonio.

2206 AK–Andras Adorjan:
FR3: 23 July:

Grünfeld

**1 P–Q4 N–KB3 2 P–QB4 P–KN3
3 N–QB3 P–Q4 4 P×P N×P 5
P–K4 N×N 6 P×N P–QB4 7
B–QB4 B–N2 8 N–K2 N–B3 9
B–K3 0–0 10 0–0 P×P 11 P×P
N–R4 12 R–B1** Or 12 B–Q3 N–B3
(also 12 . . . P–N3!?) 13 B–QN5 (13
B–QB4=) 13 . . . B–N5! 14 P–B3 (If
14 B×N P×B 15 P–B3 B–Q2 16
R–B1 Q–R4 17 R–B2 KR–Q1 with
18 . . . B–K1 to follow) 14 . . . B–Q2
15 R–N1 N–R4 16 Q–R4 B×B 17
R×B P–N3 18 R–B1 R–B1 19 R–Q5
R×R+ 20 N×R Q–B1∓ Timman–
Lewi, Groningen 1968/9 **12 . . . N×B
13 R×N P–N3 14 Q–R4 Q–Q2**
Also possible is 14 . . . P–QR4!? 15
R–B2 B–QR3 16 R–Q2 P–QN4=
15 Q–R3! Not 15 Q×Q? B×Q 16
R–B7 B–N4 17 R–K1 KR–B1 18
R×R+ (18 R×KP? B–KB3) 18
. . . R×R 19 R–QB1 R×R+ 20
N×R P–K3 with a clear advantage
to Black. **15 . . . Q–N4! 16 R1–B1
P–K3** If 16 . . . B–QR3 17 R4–B2
P–K3. 17 . . . KR–B1? would be a
horrible error: 18 N–B3 Q–Q6 19
R–Q2 Q–B5 20 R2–Q1!±± **17
N–B4 B–N2??** (*237*) 17 . . . R–Q1
was necessary: 18 P–Q5!? (18
P–B3 B–N2 19 R–B7 B–KB1!∓) 18
. . . P×P (18 . . . B–N7? 19 Q–K7
R–Q2 20 Q–N5±) 19 N×QP
B–K3 20 R–N4 Q–Q2 21 R–Q1=
18 R–B7?!± Missing 18 N×KP!!
P×N 19 R–B7±± **18 . . . B×KP 19
N×KP KR–K1** Necessary. 19 . . .
Q–KB4? fails to 20 N×R Q–N5 21
P–B3 B×BP 22 Q–N2 B×N 23

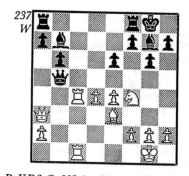

237
W

P–KR3 Q–N6 (or 23 . . . Q–K5) 24
Q–KB2±± **20 N×B K×N 21
B–B4 Q–KB4 22 B–K5+ K–N1 23
P–R4** If 23 Q–K3 then 23 . . .
P–KN4 24 P–KR4 P–KR3 (not
24 . . . P–B3? 25 Q–QN3+ R–K3
26 R–K7±±) 25 P×P P×P 26
P–B3 B–Q4 27 K–B2 P–B3 28
P–N4 Q–N3 29 R–KR1 QR–B1!
30 R×R R×R 31 B–Q6 B×RP!∓
**23 . . . B–Q4 24 P–B3 P–B3 25
B–N3 R–K7 26 R–K7 R×R 27
Q×R Q–K3 28 Q–QB7!** Q–B2
Black has no time to go pawn-hunt-
ing: 28 . . . B×RP 29 R–B6 Q–B2
30 Q–B4 B–K3 31 P–Q5!± **29
Q–KB4 R–K1 30 R–B7 R–K2 31
R–B8+** (*238*)

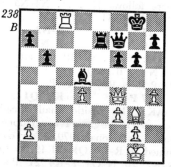

238
B

31 . . . R–K1?? The right way was
31 . . .K–N2 32 Q–N8 R–N2
33 Q–Q6 R–Q2= **32 R×R+
Q×R 33 Q×P Q–KB1 34 Q–K5
B×RP 35 Q–B7 B–B2 36 Q×RP**

P–QN4 37 Q–N6 B–B5 38 Q–QB6?!
Again Karpov overlooks a quick
win, this time with 38 B–K5. **38 . . .
Q–Q1! 39 Q–B5?** White can still
maintain winning chances with 39
B–K5! K–B2!± **39 . . . K–B2 40
P–R5?** Throwing away the rem-
nants of his advantage. Better 40
K–R2±. **40 . . . Q–K2!= 41 Q–B6
Q–K6+ ½–½** In view of 42 K–R2
Q×QP 43 Q–B7+ K–N1 with 44
. . . P–N4 to follow, or 42 B–B2
Q–B8+ 43 K–R2 Q–B5+ 44
P–N3 Q–N4.

2207 Guillermo Estevez–AK:
FR4: 24 July:

Sicilian

**1 P–K4 P–QB4 2 N–KB3 N–QB3
3 P–Q4 P×P 4 N×P P–K3 5 N–N5
P–Q3 6 P–QB4 N–B3 7 N1–B3
P–QR3 8 N–R3 B–K2 9 B–K2 0–0
10 0–0 Q–R4 11 N–B2?!** Better 11
B–K3 **11 . . . R–Q1 12 B–Q2** Now
if 12 B–K3 P–Q4!∓ **12 . . . Q–B2 13
R–B1 B–Q2 14 B–K3 B–K1 15
P–B3 P–QN3 16 Q–Q2 R–R2! 17
KR–Q1 Q–N1 18 B–B1 R–N2** The
position is approximately equal. **19
Q–B2** Not 19 P–QR4? N–QR4 **19
. . . R–B1 20 N–Q4 N–K4 21
P–QN3 P–R3 22 P–QR4 N3–Q2
23 Q–N3 K–R1 24 P–B4 N–QB3**
(*239*)

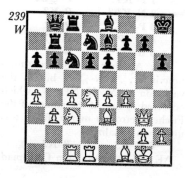

239
W

25 P–KB5? White had two good choices in 25 B–K2! with 26 N×N and 27 B–B3 to follow, and 25 N×N! R×N 26 B–K2 with P–K5 to come. **25 . . . N×N 26 B×N N–K4∓ 27 P×P P×P 28 Q–R3 B–N4 29 R–B2 P–N4!? 30 RP×P P×P 31 R–B2?** Also bad is 31 Q×KP? R–K2 32 Q–B5 R–KB2 33 Q–K6 R–KB3 34 Q–R3 B–Q2 35 Q–R5 B–N5 winning the queen, but White may be able to hang on with 31 P×P!? with the idea of 32 B×N P×B 33 B–B4. **31 . . . P–N5 32 N–N5 B×N 33 P×B R–K2∓ 34 B–K2 Q–N2 35 B–Q3 N×B 36 Q×N P–K4 37 B–N2 Q–N3 38 K–B1 B–K6 39 R–B3 B–B4 40 B–B1 R–QN1 41 K–K2 R–R2 42 R1–B1 Q×P∓∓ 43 R–B8+ K–R2 44 R×R Q×R 45 Q–R3 Q–K1 46 B–Q2 R–R7 47 Q–B5+ K–N1 48 R–B3 B–Q5 49 R–Q3 R–R2! 50 B–K3 B×B 51 K×B R–KB2 52 Q–N4 R–B5 53 Q–R3 Q–N3 54 Q–B8+ K–R2 55 Q–B6 Q×NP 0–1**

2208 AK–Robert Hübner:
FR6: 26 July:

Sicilian

The notes to this game are by Karpov (AK) from *64* and Robert Hübner (RH) from *The Chess Player 3*.

1 P–K4	**P–QB4**
2 N–KB3	**P–K3**
3 P–Q4	**P×P**
4 N×P	**P–QR3**
5 B–Q3	**B–B4**

AK: Another possible continuation is 5 . . . N–QB3, but in the variation 6 N×N NP×N, which occurred in one of the games of the Fischer–Petrosian match, Black was unable to equalize.

6 N–N3   B–R2

AK: In the All-Union Olympiad Taimanov played 6 . . . B–N3 against me. In the variation chosen by White there is no real difference between these two lines.

7 0–0	**N–QB3**
8 Q–K2	**P–Q3**
9 B–K3	**B×B**
10 Q×B	**N–B3**
11 P–QB4	**0–0**
12 R–Q1	

AK: Hindering the freeing . . . P–Q4. The opening stage is concluded. White has a space advantage, but Black's position is solid.

12 . . .   Q–B2
13 N–B3

AK: The knight manoeuvre N1–Q2–B3 comes into consideration. But in that case one must carefully watch for the possibility of . . . P–Q4. With the text move White consolidates his space advantage.

13 . . .   N–K4
14 QR–B1

AK: Indirectly defending the QBP.

14 . . .   P–QN3
15 B–K2

AK: It is useful to preserve the bishop. If immediately 15 P–B4 there follows 15 . . . N4–N5 16 Q–B3 P–QN4!

15 . . .	**B–N2**
16 P–B4	**N–N3**

AK: 16 . . . N×BP loses after 17 B×N Q×B 18 Q×P Q–B3 (18 . . . B×P 19 N–R5) 19 R×P.

17 P–N3   KR–Q1 (*240*)

AK: This position had already occurred in the game Ivkov–Hübner, Palma Interzonal 1970. Ivkov continued 18 R–Q2 QR–B1 19 R1–Q1 N–K2 20 N–Q4 P–K4 21 P×P P×P 22 N4–N5!±. I think that instead of 20 . . . P–K4, Hübner would have got an adequate game by means of 20 . . . Q–B4 with the threat of . . . P–K4.

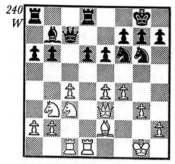

240
W

18 P–QR3

AK: Securing the knight transfer to Q4, since . . . Q–B4 can be met by P–QN4.

18 . .   QR–B1

RH: 18 . . . QR–N1!? ±

19 N–Q4   B–R1
20 P–N3

AK: Necessary in order to transfer the bishop to the long diagonal.

20 . .   N–K2

RH: With the idea of 21 . . . P–K4

21 B–B3   R–N1

RH: 21 . . . P–K4 22 P×P P×P 23 N–B2 with 24 N–Q5 to follow.

22 P–QR4

AK: Warding off the possibility of a later . . . P–QN4. Having consolidated his centre, White is ready to proceed, after appropriate piece regrouping, with the storming of Black's K-side and centre. Not wanting to passively await events, Hübner endeavours to start play in the centre, but nothing comes of this.

22 . . .   Q–B4
23 R–Q3!   P–K4?!

RH: 23 . . . N–B3 =

24 N4–K2

AK/RH: Of course not 24 N–B2 P×P 25 P×P N–N3! ∓.

AK: Having thought for 40 minutes, Hübner could find nothing better than to exchange queens and offer a draw. After the game

Hübner was in favour of 24 . . . N–B3, but 25 N–Q5 gives White an appreciable advantage.

24 . . .   P×P?!

RH: 24 . . . N–B3 25 N–Q5 N–QN5 26 N×N/4 Q×N 27 R1–Q1 R–K1 28 P–KB5 ±

25 P×P

RH: 25 N×P? N–B3 with the idea 26 . . . N–K4 ∓.

25 . . .   Q×Q+
26 R×Q

AK: It is clear that the draw is declined since the game had decisive significance for the award of the first board prize, and, besides that, I had enough foundation (purely in the chess sense) to continue the fight.

26 . . .   N–N3?

RH: 26 . . . R–K1 27 R–Q1 N–B1 28 N–N3 P–N3 with 29 . . . B–B3 and 30 . . . R–N2 to follow.

27 R–Q1   K–B1?!

AK: During the game I thought that Black's best continuation was 27 . . . R–K1 28 R×P N–R5 29 K–B2 N×B 30 K×N N×P 31 N×N P–B4 32 N2–B3 P×N+ 33 K–N4. But in that case also, White has the advantage.

RH: Better 27 . . . N–B1!? with the idea 28 . . . N–K3.

28 R3–Q3   N–K1

AK: The only move – on 28 . . . K–K2 there follows 29 P–K5 P×P 30 R×R R×R 31 R×R.

29 K–B2   R/Q1–B1

AK: Essential–the threat was P–K5.

30 K–N3   N–K2
31 N–Q4   R–B4
32 R1–Q2

AK: Preparing 33 N–B2. If 32 N–B2 then 32 . . . P–QN4 is unpleasant.

32 . . .   B–N2
33 N–B2?

RH: 33 P–R4 ±

33 . . .   P–KN4

AK: A questionable decision. Of course White could have prevented this move by means of 33 P–R4, but ... you see Black is adding many weaknesses on the K-side. Though, in all truth, Black's pieces do obtain the ... K4 square.

34 P×P	R×NP+
35 K–B2	N–N3
36 B–R1	

AK: Defending against the threat of 36 ... N–K4 and at the same time clearing the third rank for manoeuvres.

36 ...   **R–B1**

RH: 36 ... N–K4 37 R–N3 R×R 38 P×R P–B4 39 N–Q4±

| 37 R–N3 | R1–B4 |
| 38 N–K3 | N–K2 |

AK: Black was unable to appropriate the ... K4 square, since that would have involved diverting the knight from the defence of ... Q4.

39 B–B3   **R×R**

RH: 39 ... R–N3!?

40 P×R   **R–K4**

RH: 40 ... P–B4!?

41 P–KN4

AK: The sealed move. It seems illogical, because the pawn advances on to a square of the same colour as the bishop, but in return White anchors the KB5 square and further hampers his opponent.

41 ...   **P–QR4**

AK: Relinquishing the struggle for ... P–QN4 and putting the initiative completely in White's hands.

Truly Black's position is already very difficult, and in the event of him waiting passively, White will advance his QNP to QN5, then occupy Q5 with the knight at present on QB3, so that after the exchange the knight on K3 can attack Black's pawns from QB4 or KB5.

42 R–Q1

AK: 42 N–B5 is no good on account of 42 ... N×N 43 NP×N B×B 44 K×B P–R4 45 N–Q5 N–N2! White waits for a more opportune moment and for the time being withdraws his rook to the empty first rank.

RH: 42 N–B5?! N×N 43 NP×N B×B 44 K×B P–R4 is unclear.

42 ...   **B–B3**

43 N/B3–Q5 (*241*)

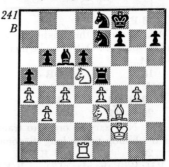

AK: A move earlier this move brought nothing because of 42 ... N×N 43 BP×N B–R3. Now Black cannot capture the knight because of the unfortunate placing of the bishop.

43 ...   **N–B1**

RH: 43 ... B×N 44 BP×B with 45 N–B4±± to follow.

44 N–B5   **B×N**

AK: The knight can no longer be endured. It would be bad to exchange the knight on ... KB4 because of NP×N.

RH: 44 ... B–Q2 45 R–KR1 K–N1 46 K–N3 B–K3±

| 45 BP×B | N–K2 |
| 46 N–K3 | |

AK: Directed towards QB4.

46 ...   **N–N1**

AK: If 46 ... N–KB3 47 N–B4 N×KP+ 48 K–N2 N–B6 49 N×R N×R 50 N–Q7+ K–K1 51 N–B6+ and 52 B×N wins.

| 47 N–B4 | R–K2 |
| 48 N×NP | |

AK: 48 P–K5 also gave a great advantage.

48 ...	R–N2
49 N–B4	R×P
50 R–QR1!	

AK: In the ending the rook should be behind the passed pawn. There is no defence against 51 N×RP.

50 ...	N/N1–B3
51 N×RP	R–N7+
52 K–K3	N–Q2
53 N–B6	R–N6+
54 K–B4	N–K4
55 N×N	P×N+
56 K–N3	

AK: The rest is, as they say, a matter of technique. 56 ... N–Q3 57 K–B2 R–N7+ 58 K–N1 R–N2 59 P–R5 R–R2 60 P–R6 K–K2

RH: 60 . . . N–N2 61 K–B2 N–B4 62 R–R5

AK: In the case of 60 . . . N–N2, White wins with 61 B–K2 N–B4 62 R–N1 N×KP 63 R–N7 R–R1 64 P–R7 K–N2 65 R–B7.

61 K–B2 K–Q2 62 K–K3 N–B5+ 63 K–Q3 N–N3 64 B–K2 K–Q3 65 K–K3 N–Q2 66 R–R1 N–B1 67 R–R6+ K–K2 68 P–Q6+ K–Q1 69 B–N5 R–R1 70 R–R5 P–B3 71 R–R6 R–N1 72 B–B6 R–N6+ 73 K–Q2 R–QR6 74 R×BP R–R7+ 1–0

2209 AK–Peter Markland:
FR8: 28 July:

Sicilian

1 N–KB3 P–QB4 2 P–K4 N–QB3 3 P–Q4 P×P 4 N×P N–B3 5 N–QB3 P–Q3 6 B–KN5 B–Q2 7 Q–Q2 R–B1 8 0–0–0 N×N 9 Q×N Q–R4 10 B–Q2 P–QR3 11 P–B3 Q–QB4 12 Q–Q3 P–KN3 (*242*)

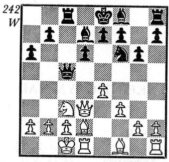

13 P–KN4 B–N2 14 P–KR4 It's a favourite tactic of Karpov to push up the K-side pawns, which usually results in the opening of attacking lines as well as weakening the opponent's defensive pawn formation. 14 ... P–R3 15 K–N1 B–K3 16 B–K3 Q–QR4 17 B–Q4! Even when Karpov is undertaking a K-side attack, he never seems to lose sight of the rest of the board – to be accurate, he tends to keep control over the whole position – see his games against Vujakovic and D. Byrne. 17 . . . 0–0 18 Q–Q2! Threatening 19 N–Q5 and 18 . . . R×N 19 Q×R Q×P+ 20 K–B1 R–B1 21 Q–R3 leads to (a) nothing for Black. 18 . . . N–Q2 19 N–Q5 Q–Q1 20 B×B K×B 21 N–K3 N–K4 22 B–K2! To play simply 23 P–KB4. Karpov's attack is simple, strong and deadly. 22 . . . P–B3 23 P–KB4 N–B5 24 B×N B×B 25 P–N5! Forcing the opening of lines to Black's king. 25 . . . RP×P 26 RP×P P×P This loses, but if 26 . . . R–KR1 or 26 . . . B–B2 then 27 P×P+, or 26 . . . B–N1 27 QR–N1 and there is no real hope. 27 Q–B3+ P–K4 28 N×B P–N4 29 P×KP R×N 30 Q–KR3! 1–0 Black is shattered: if 30 . . . R–R1 simply 31 Q×R+ followed by capture of the QP, and if 30 . . . K–B2 31 Q–R7+ wins.

Final A	1	2	3	4	5	6	7	8	9	0	1	2	3	4	5	6	
1 USSR	×	1½	2½	2	2½	2½	3	2½	3	3½	3½	3	3½	2	3	4	**42**
2 Hungary	2½	×	2½	2½	2	2½	2½	2½	2½	3½	3½	3	2	4	1½	3½	**40½**
3 Yugoslavia	1½	1½	×	1½	2	2	2	3	3	2½	3	3	3½	3	2½	4	**38**
4 Czechoslovakia	2	1½	2½	×	1½	2½	2½	2½	2	1½	1½	2½	3½	2½	4	3	**35½**
5 West Germany	1½	2	2	2½	×	2½	2½	2½	2½	2½	2½	2	2	3	2	3	**35**
6 Bulgaria	1½	1½	2	1½	1½	×	2½	3	2½	2½	2	2½	2½	2	2½	2	**32**
7 Romania	1	1½	2	1½	1½	1½	×	2	2	3	2½	2½	2½	3½	2	2½	**31½**
8 Holland	1½	1½	1	1½	1½	1	2	×	2½	3	3	2	2½	1½	2	2½	**29**
9 USA	1	1½	1	2	1½	1½	2	1½	×	2½	3	3	1½	2½	2½	2	**29**
10 East Germany	½	½	1½	2½	1½	1½	1	1	1½	×	2½	2	2	3	4	2½	**27½**
11 Spain	½	½	1	2½	1½	2	1½	1	1	1½	×	2	3½	3	1½	3	**26**
12 Poland	1	1	1	1½	2	1½	1½	2	1	2	2	×	2	2	2	2	**24½**
13 Denmark	½	2	½	½	2	1½	1½	1½	2½	2	½	2	×	2	2½	1½	**23**
14 Argentina	2	0	1	1	1½	2	½	2½	1½	1	1	2	2	×	2½	2	**22½**
15 Sweden	1	2½	1½	0	2	1½	2	2	1½	0	2½	2	1½	1½	×	1	**22½**
16 Switzerland	0	½	0	1	1	2	1½	1	2½	1½	1	2	2½	2	3	×	**21½**

The USSR team was Petrosian, Korchnoi, Smyslov, Tal, Karpov and Savon.

Karpov's score of 86·7 % was just bettered by Tal with 87·5 % (the absolute best result). Karpov's score was easily the best on his board (first reserve!): 13/15 ahead of Balshan 13/16 (81·3 %), Rantanen 12/15 (80·0 %) etc.

Ray Keene and David Levy devoted a section of *Chess Olympiad Skopje* 1972 to Hübner, Karpov and Ljubojević, entitled *Future World Champions?*

Keene and Levy posed the question 'which of this trio – if any – do you think will wrest the crown from King Bobby? Hübner – the realistic individuals? Karpov – the protége of the Soviet machine or the charismatic Ljubojević?'

Their concluding predictions were: 'David Levy believes that Karpov's all-round virtuosity backed up by the vast chess resources of the Soviet Union will one day carry him to the top, while . . . Raymond Keene adheres to the view that Hübner is likely to be Fischer's challenger in the not-too-distant future.'

From the above one can see that at this time opinion was still divided as to Karpov's likely prospects.

This is what Tal wrote about the youngest member of the Soviet Olympic team: 'To be quite frank, only now at Skopje, have I realized that Karpov is really capable of the highest achievements. He had excellent results before, it is true, but from the creative point of view his play did not impress me. Now, simply as a chessplayer, I am enchanted with several of Karpov's games. When we are asked to show something of interest from Skopje we (the other members of the USSR team) have difficulty finding examples, but in Karpov's case there is another difficulty: he cannot decide which of his fine games could be called the best one.'

Gligorić was, if anything, even more impressed. In his introduction to the game Karpov-Ungureanu in *Chess Life and Review* he wrote: 'At the present moment, Anatoly Karpov seems to come closest to satisfying the difficult requirements (to attempt to take the title away from Fischer). He has had steadily high results, which no other young player can boast, and the experience which only a Soviet-based player can achieve. At the same time, his knowledge of the openings is more profound and up-to-date (a particular Fischer weapon) than any other representative of the coming generation. If he has any deficiencies, they could be that he is a little too cautious and physically too frail for his age'.

2301 Sloth–AK:
> PR2 v. Denmark:
> 20 September:

English

1 N–KB3 P–QB4 2 P–KN3 P–KN3 3 B–N2 B–N2 4 P–B4 N–QB3 5 N–B3 P–Q3 If 5 . . . N–B3 6 P–Q4±, but 5 . . . N–R3= is also possible **6 P–QR3 N–R3 7 P–Q3 0–0 8 B–Q2 N–B4**

Taking control of d4 and restraining P–Q4. Q-side play is possible with 8 . . . P–QR3 9 R–QN1 R–N1 10 P–QN4 P×P 11 P×P P–QN4=. Karpov wants more.

9 R–QN1 P–QR4

Now P–QN4 has also been put under restraint.

10 0–0 B–Q2 11 P–K3 P–K3 12 N–K1± Q–K2 13 P–N3

Or 13 N–B2 P–R5 14 P–QN4 RP×Pep 15 R×P N–R4 with the idea of . . . B–QB3=.

13 . . . QR–N1 14 N–B2 KR–Q1 15 N–N5

15 P–QN4 RP×P 16 P×P N×QNP (16 . . . P×P? 17 N–N5) 17 N×N P×N 18 R×P!? (18 N–N5 B×N 19 P×B P–Q4=) 18 . . .P–Q4 19 Q–N1±.

15 . . . P–N3

15 . . . P–Q4 allows 16 P–K4!? P×KP 17 P×P N4–Q5 (17 . . . N–Q3 18 B–B4 N×N 19 P×N N–K4 20 Q–K2±) 18 N2×N P×N 19 P–QN4.

16 P–QN4 RP×P 17 P×P N–K4 18 P–K4!± N–R3

Or 18 . . . N–Q5 19 N2×N P×N 20 P–B4±.

19 N–B3 P–B4 20 P–N5 B–QB1 21 Q–K2 B–N2 22 P–B4 N–Q2 23 KR–K1 R–K1?!

23 . . . N–B1 is more appropriate.

24 R–R1 Q–Q1 25 R–R7

With the idea of 26 R×B R×R 27 P×P.

25 . . . N–B1?

Now 25 . . . Q–B1 is needed.

26 P–R3?

Missing his chance: 26 P×P B×B 27 P×KP! R–N2 28 R×R B×R 29 P–K7 wins.

26 . . . R–K2 27 K–R2?! R–KB2 28 R–R4 *(243)*

28 R–R3!? is probably better. Now Karpov takes full advantage of his unexpected chance.

28 . . . P–K4!= 29 N–Q5 KP×P 30 NP×P?

If 30 B×P P–N4 31 B–Q2 B×N

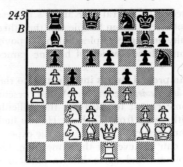

243
B

followed by . . . P–B5∓, or 30
N×BP!? P–N4 31 N–R5 B–K4 32
P×P=.

**30 . . . P×P 31 P×P N–K3∓ 32
Q–Q3**

32 P–B5 P×P 33 P×P fails to
33 . . . B–K4+ and 34 . . . N×P.
The text is the only possible way to
defend the KBP against the threat
of . . . B×N e.g. 32 R–KB1 B×N 33
KP×B N×P 34 B×N R×B 35
R×R B–K4 wins.

32 . . . Q–KB1

If 32 . . . Q–R5 33 Q–KN3 holds,
while 32 . . . B×N 33 Q×B and
Black cannot take the KBP because
of the pin on the KN1–QR7
diagonal.

33 R–KB1 K–R1 34 N×P

If 34 Q–KN3 P–N4! 35 P–B5
B–K4 36 B–QB3 N–Q5!∓∓.

34 . . . N×P 35 B×N

The alternative is 35 R×N B–K4
36 B–QB3 Q–N2! 37 K–R1 R×R
38 N–Q7! B×B 39 N×R B–K4 40
N–B6 B×N∓.

**35 . . . R×B 36 N–Q7 R×R! 37
Q×R**

Or 37 N×Q B–K4+ 38 Q–KN3
B×Q+ 39 K×B R8×N.

**37 . . . Q×Q 38 B×Q R–Q1 39
N–N6 B×P 40 N–K3**

If 40 N–K1 B–K4+ 41 K–N1
B–Q5+ 42 K–R2 R–KB1 43 B–N2
R–B7 wins.

40 . . . B–K4+ 41 K–N1 B–Q5 0–1

Because of 42 K–B2 N–B4 43 R–R3
R–KB1.

2302 AK–Eldis Cobo:
  PR3 v. Cuba:
  21 September:

Sicilian

**1 P–K4 P–QB4 2 N–KB3 P–Q3
3 P–Q4 P×P 4 N×P N–KB3 5
N–QB3 P–QR3 6 P–B4 P–K3 7
B–K2 Q–B2 8 0–0 N–B3 9 K–R1
B–Q2**

Black's position perhaps suffers
from the slight disadvantage that the
queen has gone to QB2 too soon.

10 P–QR4

10 B–K3 is also good.

10 . . .	**B–K2**
11 N–N3	**0–0**

12 B–K3

There was no point trying to tie
up the Q-side with 12 P–R5 as Black
could break out with 12 . . . P–QN4
13 P×Pep Q×P. However, 13
P–R5 is now an unpleasant threat.

12 . . .   N–QN5

Black ignores his opponent's plan
He had to play 12 . . . P–QN3!?
and only then 13 . . . N–QR4 or
13 . . . N–QN5. The alternative
12 . . . N–QR4 would give White a
slight advantage after 13 P–K5
N–K1 (Not 13 . . . P×P 14 P×P
Q×P 15 B–Q4 Q–B2 16 N×N
Q×N/R4 17 B×N±±) 14 N×N
Q×N/R4 15 Q–Q2 and 16 B–Q4.

13 P–R5±   B–B3

If 13 . . . P–Q4 14 B–N6 Q–B1 15
P–K5 N–K5 16 N×N P×N 17
P–B4.

14 B–N6   Q–N1

The logical continuation. Black
prepares to drive the bishop away
by . . . N–Q2 and follow up with
. . . P–QN4. But this plan is too slow
and Black should have played 14
. . . Q–Q2 after which I intended to

play 15 B–B3 preventing the freeing move . . . P–Q4.

15 Q–Q2

An important move. White defends the KP indirectly and threatens to win Black's advanced QN by 16 N–Q1 P–Q4 17 P–B3 N×KP 18 Q–B1.

15 . . .   **P–Q4**

16 P–K5   **N–Q2**

16 . . . N–K5 17 N×N P×N 18 P–B4 (with the threat 19 N–B5±±) is horrible for Black.

17 B–Q4   **P–QN4**

18 B–N4

Preparing P–B5 and preventing Black from advancing his BP. White would have achieved nothing concrete with 18 P×Pep N×NP 19 P–B5 because of 19 . . . P×P 20 R×BP N–B5.

18 . . .   **P–N3**

19 QR–K1

Played with the idea of 20 P–B5. Black's pieces are clustered on the Q-side and he takes no steps to transfer them to the defence of his king. He even removes his KR from the vital KB1 square to make room for the knight.

19 . . .   **R–B1** *(244)*

20 P–B5

Decisive.

20 . . .   **NP×P**

If 20 . . . KP×P 21 P–K6.

21 B×P   **N–B1**

Again if 21 . . . P×B 22 P–K6 wins.

22 Q–R6   **N–N3**

After 22 . . . P×B White breaks through with 23 P–K6 P–B3 24 R×P N×BP (24 . . . B–K1 25 R×BP and 26 R–B7) 25 R–N5+ N–N3 26 R×N+ P×R 27 Q×P+ K–R1 28 B×P+ B×B 29 Q×B+ K–R2 (or 29 . . . K–N1) 30 R–K5!

30 N–Q4 (instead of 30 R–K5!) is tempting e.g. 30 . . . N×R (30 . . . N×N 31 R–K3) 31 N–B5 R–R2 32 P–K7 R×P 33 Q×R+ K–N3 34 Q–K6+ K–N4 (34 . . . K–R4 35 Q–R6+ K–N5 36 N–K3 mate) 35 P–R4+ K–N5 (35 . . . K–R4 36 Q–R6+ K–N5 37 Q–N5 mate) 36 N–K3+ K–N6 (36 . . . K–R4 37 Q–N4+ K–R3 38 N–B5+ K–R2 39 Q–N7 mate; or 36 . . . K×P 37 Q–N4 mate) 37 Q–N4+ K–B7 38 N/B3–Q1 mate. However, Black can avoid mate by 30 . . . R–B1 when White has to fight to win.

23 B×N   **RP×B**

Eldis Cobo overlooks that after 24 . . . B–B1 he loses control of KR4 and White's major pieces are able to attack his king along the open KR-file. If 23 . . . BP×B the immediate 24 R–B7 does not work because the black king can escape to the Q-side via K1 and Q2. So I had intended to play 24 Q–R3 B–Q2 25 R–B7! K×R 26 Q×RP+ K–K1 27 Q–N8+ B–B1 28 R–KB1 K–Q1 29 Q×B+ B–K1 (29 . . . K–B2 30 Q–Q6+ K–N2 31 Q–N6 mate) 30 B–N6+ K–Q2 (30 . . . R–B2 31 N–B5) 31 R–B7+ B×R 32 Q×B+ K–B3 33 N–Q4 mate.

24 R–K3   **B–B1**

25 Q–R4   **B–KN2**

26 R–R3   **B–K1**

27 Q–R7+   **K–B1**

28 Q×NP   **P–B3**

If 28 . . . B×P 29 Q×KP with an easy win, and if 28 . . . N×P 29 R–R7 forces mate.

29 R×P+   1–0

2303 Alvarez–AK:
PR6 v. Dominica:
24 September:

Sicilian

1 P–K4 P–QB4 2 N–KB3 P–K3 3 P–Q4 P×P 4 N×P P–QR3 5 N–QB3 Q–B2 6 B–K3 B–N5 7 B–Q2 N–KB3 8 B–Q3 P–Q3 9 0–0 B–B4 10 N–N3 B–R2 11 K–R1 0–0 12 B–KN5 QN–Q2 13 P–B4 P–QN4 14 P–QR3 B–N2 15 Q–K2 KR–K1 16 QR–Q1 P–K4 17 Q–B3 P–R3 18 B–R4 P×P 19 Q×P R–K4 20 Q–B3 R1–K1 21 B–N3 R4–K3 22 N–Q5 B×N 23 P×B R–K6 24 Q–B4 N–K4 25 Q–B5 (*245*)

245
B

Now Karpov wins with a neat combination: **25 . . . R×B/N6! 26 P×R N4–N5 27 QR–K1 R×R 28 R×R N–B7+ 29 K–R2 N3–N5+ 30 K–N1 N–K5+ 0–1**

2304 Saren–AK: PR7 v. Finland:
25 September:

Sicilian

1 P–K4 P–QB4 2 N–KB3 P–K3 3 P–Q4 P×P 4 N×P N–QB3 5 N–N5 P–Q3 6 P–QB4 N–B3 7 N1–B3

P–QR3 8 N–R3 8 N–Q4!? 8 . . . B–K2 9 B–K2 0–0 10 0–0 P–QN3 10 . . . R–K1 is out of favour, but 10 . . . B–Q2 is interesting. **11 B–K3 B–N2** For 11 . . . B–Q2!? see Karpov–Hartston, game 2004 **12 P–B3?!** 12 R–B1 seems to be White's strongest here. **12 . . . R–N1!?** 12 . . . R–K1! and then 13 Q–N3 N–Q2 14 KR–Q1 N–B4! or 13 N–B2 R–QB1 are perfectly satisfactory for Black. **13 Q–K1 N–Q2** 13 . . . N–K4 14 Q–B2 B–B3± **14 Q–B2 N–B4 15 KR–Q1 P–B4?!** 15 . . . B–R5 16 P–KN3 B–B3 or 16 Q–B1 Q–K2 are both sound for Black. **16 P×P R×P 17 N–B2** to be able to kick one of Black's knights away with 18 P–QN4 **17 . . . B–R5 18 P–KN3 B–K2** Now if 18 . . . B–B3 19 P–KN4 B–R5 20 Q–N2 R–B2 21 P–N3 **19 P–QN4 N–Q2 20 P–B4 Q–KB1** (*246*)

246
W

21 P–N5? 21 B–N4 is correct: 21 . . . R–B3 22 N–K4 R–N3 23 B–R5 (23 N–N5!? B×N 24 P×B N3–K4 25 Q×Q+ R×Q 26 B–R5 N×P!∓) 23 . . . R–R3 24 B–B3± **21 . . . P×P 22 P×P N–R4 23 B×P?** This suddenly leaves White in terrible trouble thanks to Black's fine 24th move. **23 . . . N×B 24 Q×N B–Q1! 25 Q–R7** If 25 Q×QP Q×Q 26 R×Q R–B4 with 27 . . . R1–B1 to follow, or

25 Q–K3 P–K4 **25 . . . R–B1 26
Q–K3 P–K4 27 B–N4 N–B5 28
Q–Q3?!** 28 Q–K2 lasts a little
longer, though 28 . . . B–N3+ 29
K–B1 R×P+ 30 P×R Q×P+ 31
K–K1 R–B1 with 32 . . . B–B7+ to
follow wins. **28 . . . B–N3+ 29
K–B1 R×P+ 30 P×R Q×P+ 0–1**

2305 AK–Jürgen Dueball:
FR2 v. West Germany:
28 September:

Sicilian

**1 P–K4 P–QB4 2 N–KB3 P–Q3
3 P–Q4 P×P 4 N×P N–KB3 5
N–QB3 P–KN3 6 B–K3 N–B3 7
P–B3 B–N2 8 Q–Q2 0–0 9 P–KN4** 9
B–QB4 or 9 0–0–0 is more usual **9 . . .
N×N 10 B×N B–K3 11 0–0–0
Q–R4** Black has transposed into a
bad variation against 9 0–0–0. **12
K–N1** Also 12 P–QR3 could be
played. **12 . . . KR–B1 13 P–QR3
QR–N1 14 P–N5!** 14 P–KR4
allows 14 . . . P–QN4= **14 . . . N–R4
15 N–Q5 Q×Q 16 R×Q B×N 17
P×B± P–QR3 18 R–N1! P–N4 19
P–B3 P–R4 20 B–R7 R–N2 21
B–K3 B–K4!** 22 K–R2 Not 22
P–QR4? P×P! 23 B–R6 R×BP∓
**22 . . . R/N2–B2 23 K–N3 R–N1 24
B–Q3** This is more accurate than
24 R–N4 P–B4 25 P×Pep P×P 26
P–KB4 P–B4 27 P×B P×R 28
P×P R–B2 29 B–K2 N–B3 which
gives rise to an unclear position.
24 . . . N–B5 25 B–K4 P–B4 Here
Black misses the opportunity for
25 . . . R–B5! 26 R–N4 P–R5+ 27
K–R2 N–R4 28 B–Q3 R×R 29
P×R N–B5 30 B–K4 R–QB1 with
the idea of 31 . . .R–B5=. **26
P×Pep P×P 27 R–N4 P–N4** (*247*)
28 R–N1?

It is better to retain the bishop
pair with 28 B–KB5± though after
28 . . . P–R4 29 R–N1 P–KR5 it is

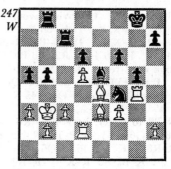

not easy to see how White would
make progress.
28 . . . N–R6!
28 . . . P–QN5? 29 RP×P! (29
BP×P? P×P 30 P–QR4 R–
B6+!∓) 29 . . . P×P 30 P–B4 (30
P×P? R2–QN2) 30 . . . R–R1 31
R2–Q1± only succeeds in weakening Black's Q-side pawn structure.
**29 R–K1 B–B5 30 B–KB5 B×B 31
R×B N–B5= 32 K–R2 K–B1?!**
32 . . . P–QN5 33 BP×P P×P 34
R–N3 R2–QN2 35 P×P R×P 36
R×R R×R 37 K–R3 only serves to
open up the position, giving White
excellent winning chances thanks to
his passed QNP.

However, 32 . . . P–R5, fixing the
Q-side pawns, is much better.
33 P–N4 P–R3 34 K–N2 R–K2?
Black's best chance of counterplay
lay in occupying the QR–file immediately by 34 . . . R–R1 followed
by 35 . . . R2–QR2, allowing the
white pieces as little scope as
possible, and constantly threatening
to penetrate to a3.
35 R×R K×R 36 K–N3± R–QR1
Better than both 36 . . . P–R5+?
and 36 . . . P×P 37 K×P, both of
which would only further weaken
Black's pawns.
**37 P–B4 RP×P 38 RP×P P×P+
39 K×P K–Q1 40 K–N5 K–B2**
If 40 . . . R–N1+ White can

abandon the QNP in favour of direct attack, e.g. 41 K–B6 R×P 42 K×P R–N3+ 43 K–B5 R–N1 (43 . . . R–N6 44 R–R2 and Black's rook must retreat to QN1 since 44 . . .R×P 45 R–R8+ and 46 P–Q6+ wins, while 44 . . . N–Q6+ 45 K–B4 – 45 *K–Q6?? R–N3 mate* – 45 . . . N–B8 46 R–R7 R×P 47 B–K6 and 48 P–Q6±±) 44 R–R2 R–N2 45 R–R8+ K–K2 46 P–Q6+ or 44 . . . K–B2 45 R–R7+ R–N2 46 P–Q6+ K–N1 47 P–Q7!

41 R–QB2+ K–N2 42 B–Q7!

42 R–B6? allows Black strong counterplay with 41 . . . N–K7!

42 . . . R–R6 43 R–B6! R–Q6

If 43 . . . N–K7 44 B–B8+ K–N1 45 K–N6 wins, e.g. 45 . . . N–B6 46 B–K6 N–R5+ 47 K–N5 N–B6+ 48 K–B4 N–K7 49 R×P R×P 50 R–N6+ and the advanced pawns win easily.

43 . . . N×P!? 44 R×P N×P! 45 K×N R×P± or 45 R×P!?±, though interesting, would not help Black survive in the long run. Also 43 . . . R×P 44 R–R6 N–Q6 45 B–B6+ K–B2 46 R–R7+ K–B1 47 K–R5 N–K4 (47 . . . R–B7 48 P–N5 R–R7+ 49 K–N6±±) 48 P–N5 leads to a win for White.

44 R–N6+ K–B2 45 B–B6 N×P 46 R–N7+ K–B1

46 . . . K–Q1 is no better: 47 R–Q7+ K–B1 48 R–KR7±±.

47 R–KB7

47 R–KR7! wins more quickly: (a) 47 . . . N–B5 48 R×P P–B4 49 R–B6 R–Q7 50 R×BP R×P 51 R×P±±. (b) 47 . . . K–Q1 48 R×P K–K2 49 K–B4 N–B5 50 R–R7+ K–Q1 (50 . . . K–K3? 51 B–Q7+; 50 . . . K–B1 51 P–N5) 51 R–KB7±±. (c) 47 . . . N–B2+ 48 K–N6 wins the knight. (d) 47 . . . N–B6+ 48 K–B4 R–K6 (48 . . . R–Q8 49 B–N7+ and 50 K×N) 49

K–Q4 N–Q8 50 B–R4 R–K8 51 R×P±±.

47 . . . K–Q1 48 R–Q7+ K–B1 49 R–KB7

Again 49 R–KR7!

49 . . . K–Q1 50 K–B4 N–B5 (*248*)

51 R×P

Not 51 P–N5 N–N3! and it is not clear any more that White is winning, e.g. 52 K×R (52 R–Q7+ K–B1 53 K×R N–K4+ 54 K–K4 N×R 55 K–B5 N–K4 56 B–Q5 K–B2 57 K×BP K–N3 and Black survives) 52 . . . N–K4+ 53 K–K4 N×R 54 K–B5 K–K2 55 P–N6 N–K456B–Q5N–Q2 57 P–N7 P–R4.

51 . . P–Q4+

If 51 . . . K–B2 52 K–N5! wins, but not 52 R×N? R–R6!=.

52 K–B5

And now not 52 B×P? N×B!=.

52 . . . K–K2 53 R×P R–B6+

If 53 . . . R×P 54 B×P wins.

54 K–N6 R×P 55 P–N5 P–N5?

After 55 . . . R–K6 or 55 . . . R–QN6± White still has clear winning chances, but now he has a clear win.

56 R–R4! R–KR6 57 R×P N–K7

There is no longer anything better: 57 . . . N–K3 58 B×P R×P 59 R–K4±±, or 57 . . . N–Q6 58 R–N3±±.

58 K–B7

White, though, could still go

wrong with 58 B×P? N–B6!= since Black can give up the knight for both the white pawns.
58 ... R–R2 59 P–N6 K–K3+ 60 K–Q8! N–Q5!

Ingenious, better than 60 ... K–Q3 61 R–N6+ K–B4 62 P–N7±±, but inadequate.
61 R×N K–Q3 62 B×P! K–B4

White's last move prevented the mate threat, now Black would be on the receiving end: 62 ... R–R1+ 63 B–N8+ K–B3 64 R–KN4±±, or 62 ... R×P 63 P–N7 R–R1+ 64 B–N8+ K–B3 65 P–N8=N+! K–N2 66 R–QN4+ K–R2 67 K–B7 wins.
63 R–Q2 K×P 64 R–QB2 1–0

2306 Nicolai Padevsky–AK:
FR4 v. Bulgaria:
30 September:

French

Karpov's only loss from this event:
1 P–K4 P–QB4 2 N–KB3 P–K3 3 P–B3 P–Q4 4 P×P P×P 5 P–Q4 B–Q3 6 P×P B×BP 7 B–K2?!
7 B–QN5 is preferable. **7 ... N–QB3 8 0–0 KN–K2 9 QN–Q2 0–0 10 N–N3 B–N3 11 N/B3–Q4?** 11 N/N3–Q4!= **11 ... N–N3 12 B–K3 R–K1 13 Q–B2 N/B3–K4 14 QR–Q1 B–Q2 15 N–Q2 N–N5 16 B×N B×B 17 QR–K1 R–QB1**
Also 17 ... N–R5 18 P–B3 B–KB4 **18 N2–B3 R–K5 19 Q–N3 Q–Q2 20 N–Q2 R5–K1 21 P–B3 B–K3 22 Q–Q1 B–B2 23 R–B2 Q–Q3 24 N–B1 Q–R3 25 P–KB4 B–Q2 26 Q–N1 B–N4!∓ 27 N×B Q×N 28 P–KN3 R–K5 29 B–Q4 R×R?!**
29 ... R1–K1 was much stronger: 30 R×R P×R 31 N–K3 N–B1! 32 P–B5 N–Q2 with ... N–B4∓ to follow. **30 Q×R R–K1 31 Q–Q1= P–QR4 32 N–K3 R–K5 33 Q–N3 Q×Q** Perhaps it was better to go for a draw by 33 ... Q–Q6 34 Q×NP

R×N 35 B×R Q×B 36 Q–B8+ N–B1 37 Q×B Q–K8+ with a draw by perpetual check. **34 P×Q** Now White is better – Black's weak isolated QP is the most important feature of the position. **34 ... N–K2 35 R–Q2 P–R4 36 K–B2 R–K3 37 K–B3 P–KN3 38 B–B5 B–N3?** The last chance to keep the game level was 38 ... B–Q3!= **39 P–QN4 P×P 40 P×P** (*249*)

40 ... B×B 41 P×B P–N3 42 P–QN4 P×P 43 P×P K–B1 There is nothing better as 43 ... R–QB3 44 N×P N–B4 fails to 45 R–QB2! N–Q5+ 46 K–K4 N×R 47 N–K7+ and wins. **44 N×P R–QB3** But now Black should follow the plan of the previous note with 44 ... N–B4 (with the idea 45 ... R–QB3) 45 K–B2! R–R3 46 N–N6 K–K2! making White's task more difficult. **45 N×N K×N 46 R–QB2±± K–Q2 47 K–K4 R–B3** Or 47 ... R–R3 48 P–B6+ R×P 49 R×R K×R 50 K–K5 K–Q2 51 K–B6 K–K1 52 P–B5 P×P 53 P–R4!±± **48 R–R2 R–B4 49 R–R7+! K–K1 50 R–R5 K–Q1 51 K–Q4** 51 P–R4 is more accurate. **51 ... P–R5 52 R–R8+ K–B2 53 R–R7+ K–B3** If 53 ... K–B1 then 54 R–K7±± **54 K–K4! R×QBP 55 R×P R–B7 56 R–B6+ K–Q2 57 R×P R×P 58 P–N4 P–R6 59 R–KR6 R–R8 60**

**K–B5 P–R7 61 P–N5 K–K2 62
P–N6 R–R8** The black king can do
no more: if 62 . . . K–B1 63 K–B6
K–N1 64 P–N7 and mates. **63
R–R7+ K–B1 64 R×P R–R4+
65 K–B6 1–0**

2307 Alexander Sznapik–AK:
FR6 v. Poland: 2 October:

King's Indian Attack

**1 P–K4 P–QB4 2 N–KB3 P–K3
3 P–Q3 N–QB3 4 P–KN3 P–Q4 5
QN–Q2 B–Q3 6 B–N2 KN–K2 7
0–0 0–0 8 R–K1** 8 N–KR4! is more
aggressive, e.g. 8 . . . P–QN3?!
(better 8 . . . P×P) 9 P–KB4 P×P
10 P×P B–R3 11 R–K1 P–B5 12
P–B3 N–R4 13 P–K5 B–B4+ 14
K–R1 N–Q4 15 N–K4± Fischer–
Ivkov, Santa Monica 1966. **8 . . .
B–B2 9 P–B3** 9 N–R4! is still
correct, e.g. 9 . . . P–QN3?! 10
P–KB4 B–N2 11 P–B3 Q–Q2 12
P–K5 P–QN4? (12 . . . N–N3 and if
13 Q–R5 N×N 14 Q×N P–B3!
still gave chances of holding out) 13
Q–R5±± Ciocaltea-Jansa, Tel
Aviv 1964. **9 . . . P–QN3** The most
logical, though 9 . . . P–QN4 and
9 . . . P–QR4 have both been tried.
10 P–K5 Ciocaltea-Ivkov, Sarajevo
1964 continued 10 P–QR3 B–R3 11
P×P N×P 12 N–B4 Q–Q2 13
Q–B2 QR–Q1= **10 . . . P–QR4**
Avoiding the dubious line 10 . . .
N–N3?! 11 P–Q4 P×P 12 P×P
N–N5 13 N–B1± **11 N–B1 B–R3 12
P–KR4 P–Q5 13 P–B4 Q–Q2!** It
is best to ignore the KP for the time
being: 13 . . . N–N3 14 P–R5
N/N3×P 15 N×N N×N 16 B–B4!
N–Q2 (16 . . . P–B3 is even worse:
17 B×R Q×B 18 B×N B×B 19
P–B4 B–B2 20 R×P wins) 17 B×R
B×B 18 B–N2± **14 N1–R2** 14
P–R5!? is worth playing first. **14 . . .
P–B4** (*250*) Other possibilities are

14 . . . N–N3 15 N–N4 P–R4 16
N–N5 unclear, and also tackling the
KP by 14 . . . P–B3!?

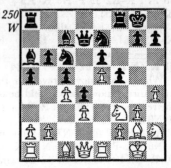

250
W

15 P×Pep? Now Black's pieces
begin to flood into active positions.
Better 15 P–R4!± keeping the
position closed. **15 . . . P×P∓ 16 N–
N4** If 16 B–R3 N–B4 17 N–N4 K–R1
is more than adequate **16 . . . P–K4!
17 B–R3 Q–K1** 17 . . . Q–Q3 is
also possible. **18 B–R6 R–B2 19
B–Q2** 19 B–N5 doesn't work: 19 . . .
P×B 20 N–R6+ K–R1 21 N×R+
Q×N 22 N×NP Q–N3 23 Q–B3
B–N2 **19 . . . K–R1∓ 20 K–R2
B–B1** Threatening to embarrass the
advanced white knight by 21 . . .
P–R4 **21 Q–K2 B–Q2 22 N–N1
P–B4 23 N–R6 R–N2 24 B–N5
Q–N3 25 B–N2 N–KN1 26 N×N** If
26 Q–Q2 then simply 26 . . . N–B3.
26 . . . R1×N 27 Q–Q2 (*251*)

251
B

27 . . . P–B5 Winning **28 B–K4 Q–Q3 29 Q–K2 B–K1 30 B–Q5 R–B1 31 P×P** If 31 N–B3 then 31 . . . P–R3 32 K–N2 B–R4 is decisive. **31 . . . P–R3** 31 . . . P×P would be too hasty: 32 N–B3 with 33 Q×B to follow **32 P×P Q×P! 33 Q×Q N×Q 34 P–B4 N–N5+ 35 K–N3** Or 35 K–R3 N–B7+ **35 . . . N–K6 0–1**

2308 AK–Dan Uddenfeldt:
FR7 v. Sweden: 3 October:

Sicilian

1 P–K4 P–QB4 2 N–KB3 P–Q3 3 P–Q4 P×P 4 N×P N–KB3 5 N–QB3 P–QR3 6 P–B4 It just does not pay to use the same line *every* time, so 6 B–K2 is given a rest. **6 . . . Q–B2 7 B–Q3 P–K3**

Zandor Nilsson criticizes this as being passive, suggesting as better 7 . . . P–K4 or 7 . . . QN–Q2 and 8 . . . P–K4. Karpov and Gufeld, however, consider that against 7 . . . P–K4 8 N–B3 followed by K–side castling is favourable for White. **8 0–0 B–K2 9 N–B3!**

Another popular treatment is 9 B–K3 followed by 10 Q–B3. **9 . . . QN–Q2** 9 . . . N–B3!? **10 Q–K1**

Supporting 11 P–K5 and also ready to move out on to the K–side. **10 . . . N–B4!? 11 P–K5! N3–Q2 12 Q–N3 P–KN3**

12 . . . 0–0!? is asking for trouble: 13 P–B5 and now:
(a) 13 . . . N×B 14 P–B6 and it's all over;
(b) 13 . . . N×P 14 N×N P×N 15 P–B6 and, again, it's all over;
(c) 13 . . . QP×P 14 B–R6 B–B3 15 B–K3 P–QN4 16 QR–Q1±;
(d) 13 . . . KP×P? 14 B–R6 B–B3 15 N–Q5 and the pieces are ready to be set up for another game.

12 . . . N×B also loses, this time to

13 Q×P Q–N3+ 14 K–R1 N–B7+ 15 R×N Q×R 16 Q×R+ and 17 B–Q2.

13 B–K3

Now if 13 P–B5 Black can hold out with possibility (d) below:
(a) 13 . . . QP×P 14 P×NP RP×P 15 B×NP P×B 16 Q×NP+ K–Q1 17 N–KN5±±;
(b) 13 . . . NP×P 14 Q–N7±;
(c) 13 . . . KP×P 14 N–Q5±;
(d) 13 . . . N×B! 14 P×KP N6×KP 15 P×N+ B×P.

13 . . . P–QN4

13 . . . 0–0 is jumping straight from the frying pan into the fire: 14 P–B5 N×B 15 P–B6 N6×KP 16 P×B R–K1 17 Q–R4± with a fierce attack.

14 B–Q4!

Stronger than 14 QR–Q1 (the idea behind which is 15 P×P B×P 16 B×QNP) 14 . . . P×P meeting the threat very simply, or 14 P×P!? B×P 15 QR–Q1. The latter, though is quite strong.

14 . . . N×B 15 P×N

Now if 15 P×P B×P 16 B×R then 16 . . . N×BP 17 Q–R4 B–N2 lets Black off the hook.

15 . . . P–Q4?

This makes matters even worse, but 15 . . . P×P, the only alternative, is not very appetizing: 16 N×KP (16 P×P is also good: 16 . . . B–N2 17 QR–B1±) and now:
(a) 16 . . . N–B3 17 N–N4 Q–Q1 18 B–K5±;
(b) 16 . . . B–B3 17 N–K4±;
(c) 16 . . . B–B4 17 B×Q Q×B+ 18 K–R1 N×N 19 N–K4±;
(d) 16 . . . N×N 17 B×N Q–N3+; 17 P×N B–N2 is probably the best of a bad lot.

16 QR–B1 Q–N2 (*252*)
17 P–B5!±± NP×P

17 . . . KP×P is no better: 18 P–K6 N–B3 19 P×P+ K×P 20

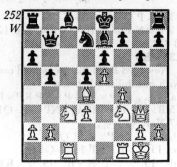

252
W

N–N5+   K–N2   21   KR–K1±±
R–K1 22 R×B+ R×R 23 Q–Q6
**18 Q–N7 R–B1 19 N–N5 B×N 20
Q×B Q–N1 21 N–K2 B–N2**
    If 21 . . . N×P? 22 R×B+ Q×R
23 B×N
22 N–B4 Q–Q1 23 Q–R5!
    Threatening 24 N×KP
23 . . . K–K2 24 Q×RP
    Now the threat is 25 N–N6+
24 . . . K–K1
    24 . . . R–KN1 allows 25 N×KP!
K×N 26 Q×P/B5+ K–K2 27
Q×P mate.
25 N–R5 Q–N4 26 R–B7 R–N1 (*253*)
    26 . . . B–B1 doesn't help: 27
R1–B1, nor does 26 . . . R–KN1 27
N–B6+.

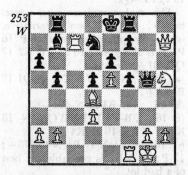

253
W

27 N–N7+ 1–0 27 . . . K–K2 (27
. . . K–Q1 28 N×KP+) 28 B–B5+
K–Q1 29 N×KP+ P×N 30 Q×N
mate.

2309 AK–Heinz Wirtensohn:
    FR8 v. Switzerland:
    4 October:

Sicilian

**1 P–K4 P–QB4 2 N–KB3 P–Q3
3 P–Q4 P×P 4 N×P N–KB3 5
N–QB3 P–QR3 6 P–B4 P–K4 7
N–B3 QN–Q2**
    Better 7 . . . Q–B2 to prevent . . .
**8 B–B4 B–K2 9 P–QR4 0–0 10
P–B5?!**
    10 0–0!? is probably better.
10 . . . P–QN3 11 B–K3
    Alternatives do not work out well
for White:
(a) 11 B–KN5 B–N2 12 B×N N×B
13 Q–K2 P–QN4! (Not 13 . . .
N×KP? 14 N×N P–Q4 15 R–Q1
or 13 . . . Q–B2 14 0–0 N×KP 15
N×N P–Q4 16 B–Q3 P×N 17
B×KP=) 14 B–N3 Q–N3∓;
(b) 11 B–Q5 N×B 12 N×N B–N2
13 P–B4 and 13 . . . N–B4 with 14 . . .
P–QN4 to follow is comfortable for
Black.
11 . . . B–N2 12 N–Q2 P–Q4
    An interesting possibility, pointed
out by Karpov, is 12 . . . Q–B2!?
13 Q–K2 P–QN4 (also 13 . . . N–B4
14 B–B2 KR–B1 or 14 B×N
Q×B∓) 14 B–N3 N–B4 (and here
14 . . . P–N5!? 15 N–Q5 N×N 16
P×N N–B3 is not bad) 15 B×N
P×B (15 . . . Q×B is correct) 16
P×P P×P 17 R×R R×R 18
N×P Q–B3 19 0–0 N×P 20 N×N
Q×N/K5 21 Q×Q B×Q 22 R–K1.
**13 N×P N×N 14 B×N B×B 15
P×B B–B4**
    If 15 . . . N–B4 then White has 16
P–B4! (but not 16 Q–B3? P–K5 17
N×P N×N 18 Q×N R–K1 and
Black wins) 16 . . . N–Q6+ 17
K–K2 N–B5+ (or 17 . . . N×P 18
Q–N3±±) 18 K–B3 with an
excellent game.

16 Q–K2 Q–R5+ 17 P–KN3 Q–QN5∓ 18 0–0

If 18 R–R2 B×B 19 Q×B N–B3 20 P–B4 KR–B1 21 0–0 N–N5 22 Q–K2 Q–B4+ 23 K–R1 N–K6 is clearly very good for Black.

18 . . . Q×NP 19 P–B4 P–B3

19 . . . P–QN4!? was a possibility.

20 K–R1

Avoiding 20 Q–Q3? P–K5!

20 . . . KR–B1

Now 20 . . . Q–B6!? could be tried.

21 Q–Q3 B×B 22 Q×B P–QR4 23 KR–B1

Or 23 QR–N1 Q–B7

23 . . . Q–N5

And here 23 . . . Q–Q5!?

24 R/B1–QN1 Q–B4 25 Q×Q R×Q 26 K–N2 = (254)

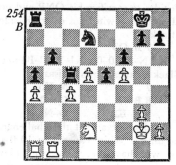

26 . . . K–B1

Black should probably try one of the alternatives: 26 . . . P–K5 27 K–B2 N–K4, or 26 . . . P–R4!?

27 K–B3 K–K2 28 P–N4 R–R1 29 P–R4± R–KB1 30 K–K3 P–R3 31 R–N1 R4–B1 32 R/R1–N1 R–QN1 33 N–K4± R/N1–B1

If 33 . . . R/B1–B1 then not 34 P–N5?! RP×P 35 P×P R×P 36 P–Q6+ (or 36 P×P+ N×P! 37 R×KNP+ K–B1) 36 . . . K–B2 37 P–N6+ K–B1, but simply 34 R/KN1–QB1±.

34 R/KN1–QB1 R/KB1–K1 35

R–N5 R/K1–Q1 36 K–Q3 K–B1? **37 P–N5 RP×P 38 P×P K–K2 39 R–KN1 R–KR1**

If 39 . . . R–KN1 then 40 P–Q6+ K–B1 41 P×P P×P 42 R×R+ K×R 43 P–B5 wins.

40 P×P+ P×P 41 R–N7+ K–Q1 42 N–Q6 R–R6+ 43 K–K2 R–R7+ 44 K–K3 1–0 44 . . . R–B2 (44 . . . R–N1 45 R–QN1 with R1/N1 to follow) 45 R–N8+ K–K2 46 R–K8+ K×N 47 R–K6 mate.

2310 AK–Vlastimil Jansa:

FR9 v. Czechoslovakia:

5 October:

Sicilian

1 P–K4 P–QB4 2 N–KB3 P–K3 3 P–Q4 P×P 4 N×P N–QB3 5 N–N5 P–Q3 6 P–QB4 N–B3 7 N1–B3 P–QR3 8 N–R3 B–K2 9 B–K2 0–0 10 0–0 P–QN3 11 B–K3 B–N2 12 R–B1

Better than 12 Q–Q2!? N–K4 13 P–B3 R–K1=.

12 . . . N–K4 13 Q–Q4 N4–Q2 14 KR–Q1!?

Stronger than 14 P–B3?! when Black can free himself with 14 . . . P–Q4! 15 KP×P P×P 16 P×P B–B4 17 Q–Q2 B×B+ 18 Q×B N×P=.

14 . . . Q–B2

Better than 14 . . . P–K4? 15 Q–Q3 N–B4 16 B×N±. However, 14 . . . R–K1 and 14 . . . R–B1 were also possible.

15 P–B3 KR–K1 16 P–QN4!±

On 16 Q–Q2 Black gets a good game from 16 . . . QR–B1 followed by . . . Q–N1.

16 . . . QR–N1

Or 16 . . . QR–B1 17 N/R3–N1 Q–N1 18 N–R4±.

17 N/R3–N1 B–R1 18 P–QR3 B–B1 19 N–Q2 P–R3 20 P–B4?! R/N1–B1?! 21 Q–Q3

White may also get an advantage from 21 P–K5 P×P 22 P×P N×P 23 Q×P, but it is not very clear.

21 . . . Q–N1 22 R–B2 R/K1–Q1 23 B–B3 B–N2 24 R1–QB1 K–R1! 25 Q–K2 B–K2 26 P–KR4 R–K1 27 Q–B2 B–R1

Black aims for . . . P–QN4.

28 Q–K2

28 P–N4 P–KN4!? 29 BP×P P×P 30 B×KNP R–N1 is unclear

28 . . . N–N1 29 P–N3 B–KB3 30 Q–Q3 R/K1–Q1 31 K–N2 B–K2 32 N–Q1 R–B2 33 B–Q4 B–KB3 (255)

Not 33 . . . P–K4? 34 B–B2±, but 33 . . . R1–QB1 with . . . P–QN4 to follow could be tried

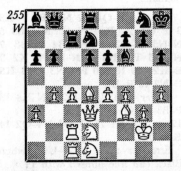

34 B×B N1×B 35 N–B2 R2–B1 36 N–B1

36 P–N4 P–KN4 leads to an unclear position.

36 . . . B–B3± 37 N–K3 P–QN4 38 P–N4

Or 38 P×P B×NP 39 R×R R×R 40 R×R+ Q×R 41 Q×P Q–B8.

38 . . . N–N3= 39 P–N5 NP×P 40 N×P N–N1 ½–½

2311 AK–Jens Enevoldsen:

FR10 v. Denmark: 7 October:

French

1 P–K4	**P–K3**
2 P–Q4	**P–Q4**

3 N–Q2   **P–KB4?!**

This move is rare in tournament play. The theoretical continuation is now 4 P×BP P×P 5 Q–R5+ P–KN3 6 Q–K2+ Q–K2 7 N2–B3 with an advantage in the coming endgame. 4 P–K5 also gives White the advantage, but Karpov did not want a blocked position.

4 P×BP	**P×P**
5 N2–B3	**N–KB3**
6 B–KN5	

The characteristic move of this variation. Of course 6 B–Q3!? followed by 7 N–K2 and 8 0–0 also gives White a clear advantage.

6 . . .   **B–K2**

The only satisfactory move. White was threatening Q–K2+ followed by capturing on KB6. Now Karpov decides to sacrifice his QNP and go all out for a win by a direct K-side attack.

7 B–Q3

If 7 N–K5 0–0 8 N1–B3 P–B4 and Black escapes a quick disaster.

7 . . .	**N–K5**
8 B×B	**Q×B**
9 N–K2	**Q–N5+**

Black must accept the challenge, because if White can get in 10 0–0 he will have very powerful play against Black's weak squares on the K-side. Thus 9 . . . 0–0 10 0–0 with 11 P–QB4± is very good for White.

10 P–B3	**Q×NP**
11 0–0	**0–0**

If Black takes the second pawn he gets taken apart: 11 . . . N×QBP 12 N×N Q×N 13 R–B1 and 14 R–K1+. The black knight at K5 is the bulwark of his position and cannot be exchanged for such a small material gain.

12 P–B4±   **P×P**

With 12 . . . P–B3 13 N–B4, Black ties himself down to the defence of the QP. He could still defend it by:

(a) 13 . . . R–Q1 14 R–B1±;

(b) 13 . . . P–KN4? 14 B×N BP×B 15 N×NP R×N 16 Q–R5 Q×QP (16 . . . B–B4 17 Q–B7+ K–R1 18 Q–B8 mate) 17 Q×RP+ K–B1 18 Q–QB7!;

(c) 13 . . . N–KB3, but then 14 R–B1 is very strong, giving White play on the QB-file after the exchange of pawns on d5.

13 B×P+   K–R1
14 R–N1

The alternatives are:

(a) 14 Q–Q3 Q–N3;

(b) 14 N–K5 N–QB3 15 N–B7+ K–N1 16 R–N1 Q–Q7 17 Q–N3 N–R4.

14 . . .   Q–R6
15 N–K5   P–KN3

The only defence against the threat of N–N6+ followed by R–N3 and mate at KR3; e.g. 15 . . . N–QB3?? 16 N–N6+ P×N 17 R–N3±± with 18 R–KR3 mate to follow.

16 R–N3   Q–K2
17 N–B4   K–N2
18 R–KR3! (*256*)

White has two threats: 19 R×P+ and 19 N4×P.

18 . . .   N–QB3

Black can defend against both threats by 18 . . . N–N4 but after 19 R–K3 Q–Q1 20 R1–K1 his position is hopeless. Also 18 . . . Q–N4 19 Q–B1 wins.

19 N4×P

An inaccuracy. White misses a beautiful win: 19 R×P+ K×R 20 N4×P (20 N5×P Q–Q3 21 N×R+ Q×N/1 22 Q–R5+ fails to mate after 22 . . . K–N2) 20 . . . Q–Q3 (or 20 . . . N×N 21 N×Q N×B 22 Q–R5+ K–N2 23 Q–N6+ K–R1 24 Q–R6 mate) 21 N×R+ K–N2 (if 21 . . . Q×N/1 then 22 Q–R5+ Q–R3 23 B–N8+ K–N2 24 Q–B7+ K–R1 25 N–N6+) 22 Q–R5 N×N 23 Q–R7+ K×N 24 P×N! (the move that Karpov missed over the board) 24 . . . Q–Q2 25 Q–N8+ K–K2 26 Q–B7+ K–Q1 27 Q–B8+ Q–K1 28 R–Q1+ B–Q2 29 Q×P followed by P–K6.

19 . . .   P×N
20 N×P   Q–B3!

The only way to keep control of KR1. If 20 . . . Q–N4 21 N×R K×N 22 R–R8+ K–K2 23 R–K1.

21 N×R   K×N
22 R–R7   N–K2?

A better try was 22 . . . N–N4 when 23 R×P does not work because of 23 . . . Q–Q3 and so Karpov had intended to play 23 R–R5 B–K3 and now:

(a) not 24 R×N B×B 25 Q–R5 N–K2∓;

(b) and not 24 P–Q5 B–B2 25 P×N B×B 26 P×P R–N1 27 Q–B1 B×R 28 Q×P R×P 29 Q×R B–K7 when Black has defended himself successfully;

(c) but 24 B×B N×B 25 P–Q5 R–Q1 26 Q–N3 N/K3–Q5 27 Q×P R×P 28 Q×BP±.

23 R–K1

There was no point to winning the queen by 23 R–B7+.

23 . . .   Q–N3
24 R–B7+   Q×R

If 24 . . . K–K1 25 P–B3 B–K3 26 B×B Q×B 27 R–R7.

25 B×Q   K×B

26 Q–R5+   K–B1
27 Q–R6+   K–B2

Or 27 . . . K–K1 28 P–B3 N–QB6
29 R×N+ K×R 30 Q–K3+
K–B2 31 Q×N wins.

28 Q–R7+   1–0

2312 Arthur Bisguier–AK:
FR12 v. USA: 9 October:

English

**1 P–QB4 P–QB4 2 N–QB3
P–KN3 3 N–B3 B–N2 4 P–K3** If 4
P–Q4 then 4 . . . P×P 5 N×P
N–QB3 is all right for Black. **4 . . .
N–KB3 5 P–Q4 0–0 6 B–K2 P×P
7 P×P P–Q4 8 0–0** 8 B–N5?! is not
so good because of 8 . . . P×P 9
B×P B–N5 and 10 . . . N–B3. **8 . . .
N–B3 9 P–KR3** If 9 P–B5 then 9 . . .
N–K5!? – Gufeld **9 . . . B–B4** Or
9 . . . P×P 10 B×P N–QR4 11
B–K2 B–K3± **10 B–K3 P×P 11
B×P R–B1± 12 B–K2 B–K3**
Gufeld gives this an exclamation
mark and assesses the position as
already slightly better for Black,
while Karpov in *Informator* gives 12
. . . N–Q4 13 Q–N3 N×N 14 P×N
N–R4 15 Q–N4 B–K3; 13 . . .
N×B 14 P×B±; or 12 . . . N–QN5
13 Q–N3. **13 Q–Q2** If 13 N–KN5
then 13 . . . B–Q4 is good for Black.
13 . . . Q–R4 Stronger than 13 . . .
N–QR4 14 P–QN3. **14 B–KR6?!
KR–Q1 15 B×B K×B 16 KR–Q1
R–Q3! 17 Q–K3 R1–Q1 18 P–R3**
Already White must be careful, e.g.
18 N–QN5 R–Q4 19 N–B3 R4–Q2
20 N–K5? R×P 21 N×N
R×R+∓∓. A sharp tactical strug-
gle is beginning. **18 . . . B–N6∓ 19
R–Q2** 19 N–QN5 fails to 19 . . .
B×N 20 N×R B×B 21 N×NP
Q–N3 22 N×R B×N. **19 . . . R–K3
20 Q–B4 N–Q4 21 N×N R×N 22
P–N4** White defends against the
threat of 23 . . . R–KB4 followed by

24 . . . R×N and 25 . . . Q×R. If
22 B–Q3 Black gets the advantage by
22 . . . R–B3 23 Q–K3 R×N 24
P×R N×QP. This threatens 25 . . .
Q×R and 26 . . . N×P+ and if
25 B–K4 there comes the bone-
crusher 25 . . . Q×R 26 B×R B×B!
27 Q–K5+ (27 Q×Q N×P+)
27 . . . K–R3. **22 . . . P–KN4 23
Q–N3 R–B3 24 B–Q1** White loses
a pawn after 24 R–Q3 B–B5 25
R–K3 B×B 26 R×B R×N 27
Q×R N×P followed by 28 . . .
N×R+. **24 . . . B–B5** After 24 . . .
R×N 25 Q×R Q×R 26 B×B the
weakness of Black's KB2 is fatally
exposed. **25 P–N3 B–R3** Of course I
would have liked to have taken the
knight but after 25 . . . R×N 26
B×R Q×R White does not play 27
R–Q1 allowing Black to finish him
off with 27 . . . Q–B6 28 P×B R×P
29 R×R N×R 30 Q–K5+ K–R3!
but instead hurries to exchange his
bishop and draws by 27 P×B R×P
28 B×N P×B 29 Q–K5+.
26 P–N4 Q–Q1 27 B–N3 (*257*)

257
B

It looks as though the American
grandmaster is winning, but Black
has a powerful tactical riposte. **27
. . . N×QP 28 R×N** Bisguier does
not wish to lose in a long and
gruelling endgame a pawn down
after 28 B×R N×N+ 29 B×N
Q×R 30 R–Q1 Q–B6 and rushes

precipitously to his doom. **28 . . .
R×R 29 N×P R–Q6 30 Q–R4
P–R3 31 N×P Q–Q5 32 R–K1
R×RP! 0–1**

2313 AK–Fernando Visier:
FR13 v. Spain: 10 October:

Sicilian:

**1 P–K4 P–QB4 2 N–KB3 P–K3 3
P–Q4 P×P 4 N×P P–QR3 5
B–Q3 Q–B2 6 0–0 N–QB3 7 N×N
NP×N 8 P–KB4 P–Q4 9 N–Q2
N–B3 10 Q–K2 B–K2 11 P–QN3
0–0 12 B–N2 P–QR4 13 R–B3
B–R3 14 P–B3 KR–K1 15 R1–KB1
P–N3 16 K–R1 P–R5 17 R–R3
RP×P 18 RP×P B–N2 19 B–N1
P×P 20 N×P N×N 21 B×N
R–R7 22 B–N1** (*258*)

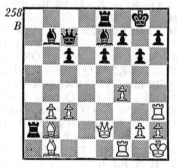

**22 . . . R×B 23 Q×R P–QB4 24
Q–K2 R–Q1 25 R–Q3 R×R 26
B×R Q–B3 27 R–K1 B–R5 28
B–K4 Q–N3 29 R–QN1 B–KB3 30
B×B Q×B 31 Q–Q3 Q–N3 32
P–B4 B–K2 33 Q–B3 Q–B2 34
R–KB1 B–Q3 35 Q–K3 P–R4
36 P–N3 B–K2 37 P–R3 B–B3 38
P–KN4 P×P 39 P×P K–N2 40
Q–KB3 Q–B1 41 K–N2 Q–R3 42
K–R3 Q–B1 43 R–Q1 Q–KR1+ 44
K–N2 Q–QB1 45 R–Q6 Q–QN1 46
R–Q7 B–Q5 47 P–B5 KP×P 48
P×P 1–0**

2314 Hase–AK: FR14 v. Argentine:
11 October:

Centre Game

**1 P–K4 P–K4 2 P–Q4 P×P 3
Q×P N–QB3 4 Q–K3 P–Q3?!** 4
. . . N–KB3 is best. Also 4 . . .
P–KN3 and 4 . . . B–N5+ are
acceptable. **5 N–QB3 N–B3 6
B–Q2 B–K2 7 0–0–0 0–0 8
Q–N3**±/± **P–QR3 9 P–B4 P–QN4
10 P–K5 N–Q2 11 N–B3 R–N1?!**
Better 11 . . . N–N3!? **12 N–Q5**
Interesting would be 12 P–KR4!?
**12 . . . N–B4 13 B–K3 N–K5 14
Q–K1 P–B4 15 P–KR3 B–K3 16
R–N1 K–R1 17 P–KN4 QP×P
18 N×B Q×N 19 N×P N×N 20
P×N R/N1–Q1 21 B–Q3 B–Q4**
(*259*) ½–½

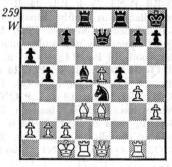

White could well continue with 22
P×P Q×P 23 Q–R4±.

2315 AK–Ungureanu:
FR15 v. Romania: 12 October:
Sicilian

**1 P–K4 P–QB4 2 N–KB3 N–QB3
3 P–Q4 P×P 4 N×P N–B3 5
N–QB3 P–Q3 6 B–KN5 P–K3 7
Q–Q2 B–K2 8 0–0–0 0–0 9 P–B4
N×N 10 Q×N Q–R4** Nowadays
10 . . . P–KR3 is thought best. **11
B–B4**± More promising than 11
P–K5 P×P 12 Q×KP Q×Q 13
P×Q N–Q4 14 B×B N×B=. **11**

... B–Q2 12 P–K5 P×P 13 P×P B–B3 14 B–Q2! During the past few years this move has taken over from 14 Q–KB4 N–R4 15 Q–KR4 B×B+ 16 Q×B P–KN3 with an unclear position. 'Also ran' possibilities are 14 B×N P×B which is probably good for Black, and 14 P–KR4 KR–Q1 unclear. **14 ... N–Q2** Not 14 ... KR–Q1? when 15 N–Q5 R×N 16 B×Q wins. **15 N–Q5 Q–Q1 16 N×B+ Q×N 17 KR–K1** 17 P–KR4!? is interesting, but the text is probably the strongest move here. **17 ... KR–B1** Or 17 ... Q–B4 18 Q–B4 B–N4 19 B–N3 P–QR4 20 P–QR4 B–B3 and White's K-side attack is again irresistible: 21 R–K3 QR–B1 22 B–B3 P–QN4 23 R–N3 KR–K1 (23 ... P×P 24 Q–R6 P–N3 25 R–R3) 24 R–B1 and Black was swiftly dispatched, Kavalek-Benko, Netanya 1969. **18 Q–B4** Apparently new and stronger than both 18 P–KR4± Q–B4 and 18 Q–N4 Q–B4. **18 ... P–QR4** If 18 ... Q–B4 then 19 B–Q3. **19 K–N1 N–N3** After 19 ... P–QN4 White has a choice between 20 B–KB1± and 20 B–Q3 N–B4 with unclear complications looming. **20 B–Q3 N–Q4 21 Q–KN4 Q–B4?!** Black should try 21 ... P–QN4 or 21 ... N–N5!? 22 B–KR6 Q–B1±. **22 R–K4! P–QN4** Now it is too late, e.g. 22 ... N–N5 23 R–QB4 Q–K2 (23 ... Q×KP 24 B–B3 P–R4 25 Q–R4±) 24 B×N and

White is well on top. **23 Q–R3!** Threatening simply 24 R–KR4, and also 24 Q×RP+ K×Q 25 R–QB4+. **23 ... N–N5** *(260)*

260
W

24 B–K3! This wins and is therefore better than retaining a large advantage with 24 R×N P×R 25 Q×RP+ K–B1 26 Q–R8+ K–K2 27 Q–R4+ P–N4 or 24 B×N P×B 25 Q×RP+ K×Q 26 R–QB4+. **24 ... B×R** If 24 ... Q–K2 (or 24 ... Q–Q4 25 R×N P×R 26 B×RP+ K–B1 27 R×Q±±) 25 R×N Q×R 26 P–R3! Q–QR5 (or 26 ... Q–K2 27 Q×RP+ K–B1 Q–R8 mate) 27 Q×RP+ K–B1 28 B–QB5+ K–K1 29 Q–N8+ K–Q2 30 Q×BP+ K–Q1 31 Q–K7 mate. **25 B×B** Stronger than 25 B×Q B×B 26 P×B R×B±. **25 ... Q×KP 26 Q×RP+ K–B1 27 B×R K–K2** If 27 ... P–N3 28 R–KB1 wins, or 27 ... R×B 28 Q–R8+ K–K2 29 Q×R Q×B 30 Q–Q8 mate. **28 Q–K4 Q–B2 29 Q–N7 1–0**

24 SAN ANTONIO

Church's Fried Chicken

		1	2	3	4	5	6	7	8	9	0	1	2	3	4	5	6	
1	**Karpov**	×	½	0	1	½	½	1	½	½	1	1	½	½	1	1	1	10½
2	Petrosian	½	×	½	1	½	½	½	1	1	½	½	½	1	½	1	1	10½
3	Portisch	1	½	×	0	1	1	½	1	½	½	½	½	1	½	1	1	10½
4	Gligorić	0	0	1	×	½	½	1	½	½	1	1	½	½	1	1	1	10
5	Keres	½	½	0	½	×	1	½	1	1	1	½	0	½	1	1	½	9½
6	Hort	½	½	0	½	0	×	½	0	1	½	1	½	1	1	1	1	9
7	Suttles	0	½	½	0	½	½	×	½	½	½	½	1	1	1	1	1	9
8	Larsen	½	0	0	½	0	1	½	×	0	1	0	1	1	1	1	1	8½
9	Mecking	½	0	½	½	0	0	½	1	×	½	1	½	1	1	½	1	8½
10	D. Byrne	0	½	½	0	0	½	½	0	½	×	0	1	½	1	1	1	7
11	Browne	0	½	½	0	½	0	½	1	0	1	×	½	1	0	0	1	6½
12	Evans	½	½	½	½	1	½	0	0	½	0	½	×	0	½	½	1	6½
13	Kaplan	½	½	0	½	½	0	0	0	0	½	0	1	×	1	½	0	5
14	Campos-Lopez	0	0	½	0	0	0	0	0	0	0	1	½	0	×	1	½	3½
15	Saidy	0	0	0	0	0	0	0	0	½	0	1	½	½	0	×	1	3½
16	Smith	0	0	0	0	½	0	0	0	0	0	0	0	1	½	0	×	2

The growing interest in Karpov, and his future potential, was noted by the late Kühnle -Woods in *Chess Express*: 'The chess world was eager to see how Karpov would fare, who is already now and somewhat prematurely labelled as opponent for Fischer in 1975. He did not disappoint and captured first place.'

Karpov's share of the prize money was $2,333.30.

2401 Anthony Saidy–AK:
R1: 19 November:

King's Indian Reversed

1 N–KB3 N–KB3 2 P–KN3 P–QN4 3 B–N2 B–N2 4 0–0 There is nothing wrong with this, but perhaps better is 4 P–Q4 P–K3 5 P–B3 P–B4 6 0–0 Q–N3!? 7 P–QR4 P–N5 8 QN–Q2 BP×P 9 P–R5! Q–N4! 10 N×P Q–R3 11 P–K4!± **4 . . . P–K3 5 P–Q3 B–K2** 5 . . . P–Q4 6 QN–Q2 B–K2 7 P–K4 0–0 8 Q–K2 P–B4 9 R–K1 N–B3 10 P–B3 P–QR4 11 P×P P×P 12 P–Q4 Q–N3 has not had a good reputation since Bilek-Tal, Moscow 1967, which Tal won . . . but probably from a lost position. 6 **P–K4** 6 P–N3!? is interesting – Keene used it to draw with Spassky at Lugano 1968. **6 . . .P–Q3! 7 P–QR4** Departing from previously known theory which was 7 R–K1 0–0 8 QN–Q2 QN–Q2 9 P–B3 P–QR3 10 Q–K2 P–B4 11 N–B1

Q–B2 12 N–K3 KR–K1 13 N–Q2 P–Q4! Rubinetti–Larsen, Palma 1970. **7 . . . P–QR3** 7 . . . P–N5 might also be played. **8 P×P P×P 9 R×R B×R 10 N–R3 P–N5 11 N–B4± 0–0 12 B–Q2 N–B3** If 12 . . . P–B4 13 P–K5 is good for White. **13 Q–R1?!** This seems too artificial, better 13 R–K1. **13 . . . P–Q4! 14 P×P** If 14 P–K5? N–Q2 wins the KP. **14 . . . N×P 15 Q–R6 B–B3 16 R–R1?** Again 16 R–K1 was the right move. **16 . . . P–R3 17 R–K1 Q–K2 18 N–R5 Q–Q3 19 N–B4 Q–B4 20 B–K3?!** N×B 21 P×N⊤ N–K2 22 N3–Q2 B–Q4! **23 N–K4 B×N/K5 24 B×B P–R4 25 Q–R1 P–N3 26 Q–Q1 P–R5 27 Q–K2 Q–KN4 28 Q–B3 K–N2 29 Q–B4 Q–QB4 30 R–R1 N–Q4 31 Q–B2 P–B3** White is being gradually outplayed. **32 R–R5 Q–K2 33 P–N4?!** Q–B2 34 R–R1 B–N4 35 K–R1 K–R3 36 R–KN1 N–B3 37 B–B3 R–Q1 38 R–R1?! Better 38 Q–K2, 38 B–K2 or even 38 P–N3 which, though making his bishop even worse and weakening more dark squares, would have prevented . . . 38 . . . P–N6!⊤ **39 R–R6 P×P 40 Q×BP N–Q4 41 Q–Q2 P–QB4! 42 Q–K2 N–N5 43 R–R3 K–N2 44 B–N2 B–B3 45 B–B1 N–B3 46 Q–KB2 N–K4 47 N×N Q×N 48 P–N3?!** Better would have been 48 R–B3 R–QR1 49 R–B1, though

261
W

Black preserves his advantage all the same. **48 . . . R–Q2 49 P–K4 Q–N4 50 Q–K2 R–N2 51 Q–B3 B–K4** (261) **52 R–R5??** This hastens the end, though White is probably lost anyway. **52 . . . Q–Q7 0–1.**

2402 AK–Walter Browne:

R2: 20 November:

Nimzowitsch/Larsen

1 P–QB4 P–QB4 2 P–QN3 An unusual experiment for Karpov. The note at the end of game 2205 may shed some light on this. **2 . . . N–KB3 3 B–N2 P–KN3 4 B×N!? P×B 5 N–QB3 B–N2** Ivkov, in *Informator* 14 suggests the amusing 5 . . . P–N3 6 N–B3 B–QN2 7 P–N3 B×N!! 8 P×B N–B3=. **6 P–N3 N–B3 7 B–N2 P–B4 8 P–K3 0–0 9 KN–K2 P–QR3** Black might do better with the solid 9 . . . P–Q3 to be followed by . . . B–K3. **10 R–QB1 P–QN4 11 P–Q3± B–N2 12 0–0 P–Q3 13 Q–Q2 Q–R4** Black would probably do better trying to get Q–side play with 13 . . . P–N5 14 N–Q5 P–QR4 with . . . P–R5 to follow. **14 KR–Q1 QR–N1 15 N–Q5 Q×Q 16 R×Q± P–N5** 16 . . . KR–K1 17 P×P P×P 18 N–B7 and 16 . . . QR–B1 17 N–K7+ N×N 18 B×B both lose a pawn, but 16 . . . KR–Q1 was probably better. **17 P–Q4 KR–Q1 18 R1–Q1 P×P 19 P×P K–B1 20 P–B5!** White succeeds in utilizing his Q–side majority. **20 . . . N–R2 21 N–K3 B×B 22 K×B P×P 23 P×P R×R 24 R×R R–B1 25 N–Q5 R×P** If 25 . . . P–QR4 26 N–N6 increases White's pressure. **26 N×P P–QR4 27 N–Q5 R–B3 28 N–K3 R–B4 29 N–KB4 B–R3 30 R–Q5! R×R 31 N4×R B×N 32 N×B** (262)

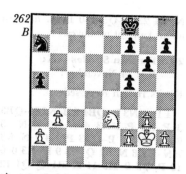

262
B

As a youngster, Karpov preferred to study endings rather than opening theory and recommends other would-be grandmasters to do the same. **32 . . . K–K2 33 K–B3 N–B3 34 N–B4 K–K3 35 K–K3 K–Q4 36 P–QR3 K–K3 37 K–Q3 K–Q4 38 P–B3 P–R3 39 K–B3 P–R4 40 K–Q3 P–B3 41 P–B4!** This places Black in zugzwang! If 41 . . . K–B4 42 N×P! N×N 43 P–QN4+ K–N4 44 P×N and the ending is won since while Black is using his king to deal with the passed pawn, White's own will plunder the other wing. Or if 41 . . . K–K3 42 N–K3! followed by 43 K–B4 forces a decisive penetration and the black QRP will be the first casualty. **41 . . . P–N4 42 N–K3+! K–K3** Forced to cover the BP. **43 P–KR4!** Putting the brake on Black's K-side operations. **43 . . . P×RP 44 P×P N–K2** What else? **45 K–B4** The beginning of the end. White wins the QRP and proves that his passed pawns are the fastest runners. **45 . . . N–N3** If 45 . . . N–B3 46 K–B5! N–K2 47 K–N5 wins. **46 N–N2!** Now Black's ambition of creating a passed pawn is considerably delayed. **46 . . . K–Q3 47 K–N5 K–Q4** Black must go after the K-side pawns but he is too late. **48 K×P K–K5 49 P–N4** Out on the freeway at last – and there is no speed limit! **49 . . .**

K–B6 50 P–N5! K×N 51 P–N6 N–B1 52 K–N5! The simplest way. **52 . . . N–Q2 53 P–R4!** The point – it's the QRP that is going to queen. **53 . . . N×P** Black didn't want his opponent to get *two* queens. **54 K×N K–B6 55 P–R5 K×P 56 P–R6 K–K6 57 P–R7 P–B5 58 P–R8=Q P–B6 59 Q–K8+ 1–0**

2403 Bent Larsen–AK:
R3: 21 November:

Queen's Indian

1 P–Q4 N–KB3 2 N–KB3 P–K3 3 P–B4 P–QN3 4 P–KN3 B–N2 5 B–N2 B–K2 6 0–0 0–0 7 P–N3 P–B4 8 B–N2 P×P 9 Q×P Or 9 N×P B×B 10 K×B P–Q4= **9 . . . N–B3 10 Q–B4 P–Q4 11 R–Q1 Q–B1** Matanović queries this and suggests 11 . . . Q–N1. **12 QN–Q2** Theory, until this game, gave only 12 N–B3 P×P 13 Q×P N–QN5=. **12 . . . R–Q1 13 QR–B1 Q–N1 14 N–K5 B–Q3 15 N×N± B×N 16 Q–R4 B–K4! 17 B×N Q×B 18 N–B3 Q–N1** If 18 . . . Q×P 19 N–Q4 picks up the bishop. **19 N–Q4 B–N2 20 P×P N×P** (263)

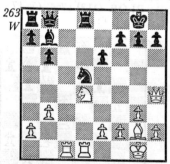

263
W

21 N–B6 B×N 22 R×B Q–K4 23 Q–K4 Q×Q 24 B×Q N–B3 25 R×R+ R×R 26 B–Q3 Also 26 B–B3!? **26 . . . N–Q4 27 P–QR3 K–B1 28 B–N5 P–N4 29 K–B1**

N–K2 30 R–B7 R–Q8+ 31 K–N2 R–QN8 32 B–B4 P–QR3 33 P–QR4 ½–½.

2404 AK—Campos-Lopez:
R4: 23 November:

Alekhine

1 P–K4 N–KB3 2 P–K5 N–Q4 3 P–Q4 P–Q3 4 N–KB3 P–KN3 5 B–QB4 P–QB3 6 0–0 B–N2 7 P×P! Q×P 8 P–KR3 This move has a poor reputation. 8 R–K1 or 8 QN–Q2 are usual. **8 . . . 0–0 9 B–N3 B–B4 10 R–K1 R–K1** Theory gives 10 . . . Q–Q1 11 QN–Q2 N–R3 12 N–K4 N3–B2 13 P–B4 N–B3 14 N×N+ P×N!? 15 P–Q5 P×P 16 P×P R–K1 17 R×R+ N×R and the knight goes to . . . Q3, maintaining equality, Kavalek-Kupka, Czechoslovakia 1968. However, Karpov probably knows more about this line than anyone else in the world and it is quite likely that he had an improvement available. **11 QN–Q2 P–QN4?! 12 P–QR4! N–Q2 13 P–B4 N–N5 14 P–B5 Q–B3 15 N–K4 B×N 16 R×N** P–K4 17 B–N5 was a threat. **17 RP×P! QR–Q1?!** (*264*) Or 17 . . . BP×P 18 B–Q2!

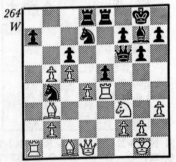

264
W

18 B–N5 Q–B4 19 B×R R×B If 19 . . . Q×R 20 N–N5 wins. **20 Q–K2 BP×P 21 R×RP N–QB3 22 R–B7**

N–R4 23 B–Q5 1–0 Black has just about run out of moves.

2405 Duncan Suttles–AK:
R5: 24 November:

King's Indian Reversed

1 P–KN3 P–QB4 2 B–N2 N–QB3 3 P–K4 P–KN3 4 N–K2 B–N2 5 0–0 P–Q3 6 P–QB3 P–K4 7 N–R3 KN–K2 8 N–B2 Q–N3 9 N–K3 0–0 10 P–Q3 B–K3 11 K–R1 Q–Q1 12 P–KB4 P–B4 13 N–Q5 K–R1 14 BP×P QP×P 15 B–N5 P–KR3 16 N×N N×N 17 B–K3 Q–B2 18 Q–Q2 K–R2 19 P–N3 QR–Q1 20 P–B4 P–KN4 21 P×P B×KBP (*265*)

265
W

White cannot defend the QP: 22 N–B1 P–K5. **22 R×B N×R 23 B–K4 K–R1 24 N–B3 N–Q3 25 N–Q5 N×B 26 P×N Q–B1 27 Q–K2 P–N5 28 K–N2 R–B6 29 R–Q1 R–Q2 30 P–KR4 P–KR4 31 B–N5 Q–B1 32 N–B4!? Q–K1 33 R×R Q×R 34 N–Q5 Q–B3 35 B–K3 K–R2 36 B–B2 P–N3 37 B–K1 Q–N2 38 B–B3 R–B1 39 B–K1 Q–KB2** (*266*) Now Black starts to make real progress. **40 B–Q2 Q–B6+! 41 Q×Q R×Q 42 B–B3 R–Q6 43 K–B2 R–B6+ 44 K–N2 K–N3 45 P–N4** If White sits still, the black king walks round to Q3 allowing the

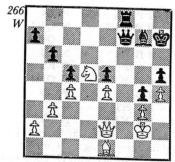

manoeuvre . . . B–R3–K6–B7. 45
. . . P×P 46 B×NP R–Q6 47
N–K7+ K–B2 48 N–B8 K–K3 49
N×RP R–Q5 50 P–R3 R×BP 51
N–N5 B–R3 52 K–B2 R–B7+ 53
K–K1 B–K6 54 K–Q1 R–KN7 55
N–B7+ K–B2 56 N–Q5 R×P 57
P–R4 B–Q5 58 P–R5 P×P 59 B×P
R–KR6 60 B–Q8 P–N6 0–1

2406 AK–Donald Byrne: R6:
26 November:

Sicilian

1 P–K4 P–QB4 2 N–KB3 P–Q3
3 P–Q4 P×P 4 N×P N–KB3 5
N–QB3 P–KN3 6 B–K3 B–N2 7
P–B3 0–0 8 Q–Q2 N–B3 9 B–QB4
P–QR4 This is a Donald Byrne
patent. 10 P–QR4! 10 P–KR4!?
is risky, though it worked well in
Fischer–D. Byrne, Western Open
1963: 10 . . . N–K4 11 B–K2! P–Q4
12 B–KB4 N–B5?!± though 12 . . .
N–R4!? would have been rather
better. 10 . . . N×N Or 10 . . .
N–QN5 11 N–Q5 N3×N 12 P×N
B×N 13 B×B P–K4 14 B–B2!±
Bodganović–Mestrović, Sarajevo
1968. 11 B×N B–K3 12 B–N5!?
TN Theory gives only 12 B–N3
B×B 13 P×B± and White gets a
strong grip on the centre. 12 . . .
R–B1 13 0–0–0 13 0–0 is also
possible e.g. 13 . . . B–B5 14 KR–
Q1!±. 13 . . . N–Q2?! Better 13 . . .

Q–B2 14 B×B K×B 15 P–B4±
N–B3 16 KR–K1 Q–B2 17 Q–Q4
KR–Q1 18 R–Q2 P–Q4?? (267)

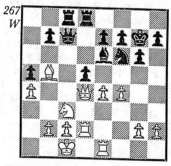

Usually admirable, here this only
results in Black having insoluble
problems on the Q–file. 19 P×P
B×P 20 Q–K5!±± P–K3 21
R1–Q1 P–N3 If 21 . . . Q–B4 22
P–KN4 will win the knight, also 21
. . . R–Q3?! 22 P–KN4. 22 B–R6
P–R4 23 B×R R×B 24 P–R3
Q×Q 25 P×Q N–K5 26 N×N
B×N 27 R–K2 B–Q4 28 R–Q4
R–B4 29 P–R4 P–B4 30 P×Pep+
K×P 31 R–KB4+ K–N2 32 R–K5
R–B2 33 P–KN3 R–B3 34 K–Q2
R–B2 35 P–N3 R–Q2 36 K–K3
R–K2 37 P–KN4 P×P 38 R×NP
K–B3 39 R5–N5 R–KR2 Or 39 . . .
R–KN2 40 P–R5 40 R×P+ K–K4
1–0

2407 Tigran Petrosian–AK:
R7: 27 November:

Queen's Indian

1 P–Q4 N–KB3 2 P–QB4 P–K3 3
N–KB3 P–QN3 4 P–K3 B–N2 5
N–B3 P–Q4 6 B–Q3 B–K2 7 0–0
0–0 8 P–QN3 P–B4 9 B–N2 BP×P
Or 9 . . . N–B3 10 R–B1 R–B1 11
Q–K2 QP×P 12 NP×P P×P 13
P×P R–K1?! (13 . . . N–QN5 is
unclear) 14 KR–Q1 Q–Q3 15 B–N1
Q–B5 16 P–Q5! Keres–Taimanov,

19 USSR Ch 1951. **10 KN×P?!**
10 KP×P is more in accordance
with the nature of the position. **10
. . . P×P 11 B×BP P–QR3!?** A
good alternative is 11 . . . N–B3 12
N×N B×N 13 B–K2=. **12 B–K2
P–QN4 13 B–B3 R–R2! 14 B×B
R×B 15 Q–B3± R–Q2 16 P–QR4
P×P!** If 16 . . . P–N5 then 17
N3–K2± **17 N×RP Q–B2 18
KR–B1 Q–N2 19 N–QB5 Q×Q 20
P×Q B×N 21 R×B P–R3 22
K–N2 R–N2** (*268*) with the idea of
. . . P–K4 to drive the knight away
from its role of guardian of the QNP

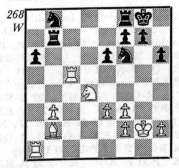

268
W

**23 P–B4 K–R2 24 R1–QB1 R–Q1
25 R1–B2 N–K5 26 R–B7 R–Q2
27 R×R/N7 R×R 28 B–R3 P–N4=
29 K–B3 N–KB3** ½–½

2408 AK–Svetozar Gligorić:

R8: 29 November:

Ruy Lopez

It is hoped that the notes to this
game will provide an especially
good insight into the game and into
the characteristics of Karpov's 'style'.
The notes by Karpov are selected
from those that he contributed to a
special article in the February 1973
issue of *Chess Life and Review*, while
the notes by grandmaster Semyon
Furman (Karpov's trainer) are from
Shakhmaty v SSSR No. 4 1973.

1 P–K4	P–K4
2 N–KB3	N–QB3
3 B–N5	P–QR3
4 B–R4	N–B3
5 0–0	B–K2
6 R–K1	P–QN4
7 B–N3	P–Q3
8 P–B3	0–0
9 P–KR3	N–N1

SF: This move was suggested by
the talented Hungarian master G.
Breyer. Together with G. Borisenko,
I have analysed this continuation a
great deal and, to that extent,
promoted its popularity in contemporary competitions.

10 P–Q3

SF: At first sight 10 P–Q4 is more
logical. After 10 . . . QN–Q2 11
QN–Q2 B–N2, White has to play 12
B–B2 to defend the KP and realize
the traditional 'Spanish' manoeuvre
N–Q2–B1–N3. In reply Black carries
out a regrouping with 12 . . . R–K1
13 N–B1 B–KB1 14 N–N3 P–N3,
neutralizing White's potential K-
side initiative. In this manoeuvre
lies the main idea of the variation. In
the tenth match game Fischer-
Spassky there followed 13 P–QN4
B–KB1 14 P–QR4 N–N3 15 P–R5
N/N3–Q2 16 B–N2 Q–N1 17 R–N1
(more convincing is 17 P–B4!
suggested by Smyslov and already
tried by Savon against Mukhin in
the USSR zonal play-off, Moscow
1973) 17 . . . P–B4 18 NP×P
QP×P 19 P×KP N2×P 20 N×N
Q×N 21 P–QB4 with better chances
for White.

A good defensive plan was demonstrated by Black in Razuvayev-
Furman in the last (40th) USSR
Championship: 14 . . . P–QR4!
(this defensive idea had already been
played by Portisch at Wijk aan Zee
in 1969 – eds.) 15 NP×P R×P 16
R–N1 B–QR3 17 RP×P R×P 18

B–N3 R–K2 19 Q–B2 R–R4 20 N–B4 B×N 21 B×B Q–R1 with equal chances.

    10 . . .   **QN–Q2**
    11 QN–Q2   **B–N2**
    12 N–B1   **N–B4**

SF: The advantages of the quiet 10 P–Q3 are already evident. White can carry out the knight manoeuvre without moving the bishop from the important a2–g8 diagonal – the KP is now obviously defended. Black, however, in order to carry out his regrouping, must drive the bishop off this diagonal. However, his QN is in an unfortunate position to attempt such a task.

    13 B–B2   **R–K1**
    14 N–N3

SF: Tal–Furman, 40 USSR Ch 1972, went 14 N–K3 B–KB1 15 P–QN4 N–K3! and Black had a good game; 16 P–Q4 is not possible – the KP being left undefended.

    14 . . .   **B–KB1**
    15 P–N4

AK: This is the only way to drive away Black's knight. 15 P–Q4 is impossible because of the insufficient defence of White's K4.

    15 . . .   **N4–Q2**

SF: The knight has to go here since 15 . . . N–K3 16 P–Q4 is clearly good for White.

    16 P–Q4 *(269)*

SF: In comparison with the 10

P–Q4 line, White has an extra tempo (the QNP has gone to QN4). It is clear that Black cannot make use of the QNP as a target for counterplay with 16 . . . P–QR4? For example: 17 P–R3 RP×P 18 BP×P P×P 19 N×P P–Q4 20 B–B4! with advantage to White, Gufeld–Holmov, Leningrad 1963. Or 17 P–R3 RP×P 18 BP×P P–B4 19 NP×P QP×P 20 P×KP N2×P 21 N×N Q×Q 22 R×Q R×N 23 B–N2 R–K3 24 P–K5 N–K1 25 P–QR4! also with advantage to White, Vasyukov–Averbakh, Moscow 1964.

    16 . .   **P–R3**
    17 B–Q2

SF: Thus White connects his rooks. Also 17 P–QR4 deserved attention.

AK: Defending against the possibility of . . . P–Q4.

    17 . . .   **N–N3**

AK: For some reason Gligorić declined to play the known 17 . . . P–QR4 which gives Black a completely equal game. Nevertheless, his move merits consideration.

    18 B–Q3

AK: This move blocks the incursion of Black's knight at White's QB4 and halts the advance of Black's QRP at the same time.

    18 . . .   **R–B1**
    19 Q–B2!? *(270)*

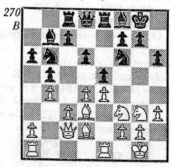

AK: At first glance a strange continuation – White places his queen on the same file as Black's rook. But the QB-file will not in fact be opened, either by the immediate 19 . . . P–B4 20 NP×P QP×P 21 P–Q5, or after the preliminary exchange 19 . . . P×P 20 P×P P–B4 21 NP×P by 21 . . . P×P 22 P–Q5 with a very sharp position.

19 . . .   Q–Q2

AK: For the present White has no direct threat, so Black continues to manoeuvre. However, already now it was necessary for him to think of counterplay. 19 . . . P×P deserved serious consideration. After 20 N×P P–N3 with 21 . . . P–B4 to follow Black stands well. While 20 P×P P–B4 gives a sharp position with chances for both sides.

AK: A lethargic move that will cost Black dearly. Not only does it lose an important tempo, but the queen has taken the . . . Q2 square away from Black's knights, limiting their manoeuvrability.

20 QR–Q1   Q–B3
21 B–K3   N–R5

AK: This is the only way to gain time to defend against the threatened N–Q2–N3–R5. 21 . . . N–B5 was impossible in view of 22 P–Q5 Q–Q2 23 B×N P×B 24 N–Q2 and 25 N×P.

22 R–QB1   N–N3
23 Q–N1

AK: Better is the immediate 23 N–Q2; then 23 . . . P–Q4 is not dangerous since White's K4 is safely defended, e.g. 24 QP×P R×P 25 B–Q4! (25 P–KB4? P×P with a winning position for Black) 25 . . . P×P 26 N2×P. There is no defence against N–Q2–N3–R5.

23 . . .   Q–Q2
24 N–Q2   P–B4

SF: Now Black is obliged to resort to this advance in less favourable circumstances. White has already prepared P–QB4.

AK: A forced action. Now White gets a strong, defended passed pawn on Q5.

25 NP×P   QP×P
26 P–Q5

SF: The location of the pawn on Q5 defines White's spatial advantage. If Black could now advance his pawn to . . . QB5, his position would be satisfactory. However, that is not possible as the knight on QN3 would be left undefended.

26 . . .   N–R5
27 P–QB4   P–N5
28 R–B1

SF: White prepares K-side play. Black's Q-side pawn majority could tell in the long run in an ending.

AK: Black's trouble is that he cannot find a satisfactory defence against the breakthrough P–B4, initiating a fearsome assault on the king's position. Q-side counterplay is hopelessly late.

28 . .   Q–B2
29 P–B4   N–Q2
30 Q–B2   N–B6 (271)

AK: This advance of Black's knight loses a pawn by force after the transfer of White's bishop to Q2, but a retreat to N3 would be even gloomier.

31 P–B5!

SF: White increases his space advantage and prepares a K-side pawn storm.

31 ..   N–B3

32 N–K2?!

AK: Of course it would have been better to win the pawn by 32 N–B3, 33 B–Q2 and 34 B×N, but it seemed to me that Black was defenceless against a K-side pawn storm. However, it turns out that Black's king is able, a little at a time, to escape from its insecure refuge.

32 ...   N×N+

33 B×N   B–Q3

34 P–N4   K–B1

SF: The beginning of the evacuation, not without difficulty, of the king to the Q-side. However it is very difficult to suggest something better for Black – he is completely devoid of counterplay.

35 P–KR4   K–K2

36 P–N5   ♦ P×P

37 P×P   N–Q2

38 B–N4

AK: White's pieces have turned out to be unprepared for such a swift unfolding of events. The decisive thrust requires regrouping and the supply of new pieces to the K-side.

38 ..   R–KN1

AK: White was threatening 39 P–B6+ P×P 40 P×P+ N×P 41 B–N5. But without the advance ... P–B3, Black will hardly be able to manage. Thus 38 . . . P–B3 was better here.

39 K–B2   R–KR1

40 R–KR1   QR–KN1
                          (272)

AK: It is vital for the black king to be able to escape to the Q-side without interference. Now White has an excellent chance to resolve the struggle in his favour by 41 P–R3

272
W

P–R4 42 Q–R4! N–N3 43 Q–N5! and Black cannot trap the queen since on 43 . . . R×R 44 R×R R–QR1 there follows the deadly P–B6+ and Black has no time for . . . P–B3 because of the manoeuvre N–N3 with attacks on Black's QR4 and QB4. But I bypassed this opportunity and made a not completely unsuccessful move.

41 Q–Q1   K–Q1

AK: The sealed move. Gligorić, as previously, refrains from advancing . . . P–B3. 41 . . . N–N3 loses because of 42 P–B6+ P×P 43 Q–B3 N–Q2 44 N–N3 with the threats B×N and N×P. Also bad is 41 . . . P–R4 42 Q–R4 N–N3 43 Q–N5.

42 Q–N1   N–N3

43 R–R2   Q–K2?

AK: This is a serious mistake. It is necessary to push the Q-side pawns. White's knight immediately occupies QR5 and the game ends quickly.

44 N–N3   K–B2

45 K–B3

AK: Yet another little stratagem: White's king move frees the second rank for his rooks and opens the KN1–QR7 diagonal for his queen.

45 ...   N–Q2 *(273)*

46 P–R3!

SF: Black's 'late Q-side' (now 'K-side') is fragile, and White opens lines for attack.

273
W

46 ...   P×P
47 R–R2

SF: White no longer needs the
KR-file.

47 ...   R–R5
48 R×P   R1–KR1
49 R–QN1

AK: Black lacks the strength to
defend all his weak points, and the
game ends very quickly.

49 ...   R–QN1?

AK: An error which does not
change matters. All the same, 49 . . .
P–B3 was more tenacious.

50 Q–K1   R×B

AK: On 50 . . . R5–R1 there
would follow 51 Q–R5+ K–B1
52 P–B6 P×P 53 N×P.

51 K×R   B–B1
52 Q–R5+   1–0

AK: On 52 . . . R–N3, decisive is
53 N×P B×N 54 R×R B×R 55
B×B+ N×B 56 P–B5.

SF: A game characteristic of
Karpov's style.

2409 Lajos Portisch–AK:
R9: 30 November:
Nimzo-Indian

**1 P–Q4 N–KB3 2 P–QB4 P–K3
3 N–QB3 B–N5 4 P–K3 P–B4 5
B–Q3 0–0 6 N–B3 P–Q4 7 0–0
QP×P 8 B×BP QN–Q2 9 Q–K2
P×P** Both 9 . . . P–QR3 and 9 . . .
P–QN3 are better. **10 P×P
P–QN3?!** New, but no improvement

on 10 . . . N–N3 11 B–N3 B–Q2 12
B–N5 B–B3 13 N–K5 B–K2 14
QR–Q1 N/N3–Q4 15 KR–K1
Panno–Bolbochan, Buenos Aires
1965. Now White solves any prob-
lem concerning his IQP. **11 P–Q5
B×N 12 P×P B–N5 13 P×N
Q×P 14 P–QR3!** Freeing the K1
square for use and forcing the bishop
to a less active square. 14 N–K5
would allow 14 . . . Q–B4!= **14 ...
B–Q3 15 R–Q1?** Better 15
B–KN5!± e.g. 15 . . . Q–K2 16
Q×Q B×Q 17 KR–K1 and Black
is in trouble.

David Levy, in his report on the
tournament for *Chess*, relates the
reason for Portisch not playing the
above line: '. . . but after 17 . . .
B–Q3 he had a position in his mind
in which his bishop was on QB1 and
so the move 18 QR–Q1 was "impossible". Had he realized that his
rooks were already united in that
variation, he would have played it
and got a very good game.'

15 ... Q–B2! 16 P–R3 16 B–KN5
is now too late: 16 . . . B–KN5! 17
B×N P×B 18 R–Q4 B–R4! **16 ...
B–N2= 17 B–K3 QR–K1 18
QR–B1 Q–N1 19 B–QN5 R–K2?!**
19 . . . R–B1 is safer and more
correct. **20 B–B6 B×B** If 20 . . .
B–B4 then White gets the advantage
with 21 N–Q4! B×N 22 R×B R–B1
23 R4–QB4 B–R3 24 B–QN5!±
21 R×B B–B4 22 R×N!? If 22
N–Q4?! Q–K4! leaves White with
problems. **22 . . . P×R** Black's
position would be tenable after 22
. . . B×B 23 R6–Q6 B–N4 24 Q–Q3
B–B3 25 P–QN4. **23 N–Q4 B×N 24
R×B Q–K4 25 Q–B3** (*274*)
Compare this position with that after
White's 42nd move in game 2103
25 . . . K–R1?? 25 . . . P–B4! 26
R–Q5 Q×P 27 B–Q4 Q–B8+ 28
K–R2 R–K3 29 R×P R–N3 30

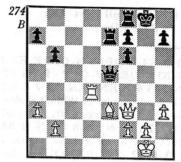

274
B

P–KR4 and White's control of the dark squares and Black's K-side weaknesses are probably adequate compensation for the exchange. **26 R–Q5 1–0** If 26 ... Q–K3 27 B–Q4.

2410 AK–Kenneth Smith:
R10: 1 December:

Sicilian

1 P–K4 P–QB4 2 N–KB3 P–Q3 3 P–Q4 P×P 4 N×P N–KB3 5 N–QB3 P–K3 6 P–KN4 P–KR3 7 P–N5 P×P 8 B×P P–QR3 An interesting possibility here is 8 ... N–B3 9 Q–Q2 Q–N3!? **9 Q–Q2 B–Q2 10 0–0–0 N–B3 11 P–KR4 Q–B2 12 B–K2** 12 B–R3 is also good. **12 ... 0–0–0 13 P–B4± B–K2 14 P–R5 K–N1 15 K–N1 B–K1 16 B–B3 N–R4!? 17 Q–K2 N–B5 18 KR–K1 R–QB1 19 R–Q3 N–N1 20 Q–N2 B–B1?! 21 R–R1 N–K2 22 P–N3 N–R6+!?** This leads to a serious weakening of Black's Q-side which would be avoided with 22 ... N–R4 or 22 ... N–QN3. **23 K–N2 N–N4 24 N3×N P×N 25 Q–Q2 Q–N3 26 B–R4 P–N5 27 B–B2 Q–R4 28 B–K1 P–K4 29 N–K2 N–B3 30 P–B5! P–B3 31 R–Q5 Q–R6+ 32 K–N1 B–B2 33 R–Q3 P–QN3?!** Further weakening of the Q-side is involved by this. **34 B–B2 K–N2 35 P–B3 P×P 36 R×BP B–K2 37 R–N1 KR–N1 38 Q–N2**

Q×Q+ 39 K×Q N–R2 40 R×R N×R 41 N–B3 B–Q1 42 B–K2 N–K2 43 B–B4! B×B 44 P×B± (*275*)

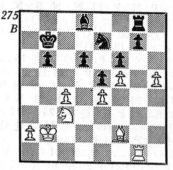

275
B

44 ...R–R1 45 R–KR1 K–B3 46 K–N3 R–R2 47 B–K3 R–R1 48 K–N4 R–R2? Better 48 ... K–N2 with 49 ... N–B3 to follow, after which White's king can always be repulsed by ... N–R2+. **49 N–Q5 N×N?** Tantamount to resignation. 49 ... N–B1 was the only move. Now White's king is free to advance further, blockading the QNP and thus completely incarcerating Black's bishop. **50 BP×N+ K–N2 51 K–N5 B–B2 52 P–R4 R–R1 53 B–Q2 R–R2 54 B–N4 R–R1 55 R–KN1 R–R2 56 R–N6!** The start of the final winning idea. **56 ... B–N1 57 P–R6! P×P 58 R×BP P–R4 59 B×P B×B 60 R×B P–R5 61 R×P+ K–R2 62 R–N6 P–R6 63 R–N1 R–R5 64 R–N7+ K–R1 65 P–B6 R–B5 66 P–B7 P–R7 67 R–R7 R×BP 68 R×P R–B5 69 P–Q6 R×P 70 R–R8+ 1–0**

2411 Larry Evans–AK:
R11: 3 December:

English

1 P–QB4 P–QB4 2 N–QB3 N–QB3 3 P–KN3 P–KN3 4 B–N2

B–N2 5 P–QR3 P–Q3 6 R–N1
P–QR4 7 N–B3 P–K4 8 0–0 KN–K2
9 P–Q3 0–0 10 B–Q2 R–N1 11
N–K1 B–K3 12 N–B2 P–Q4 13
P×P N×P 14 N×N B×N 15
P–QN4 Better 15 B×B! Q×B 16
P–QN4 RP×P 17 P×P P×P (17
. . . P–K5 18 B–B4!) 18 N×P N×N
19 B×N KR–B1 20 Q–N3± 15 . . .
B×B 16 K×B P–QN4 17 P×RP
N×P 18 N–K3 R–K1 19 Q–B1
B–B1 20 B×N Q×B 21 N–Q5
R–K3 22 P–K4 Q–R5 23 P–B4 23
Q–B3 was worth trying. 23 . . . Q–Q5
24 P×P If 24 P–B5 simply 24 . . .
R–Q3 24 . . . Q×P/K4 (*276*) Not
24 . . . Q×QP 25 Q–B4 R–N2 26
R/N1–Q1!

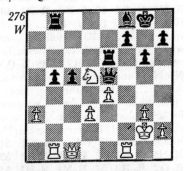

276
W

25 R–B3 R–R3 26 R–N3 P–B4 27
Q–QN1 R1–R1 28 R×NP R×P 29
R–N7 29 R–B2 is needed. 29 . . .
R–R7+ 30 R–B2 30 K–R3 would
be wrong because of 30 . . . K–R1!
with the terrible threat . . . P×P and
. . . Q–R4 mate. 30 . . . R×R+
31 K×R P×P 32 P×P P–B5 33
K–N2 R–B1 33 . . . R–R8 looks
tempting, but loses to 34 Q–B2
Q–Q5 35 Q×P! Q×Q 36 N–B6+
K–R1 37 R×P mate. 33 . . . B–B4
is also no good on account of 34
R–QB7 Q–Q5 35 N–B6+! 34 N–N6
R–K1 ½–½ 35 N×P Q×KP+ 36
Q×Q R×Q=.

2412 Vlastimil Hort–AK:

R12: 4 December:

Sicilian

1 P–K4 P–QB4 2 N–QB3 P–K3 3
N–B3 N–QB3 4 P–Q4 P×P 5 N×P
P–QR3 6 P–KN3 KN–K2 7 B–N2
The least popular of White's choices
here. See also games 1501, 1704 and
2007. 7 . . . N×N 8 Q×N N–B3
Black has a comfortable position.
9 Q–K3!? (277) 9 Q–Q1!? is discussed in game 1501.

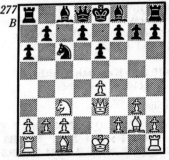

277
B

9 . . . P–Q3 9 . . . P–QN3! is prob-
ably stronger. 10 P–N3 B–K2 11
B–N2 0–0 12 0–0 R–N1 13 N–K2
P–QN4 14 QR–B1 Q–R4 15 P–QR3
Q–N3 16 Q–Q2 P–QR4 17 KR–Q1
R–Q1 18 N–B4 ½–½

2413 AK–Julio Kaplan:

R13: 5 December:

Sicilian

1 P–K4 P–QB4 2 N–KB3 N–QB3
3 P–Q4 P×P 4 N×P P–KN3 5
P–QB4 N–B3 6 N–QB3 P–Q3 7
N–B2 B–N2 8 B–K2 0–0 9 0–0?!
9 B–K3! N–Q2 10 Q–Q2 is stronger.
9 . . . N–Q2∓ 10 Q–Q2?! 10 B–Q2
is better, but not 10 B–K3 B×N!
10 . . . N–B4 11 P–B3 P–B4 12 P×P
B×P 13 N–K3 N–Q5 Also 13 . . .
P–QR4 is good. 14 N×B N×N 15
R–N1 P–K3 Preparing . . . P–Q4 16
Q–K1 (*278*)

278
B

... R–K7∓ 32 R×P+?! K–K3 33
R–R5 P×P 34 P×P B×P 35
P–QR4∓ but Black is in time-
trouble, so ... ½–½

16 ... P–QR3? Securing ... Q5 so
that ... B–Q5+ will be available,
but much stronger is 16 ... P–QR4!
17 B–Q2 P–Q4∓. **17 K–R1 B–Q5
18 B–Q2 Q–K2 19 P–B4 QR–K1?!**
Still 19 ... P–QR4 should be played.
**20 P–QN4!± N–Q2 21 B–Q3
P–K4!? 22 P×P N×P 23 Q–K4!
B–R2 24 Q–Q5+ K–N2** (279)

2414 Paul Keres–AK:
R14: 8 December:

Nimzo-Indian

**1 P–Q4 N–KB3 2 P–QB4 P–K3 3
N–QB3 B–N5 4 P–K3 P–B4 5
B–Q3 0–0 6 N–B3 P–Q4 7 0–0
QP×P 8 B×BP P×P 9 P×P
P–QN3 10 B–KN5 B–N2 11 Q–K2
QN–Q2 12 QR–B1 R–B1 13
N–K5!± P–KR3** (280)

279
W

280
W

25 R/N1–K1? White should con-
solidate with 25 B×N R×B 26
R×R P×R 27 R–KB1± **25 ...
Q–KB2!±** Not 25 ... Q–R5? 26
B×N N–N5 27 Q×NP+ K–N1 28
P–KR3! and White wins, but not 28
B×N?? Q×R! and Black wins.
26 B×N Q×Q 27 N×Q 27 P×Q!?
is the alternative. **27 ... R×B 28
B–B3 K–B2 29 R×R+ P×R 30
P–B5 N–Q6! 31 R–KB1?** White
still has the advantage if he plays 31
R×R K K×R 32 N–B6+! but not 32
P×P N–B7+ 33 K–N1 N–K5+ 34
K–B1 N×B 35 N×N K–Q2∓. **31**

14 B–B4 This is not the best. 14
N×N! (14 B–R4 N×N 15 P×N
Q–Q5!) 14 ... Q×N 15 B×N P×B
is good for White after both 16
P–Q5!? P×P 17 B–Q3! and 16
KR–Q1!± **14 ... N×N 15 B×N**
If 15 P×N then Black has 15 ...
Q–Q5! **15 ... Q–K2 16 B–R6 B×B
17 Q×B B×N 18 P×B N–Q4 19
P–QB4 N–N5 20 Q–R3 P–B3 21
B–N3 ½–½**

2415 AK–Henrique Mecking:
R15: 10 December:

Sicilian

**1 P–K4 P–QB4 2 N–KB3 P–Q3
3 B–N5+ B–Q2 4 B×B+ Q×B 5
0–0 N–QB3 6 P–B4 N–B3 7 N–B3
P–KN3 8 P–Q4 P×P 9 N×P ½–½**

25 BUDAPEST 13.2–2.3.1973

		1	2	3	4	5	6	7	8	9	0	1	2	3	4	5	6	
1	Geller	×	½	½	1	1	½	½	½	1	½	½	1	1	½	½	1	**10½**
2	**Karpov**	½	×	1	½	1	1	½	½	½	½	½	1	½	½	½	½	**9½**
3	Vaganian	½	0	×	½	½	½	½	1	½	½	1	½	½	½	½	1	**8½**
4	Szabo	0	½	½	×	½	1	½	½	½	½	½	½	1	1	½	½	**8½**
5	Adorjan	0	0	½	½	×	½	½	½	½	½	1	1	½	1	1	½	**8½**
6	Hort	½	0	½	0	½	×	½	1	½	1	1	0	1	1	½	½	**8½**
7	Bilek	½	½	½	½	½	½	×	½	½	½	½	½	½	1	½	½	**8**
8	Antoshin	½	½	0	½	½	0	½	×	1	½	½	0	½	1	1	1	**8**
9	Csom	0	½	½	½	½	½	½	0	×	½	½	1	½	½	½	1	**7½**
10	Ribli	½	½	½	½	0	½	½	½	½	×	½	½	1	0	½	½	**7**
11	Ciocaltea	½	½	0	½	0	0	½	½	½	½	×	1	½	½	½	½	**6½**
12	Sax	0	0	½	½	0	1	½	1	0	½	0	×	½	0	1	½	**6**
13	Hecht	0	½	½	0	½	0	½	½	½	0	½	½	×	1	1	0	**6**
14	Velimirović	½	½	½	0	0	0	0	0	½	1	½	1	0	×	½	1	**6**
15	Forintos	½	½	½	½	0	½	½	0	½	½	½	0	0	½	×	½	**5½**
16	Lengyel	0	½	0	½	½	½	½	0	0	½	½	½	1	0	½	×	**5½**

Geller, in *65* No. 11 1973, tells the story of Karpov at Budapest: 'After six rounds he was one point behind me. In the remaining eight rounds a real race developed with the interesting consequence that we, one with the other, as if by agreement, began to play in synchronisation: if one day one of us won, then the other was also victorious.

'A. Karpov's play is distinguished by the confidence in his strength for rapid and correct calculation of variations, the highest technique in playing typical endings (for example in his game against Hort). And here, in Budapest, Anatoly played confidently, easily, was boldly combinative, but sometimes he showed, I dare say, insufficient sporting staying-power. He sometimes let slip an advantage in the struggle against stubborn opponents. (Geller here points out the win Karpov missed against Ribli – eds).

'Usually Karpov goes straight towards the goal by simple means. However, when that does not work, he can abruptly switch to a sharp combinative struggle.'

2501 AK–Hans Hecht:
R1: 13 February:

English

1 P–QB4 P–K4 2 N–QB3 N–KB3 3 N–B3 N–B3 4 P–KN3 B–N5 5 N–Q5 P–K5 Not 5 . . . N×N 6 P×N P–K5? 7 P×N P×N 8 Q–N3 1–0 Petrosian–Ree, Wijk aan Zee 1971. **6 N–R4 B–B4 7 B–N2 P–Q3** 7 . . . 0–0 8 0–0 R–K1 would transpose to Gheorghiu–Hecht, Teesside 1972, which continued 9 P–Q3! P×P 10 Q×P N–K4 11 Q–B2 N×N 12 P×N P–Q3 13 P–N3!±. **8 0–0!?** Annotating his game against Kushnir from Wijk aan Zee II (played the previous month), Hecht gave 8 P–Q3 as better. **8 . . . B–K3** Better than 8 . . . P–KN4!? 9 P–Q4! Kushnir–Hecht. **9 P–Q3** Antunac–Hecht, also from Wijk aan Zee II, had gone 9 N×N+ Q×N 10 B×P B×QBP 11 Q–R4! P–Q4 12 B–B3 0–0 13 P–Q3 B–R3 14 B×P N–Q5 15 Q–Q1 ½–½. **9 . . . N×N 10 P×N B×QP 11 P×P B–K3 12 B–Q2 Q–Q2 13 B–QB3 0–0 14 N–B3 B–KR6 15 Q–Q5 B×B 16 K×B QR–K1 17 P–K5 Q–K3 18 QR–Q1 Q×Q 19 R×Q N–K2 20 R–Q3 N–B3 21 P×P B×QP 22 P–K3 P–B3 23 R1–Q1 R–Q1 24 N–R4 P–KN3 25 P–B4 P–B4 26 N–B3 B–B4 27 R–Q7 R×R 28 R×R R–B2 29 R×R K×R 30 P–K4 B–K2 31 P×P P×P** (*281*)

281
W

32 N–N5+ K–N3 33 N–K6 B–Q3 34 K–B3 P–KR4 35 P–KR3 N–K2 36 B–K5 N–B3 37 B–B3 K–B2 38 N–N7 K–N3 39 P–R3 P–R3 40 N–K8 K–B2 41 N–B6 K–N3 42 N–Q5 N–K2 43 N–B6 N–B3 44 K–K2 P–N4 45 K–Q3 P–R5 46 P×P B×BP 47 P–R5+ K–N4 48 P–KR4+ K×P/R5 49 N–Q5 B–R3 50 N×P K×P 51 N×RP B–B1 52 N–B7 P–N5 53 P×P N×P+ ½–½

2502 AK–Vlastimil Hort:

R2: 14 February:

French

The notes to this game are by Karpov from *Informator 15*, Victor Ciocaltea (VC) from *The Chess Player 4* and Ervin Haag (EH) from *Magyar Sakkelet*.

1 P–K4	**P–K3**
2 P–Q4	**P–Q4**
3 N–Q2	**N–KB3**
4 P–K5	**N3–Q2**
5 P–QB3	

VC suggests 5 P–KB4!?

5 . . .	**P–QB4**
6 B–Q3	**N–QB3**
7 N–K2	

VC: 7 KN–B3!? Q–N3 8 0–0 P×P 9 P×P N×QP 10 N×N Q×N 11 N–B3 Q–N3! 12 Q–B2 (12 Q–R4!?) 12 . . . Q–B4 (12 . . . P–KR3?) 13 Q–R4 (13 B×P=) 13 . . . Q–N5 14 Q–B2 and now not 14 . . . P–KR3!? 15 B–Q2 Q–N3 16 QR–B1 B–K2 17 Q–R4!± Korchnoi–Udović, Leningrad 1967, but 14 . . . Q–B4= Nunn–Moles, England 1971.

7 . . .	**Q–N3**

EH: a good alternative is 7 . . . P×P 8 P×P P–B3! 9 P×P Q×P 10 N–KB3 P–K4!

8 N–B3	

AK: Or 8 0–0!? P×P 9 P×P N×QP 10 N×N Q×N 11 N–B3.

8 . .	**P×P**
9 P×P	**P–B3**
10 P×P	**N×BP**
11 0–0	**B–Q3**
12 N–B3!?	

VC: Or 12 R–K1?! 0–0 13 N–N3 B–Q2 14 P–N3± Georgadze–Doroshkevich, RSFR–Georgia 1972; or 12 N–B4 0–0 13 R–K1 B–Q2∓ Georgadze–Doroshkevich, same event.

12 . . .	**0–0**

13 B–K3

EH apparently prefers 13 B–KN5.

13 ...   Q–Q1

AK/VC: 13 ... Q×NP? 14 N–QN5! B–K2 15 R–N1 Q×RP 16 R–R1 Q–N7 17 R–R4! with 18 B–B1! to follow wins for White.

14 B–KN5   B–Q2

EH: Or 14 ... Q–K1 (heading for R4) 15 B–R4! Q–R4 16 B–N3! and if 16 ... B×B 17 BP×B!

15 R–K1   Q–N1

AK/VC: If 15 ... R–B1 then 16 R–B1! with the idea of B–N1 (± – VC; and Q–Q3± – AK), or 15 ... Q–K1 16 B×N with 17 N×P±± to follow.

16 B–R4!   P–QR3

17 R–QB1   P–QN4

EH queries this and suggests instead 17 ... Q–R2.

18 B–N1   B–B5

19 B–N3

VC: 19 R–B2!? with 20 R2–K2± to follow.

AK: 19 R–B2 Q–Q3 20 R2–K2=.

19 ..   B×B

20 RP×B±   Q–N3

VC: Or 20 ... Q–Q3 21 N–K5 with P–B4 to follow with a clear advantage for White.

21 N–K2

Better 21 Q–Q3! and if 21 ... QR–K1 22 N–K5! VC continues the line with 22 ... Q×P 23 N×B!±±.

21 ...   QR–K1

AK: Aiming for 22 ... P–K4±.

22 N–B4   N×P

EH queries this and suggests 22 ... R–K2.

23 Q×N?;

AK/VC: Overlooking 23 N×N! P–K4 24 N×QP Q×N! (24 ... N×N?! 25 N–B3±) 25 N×N+ R×N 26 Q×Q P×Q 27 R×R+ B×R 28 R–B8 K–B2 29 R–Q8±.

23 ..   Q×Q

24 N×Q   P–K4 (*282*)

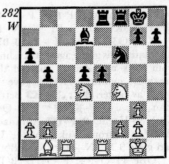

25 N/B4–K6!   B×N

26 R×P   B–Q2

27 R×R   R×R

28 P–B3   R–QB1

29 R×R+   B×R±

30 K–B2   K–B2

31 K–K3   K–K2

32 P–QN4   P–N3

33 P–N4   N–Q2

34 P–B4 (*283*)

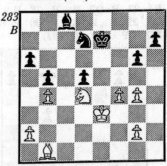

34 ...   N–B1?

Both AK and VC point out that more resistance was offered by 34 ... K–Q3!? (Stronger than 34 ... N–N3 which allows 35 N–B6+! K–Q3 36 N–K5 N–B5+ 37 K–Q4±) 35 P–N5! (But not 35 N–B3? which allows Black to draw the ending after 35 ... N–B3! 36 P–N5 P–Q5+! and 37 ...N–Q4.) 35 ... N–N3 36 B–Q3 with the idea of B–K2–N4 with an edge for White.

35 P–N5	K–Q3
36 K–B3±	N–K3?

VC points out that both 36 . . . B–N2!? and 36 . . . N–Q2!? are better, though White should still win.

37 N×N	B×N
38 K–K3±±	B–N5
39 B–Q3	B–K3
40 K–Q4	B–N5
41 B–B2	B–K3
42 B–N3	B–B2
43 B–Q1	B–K3
44 B–B3	B–B2
45 B–N4	1–0

AK: White follows up with B–B8×RP.

EH: 45 . . . B–K3 46 B×B K×B 47 P–N4 K–Q3 48 P–B5.

2503 Efim Geller–AK:
R3: 15 February:

Ruy Lopez

1 P–K4 P–K4 2 N–KB3 N–QB3 3 B–N5 P–QR3 4 B–R4 N–B3 5 0–0 B–K2 6 R–K1 P–QN4 7 B–N3 P–Q3 8 P–B3 0–0 9 P–KR3 N–N1 10 P–Q4 QN–Q2 11 QN–Q2 B–N2 12 B–B2 R–K1 13 N–B1 13 P–QN4 B–KB1 14 P–QR4 is still widely regarded as strongest, despite Portisch's idea of 14 . . . P–QR4! **13 . . . B–KB1 14 N–N3 P–N3 15 P–QR4** Or 15 P–N4 P–QR4 16 P–R3 P×P 17 BP×P P–Q4! and Black has equalized. **15 . . . P–B4 16 P–Q5 P–B5 17 B–N5 P–R3 18 B–K3 N–B4 19 Q–Q2 K–R2 20 R–R3± Q–B2 21 R1–R1 B–N2 22 Q–Q1!** With the idea of trebling on the QR–file by R1–R2 and Q–R1. **22 . . . QR–N1 23 P×P P×P 24 R–R7** *(284)*

24 . . . Q–N3 The immediate attempt to contest the QR–file by 24 . . . R–R1 fails to 25 B×N P×B 26 P–Q6! and White's advanced pawn costs Black at least the

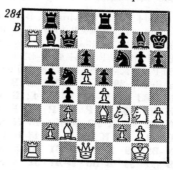

284
B

exchange. **25 R1–R5 R–QR1 26 Q–R1 R×R 27 R×R N3–Q2 28 P–R4** An interesting alternative is 28 N–Q2, planning P–QN4. **28 . . . R–QN1! 29 P–R5 Q–Q1 30 N–Q2 R–R1 31 P–N4** White might try 31 R×R!? Q×R 32 Q×Q B×Q 33 N–N1 B–N2 34 N–R3 B–R3 35 P×P+ P×P 36 N–K2 planning the manoeuvre N–B1–R2–N4 with extremely strong pressure against Black's Q-side pawn structure. **31 . . . BP×Pep 32 N×P N×N 33 B×N R×R 34 Q×R Q–QR1 35 Q×Q B×Q 36 P–QB4 P×BP 37 B–R4 N–N1 38 B–R7 N–R3** *(285)*

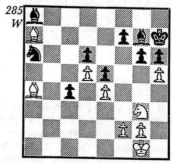

285
W

39 B–N5 White can make no progress in the ending, e.g. 39 B–B6 B×B 40 P×B P–B6 41 B–N8 P–B7 (The White bishop is immune from capture.) 42 P×P+ (or 42 N–K2 P×P 43 B×P B–B3=) 42 . . . K×P 43 N–K2 P–R4 44 P–B7 (if 44 B×P then 44 ... P–B3 with ... B–R3 to follow) 44 ... N×P 45 B×N B–R3 46 B×P P–B8=Q+ 47 N×Q B×N 48 B×P P–B4 49 P–B3 P×P 50 P×P K–N4 51 K–B2 K–N5 with a draw. **39 ... B–N2 40 B×P B–KB3 41 N–B1 B–N4 42 B–N5 K–N2 43 P×P P×P 44 P–B3 K–B2 45 K–B2 K–K2 46 N–K3 B×N+ 47 K×B P–N4 48 K–Q3 N–B2 49 K–B4 B–B1 50 B–K3 B–Q2 51 B–B6 B–B1 52 B–N5 B–Q2 53 B–B6 B–B1** ½–½

22504 AK–Laszlo Szabo:

R4: 16 February:

Sicilian

1 P–K4 P–QB4 2 N–KB3 P–Q3 3 P–Q4 P×P 4 Q×P N–QB3 5 B–QN5 P–QR3 5 ... B–Q2 is the most natural, e.g. 6 B×N B×B 7 N–B3 N–B3 8 B–N5 P–K3 9 0–0–0 B–K2 10 KR–K1 0–0 11 P–K5 P×P 12 Q–KR4 Q–B2 13 N×P KR–Q1 and Black can equalize as in Vasyukov–Tal, 40 USSR Ch 1972. Velimirović gives 13 ... P–KR3. This allows the sacrifice 14 B×P, but Black can then probably force a draw with 14 ... N–K5 15 Q–R5 N×N 16 B×P N×P+ 17 K–N1 N–B6+ Gipslis–Tukmakov, ½-final 40 USSR Ch 1972. Another unusual fifth move was tried by Csom against Karpov in round 14. **6 B×N+ P×B 7 0–0 P–K4 8 Q–Q3 B–K2 9 P–B4 N–B3 10 N–B3 N–Q2 11 P–QN4!** Preparing to monopolize the Q-side. 11 ... 0–0 with 11 ... P–QR4 gets Black nowhere after 12 P–N5±. **12 B–K3 P–QR4 13 P–N5 B–N2 14 P–QR4 P–QB4 15 N–Q2 N–N3** (*286*) **16 KR–Q1?!** White has a clear advantage on the Q-side, but there is a danger that it will come to nothing if the position remains

blocked, therefore White would do better to open the game up a little with 16 P–B4!±. **16 ... Q–B1 17 P–B3 Q–K3 18 N–Q5 B×N 19 BP×B Q–N3 20 N–B4 N×N 21 Q×N B–N4 22 B–B2 QR–N1** 22 ... P–B4!?, beginning active operations on the K-side, was worth a try. **23 P–N4 P–R4 24 P–R3 Q–R3 25 K–N2 B–K6 26 B×B Q×B 27 Q–Q3 Q×Q 28 R×Q P–R5 29 R–N3 R–N3 30 P–N5 P–B4 31 NP×Pep R×BP 32 K–B2 R–N3 33 R3–N1 K–B2** 33 ... R–N6 can be repulsed by 34 R–R1 and 35 QR–KN1. **34 R–N1 R×R 35 R×R K–B3 36 K–K3 P–N4 37 K–Q3 R–N1 38 R–N1 R–N3** ½–½

2505 Victor Ciocaltea–AK:

R5: 18 February:

King's Indian Attack

1 P–K4 P–QB4 2 N–KB3 P–K3 3 P–Q3 N–QB3 4 P–KN3 P–KN3 5 B–N2 B–N2 6 0–0 KN–K2 7 P–B3 0–0 8 N–R4 P–Q4 9 P–KB4 P–KB4 10 P×BP KP×P 11 N–R3 R–N1 12 N–B3 ½–½

2506 AK–Levente Lengyel:

R6: 19 February:

Ruy Lopez

1 P–K4 P–K4 2 N–KB3 N–QB3 3 B–N5 P–QR3 4 B–R4 N–B3 5 0–0

B–K2 6 R–K1 P–QN4 7 B–N3 P–Q3
8 P–B3 0–0 9 P–KR3 N–N1 10
P–Q3 QN–Q2 11 QN–Q2 N–B4 12
N–B1 An unusual move-order. 12
B–B2, and if 12 . . . B–N2 13 P–Q4!,
is more usual. **12 . . . R–K1 13
N–N3 B–N2 14 B–B2 B–KB1 15
P–N4 N4–Q2 16 P–Q4± P–N3** At
San Antonio Gligorić had played
16 . . . P–R3, the move also favoured
by Spassky (game 2602). **17 P–QR4
B–N2 18 B–Q3 P–B3 19 B–N5
P–R3 20 B–K3 Q–B2 21 R–QB1
QR–Q1 22 Q–Q2 K–R2 23 Q–R2
R–K2 24 P–B4 KP×P 25 B×QP
N–K4 26 B–K2 N×BP 27 B2×N
P×B 28 Q×P R1–K1 29 P–K5
N–Q4 30 P×P R×R+ 31 N×R
Q×P 32 B×B K×B 33 N–Q3
N–N3 34 Q–B3+ Q–B3 35 Q–B2
N–Q2 36 P–R5 P–B4 37 P×P
R–QB1 38 Q–N3 B–B3 39 N–N4
R–QN1 40 Q–R3 N–K4 41 R–Q1**
(*287*) 41 N×B was better

287
B

**41 . . . B×P 42 K×B R×N 43
Q×R Q–B6+ 44 K–N1 Q×R+ 45
N–B1 N–B6+ 46 K–N2 N–K8+ 47
K–N1 N–B6+ 48 K–N2 N–K8+ 49
K–N1** ½–½

2507 Vladimir Antoshin–AK:
R7: 20 February:

Queen's Indian

**1 P–Q4 N–KB3 2 P–QB4 P–K3
3 N–KB3 P–QN3 4 P–KN3 B–N2**

5 B–N2 B–K2 6 0–0 0–0 7 N–B3
N–K5 8 N×N B×N 9 N–K1
B×B 10 N×B P–Q4 11 Q–R4
Q–Q2 12 Q×Q N×Q 13 P×P
P×P 14 N–B4 N–B3 15 B–K3
P–B4 16 P×P P P×P ½–½

2508 AK–Gyula Sax:
R8: 21 February:

King's Indian

**1 P–Q4 N–KB3 2 P–QB4 P–KN3
3 N–QB3 P–Q3 4 P–KN3 B–N2 5
B–N2 0–0 6 N–B3 P–B4 7 P–Q5
P–K4 8 0–0** 8 P×Pep?! B×P 9
N–KN5 B×P! 10 B×P QN–Q2
gives Black a good game. **8 . . .
N–R3** Also 8 . . . QN–Q2 9 P–QR3
N–K1 10 P–K4 P–KR3! 11 N–K1
P–B4 12 N–Q3 N1–B3 13 P–B4?!
BP×P 14 N/B3×P N×N 15 B×N
Q–K1∓/∓ Rajković–Jansa, Orebro
1966. **9 P–K4 N–B2 10 P–QR4
P–N3 11 N–K1 N–R4 12 N–Q3**
White must avoid 12 P–B4 P×P 13
P×P? B–Q5+ 14 K–R1 Q–R5∓ ∓.
**12 . . . P–B4 13 P×P B×P 14
N–K4 Q–Q2 15 P–B3 N–B3 16
N3–B2 B×N 17 P×B! P–QR3 18
B–K3 KR–N1** 18 . . . P–QN4 may
be better, e.g. 19 B–R3 Q–K2 20
P–QN4 BP×P 21 RP×P RP×P 22
R×R R×R 23 P–B5 R–R6!, or,
in this line, 21 P–B5 NP×P 22
R×P N–N4! **19 B–R3 Q–K2 20
Q–Q2 P–QN4** (*288*)

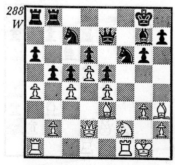

288
W

21 P–QN4!? BP×**P 22 RP**×**P P**×**P 23 P–B5 R–R5 24 QR–B1 N2–K1** 24 . . . N3–K1 loses to 25 N–N4 N–B3 26 B–N5! **25 P–B6 N–B2 26 R–R1 N–R3** Perhaps 26 . . . R1–R1 is better. **27 Q–Q3 N–B2 28 R/R1–N1 N–R3 29 R–R1 N–B2 30 Q–N3 R1–R1 31 R**×**R R**×**R 32 B–Q2 N–R3 33 Q–Q3 R–R4** 33 . . . N–B2!? **34 Q–K2 Q–R2 35 B–K3 N–B4? 36 R–B1 N–K1** to cover the QP after 1 B×N P×B 2 P–Q6 at some point. **37 Q–N4! P–N6 38 K–N2 P–N7 39 R–QN1 R–R6?** 39 . . . Q–N1 provides the basis for a more tenacious resistance. **40 B**×**N P**×**B 41 R**×**P Q–N1 42 Q–K6+ 1–0** If 42 . . . K–R1 then 43 R×P!, or 42 . . . K–B1 43 N–N4.

2509 Gyozo Forintos–AK:
R9: 23 February:

Queen's Gambit Declined

1 P–Q4 N–KB3 2 P–QB4 P–K3 3 N–KB3 P–Q4 4 N–QB3 B–K2 5 B–B4 0–0 6 P–K3 P–QN3 7 B–Q3 B–N2 8 0–0 P–B4 9 Q–K2 N–B3 10 QP×**P NP**×**P 11 P**×**P P**×**P 12 KR–Q1 Q–R4 13 P–QR3 KR–Q1 14 Q–B2 P–B5 15 B–K2 B–QB1 16 N–K5 N**×**N 17 B**×**N B–K3 18 B–B3 R–Q2 19 P–R3 R1–Q1 20 N–K2 N–K1 21 N–B4 B–B3 22 B**×**B N**×**B** (*289*)

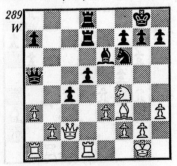

289
W

---

23 P–QN3 P×**P 24 Q**×**NP P–KR3 25 R–Q4 R–QB1 26 R–R4 Q–B4 27 Q–Q3 Q–B6 28 Q**×**Q R**×**Q 29 R–R5 K–B1 30 R–N1 R–B1 31 R–Q1 P–N4 32 N–R5 N**×**N 33 B**×**N K–K2 34 B–B3 R–B6 35 R–Q4 K–B3 36 K–R2 R–B7 37 K–N3 R–N2 38 R–N4 R**×**R 39 P**×**R R–B5 40 B**×**P B**×**B 41 R**×**B R**×**P 42 R–Q6+ K–N2 43 R–R6 R–N2 44 P–R4 R–N5 45 P**×**P P**×**P 46 R**×**P K–N3 47 R–R6+ P–B3 48 P–B3 R–N7 49 P–K4 R–K7 50 K–R3 K–N2 51 P–N3 K–N3 52 R–R3 R–K8 53 K–N4 R–K7 54 R–N3 R–K8 55 R–N4 R–K6 56 R–N6 R–K7 57 K–R3 R–K6 58 K–N4 R–K7 59 R–N3 R–K8 60 R–N4 R–K6 61 P–B4 R**×**KP 62 R**×**R P–B4+ 63 K–B3 P**×**R+ 64 K**×**P ½–½**

2510 AK–Andras Adorjan:
R10: 24 February:

Grünfeld

1 P–QB4 P–KN3 2 P–Q4 N–KB3 3 N–QB3 P–Q4 4 N–B3 B–N2 5 B–N5 N–K5 6 P×**P N**×**N 7 N**×**N P–K3 8 Q–Q2 P–KR3 9 N–R3 P**×**P 10 N–B4** 10 Q–K3+ K–B1 11 N–B4 P–QB4! 12 P×P P–Q5 is unclear. **10 . . . 0–0! 11 P–KN3** Alternatives are weaker, e.g. 11 N4×QP P–QB3∓, or 11 P–K3 P–QB4! 12 P×P P–Q5 13 P×P (13 0–0–0? P×N 14 Q×Q P×P+ 15 K–N1 B–B4+ 16 Q–Q3 B×Q+ 17 N×B N–R3∓) 13 . . . Q×P 14 Q×Q B×Q 15 B–N5 N–R3! 16 N4–K2 B×QBP 17 0–0 N–B2 18 B–R4 B–B4∓ Pytel–Adorjan, Polanica Zdroj 1971. **11 . . . N–B3!?** Black can equalize here with 11 . . . P–QB3 12 B–N2 B–B4 13 0–0 N–Q2. **12 P–K3 N–K2 13 B–N2 P–QB4! 14 P**×**P** 14 0–0 is good for Black after 14 . . . P×P 15 P×P N–B3 16

N3–K2 P–KN4! 17 N–R5 B–R1 18 P–B4 B–N5 19 B–B3 B×B 20 R×B P–N5∓, while 14 N3×QP leads to equality after 14 . . . P×P 15 0–0. but not 15 P×P? N×N 16 N×N R–K1+. **14 . . . P–Q5 15 N–Q1** This seems best. The alternatives are 15 R–Q1 B–N5! 16 N3–K2 P×P 17 P×P (17 Q×P Q–R4+∓; 17 Q×Q P×P+∓) 17 . . . Q–B2, and 15 0–0–0 P×N!? 16 Q×Q P×P+ 17 K–N1 B–B4+ 18 Q–Q3 B×Q+ 19 N×Q QR–N1 20 N×P KR–B1 21 R–QB1 (21 R–Q7 R×P!) 21 . . . N–B3 with 22 . . . P–N3 to follow in an unclear position. **15 . . . P×P 16 N×KP Q×Q+ 17 K×Q B×P 18 QR–QN1 B–QR6!** This is better than both 18 . . . B–Q5 19 KR–QB1± and 18 . . . R–Q1+ 19 K–K2 B–QR6 20 B×P (20 N–Q3 N–B4!) 20 . . . B×B 21 R×B B×P 22 R–QB1 B–Q3 (22 . . . B×N? 23 P×B N–B4 24 R1–B7 N–Q3 25 R×RP N–N4 26 R×R R×R 27 R–B2± and if now 27 . . . R×P? White wins with 28 R×R N–B6+ 29 K–Q2 N×R 30 N–Q5) 23 N–Q3±. **19 N–Q3 R–Q1 20 K–B3!** Both 20 K–B2 and 20 K–K2 allow 20 . . . N–B4! **20 . . . P–QR4** 20 . . . B–K3 allows White a big advantage after 21 R×P N–Q4+ 22 B×N B×B 23 N×B R×N 24 K–B4 R1–Q1 25 N–N4. **21 KR–Q1 B–K3 22 B×P** Not 22 N–B2? B×BP!, while the other alternatives promise White nothing: 22 N–QB4 R×N+! (22 . . . B–QN5+?! 23 N×B P×N+ 24 K×P R×R 25 R×R R×P and the position is roughly equal.) 23 R×R B×P; or 22 R×P N–Q4+ 23 N×N B×N 24 B×B R×B=. **22 . . . QR–N1 23 P–B6 B–Q3 24 N–QB4 N–Q4+ 25 K–N2 N–K2 26 K–B3** Or 26 N×P N×P! **26 . . . N–Q4+ 27 K–B2?** Better 27 K–N2= **27 . . . B–KB4 28**

P–QR3 B–B2 29 R–N5 N–K2 30 P–B3 P–R4? Adorjan was in time-trouble and overlooks 30 . . . R–Q5! 31 K–B3 (31 N–K3?! R1–Q1 with a probably winning position) 31 . . . R1–Q1 32 N4–N2 ∓. **31 K–B3 N–Q4+ 32 K–N2 N–K2 33 N–B2 R×R 34 N×R P–KR5! 35 P×P B–Q6 36 N1–K3 B–K7 37 K–B3 B×BP 38 N×P** (*290*)

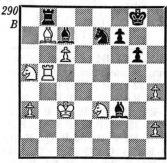

38 . . . B×N?? 38 . . . P–B4 would keep Black alive, but now he is dead. **39 R×B N×P** 39 . . . B×P may be a little better. **40 R–R8! R×R 41 B×R N–K4 42 B×B N×B 43 P–R4 1–0**

2511 Zoltan Ribli–AK:
R11: 25 February:

Sicilian

1 P–K4 P–QB4 2 N–KB3 P–K3 3 P–Q4 P×P 4 N×P N–QB3 5 N–QB3 Q–B2 6 B–K2 N–B3 7 0–0 P–QR3 8 B–K3 B–N5 9 N–R4 0–0 10 N×N QP×N 11 B–N6 Q–B5 12 B–Q3 N–Q2 13 P–KN3 Q–B3 14 P–QR3 B–K2 15 B–B7 P–K4 16 P–QN4 P–QN4 17 N–N6 N×N 18 B×N B–R6 19 R–K1 KR–N1 20 B–K3 P–QR4 21 P–QB3 P×P 22 BP×P R–Q1 23 B–N6 R–Q2 24 Q–B2 R–N1 25 B–R5 P–B4 26 B–K2 P–B5 27 P–R4 P×P 28 R×P R–Q5 29 P–N5 R×NP 30

B–QB3 R–Q1 31 R–Q1 R–QB1 32 R × P (*291*)

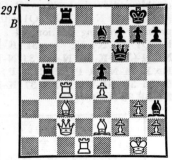

32 . . . R4–B4 Overlooking an easy win, pointed out by Geller in *64*, with 32 . . . R × R 33 B × R Q–B6 34 B–B1 B × B 35 R × B R–B4 36 R–B1 P–R4! **33 R × R B × R 34 B–B1 B × B 35 K × B B B × P 36 Q × B R × B 37 K–N2 P–R4 38 R–Q5 K–R2 39 Q–KB5+ Q × Q 40 P × Q P–B3 41 P–R4 R–B3 42 K–B3 P–N3 43 P × P+ K × P 44 R–Q8 R–B6+ 45 K–B2 K–B4** The sealed move. **46 R–KR8 R–B7+ 47 K–K3 K–N5 48 R–KN8+ K–B4 49 R–KR8 R–B6+ 50 K–B2 P–K5 51 R–KN8 R–R6 52 R–K8 R–R5 53 R–KN8 R–R7+ 54 K–K3 R–KN7 55 R–N7 K–K4 56 R–K7+ K–Q4 57 R–Q7+ K–K3 58 R–QR7 R × P+ 59 K × P R–N5+ 60 K–B3 K–B4 61 R–R5+ K–N3 62 R–QN5 R × P 63 R–R5 R–R8 64 K–N2 R–R5 65 K–B3 R–QN5 66 R–QB5 R–N1 67 R–B4 K–N4 68 R–B5+ P–B4 69 R–B4 P–R5 70 K–N2 R–N7+ 71 K–R3 R–N6+ 72 K–N2 R–N6+ 73 K–B2 R–N5 74 R–B8 P–R6 75 R–QR8 R–N5 76 K–N3 R–N6+ 77 K–R2 P–B5 78 R–KN8+ K–R5 79 R–KR8+ K–N5 80 R–KN8+ K–B4 81 R–KB8+ K–K5 82 R–K8+ K–B6 83 R–KB8 R–N2 84 R–QR8 R–K2 85 R–R6 R–K8 86 R–R8 K–B7 87 K × P P–B6 88 R–R2+ R–K7 89 R–R1 ½–½**

2512 AK–Rafael Vaniagan:
R12: 26 February:

French

1 P–K4 P–K3 2 P–Q4 P–Q4 3 N–Q2 P–QB4 4 KN–B3 N–QB3 5 KP × P KP × P 6 B–N5 B–Q3 7 P × P B × BP 7 . . . Q–K2+ is unclear. **8 0–0 KN–K2 9 N–N3 B–N3** Or 9 . . . B–Q3± **10 R–K1 0–0 11 B–N5!?** The alternative is 11 B–K3± **11 . . . P–KR3 12 B–KR4** Not 12 B/QN5 × N?! RP × B 13 B–N5 P–N5∓, but 12 B–K3 was also possible. **12 . . . P–N4** 12 . . . P–B3!? 13 B–N3 N–B4 is unclear. **13 B–N3 N–B4** If 13 . . . B–N5 then 14 Q–Q3± with N/B3–Q4 to follow. **14 Q–Q2 N × B 15 RP × N Q–B3 16 P–B3 B–KB4 17 Q × QP QR–Q1 18 Q–B4 B–Q6 19 Q–QR4 B × B 20 Q × B P–N5 21 N/B3–Q4 N × N 22 P × N** Not 22 N × N? which allows Black to obtain equality after 22 . . . P–R3 23 Q–KR5 B × N. **22 . . . P–R3** If 22 . . . B × P White obtains a clear advantage with 23 N × B R × N 24 Q × P R–Q7 25 Q × RP R × NP 26 P–R4±. **23 Q–KR5** Not 23 Q–K5? B × P= **23 . . . B × P 24 Q × NP+ Q–N2 25 Q–B3** If 25 Q × Q+ Black is all right after 25 . . . B × Q 26 R–K2 (26 R–K7 KR–K1 27 R × NP R–K7) 26 . . . KR–K1 27 R1–K1 R × R 28 R × R P–N3. **25 . . . B × NP 26 QR–Q1** Probably more accurate than 26 QR–N1 P–N4! (26 . . . P–N3? 27 R–K4 K–R1 28 Q–K2±±) 27 R–K4 K–R1± **26 . . . P–N3 27 Q–N7** 27 R–K4!? **27 . . . R × R! 28 R × R Q–N5 29 R–N1 R–Q1 30 Q × RP R–Q8+ 31 R × R Q × R+ 32 Q–B1** 32 K–R2 leads to a perpetual by 32 . . . Q–R4+ 33 K–N1 Q–Q8+. **32 . . . Q–B7 33 Q–N5 B–R6 34 Q–Q5±** (*292*)

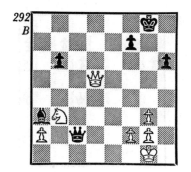

292
B

34 . . . **B–B1** Or 34 . . . Q×RP 35
Q–Q8+ K–N2 36 Q×P±, but
34 . . . B–B4! is better. **35 Q–Q2**
Not 35 P–R4? Q–N8+ 36 K–R2
Q–R7 **35 . . . Q–K5 36 K–R2 B–B4
37 N–B1 K–N2 38 N–Q3 Q–Q5 39
Q–K2 B–Q3?!** 39 . . . Q–QB5!?
is safer, **40 K–R3 Q–Q4 41 N–B4
B×N 42 P×P± K–B1 43 K–N3
P–N4 44 Q–N2 Q–Q6+ 45 K–R4
Q–Q1+ 46 K–N3 Q–Q6+ 47 K–
R2 K–N1 48 P–R3 Q–Q3 49 Q–N4
Q–KB3 50 P–B3! Q–R5+ 51 K–N1
Q–R4?** This lightens White's task.
Better 51 . . . Q–B3 **52 Q–K7 K–
R2** Black also loses after 52 . . . Q–
KB4 53 Q–K8+ K–N2 54 Q–K5+
Q×Q 55 P×Q K–N3 56 P–B4 K–
B4 57 P–N3 P–R4 58 K–B2 K–N5 59
K–K3! K×NP 60 P–B5 P–R5 61
P–K6 P×P 62 P×P P–R6 63 P–K7
P–R7 64 P–K8=Q P–R8=Q 65
Q–KN8+, and after 52 . . . Q–N3 53
Q–K8+ K–N2 54 Q×NP. **53
P–N4 Q–R6** 53 . . . Q–N3 is met by
54 Q–K4 and if 54 . . . P–B4 55
Q–Q3±± or 54 . . . K–N2 55
Q–K5+ and 56 Q×P±±. **54
Q×P+ K–R1 55 Q–K8+ K–R2 56
Q–K4+ K–N1 57 P–B5 Q–N6+ 58
K–B1 Q–R6+ 59 K–K2 Q–N7+
1–0**

2513 Istvan Bilek–AK:
R13: 27 February:

English

**1 P–QB4 P–QB4 2 P–KN3 P–KN3
3 B–N2 B–N2 4 N–QB3 N–QB3
5 P–K3 P–K3 6 KN–K2 KN–K2 7
0–0 0–0 8 P–Q4 P×P 9 N×P
P–Q4 10 P×P N×N 11 P×N N×P
12 N×N P×N 13 B–K3 B–K3 14
Q–Q2 Q–Q2 ½–½**

2514 AK–Istvan Csom:
R14: 1 March:

Sicilian

The notes to this game are by
Geller from *64*.

1 P–K4	P–QB4
2 N–KB3	P–Q3
3 P–Q4	P×P
4 Q×P	

In this comparatively quiet variation White can hardly count on
gaining any opening advantage.

| 4 . . . | N–QB3 |
| 5 B–QN5 | Q–Q2!? |

As a rule 5 . . . B–Q2 is played
here. I considered the text move a
theoretical novelty, although these
days it is difficult to think up a new
continuation on move five, let alone
in the well-studied Sicilian. Only
after the tournament ended, when I
was already back in Moscow, did
I learn that the move 5 . . . Q–Q2
had been suggested in the article
Theoretical Notes by the international
master I. Zaitsev (*64* 1972 No. 40),
although, apparently, it had not
been seen in a major tournament. It
is possible that it was independently
examined, even earlier, by
Hungarian players, but maybe they
noticed that article.

6 Q–K3

An artificial move. Simpler and
better is 6 B×N and if 6 . . . P×B

then 7 P–B4, getting into a known set-up, while in the case of 6 . . . Q×B, as recommended by Zaitsev, 7 N–B3 with a big advantage in development.

| 6 . . . | P–QR3 |
| 7 B–R4 | |

And here 7 B×N deserved consideration, although on K3 the white queen occupies a less apt position. Now Black's light-squared bishop stands to be very strong and may play a major role both in attack and defence

7 . .	P–QN4
8 B–N3	N–R4
9 0–0	P–K3
10 R–Q1	B–N2
11 N–B3	B–K2
12 P–K5	N×B
13 RP×N	

It is possible that after 13 BP×N the QB-file might come in handy for White.

13 . . .   R–Q1

A questionable decision. He should have played 13 . . . Q–B3, creating pressure on the a8–h1 diagonal and controlling the e4 square. In that case 14 P×P B×P 15 Q–Q4 is not difficult on account of 15 . . . 0–0–0 and the line 16 Q×P N–K2 17 Q×BP KR–N1 leads to a suspect position for White.

14 N–K4!	Q–B3
15 N×P+	B×N
16 P×B	R×P
17 B–Q2	N–K2
18 B–N4	R–Q4

18 . . . R–Q2 is more reliable.

Barczay points out that if 18 . . . R×R 19 R×R N–Q4 20 Q–Q4.

19 P–B4!	P×P
20 P×P	Q×P
21 B×N	K×B
22 N–K5	Q–K5? (293)

A mistake. He should have defended by means of 22 . . . Q–N4

293
W

| 23 Q–N5+ | K–B1 |
| 24 P–B3 | |

White wins the exchange, but now he obtains a technically difficult ending, ultimately ending up as a draw.

A win is reached with 24 N–Q7+ K–K1 25 Q×P K×N 26 Q×R Q×P+ 27 K×Q R×R+ 28 P–B3 R×R 29 Q×P and the KRP decides the game's outcome.

24 . . . Q×N 25 Q×Q R×Q 26 R–Q8+ K–K2 27 R×R R–KN4! 28 R–R3 R–N4 (?) 28 . . . P–KR4! 29 R×KRP K–B3 30 P–QN3 R–N3 31 R–KR4 B–Q4 32 P–QN4 P–N4 33 R–N4 K–B4 34 R–R5 P–B3 35 K–B2 K–K4 36 K–K3 R–B3 37 R–B5 R–N3 38 R–Q4 P–B4 39 P–R4 (?) P–B5+ 40 K–Q3 P×P 41 K–B3 R–N2 42 R–Q2 R–KR2 ½–½

2515 **Dragun Velimirović–AK:**
    R15: 2 March:

Ruy Lopez

1 P–K4 P–K4 2 N–KB3 N–QB3 3 B–N5 P–QR3 4 B–R4 N–B3 5 0–0 B–K2 6 R–K1 P–QN4 7 B–N3 P–Q3 8 P–B3 0–0 9 P–KR3 N–QR4 10 B–B2 P–B4 11 P–Q4 Q–B2 12 QN–Q2 N–B3 13 N–N3 B–N2 14 P–Q5 N–N1 15 P–B4 N1–Q2 16 B–Q2 P–N5 17 N–B1 N–K1 18 N–Q3 P–N3 19 B–R6 N–N2 20 P–N4 ½–½

Moscow, 24–30.4.1973

Karpov	1	$\frac{1}{2}$	Karpov	1	$\frac{1}{2}$
Spassky	0	$\frac{1}{2}$	Taimanov	0	$\frac{1}{2}$

Karpov played on board one for the USSR Youth team (the other two teams in the event were USSR–1 and USSR–2), and captured the board prize with 3/4 (this was jointly the absolute best result). Karpov also won the best game prize for his win over Spassky. Team results: USSR–1 23½, USSR Youth 18½, USSR–2 18.

2601 Mark Taimanov–AK:
R1: 24 April:

Nimzo-Indian

In single combat on the first board, the two Leningrad grandmasters were the only ones in the entire match to keep both queens on the board for nearly forty moves. In all the other first round games the queen was the most short-lived piece, and several grandmaster pairs managed to cross the bridge from opening to endgame in double-quick time.

The leader of the country's youth team went to play on this day feeling slightly unwell, but that didn't have any effect on his fighting frame of mind. As always, Mark Taimanov played actively and optimistically. As a result, though not without errors, a heavy-weight grandmaster duel evolved.

1 P–Q4 N–KB3 2 P–QB4 P–K3 3 N–QB3 B–N5 4 P–K3 P–B4 5 B–Q3 0–0 6 N–B3 P–Q4 7 0–0 QP×P 8 B×BP P×P 9 P×P P–QN3 10 Q–K2 B–N2 11 R–Q1 QN–Q2 12 B–Q2 R–B1 13 B–QR6 B×B 14 Q×B B×N 15 P×B R–B2 16 QR–B1 Q–B1 17 Q–R4 (*294*)

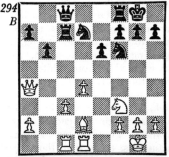

294
B

At first the struggle flows smoothly enough and, it seems, is on the point of rolling along a peaceful channel. But the main events unfold after Black's next move.

17 . . . R–B5!

The moves P–QB4 and B–B4 pose Black definite threats, and so he hurries to block the c4 square, even at the cost of a dead pawn.

18 Q×P

Now White has a material advantage, Black a positional advantage.
18 . . . Q–B3 19 Q–R3 R–B1 20 P–R3 P–R3 21 R–N1 R–R5

Black, not without foundation, counts on winning one of the Q-side pawns.
22 Q–N3 N–Q4 23 R/Q1–QB1 R–B5

Black's concentrated force oscillates; as a whole compensating the sacrificed pawn, but hardly sufficient to gain a palpable advantage.

After the game, in analysis, both players, at almost every move, solved the problems of the ending at once. Thus, for example, here Anatoly Karpov, on 24 Q–N5, intended to carry out approximately the following plan: 24 . . . Q×Q 25 R×Q R–R1 26 R–B2 P–B3 27 K–B1 K–B2 28 K–K2 P–K4 29 K–Q3 R1–R5 30 R–N3 K–K3 and White's position is suddenly threatened with the piquant threat 31 P–N4 P–K5+! 32 K×P N–B4 mate! Of course, this line is far from forced, but it serves to illustrate that, in the ending, disregarding the extra pawn, exact play is called for from White. On the whole the rivals' chances must now be counted as level, and, one should think, that White will, in the final analysis, reach a peaceful haven. However, grandmaster Taimanov has nothing to do with those chess-players who, having an extra pawn, will think about a quick draw.
24 R–N2 P–B3

On 24 . . . N×P 25 B×N R×B 26 R×R Q×R 27 Q×Q R×Q 28 N–K5 N×N 29 P×N both players will cross the 30-move barrier with preparations for a draw. (Reference to the ill-starred but immortal rule that games may not be drawn in less than thirty moves – eds).

25 R–K1 K–B2 26 Q–Q1

'I cannot be worse here', Taimanov stated definitely. At this moment White's position already seems more attractive than it did a few moves ago. In the press bureau, opinion was divided – one preferred Black's chances, another White's.
26 . . .N–B1 27 R–N3 N–N3 28 Q–N1 R–QR1 29 R–K4

The white queen is tied down to defence. Perhaps now is exactly the right time to 'stir up trouble': 29 Q–Q3 R×RP 30 R×KP!? K×R 31 Q×N.
29 . . . R5–R5 30 R–N2 N–B1 31 Q–Q3 R–B5 32 R–K1

A 'polite' invitation to the black knight to return to KN3, in which case, clearly, 33 R×KP!? would follow without fail. White, as before, does not fear for his QBP: 32 . . . N×P 33 B×N R×B 34 R×NP R×Q 35 R×Q etc.
32 . . . R–R6

The battery of black pieces strengthens to the maximum its fire upon White's Q-side. All the same, the following denouement is largely attributable to the time-trouble in which White now finds himself.
33 Q–N1 N–N3 34 R–QB1

White, in vain, switches wholly to defence. 34 Q–Q3 deserved consideration – setting a trap: 34 . . . N×P? 35 R–N3! and intending to strike a blow against K6 – 36 R×KP.
34 . . . N×P

Black denied himself this dainty morsel for a good fifteen moves.
35 Q–Q3 N–K7+ 36 Q×N/2 R×R 37 B×R Q×B+ 38 K–R2 (*295*)

The decisive mistake. 38 N–K1 was essential.
38 . . . R×N!

295
B

A well-thought-out blow. After 38 . . . N–B5 39 Q–Q2 the worst is over for White.

39 P×R N–R5!

At this moment the flag on White's clock quivered and tumbled down. Truth to tell, it is already none too easy to find an acceptable defence, e.g. 40 R×P? Q–B2+; 40 K–N3 Q–N4+; that leaves 40 R–N3 but also then with 40 . . . Q–N4! 41 Q–B1 Q–B5+ 42 K–N1 N×P+ or 42 . . . Q×QP, Black has excellent chances of realizing his advantage. **0–1** (time)

2602 AK–Boris Spassky:
R3: 26 April:

Ruy Lopez

The prize of the weekly *64* for the best game of the match tournament was awarded to grandmaster Anatoly Karpov. The prize was a cut crystal (or glass) bowl. The presentation was made by Tigran Petrosian!

1	P–K4	P–K4
2	N–KB3	N–QB3
3	B–N5	P–QR3
4	B–R4	N–B3
5	0–0	B–K2
6	R–K1	P–QN4
7	B–N3	P–Q3
8	P–B3	0–0
9	P–KR3	N–N1

Both players are ardent supporters of the Spanish game. They not infrequently employ it in the most crucial competitions and have successfully passed through theoretical duels. It is not surprising that on this occasion the subject of the argument was the frequently met Breyer variation.

10 P–Q3

The main line continuation is 10 P–Q4. The line employed in the game hardly gives White any advantage. But in return it leads to a tense, protracted struggle.

10	...	B–N2
11	QN–Q2	N1–Q2
12	N–B1	N–B4
13	B–B2	R–K1
14	N–N3	B–KB1
15	P–N4	N4–Q2
16	P–Q4	

All this has been met with more than once. Now White is forced to push the QP, otherwise Black will intercept the initiative with the liberating pawn advance . . . P–Q4.

16	...	P–R3
17	B–Q2	N–N3
18	B–Q3	P–N3

Spassky deviates from the game Karpov–Gligorić (No. 2408) in which 18 . . . R–B1 was played.

19 Q–B2

A regrouping of forces. The queen frees the Q1 square for the rooks and at the same time protects the K4 square.

19 ... N/B3–Q2

If White has surplus defence of his QB4 square, it is essential to organize rapid pressure against the neighbouring . . . Q5 square with the help of the bishop on . . . KN2.

20	QR–Q1	B–N2
21	P×P	

Here I thought for more than 30 minutes. Black has disposed his pieces very adroitly and, therefore, it is not easy to set up an advantageous game. The standard plan, with an attempt at a K-side attack, or undermining the centre with P–KB4, will not do, since in each case Black has time to strike a counter-blow in the centre – . . . P–Q4. I came to the conclusion that White is almost forced to carry out this central exchange.

21 . . .   **P×P**

This move, undoubtedly, cannot be called a mistake, but maybe one should exchange knights.

22 P–B4

This follows rapidly; there is no time to prepare this advance, for example, 22 B–K3 Q–K2 23 N–Q2 P–QB4 with quality.

22 . . .   **P×P**

On 22 . . . P–QB4 a piece sacrifice was possible: 23 BP×P P–B5 24 B×BP R–QB1 25 B×BP+ K×B 26 Q–N3+.

23 B×BP   **Q–K2** (*296*)

But this is already an inaccuracy. Allowing the dangerous white 'Spanish bishop' to escape with his life, Black subjects himself to great difficulties. After 23 . . . N×B 24 Q×N chances would have been level.

24 B–N3!   **P–QB4**
25 P–QR4

Of course, in making this move, I

foresaw the exchange sacrifice and considered its consequences. As a matter of fact, White had decided on the exchange sacrifice a move earlier (24 B–N3), and now there is no going back, nor is there any need.

25 . . .   **P–B5**

25 . . . P×P and 25 . . . R–QB1 were both bad on account of 26 P–R5, Black replying, according to his 25th move, either 26 . . . R–QB1 or 26 . . . P×P 27 Q–R2 N–R1 28 B×NP!

26 B–R2   **B–QB3**
27 P–R5   **B–R5**
28 Q–B1   **N–QB1**

Hardly better for Black was 28 . . . B×R 29 R×B N–R5 30 B×RP B×B 31 Q×B and not 31 . . . N–B6 because of 32 B×P with the threat of 33 Q×P+, while on 31 . . . N–B1 White has excellent attacking prospects with 32 R–QB1.

29 B×RP   **B×R**
30 R×B   **N–Q3?**

After this move there follows an utterly unexpected denouement. 30 . . . B×B also loses: 31 Q×B N–Q3 32 N–N5 N–KB1 33 N–R5 P×N 34 R×N QR–B1 35 R–KB6.

The best appears to be 30 . . . R–R2. but even in that case, after 31 B×B K×B 32 Q×P, White gets more than enough compensation for the exchange.

31 B×B   **K×B** (*297*)

32 Q–N5!

And here is the surprise! White quite unexpectedly offers the exchange of queens, which Black cannot accept in view of the piece that would be lost.

Black would suddenly be winning after 32 Q–Q2 QR–Q1 33 Q×N? N–B1.

32 . . .   P–B3

32 . . . QR–B1 only drags out the struggle; after 33 R×N Q×Q 34 N×Q N–B3 35 N–K2 P–B6 36 B×P, White ought to realize his material advantage.

33 Q–N4   K–R2

The only defence against 34 R×N and N–B5+, but the position is already hopeless.

34 N–R4   1–0

Some might think this a somewhat premature surrender, but, with a survey of the following variations, they will be convinced that Black's position is hopelessly indefensible: (a) 34 . . . R–KN1 35 B×P R–N2 36 R×N Q×R 37 N4–B5 and mate can only be avoided at the cost of the queen – 37 . . . Q–Q8+, or (b) 34 . . . N–KB1 35 N×NP with 36 Q–R5+ and 37 R×N to follow.

2603 AK–Mark Taimanov:
R4: 27 April:

Sicilian

1 P–K4 P–QB4 2 N–KB3 N–QB3 3 P–Q4 P×P 4 N×P P–K3 5 N–N5 P–Q3 6 P–QB4 N–B3 7 N1–B3 P–QR3 8 N–R3 B–K2 9 B–K2 0–0 10 0–0 P–QN3 11 B–K3 B–N2 12 R–B1 R–B1 13 Q–Q2 N–K4 14 Q–Q4 N4–Q2 15 KR–Q1

R–K1 16 N–B2 Q–B2 17 K–R1 P–R3 18 P–B3 (*298*)

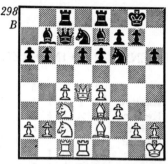

298
B

18 . . . P–Q4 19 BP×P P×P 20 P×P B–B4 21 Q–Q2 B×B 22 N×B Q–KB5 23 N–N4 N×P 24 B×P B×B 25 Q×N N–B4 26 R–QN1 B–N2 27 Q–Q2 N–K3 28 N–N5 P–R4 29 N–B2 Q–QR5 30 N–B3 Q–R5 31 N2–K4 B×N 32 N×B R/K1–Q1 33 Q–K3 P–QN4 34 R/Q1–QB1 R–R1 35 P–QR3 R–Q5 36 R–Q1 R1–Q1 37 N–B3 P–N5 38 P×P R×P 39 N–Q5 R–N4 40 Q–K4 Q×Q 41 P×Q R–N6 42 N–K7+ K–B1 43 R×R+ N×R 44 N–Q5 K–K1 ½–½

2604 Boris Spassky–AK:
R6: 29 April:

English

1 P–QB4 N–KB3 2 N–QB3 P–B4 3 N–B3 P–Q4 4 P×P N×P 5 P–K3 N×N 6 NP×N P–KN3 7 P–Q4 B–N2 8 B–Q3 Q–B2 9 0–0 0–0 10 B–R3 N–Q2 11 P–K4 P–K4 12 B–N5 P–QR3 13 B×N B×B 14 B×P KR–K1 15 N×P B–N4 16 P–QB4 B×N 17 QP×B Q×B 18 P×B P×P ½–½

27 LENINGRAD INTERZONAL 2–27.6.1973

	1	2	3	4	5	6	7	8	9	0	1	2	3	4	5	6	7	8	
1 **Karpov**	×	½	½	1	½	½	1	1	½	½	1	½	1	1	1	1	1	1	**13½**
2 Korchnoi	½	×	1	½	1	1	½	½	1	1	1	1	1	½	0	1	1	1	**13½**
3 R. Byrne	½	0	×	½	1	½	½	½	1	½	1	1	1	½	1	1	1	1	**12½**
4 Smejkal	0	½	½	×	0	0	½	1	1	½	0	1	1	1	1	1	1	1	**11**
5 Larsen	½	0	0	1	×	1	1	0	½	0	0	1	½	1	1	½	1	1	**10**
6 Hübner	½	0	½	1	0	×	½	1	½	1	½	1	1	½	½	½	0	1	**10**
7 Kuzmin	0	½	½	½	0	½	×	0	½	1	½	½	½	1	1	1	1	½	**9½**
8 Gligorić	0	½	½	0	1	0	1	×	½	0	½	½	1	½	½	0	1	1	**8½**
9 Taimanov	½	0	0	0	½	½	½	½	×	½	½	1	½	½	1	½	1	½	**8½**
10 Tal	½	0	½	½	1	0	0	1	½	×	1	1	0	½	0	1	0	1	**8½**
11 Quinteros	0	0	0	1	1	½	½	½	½	0	×	0	½	0	½	1	½	1	**7½**
12 Radulov	½	0	0	0	0	0	½	½	0	0	1	×	1	1	½	½	1	1	**7½**
13 Torre	0	0	0	0	½	0	½	0	½	1	½	0	×	½	½	1	1	1	**7**
14 Uhlmann	0	½	½	0	0	½	0	½	½	½	1	0	½	×	½	½	½	1	**7**
15 Rukavina	0	1	0	0	0	½	0	½	0	1	½	½	½	½	×	0	1	½	**6½**
16 Tukmakov	0	0	0	0	½	½	0	1	½	0	0	½	0	½	1	×	½	1	**6**
17 Estevez	0	0	0	0	0	1	0	0	0	1	½	0	0	½	0	½	×	1	**4½**
18 Cuellar	0	0	0	0	0	0	½	0	½	0	0	0	0	0	½	0	0	×	**1½**

The tournament, played in the Dzerzhinsky House of Culture, was a very great success for Karpov.

2701 Guillermo Estevez–AK:
R1: 3 June:

Queen's Gambit Declined

1 P–Q4 N–KB3 2 P–QB4 P–K3 3 N–KB3 P–Q4 4 N–B3 B–K2 5 B–N5 0–0 6 P–K3 P–KR3 7 B–R4 P–QN3 8 B–K2 B–N2 9 B×N B×B 10 P×P P×P 11 P–QN4 P–B3 12 0–0 P–QR4 13 P–QR3 Q–Q3 14 Q–N3 P×P 15 P×P N–Q2= **16 KR–Q1 R×R 17 R×R B–K2 18 R–R7 R–N1 19 N–R2 B–QB1 20 Q–B2 B–B3 21 N–B1 N–B1 22 N–Q3 B–B4 23 Q–R4 N–Q2 24 R–R8 R×R 25 Q×R+ K–R2 26 Q–R6 P–N3 27 Q–N7 K–N2 28 P–R3 P–R4 29 Q–R7 B–Q1 30 Q–N7 Q–B2 31 Q–R8 B–K2 32 N/Q3–K5 B×NP 33 Q×P?!** Better 33 N×QBP! B–Q3 34 B–N5= **33 . . . Q×Q 34 N×Q B–Q3 35 B–N5 N–B3 36 N–Q2 N–K1 37 P–B3 N–B2 38 B–K2 B–B7 39 K–B2 B–R5 40 N–K5 P–QN4** Here the game was adjourned and White sealed **41 N–Q3** Better 41 N–B6! P–N5 42 N–R5= White was certainly not losing up to this point, but from here on White goes unnecessarily on to the defensive . . . **41 . . . P–R5! 42 N–N2** And here it was better to play 42 N–QB1 to regroup by 43 B–Q3 and 44 N2–N3. **42 . . . B–N5 43 N–N1 B–N6** *(299)*

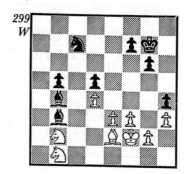

299
W

44 B–Q3 B–B5 45 P–K4 P–N4 46 P×P B×P 47 N–Q1 B–B3 48 N/N1–B3 B–Q2 49 N–K4 B–K2 50 N–B5? This is a definite error. Estevez should have played 50 K–K2. The text allows Black to win a pawn. **50 . . . B×N! 51 P×B N–K3 52 N–B3 P–N5 53 N–K4 P–N6 54 N–Q2** Other moves allow 54 . . . P–B4 and 55 . . . N×P. **54 . . . N×P 55 B–N1 K–B3 0–1** (time) 3.30 – 2.56

2702 AK–Robert Hübner:
R2: 4 June:

Sicilian

The notes to this game are based on those by Robert Hübner (RH) in *The Chess Player* and those by Pavel Kondratiev (PK) in the tournament bulletin.

The figures after the moves indicate the amount of time (in minutes) taken.

1 P–K4 0		**P–QB4** 0
2 N–KB3 0		**P–K3** 0
3 P–Q4 0		**P×P** 0
4 N×P 0		**P–QR3** 0

5 B–Q3 0		**N–KB3** 1
6 0–0 1		**Q–B2** 1
7 Q–K2 8		**P–Q3** 2
8 P–QB4 4		**P–KN3** 8

PK: The German player tries an original opening system, the originator of which seems to be the Riga grandmaster Aivar Gipslis. Black boldly goes in for a considerable weakening of his dark squares and, at the same time, his QP, hoping that White will not find it so simple to utilize these circumstances in the given concrete situation.

9 N–QB3 8

RH: An interesting alternative is 9 P–QN3!? with the follow-up B–N2, P–B4 and N–Q2–B3.

9 . . . **B–N2** 0
10 B–K3 1

PK: In the game Holmov–Gipslis, 34 USSR Ch 1967, White tried the plan of a K-side attack: 10 B–N5 0–0 11 QR–Q1 P–N3 12 K–R1 B–N2 13 P–B4 QN–Q2 14 P–KB5. However, after 14 . . . QR–K1 15 P×KP P×P 16 B–B2 N–K4 17 B–QR4 R–K2 18 B–N3 B–B1 Black, having beaten off the attack, had an excellent game.

10 . . **0–0** 1
11 QR–B1 9

RH: Better 11 P–B4! (Hübner only gave this a '!?' in *Informator 15*) and if 11 . . . N–B3 then 12 N×N P×N 13 P–KB5!

11 . . . **N–B3** 6
12 N×N 4

PK: A courageous, unstereotyped decision, marking the start of an interesting and deep plan. The standard tactical lunge 12 N–Q5? would have been bad in view of 12 . . . P×N 13 BP×P N×N.

12 . . . **P×N** 4
13 P–B4 3

RH: Not 13 P–B5? P–Q4 14 P×P N×P (in *Informator* RH gives this as equal) 15 N×N KP×N∓

13 ...   **P–B4** 4

14 KR–Q1 16

PK: Another unexpected move. White, apparently having prepared a K-side attack, moves the rook off the KB-file. The thought behind this becomes clear later.

14 ...   **B–N2** 1

Hübner now prefers 14 ... R–N1 which he gives '!?' in *The Chess Player 4*, while in *Informator 15* he gives the text a '?!' and 14 ... R–N1 an exclamation mark.

15 P–QR3 5   **B–B3** 18

16 P–QN4! 9

RH: Weaker is 16 P–K5 P×P 17 B×BP B–B6 18 Q×B Q×B+ 19 K–R1 P×P 20 Q×P P–QR4∓.

PK: White rapidly utilizes his better Q-side pawns and here generates a passed pawn – an untypical plan for a Sicilian middle-game, for this is usually Black's sphere of influence.

16 ...   **P×P** 4

17 P×P 0   **Q–N2** 1

PK: Pressure along the long diagonal – Black's only counter-chance. The text move is also played against the threat of N–Q5.

18 P–K5 1

RH: Alternatives are weaker:

(a) 18 P–N5 P×P 19 P×P B×KP 20 N×B N×N 21 B×N Q×B 22 R×P R–R7 23 R–Q2 B–Q5! and Black wins.

(b) 18 B–Q2 Q×P and now:

(b1) 19 N–N5 Q–B4+ 20 B–K3 Q–R4∓ and

(b2) 19 N–Q5 Q–N1 20 N–K7+ K–R1 21 N×B Q–N3+ 22 N–Q4! N–Q2 23 P–K5 P×P 24 P–QB5 N×P 25 R–N1 Q–Q1 are both good for Black.

18 ..   **P×P** 0

19 P×P 0   **N–Q2** 1

PK: 19 ... N–K5 is bad on account of 20 B×N B×B 21 B–B5.

20 P–N5 1   **P×P** 1

21 P×P 0   **B–Q4** 1

22 B–Q4 8 (*300*)

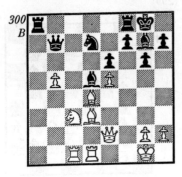

PK: Here is the position Karpov has been aiming for. In spite of the fact that there are many pieces on the board, the passed QNP is dangerous enough; in the first place its further advance greatly restricts Black. It is interesting that this is not the first time that Karpov has followed such an original plan in the Sicilian.

Compare the present position with that after White's 27th move in the game Karpov-Stein (diagram *171*, p. 162).

22 ...   **Q–N1** 27

23 R–K1 1   **B–N2** 1

24 P–N6 16   **R–Q1** 15

RH: Or 24 ... R–B1 25 B–N5 N–B4 26 R–N1±.

PK: Black prevents the manoeuvre 25 N–N5 on which would follow 25 ... N×KP!

25 B–N5 2   **R–R4!** 1

26 Q–K3 1   **Q–R1?** 18

RH: I should have played 26 ... B–QR1 with 27 ... Q–N2 to follow.

27 Q–B2 8   **B–QR3** 3

PK: An interesting continuation was 27 ... N–N1!? with the threat of 28 ... N–B3.

28 R–N1 9   **B×B** 8 (*301*)

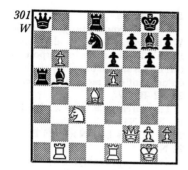

301
W

PK: The critical moment of the struggle. How to take on QN5? The answer to that question demanded great expenditure of energy and time, but that is just exactly what both players no longer had too much of. Karpov decided to exchange rooks, in order to reduce the pressure against his KP, but, all the same, 29 N×B was stronger. After that 29 ... R–R7 would be bad because of 30 P–N7!

Also after 29 ... Q–Q4 30 N–Q6 R–R7 (30 ... N×KP is bad: 31 B×N B×B 32 Q×P+ K–R1 33 N–K8. Hübner, in *Informator 15*, also mentions 30 ... R–KB1 31 P–N7±±.) 31 Q×P+ K–R1 32 B–N2 White has the better prospects, for example:

(a) 32 ... N×KP 33 Q–K7! Q×N 34 Q×Q R×Q 35 B×N B×B 36 R×B R–R1 37 P–N7 R–QN1 38 R–QB5 R3–Q1 39 R–B7 with R–KB1–B7 to follow;
(b) 32 ... N×NP 33 Q–B7;
(c) 32 ... R×B 33 R×R N×KP 34 Q–K7! or
(d) 32 ... Q–B4+ 33 K–R1 N×NP 34 Q×KP.

29 R×B? 5   R×R 9
30 N×R 1   Q–R4 1
31 N–Q6 3   N×KP! 6
PK: A tactical blow, saving Black.
32 B×N 12

Not 32 N–N7? on account of 32 ... N–B6+! (but not 32 ... N–N5? 33 N×Q B×B 34 Q×B R×Q 35 R–N1±± – Hübner) 33 P×N Q–KN4+ 34 K–R1 B×B 35 Q–B2 R–Q4 and Black wins.

32 ...   R×N! 0
Not 32 ... B×B 33 N–B4.
33 B×B 1
White has a lot of promising looking moves, but none of them work:

(a) 33 B×R? B–Q5∓∓ 34 R–K3 Q–R8+;
(b) 33 R–KB1? Q×P∓∓;
(c) 33 P–N7? and now
(c1) Kondratiev gives 33 ... R–Q1 and 34 P–N8=Q is no good because of 34 ... R×Q 35 B×R B–Q5 – this is where the weakness of White's back rank becomes apparent after the exchange of rooks on move 29.
(c2) Hübner, however, chooses 33 ... R–N3! with the same idea as in c1, while after 34 R–R1 there would follow 34 ... B×B 35 R×Q R–N8+ 36 Q–B1 B–Q5+ 37 K–R1 R×Q mate.

33 ...   K×B 1
34 R–N1 2   R–Q1 0
35 Q–N2+ 2   K–N1 0
RH: Also 35 ... P–K4!?
36 P–N7 0   R–N1?! 1
RH: More accurate is 36 ... Q–QB4+ 37 K–R1 R–N1 and then 38 R–QB1? allows 38 ... R×P, or 38 R–R1 Q–B3.
37 Q–QB2 1
Of course not 37 R–R1? R×P.
37 ...   K–N2 3
38 Q–B8 2   Q–R7 1
39 Q–B3+ 2   K–N1 3
40 R–R1 2   Q–Q4 2
41 Q–B8+   ½–½
After 41 ... K–N2 42 Q×R Black has a perpetual with 42 ... Q–Q5+ 43 K–B1 Q×R+ 44 K–B2 Q–Q5+. 2.37 – 2.27.

2703 Vladimir Tukmakov–AK:
R3: 5 June:

Ruy Lopez

1 P–K4 P–K4 2 N–KB3 N–QB3 3
B–N5 P–QR3 4 B–R4 N–B3 5
0–0 B–K2 6 R–K1 P–QN4 7 B–N3
P–Q3 8 P–B3 1 0–0 9 P–KR3 N–N1
10 P–Q4 2 N1–Q2 3 11 P–B4 4

This plan in the Breyer variation
is seen much less than the usual 11
QN–Q2.

11 . . . P–B3 12 B–N5 2

This move turns out to be rather
harmless. The tried path is 12 P–B5
Q–B2 13 BP×P B×P 14 B–N5
P×P 15 B×N P×B 16 N×P or 16
Q×P.

12 . . . P–R3 15 13 B–KR4 4 N–R4 8

A typical Lopez method of exchanging dark-squared bishops,
allowing Black to equalize.

**14 B×B 4 Q×B 15 BP×P RP×P
2 16 N–B3 1**

More circumspect would be 16
QN–Q2 or 16 Q–B1 B–N2 17 Q–B3
N–B5 18 QN–Q2.

16 . . . P–N5 5 17 N–N1 5

Played too optimistically. 17
N–K2 is safer. White is still counting
on having the advantage, but only
collides with difficulties.

**17 . . . N–B5 3 18 N1–Q2 5 P×P 21
19 N×P 1** (302)

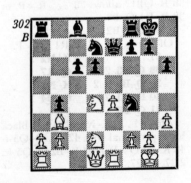

302
B

19 . . . N–K4

Clearly, going into this position,
White was hoping to drive away
Black's knight from its outpost, but
this task is shown to be impracticable
on account of a tactical nuance.

20 N2–B3 17

The threat was 20 . . . B×P 21
P×B Q–N4+.

**20 . . . Q–B3 1 21 N×N 35 P×N 2
22 N–B5**

'It was probably only at this
point that the grandmaster from
Odessa realized that on 22 N–K2
there would follow 22 . . . R–Q1
23 Q–B2 N×RP 24 P×N Q–B6 and
in order to avoid the threat of mate,
White would have to play 25 B×P+,
but that does not bring him any
appreciable relief.'

To judge from Bronstein's time
record of the game it would seem
that Tukmakov has been only too well
aware of his difficulties over the last
two moves.

**22 . . . B×N 8 23 P×B QR–Q1 1
24 Q–B3 7**

After 24 Q–B2 there is the
extremely unpleasant 24 . . . R–Q7!
25 Q×R Q–N4 and White must
part with his queen.

24 . . . R–Q7 6 25 R–K3 21

Very likely the best. 25 QR–B1 is a
blank shot: 25 . . . Q×P 26 R×BP
N×RP+! 27 Q×N Q×P+.

25 . . . R×NP 26

25 . . . Q×P deserved consideration (and, again judging from the
time record, got it – eds): 26 R1–K1
Q–N3! and the days of White's
QNP are numbered.

**26 R1–K1 4 R–K1 4 27 R–K4 4
N–Q4 2**

The knight retreats from its
advantageous post in view of the
threat 28 R×N.

28 Q–N3 3 N–B6 5 29 R×NP 12

29 R–N4, calculating on 29 . . .

N–K7+ 30 R×N R×R 31 R–N6, is countered by 29 . . . K–R1.
29 . . . N–K7+ 30 R×N R×R 1 31 R–N7?

This move was played almost instantly (White had only 12 minutes left for 10 moves). Had he had time, White could only have tried to exploit Black's inaccuracy at move 25 with 31 Q–N6. For example: 31 . . . K–B1 32 Q–R7; 31 . . . Q–K2? 32 R–N4! The variation 31 . . . P–K5 32 R–N7 Q–R8+ 33 K–R2 Q–K4+ 34 P–N3 R×BP+ 35 K–N1 P–K6 ends lamentably for White, but 32 Q×Q P×Q 33 K–B1 R–Q7 34 R–N7 R–KB1 35 R–B7 leaves the question open. . . .
31 . . . R–K2 1 32 R–N8+ 2 K–R2 33 K–B1 2 R–Q7! 1

The only square for the rook. After 33 . . . R–K5 or 33 . . . R–N7 White has a miraculous saving clause: 34 Q–N6+!! Q×Q (if 34 . . . P×Q White announces perpetual check) 35 P×Q+ K×P and now, accordingly, 36 B–B2 or 36 B×P+.
0–1 2.22 – 1.55.

2704 AK–Viktor Korchnoi:
R4: 7 June:

Pirc

1 P–K4 P–Q3 2 P–Q4 N–KB3 3 N–QB3 P–KN3 4 N–B3 B–N2 5 B–K2 0–0 6 0–0 N–B3 7 P–Q5 N–N1 8 P–KR3 P–B3 9 P–QR4!± ** White's advantage is kept to a minimum. **10 B–KN5 B–Q2!? 11 R–K1 N–R3 12 P×P?! Better 12 P–K5! QP×P 13 N×P± – Kotov **12 . . . B×BP 13 B–N5 N–QN5!** Gufeld assesses the position as unclear while Igor Zaitsev considers that Black is already better. **14 Q–K2 P–R3 15 B–KB4 P–K4!** The position is level – Kotov. **16 B–R2** *(303)*

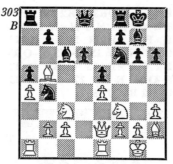

303 B

16 . . . R–B1?! Better 16 . . . N–Q2! e.g. 17 QR–Q1 N–B4 18 R–Q2 Q–K2 with a rather unclear position that is probably better for Black; or 18 Q–Q2 Q–N3∓. Also quite good for Black is 16 . . . Q–K2 17 QR–Q1 N–Q2 18 R–Q2 N–B4 19 R1–Q1 QR–Q1 with . . . P–B4 to follow. **17 QR–Q1 Q–K2 18 R–Q2= P–R4!?**

Not only with the idea of playing . . . B–R3, but also with the idea of meeting 19 Q–K3! (threatening B–N3–R4) with 19 . . . N–N5!? 20 P×N P×P 21 Q–N5 Q×Q 22 N×Q B–R3 23 P–B4 NP×Pep 24 N×P/3 B×R 25 N×B B×B 26 P×B N×P. But here tournament wisdom (or perhaps simply caution) prompted the players to consider that the time to operate on the principle 'double or bust', perhaps still had not come, and they signed a peace treaty.

On 19 R1–Q1 KR–Q1 20 Q–K3 Black has at his disposal the reply 20 . . . Q–B1! 21 Q–N6 B–R3 22 Q×RP B×R 23 R×B P–Q4∓.
½–½ 1.45 – 1.40.

2705 Mark Taimanov–AK:
R5: 8 June:

Nimzo-Indian

1 P–Q4 N–KB3 2 P–QB4 P–K3 3 N–QB3 B–N5 4 P–K3 0–0 5 KN–K2

P–Q4 6 P–QR3 B–K2 7 P×P N×P
8 B–Q2 N×N 9 N×N P–QB4 10
P×P B×P 11 N–K4 B–K2 12
B–B3 N–B3 13 B–N5 P–QR3 14
B×N P×B 15 Q–B3 Q–B2 16
R–QB1 R–N1 17 0–0 P–B3 18
Q–K2 R–Q1 (*304*)

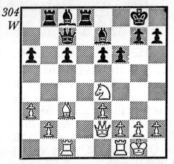

304 W

19 R–B2 Q–N3 20 R1–B1 Q–N4 21
Q–K1 P–KB4 22 N–Q2 B–N2 23
P–B3 B–KB1 24 Q–N3 R/N1–B1
25 B–K5 R–Q4 26 N–B4 R1–Q1 27
P–KR4 P–B4 28 K–R2 R–Q8 29
Q–B4 R×R 30 R×R B–Q4 31
R–B3 R–Q2 32 P–QN3 B×N! 33
Q×B Q×Q 34 R×Q R–Q6 35
R–B3 P–QB5 36 R×P R×KP 37
P–B4 R×P 38 P–R4 B–K2 39
R–B7 B–B3 40 B×B ½–½ 2.26 –
2.27

2706 Miguel Cuellar–AK:

R6: 9 June:

English

1 P–Q4 N–KB3 2 N–KB3 P–B4
3 P–B4 P×P 4 N×P N–B3 5
N–QB3 Q–N3 6 P–K3 P–K3 7
B–K2 B–K2 8 0–0 0–0 9 P–QN3
P–QR3 10 B–N2 P–Q3 11 Q–Q2
B–Q2= 12 QR–Q1 KR–Q1 13
P–KN4!? The Colombian played
just like a Canadian hockey player:
hammering the puck into another's
zone, and all the other men hurling
themselves there after it. This com-

parison came to mind when White
unexpectedly played 13 P–KN4.
Only do not think that Karpov's
task of parrying this puck seems very
simple. 13 . . . Q–R2 14 P–N5
N–K1 15 N–B3 QR–N1 16 P–K4
B–KB1 17 Q–B4 N–K2 18 N–KR4
P–N4! 19 R–Q2 B–B3 20 R1–Q1
Q–R1 21 B–Q3 R–Q2 22 Q–N4
N–B2 Kotov, in *Informator 15*, pre-
fers 22 . . . P×P 23 B×P Q–N2. 23
N–Q5! Karpov quite quickly played
23 . . . P×P since any capture of the
knight gets nowhere after 24 KP×X
and White's light-squared bishop
has a strong diagonal. 24 N×N/K7+
B×N 25 P×P P–N3 26 B–B3
P–QR4 (*305*)

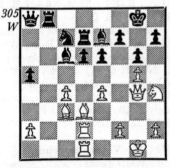

305 W

Is the sacrifice 27 N–B5 'on' here?
To take with 27 . . . NP×N is
patently bad on account of 28 P×P
B–B6 29 Q–R3. Correct is 27 . . .
KP×N 28 P×P Q–R2 (otherwise
29 Q–Q4) 29 P×P BP×P (29 . . .
RP×P 30 Q–R4) 30 B–K4 B×B 31
Q×R B–B1 32 B–Q4 Q–N2 (32 . . .
Q–R1 is also good enough: 33
Q×N R–N2) 32 R–N2 Q–B1.

27 B–B2

27 N–B3 was an interesting idea
with 28 Q–B4 to follow, threatening
29 N–K5 P×N 30 Q×KP. It is not
easy for Black to organize a defence,
since his light-squared bishop is
awkwardly placed e.g. 27 . . . B–B1

28 Q–B4 N–K1 (bad is 28 . . . R2–Q1 29 N–K5 B–K1 30 N–N4) 29 N–Q4. **27 . . . N–K1 28 N–B3 R2–Q1** White has assembled his pieces for N–Q4 and N×P. **29 N–Q4 B–Q2 30 P–K5 B–KB1** If 30 . . . P×P then 31 N–B3. **31 N–K2 P–Q4 32 R–Q3?** Karpov, without delay, played **32 . . . R/N1–B1**, won a pawn and took over the initiative. **33 P×P P×P 34 Q–R4 B–KB4 35 P–K6?** Better 35 R3–Q2 N–N2 36 B–N3 or 35 . . . B×B 36 R×B N–N2 37 R2–Q2 – Kotov in *Informator 15* **35 . . . P×P 36 N–Q4 N–N2 37 N×B N×N 38 Q–R4 B–N2 39 B×B K×B∓∓ 40 B–N3 R–B4 41 R–K1 Q–B3 42 Q–KB4 Q–Q3 43 Q–Q2 K–N1 44 P–B4 N–N2** The game was adjourned here and White sealed **45 R–Q4 Q–N3 46 K–R1 R–N4 47 R–QB1 R–KB1 48 R–Q3 R–N5 49 R–KB3 Q–Q3 50 P–B5 N×P 51 P–QR3 N–KR5 52 B–Q1 Q–K4 53 Q–KB2 R–K5 54 K–N2 N–R5+ 55 K–R3 N×R 56 B×N 0–1** 3.00 – 3.05

2707 AK–Gennady Kuzmin:
R7: 12 June:
French

1 P–K4	**P–K3**
2 P–Q4	**P–Q4**
3 N–Q2	

The World Champion, Robert Fischer, prefers 3 N–QB3.

3 . . .	**P–QB4**
4 KP×P	**KP×P**
5 KN–B3	**N–QB3**
6 B–QN5	**B–Q3**

Possibly 6 . . . P×P 7 0–0 B–Q3 8 N–N3 (8 N×P B×P+!) 8 . . . KN–K2 9 N/N3×P 0–0 10 B–N5 P–B3 is more exact, and after 11 B–K3 N–K4! 12 R–K1 P–QR3 13 B–KB1 K–R1 Black's chances are no worse, Geller–Uhlmann, Amsterdam 1970.

7 P×P	**B×BP**
8 0–0	**KN–K2**
9 N–N3	**B–Q3**

Vaganian, at Budapest (No. 2512), played 9 . . . B–N3 and was soon in trouble.

10 B–N5
The idea of this move is based on the idea of countering the influence of Black's dark-squared bishop with the manoeuvre B–KR4–KN3.

10 . .	**0–0**
11 B–KR4	**Q–B2?**

A waste of time, helping White's plan: the exchange of dark-squared bishops strengthens White's control of Q4. It was necessary to start fighting for central squares with 11 . . . B–KN5 12 B–N3 (In the final round Robert Byrne–Uhlmann went 12 B–K2 R–K1 13 R–K1 ½–½, but for a real game with 12 B–K2 see Karpov–Uhlmann, No. 3012) 12 . . . B×B 13 RP×B Q–N3 14 B–Q3 N–B4.

12 B–N3	**B×B**
13 RP×B	**B–N5**
14 R–K1	**QR–Q1**
15 P–B3	**Q–N3**

Now the attempt at getting rid of the isolated pawn is already too late.

16 B–Q3	**N–N3**
17 Q–B2	**B×N**
18 P×B±	**R–Q3**

After 18 . . . P–Q5 19 P–QB4 N–N5 20 Q–Q2 N×B 21 Q×N the QP is even weaker. 18 . . . KR–K1 was better, making defence easier by exchanging a pair of rooks.

19 P–KB4	**R1–Q1**
20 P–R3! (*306*)	

White prepares to build up with 21 K–N2, 22 R–K2 and 23 R1–K1 or 23 R–QN1. Another point is that after 20 . . . P–Q5 21 P–B4 is even stronger than in the previous note.

20 . . .	**P–KR4?!**

This is only a gesture – Black is

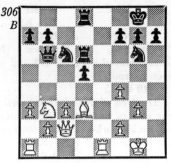

306
B

unable to funnel pieces over to the K-side to support an attack.

21 K–N2	P–R5
22 R–K2±	N–B1
23 N–Q2	

This knight is now needed on the other flank.

23 ..	R–R3
24 N–B3	P×P
25 P×P	N–Q2
26 R1–K1	K–B1 (*307*)

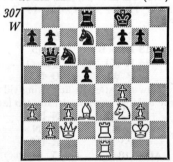

307
W

The complete triumph of White's strategy. Black's attempted counter-attack has wound up in a dead-end.

27 P–KN4!±±	Q–B2
28 P–N5	R–KR1
29 K–N3!	N–B4
30 B–B5	P–KN3
31 P–N4!	N–K5+

Black gives up a pawn. 31 . . . N–Q2 allows White a decisive attack after the bishop sacrifice 32 B×P P×B 33 Q×P. Also 31 . . . P×B 32 P×N±±.

32 B×N	P×B
33 Q×P	K–N2
34 P–N5	N–R4
35 Q–K7!	

White forces the transition to an easily won ending. If 35 . . . Q×QBP then 36 R–K3 (but not 36 R–K5? R–R6+!) 36 . . . Q–N7 37 R–K5 winning easily.

35 . . .	Q×Q
36 R×Q	R–Q6
37 R–B7	N–N6
38 K–N4	

Preparing for the decisive N–K5.

| 38 . . . | R–KB1 |
| 39 R1–K7 | 1–0 |

Black anticipates 40 N–K5. 1.41 – 2.29

2708 Mikhail Tal–AK:
R8: 15* June:

Ruy Lopez

1 P–K4 P–K4 2 N–KB3 N–QB3 3 B–N5 P–QR3 4 B–R4 N–B3 5 0–0 B–K2 6 R–K1 P–QN4 7 B–N3 P–Q3 8 P–B3 0–0 9 P–KR3 N–N1 10 P–Q4 N1–Q2 11 QN–Q2 B–N2 12 B–B2 R–K1 13 P–QN4 B–KB1 14 B–N2 P–QR4 15 B–Q3 Stronger than 15 P–R3 Q–N1 16 QP×P QP×P 17 N–N3 P×P 18 BP×P P–B4 19 P×P N×BP 20 N×N B×N= Gufeld–Dely, Kecskemet 1968. 15 . . . P–B3 16 P–R3 N–N3 17 R–QB1 KP×P 18 N×P N/B3–Q2 19 N2–N3 N–K4! 20 N×RP R×N! 21 P×R N3–B5 22 R–B2 Q×P 23 B–KB1 Also 23 B–QB1 deserved consideration e.g. 23 . . . N×B 24 Q×N P–Q4 25 R2–K2 P–QB4 26 N–N3± – Kotov in *Informator 15*. 23 . . . N×B 24 R×N Q×BP 25 R–N3 Q–R4 26 Q–N1 Q–R2 27

*The eighth round took place on June 13. This game was postponed because of Tal being ill.

R–Q1 N–Q2 28 N–B5 R–K3 29 N–Q4 R–K1 (*308*)

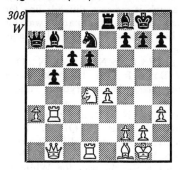

30 B×P! P×B 31 N×P Q–B4 32 N×P B×N 33 R3×B N–B3 34 Q–N3 B–B2 34 . . . R–K3 looks stronger, not fearing the spectral attack 35 R–N6 (with the threat 36 R6×B R×R 37 Q–N8+), since Black has 35 . . . K–B1! **35 Q–N5! Q–B7 36 Q–N1! Q×Q 37 R1×Q B–Q3 38 P–QR4 R×P 39 R–Q1** 39 P–R5 gave much better winning chances. **39 . . . N–K1 40 P–R5 K–B1** Here the game was adjourned and White sealed the obvious **41 P–R6** (*309*)

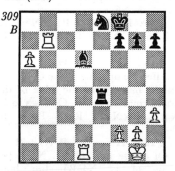

We now follow grandmaster Furman's explanation of what happened during the adjournment: 'We looked a little at the position and then Anatoly went to bed. In his dreams he saw an awful move for

White after 41 . . . R–QR5 in 42 R–R7. He began to seek a defence and, in his dream, he found it in 42 . . . P–N4. His brain continued to work. Again he saw a terrible continuation for White in 43 R–R8 B–K4 44 P–B4 when, if Black takes on B5 with bishop or pawn, 45 R1–Q8 is decisive. After he woke up we found the best defence was 44 . . . R×BP, but Tal did not play this dangerous move.'

41 . . .	**R–QR5**
42 R–R7!	**P–N4!**

42 . . . B–K4 loses quickly on account of 43 P–N3 N–Q3 44 R–K1! P–B3 45 R–N1 and there is no visible defence.

43 R–R8	**B–K4**
44 P–N3?	

Had the dream become reality Black would have been in trouble: 44 P–B4! R×BP and now:

(a) 45 P–R7 R–QR5 46 R1–Q8 K–N2 47 R×N R×P leads to a theoretical draw – I. Zaitsev.

(b) 45 R1–Q8 B–Q5+ 46 K–R2 R–K5 47 P–R7 B×P 48 R×B reaching an ending in which Black would not find it easy to make a draw – Kotov.

44 . . .	**K–K2**
45 R–K1	**P–B3**
46 P–R7	**N–B2**
47 R–R8	**R×P**
$\frac{1}{2}\text{–}\frac{1}{2}$	

After 48 P–B4 R–R8 the draw is inevitable. 2.57 – 2.25.

2709 AK–Miguel Quinteros:
R9: 14 June:

Sicilian

1 P–K4	P–QB4
2 N–KB3	P–Q3
3 P–Q4	P×P
4 N×P	N–KB3

5 N–QB3	P–QR3
6 B–KN5	P–K3
7 P–B4	Q–N3

This sharp line has been seen quite frequently in recent years, notably in two of the Spassky–Fischer match games.

8 N–N3

8 Q–Q2 is usual. Theory does not regard the text as being difficult for Black.

8 ...	B–K2

The ending after 8 ... Q–K6+ 9 Q–K2 Q×Q+ 10 B×Q is rather better for White; he not only has the better development, but also the possibility of directing fire at Black's QP.

9 Q–B3	P–R3
10 B–R4	QN–Q2

10 ... N×P is no good: 11 B×B N×N 12 Q×N K×B 13 Q×P±.

11 0–0–0	Q–B2

12 B–N3!

One would like to play P–N4 first and then B–N3, but after 12 P–N4 a reply typical of such positions is available in the form of 12 ... P–KN4, capturing the dark squares. After the text move it is difficult for Black to prevent the advance of White's KP.

12 ...	P–QN4
13 P–K5	B–N2
14 Q–K2	(*310*)

14 ...	P×P?

14 ... N–Q4 was necessary. Though it seems a difficult line for Black, there is no apparent way for White to extract any real advantage, e.g.:

(a) 15 P×P N×N! 16 P×Q N×Q+ 17 B×N R–QB1 18 P–B5 P–K4 and Black has everything under control.

(b) 15 N×N B×N and now:

(b1) 16 P×P Q×QP 17 P–B5 seems to pose more difficult problems, but after 17 ... P–K4! there seems to be no way for White to capitalize on the Q–file, e.g.

(b11) 18 Q–Q3 N–B3 19 Q–QB3 N–K5 20 Q×P Q×Q 21 B×Q N–B7 with unclear complications.

(b12) 18 P–KR4! 0–0 19 R–R3 QR–B1 20 B–R2 Q–QB3 21 N–R5 Q–R1 (21 ... Q–B4 22 R–QB3) 22 R3–Q3 with sharp double-edged play is White's most promising line here – I. Zaitsev.

(b2) 16 P–B5 N×P 17 P×P B×KP and the manoeuvre 18 N–Q4 0–0 19 B×N P×B 20 N×B P×N 21 Q–K4 is nipped in the bud by 18 ... B–N5.

(c) 15 N–K4 P×P 16 P×P N×P 17 N4–B5 B×N 18 B×N B–Q3 19 B×P R–KN1.

15 P×P	N–R2

After the opening of the Q-file the knight must go to the edge of the board since 15 ... N–Q4 loses to 16 N×N B×N 17 R×B P×R 18 P–K6.

16 N–K4	B–N4+?!

Of course not 16 ... N×P because of 17 N4–B5, but both Tseitlin and Kotov regard 16 ... N–N4 17 N–B6+ P×N 18 P×P Q–QB5! as better, though Igor Zaitsev points out that White is probably still winning with 19 Q–Q2. Tseitlin also gives 17 N–Q6+ B×N

18 P×B Q–Q1 and Black seems to be surviving.

17 K–N1	**0–0**
18 P–KR4	**B–K2**
19 N–Q6	**B–Q4?** *(311)*

This allows White to sacrifice the exchange for a raging K-side attack. Better 19 . . . QR–Q1 or 19 . . . B–QB3.

20 R×B!	**P×R**
21 N–KB5	**Q–Q1**
22 Q–N4	**P–N3**
23 N×P+	**K–N2**
24 N–KB5+	

White's advantage is so great that he even has a choice of winning methods. 24 N–Q4 is also winning, e.g. 24 . . . K×N 25 N–B5+! P×N 26 B–KB4+ N–N4 27 Q×P K–N2 28 P×N R–R1 29 R–R6! and the rook cannot be taken. Black is apparently unable to meet the host of mating threats (B–Q3, P–K6, P–N6 etc.) e.g. 29 . . . N–B1 30 P–K6. Karpov uses what looks to be the safer winning method.

24 . . .	**K–R1**
25 B–Q3	**R–KN1**

Black cannot take the knight: 25 . . . P×N 26 Q×P N/Q2–B3 27 P×N N×P 28 B–K5 and mate is inevitable.

26 N–R6	**R–N2**
27 P–R5	**Q–K1**

Black has no defence against the multiple threats. Opening the KR-file would lose even more rapidly.

28 P–K6!	**N/Q2–B3**
29 KP×P	**Q–Q1**

After 29 . . . Q–KB1 White would win with the pretty queen sacrifice 30 P×P! N×Q 31 N×N B–Q3 (the threat was 32 B–K5) 32 N–B6! B×B 33 N×N Q–Q3 34 N–B6+ B–R7 35 N–K8! *(312)*

35 . . . R×NP 36 B×R.

30 Q–Q4	**N×P**
31 B–K5	**B–B3**
32 R–K1	

Another possibility was 32 N–N4 R×P 33 B×KNP.

32 . .	**B×B**
33 R×B	**N4–B3**
34 P–N4	**Q–KB1**
35 P–N5	**N–K5**
36 B×N	**P×B**
37 Q×P	**1–0**

2.04 – 1.58

38 R–K8 and 38 Q×R are unanswerable threats.

2710 Bent Larsen–AK:
R10: 16 June:

English

1 P–QB4 P–QB4 2 P–KN3 P–KN3 3 B–N2 B–N2 4 N–QB3 N–QB3 5 P–QR3 P–K3 6 R–N1 P–QR4 7 N–R3 KN–K2 8 N–B4 0–0 9 P–Q3 R–N1 10 B–Q2 P–N3 11

0–0 B–N2 12 R–K1 P–Q3 13 N–N5
N–Q5 14 N×N B×N 15 B×B
R×B 16 Q–R4 Q–Q2 17 Q×Q
R×Q 18 B–B3 B–N2 19 B×B
K×B 20 P–QN4 RP×P 21 P×P
R–QR1 ½–½ 0.55 – 0.57

2711 AK–Robert Byrne:
R11: 17 June:

Sicilian

1 P–K4 P–QB4 2 N–KB3 P–Q3 3
P–Q4 P×P 4 N×P N–KB3 5
N–QB3 P–QR3 6 B–K2 P–K4 7
N–N3 B–K3 8 P–B4 Q–B2 9 P–B5
B–B5 10 P–QR4 QN–Q2 11 B–K3
B–K2 12 P–R5 0–0 13 0–0 P–QN4
14 P×Pep N×NP 15 K–R1 KR–B1
16 B×N Q×B 17 B×B R×B 18
Q–K2 R1–QB1 19 R–R2 B–Q1 20
R1–R1 Q–N2 21 R–R4 (313)

313
B

21 ... R×R ½–½ 0.37 – 0.31 Leaving
questions unanswered. See Karpov–
Stoica (No. 2205) for a continuation.

2712 Wolfgang Uhlmann–AK:
R12: 19 June:

Semi-Tarrasch

1   P–QB4   P–QB4   2   N–KB3
N–KB3 3 N–B3 P–Q4 4 P×P N×P
5 P–K3 P–K3 6 P–Q4 N–QB3 7

B–Q3 P×P 8 P×P B–K2 9 0–0
0–0 10 R–K1 N–B3 11 P–QR3
P–QN3 12 B–K3 B–N2 13 R–QB1
R–B1 14 B–N1 R–B2 15 Q–Q3
R–Q2 16 Q–B2 P–N3 17 B–R2?!
N–KN5?! Gaining the two bishops,
but at some positional cost –
allowing Uhlmann to build up along
the KB-file. 18 R/B1–Q1 N×B 19
P×N B–B3 20 Q–B2 B–N2 21
R–Q2 N–K2= 22 P–K4 P–KR3 23
R1–Q1 Q–N1 24 Q–K3 R1–Q1 25
P–R3 K–R2 26 K–R1 P–R3 27
R–KB2 N–N1 28 R1–KB1 P–QN4
(314)

314
W

The critical moment 29 P–KR4?
This is bad. Both 29 B–N1 (Kotov)
and 29 P–Q5 (Zaitsev) are better.
29 . . . N–B3! 30 N–K5 R×P 31
R×N! Q×N! 32 R×BP R1–Q2
33 R×R R R×R 34 Q–R3 R–Q3 35
B–N1 R–Q7 36 P–R5 P×P 37
N–Q1 B–QB3! The bishop heads
for KN3 to fill the hole in Black's
K-side. 'Typical of Karpov's chess
art' – Kotov. 38 Q–KB3 B–K1 39
P–QN4 B–N3 40 N–B2 Q–Q5∓
The game was adjourned here and
White sealed 41 N–R3 and resumed
for a few moves 41 . . . P–K4 42
N–B2 R–N7 43 K–R2 Q–B5 44
R–Q1 R–N6 45 N–Q3 Q×KP 0–1
3.04 – 2.54

2713 AK–Svetozar Gligorić:
R13: 21 June:

Ruy Lopez

1 P–K4 P–K4 2 N–KB3 N–QB3 3
B–N5 P–QR3 4 B–R4 N–B3 5 0–0
B–K2 6 R–K1 P–QN4 7 B–N3
P–Q3 8 P–B3 0–0 9 P–KR3 N–N1
10 P–Q4 N1–Q2 11 QN–Q2 B–N2
12 B–B2 P–B4 13 P–Q5 13 N–B1!?
13 . . . N–K1 14 N–B1 P–N3 15
B–R6 N–N2 16 N–K3 N–B3 17
P–QR4 K–R1 18 P–QN3 18 Q–K2
P–B5 = 18 . . . R–QN1 19 Q–K2
B–B1 19 . . . Q–N3 20 P×P P×P
21 R–R7 N–N1 22 B×N+ K×B
23 R1–R1 N–B3 24 B–Q3 B–Q2 25
Q–R2 N–K1?! (*315*)

315
W

25 . . . Q–N3!? 26 Q–R6! 26 Q–R5
Q–B1 27 Q–R6 B–Q1 = 26 . . .
R–N3 26 . . . N–B2 27 Q–R5 R–QR1
(27 . . . R–B1 28 Q–N6, 29 R–N7±)
28 R×R Q×R 29 Q×N! Q×R+
30 K–R2 R–Q1 31 B×P B×B 32
Q×B R–Q2 33 Q–R4 with the idea
34 P–B4 or 34 N–N4± 27 Q–R5
N–B3 28 N–N4! R–QN1 29 N×N
29 Q–B7?! B×N 30 P×B Q×Q 31
R×Q B–Q1 32 R–B6 P–B5 33
P×P P×P 34 R×BP N×NP= 29
. . . B×N 30 Q–B7 Q×Q 31 R×Q
KR–Q1 32 R1–R7 B–K1 33 R/R7–
N7 With the idea 34 B×P B×B 35
R×KBP+ K–N1 36 R×R 33 . . .
K–N1 34 P–KN4 P–R3 35 P–R4

R×R 36 R×R P–B5 37 P×P
P×P 38 B–K2 38 B×P B–Q2 39
P–N5 B–N5! (39 . . . P×P 40
N×NP±) 40 P×B B×N 41 B–Q3
P–N4 38 . . . R–R1 39 B×P B–R5
39 . . . R–B1 40 B–K2 B–R5 41
P–N5 P×P 42 N×NP B×N 43
P×B R×P 44 R–N6± 40 B–N3!
B×B 41 R×B R–QB1 41 . . . R–R5
42 R–N4±± 42 K–N2 P–R4 43
P×P P×P 44 R–N6 R×P 45
R×P K–N2 46 R–B6 R–Q6 46 . . .
R–R6 47 R–B7 K–N3 48 R–B8
With the idea that if 48 . . . R–R6
then 49 R–K8 R–R5 50 N×P+
48 . . . B–N2 49 R–B6+ K–R2 50
N–N5+ K–N1 51 R–B8+ B–B1
52 R–B7 P–B3 53 N–K6 B–R3 54
R–Q7±± R–Q7 55 K–B1 R–Q8+
56 K–K2 R–Q7+ 57 K–K1 R–B7
58 P–Q6 R–B8+ 59 K–K2 R–B7+
60 K–B1 R–B3 61 K–N2 R–N3 Or
61 . . . B–Q7 62 R–KN7+ K–R1
63 P–Q7 R–Q3 64 R–K7 B–R4 65
P–Q8=Q+ B×Q 66 R–K8+±±
62 N–B7 R–N2 62 . . . B–B1 63
N–K8 63 N–Q5 1–0 3.00 – 4.00

2714 Josip Rukavina–AK:
R14: 22 June:

English

1 P–QB4 N–KB3 2 N–QB3 P–K3
3 N–B3 P–B4 4 P–Q4 P×P 5 N×P
B–N5 6 N–B2!? B×N+ 7 P×B
Q–R4 8 N–N4 0–0 9 P–K3 P–QN3
10 B–K2 B–N2 11 0–0 R–B1∓ 12
P–B3 N–B3 13 Q–N3 Q–K4 14
N×N R×N 15 B–Q2 Q–B2 16
Q–R4 P–QR4 17 KR–N1 B–R3 18
R–N2 B×P 19 B×B R×B 20
Q–N5 R–B3∓ (*316*)
21 P–K4 P–Q3 22 Q–N5 N–Q2 23
Q–K7 N–K4 24 Q×Q R×Q 25
R–N5 N–B5 26 B–B1 R1–QB1 27
R1–N1 R–B4 28 K–B1 K–B1 29
K–K2 K–K2 30 R5–N3 K–Q2 31
P–QR4 K–B2 32 B–B4 K–N2 33

B–K3 R4–B3 34 B–Q4 P–B3 35
R–Q1 R–Q1 36 P–B4 P–Q4! 37
B–B2 R3–Q3 38 B–B5 R–B3 39
B–B2 R1–Q3 40 P×P R×P 41
R×R P×R 42 R–N5 R–K3+
43 K–Q3 K–B3 44 P–N3 R–K2 45
R–N1 R–N2 46 R–N5 N–Q3 47
R–N2 P–QN4 48 P×P+ R×P
White sealed his 49th move 49
R–K2 0–1 2.56 – 2.11

2715 AK–Ivan Radulov:
R15: 23 June:

English

1 P–QB4 P–K4 2 N–QB3 P–QB4
3 P–KN3 P–KN3 4 B–N2 B–N2 5
N–B3 N–K2 6 0–0 0–0 7 N–K1
QN–B3 8 N–B2 P–Q3 9 N–K3
B–K3 10 P–QR3 Q–Q2 11 P–Q3
B–R6! 12 N/K3–Q5 B×B 13 K×B
N×N 14 N×N N–K2 15 N×N+
Q×N= 16 P–K4 P–B4! 17 P–B3
P–KR4 18 B–Q2 K–R2 19 P–QN4

B–R3 20 KP×P R×P 21 B×B
K×B 22 Q–Q2+ K–N2 23 P×P
P×P 24 QR–K1 R–Q1 (*317*)
25 R–K3 R–Q5 26 Q–K2= Q–Q3
27 R–QN1 R–B2 28 P–QR4 P–N3
29 R–K1 R–Q2 30 P–R4 R×QP 31
R×R Q×R 32 Q×P+ K–R2 33
Q–K6 Q–B4 34 Q×Q P×Q 35
K–B2 K–N2 36 P–R5 R–Q5 37
P×P P×P 38 R–K6 R×BP 39
R×P P–B5 ½–½ 2.06 – 1.42

2716 Jan Smejkal–AK:
R16: June:

Sicilian

1 P–K4	P–QB4
2 N–KB3	P–K3
3 P–Q4	P×P
4 N×P	N–QB3
5 N–QB3	P–QR3
6 B–K2	Q–B2
7 0–0	N–B3
8 B–K3	B–N5

One of the most analysed variations of the Paulsen, in which forced
theoretical variations sometimes
stretch right up to the 25th move.
9 N–R4
The popular continuation, though
9 N×N NP×N also, quite clearly,
gives White some advantage.
9 . . .   0–0
Of the five replies which theory
considers for Black (9 . . . N–K2,
9 . . . B–K2, 9 . . . B–Q3 and 9 . . .
P–QN4) this, undoubtedly, is the
most solid.

10 N×N	NP×N
11 N–N6	

The tempting 11 Q–Q4 does not
work on account of 11 . . . B–Q3 12
N–N6 R–N1 13 N–B4 B×P+ 14
K–R1 P–Q4 15 P–K5 P×N 16
K×B R–Q1.

11 . . .	R–N1
12 N×B	KR×N
13 B×P	R–Q1! (*318*)

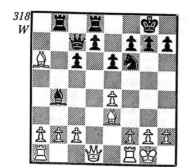

318
W

An innovation. Though, in all honesty, this move has already been seen some time ago in Leningrad events, but little known on a wider scale.

Previously 13 . . . R–K1 was always chosen. In connection with this it is important to have the knowledge of two circumstances: There is the black knight's lack of squares, which, for example, gave grounds for Geller, in the 39th USSR Championship, to start a blunt chase after it with 14 B–Q3 B–Q3 15 P–KN4!? The second, less striking consideration, is that the black rook on K1 can come under attack from the queen.

Black's last move has as its object the avoidance of such unpleasant consequences.

14 B–Q3   B–Q3
15 K–R1!

The best. After 15 P–KB4 P–K4 16 P–B5 R×P 17 P–N4 Q–R4 18 K–R1 B–B4 19 B–B1 R×RP 20 R×R Q×R 21 P–N5 N–K1 22 Q–R5 P–Q4 Black successfully defends himself.

15 . . .   B–K4

The KRP, of course, is inviolate: after 15 . . . B×P 16 P–KB4 B–N6 17 Q–B3 White wins quickly.

Winning back material with 15 . . . R×P, Black risks falling under

attack: 16 B–Q4 R7–N1 17 B×N P×B 18 Q–R5.

16 P–QB3

16 P–KB4 does not promise anything more: 16 . . . B×NP 17 R–QN1 P–Q4 18 P–K5 N–Q2 19 Q–N4, though, all the same, White does have some initiative on the K-side.

16 . . .   R×P
17 Q–B1!

It is in just this way (with the black rook on K1) that White, time and again, gets good chances in this variation.

17 . .   N–N5
18 P–KB4

The rook is untouchable: 18 Q×R? B×BP! and Black mates or wins the queen.

18 . . .   N×B
19 Q×R

19 P×B is wrong – 19 . . . Q–N3 and the advantage is in Black's hands.

19 . . .   B×KBP
20 Q–KB2!

The attempt to hang on to the exchange, 20 R–B3 N–N5, does not work in White's favour because of Black's many threats: 21 P–KR3 (21 R1–B1) 21 . . . B–B8!, 21 P–N3 N–K4 – highly unpleasant.

20 . .   N×R
21 R×N   P–K4 (*319*)

319
W

Finally the idea behind the innovation on move 13 is revealed! With the rook on Q1, the threat against KB2 is not so deadly.

Black has a bad game after 21 ... P–N4?! 22 P–N3 Q–Q3 23 B–K2 or 23 B–B2.

22 P–N3   Q–Q3

The black bishop cannot move because of mate.

23 B–K2

23 B–B4 also looks interesting. In that case after 23 . . . B–N4 24 Q×P+ K–R1 25 P–QR4 B–B3 26 P–R5 R–KB1 27 Q–R5 Q–Q7 28 Q×KP P–R3 29 Q–QB5 Q×BP 30 P–K5 White achieves his goal (and retains chances of qualifying for the Candidates). A more convincing defence is 27 . . . Q–B4 28 B–B7 B–Q1 in the above, or 25 . . . P–R3 26 P–R5 Q–B4 27 P–R6 P–Q4 28 B–Q3 Q×P.

23 . . .   B–N4
24 Q×P+   K–R1
25 P–QR4

The alternative (25 B–N4) also turns out in his favour.

25 . . .   B–K2

Variations on the theme of a flight-square are weaker, e.g. 25 . . . P–R3 26 B–R5! Q–Q6 27 B–N6.

26 P–R5   R–KB1
27 Q–QB4   R×R+
28 B×R   Q–B3
29 K–N2   Q–B1!
30 B–K2   B–B4
31 B–N4   Q–B7+

On 31 . . . Q–Q3 32 Q–B7 is possible: 32 . . . Q–Q7+ 33 K–R3 Q–R3+ 34 B–R5 Q–K3+ (34 . . . P–N3? 35 Q–K8+) 35 Q×Q with winning chances.

32 K–R3   P–Q3
33 B–Q7

According to Petrosian and Keres, analysing this position in the press-bureau, here White should play 33 Q–K6! The endgame after 33 . . . Q–B8+ 34 K–R4 Q–B3+ 35 Q×Q

being considered as highly promising for White. Now the black pieces become active.

33 . . .   P–N3
34 B×P   K–N2
35 B–N5   Q–QN7!
36 P–R6   B–N8
37 Q–K2   Q×P
38 B–B4   Q–B8
39 Q–B1

39 K–N2 looks better; now Black gets some initiative.

39 . . .   Q–R3+
40 K–N2   Q×P+
41 K–B3   Q–R4+
42 K–N2 *(320)*

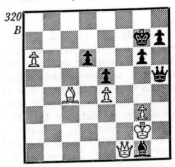

320
B

Here the game was adjourned and Black sealed his move.

We now follow the comments made by Furman in a newspaper article under the title of *The Knight's Move.*

There is a knight's move *here?* the reader asks in astonishment – there is no such piece left on the board.

It turns out that a 'knight's move' can be made by other pieces. Here is how the continuation went:

42 . . .   Q–R7+
43 K–B3   B–Q5
44 B–Q5   B–B4
45 B–B6

The advantage is on Black's side. It consists not only of an extra pawn, but also of the unhappy position of the white king. Black has at his disposal two plans of campaign. However, with correct defence neither of these lead to a win. But one cannot utilize both possibilities. How to guess which one the opponent is least ready for? Which would be the most unexpected for him?

45 ...   **B–Q5 (!)**

Here it is, the 'knight's move'. With this aimless bishop move Karpov demonstrates the lack of any kind of plan and dulls the opponent's vigilance.

46 B–N7?

This bishop move is the decisive error. On the best continuation, 46 B–Q5, Black can play 46 . . . B–N3 with the theme that the bishop can, when the opportunity arises, take part in an attack on the white king from the square . . . Q1, later transferring the queen to . . . Q7 and advancing the K-side pawns. During the construction of this plan White would have to speed the withdrawal of his king to a safe place.

46 ...   **P–N4!**
47 K–N4   **P–R4+!**
48 K–B5

After 48 K×NP Q×P+ 49 K×P B–B7 White gets mated.

48 ...   **Q×P**
49 K–K6   **Q–B7**

Now one might ask why Karpov did not follow this plan at once. The reason is that the ending is won only with White's bishop on N7.

50 Q–N5

After 50 Q×Q B×Q 51 K–B5 P–N5 White, in order to prevent the further advance of Black's KNP, would have to play 52 P–R7, giving up his important passed pawn. With the bishop on Q5 or B6 White draws by 52 B–B4 and 52 B–N5 respectively.

50 ...   **Q–B3+**
51 K–Q5   **P–N5**
52 B–B8   **Q–K2**

Now Black wins, gradually preparing the advance of his passed pawns.

53 B–B5 K–R3 54 Q–B1 Q–QB2 55 Q–K2 Q–B4+ 56 K–K6 K–N4 57 Q–B1 Q–R6 58 Q–K2 B–B4 59 Q–Q2+ Q–K6 60 Q–R5 B–N3 61 Q–R2 Q–B7 62 Q–N1 P–N6 63 B–R3 K–R5 64 B–N2 Q–N8 65 Q×Q B×Q 66 K×QP

After 66 K–B5 B–B4 White is in zugzwang: 67 B–B1 P–N7 68 B×P K–N6 securing the advance of the KRP.

66 ... B–Q5 67 P–R7 B×P 68 K×P K–N5 69 K–Q5 P–R5 70 P–K5 P–R6 71 B×P+ K×B 72 P–K6 B–B4 0–1 4.06 – 4.02

2717 AK–Eugenio Torre:
     R17: 27 June:

Alekhine

1 P–K4 N–KB3 2 P–K5 N–Q4 3 P–Q4 P–Q3 4 N–KB3 P–KN3 5 B–QB4 N–N3 6 B–N3 B–N2 7 N–N5 P–Q4 8 P–KB4 N–B3 9 P–B3 So that if 9 . . . N–R4 White can preserve his good white-square bishop with 10 B–B2. **9 ... P–B3 10 N–B3 B–B4 11 0–0 Q–Q2** Or 11 . . . 0–0 12 QN–Q2± **12 QN–Q2** 12 N–R4?! is dubious on account of 12 . . . B–N5 13 Q–K1 0–0–0 with 14 . . . P–N4 to follow. **12 ... P×P** Or 12 . . . B–R3 13 N–R4 **13 BP×P 0–0 14 R–B2! N–R4 15 B–B2 B×B 16 Q×B Q–B4?!** Having the queen on this square has disastrous consequences later. 16 . . . P–K3 was preferable. **17 Q–Q1 P–K3** If 17 . . . Q–Q6 White gets a big advantage with 18 N–K1 and if 18 . . . Q–K6 19 N2–B3. **18 N–B1 P–B4** (*321*)

321
W

19 P–KR3! The position of the black queen cannot be exploited immediately, e.g. 19 N–K3 Q–R4 (but not 19 . . . Q–K5 20 N–N5 Q–R5 21 R×R+ R×R 22 N×KP Q–B7+

23 K–R1±±) 20 P–KN4 Q–R6 21 N–N5 Q–R5. **19 . . . P×P 20 P×P N–B3 21 P–QN3 N–Q2 22 B–R3±± R–B2** This appears to be the decisive error, but Black is already quite lost, e.g. 22 . . . KR–Q1 23 N–N3 Q–B5 24 N–K2 Q–B2 (24 . . .Q–K5 25 N–N5 Q–K6 26 B–B1±±) 25 N–N5. **23 P–KN4!** 23 N–N3 is less accurate: 23 . . . Q–B5 24 N–K2 Q–B4 (24 . . . Q–K6? 25 B–B1 Q–K5 26 N–N3±±) 25 P–KN4 Q×N 26 R×Q R×R± and Black, though in a bad way, is better off than in the game. **23 . . . Q–K5** White also wins after 23 . . . Q–B5 24 B–B1 Q–K5 25 N–N3. **24 N–N5 1–0** 1.23 – 2.26

28 EUROPEAN TEAM CHAMPIONSHIP

Bath, 6–13.7.1973

	1	2	3	4	5	6	7	8	
1 USSR	×	5½	5	5½	5½	6½	5½	7	**40½**
2 Yugoslavia	2½	×	4½	6	6½	4½	4½	5½	**34**
3 Hungary	3	3½	×	6½	5½	5½	5½	3½	**33**
4 Poland	2½	2	1½	×	5	4	5½	4½	**25**
5 W. Germany	2½	1½	2½	3	×	4½	4½	5½	**24**
6 England	1½	3½	2½	4	3½	×	4½	4½	**24**
7 Romania	2½	3½	2½	2½	3½	3½	×	5	**23**
8 Switzerland	1	2½	4½	3½	2½	3½	3	×	**20½**

Once again Karpov received a board prize (his score was 5/6) and registered an advance within his own team of two boards compared with Skopje. The USSR team was Spassky, Petrosian, Korchnoi, Karpov, Tal, Smyslov, Geller, Kuzmin, Tukmakov and Balashov.

2801 AK–Andrew Whiteley:
R1: 6 July:

Sicilian

1 P–K4 P–QB4 2 N–KB3 P–Q3 3 N–B3 P–KN3 4 P–Q4 P×P 5 N×P Black can equalize after 5 Q×P N–KB3 6 P–K5 N–B3 7 B–QN5 P×P 8 Q×Q+ K×Q 9 B×N P×B 10 N×P K–K1 e.g. 11 N×QBP B–N2 12 N–K5 B×P. **5 ... N–KB3 6 B–K3 B–N2 7 B–QB4 N–B3 8 P–B3 0–0 9 Q–Q2 B–Q2 10 0–0–0 Q–R4 11 B–N3 KR–B1 12 P–KR4 N–K4 13 K–N1** The immediate 13 P–R5 is dangerous on account of 13 ... N×RP 14 B–R6 N–Q6+ 15 K–N1 N×P 16 K×N B×B 17 Q×B R×N! **13 ... N–B5 14 B×N R×B 15 N–N3 Q–Q1** Not 15 ... Q–R3? 16 P–K5 N–K1 (even worse is 16 ... P×P 17 N–B5±±) 17 N–Q5± **16 B–R6 Q–KB1?!**

Better 16 ... B–R1 **17 B×B± Q×B 18 P–N4** with the idea of 19 P–K5 P×P 20 P–N5 netting a piece **18 ... B–K3 19 N–Q4 N–Q2 20 P–R5 R1–QB1 21 P×P RP×P** (*322*)

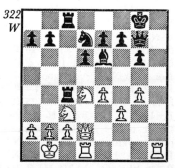

322
W

22 N3–K2! Black can defend against the immediate 22 N–B5 with 22 ... B×N 23 NP×B R×N 24 P×R Q×P 25 P×P P×P. **22 ... R5–B4**

22 ... N-K4 is also met by 23 P-B3.
23 P-B3 N-B1 24 QR-N1 Building
up for 25 N-B5 **24 ... Q-K4 25
N-KN3±± P-KN4** If 25 ...
R-R4 then 26 P-R3 with 27 P-KB4
and/or N3-B5 to follow. **26 N3-B5
B×N 27 NP×B P-B3 28 P-KB4
Q×KP+ 29 K-R1 K-B2** Or 29 ...
N-R2 30 Q-R2±± **30 P×P P×P
31 Q×P R-K4** 31 ... K-K1 brings
retribution on the K-file in the form
of 32 R-K1. **32 Q-R5+ 1-0**

2802 Dimitri Ghizdavu–AK:
R2: 7 July:

Sicilian

**1 P-K4 P-QB4 2 N-KB3 P-Q3 3
P-Q4 P×P 4 N×P N-KB3 5
N-QB3 P-QR3 6 P-B4 QN-Q2
7 P-QR4 P-KN3 8 B-Q3 B-N2 9
N-B3 0-0 10 0-0 N-B4!?** Safer
would have been 10 ... P-K4 and
... Q-B2 and ... P-N3. **11 Q-K1
R-N1** Not 11 ... B-N5?! 12 Q-R4
B×N 13 R×B and 14 R-KR3±
**12 Q-R4 P-QN4 13 P×P P P×P 14
P-K5?!** Better 14 K-R1 **14 ...
N×B 15 BP×N** 15 KP×N? loses
to 15 ... B×P 16 N-N5 B×N/4 17
P×B N×B, and 15 N-N5 is well
met by 15 ... P×P 16 P×P P-R3.
15 ... N-K1 Also possible is 15 ...
P-N5 16 P×N B×P 17 N-KN5
B×N/4 18 P×B P×N∓ **16 P-Q4**
Not 16 N-Q4? P×P 17 P×P P-N5.
Nor is 16 N-Q5 very good: 16 ...
R-N2 (16 ... P-B3?! 17 N-Q4 and
if 17 ... P×P 18 N-QB6) 17 R-R8
P×P. **16 ... N-B2 17 N-K4 P-B4!**
Other moves hand the advantage
over to White, e.g. 17 ... B-N2 18
P-B5! or 17 ... B-B4 18 N-N3
B-Q6 19 R-Q1. **18 N4-N5 P-R3 19
N-R3 B-K3 20 Q-N3 B-B2 21
R-K1 P-N5 22 K-R1** 22 N-R4 is
met by 22 ... P×P **22 ... N-Q4?!**
Better 22 ... R-N2, but not 22 ...

Q-Q2? 23 N-R4 K-R2 24 R-R7±
23 Q-R4 Or 23 N-R4 K-R2 24
N-B3 P-K3∓ **23 ... R-N2 24
N/R3-N5 P-K3 25 N×B** 25 R-R6
is answered by 25 ... P×N 26 N×P
R-K1 27 R×P Q-B1∓. **25 ...
Q×Q 26 N×Q K×N 27 N-B3
P×P 28 QP×P R-B1∓ 29 N-Q4
B-B1 30 R-R6** (*323*)

30 ... R-N3 Much better 30 ...
B-B4! e.g. 31 N×KP B-N3∓∓ or
31 N-N3 B-N3∓ **31 R-R7+ R-B2
32 R-R8 P-N6 33 R-R4 B-B4 34
N-K2 B-N5?!** And here 34 ...
B-K6! was right. **35 R-Q1 R3-B3
36 R-R1 R-N3** 36 ... R-B7 37
N-Q4 R-B7 would be a terrible
error: 38 K-N1 wins. **37 R-Q3
B-K2 38 P-N3 R-B5 39 K-N2
R-B7 40 K-B3 R-N5** An interesting
try would be 40 ... R-N2!? in order
to play 41 ... B-B4. **41 P-R4?**
Correct was 41 R-R7 R-K5 (41
... R5-B5 42 R×P R×N 43 K×R
R×B 44 P-R4!=) 42 B-Q2 R×NP
43 R-N7 with only a small advan-
tage to Black. **41 ... B-B4?** Black,
in turn, goes wrong. Correct was 41
... R-K5∓∓ e.g. 42 B-Q2 R×NP
43 N-Q4 R-R7, or 42 N-Q4
R-R7 with 43 ... B-B4 or 43 ...
R-K8 to follow. **42 B-Q2 R-K5 43
R-QB1 B-N5 44 R×R P×R 45
B-B1** 45 B×B is answered not by 45
... N×B but by 45 ... R×N. **45**

... **R–B5 46 R–Q4 R–B2 47 P–N3 B–K8** If 47 ... B–B6 then 48 R–B4 R–N2 49 P–QN4, but another way is 47 ... B–R4!? and after 48 R–B4 R×R 49 P×R N–B6 50 N×N B×N Black wins. **48 R–B4 R×R 49 P×R** Now 49 ... N–N5 can be met by 50 K–K3 N–R7 51 B–Q2, so **49 ... N–B6** (*324*)

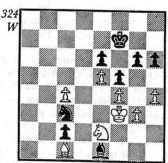

324
W

50 N×N? Ghizdavu could have preserved very good drawing chances with 50 N–Q4 N–K5 51 N×QBP B×P 52 P–R5∓, but the text loses rapidly. **50 ... B×N 51 P–N4 P×P+ 52 K×P P–R4+ 53 K–B3 B–K8 54 K–K2 B×P 55 K–Q3 B–B7 56 K×P P–R5 57 K–Q3 P–R6 0–1**

2803 Alexander Matanović–AK:
R4: 9 July:

Ruy Lopez

1 P–K4 P–K4 2 N–KB3 N–QB3 3 B–N5 P–QR3 4 B–R4 N–B3 5 0–0 B–K2 6 R–K1 P–QN4 7 B–N3 P–Q3 8 P–B3 0–0 9 P–KR3 N–N1 10 P–Q4 QN–Q2 11 QN–Q2 B–N2 12 B–B2 R–K1 13 P–QN4 B–KB1 14 P–QR4 P–QR4! 15 NP×P The stem game of this line, Kavalek–Portisch, Beverwijk 1969, went 15 RP×P RP×P 16 B–N2 NP×P 17 B×P P–B3 ½–½. **15 ... R×P 16 R–N1 B–QR3 17 RP×P R×P 18 R–R1** Varying

from 18 B–N3 R–K2 19 Q–B2 R–R4 20 N–B4 B×N 21 B×B Q–R1 'with equal chances' – Furman, Razuvayev–Furman, 40 USSR Ch 1972. **18 ... R–N3 19 B–N3 P–R3 20 Q–K2 B–N2 21 B–R4 R–R3 22 B–N2 Q–R1 23 B–N5 R×R 24 R×R Q–B1 25 R–K1 Q–R1 26 R–R1 Q–B1 27 R–K1** (*325*) ½–½

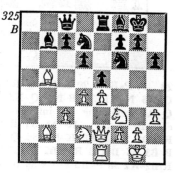

325
B

2804 AK–Schauwecker:
R5: 10 July:

English

1 N–KB3 N–KB3 2 P–B4 P–B4 3 N–B3 P–K3 4 P–KN3 N–B3 5 B–N2 P–Q3?! Rather passive **6 0–0 B–Q2 7 P–Q4 P×P 8 N×P P–QR3 9 P–N3± B–K2 10 P–QR4 0–0 11 B–QR3 Q–N1 12 R–R2! R–Q1 13 R–Q2 N×N 13** ... B–K1!? **14 R×N B–B3 15 Q–Q2 N–K1 16 R–Q3 Q–B2 17 R–Q1 R–Q2?** This allows White to increase the pressures but 17 ... B×B 18 K×B R–Q2 19 P–K4 is also good for White. **18 N–Q5! P×N 18** ... B×N 19 P×B P–K4 20 R–QB1 Q–N3 21 B–R3 R2–Q1 22 P–K3± **19 P×P B×RP** A desperado to regain the pawn, but White now has complete control of the QN-file. **20 P×B B–B3 21 Q–N4 R–K2 22 B–B3 B–K4 23 R–N3 P–KN3 24 R1–N1 R–N1 25 P–K4 N–B3 26 B–KN2± Q–B7 27**

**R–QB1 27 P–B4?! P–QR4! 27 . . .
Q–K7 28 P–R3!** (*326*)

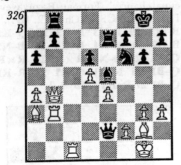

326
B

**28 . . . P–KN4 29 R–K3 Q–R4 30
Q–N6 N–K1 31 B–N4 Q–N3 32
Q–R7** beginning to infiltrate in
earnest **32 . . . R–Q1 33 B–R5
R1–Q2 34 R–B8 K–N2 35 Q–N8
P–B3 36 B–Q8 R–KB2 37 B–N6
R/B2–K2 38 P–R5 P–R4 39 B–B3!
K–R3 40 B–Q1 P–B4** trying to
create a little space within which to
manoeuvre **41 P×P Q–B2 42
B–R4 N–B3 43 R–B8! Q–N2 44
R–R8+ N–R2 45 R–KN8** (*327*) **1–0**

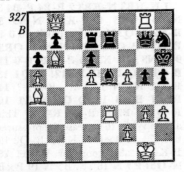

327
B

2805 Hans–Joachim Hecht—AK:
R6: 11 July:

French

**1 P–K4 P–QB4 2 N–KB3 P–K3
3 P–B3 P–Q4 4 P–K5 B–Q2** Hecht
got an excellent game against

Gerusel at Bad Pyrmont 1970 after
4 . . . N–K2!? 5 N–R3 N–B4 6
N–B2 N–B3 (6 . . . P–Q5!?) 7
P–Q4. **5 P–Q4 Q–N3** Dueball
recommends 5 . . . Q–R4!? **6 B–K2
B–N4 7 0–0 B×B 8 Q×B Q–R3 9
Q–Q1 P–B5** 9 . . . N–QB3 was
played in Hecht–Tröger, Bad
Pyrmont 1963, which game resulted
in a beautiful win for White.
Annotating the game at the time in
Deutsche Schachzeitung, Hecht suggested 9 . . . N–Q2 followed by . . .
N–K2–QB3 as better. **10 R–K1
N–QB3 11 QN–Q2 0–0–0** Hecht
suggests 11 . . . KN–K2. **12 N–B1
R–Q2!** An important move which
facilitates a number of plans, e.g.
. . . N–Q1 and . . . P–B3, . . . P–QN4
and . . . R–N2, and a recentraliza-
tion of the queen by . . . Q–N3–Q1.
13 B–B4!? More accurate would be
13 P–KR4 and if 13 . . . N–Q1 then
14 B–B4. **13 . . . KN–K2! 14
P–KR4 P–R4** If 14 . . . N–N3 then
not 15 B–N5? P–R3 16 P–R5
N/N3×P!∓, but simply 15 B–N3!
with N–K3 to follow. **15 N–N3
N–N3 16 B–N5 B–K2 17 Q–Q2
Q–N3! 18 B×B R×B 19 R–K2**
preparing Q–N5 19 . . . **Q–Q1!**
Black prepares . . . R–B2 threatening
the KRP, and if 20 P–N3?! then not
20 . . . P×P 21 P×P R–B2 22
P–N4 N×RP 23 N×N Q×N 24
P–N5 N–N1 25 R×P with an unclear
position, but 20 . . . N–R4! and
Black emerges with the better
position: 21 P–N4 N–B3 22 P–N5
N–N1∓. **20 N–B1 P–B3 21 N1–R2!
P×P 22 N×P! N×RP?** Or 22 . . .
N/B3×N 23 P×N R–B1 24 P–KN3
with P–B4 to follow, but correct was
22 . . . N/N3×N 23 P×N R–Q2
and Black achieves equality by
forcing through . . . P–Q5. **23 N×N
P×N 24 P–QN3!** The position is
now unclear. **24 . . . P×P 25 P×P**

K–N2?! The king heads towards the danger zone. Hecht suggests 25 . . . R–R3!? 26 Q–Q3 K–N1 27 P–N3 N–N3. **26 Q–Q3 K–R1 27 P–N3 N–B4 28 N–B3± P–R5 29 P–KN4** 29 N–K5 R–QB2 **29 . . . N–Q3 30 N–K5 R–QB2 31 R2–R2 N–B1** White threatened 32 R×P+ R×R 33 R×R+ K×R 34 N×P+. **32 R–R6 Q–K1 33 Q–Q2** To put more pressure on Black's weak points at c6 and a7 by Q–R2–R4, or by Q–B4. Another possibility was 33 P–QB4!? **33 . . . P–R6 34 K–R2 P–B4** If 34 . . . R–B1 then 35 R1–R2 with Q–K3–N3 to follow. **35 P×P R×P 36 Q–Q4 R–B2** (*328*)

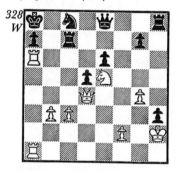

328
W

37 P–KB4?? The wrong B-file! 37 P–QB4! R–B1!? (37 . . . P×P? 38 Q–K4+ R–N2 39 N×P and N–R5 wins) 38 P×P P×P 39 Q×QP+ R–N2 40 R1–R2± **37 . . . Q–N4!=** The defect of White's last move is made painfully evident – the second rank in particular and White's king position in general have been seriously weakened. Black now threatens 38 . . . Q–K7+. **38 R6–R2** Preventing the incursion of the black queen on K2 and threatening P–B4. **38 . . . Q×P 39 N–B6!** Q–N2 Black can easily lose if he gets careless with 39 . . . R×N 40 R×P+ K–N1 41 R–R8+ K–B2 42 Q×NP+ K–Q3 43 Q–K5+ K–Q2

44 R1–R7+. **40 N×P N×N 41 R×N+ Q×R 42 R×Q+ R×R 43 Q–N6!** ½–½ White can draw comfortably despite his material disadvantage, e.g. 43 . . . R–KR3 44 Q–Q8+ K–N2 45 Q–Q7+ K–N3 46 Q–Q6+ K–N4 47 Q–N8+=.

2806 AK–Zoltan Ribli:
R7: 12 July:

Sicilian

1 P–K4 P–QB4 2 N–KB3 P–Q3 3 B–N5+ B–Q2 4 B×B+ Q×B 5 P–B4 P–K4 6 N–B3 N–QB3 7 0–0 KN–K2 8 N–Q5 N×N 9 BP×N N–Q5 10 N×N BP×N 11 P–Q3 B–K2 12 Q–N3 0–0 13 P–B4 QR–B1 14 B–Q2 Unzicker–Gheorghiu, round four, was agreed drawn at this point. **14 . . . P–B3 15 P–KR3 R–QB2 16 R–B2 R1–B1 17 R1–KB1 R–B7 18 P–N4 P–QR3 19 P–QR4 R1–B4 20 B–N4 R×R 21 K×R R–B2 22 B–Q2 Q–B1 23 K–K2 R–B4 24 P–B5 B–Q1 25 Q–R3 K–B2 26 R–QN1 K–K2 27 K–Q1 Q–Q2 28 P–N4 R–B1 29 Q–R2 B–N3 30 B–K1 K–B2 31 R–R1 B–Q1 32 B–Q2 B–N3 33 P–R5 B–Q1 34 Q–R4 Q×Q+ 35 R×Q K–K1 36 P–R4 P–R3 37 R–R2 K–Q2 38 B–K1 B–K2 39 R–KN2 B–Q1 40 B–Q2 B–K2 41 R–N3 R–KR1 42 K–B2 R–QB1+**

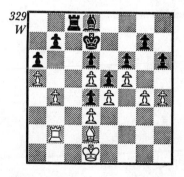

329
W

43 K–N2 R–KR1 44 R–N2 R–QB1
45 R–N1 R–KR1 46 K–B2
R–QB1+ 47 K–Q1 R–KR1 48
B–K1 R–QB1 49 R–N2 R–KR1 50
R–N2 R–QB1 51 B–Q2 B–Q1 (*329*)
52 P–QN5 P×P 53 R×P K–B2 54
K–K2 K–N1 55 B–N4 B–B2 56
P–R6 K–R2 57 P×P R–QN1 58
B–Q2 R×P 59 R×R+ K×R 60

P–N5 RP×P 61 P×P B–Q1 62
K–B3 K–B1 63 K–N4 K–Q2 64
K–R5 K–K1 65 B–N4 P×P 66
B×P B–B3 67 B–N4 K–B2 68
B–Q2 B–K2 69 B×P B–R6 70
B–Q8 B–Q3 71 K–N5 1–0 71 . . .
B–N1 72 P–B6 P–N3 (72 . . . P×P+
73 B×P and 74 K–B5) 73 B–K7
B–B2 74 P–Q6±±

29 41 USSR CHAMPIONSHIP Moscow, 2–26.10.1973

		1	2	3	4	5	6	7	8	9	0	1	2	3	4	5	6	7	8	
1	Spassky	×	½	½	½	½	½	½	½	½	1	0	½	1	1	1	1	1	1	**11½**
2	**Karpov**	½	×	1	1	0	½	½	½	½	½	1	½	1	½	½	½	½	1	**10½**
3	Korchnoi	½	0	×	½	½	½	½	½	½	½	1	½	1	1	½	1	1	½	**10½**
4	Kuzmin	½	0	½	×	½	½	½	½	½	1	½	½	½	1	1	1	1	½	**10½**
5	Petrosian	½	1	½	½	×	½	½	½	1	½	½	½	½	½	½	½	1	1	**10½**
6	Polugayevsky	½	½	½	½	½	×	½	1	1	½	½	½	1	½	½	½	½	1	**10½**
7	Geller	½	½	½	½	½	½	×	½	½	0	½	1	½	0	½	1	1	0	**8½**
8	K. Grigorian	½	½	½	½	½	0	½	×	1	½	+	½	½	1	½	0	0	½	**8½**
9	Tal	½	½	½	½	0	0	½	0	×	0	½	1	½	½	1	½	½	1	**8**
10	Taimanov	0	½	½	0	½	½	1	½	1	×	½	½	0	½	½	½	½	½	**8**
11	Savon	1	0	0	½	½	½	½	–	½	½	×	½	½	½	½	½	½	1	**8**
12	Keres	½	½	½	½	½	½	0	½	0	½	½	×	½	½	½	½	½	1	**8**
13	Rashkovsky	0	0	0	½	½	0	½	½	½	1	½	½	×	½	½	½	½	1	**7½**
14	Tukmakov	0	½	0	0	½	½	1	0	½	½	½	½	½	×	½	½	½	1	**7½**
15	Averkin	0	½	½	0	½	½	½	½	0	½	½	½	½	½	×	½	0	1	**7**
16	Smyslov	0	½	0	0	½	½	0	1	½	½	½	½	½	½	½	×	½	½	**7**
17	Sveshnikov	0	½	0	0	0	½	0	1	½	½	½	½	½	½	1	½	×	0	**6½**
18	Belyavsky	0	0	½	½	0	0	1	½	0	½	0	0	0	0	0	½	1	×	**4½**

Karpov's impressions of the tournament (from *64*):

'Spassky played excellently throughout the whole tournament and completely deserved his success. As usual Korchnoi played in a fighting spirit and also at a high level.

'I began the tournament, if you take the number of points obtained as the criterion, like never before. But all the same, even in those games which I won, such as those against Savon and Belyavsky, a feeling of dissatisfaction with my play never left me. I never felt that my game got going. When, in the all-important meeting with Spassky, I not only let slip a tremendous advantage, but even obtained the inferior position, it became clear to me that I could have wished for better form.

'Although I was not very satisfied with the place I obtained, nevertheless I consider my overall result satisfactory, the more so because towards the end I succeeded in overcoming the slump in my play. Although in the later stages I scored fewer points than at the start, nevertheless the quality of my play was higher.'

2901 AK–Vladimir Savon:
R1: 2 October:

English

1 N–KB3 N–KB3 2 P–B4 P–QN3 3 P–KN3 B–N2 4 B–N2 P–B4 5 0–0 P–N3 6 P–Q3 B–N2 7 P–K4 0–0 8 N–B3 N–B3 9 R–N1 N–K1 10 B–K3 N–Q5 11 N–K2 P–K4 One of the complicated contemporary strategic patterns. Apart from the text, 11 . . . N×N/6+ clearly deserves consideration: 12 B×N P–B4 and if 13 P–QN4 then 13 . . . N–Q3. **12 P–QN4 P–Q3 13 P×P QP×P 14 N2×N!** The start of a far-reaching plan, which Karpov succeeds in bringing to life. Now the centre is hermetically sealed and both players' attention is focused on flank operations. **14 . . . BP×N** Also possible is 14 . . . KP×N 15 B–B4 P–KR3. **15 B–Q2 N–B2 16 N–K1 N–K3 17 B–N4 R–K1 18 P–B4 P×P 19 P×P Q–B2 20 Q–N4 N–B4 21 B×N** A concrete approach to the position prompted this exchange and ceding the two bishops; that pair remain inactive for a long time and Black just cannot find a use for them. **21 . . . P×B 22 R–N2 QR–N1 23 R2–KB2 B–QB1 24 Q–N3 R–N8 25 P–KR4 P–KR4 26 N–B3 R×R+ 27 B×R B–KR3 28 N–Q2 K–R2 29 K–R2 B–N5 30 P–K5 P–B4** On 30 . . . P–B3 31 N–K4 is very unpleasant, but now Black's light-square bishop is imprisoned, and, not finding any opposition on the light squares, the white pieces threaten to infiltrate into the enemy camp. **31 Q–N2** *(330)* **31 . . . R–QN1** One would think that Black should now concentrate most of his attention on the tactical peculiarities of the position, weighing up variations such as 31 . . . Q–Q1

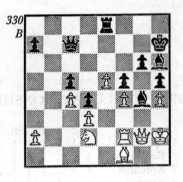

330
B

(31 . . . Q–K2 32 K–N3 P–N4?! 33 RP×P B×P 34 P×B Q×KP+ 35 K–R4!) 32 K–N3 B–N2 (threat 33 . . . R×P 34 P×R B×P+ 35 R–B4 B×R+ 36 K×B Q–Q3+ 37 K–N5 Q–K2+ 38 K–B4 Q–K6 mate) 33 N–B3 (or 33 Q–Q5 Q–B2) 33 . . . B×N 34 Q×B B–B3 35 R–R2 R×P 36 P×R B×KP+ 37 K–R3 B×R 38 K×B Q×P+. Of course all this is very rough, and White, clearly, could find a way to preserve his advantage. But Black should be trying to create at least the illusion of counter-threats. **32 K–N3** Karpov frequently and readily enlists the services of his king as an active participant in the game. Two successful examples come readily to mind: v. Gligorić (No. 2408) and v. A. Zaitsev (No. 1103), as does Nimzowitsch's saying 'My king likes to go for walks'. **32 . . . R–Q1 33 N–B3 R–Q2 34 R–N2 Q–R4 35 Q–Q2 Q–B6 36 B–N2 R–Q1 37 R–N3 Q–R8 38 R–N7+ K–R1** Black loses a piece after 38 . . . B–N2 39 N–N5+ K–N1 40 R×B+. **39 Q–K1! Q–B6 40 P–K6 Q×Q+ 41 N×Q 1–0** 2.27 – 2.34 There is no defence against the threat of 42 P–K7 R–K1 43 B–B6.

2902 Mark Taimanov–AK:
R2: 3 October:

Nimzo–Indian

1 P–Q4 1 N–KB3 2 P–QB4 P–K3
3 N–QB3 B–N5 4 P–K3 P–B4 5
N–B3 0–0 6 B–Q3 1 P–Q4 1 7 0–0
QP×P 2 8 B×BP 1 N–B3 9 P–QR3
1 B–R4 10 B–R2 2 P–QR3 7 11
N–K2 8 P×P 2 12 N2×P 1 N×N 2
13 N×N 1 B–B2 4 14 B–Q2 7
B–Q3 11 15 R–B1 12 B–Q2 4 16
B–N1 9 R–B1 8 17 Q–N3 5 R×R
18 R×R 1 Q–N1 5 19 P–R3 5
R–B1 2 20 R×R+ ½–½ 0.55 – 0.50

2903 AK–Evgenny Sveshnikov:
R3: 4–5 October:

Sicilian

1 P–K4 2 P–QB4 2 N–KB3 P–K3
1 3 P–Q4 P×P 4 N×P N–QB3 1
5 N–N5 N–B3 6 N1–B3 P–Q3 7
B–KB4 1 P–K4 8 B–N5 2 P–QR3 9
N–R3 P–N4 10 N–Q5 2 B–K2 11
B×N B×B 12 P–QB3 1 0–0 1 13
N–B2 4 B–N4 14 P–QR4 3 P×P 15
R×P P–QR4 2 16 B–B4 3 R–N1 3
17 P–QN3 2 B–K3 4 18 Q–R1 8
P–N3 5 19 0–0 Q–Q2 27 20 R–Q1 18
P–B4 2 21 P×P 3 P×P 6 22
P–QN4 1

It seems clear that White, who has
some potential advantage, can do
without this advance. 22 N–R3
deserved consideration.

22 . . . P×P 8 **23 P×P K–R1 24
P–N5** 6

This is rather rash. 24 Q–R2
makes a better impression.

24 . . . B×N! 29

This is more accurate than 24 . . .
N–K2 25 R–R7 R–N2 26 P–N6
when the chances are in White's
favour.

25 R×B 1 **N–K2** (*331*)

26 Q×P+ 9

White wins a pawn, but loses the
initiative. The quieter 26 R–Q1 was

331
W

also very likely the strongest. Also
tempting is 26 R–R7 Q–Q1 (26 . . .
Q–K3 27 R–B5 Q–N3 28 R5–B7 is
good for White) and then 27 R–Q1
(27 Q–Q1?! N×R 28 Q–R5 is
weak on account of 28 . . . N–B2,
while the consequences of 27 N–N4!?
N×R 28 N×N Q–B1 29 R–QB7
R–R1 are far from clear).

Shamkovich, in the Soviet bulletins of the event, suggested 26 R–Q3!
e.g. 26 . . . B–B3 27 R–R7 Q–Q1
(now the pawn sacrifice is unjusti-
fiable after 27 . . . R–N2 28 R×R
Q×R 29 R×P) 28 Q–Q1! N–B1
29 R–R6 with a big positional
advantage.

26 . . . P×Q 2 **27 R×Q 1 N–B1** 2

An accurate manoeuvre which
completely equalizes.

28 R–QB7 B–Q1 14 **29 R–B6** 3
N–N3 30 R–N4 1 **N×B** 1 **31
R6×N** 1 **B–N3 32 K–B1**

32 P–N3 P–B5! and the activity of
Black's pieces is sufficient to draw,
e.g. 33 P×P P×P 34 R×P R×R 35
R×R B–B4 36 R–B5 R×P 37
K–N2 R–R4.

32 . . . KR–Q1 1 **33 K–K2** 1 **B–R4**
10 **34 R–N3** 8 **R–Q7+** 2 **35 K–K3** 2
P–B5+ 1 **36 K–K4 R×BP** 2 **37
K×KP** 1 **R×KNP 38 N–Q4
R×RP** 5 **39 R–B6 2 B–N3** 9 **40
N–K6** 4 **P–B6** 3 **41 R×P R–R4+ 42
K–B6 R×P** 2 **43 R–Q6** 1 **R–N7** 5
44 K–K7 3 **B–R4** 5 ½–½ 1.35 – 2.34

2904 Alexander Belyavsky–AK:
R4: 6 + 9 October:

Nimzo-Indian

1 P–Q4 N–KB3 2 P–QB4 P–K3 3 N–QB3 B–N5 4 P–K3 2 P–B4 5 B–Q3 1 0–0 1 6 N–B3 P–Q4 7 0–0 1 QP×P 8 B×BP 1 P×P 1 9 P×P 5 P–QN3 10 B–KN5 4 B–N2 2 11 Q–K2 1 QN–Q2 6 12 QR–B1 2 R–B1 6 13 N–K5 29 Q–B2 35 14 B–N5 21 Q–Q3 20 15 KR–Q1 6 B×N 1 16 P×B 1 Q–Q4 16 17 P–KB4 4 Q–Q3 8 18 P–B4 18 Q–B2 1 19 B–QR4 7 P–QR3 5 20 B–B2 2 P–N3 3 21 Q–K1 3 K–N2 6 22 B–QR4 10 P–R3 1 23 B–R4 P–QN4 4 24 P×P 5 Q–Q3 25 P×P 8 B×RP 2 26 P–Q5 R×R 2 27 R×R 1 B–B1 1 (*332*)

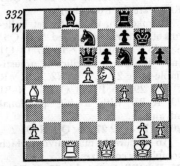

332
W

28 B×N/7 9
Here 28 N×N! wins: 28 . . . B×N 29 B×N+ K×B 30 B×B Q×B 31 Q–K5+ K–K2 32 R–B7 winning the queen, while if 28 . . . N×N then 29 P×P P×P (Black loses a piece after 29 . . . Q×KP 30 Q×Q P×Q 31 R–B7) 30 R–Q1 and then Q×KP with two good plus pawns.
28 . . . N×B 29 P×P 1 Q×P 1 30 N–B4 2 B–R3 31 Q×Q 2 P×Q 10 32 B–N3 1 R–B1 2 33 R–Q1 B×N 34 R×N+ K–B3 1 35 P–QR3 1 B–Q4 36 P–R3 R–B8+ 37 K–B2

R–B7+ 1 38 K–K3 1 R–B6+ 39 K–B2 R×P 40 B–R4+ P–N4 41 P×P+ P×P 42 B–N3 R–R7+ 43 K–K3 R×P Here the game was adjourned and White sealed 44 B–B7 R–QR7 45 R–R7 R–R1 46 K–B2 K–N3 47 R–Q7 R–R6 48 R–Q8 R–KB6+ 49 K–N1 R×P 50 R–KB8 R–QB6 51 B–Q6 R–B7 52 R–B2 R–B3 53 B–K5 P–N5 54 R–B6+ K–N4 55 R–B8 B–B6 56 B–B4+ K–N3 57 K–B2 R–B7+ 58 K–N3 R–KN7+ 59 K–R4 R–K7 60 B–N3 P–K4 61 R–QN8 P–K5 62 R–N5 R–K6 63 R–N6+ K–B2 64 K–N5 R–Q6 65 K–B5 P–K6 66 R–Q6 R–N6 67 R–Q7+ K–K1 68 K–K6 P–K7 69 R×K7 R–K6 70 K–B6 B–Q4 71 B–R4 R–KB6+ 72 K–N6 B–B2+ 0–1 4.25 – 3.15

2905 AK–Mikhail Tal:
R5: 7 October:

Slav

1 N–KB3 P–Q4 2 P–B4 P–QB3 3 P–Q4 1 N–B3 1 4 N–B3 1 P–K3 5 P–K3 5 QN–Q2 3 6 B–Q3 B–N5 7 0–0 4 0–0 1 8 P–QR3 3 B–Q3 9 Q–B2 6 P×P 16 10 B×BP 1 Q–K2 11 P–R3 7 P–K4 2 12 B–R2 1 P–QR4 22 13 P–QR4 31 B–N5 19 14 R–Q1 5 P–QN3 10 15 P×P 4 N×P 16 N–Q4 B–Q2 14 17 B–Q2 3 QR–Q1 2 18 B–K1 3 N–N3 2 19 N–B3 12 N–K4 20 20N–Q4 1 N–N3 1 21 N–B3 2 N–K4 2 ½–½ 1.30 – 1.40

2906 Viktor Korchnoi–AK:
R6: 8 October:

King's Indian Reversed

1 N–KB3 7 N–KB3 3 2 P–KN3 1 P–QN4 1 3 P–B3 6 (*333*)
This line is rarely seen, and on its infrequent outings 3 B–N2 is invariably played. The text is the start of an attack on the QNP of a type

333
B

which is familiar from the Sokolsky e.g. 1 P–QN4 P–QB3 2 B–N2 P–QR4. Strangely there was an article by T. D. Harding entitled *The Refutation of the Sokolsky?* in the May 1973 issue of *Chess* which included the opening of a game Harding–Alldridge, Birmingham University Open 1973: 1 N–KB3 N–KB3 2 P–KN3 P–QN4 3 P–B3 P–N3. It is interesting to speculate as to whether Korchnoi and/or Karpov had seen this article when they were at the European Team Championship in Bath.

3 . . . B–N2 3 4 P–QR4 P–QR3 3 5 P–K3 3 A rather dubious move; now White's position has many weaknesses: the squares KB3, Q3 and QN3. **5 . . . N–B3 6 6 P–Q4 P–K3 7 P–QN4** 10 **B–K2** 4 **8 QN–Q2** 1 It is clear that White could not take the QNP neither now nor earlier. Now Black's QN is driven back to the edge of the board and White stabilizes his position. **8 . . . N–R2** 1 **9 B–Q3** 1 **0–0** 4 **10 P–K4** 3 **P–Q3** 1 Preparing the advance . . . P–QB4 to open up the centre. **11 0–0** 12 **P–B4** 7 **12 NP×P** 2 Otherwise, for example after 12 B–N2, there can follow 12 . . . P×NP 13 BP×P P–Q4. **12 . . . QP×P** 1 **13 B–N2** 3 **N–B3** 31 The pawn sacrifice leads to a sharp game. Now after 14 RP×P RP×P 15 B×P Q–N3 16 Q–K2 N–R2 17

B–Q3 Q×B 18 QR–N1 Q×P there is material equality on the board. **14 P–K5** 11 **N–Q4** 2 **15 RP×P** 7 **RP×P** 1 **16 Q–N1** 1 **P×P** 4 **17 P×P** 1 **P–R3** 2 **18 B×P** 1 **Q–N3** 3 **19 B–K2** 11 19 B–Q3, transferring the bishop to K4, was not bad. **19 . . . R×R** 1 **20 B×R** 1 **Q–R2** 1 Black has compensation for the sacrificed pawn: a strong knight on Q4 and rich possibilities for piece-play. Besides that the white bishop is very unfortunately placed on QR1. **21 N–B4** 6 **R–N1** 11 **22 B–N2** 9 **B–R3** 4 **23 Q–B2** 5 **Q–N2** 8 **24 B–R1** 16 **N3–N5** 12 **25 Q–Q2** 2 **R–QB1** 3 **26 N–K3** 10 **N×N** 9 **27 Q×N/3** Not 27 B×B N×R, while if 27 P×N then 27 . . . R–B7 is good. **27 . . . B×B** 4 **28 Q×B** 1 **R–B7** 1 **29 Q–Q1** 1 **Q–B3** 2 **30 P–R3** 3 **N–Q4** 2 **31 Q–Q3** 4 **Q–R5** 1 **32 N–Q2** 3 **R–R7** 3 **33 N–N3** **N–N5** 2 **34 Q–N1** 1 **N–Q4** 1 **35 R–B1** 1 **Q–R1** 1 **36 R–B8+** 1 **Q×R** 37 **Q×R** 1 **Q–B5** 1 **38 Q–N1** 1 **Q–K7** 39 **Q–QB1** 1 **B–N4** 40 **Q–B1** 1 **Q–B6** (*334*)

334
W

Here the game was adjourned. The threat is 41 . . . Q×N and if the knight moves then 41 . . . N–K6 is decisive. If 41 Q–N1 there follows 41 . . . N–K6 42 P×N B×P+ 43 K–R2 B–B7.

Korchnoi sealed **41 P–R4** 1,

however in this case 41 . . . B–K6 is strong and if 42 Q–N2 (42 P×B Q×NP+ 43 K–R1 Q×RP+ 44 K–N1 Q–N6+ 45 K–R1 N×P) then both 42 . . . Q–Q8+ and 42 . . . B×BP+ are possible.

0–1 without further play. 2.30 – 2.28

2907 AK–Boris Spassky:
R7: 11 + 14 October:

Ruy Lopez

The notes are Karpov's from *64*.

1 P–K4 P–K4 2 N–KB3 N–QB3 3 B–N5 1 **P–QR3** 1 **4 B–R4 N–B3 5 0–0 B–K2 6 R–K1** 1 **P–QN4** 1 **7 B–N3 P–Q3 8 P–B3 0–0** 1 **9 P–KR3 N–QR4 10 B–B2** 1 **P–B4** 1 **11 P–Q4 Q–B2 12 QN–Q2 N–B3** 1 **13 P–Q5 N–Q1** 1 **14 P–QR4** 9 **R–N1** 6

It is interesting that this same line was employed in the first game of the Spassky–Korchnoi match (Kiev 1968).

15 P×P 3

The immediate 15 P–QN4 is good here, but the text move is also not bad.

15 . . .	**P×P** 1
16 P–QN4	**P–B5** 7
17 N–B1 1	**N–K1** 21

In my opinion this is an inaccuracy, since Black shows his hand too soon, declaring his intentions. It is not advisable to take away the . . . K1 square from the black rook at such an early stage. Taking advantage of this I succeeded in thinking up a comparatively new plan involving the moves N3–R2 and P–B4.

Apparently Black should have played 17 . . . B–Q2.

18 N3–R2 18	**P–B3** 9

In my opinion 18 . . . B–B3 was better.

19 P–B4 2	**N–B2** 1
20 N–B3 5	

Here White has many varied possibilities. Thus 20 P–B5 P–N3 21 P–N4 N–N2 seems natural, and now, by playing 22 B–K3, White firmly seizes the QR-file. This is perfectly sound, but it is true that it remains unclear what domination of the only open file would have given.

20 . . .	**P–N3** 2
21 P–B5 2	**N–N2** 1
22 P–N4 4	**B–Q2** 1
23 B–K3 1	**R–R1** 3
24 Q–Q2 3	

Seemingly not the best, although by this move White forces the black queen to go to . . . QN2. More consistent, however, was 24 R–B1, so that if 24 . . . R–R7 the rook can be repelled from the second rank with 25 B–N1 and only then play 26 Q–Q2.

24 . . .	**Q–N2** 1
25 QR–B1 5	

A crucial decision – to concede the QR-file to the opponent. On the other hand, if one pair of rooks is exchanged then White is left with fewer winning chances. If you want to win – give your opponent counterplay!

25 . . .	**R–R7** 6
26 N–N3 7	**R1–R1** 7
27 P–R4 12	**B–Q1** 35
28 K–R1 11	**B–N3** 4
29 R–KN1 7	**B×B** 10
30 Q×B	**Q–R2** 6
31 Q–Q2 3	**B–K1** 1

I do not think very much of this manoeuvre – the black pieces have become very passive. In guarding . . . KN3 an extra time, Black finally unties his opponent's hands for a K-side attack. I think that transferring the queen to . . . Q1 by . . . Q–N3–Q1 was more useful here.

32 P–N5 10	**Q–K2** 7

33 R/B1–B1 5   **BP ✕ P** 7

Black must go in for this exchange immediately, otherwise White plays 34 N–R2 and eliminates even this possibility.

34 RP ✕ P 1   **Q–Q2**

35 N–R2 6

I dare say the simplest move was 35 R–B2 keeping in reserve the threat P–B6. That would have posed Black very difficult problems, the more so because at this moment there were only four minutes left on Spassky's clock. But instead of this I myself made some unimportant moves.

35 . . .   **Q–Q1** 3
(335)

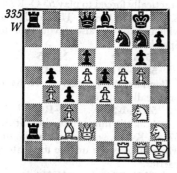

36 P–B6 1

It seemed to me that after 36 P ✕ P P ✕ P 37 N–N4 Q ✕ P 38 N–B6+ K–R1 39 Q–R2+ Q–R3 40 R–N2 (not diverting the other rook which can still prove useful on the KB-file) 40 . . . R–R8 41 B–N1 Q ✕ Q+ 42 R ✕ Q+ N–R4 43 N3 ✕ N P ✕ N there is nothing clearly forced and Black's position is holding. If, all the same, White plays 40 R–B2 then again 40 . . . R–R8 41 Q ✕ Q+ N ✕ Q 42 R–R2 N–R4 43 N3 ✕ N P ✕ N and the . . . KN1 square is protected. It is true that in all circumstances Black's position remains shaky, and it was

necessary to seek a strengthening of the play in one of these variations.

36 . . .   **B–Q2**

Black, on the other hand, has no pretensions, he just makes the best moves.

37 P ✕ N 1

Bondarevsky suggested sacrificing a piece instead of taking one: 37 R–B2 N–K1 38 N–B5 with an attack.

37 . . .   **Q ✕ P**

38 Q–N2 15

38 Q–B2 was stronger, and after the forced 38 . . . Q–B5 then 39 N–B5, and White again has the advantage, and a significant one at that.

38 . . .   **R–N7** 1

39 R–N1 7

Again 39 Q–B2 was better here. The variations arising from that I analysed at home because they could have a bearing on the adjourned position.

39 . . . Q–K2 40 N–B5 P ✕ N 41 P ✕ P R1–R7 (41 . . . Q–B3 42 N–N4 Q–N4 43 R–N2±) 42 P–B6 Q–K1 43 R–B1 N–R3 44 R–N5 (preventing the bishop from going to . . . KB4) 44 . . . Q–B2 45 K–N1 B–B4 (45 . . . N–B4 46 N–N4; 45 . . . P–K5 46 Q–R4 Q–B3 47 R–B1) 46 Q–N6 (The tempting 46 R ✕ B Q–N3+ 47 K–R1 N ✕ R 48 B ✕ N R ✕ Q 49 B–K6+ Q–B2 50 N–N4 unfortunately does not work because of 47 . . . R ✕ B 48 R ✕ R R–R8+).

It is clear that 45 . . . B–B1 is preferable (instead of 45 . . . B–B4): 46 N–B1 R ✕ B 47 R ✕ R R ✕ R 48 Q ✕ R Q ✕ BP 49 R–N2 N–N5 50 N–K3 P–R4 (50 . . . N ✕ N 51 Q ✕ P+ K ✕ Q 52 P–N8=Q+) 51 N ✕ N B ✕ N 52 Q–B2 K ✕ P 53 Q–K3 and White's position is slightly better.

Instead of 39 ... Q–K2, 39 ... Q–B5 deserves consideration. Also in this case it seems possible to play 40 N–B5 Q×Q 41 R×Q P×N 42 P×P and, with P–B6 to follow, White sets his opponent difficult problems. If Black prevents this then the following piquant ending arises: 42 ... R1–R7 43 N–N4 K×P 44 N–R6+ and all the king's retreats lead to mate. If he plays immediately 41 ... R1–R7, then 42 N–K3 in conjunction with N–B3–N5–K6, also gives White the advantage.

Finally, I was aware that all the preceding variations were similar and required further checking.

39 ...	**R7–R7**
40 Q–K2 3	**Q–R5**
41 R/QN1–KB1	

The sealed move. In the adjourned position, despite White's extra piece, Black already has some advantage.

41 ..	**B–R6**
42 R–B2	**N–N4**
43 Q–K3	**B–N5**

Move by move Black introduces threats, each time forcing White to make practically the only reply.

44 R1–KB1	**K×P**
45 B–Q1	

I do not see any other satisfactory reply.

45 ...	**B×B**
46 R×B	**R–R8**
47 R1–KB1	

47 R2–B1 is unsatisfactory on account of 47 ... R1–R7 and 47 R2–Q2 because of the same reply.

47 ...	**R×R+**
48 R×R	**R–R7**
49 R–B2	**R–R8+**
50 R–B1	**R–R7**
51 R–B2	**R–R8+**
52 R–B1	**R×R+**
53 N3×R	**Q×P+**
54 K–N1 (*336*)	
54 ...	**Q×Q+**

336
B

In my opinion not a forced exchange. Black had the useful 54 ... Q–R5 (54 ... P–R3 is not possible in view of 55 Q–R7+ K–B3 56 Q–Q7) with the idea of the manoeuvre ... N–R6–B5. White is practically forced to play 55 Q–R7+ K–R3 56 Q–K3. The endgame which arises is also favourable to Spassky.

55 N×Q	**N–K5**
56 N–Q1	**N–B3**

Bondarevsky gave 56 ... K–B3 as practically winning.

57 N–K3	**P–R4**

I think the immediate king thrust, 57 ... K–R3, was better – while the white knights are unable to create a barrier.

58 N–B3	**N–K5**
59 N–Q1	½–½

3.23 – 3.54

The ending still retains its tension e.g.:

59 ... P–N4 60 N–K1 N–B3 61 N–K3 (61 ... N–K1 62 N–B3 K–N3 63 N–Q2 N–B3 64 N2×P P×N 65 P–N5 K–B2 66 P–N6 N–Q2 67 P–N7 and the QP is lost all the same.) 61 ... K–N3 62 N1–B2 N–K1 63 N–R3 (Possibly better is the immediate 63 N×P) 63 ... N–B2 64 K–N2 P–N5 65 N/K3×BP P×N 66 P–N5 N×QP 67 N×P P–R5 68 N×QP and although Black is certainly not risking defeat,

the white pawns, in certain circumstances, can become strong.

2908 Tigran Petrosian–AK:
R8: 12 + 14 October:

Queen's Indian

1 P–Q4 1 **N–KB3** 4 **2 N–KB3** 1 **P–K3 3 P–QB4** 1 **P–QN3** 1 **4 P–K3 B–N2 5 N–B3 B–K2** 2 **6 B–Q3** 1 **P–Q4** 7 **0–0 0–0 8 Q–K2** 1 **P–B4** 8 **9 QP×P** 2 **QP×P** 22 **10 B×BP B×P 11 P–K4** 26 **QN–Q2** 8 **12 P–K5** 9 **B×N 13 P×B N–R4** 14 **R–Q1** 2 **Q–K2** 1 **15 P–B4** 4 **P–N3** 16 **P–B5!** 2 **KP×P** *(337)*

337
W

17 P–K6 N2–B3 1 **18 P×P+** 5 **K–N2** 7 **19 Q×Q** 3 **B×Q 20 N–N5** 6 **QR–B1** 12 **21 B–N3** 2 **P–QR3** 2 **22 N–Q4** 2 **R×P** 1 In the face of N–K6+ there is no choice. **23 B–K3** 2 **N–N5** 5 **24 B×R** 25 **K×B 25 QR–B1** 1 **R–B4** 6 **26 K–N2** 4 **N4–B3** 13 **27 B–Q2** 8 **R–Q4** 13 **28 B–K1** 4 **P–QR4** 3 **29 N–B3** 5 **R×R** 1 **30 R×R N–K5 31 N–Q2** 5 **N–Q3 32 P–N3** 3 **N–K4** 11 **33 N–N1** 1 **K–K3** 12 **34 N–B3** 1 **N4–B2** 4 **35 P–B3** 8 **B–Q1** 3 **36 B–B2** 5 **N–B1** 4 **37 N–N5** 2 **N1–Q3** 3 **38 N–Q4+** 1 **K–Q2 39 B–N3** 1 **B–K2 40 K–B1** 1 **B–B3** 1 *(338)* **41 N–N5** The sealed move **41 . . . B–K2 42 P–KR4 K–K3 43 N–Q4+ K–Q2 44 K–N2 B–B3 45 N–N5**

338
W

B–K2 46 P–R4 P–R3 47 P–R5! This forces a decisive weakening. **47 . . . P×P 48 B–B2 B–Q1 49 N–Q4 P–B5 50 N–K2 K–B3 51 N×P P–R5 52 N–N6 N–N2 53 P–B4 B–B3 54 R–QB1+ N–B4 55 K–R3 N–Q3 56 B×N P×B 57 N×P P–R4 58 N–B3 K–Q4 59 R–Q1+ B–Q5 60 N–Q2 K–K3 61 K–N3 N–B4+ 62 K–B3 P–R5 63 N–B4 B–B6 64 K–N4 B–N5 65 R–Q3 1–0** 3.47 – 3.05

Black is in zugswang e.g. 65 . . . B–K8 66 N–K3! wins a piece, while after 65 . . . K–B3 66 R–Q5 picks up the KRP (66 . . . N–K2 67 R–Q6+ K–B2 68 N–K5+ K–K1 69 R–K6 and there is no longer a troublesome check on . . . KB4).

2909 AK–Gennady Kuzmin:
R9: 13 October:

Sicilian

1 P–K4 P–QB4 2 N–KB3 P–Q3 3 P–Q4 P×P 4 N×P 1 **N–KB3** 5 **N–QB3** 1 **P–QR3** 1 **6 P–B4** 1 **Q–B2 7 P–QR4** 1 **P–KN3** 18 **8 N–B3** 3 **B–N5** 9 **9 B–Q3** 8 **N–B3** 4 **10 P–R3** 2 **B×N 11 Q×B B–N2** 1 **12 0–0** 1 **0–0** 1 **13 B–Q2** 12 **P–K3** 4 **14 N–K2** 8 **QR–B1** 14 Black might do better with 14 . . . N–QN5 and if 15 B×N Q–N3+ and 16 . . . Q×B with a good game, or 14 . . . N–Q2 15 B–B3 B×B 16 P×B (16 N×B

Q–N3+ and 17 . . . Q×P) 16 . . .
16 . . . Q–Q1! and it would be difficult for White to take the initiative on the K-side. **15 K–R1** 6 **P–K4** 12 **16 N–B3** 11 **P×P** 2 **17 B×BP** 2 **N–QN5** 3 **18 B–Q2** 6 **N–Q2** 9 **19 Q–N3** 12 **Q–B3** 16 **20 B–KN5** 5 **R/QB1–K1** 11 **21 QR–Q1** 12 **N–K4** 9 better **21** . . .**P–R3 22 Q–R4** 4 **N4×B** 1 **23 P×N Q–Q2** 5 **24 B–B6** 6 **P–QR4** 1 **25 P–Q4** 3 **R–K3** 3 (*339*)

339
W

26 P–K5 7 **P–Q4** 7 **27 B×B** 1 **K×B 28 R–B6 P–R3** 4 **29 R1–KB1** 1 **R×R** 2 **30 R×R** 1 **R–K1** 1 **31 N–K2** 7 **N–B3** 2 if 31 . . . R–K3 then 32 N–B4 R×R 33 Q×R+ and 34 P–K6±± **32 R–Q6** 3 **Q–B4** 4 **33 N–N3 Q–Q6** 1 **34 R×QP R–K3 35 Q–B4** 5 **R–K2** 2 **36 K–R2** 1 **K–N1 37 Q×RP** 1 **Q–B5 38 N–K4 1–0**
2.10 – 2.25

2910 Orest Averkin–AK:
R10: 15 October:

Reti

1 N–KB3 N–KB3 2 **P–B4** 1 **P–QN3** 1 3 **P–QN3** 3 **B–N2** 1 4 **B–N2 P–K3** 1 5 **P–K3** 1 **B–K2** 1 6 **B–K2** 2 **0–0** 7 **0–0** 1 **P–Q4** 5 8 **N–B3** 1 **P–B4** 1 9 **P×P N×P** 1 **10 P–Q4** 1 **N×N** 2 **11 B×N N–B3** **12 R–B1** 8 **R–B1** 13 **P×P** 11 **B×P** 1 **14 Q×Q** 2 **KR×Q** 2 **15 B–N2** 3 **N–N5** 4 (*340*)

340
W

16 KR–Q1 11 **N×P** 14 **17 R×R+ R×R 18 R–R1 N–N5 19 R×P** 2 **B–Q4** 1 **20 N–Q4** 3 **P–R3** 12 **21 R–B7** 7 **R–R1** 2 **22 B–KB1** 4 **B–Q3** 44 **23 R–B1** 2 **B–K4** 1 **24 R–R1 R×R** 1 **25 B×R B–KB3** 4 **26 B–B4** 2 **B×B** 6 **27 P×B K–B1** 1 **28 K–B1** 2 **K–K2** 5 **29 B–B3** ½–½
1.10 – 1.55

2911 AK–Efim Geller:
R11: 16 October

Ruy Lopez

1 P–K4 P–K4 2 **N–KB3 N–QB3** 3 **B–N5 P–QR3** 4 **B–R4 N–B3** 5 **0–0 B–K2** 6 **R–K1 P–QN4** 7 **B–N3 0–0** 8 **P–QR4 B–N2** 9 **P–Q3 P–Q3** 10 **N–B3 N–QR4!** 11 **B–R2 P–N5** 12 **N–K2 P–B4!** 13 **P–B3** This has been thought to be unsatisfactory, but White can only obtain equality from 13 N–N3 P–N6! 14 P×P N–B3 15 P–N4! N×NP 16 B–QB4= **13** . . . **P–B5! 14 N–N3 BP×P 15 B–N5** (*341*) The reason for dissatisfaction with White's game is to be found in 15 Q×P P–N6 16 B–N1 N–Q2 17 B–K3 P–N3 and White had been driven on to the defensive in Liberzon–Jansa, Luhacovice 1971. **15** . . . **P–R3 16 B×N B×B 17 R–K3 P×P 18 P×P Q–B2 19 R×P QR–Q1 20 N–K1 P–N3 21 N–B2 B–N2 22 N–K3 K–R1 23 R–N1 B–B1 24 R–N2 N–N2 25 N–Q5 Q–Q2 26 N–N6 Q–B2 27**

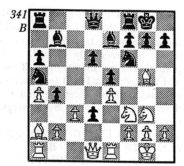

341
B

N×B R×N 28 P-R4 N-B4 29
R-Q5 P-KR4 30 R2-Q2 Q-K2
½-½ 2.20 – 2.22

2912 Vladimir Tukmakov–AK:
R12: 17 October:
Sicilian

The notes are Tukmakov's from
64.

**1 P-K4 P-QB4 3 2 N-KB3 P-K3
1 3 P-Q4 P×P 4 N×P 1 P-QR3 5
B-Q3 1 N-KB3 1 6 0-0 Q-B2 7
N-Q2** 23

Here, against 7 P-QB4, 7 . . .
N-B3 8 B-K3 N-K4 is possible,
while against 8 N×N Black is
perfectly able to play 8 . . . NP×N.
**7 . . . N-B3 2 8 N×N 3 NP×N 9
P-KB4 17 P-Q4 2 10 P-QN3 7
B-K2 8 11 B-N2 3 P-QR4 12 P-B4**
11

The first controversial moment.
Black wants, by means of . . . P-R5
and . . . B-R3, to rid himself of his
bad pieces – the QRP and the light-
squared bishop.

12 P-QR4 does not achieve anything for White after 12 . . . B-R3,
but 12 P-B4 also suffers from
weakening the QN4 square.

12 Q-K2 deserved consideration –
a more natural place for the queen
than the one I chose.

12 . . . 0-0 36

Karpov made this move after long
thought. Here 12 . . . P-R5 is no

longer so good: White replies 13
R-B1 or 13 Q-B2 and the evacuation
of the black king is again delayed.

In castling Black was obliged to
look at the consequences of the
sacrifice 13 P-K5 N-Q2 (on . . . K1
the knight is not doing anything) 14
B×P+ K×B 15 Q-R5+ K-N1 16
R-B3 P-KB4 17 R-R3. After 17 . . .
R-Q1 White has a draw but no
more. I was attracted by a different
plan of attack

13 Q-B2 20 P-R3! 8

Here this is better than the
traditional Sicilian reaction . . .
P-N3.

14 K-R1 1 Q-N3 6

15 BP×P was threatened.

15 QR-K1?! 13

I thought for a long time about the
position after the exchange sacrifice
and it seemed to me very terrible (in
the sense of awe-inspiring – eds); in
reality it was not so simple. Quieter
and better was 15 N-B3.

15 . . . N-N5 10 (*342*)

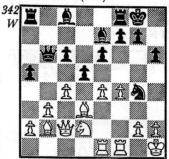

342
W

16 KP×P 20

Now 16 N-B3 will no longer do
because of 16 . . . B-B4. **16 . . .
BP×P 2 17 P×P 2 N-B7+ 1 18
R×N Q×R 19 R-K2** 3

After 19 R-KB1 Q-B4 White has
no compensation for the exchange
because 20 N-B4 P×P 21 B-R3
Q-B2 does not work – the bishop on
. . . K2 is defended.

19 . . . Q×BP 10

19 . . . Q–B4 is bad: 20 N–B4 (also possible is 20 P×P Q×Q 21 P×P+ with sufficient compensation) 20 . . . P×P 21 B–R3 P×N 22 B–R7+! K–R1 23 B×Q.

20 R–K4 3 **Q–Q3** 22

The queen cannot go to . . . B7 because after 21 B–Q4 she is trapped, but 20 . . . Q–N4 was possible. White can then draw with 21 R–K5 Q–B5 (21 . . . P–B4 is too dangerous) 22 R–K4, but it is not so easy to find more, if indeed it is possible. However, the text move is better.

21 N–B4 11 **Q×QP** 22 **R–N4!** 6

Immediately regaining the exchange does not work: 22 N–N6 Q–N2 23 Q–B3 P–K4! (also possible is 23 . . . P–B3, but not 23 . . . B–B3?? 24 Q×B±±) 24 N×R Q×N and Black has an extra pawn.

22 . . . P–K4 3 **23 R–N3 R–R3** 1

Here Black has a wide choice of moves. As well as the game continuation the moves 23 . . . Q–K3, 23 . . . Q–Q1 and 23 . . . R–Q1 are possible.

24 N×P 2 (*343*)

343
B

Here my opponent thought for a long time, and it seemed to me that in playing 23 . . . R–R3 Karpov had overlooked, in the variation 24 N×P R–K3 25 B–B4 R×N, the move 26 R×P+!±±.

Against 24 . . . R–KB3 25 N–B6 is possible. 25 N–B6! is a solid threat anyway, therefore the text move is practically forced. The position is most interesting – if you add the fact that I had ten minutes left and Karpov, twenty, then the drama of the following struggle increases.

24 . . . B–B3 12 **25 B–B4** 4 **Q–Q3** 4 **26 N×P! R×N** 1 **27 B×B** 1

27 B×R/7+ loses to 27 . . . K×B 28 B×B B–B4 (but not 28 . . . Q×B 29 R–KB3 or 28 . . . P×B 29 Q–R7+) 29 R×P+ K–B1!

27 . . . B–K3! 1

Or 27 . . . Q×B 28 B×R/7+ Q×B (28 . . . K×B 29 R–KB3) 29 Q×B+.

28 R–Q3 1 **Q–B2** 4

After 28 . . . B×B 29 R×Q R×R 30 P×B White is not risking anything.

29 R–Q8+ 1 **Q×R!** 1

If 29 . . . R–B1 there follows the stunning blow 30 R×R+ K×R 31 B×P+!. The bishop is immune: 31 . . . Q×B/2 32 Q–B2+ and 33 B×R or 31 . . . K×B 32 Q–N2+ and 33 B×R. There remains 31 . . . K–N1 but then 32 B–N2 and White has two pawns for the exchange which, together with the position of the black king, gives White at least equal chances.

30 B×Q 1 **B×B** 4 **31 P–KR3!**

If 31 Q×B then 31 . . . R–QB3! – it is impossible to defend against the two mate threats on KB1 and QB1 and the endgame after 32 Q×R/7+ is lost for White.

Now there remained not more than a minute on my clock, and on my opponent's, about five.

The smoke of battle has cleared somewhat and it has become clear that the chances are on the side of Black, to whom the presence of opposite coloured bishops gives good attacking chances.

31 ... B–B8 !

In this position best of all was 31 ... B–Q4 and both 32 Q–Q3 R–Q3! and 32 Q–QB5 B–N2 are bad. 32 K–R2 should be played and a similar position is obtained to that which arises after several moves in the game.

32 Q–K4! P–R5 33 P×P R–Q3 34 B–R5 R3–KB3 ! 35 B–K1 B–R3 36 K–R2 B–N2 1 37 Q–QB4 R–B3 38 Q–N3 R–KN3 39 B–N3 R–N4 1 40 Q–B4 B–Q4

Here the game was adjourned and I sealed . . . **41 Q–B8+**

On analysis it was clear that Black's advantage was not sufficient to play for a win. The passed QRP gives sufficient counterchances.

41 ... R–B1 42 Q–B2 P–R4 43 P–R5! ½–½ 2.55 – 3.00

The ending after 43 . . . P–R5 44 B×P R×P+ 45 Q×R B×Q 46 K×B cannot be won.

2913 AK–Lev Polugayevsky:
R13: 20 October:

Slav

1 P–Q4 5 P–Q4 2 2 P–QB4 P–QB3 3 3 N–KB3 1 N–KB3 1 4 N–B3 1 P–K3 5 P–K3 1 QN–Q2 1 6 B–Q3 2 P×P 7 B×BP P–QN4 8 B–Q3 2 B–N2 1 9 P–K4 7 P–N5 1 10 N–QR4 3 P–B4 1 11 P–K5 N–Q4 Following the game Ivkov–Larsen, Candidates ¼-final, Bled 1965. **12 P×P 4 N×BP 4 13 N×N 2 B×N** Larsen in the afore-mentioned match (both in the fourth and sixth games) exchanged his dark-squared bishop, retaining the two knights. **14 0–0 1 P–KR3 1 15 Q–K2 4 Q–N3 9 16 B–Q2 13 K–B1 13 17 QR–B1 12 R–Q1 35 18 R–B2 27 P–N3 8** (*344*)

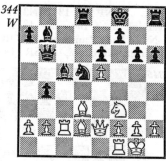

344
W

Both the advance of Black's KRP and KNP and the king manoeuvre ... K–B1–N2 are to be found in the Danish grandmaster's analysis. **19 R1–B1 1 B–K2 20 B–QB4 10 R–B1 22 21 B×N 9 R×R 3 22 R×R B×B 23 R–B8+ K–N2 24 R×R K×R 25 B×RP Q–B2 2 26 P–QN3 5 Q–B6 6 27 P–KR4 3 P–R4 17 28 B–N5 24 B×N 2 29 Q×B 1 B×B 2 30 P×B Q–K8+ 31 K–R2 2 Q×KP+ 1 32 Q–N3 2 Q–N7 33 Q–N8+ K–N2 34 P–B4 1 Q×RP 3 35 Q–K5+ 4** ½–½ 2.27 – 2.17

2914 Paul Keres–AK:
R14: 21 October:

Queen's Indian

1 P–Q4 N–KB3 2 P–QB4 1 P–K3 3 N–KB3 3 P–QN3 1 4 P–KN3 1 B–N2 5 B–N2 B–K2 1 6 0–0 1 0–0 7 N–B3 3 N–K5 1 8 Q–B2 3 N×N 9 Q×N P–QB4 2 10 R–Q1 4 P–Q3 2 11 Q–B2 9 N–B3 8 12 P×P 30

Keres was probably mulling over the alternatives: 12 P–K3 and 12 B–K3 P×P (12 ... Q–B2 13 QR–B1 P–K4 14 P×KP P×P 15 N–K1 N–Q5 ½–½ O'Kelly–Mecking, Buenos Aires 1970) 13 N×P N×N 14 B×N B×B 15 K×B Q–B2 16 Q–Q3 QR–B1 17 P–N3 Q–B3+ 18 Q–KB3 Q×Q+ 19 K×Q KR–Q1 with an equal ending, Smyslov–Reshevsky, Buenos Aires 1970.

12 . . . NP×P 13 P–N3 (*345*)
diverging from theory – 13 B–B4
R–N1 14 R–Q2! and not 14 P–QR3?
Podgayets–Korchnoi, USSR 1969.

345
B

**13 . . . P–QR4 11 14 B–N2 Q–B2 15
Q–B3 3 B–B3 1 16 Q–Q2 1 B×B 1
17 Q×B P–R5 1 18 P–K3 5 P–R3 6
19 R–Q2 4 P×P 2 20 P×P R×R+
21 Q×R R–R1 1 22 R–R2 1 R×R
2 23 Q×R ½–½** 1.10 – 0.50

2915 AK–Karen Grigorian:
R15: 23 + 25 October:

Semi-Tarrasch

**1 N–KB3 P–QB4 2 P–B4 5
N–KB3 1 3 N–B3 1 P–Q4 1 4 P×P
N×P 1 5 P–Q4 1 P–K3 1 6 P–K4 1
N×N 1 7 P×N P×P 2 8 P×P
N–B3 2 9 B–QB4 B–N5+ 5 10
B–Q2 Q–R4** 43 **11 P–Q5** 14 if 11
R–QN1 then 11 . . . B×B+ 12
Q×B K–K2 with . . . R–Q1 to
follow **11 . . . B×B+ 3 12 N×B 3**
or 12 Q×B Q×Q+ 13 K×Q
N–R4 14 B–N5+ K–K2 15 KR–QB1
P–QR3 16 B–Q3 B–Q2= **12 . . .
N–K2!** 32 Other moves are weaker:
12 . . . N–Q5 13 0–0 0–0 14 N–N3
N×N 15 P×N and 16 P–Q6 or
12 . . . P×P 13 P×P N–K2 14
Q–K2. **13 0–0 5 P×P 14 P×P 1
0–0 2 15 R–K1 9 N–B4 6 16 B–N3 5
N–Q3 2 17 N–K4 Q–N5!** 18 (*346*)

346
W

18 Q–B3 62 **R–K1 5 19 P–QR3 2
Q–R4 20 R–K3 1 N×N 21 R×N
R×R 22 Q×R 1 B–Q2 1 23 P–R3
Q–B6 4 24 Q–N1! 1 Q–B4** if 24 . . .
R–K1 then 25 Q–Q1 followed by
26 R–B1 and 27 P–Q6 is very strong.
**25 B–B2 1 Q×QP 26 B×P+ 1
K–R1 27 B–K4 2 Q–Q5 28 R–R2
R–K1 5 29 B×P 3 R–QN1 8 30
Q–K4 11 Q–Q8+ 31 K–R2 B–K3
32 R–N2 Q–Q3+ 1 33 P–N3 1
Q×RP 34 Q–K5 2 R–Q1 35 B–K4
1 K–N1 36 R–N8 2 Q–K2 1 37
P–R4 3 P–R4 38 Q–R5 P–B4 39
R×R+ 4 Q×R 1 40 B×P 2 B×B
3 41 Q×B** (*347*)

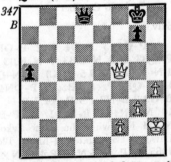

347
B

41 . . . P–R5 the sealed move **42
Q–B2 Q–R4 ½–½** 2.40 – 2.40

2916 AK–Naum Rashkovsky:
R16: 24 + 25 October:

Benoni

**1 P–QB4 P–KN3 2 2 P–Q4 N–
KB3 2 3 N–QB3 P–B4 3 4 P–Q5 3 P–**

Q3 5 N–B3 1 B–N6 P–K4 1 0–0 7
B–K2 P–K3 1 8 0–0 2 R–K1 9
P–KR3 3 P×P 6 10 KP×P N–K5?
10 **11** N×N 1 R×N **12** B–Q3 2
R–K1 **13** B–N5 5 Q–N3 20 **14** R–N1
7 B–Q2 30 Rashkovsky consumes
great quantities of time trying to
find a way to develop his pieces. The
position is very bleak for Black. **15**
P–R3 7 P–QR4 13 **16** P–QN3
Q–B2 2 **17** Q–Q2 10 P–R5 4 **18**
B–R6 16 P×P 2 **19** B×B 8 K×B 20
R×P 3 B–B1 **21** Q–N2+ K–N1 **22**
N–Q2 4 P–B4 7 (*348*)

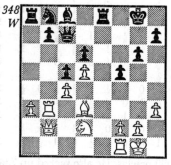

348
W

23 N–B3 8 Missing 23 B×P! B×B
24 R×P±± or 23 . . . P×B 24
R–N3+ K–B1 25 Q–R8+ K–K2 26
R–K1+±± **23** . . . N–Q2 1 **24**
N–N5 7 N–B1 **25** Q–Q2 Q–K2 6
26 P–B4 3 Q–K6+ 11 **27** Q×Q 3
R×Q **28** K–B2 R–K2 **29** R–QR1 4
N–Q2 9 **30** N–B3 1 K–B1 3 **31** N–Q2
N–B3 1 **32** P–QR4 3 R–R4 5 **33**
B–B2 2 K–K1 **34** K–B3 6 K–Q1 1
35 R3–N1 R–R3 **36** P–R5 6 R–R2 3
37 R–N1 5 R–R3 **38** N–N3 2 B–Q3
3 **39** R/N1–N1 5 R–R2 **40** N–Q2 2
B–B1 1 **41** N–B1 4 R–R3? the
sealed move **42** R–N6! P–R3 42 . . .
R×R 43 P×R N–Q2 44 R–N1 and
White will be able to infiltrate the
black position. **43** R×R P×R **44**
R–N1 P–N4 **45** N–N3 P–N5+ **46**

P×P P×P+ **47** K–B2 N–K1 **48**
B–N6 R–KN2 **49** B×N K×B **50**
N–K4 K–K2 **51** R–N8 B–Q2 **52**
K–N3 R–N3 **53** R–N7 K–Q1 **54**
R–N6 1–0 3.03 – 3.25

2917 Vasily Smyslov–AK:
   R17: 26 October:

Sicilian

1 P–K4 1 P–QB4 2 N–KB3 P–Q3
3 P–Q4 1 P×P 4 N×P N–KB3 1
5 N–QB3 1 P–QR3 1 6 B–K2 2
P–K4 1 7 N–B3 1 With no intention
of testing for improvements by
Black on Karpov–Bronstein or
Karpov–R. Byrne. **7** . . . B–K2 1
8 0–0 0–0 1 **9** R–K1 1 QN–Q2 4
10 P–QR4 5 Q–B2 5 **11** N–Q2 15
N–B4 4 **12** B–B3 4 R–N1 12 **13**
P–R5 4 N–K3 14 **14** N–N3 10
P–QN4 1 **15** P×Pep 2 R×P 9
16 B–K3 8 R–N5 7 **17** B–K2 14
B–N2 5 **18** P–B3 17 (*349*)

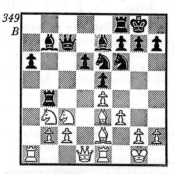

349
B

18 . . . P–Q4 9 **19** N×P 1 N×N 2
20 P×N 2 N–Q5 2 **21** N×N 17
P×N **22** P–B3 6 not 22 B×QP??
22 . . . P×P 4 **23** P×P 3 Q×BP 2
24 B×P 1 B–B4 4 **25** B3×B 1
Q×B+ 3 **26** K–R1 2 B×B 1 **27**
R×B 3 R–Q5 1 **28** Q–R1 3 Q×P
29 R–R5 2 ½–½ 2.06 – 1.36

30 MADRID 25.11–15.12.1973

		1	2	3	4	5	6	7	8	9	0	1	2	3	4	5	6	
1	**Karpov**	×	½	½	½	1	1	½	½	½	1	½	1	1	1	1	½	**11**
2	Tukmakov	½	×	½	½	½	½	1	0	1	1	1	½	1	1	½	1	**10½**
3	Furman	½	½	×	½	1	1	½	½	½	½	1	0	1	½	1	1	**10**
4	Hort	½	½	½	×	½	½	1	1	½	½	½	½	½	1	½	1	**9½**
5	Uhlmann	0	½	0	½	×	½	½	½	1	1	½	1	½	1	1	1	**9½**
6	Andersson	0	½	0	½	½	×	½	½	1	½	½	1	1	1	½	1	**9**
7	Portisch	½	0	½	0	½	½	×	½	½	1	1	1	½	½	1	1	**9**
8	Browne	½	1	½	0	½	½	½	×	½	½	½	1	1	½	1	0	**8½**
9	Ljubojević	½	0	½	½	0	0	½	½	×	½	1	1	½	1	1	1	**8½**
10	Planinc	0	0	½	½	0	½	0	½	½	×	1	0	1	0	1	1	**6½**
11	Panno	½	0	0	½	½	½	0	½	0	0	×	½	1	½	1	½	**6**
12	Calvo	0	½	1	½	0	0	0	0	0	1	½	×	½	½	0	½	**5**
13	Kaplan	0	0	0	½	½	0	½	0	½	0	0	½	×	1	½	1	**5**
14	Pomar	0	0	½	0	0	0	½	½	0	1	½	½	0	×	½	1	**5**
15	S. Garcia	0	½	0	½	0	½	0	0	0	0	0	1	½	½	×	½	**4**
16	Bellon	½	0	0	0	0	0	0	1	0	0	½	½	0	0	½	×	**3**

Karpov's first prize amounted to 125,000 pesetas. He also picked up 7,000 pesetas for the Best Game Prize and a further 5,000 pesetas for scoring the best result in the last four rounds (3½/4).

This tournament re-inforced Karpov's position as number two in the world (after Fischer), though Spassky still has some claims to share this place. Golombek, the tournament arbiter, made some interesting comments in *The Times*: 'Anyone who had watched his play at Madrid would have come away with the conviction that if he does manage to make his way successfully through the series of Candidates' matches then Karpov will give the world champion a really hard fight for the title. His play at Madrid had that sort of universal quality that characterizes the really great player and, in a tournament which was toughly contested he, as far as I could distinguish, made only one mistake, in his draw with Portisch.'

3001 AK–Arturo Pomar:
R1: 26 November:

Caro Kann

1 P–K4 P–QB3 2 N–QB3 P–Q4 3 N–B3 B–N5 4 P–KR3 B×N 5 Q×B P–K3 6 P–R3 P×P 7 N×P N–B3 8 N–B3 N–Q4 9 B–K2 N–Q2 10 0–0 Q–B3 11 Q×Q N2×Q 12 B–B3 B–Q3 13 P–Q3 0–0 14 P–KN3 KR–K1 15 R–K1 R–K2 16 N–N1 R1–K1 17 N–Q2 P–K4 18 P–N3 P–K5 19 N×P B–K4 20 B–N5

B×R 21 R×B P–KR3 22 N×N+
N×N 23 B–Q2 (*350*)

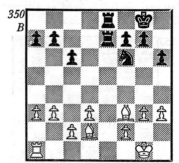

350
B

23 ... N–Q2 24 P–QR4 N–K4 25
B–N2 P–QB4 26 B–K3 N–B3 27
B×N P×B 28 P–R5 R–K4 29
P–R6 R–Q4 30 K–B1 K–B1 31
K–K2 K–K2 32 K–Q2 K–Q2 33
P–QB4 R–R4 34 P–R4 K–B2 35
P–B4 R–B4 36 R–R5 P–N4 37
RP×P P×P 38 P–QN4 NP×P 39
KNP×P K–N1 40 R×P R×R 41
B×R R–R1 42 K–B3 R–R8 43
P–N5 R–QN8 44 P×P K–B2 45
P–Q4 K×P 46 B×P R–QR8 47
P–Q5+ K–Q2 48 B–N8 R×P 49
P–QB5 R–R5 50 P–B6+ K–B1 51
B–Q6 P–B3 52 B–N4 K–B2 53
K–N3 R–R8 54 K–B4 K–N3 55
B–B5+ K–B2 56 K–N5 R–QN8+
57 B–N4 1–0 2.28 – 3.32

3002 Oscar Panno–AK:
R2: 27 November:

Reti

1 P–QB4 N–KB3 2 P–KN3 P–B3
3 N–KB3 P–Q4 4 P–N3 B–B4 5
B–KN2 P–K3 6 0–0 B–K2 7 B–N2
P–KR3 8 P–Q3 0–0 9 QN–Q2
B–R2 10 P–QR3 QN–Q2 11 P–QN4
P–QR4 12 Q–N3 RP×P 13 RP×P
Q–N3 14 B–B3 KR–B1 (*351*)

15 Q–N2 B–B1 16 P–R3 Q–Q1 17
R–R5 R×R 18 P×R P–QN3 19
P×P Q×P 20 R–R1 Q×Q 21

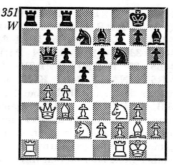

351
W

B×Q B–N5 22 P×P BP×P 23
R–QB1 ½–½ 2.22 – 1.27

3003 AK–Ulf Andersson:
R3: 28 November:

Queen's Indian

1 P–Q4 N–KB3 2 P–QB4 P–K3
3 N–KB3 P–QN3 4 P–KN3 B–N5+
5 QN–Q2 B–N2 6 B–N2 0–0 7 0–0
P–B4 8 P–QR3 B5×N 9 B×B
P×P 10 B–N4 R–K1 11 B–Q6 An
original manoeuvre in this position.
11 ... N–K5 12 Q×P N–R3 13
P–QN4 R–QB1 14 QR–B1 N×B
15 Q×N N–B2 16 KR–Q1 R–K2 17
Q–Q3 B×N 18 B×B N–K1 19
B–N7 R–B2 (*352*)

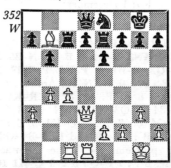

352
W

20 B–R6! The bishop leaves the long
diagonal of its own free will! 20 ...
R–B3 21 Q–N3 Q–N1 22 Q–R4
R–B2 23 Q–N5 N–B3 24 P–B3
P–Q4 25 P–B5 P–R4 26 P–QR4

R-K1 27 P×P P×P 28 P-R5
R×R 29 R×R Q-K4 30 Q×NP
P-Q5 31 K-R1 Q-K6 32 R-B1
P-K4 33 B-Q3 P-R5 34 P×P
Q-B5 35 R-KN1 Q×P/R5 36
P-R6 P-N3 37 P-R7 K-N2 intending 38 . . . R-KR1, but . . .
38 B×P! 1-0 1.52 – 2.28 'This game
came very much into the reckoning
for the best game prize, but, in the
opinion of the judges, Karpov played
another game later on that was even
more worthy of the prize' – Golombek (tournament arbiter).

3004 Vladimir Tukmakov-AK:
R4: 30 November:

Queen's Indian

**1 N-KB3 N-KB3 2 P-QB4
P-K3 3 P-Q4 P-QN3 4 P-KN3
B-N2 5 B-N2 B-K2 6 0-0 0-0 7
N-B3 N-K5 8 Q-B2 N×N 9
Q×N P-Q3 10 P-N3 N-Q2 11
B-N2 N-B3 12 KR-Q1 P-B4 13
N-K1 B×B 14 N×B P×P 15
Q×P Q-N1 16 QR-B1 R-Q1 17
N-K3 ½-½** 0.15 – 0.17

3005 AK-Juan Bellon:
R5: 1 December:

English

**1 P-QB4 P-K4 2 N-QB3 N-QB3
3 P-KN3 P-B4 4 B-N2 N-B3 5
P-Q3 B-B4 6 P-K3 P-B5!?** 7
KP×P 0-0 8 KN-K2 Aronin sug-
gested 8 P×P! e.g. 8 . . . R-K1 9
P-B4 P-Q3 10 B×N P×B 11
P-Q4 or 8 . . . Q-K1 9 B×N
QP×B 10 P-Q4 and 11 P-B4 with
no problems for White in either
case. **8 . . . P-Q3 9 0-0 Q-K1 10
N-R4** 10 B-K3 is met by 10 . . .
B×B 11 P×B P×P 12 KP×P
Q-K6+ 13 K-R1 N-KN5 and if 14
B-Q5+ K-R1 15 K-N2 Q-K1
vacating his K6 square for a knight

– Wade. **10 . . . B-Q5! 11 N×B
P×N!** White's knight is left out of
play and his QP is fixed as a target
12 P-QR3 P-QR4 (*353*)

353
W

13 P-N3 13 P-R3 P-R4! would
transpose into Saidy–Fischer, New
York Metropolitan League 1969
(that game reached this position
via 12 P-KR3 P-KR4!). **13 . . .
B-B4 14 N-N2 Q-N3 15 Q-B2
N-Q2 16 R-K1 N-B4 17 B-B1
R-R3** Following Fischer's manoeuvre. The two games are running
parallel, the only difference being
the positions of the KRPs. **18 B-Q2
R-N3 19 B×P R×P 20 B-Q2
R-R1 21 P-QR4 P-R4 22 P-R3**
Now the two games become identical! **22 . . . R-R3! 23 P-R5** (*354*)

354
B

23 . . . N-N5 Finally the games do
part company. Saidy–Fischer went
23 . . . K-R2 24 R/K1-Q1 P-N3 25

B–K1 P×P 26 N–R4 R×P 27 B×R B×B 28 Q–R2 N–N5 29 Q–R3 N–B7 30 Q–N2 N×R 31 R×N N×N 32 R×N Q–K5 33 B×P?? (better 33 B–Q2, though 33 . . . R–N3 should win – Wade) 33 . . . R×B 34 R×R Q–K8+ 35 K–R2 Q×R 0–1. One therefore assumes that Bellon's move is weaker. **24 B×N R×B 25 R–R3 P–N3 26 R1–R1 Q–K3 27 P×P R3×P 28 R–R8+ K–R2 29 Q–Q1 P–N3 30 N–R4 N×N 31 R8×N R×R 32 R×R B×RP 33 R–R7 B×B 34 R×P+ K–R3 35 Q×B P–R5 36 K–N2 R–N7 37 K–B3 P–Q4 38 NP×P R–N6 39 P×P Q×P+ 40 K–N3 Q–KB4 41 P–B3 R×P 42 R–B6 R–B6 43 R–Q6 K–R4 44 K–N2 R–B7+ 45 K–N3 R–B6 46 K–N2 Q×P 47 R–Q5+ K–R3 48 Q–K2 Q–B8 49 R–KR5+ ½–½** 2.27 – 3.01

3006 Ljubomir Ljubojević–AK: R6: 2 December:

Sicilian

1 P–K4 P–QB4 2 N–KB3 P–K3 3 P–Q4 P×P 4 N×P N–QB3 5 N–N5 P–Q3 6 P–QB4 N–B3 7 N5–B3 B–K2 8 B–K2 0–0 9 0–0 P–QN3 10 B–B4 B–N2 11 N–Q2 P–QR3 12 P–QR3 N–Q5 13 B–Q3 N–Q2 14 B–K3 B–KB3 15 R–B1 N–K4 16 B–N1 N4–B3 17 R–K1

R–N1 18 P–QN4 P–QN4 19 B–R2 **B–R1** (*355*) **20 N–Q5 P×N 21 BP×P P–QR4 22 P×N N×P 23 Q–N3 P×P 24 P×P N–K4 25 P–R3 Q–K2 26 Q–N1 ½–½** 1.45 – 1.36

3007 AK–Walter Browne: R7: 4 December:

Benoni

1 P–Q4 P–QB4 2 P–Q5 N–KB3 3 N–QB3 P–Q3 4 P–K4 P–KN3 5 N–B3 B–N2 6 B–K2 0–0 7 0–0 N–R3 8 B–KB4 Perhaps stronger is 8 N–Q2! N–B2 9 P–QR4 P–N3 10 N–B4 B–QR3 11 B–B4! R–N1? (11 . . . B×N is necessary, though White clearly stands better after 12 B×B – Hartston) 12 P–QN3! N–Q2 13 Q–Q2± Smyslov–Schmid, Helsinki Olympiad 1952. **8 . . . N–B2 9 P–QR4 B–N5 10 P–R3 B×N 11 B×B± N–Q2 12 Q–Q2 P–QR3 13 B–K2 R–N1 14 B–R6 P–QN4 15 B×B K×B 16 N–Q1 N–B3 17 B–B3 P–K3 18 RP×P RP×P 19 N–K3 P×P 20 P×P R–K1 21 R–R7 R–K4 22 P–QN4! P–B5 23 Q–Q4 R–R1 24 R1–R1 R×R 25 R×R Q–QN1 26 P–N3 P–R4 27 B–N2 K–N1 28 P–N4 P×P 29 P×P** (*356*)

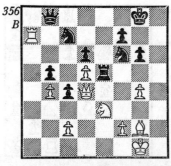

29 . . . N3×QP 30 N×N N×N 31 R–Q7 31 B×N R×B 32 Q×R

Q×R 33 Q×NP is unclear. **31 . . . Q–N3 32 Q×Q N×Q 33 R×QP N–R5 34 B–Q5 R–K8+ 35 K–R2 N–B6 36 R×P+ K–B1 37 R–N5 R–K7 38 K–N2 R×QBP 39 R–B5 N×B 40 R×N R–N7 41 R×P P–B6 42 K–N3 P–B7 43 R–QB5 R×P 44 R×P K–N2** Karpov carries on for a while. Though the position does hold winning chances, they are very slim. **45 R–B5 R–N6+ 46 K–B4 R–N7 47 P–B3 R–N2 48 R–B6 R–N5+ 49 K–N3 R–N6 50 P–N5 R–R6 51 K–N4 R–R5+ 52 P–B4 R–N5 53 R–Q6 R–R5 54 K–B5 R–R8 55 R–Q4 R–K8** ½–½ 2.45 – 3.08

3008 Silvino Garcia–AK:
R8: 5 December:

Sicilian

1 P–K4 P–QB4 2 N–KB3 P–K3 3 P–Q4 P×P 4 N×P P–QR3 5 B–Q3 N–KB3 6 0–0 Q–B2 7 P–QB4 Q–B2 8 Q–K2 P–KN3 9 P–B4 Karpov had played 9 N–QB3 against Hubner at Leningrad (2702). **9 . . . B–N2 10 K–R1 0–0 11 N–QB3 P–N3 12 B–Q2 B–N2 13 N–B3 N–B3 14 QR–B1 QR–K1 15 Q–B2 N–KN5 16 Q–N1 P–B4 17 P×P NP×P 18 P–KR3 N–B3** (357)

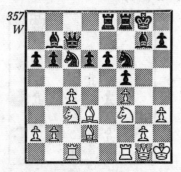

357
W

19 N–Q5!? Q–Q1! 20 Q×P Q×Q 21 N×Q N–K5! 22 B×N? P×B 23

N–N5 N–Q1! 24 KR–K1 P–Q4 25 N–Q7 P–R3 26 N×P/4 P×N 27 N×R R×N 28 P–QN4 B–QB3 29 P–QR4! B×P 30 R×P B–QB3 31 R–K2 P–RK4 32 K–R2 P–R5 33 P–N3 P×P+ 34 K×P K–R2 35 B–B3 B–R3! 36 R–B1 R–N1+ 37 K–R2 N–B2 38 B–K5 N×B 39 P×N B–KN2 40 R–B7 K–R3 41 P–R4 K–R4 42 K–R3 B–K1 43 R–R7 B–N3 44 R×P B–Q6 45 R–KB2 B×BP 46 R–R3 B–KR3? 47 R–KN3 R–QR1 48 R–B7 R–R8 49 R–KR7 R–R8+ 50 K–N2 R×P 51 K–N1 (358)

358
B

51 . . . B–K7 52 K–B2 B–N5 53 P–N5 B–B4 54 R–R8 R–QN5 55 R–N1 R–N7+ 56 K–B3 R–N6+ 57 K–B2 B–K5 58 R–N3 R–N7+ 59 K–N1 B–B4 60 R–N2 R×R+ 61 K×R B–K5+ 62 K–N3 K–N3 63 P–N6 B–Q4 64 R–QN8 K–B4 65 P–N7 K×P 66 K–N4 B–K6 67 K–N3 B–N4 68 K–B2 B–K2 0–1 4.03 – 2.30

3009 AK–Vlastimil Hort:
R9: 7 December:

Caro Kann

1 P–K4 P–QB3 2 P–Q4 P–Q4 3 N–Q2 P×P 4 N×P B–B4 5 N–N3 B–N3 6 N–B3 N–Q2 7 P–KR4 P–KR3 8 P–R5 B–R2 9 B–Q3 B×B 10 Q×B N1–B3 11 B–Q2 P–K3 12

Q–K2 Q–B2 13 0–0–0 P–B4 14
R–R4 B–K2 15 P×P N×P 16
R–Q4 0–0 17 B–B4 Q–R4 18 K–N1
KR–Q1 19 B–K5 R×R 20 B×R
½–½ 1.02 – 1.00

3010 AK–Semyon Furman:
   R10: 8 December:

Ruy Lopez

   1 P–K4 P–K4 2 N–KB3 N–QB3 3
B–N5 P–QR3 4 B×N QP×B 5
P–Q4 P×P 6 Q×P Q×Q 7 N×Q
B–Q3 8 N–QB3 N–K2 9 B–K3
B–Q2 10 0–0–0 0–0–0 11 N–N3 K–N1
12 P–B4 P–B3 13 P–B5 KR–K1 14
N–Q2 B–N5 15 N–B4 B×N 16 P×B
P–B4 17 B–B4 K–B1 18 P–N4
B–N4 19 R×R+ R×R 20 N–Q2
R–K1 21 P–KR4 N–B3 22 P–N5
N–R4 23 P×P ½–½ 0.45 – 1.02

3011 Julio Kaplan–AK:
   R11: 9 December:

Sicilian

   1 P–K4 P–QB4 2 N–KB3 P–K3 3
P–Q4 P×P 4 N×P N–QB3 5
N–QB3 P–QR3 6 B–K2 Q–B2 7
0–0 N–B3 8 K–R1 B–N5 9 N×N 9
N–R4 was played in Smejkal;
Karpov (2716). 9 . . . NP×N 10
Q–Q4 P–B4 11 Q–K3 P–Q3 12
Q–N3 B×N 13 Q×B 0–0 14 P–B3
B–N2 15 B–KB4 N–R4 16 B–KN5
P–K4 17 QR–Q1 P–B4 18 Q–Q3
P–R3 19 B–B1 QR–Q1 20 P×P
P–Q4 21 P–KB4 N×P 22 B×N
P×B 23 B–N4 P–Q5 24 Q–Q2
P–KR4 25 B×P R×P 26 B–N4
R–B3 (*359*)
27 Q–K2 B–Q4 28 R/Q1–K1
P–B5 29 Q–K5 Q×Q 30 R×Q
P–Q6 31 P×P P×P 32 P–QN3
R–KN3 33 P–KR3 P–Q7 34 R–Q1
B–B2 35 K–N1 R–QB3 36 K–B2
R–B7 37 R–QR5 R–Q3 38 B–K2
R–B8 39 B–B3 K–R1 40 R–K5

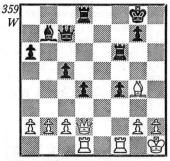

R–B7 41 R–QR5 B–N3 42 R–Q5
R×R 43 B×R B–Q6 44 P–R3
P–N4 45 B–B4 R–B8 46 B×B R×R
47 K–K2 R–KN8 48 K×P R×P+
49 K–B3 R–N6 50 K–B2 R×P 51
B×P P–N5 52 P–R4 P–N6 0–1
3.30 – 2.20

3012 AK–Wolfgang Uhlmann:
   R12: 11 December:

French

   At the start of this round Uhlmann
was tournament leader with 8½ and
Karpov was on 7½. At the end of this
round Karpov was joint leader. This
game had the added bonus of winn-
ing the best game prize of 7,000
pesetas.
   1 P–K4 P–K3 2 P–Q4 P–Q4 3
N–Q2 P–QB4 4 KP×P KP×P 5
KN–B3 N–QB3 6 B–N5 B–Q3 7
P×P B×BP 8 0–0 KN–K2 9
N–N3 B–Q3 10 B–N5 0–0 11
B–KR4 B–KN5 12 B–K2 B–R4
Varying from 12 . . . Q–N3 13 B×N
(13 B–N3 was suggested by Kotov
as an improvement) 13 . . . N×B 14
Q–Q4 Q×Q 15 N/B3×Q B–Q2=
Kuzmin–Uhlmann, Leningrad 1973,
and 12 . . . R–K1 13 R–K1 ½–½ R.
Byrne–Uhlmann, Leningrad (last
round). 13 R–K1 Q–N3 14 N/B3–
Q4 B–N3 15 P–QB3 KR–K1 16
B–B1 B–K5 17 B–N3 B×B 18
RP×B P–QR4?! This seriously
weakens his . . . QN4. 19 P–R4

N × N 'Uhlmann afterwards thought this exchange was premature and that he could have gained an important tempo by playing here 19 . . . QR–B1' – Golombek. **20 N × N! N–B3** 20 . . . Q × P allows 21 N–N5 winning material. **21 B–N5 R/K1–Q1** (*360*)

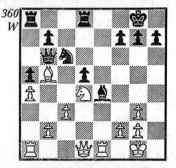

22 P–KN4! This keeps Black's bishop off the h3–c8 diagonal. **22 . . . N × N** perhaps 22 . . . QR–B1 is better. **23 Q × N Q × Q 24 P × Q QR–B1 25 P–B3 B–N3 26 R–K7 P–N3 27 R1–K1 P–R3 28 R–N7 R–Q3 29 R1–K7 P–R4 30 P × P B × P 31 P–KN4 B–N3 32 P–B4 R–B8+ 33 K–B2 R–B7+ 34 K–K3 B–K5 35 R × BP R–N3 36 P–N5 K–R2 37 R/B7–K7 R × QNP** (*361*)

38 B–K8 R–N6+ 39 K–K2 R–N7+ 40 K–K1 R–Q3 41 R × KNP+ K–R1 42 R/KN7–K7 1–0 2.31 – 2.32

3013 Ricardo Calvo–AK:
    R13: 12 December:

King's Indian Attack

1 P–K4 P–QB4 2 N–KB3 P–K3 3 P–Q3 N–QB3 4 P–KN3 P–Q4 5 QN–Q2 B–Q3 6 B–N2 KN–K2 7 0–0 0–0 8 R–K1 8 N–R4! is more aggressive. **8 . . . Q–B2 9 P–N3 B–Q2 10 B–N2 P–Q5 11 N–B4 P–K4 12 P–QR4 P–QN3 13 Q–Q2 P–B3 14 P–R4 Q–N1 15 B–QR3 B–B2 16 R/K1–N1 B–K3 17 K–R2 Q–B1 18 Q–K2 B–N5 19 Q–B1 P–B4 20 N4–Q2 P–KB5 21 B–R3 P–KR4 22 Q–N2 N–N3 23 N–N5 B–Q1 24 N5–B3 B–K2 25 R–N1 Q–K3 26 QR–KB1 R–B2 27 R–KR1 R1–KB1 28 K–N1 Q–Q3 29 K–R2 P–R3 30 K–N1 R–B3 31 B × B P × B 32 N–N5 P–B6 33 Q–R2 N–R1** (*362*)

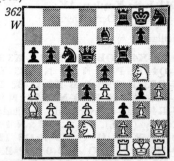

34 R–B1 R–R3 35 N–B4 Q–B2 0–1 2.00 – 1.48

3014 AK–Lajos Portisch:
    R14: 13 December:

Ruy Lopez

1 P–K4 P–K4 2 N–KB3 N–QB3 3 B–N5 P–QR3 4 B–R4 N–B3 5 0–0 B–K2 6 R–K1 P–QN4 7 B–N3 P–Q3 8 P–B3 0–0 9 P–KR3 N–N1 10 P–Q4 N1–Q2 11 QN–Q2 B–N2 12 B–B2 R–K1 13 N–B1 B–KB1 14 N–N3 P–N3 15 P–QR4 P–B4 16

P-Q5 N-N3 17 P-R5 N-B5 18
P-QN4 P×P 19 P×P R-B1 20
B-Q3 B-N2 21 R-R2 R-B1 22
R-B2 Q-Q2 23 N-R2 K-R1 24
P-R4 P-R4 25 Q-K2 K-N1 26
B×N R×B 27 R×R P×R 28
Q×BP N-K1 29 R-B1 N-B2 30
P-B4 P×P 31 B×P N-N4 32
Q-Q3 R-B1 33 B-Q2 R-B2 34
N-K2 B-QB1 35 N-KB3 Q-K2 36
B-N5 P-B3 37 B-B4 P-B4 38
N-N5 P×P 39 Q×P Q×Q 40
N×Q R-B5 41 N×P N×N 42
B×N R×RP (363)

P-Q4 P×P 4 N×P N-QB3 5
N-QB3 P-QR3 6 P-B4 Q-B2 7
N×N Q×N 8 B-Q3 P-QN4 9
Q-K2 B-N2 10 B-Q2 B-B4 11
Q-N4 P-N3 12 P-QR3 P-B4 13
Q×P KP×P 14 Q-K2+ K-B2 15
0-0-0 R-K1 16 Q-B1 N-B3 17
P-QR4 (364)

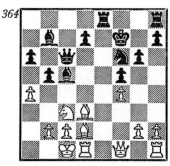

364

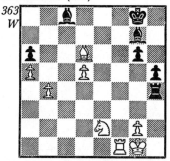

363
W

17 ... Q×P 18 Q×Q B×Q 19
KR-K1 P-N5 20 N-R2 P-QR4 21
K-N1 B-B6 22 R-QB1 N-K5 23
B×N B×B 24 K-R1 P-Q4 25
B-K3 B×B 26 R×B P-Q5 27
R-K2 B-B3 28 R-Q2 R-K5 29
R1-Q1 B×P 30 P-N3 B-B3 31
R×P R×R 32 R×R R-K1 33
R-B4 R-K8+ 34 K-N2 B-K5 35
N-B1 R-R8 36 R-B7+ K-N1 37
N-K2 R×P 38 N-Q4 P-R4 39
N-K6 P-KR5 40 N-N5 P-R6 41
R-B8+ K-N2 42 R-B7+ K-B1
0-1 2.40 - 1.25

43 B-B5 R-K5 44 N-B4 K-R2 45
N-K6 B×N 46 P×B R×KP 47
R-B7 K-R3 48 R-N7 R-K5 49
K-B2 B-Q5+ ½-½ 2.44 - 2.58

3015 Albin Planinc-AK:
R15: 15 December:

Sicilian

1 P-K4 P-QB4 2 N-KB3 P-K3 3

1973 Chess Oscar

1973 was a magnificent year for Karpov – he lost only one game (against Petrosian in the USSR Championship) and finished with the excellent overall score of +32 —1 =41 (71%) which recalls Fischer's results of 1970: +48 —3 =23 (80%).

The year's achievements were crowned when he was awarded the chess oscar at the end of the Madrid tournament (In 1972 Karpov had also been in the running for this prize: 1 Fischer, 2 Spassky, 3 Portisch, 4 Karpov).

If one can draw conclusions from history then the list of previous oscar winners is most interesting: 1967 Bent Larsen; 1968, 1969 Boris Spassky; 1970, 1971, 1972 Robert Fischer.

Karpov was also voted one of the Soviet Union's top ten sportsmen of the year (No. 1 chessplayer) in an annual poll of Soviet sports writers.

Moscow, 17.1–3.2.1974

	1	2	3	4	5	6	7	8	
Karpov	½	½	½	1	½	1	½	1	5½
Polugayevsky	½	½	½	0	½	0	½	0	2½

3101 Lev Polugayevsky–AK: G1:

Nimzo–Indian

1 P–Q4 N–KB3 2 P–QB4 P–K3 3 N–QB3 B–N5 4 P–K3 0–0 5 B–Q3 P–B4 6 N–B3 P–Q4 7 0–0 QP×P 8 B×BP N–B3 9 P–QR3 B–R4

A long-forgotten variation which has again become popular thanks to the efforts of grandmaster Larsen. Both players play this line as Black. The theoretical duel has become the more interesting in that Polugayevsky is obliged to demonstrate an advantage for White.

10 B–Q3

One of the most unpleasant continuations for Black to meet.

10 . . . P×P 11 P×P B–N3 12 B–K3 N–Q4 13 B–KN5!

An improvement on 13 N×N which gave Black easy equality in Gligorić–Karpov (2009). Polugayevsky's move is a theoretical novelty which poses Black complex problems.

13 . . . P–B3

He is obliged to make this weakening of his pawn formation because if the queen moves it is difficult for Black to complete his development. **14 B–K3 N3–K2 15 Q–B2 N×B 16 P×N P–N3**

White has some advantage be-cause of his strong pawn centre. However, Black's position is sufficiently solid, possessing the advantage of the two bishops he can count on utilizing this in the event of the game being opened up.

In the next few moves both players try to improve the position of their pieces.

17 B–B4 N–B4! 18 KR–K1 K–N2 19 QR–Q1 B–Q2 20 K–R1 R–B1 21 B–R2 N–Q3 22 Q–Q3 Q–K2 23 P–K4 N–B2 (*365*)

An important moment in the game. By the efficient manoeuvre . . . N–K2–B4–Q3–B2 Karpov prepares to defend against his opponent's possible central pawn thrusts.

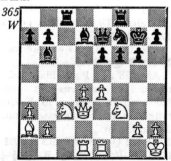

365
W

24 P–K5

Polugayevsky made this move after 36 minutes' thought. Probably he was balancing possibilities of improving the position of his pieces against Black, at the same time, gradually preparing a Q-side pawn advance.

If 24 P–Q5 then sufficiently good is 24 . . . N–K4 25 N×N P×N and possibly Black stands a little better.
24 . . . P×P 25 N×P

In the press room the opinion was expressed that by means of 25 P–Q5 White would have retained the initiative. However, after 25 . . . B–B2 26 N–K4 P×P 27 B×P B–B3 it is not clear what advantage White can extract from the position.
25 . . . N×N 26 R×N R–KB4

Black has the possibility of playing 26 . . . Q–R5 with the threats 27 . . . B–B2 and 27 . . . Q×QP. It is obvious that Karpov did not like the fact that after 26 . . . Q–R5 White could force a draw by 27 B×P Q×QP 28 Q×Q B×Q 29 B×B B×R 30 B×R R×B 31 R–Q7+ K–R3 32 R×NP B×N 33 P×B R×P 34 P–KR4 R×P.
27 N–Q5

It is very tempting to exchange off the bishop on QN6, and Polugayevsky passes over the move 27 R5–K1, suggested in the press room by David Bronstein. In this case Black would have found it difficult to neutralize White's central pressure.
27 . . . Q–Q3

Also 27 . . . Q–N4 was not bad.
28 N×B Q×N

After 28 . . . P×N Black gains a tempo but weakens his pawns. However, it is more to Karpov's taste to attack enemy pawns than to defend his own.
29 Q–K2 Q–Q3 30 P–R3 R1–B1 31 K–N1 B–R5 32 R–Q2 B–Q2 ½–½

After 32 . . . B–Q2 it is not clear that White has anything other than 33 R–Q1.

It was not good for Black to go into the ending by 32 . . . R×R 33 Q×R+ Q×Q 34 P×Q R–B4 35 R–K2 because White is the one with the chances.

3102 AK–Lev Polugayevsky: G2: Sicilian

1 P–K4 P–QB4 2 N–KB3 P–Q3 3 P–Q4 P×P 4 N×P N–KB3 5 N–QB3 P–QR3 6 B–K2 P–K4 7 N–N3 B–K2 8 0–0 B–K3 9 P–B4 Q–B2 10 P–QR4 QN–Q2 11 K–R1 0–0 12 B–K3 P×P 13 R×P KR–K1 14 N–Q4 N–K4 15 N–B5 N–N3 16 R–KB1 B–KB1 17 Q–Q4 N–K4 18 B–KN5 N3–Q2 19 QR–Q1 N–B4 20 N×QP B×N 21 Q×B Q×Q 22 R×Q B–Q2 *(366)*

366
W

White has an extra pawn which, paradoxically, it is not good to hang on to. Karpov himself considers that after, for example, 23 B–K3 N×RP 24 N–Q5 he would have had a strategically won position. But in the game something different happened and Polugayevsky's pieces became quite active.
23 P–QN3 B–B3 24 B–B3 P–B4 25 B–K3 N×KP 26 B×N P×B 27 P–R3 QR–Q1 28 R×R R×R 29 K–N1 N–N3 30 N–K2 R–KB1 31 R–Q1 N–R5 32 B–B5 R–B1 33 B–K7 N–B4 34 R–Q8+ R×R 35 B×R P–KR4 36 P–B4 P–K6 37

B–N5 B–K5 38 P–R5 K–B2 39 N–B3 B–B7 40 P–QN4 N–Q3 ½–½

3103 Lev Polugayevsky–AK: G3: Nimzo–Indian

1 P–Q4 N–KB3 2 P–QB4 P–K3 3 N–QB3 B–N5 4 P–K3 0–0 5 B–Q3 P–B4 6 N–B3 P–Q4 7 0–0 QP×P 8 B×BP N–B3 9 P–QR3 B–R4 10 B–R2

Remaining on the a2–g8 diagonal, the bishop covers the central square Q5, so that Black has to reckon with the advance P–Q5.

10 . . . P–QR3 11 N–QR4

This forces an exchange on Q4, after which the unpleasant (for Black) pin B–KN5 is threatened.

11 . . . P×P 12 P×P P–R3 13 B–KB4

Black could answer 13 B–K3 with 13 . . . N–K2 and . . . N–B4 to follow.

13 . . . B–B2 14 B×B Q×B 15 Q–K2 R–Q1 16 KR–Q1 B–Q2

Transferring the bishop to . . . K1, Black strengthens his KB2 square. If instead 16 . . . P–QN4 17 N–B3 and the threat of P–Q5 is becoming a real one.

17 QR–B1 B–K1 18 N–B3 R–Q3 (367)

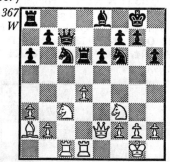

367
W

19 P–Q5

A move made after half-an-hour's thought. It leads to exchanges after which a draw becomes inevitable.

The attempt to play for a K-side attack by 19 N–K4 N×N 20 Q×N R1–Q1 21 B–N1 was not without risk. After 21 . . . P–B4 Black beats off the immediate threats and the QP is left weak.

19 . . . P×P 20 N×P N×N 21 R×N R1–Q1 ½–½

3104 AK–Lev Polugayevsky: G4: Sicilian

1 P–K4 P–QB4 2 N–KB3 P–Q3 3 P–Q4 P×P 4 N×P N–KB3 5 N–QB3 P–QR3 6 B–K2 P–K4 7 N–N3 B–K2 8 0–0 B–K3 9 P–B4 Q–B2 10 P–QR4 QN–Q2 11 K–R1 following Geller–Ivkov, Hilversum 1973 **11 . . . 0–0 12 B–K3** Spassky played 12 P–R5 in the second game of his quarter-final against Robert Byrne; that game continued 12 . . . N–B4 13 N×N Q×N 14 P–B5 B–B5? (14 . . . B–Q2= 15 B–KN5 B–B3=) 15 B×B Q×B 16 B–N5±. **12 . . . P×P 13 R×P N–K4** improving upon the weaker 13 . . . KR–K1 of the second game **14 N–Q4?!** Karpov employed the correct plan in both the sixth and eighth games. **14 . . . QR–Q1 15 Q–KN1** 'A characteristic move for Karpov' – Geller. An alternative idea was the blockading 15 P–R5 R–Q2 16 N–B5 with N–Q5 to follow. **15 . . . R–Q2 16 R–Q1 R–K1 17 N–B5** This is a waste of time. **17 . . . B–Q1!** Now 18 . . . P–Q4 is threatened and White's knight must return to Q4 to be able to meet that with 19 N×B. **18 N–Q4 N–N3** More energetic, according to Geller, was 18 . . . B–B5 with the threat of 19 . . . B×B followed by 20 . . . N–N3. **19 R4–B1 N–K4 20 B–KB4** better 20 P–R3 to prepare to transfer the queen to KN3 or KB2 **20 . . . Q–B4** 20 . . . Q–R4, with ideas of 21 . . . Q–N5 and 21 . . . B–N3, was

stronger. **21 N×B Q×Q+ 22 R×Q R×N** This threatens 23 . . . N–N3, but 22 . . . P×N also had its points – increasing control over the . . . Q4 square. **23 B–B3 N4–N5 24 R/N1–B1 B–N3 25 R–Q2 B–K6 26 B×B** Geller prefers 26 B×N, exchanging the bad bishop. **26 . . . N×B 27 R–QN1 K–B1 28 K–N1 R–B2 29 K–B2** 29 R–K2 N–B5 30 N–Q1 also came in for consideration **29 . . . N–B5 30 R–Q3** (368)

368
B

Black stands clearly better and after 30 . . . R–K4 it is unlikely that White would be able to maintain material equality, e.g. 31 N–Q5 N×N 32 R×N R×R 33 P×R N–N3. **30 . . . P–KN4** The beginning of a faulty plan. **31 P–R3 P–KR4 32 N–Q5 N×N** 32 . . . R–B4 would still retain some advantage. **33 R×N N–K4 34 P–B3 P–R5** Polugayevsky carries on playing for a win. Here he should have tried 34 . . . R–KB3 with the threat of 35 . . . P–N5. **35 R1–Q1 K–K2 36 R1–Q4 P–B3 37 P–R5 R–B3** better 37 . . . N–B5 **38 B–K2 K–Q1** another dubious plan **39 P–B4 K–B2 40 P–QN4 N–N3** (369)
41 P–N5 Here the game was adjourned. **41 . . . P×P** If 41 . . . R–B4 then 42 P–N6+ K–B3 43 B–Q1 R×R 44 R×R wins. **42 P×P R–B7 43 P–N6+ K–Q2 44**

369
W

R–Q2! R×R 45 R×R R–K4 After 45 . . . R×P White has a forcing line at hand in 46 B–N5+ K–B1 47 R–B2+ K–N1 48 P–R6 P×P 49 B×P R–K1 50 P–N7 N–K2 51 R–K2. **46 P–R6 K–B3** Or 46 . . . P×P 47 B×P and White forces the QNP through by putting his rook on QN2. **47 R–N2 N–B5 48 P–R7 R–R4 49 B–B4 1–0**

3105 Lev Polugayevsky–AK: G5: Nimzo–Indian

1 P–Q4 N–KB3 2 P–QB4 P–K3 3 N–QB3 B–N5 4 P–K3 0–0 5 B–Q3 P–B4 6 N–B3 P–Q4 7 0–0 QP×P 8 B×BP N–B3 9 P–QR3 B–R4 10 B–R2 not repeating 10 B–Q3 of the first game **10 . . . P–QR3 11 B–N1** Now Polugayevsky varies from the third game in which he played 11 N–QR4. **11 . . . B–N3 12 Q–B2 P–N3 13 P×P B×P 14 P–QN4 B–K2 15 B–N2 P–K4 16**

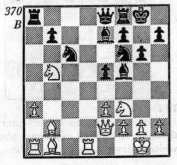

370
B

R–Q1 Q–K1 17 P–N5 P×P 18 N×NP B–KB4 19 Q–K2 (*370*)

19 . . . B×B Rather than allow White to obtain a big positional advantage, Karpov decides to sacrifice the exchange. 19 . . . P–K5 20 N–R4 B–KN5 21 P–B3 P×P 22 P×P B–R4 23 N–B7 Q–B1 24 N×R Q–R6 would lead to a similar position as occurs in the game. **20 N–B7 Q–N1 21 N×R B–KB4** If 21 . . . P–K5 then White retains his material advantage with 22 QR×B P×N 23 Q×P Q×N 24 B×N. **22 N–N6 P–K5 23 N–Q4** After 23 N–K1 B–KN5 24 P–B3 P×P 25 N×P White would avoid K–side pawn weaknesses, but Black would get a good game with 23 . . . N–KN5 24 P–B4 P×Pep 25 N×P B–B4 or 24 P–N3 N5–K4. **23 . . . N×N 24 B×N B–KN5 25 P–B3** At first sight it seems more accurate to play 25 Q–N2 B×R 26 B×N B×B 27 Q×B B–N5 28 N–Q5 R–K1 (28 . . . P–R3 29 P–R3 B–K3 30 N–K7+ K–R2 31 N×P P×N 32 Q×B) 29 Q–Q4 and Black is defenceless against the threatened 30 N–B6+. However, 27 . . . Q–Q1! would be a clear draw. **25 . . . P×P 26 P×P B–K3 27 QR–B1 R–Q1** White's K–side pawn weaknesses give Black some compensation for the exchange but it should not be enough to hold the game. **28 Q–QN2 N–K1 29 B–K5 B–Q3 30 B×B** 30 R×B looks more effective: after 30 . . . N×R 31 Q–N4 and 32 R–Q1 White keeps his extra piece, but 30 . . . R×R! 31 Q–N4 Q–Q1 32 B×R N×B merely transposes to the game continuation. **30 . . . R×B** (*371*)

31 Q–N4 Up to this point White had played very accurately, but now 31 Q–N5! would leave Black's forces overworked: 31 . . . Q–Q1 32 R×R and 32 . . . Q×R allows 33

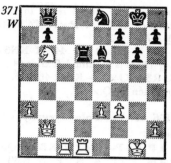

371
W

Q×N+ while 32 . . . N×R 33 R–Q1 leads to a winning ending. Also good would have been 31 R×R Q×R 32 Q–Q4 Q×QRP 33 R–R1 with 34 R–R8 to follow, and if 32 . . . Q–K2 then 33 R–Q1. The text move allows Black's queen to swing over to the K–side.

31 . . . Q–Q1 32 R×R N×R 33 R–Q1 Q–N4+ 34 K–B2 N–B4 35 Q–KB4 Q–B3 36 N–R4 White was now faced with time trouble. 36 N–Q7 would have maintained some winning chances: 36 . . . Q–N7+ 37 K–N1 Q×QRP? 38 N–B6+ K–N2 39 N–R5+! P×N 40 Q–N5+, but 37 . . . B×N 38 R×B Q×QRP would draw safely. **36 . . . B–N6 37 R–Q2** 37 R–K1 was better. **37 . . . P–KN4¡ 38 Q–N8+** 38 Q–K4 is no good on account of 38 . . . B×N 39 Q×B Q–K4. **38 . . . K–N2 39 N–N2 B–Q4 40 N–Q3 N–Q3 41 N–B4!** The only move;

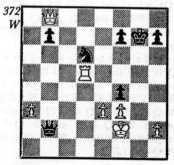

372
W

anything else would result in catastrophe. **41 . . . P×N 42 R×B Q–N7+** (*372*)

43 K–B1 P×P 44 R–KN5+ ½–½ There is nothing left after 44 . . . K–R3 45 Q×N+ K×R 46 Q–K7+ and then 47 Q×KP.

3106 AK–Lev Polugayevsky: G6: Sicilian

1 P–K4 P–QB4 2 N–KB3 P–Q3 3 P–Q4 P×P 4 N×P N–KB3 5 N–QB3 P–QR3 6 B–K2 P–K4 7 N–N3 B–K2 8 0–0 B–K3 9 P–B4 Q–B2 10 P–QR4 QN–Q2 11 K–R1 0–0 12 B–K3 P×P 13 R×P N–K4 thus far as in the fourth game **14 P–R5!** much better than 14 N–Q4 **14...N3–Q2 15 R–KB1 B–B3** (*373*)

16 N–Q5! B×N 17 Q×B! 17 P×B only eases Black's task. **17 . . . Q×BP!** otherwise Black has few prospects. **18 N–Q4 Q×NP 19 QR–N1 Q–B6 20 N–B5 Q–B7 21 R/N1–K1 N–B4** if 21 . . . Q–B3, to exchange queens, then 22 N×QP with an excellent game for White – he will always be able to pick up the QNP and then it would be difficult for Black to defend his QRP. **22 N×QP N/B4–Q6 23 B×N N×B 24 R–Q1 N–N5 25 Q×NP?!** Vasyukov prefers 25 Q–KB5 or 25 Q–R5 keeping the initiative. **25... QR–N1 26 Q–R7** (*374*)

26 . . . Q–B3? 26 . . . Q–K7!, as suggested by Shatskes, is correct, when it is very difficult for White's rooks to leave the back rank and Black threatens 27 . . . N–Q6 (or 27 . . . N–B3) followed by 28 . . . R–N7. And on 27 R/Q1–K1 Black would have the choice of 27 . . . Q–R4 (or 27 . . . Q–N5) and 27 . . . Q–R7. **27 B–B4.** There was also a possibility of 27 R×B P×R 28 B–R6, discovered by Furman in the press room, but then White would have to reckon with the possibility of 28 . . . Q–B7 e.g. 29 Q–Q4? N–Q6! or 29 R–QB1 Q–Q6 30 Q–K7 Q–Q5. Karpov prefers to strengthen his position. **27 . . . R–R1 28 Q–B2 QR–Q1 29 Q–N3 Q–B6 30 R–B3 Q–B7 31 R1–KB1 B–Q5 32 B–R6 N–B3 33 N–B5 Q–N7** if 33 . . . B–K4 then 34 B×P wins as Karpov pointed out in the postmortem: 34 . . . B×Q 35 R×B P–R4 (the threat was 36 N–R6 mate) 36 B–B6+ K–R2 37 R–N7+ K–R1 38 R×P+ K–N1 39 N–R6 mate. **34 B–B1! Q–N4 35 N–R6+ K–R1 36 N×P+ R×N 37 R×R B–B3 38 Q–B2 K–N1 39 R×B P×R 40 Q×P 1–0**

3107 Lev Polugayevsky–AK: G7: Nimzo–Indian

1 P–Q4 N–KB3 2 P–QB4 P–K3 3 N–QB3 B–N5 4 P–K3 0–0 5 B–Q3

P–B4 6 N–B3 P–Q4 7 0–0 QP×P
8 B×BP N–B3 9 P–QR3 B–R4 10
B–R2 B–N3 11 P×P 11 B–N1 was
played in the fifth game. **11 . . .**
B×P 12 P–QN4 B–Q3 13 B–N2
Q–K2 14 Q–B2 B–Q2 15 KR–Q1
N–K4 16 N–KN5 QR–B1 17 P–B4
N–N3 18 Q–K2 (*375*)

18 . . . **B–N1 19 Q–B3 P–KR3 20**
N–R3 B–B3 21 Q–N3 N–K5 22
N×N B×N 23 N–B2 B–B7 24
R–Q2 KR–Q1 25 B–Q4 P–N3 26
R–QB1 B–R5 27 R×R R×R 28
N–Q3 B–B7 29 Q–N4 B×N 30
R×B R–B8+ 31 R–Q1 Q–R5 32
Q–B3 R×R+ 33 Q×R P–K4 34
P–N3 Q–Q1 35 P×P N×P 36
Q–R5 Q–B3 37 B×N B×B 38
B×P+ Q×B 39 Q×B Q–N6 40
P–N5 Q×RP 41 K–N2 ½–½

3108 AK–Lev Polugayevsky: G8:
Sicilian

1 **P–K4 P–QB4 2 N–KB3 P–Q3**
3 P–Q4 P×P 4 N×P N–KB3 5
N–QB3 P–QR3 6 B–K2 P–K4 7
N–N3 B–K2 8 0–0 B–K3 9 P–B4
Q–B2 10 P–QR4 QN–Q2 11 K–R1

It was customary to play 11 P–B5
and after 11 . . . B–B5 12 P–R5 as in
Geller–Fischer, Curaçao 1962. After
the exchange of white square bishops,
White increases his control over Q5,
but with accurate play Black has
adequate resources. In the game
Karpov–Byrne (2711) White got

nothing from the opening and so
chose a different plan for the quarter-
final match.

11 . . . 0–0 12 B–K3

White retains the move P–KB5
as a threat and invites Black to
exchange on KB4.

12 . . . P×P

Black gains the K4 square for his
knight but cedes control of important
central squares, notably . . . Q5.

13 R×P N–K4 14 P–R5!

In the fourth game Karpov played
14 N–Q4, but Black rapidly
equalized.

The idea behind 14 P–R5 is to
prevent Black from placing a rook
on Q1, as he did in the fourth game,
after which Black gets counterplay
with . . . P–Q4.

14 . . . KR–K1

In the sixth game Polugayevsky
failed to obtain counterplay with
14 . . . N3–Q2; now he tries to
strengthen Black's play.

15 B–N6 Q–Q2 (*376*)

16 R–QR4!

Otherwise Black plays . . . P–Q4.
The alternative 16 N–Q5 is met
strongly by 16 . . . N–N3.

16 . . . QR–B1

This allows White to transfer his
rook to the Q-file, increasing the pressure on the QP, but if 16 . . . N–B3
then 17 N–Q5 is strong and 16 . . .
B–Q1 is answered by 17 R–Q4 and

Black has no time to exchange off the troublesome bishop because of 18 R×P.

17 R–Q4 Q–B3

The tactical 17 . . . R×N 18 P×R Q–B3 founders upon 19 Q–K1! and Black does not have sufficient compensation for the exchange after 19 . . . N3–Q2 20 R–QN4. If, instead, 18 . . . R–QB1 then again 19 Q–K1 and the most that Black could hope to get in return for the exchange would be one pawn.

18 R–Q2

Clearing a retreat for the bishop on QN6 and threatening N–Q4.

18 . . . B×N 19 P×B N3–Q2 20 B–N1

The bishop stands well on N1. 20 B–K3 also merited consideration; it is true that the bishop stands worse on K3 than on N1, but it would have denied Black his following tactical operation.

20 . . . B–N4!?

The best practical chance.

21 R×QP B×R 22 R×Q R×R 23 P–QN4 N–B3

23 . . . R1–QB1, uniting the rooks, was preferable to this plan of laying siege to the KP.

24 P–N5 R3–K3 25 P×P P×P (377)

377
W

26 P–KN3!

This seems to be the only way for White to realize his advantage. The straightforward P–QN4–N5 robs the knight of its support and would allow Black's rooks to penetrate along the QB-file. If 26 Q–N3 then 26 . . . B–Q7 follows with real threats against the KP. For the same reason (26 . . . B–Q7) the move 26 Q–KB1 is unjustified.

After 26 N–Q5 (apparently forcing Black to exchange knights because of the dual threats 27 N×B and 27 N–B7) Black replies 26 . . . N–N3 defending against both threats. After 27 N×B N×N 28 B–B4 R×P 29 B×RP White, with accurate play, should win. However, Black's rooks would have a great deal of scope and Karpov's task would be much more difficult than in the game.

26 . . . B–N4 27 P–R4

Forcing the bishop to occupy the worst possible square (furthest away from the Q-side).

27 . . . B–R3 28 B–N6

The start of a well-thought-out plan of attack on the QRP. The tactical solution 28 P–KN4, and on 28 . . . P–N4 then 29 B–K3, looks tempting, but after 29 . . . N–N3 30 P×P N×KP Black has counter-chances.

28 . . . N4–Q2

Now it seems that the bishop cannot be maintained on QN6, but Karpov has taken everything into account.

29 B–B4 R–K4 30 Q–N3

30 B–N1, threatening to take the QRP, was also good; the KP is immune because the knight on . . . Q2 would be left undefined, and after 30 . . . N–N1 31 Q–B3 White's clear advantage is not in any doubt. Karpov, however, chooses a more energetic method: after 30 Q–N3 both the BP and the QRP are threatened.

30 ... R–N1 31 B×BP+ K–R1 32 Q–B4! B–Q7

If 32 ... N×B 33 P×N R–K2 then 34 P–K5! and on 34 ... R×KP 35 P–N7 and 36 Q–B8+ cannot be prevented.

33 B–B7 R–QB4

The only reply. If 33 ... R–QB1 then 34 Q×P! Now White exchanges into a won ending.

34 Q×R N×Q 35 B×R B×N 36 P×B N3×P 37 P–B4 N–Q2 38 B–B7 P–N3 39 B–K6 N5–B4 40 B×N N×B 41 B–Q6 (*378*) **1–0**

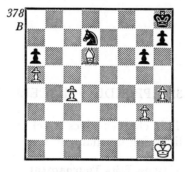

And now for Spassky!

CANDIDATES' SEMI-FINAL

Leningrad 12.4–10.5.74

	1	2	3	4	5	6	7	8	9	10	11	
Karpov	0	½	1	½	½	1	½	½	1	½	1	7
Spassky	1	½	0	½	½	0	½	½	0	½	0	4

3109–3116 – next edition

3117 AK–Boris Spassky: G9: Sicilian

1 P–K4 P–QB4 2 N–KB3 P–K3 3 P–Q4 P×P 4 N×P N–KB3 5 N–QB3 P–Q3 6 B–K2 B–K2 7 0–0 0–0 8 P–B4 N–B3 9 B–K3 B–Q2 10 N–N3 P–QR4 11 P–QR4 N–QN5 12 B–B3 B–B3 13 N–Q4 P–KN3 14 R–B2! P–K4 15 N×B P×N 16 P×P P×P 17 Q–B1! Karpov contrives to bring his pieces to the best available squares; the queen has a great future on QB4. **17 ... Q–B1 18 P–R3 N–Q2? 19 B–N4!** A bad bishop for a good knight! **19 ... P–R4 20 B×N Q×B 21 Q–B4 B–R5 22 R–Q2 Q–K2 23 R–KB1 R/B1–Q1?** (*379*)

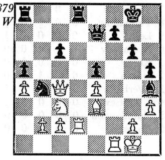

24 N–N1!! An updated version of Nimzowitsch–Rubinstein, Dresden 1926, where Nimzowitsch also focused his knight on to KN5 with an equally sensational N/KN3–R1!! **24 ... Q–N2 25 K–R2 K–N2 26 P–B3 N–R3 27 R–K2!** The rook is a real gentleman; on move 14 it made way for the queen to pass via KB1, and now it allows the knight use of Q2. **27 ... R–KB1 28 N–Q2 B–Q1 29 N–B3 P–B3 30 R–Q2 B–K2 31 Q–K6! R/R1–Q1 32 R×R B×R 33 R–Q1 N–N1 34 B–B5 R–R1 35 R×B!** 1–0 If 35 ... R×R 36 B–K7 wins easily.

The game is a fine example of Karpov's genius in bringing out the very best in each and every one of his pieces.

3118–3119 next edition.

32 APPENDIX: MISCELLANEOUS

This chapter gives a selection of games played by Karpov in lightning tournaments and simultaneous displays.

Moscow Blitz Tournament

31.3.1971

This was a 'five-minute' tournament.

		1	2	3	4	5	6	7	8	9	0	1	2	3	4	5	6	
1	Petrosian	×	1	1	1	1	1	1	1	1	½	1	1	1	1	1	1	14½
2	Korchnoi	0	×	1	0	½	1	1	1	1	0	1	1	1	1	1	1	11½
3	Balashov	0	0	×	½	1	½	1	½	1	1	1	½	½	1	1	1	10½
4	**Karpov**	0	1	½	×	1	0	0	1	1	1	0	0	1	1	1	1	9½
5	Tal	0	½	0	0	×	1	1	½	1	1	1	1	0	½	1	1	9½
6	Holmov	0	0	½	1	0	×	1	½	½	1	1	½	1	1	1	½	9½
7	Vasyukov	0	0	0	1	0	0	×	1	1	0	½	1	1	1	1	1	8½
8	Taimanov	0	0	½	0	½	½	0	×	0	1	1	1	1	1	1	1	8½
9	Lein	0	0	0	0	½	0	1	×	½	1	1	1	1	1	1	1	8
10	A. Zaitsev	½	1	0	0	0	0	1	0	½	×	1	1	0	0	1	1	7
11	Kotov	0	0	0	1	0	0	½	0	0	0	×	½	½	1	1	1	5½
12	Suetin	0	0	½	1	0	½	0	0	0	0	½	×	1	0	0	1	4½
13	Averbakh	0	0	½	0	1	0	0	0	0	1	½	0	×	0	½	0	3½
14	I. Zaitsev	0	0	0	0	½	0	0	0	0	1	0	1	1	×	0	0	3½
15	Shamkovich	0	0	0	0	0	0	0	0	0	0	1	½	1	1	×	1	3½
16	Antoshin	0	0	0	0	0	½	0	0	0	0	0	0	1	1	0	×	2½

3201 Tigran Petrosian–AK:

R7: Queen's Indian

This was the first occasion that these two players met over the board.

1 P–Q4 N–KB3 2 P–QB4 P–K3 3 N–KB3 P–QN3 4 B–N5 B–N2 5 P–K3 P–KR3 6 B–R4 P–KN4 7 B–N3 N–K5 8 QN–Q2 N×B 9 RP×N P–QB4 10 B–Q3 B–N2 11 B–K4 Q–B2 12 B×B Q×B 13 Q–N1 P–Q3 14 N–K4 K–K2 15 Q–Q3 Q–B2 (*A1*)

16 P–Q5 N–Q2 If 16 ... B×P 17 R–Q1 and not 17 ... P–K4 on

A1
W

account of 18 Q–N3 winning the bishop. 17 P×P P×P 18 0–0–0 QR–Q1 19 Q×P+ Q×Q 20

R×Q N–N1 21 R×R R×R 22
P–N3 N–B3 23 P–R3 P–N5 24
N3–Q2 N–K4 25 K–B2 R–KB1 26
N–N1 R–B4 27 N1–B3 P–R3 28
N–K2 N–B3 29 N–B4 P–N4 30
R–R5 P×P 31 P×P N–R4 32
K–Q3 N–N2 33 R×R P×R 34
N–Q5+ K–Q2 35 N–Q2 N–Q3 36
P–B3 B–K4 37 N–N3 K–B3 38
P–B4 B–N2 39 N–Q2 K–Q2 1–0
(time) 40 P–K4 is clearly winning.

3202 AK–Alexei Suetin:
R14: Budapest

1 P–Q4 N–KB3 2 P–QB4 P–K4 3
P×P N–N5 4 N–KB3 B–B4 5
P–K3 N–QB3 6 B–Q2 N5×P/K4
7 N×N N×N 8 B–B3 P–Q3 9
N–Q2 P–QR4 10 N–K4 B–QN5 11
Q–Q2 B×B 12 N×B 0–0 13 R–Q1
B–K3 14 P–QN3 P–R5 15 P–B4
N–N5 16 N×P R–K1 17 B–K2 (*A2*)

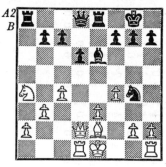

17 ... N×KP 18 K–B2 N×R+ 19
R×N Q–R5+ 20 K–N1 B–N5 21
B×B Q×B 22 N–B3 Q–K3 23
K–B2 P–QB3 24 P–QR4 QR–Q1 25
P–R3 P–R3 26 Q–Q3 R–Q2 27
K–B3 R2–K2 28 K–B2 Q–K6+ 29
Q×Q R×Q 30 R–QB1 R–Q6 31
P–R5 R1–K6 32 N–Q1 R–K5 33
N–B3 R×KBP+ 34 K–K2 R5–Q5
35 R–B2 K–B1 36 P–QN4 R–N6 37
K–B2 R–N3 38 N–K2 R–K5 39

P–N5 P×P 40 P×P R–QR5 41
R–B8+ K–K2 42 R–B7+ K–Q1 43
R×NP R×RP 44 N–B3 R–R6 45
N–Q5 R–R7+ 46 K–B3 R3×P 47
R–N8+ K–Q2 0–1 (time)

3203 Vladimir Antoshin–AK:
R15: Catalan

1 P–Q4 N–KB3 2 P–QB4 P–K3
3 N–KB3 P–Q4 4 P–KN3 P×P 5
Q–R4+ QN–Q2 6 B–N2 P–QR3 7
Q×BP P–QN4 8 Q–B6 R–QN1 9
0–0 B–N2 10 Q–B2 P–B4 11 P×P
B×P 12 N–B3 R–QB1 13 Q–N3 0–0
14 B–B4 Q–N3 15 QR–Q1 B–K2 16
B–K3 Q–R4 17 P–QR3 N–B4 18
Q–R2 N4–K5 19 N×N B×N 20
B–Q4 (*A3*)

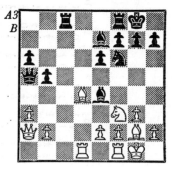

20 ... P–N5 21 R–R1 P×P 22 P×P
R–B7 23 Q–N3 R×P 24 B–B3
Q–Q4 25 Q×Q N×Q 26 B–Q4
R–B7 27 KR–B1 R1–B1 28 R×R
B×R 29 N–K5 P–B3 30 B×N P×B
31 N–N4 B–K5 32 N–K3 B–Q3 33
K–B1 B–B6 34 K–K1 B–K4 35
B×B P×B 36 K–Q2 K–B2 37
R–QN1 R–B3 38 R–N7+ K–N3 39
P–N4 B–K5 40 P–KR4 P–Q5 41
N–B5 B×N 42 P×B+ K–B3 43
K–Q3 K×P 44 R×P R–B6+ 45
K–Q2 R×P 46 R×P K–K5 47
P–R5 R–R7+ 0–1 (time)

Moscow Blitz Tournament

11–12.5.1972

	1	2	3	4	5	6	7	8	9	10	11	12	13	14	15	16	17	
1 **Karpov**	×	0 1	1 0	0 1	0 ½	½ ½	1 1	1 1	0 1	1 1	1 1	½ 1	1 1	1 1	1 1	1 1	0 1	**24**
2 Tukmakov	1 0	×	½ 0	1 ½	1 ½	1 1	1 1	0 ½	½ 1	1 1	1 ½	1 1	1 1	1 1	1 1	½ 1	0 ½	**24**
3 Korchnoi	0 1	½ 1	×	½ ½	½ ½	0 1	½ ½	1 1	½ 1	1 0	1 1	0 0	1 1	0 1	1 1	1 ½	1 0	**20½**
4 Holmov	1 0	0 ½	½ ½	×	1 0	½ 0	½ 0	½ 1	1 ½	1 1	1 1	½ 1	½ ½	0 1	1 1	1 ½	1 1	**20½**
5 Vasyukov	1 ½	0 ½	½ ½	0 1	×	½ 1	½ 1	1 ½	0 0	½ 0	½ 1	1 0	½ 0	1 1	1 1	1 ½	1 1	**19½**
6 Gufeld	½ ½	0 0	1 0	½ 1	½ 0	×	0 1	½ ½	1 1	½ 1	½ ½	½ 1	0 ½	½ 0	0 1	1 1	1 1	**18**
7 Tal	0 0	0 0	½ ½	½ 1	½ 0	1 0	×	0 0	1 0	0 1	½ 0	1 1	1 1	½ ½	1 1	1 1	1 1	**17½**
8 Stein	0 0	1 ½	0 0	½ 0	0 ½	½ ½	1 1	×	0 1	1 1	½ 1	½ 1	1 0	½ 0	0 1	½ ½	1 1	**17**
9 Bronstein	1 0	½ 0	½ 0	0 ½	1 1	0 0	0 1	1 0	×	½ 0	½ ½	1 1	1 ½	½ 1	0 ½	½ 1	0 1	**16**
10 Polugayevsky	0 0	0 0	0 1	0 0	½ 1	½ 0	1 0	0 0	½ 1	×	½ 0	1 1	0 0	1 ½	1 0	1 ½	1 1	**14**
11 Taimanov	0 0	0 ½	0 0	0 0	½ 0	½ ½	½ 1	½ 0	½ ½	½ 1	×	1 0	1 1	½ 0	0 1	0 1	1 1	**14**
12 Balashov	½ 0	0 0	1 1	½ 0	0 1	½ 0	0 0	½ 0	0 0	0 0	0 1	×	1 ½	1 1	1 1	½ ½	½ 0	**13**
13 Lutikov	0 0	0 0	0 0	½ ½	½ 1	1 ½	0 0	0 1	0 ½	1 1	0 0	0 ½	×	1 ½	1 ½	0 ½	1 ½	**13**
14 Gipslis	0 0	0 0	1 0	1 0	0 0	½ 1	½ ½	½ 1	½ 0	0 ½	½ 1	0 0	0 ½	×	0 0	½ ½	1 1	**12**
15 Vaganian	0 0	0 0	0 0	0 0	0 0	1 0	0 0	1 0	1 ½	0 1	1 0	0 0	0 ½	1 1	×	0 1	½ 1	**10½**
16 Lein	0 0	½ 0	0 ½	0 ½	0 ½	0 0	0 0	½ ½	½ 0	0 ½	1 0	½ ½	1 ½	½ ½	1 0	×	1 0	**10½**
17 Antoshin	1 0	1 ½	0 1	0 0	0 0	0 0	0 0	0 0	1 0	0 0	0 0	½ 1	0 ½	0 0	½ 0	0 1	×	**8**

3204 AK–Vladimir Tukmakov:

Sicilian

1 P–K4 P–QB4 2 N–QB3 P–Q3 3 N–KB3 P–K3 4 P–Q4 P×P 5 N×P N–KB3 6 B–K2 N–B3 7 B–K3 B–K2 8 P–B4 B–Q2 9 0–0 N×N 10 B×N B–B3 11 B–Q3 0–0 12 Q–K2 P–QR3 13 P–QR4 Q–R4 14 Q–B2 N–Q2 15 KR–N1 P–K4 16 B–K3 N–B3 17 P–R3 P×P 18 Q×P Q–K4 19 Q×Q P×Q 20 P–QN4 QR–B1 21 P–N5 B–Q2 22 N–Q1 P–QR4 23 P–N6 B–B3 24 N–B2 KR–Q1 25 K–B1 B–N5 26 K–K2 P–R3 27 P–N4 N–Q2 28 B–Q2 B×B 29 K×B N–B4 30 K–K3 N×RP 31 R–R3 R–Q5 32 P–B3 R–Q3 33 B–B2 N–B4 34 R×P N–Q2 35 N–Q3 P–B3 36 B–N3+ K–B1 37 B–R2 R–Q1 38 B–B4 K–K2 39 R–N4 N–B1 40 N–B5 N–Q2 41 N–N3 N–B1 42 R–R7 R–Q8 43 N–B5 R–N1 44 B–Q5 (*A4*)

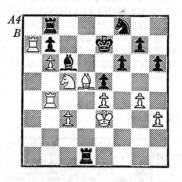

A4
B

44 ... R×B 45 P×R B×P 46 N–R6 R–B1 47 N–B7 B–B3 48 R–QB4 N–Q2 49 R×B P×R 50 P–N7 R–QN1 51 N–R6 K–Q1 52 N×R N×N 53 K–K4 P–N3 54 R–R1 N–Q2 55 R–Q1 K–B2 56 R×N+ K×R 57 P–N8=Q 1–0

3205 Vladimir Tukmakov–AK:

Ruy Lopez

1 P–K4 P–K4 2 N–KB3 N–QB3 3 B–N5 P–QR3 4 B–R4 N–B3 5 0–0 B–K2 6 R–K1 P–QN4 7 B–N3 P–Q3 8 P–B3 0–0 9 P–KR3 N–QR4 10 B–B2 P–B4 11 P–Q4 Q–B2 12 QN–Q2 N–B3 13 N–B1 BP×P 14 P×P P×P 15 B–N5 R–K1 16 R–B1 Q–N3 17 N–N3 P–R3 18 B–B4 B–K3 19 B–N1 QR–B1 20 Q–Q2 B–B1 21 R/B1–Q1 P–N4 21 ... P–Q4 is more solid. 22 B×NP P×B 23 Q×NP+ B–N2 24 P–K5! (*A5*)

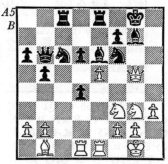

A5
B

24 ... P×P 25 N–R4 N–K2? better 25 ... Q–B4 with ... Q–KB1 to follow 26 R×KP R/K1–Q1 27 B–Q3 R–Q4 28 R×R N3×R 29 N–R5 N–N3 30 N×N P×N 31 Q×P R–B2 32 R–K1 R–K2 33 N×B R×N 34 Q–K8 mate

3206 Viktor Korchnoi–AK:

English

1 P–QB4 N–KB3 2 N–QB3 P–B4 3 N–B3 P–Q4 4 P×P N×P 5 P–K3 N×N 6 NP×N P–KN3 7 Q–R4+ N–Q2 8 B–K2 B–N2 9 0–0 0–0 10 B–N2 P–QR3 11 Q–B2 P–QN4 12 P–B4 B×B 13 Q×B P–N5 14 P–Q4 P–QR4 15 KR–Q1 Q–B2 16 P–QR3 R–N1 17 RP×P

RP×P 18 P–Q5 B–N2 19 P–K4
P–B3 20 P–N3 R–R1 21 B–B1
N–K4 22 N–Q2 P–N4 23 B–K2
P–N5 24 N–N3 R–R3 25 Q–Q2
R1–R1 26 R×R B×R 27 R–QB1
B–B1 28 Q–K3 R–R7 29 K–B1
B–R3 30 Q×P Q–Q3 31 Q–K3
R–R6 32 P–B5 B×B+ 33 Q×B
Q–B2 34 Q–B2 N–B6 35 K–N2
Q–K4 36 P–B6 Q–R4 37 P–R4
P×Pep+ 38 K–R1 (*A6*)

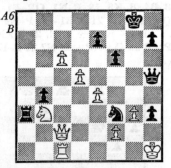

A6
B

38 . . . N–K8 39 Q–Q1 Q×Q 40
R×Q R×N 41 R×N R–QB6 42
R–QN1 P–N6 43 K–R2 K–B2 44
K×P P–K3 45 R–Q1 P×P 46
P×P P–N7 47 R–QN1 K–K2 48
R×P 1–0 (time)

3207 AK–Eduard Gufeld

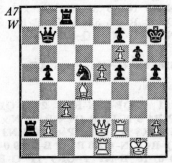

A7
W

29 R×P! N×QBP or 29 . . . R×NP
30 R×P+ P×R (30 . . . K–N1 31
Q×R) 31 Q×RP+ K–N1 32

Q–N5+ (but not 32 Q–R6 on
account of 32 . . . N×KBP) 32 . . .
K–B1 33 Q–N7+ K–K1 34 Q–N8+
K–Q2 35 Q×P+ K–B3 36 Q–K6+
K–B2 37 Q–Q6 mate **30 R×P+
K–N1 31 B×N?** 31 Q–Q2! with the
threat R–R8+ wins, e.g. 31 . . .
P×R 32 Q–R6 with mate to follow.
31 . . . R×B 32 R–N5? There was
still a win with 32 R–Q1! Q–N3+
33 K–B1 and if 33 . . . R–QN6 then
34 P–K6! P×P 35 R–Q8+! K–B2
36 R–R7+ K×P 37 R–KB8+!
K–N5 38 P–R4 mate. **32 . . . R–QN6
33 R–N1 Q–N3+ 34 K–R1 Q–B3+
35 Q–N2 Q×Q+ 36 R×Q R–K6
37 R–N5 K–R2 ½–½**

3208 David Bronstein–AK:

Queen's Indian

1 P–Q4 N–KB3 2 N–KB3 P–K3 3
B–B4 P–QN3 4 P–K3 B–N2 5
B–Q3 B–K2 6 0–0 0–0 7 P–B4
P–B4 8 N–B3 P×P 9 P×P P–Q4
10 Q–K2 N–B3 11 QR–Q1 N–QN5
12 B–N1 P×P 13 B–K5 R–B1 14
N–KN5 P–N3 15 KR–K1 B–R3
16 P–KR4 N–Q6 17 R–KB1 N–Q2
18 B–N3 B–B3 19 N–B3 B–KN2 20
P–R5 P×P 21 B–R4 Q–B2 22
N–KN5 N–B3 23 N3–K4 N–KN5
24 B–N3 Q–Q1 25 P–N3 P–R3 26
N–KB3 N–N5 (*A8*)

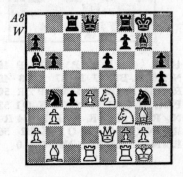

A8
W

27 Q–Q2 P–B6 28 N×P B×R 29
R×B N–Q4 30 Q–Q3 P–B4 31 N–
K2 Q–K2 32 N–R4 Q–N4 33 N–KB3
Q–B3 34 P–R3 Q–B2 35 P–N4
KR–Q1 36 B–QR2 P–B5 37 B–R4
B–B3 38 B–N1 B×B 39 N×B
R–B2 40 N–KB3 Q–B4 41 Q–Q2
Q–B3 42 Q–Q3 R–KN2 43 R–B1
P–R5 44 K–B1 N–K2 45 Q–K4
N–Q4 46 N2–N1 Q–B4 47 Q×Q
P×Q 48 B×P N5–K6+ 49 P×N
N×KP+ 50 K–K2 R×NP+ 51
K–Q3 N×B 0–1

3209 AK–Lev Polugayevsky:

Sicilian

1 P–K4 P–QB4 2 N–KB3 P–Q3
3 P–Q4 P×P 4 N×P N–KB3 5
N–QB3 P–QR3 6 B–K2 QN–Q2 7
P–B4 P–KN3 8 B–B3 B–N2 9 0–0
Q–N3 10 B–K3 Q×P 11 Q–Q2
Q–R6 12 QR–N1 Q–R4 13 P–QR4
Q–B2 14 P–N4 P–K4 15 P–N5
P×N 16 B×P 0–0 17 P×N N×P
18 P–K5 P×P 19 P×P N–Q2 20
N–Q5 Q–Q1 21 KR–K1 Q–R5 22
R–K4 Q–R6 23 N–K7+ K–R1 24
B–N4 (*A9*)

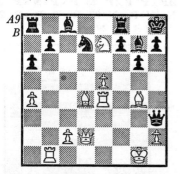

24 ... N×P 25 B×N B1×B 26
B×B+ K×B 27 Q–Q4+ P–B3 28
R×B QR–Q1 29 Q–K4 R–Q2 30
R–K1 K–R1 31 N×P+ P×N 32
R–R4+ Q×R 33 Q×Q+ 1–0

3210 Lev Polugayevsky–AK:

Nimzo-Indian

1 P–Q4 N–KB3 2 P–QB4 P–K3 3
N–QB3 B–N5 4 P–QR3 B×N+ 5
P×B P–B4 6 P–B3 P–Q3 7 P–K4
0–0 8 B–Q3 N–B3 9 N–K2 P–QN3
10 B–K3 B–R3 11 N–N3 N–QR4 12
Q–K2 P×P 13 P×P R–B1 14
R–QB1 Q–K1 15 0–0 Q–R5 (*A10*)

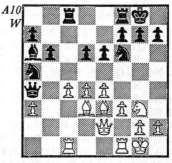

16 P–K5 P×P 17 P×P N–Q2 18
P–B4 B×P 19 N–K4 Q×P 20
R–QB3 Q–N5 21 N–Q6 Q×R 22
B×RP+ K×B 23 Q–R5+ K–N1
24 K–B2 B×R 0–1

3211 AK–Yuri Balashov:

Ruy Lopez

1 P–K4 P–K4 2 N–KB3 N–QB3
3 B–N5 P–QR3 4 B–R4 N–B3 5 0–0
P–Q3 6 R–K1 B–Q2 7 P–B3
P–KN3 8 P–Q4 Q–K2 9 QN–Q2
B–N2 10 N–B1 0–0 11 N–N3
QR–K1 12 B–Q2 P–R3 13 P–KR3
K–R2 14 P–N4 N–KN1 15 P–Q5
N–N1 16 P–B4 B×B 17 Q×B N–Q2
18 Q–B2 P–KR4 (*A11*)
19 P–B5 B–R3 20 P–B6 P×P 21
Q×P N–N1 22 Q–B2 B×B 23
Q×B P–KB3 24 P–QR4 R–B2 25
P–R5 Q–Q2 26 Q–Q3 Q–B1 27
R/K1–Q1 N–K2 28 P–N5 P×P 29
Q×P N–R3 30 N–K1 P–B3 31
P×P Q×BP 32 Q×Q N×Q 33

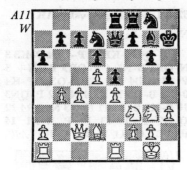

A11
W

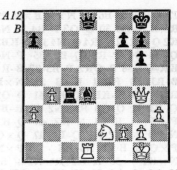

A12
B

R×P N/B3–N1 34 R–N6 R–QB1
35 R–Q1 R–B4 36 R1–Q6 R×P 37
R×P R×R 38 R×R K–N2 39
R–N6 N–Q2 40 R–Q6 N–B3 41
N–B3 N–B2 42 R–B6 N3–K1 43
N–R4 R–R3 44 R–B5 R–K3 45
N–B3 K–B3 46 N–B1 N–R3 47
R–R5 N–N5 48 N–K3 N–Q3 49
R–R4 N–Q6 50 N–Q5+ K–N2 51
R–R7+ K–R3 52 N–Q2 N–KB5
53 N–K7 P–N4 54 R–Q7 N–N3 55
N–B5+ N×N 56 P×N 1–0

3212 AK–Anatoly Lutikov:

Nimzowitsch

1 P–K4 N–QB3 2 N–KB3 P–Q3
3 P–Q4 N–B3 4 B–Q3 B–N5 5
P–B3 P–K4 6 P–Q5 N–QN1 7
P–KR3 B–R4 8 QN–Q2 N1–Q2
9 P–QN4 P–B3 10 P×P P×P 11
0–0 B–K2 12 R–K1 0–0 13 N–B1
P–Q4 14 N–N3 B–N3 15 P×P
N×P 16 B×B RP×B 17 P–R3
N×BP 18 Q–B2 N–N4 19 Q×BP
N–Q5 20 N×N P×N 21 B–N2
B–B3 22 QR–Q1 N–K4 23 Q–K4
R–K1 24 B×P N–B6+ 25 Q×N
R×R+ 26 R×R B×B 27 R–Q1
R–B1 28 Q–N4 R–B5 29 N–K2
(A*12*)
29 ... B×P+ 30 K×B Q–B3+ 31
Q–B3 Q–N3+ 32 Q–K3 Q–B2 33
R–QB1 R×R 34 Q×R Q–Q2 35
Q–K3 P–R3 36 Q–B5 Q–R5 37

Q–B3 Q–Q2 38 N–Q4 Q–Q4 39
N–B3 1–0

3213 Anatoly Lutikov–AK:

QP – Torre

1 P–Q4 N–KB3 2 N–KB3 P–K3 3
B–N5 P–B4 4 P–B3 Q–N3 5 Q–N3
N–B3 6 P–K3 P–Q4 7 QN–Q2
B–K2 8 B–K2 0–0 9 0–0 P–KR3 10
B–R4 R–K1 11 N–K5 N–Q2 12
B×B R×B 13 P–KB4 P×P 14
Q×Q N×Q 15 KP×P N–Q2 16
N–N3 B–K1 17 N–B5 P–B3 18
N×N P×N 19 B–N4 B–B2 20
QR–K1 R1–K1 21 R–B2 N–Q2 22
N–Q3 P–KR4 23 B–Q1 P–K4 24
BP×P P×P 25 P×P N×P 26
N×N R×N 27 R×R R×R 28
R–K2 R×R 29 B×R (A*13*)

A13
B

29 ... K–B1 30 K–B2 P–B4 31
P–KR4 K–K2 32 K–K3 K–B3 33
K–B4 P–N3 34 P–QN4 P–Q5 35

NP×P P×P 36 K–K3 B×P 37
P–B6 K–K2 38 B–Q3 B–B2 39
K–Q4 K–Q3 40 K×P K×P 41
K–Q4 P–R4 42 K–K5 P–R5 43
K–B6 P–R6 44 B–N1 B–K1 45
K–K7 B–Q2 46 B–R2 B–B4 47
K–B6 K–B4 48 K–K5 K–N5 49
K–Q4 B–B7 50 P–N3 B–N6 51
B–N1 P–R7 0–1

3214 AK–Aivar Gipslis:

Alekhine

1 P–K4 N–KB3 2 P–K5 N–
Q4 3 P–Q4 P–Q3 4 N–KB3
P–KN3 5 B–QB4 P–QB3 6 0–0
P×P 7 N×P B–N2 8 R–K1 0–0
9 N–Q2 N–Q2 10 N5–B3 P–QR4 11
P–QR4 N2–B3 12 P–R3 Q–N3 13
B–N3 R–K1 14 N–B4 Q–B2 15
N4–K5 B–B4 16 P–B4 N–QN5 17
B–B4 Q–Q1 18 Q–Q2 N–Q2 19
N–N4 N–Q6 20 R–K2 N×B 21
Q×N Q–N3 22 R–K3 N–B3 (*A14*)

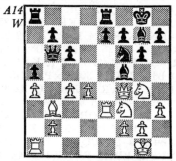

A14
W

23 N–R6+ B×N 24 Q×B/6 QR–Q1

25 R1–K1 Q–B2 26 P–B5 R–Q4 27
B×R P×B 28 N–N5 Q–B5 29
P–KN3 Q×QP 30 R×P R×R 31
R×R Q×QBP 32 R–K8+ N×R
33 Q×RP+ 1–0

3215 AK–Rafael Vaganian:

French

1 P–K4 P–K3 2 P–Q4 P–Q4 3
N–QB3 B–N5 4 P–K5 N–K2 5
N–B3 P–QB4 6 P–QR3 B×N+ 7
P×B QN–B3 8 B–K2 Q–R4 9
0–0 Q×BP 10 B–Q2 Q–N7 11
R–N1 Q×RP 12 R–N3! The move
Vaganian had overlooked. 12 . . .
Q–R7 13 Q–B1 N–B4 13 . . . N–N5
14 P×P±± 14 R–R3 N4×P (*A15*)

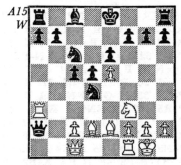

A15
W

15 B–Q3 15 N×N N×N 16
B–QN5+! is more accurate. 15 . . .
N×N+ 16 P×N Q×R 17 Q×Q
0–0 18 Q×BP N×P 19 B–K2 N–N3
20 Q–B7 P–B3 21 B–QN4 R–B2 22
Q–Q8+ N–B1 23 B–N5 1–0

Clock Simultaneous

Moscow, November 1972

Six teams of six juniors from Pioneer Palaces played, in turn, against Tal, Spassky, Petrosian, Bronstein, Smyslov and Karpov, with the exception of their team captain.

The grandmasters' scores: Tal 25½/30, Petrosian 24½, Smyslov 24½, Spassky 24, Karpov 23½, Bronstein 21.

Placings in the tournament were determined by adding the

team score to that of the captain, thus: 1 Moscow (Smyslov) 35, 2 Leningrad (Spassky) 32½, 3 Riga (Tal) 31, 4 Kiev (Bronstein) 27½, 5 Chelyabinsk (Karpov) 27½, 6 Tbilisi (Petrosian) 26½.

3216 V. Sokolov–AK

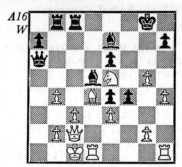

26 KR–B1! R×NP 27 R×P R×NP 28 Q×R B–R6 29 R–Q2 R–N1 30 N–N4 B×Q+ 31 K–Q1 P–K4 32 B×KP B×P 33 N–R6+ Q×N 34 P×Q B–N6+ 35 K–K2 B×B 36 R×P B–B6 37 R–Q7 P–R4 38 K–Q3 B–N7 39 R–R7 P–R5 40 R–KN4+ K–R1 41 R4×P B×R 42 R×B K–N1 43 R–KB4 R–N3 44 P–N4 R×P 45 P–N5 R–QN3 46 K–K4 R–N6 47 K–B3 B–B8 48 R–K4 K–B2 49 P–R5 R–B6 50 K–B4 R–B7 51 K–N3 B–R6 52 R–KB4+ K–N2 53 K–N4 ½–½

3217 AK–V. Chekhov:

Ruy Lopez

1 P–K4 P–K4 2 N–KB3 N–QB3 3 B–N5 P–QR3 4 B–R4 N–B3 5 O–O N×P 6 P–Q4 P–QN4 7 B–N3 P–Q4 8 P×P B–K3 9 P–B3 B–K2 10 QN–Q2 O–O 11 B–B2 P–B4 12 N–N3 Q–Q2 13 N/B3–Q4 N×N 14

N×N P–B4 15 N×B Q×N 16 P–B3 N–N4 (*A17*)

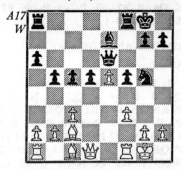

17 R–K1 In an earlier round Spassky had not been very successful against Chekhov with the alternative 17 B×N B×B 18 P–KB4 B–K2 19 Q–K2 QR–Q1 20 QR–Q1 P–B5 21 K–R1 B–B4 22 P–KR3 P–N3 23 P–KN4 K–R1 24 K–R2 R–Q2 25 R–Q2 P–N5 26 NP×P KNP×P 27 R1–Q1 P×P 28 P×P R–KN1 29 Q–B3 R2–KN2 30 R×P B–N8+ 31 R×B R×R 32 R–Q6 Q–B2 33 R–Q2 Q–N3 and Black went on to win. 17 . . . QR–Q1 18 Q–K2 P–QB5 19 K–R1 P–B5 20 P–QN3 B–B4 21 B–Q2 R/Q1–K1 22 P–QR4 Q–R3 23 RP×P RP×P 24 P–QN4 B–N3 25 R–R6 R–K3 26 R×B R×R 27 Q–B2 R–R3 28 P–N3 P×P 29 Q×P N–K5 30 B×Q N×Q+ 31 P×N P×B 32 P–B4 R–R6 33 P–K6 R×QBP 34 B–Q1 R×NP 35 P–K7 R–K1 36 P–B5 R–N4 37 P–B6 K–B2 38 R–B1 P–Q5 39 B–B3 R–KB4 0–1

Simultaneous Display   London Central YMCA, 22.1.1972

Karpov concluded a successful exhibition tour with this display (+17 −5 =4) in which he had more difficulties than in his previous two displays (20/20 and 35½/36!).

3218 AK–John Yeo:

Pirc

1 P–K4 P–Q3 2 P–Q4 N–KB3 3 N–QB3 P–KN3 4 B–KN5 B–N2 5 Q–Q2 P–KR3 6 B–KB4 N–R4 7 B–K3 N–QB3 8 0–0–0 P–K4 9 P–Q5 N–K2 10 P–KN3 P–KN4 11 B–K2 N–KB3 12 P–B3 N–N3 13 B–N5+ B–Q2 14 KN–K2 P–R3 15 B×B+ Q×B 16 P–KR4 P×P 17 P×P N–R4 18 QR–N1 0–0–0 19 K–N1 K–N1 20 N–B1 B–B1 21 N–N3 P–N3 22 P–R4 N3–B5 23 P–R5 P–N4 (*A18*)

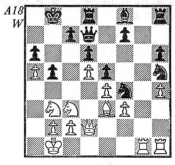

A18
W

24 N–R2 P–QB4 25 P×Pep Q×P 26 N–N4 Q–R1 27 N–B5 K–B1 28 N5×P R–Q2 29 Q–B3+ K–Q1 30 B–N6+ K–K2 31 N–B7 Q–N2 32 P–R6 N–K7 33 P×Q N×Q+ 34 P×N B–N2 35 N4–Q5+ 1–0

3219 AK–Mike Wills:

Alekhine

1 P–K4 N–KB3 2 P–K5 N–Q4 3 P–Q4 P–Q3 4 N–KB3 P–KN3 5 B–QB4 N–N3 6 B–N3 B–N2 7

N–N5 P–Q4 8 P–KB4 P–KB3 9 N–KB3 0–0 10 0–0 N–B3 11 P–B3 P×P 12 BP×P B–B4! (*A19*)

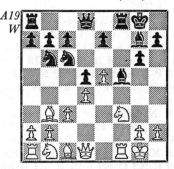

A19
W

This improves upon Karpov–Grigorian (1805). **13 QN–Q2 N–R4 14 B–B2 N3–B5 15 N×N N×N 16 P–QN3 N–N3 17 B–N5 Q–Q2 18 N–R4 B×B 19 Q×B QR–K1 20 P–R4 N–B1 21 Q–K2 P–K3 22 P–KN4 R×R+ 23 R×R R–B1 24 N–B3 P–QR3 25 Q–K3 N–K2 26 K–N2 N–B3 27 N–Q2 R×R 28 K×R Q–B2+ 29 K–K2 Q–B1 30 P–R4 P–R3 31 B–B4 N–K2 32 Q–N3 Q–B2 33 N–B3 P–B3 34 B–Q2 P–QN4 35 P×P RP×P 36 B–B1 N–B1 37 N–K1 N–N3 38 B–R3 N–Q2 39 N–Q3 B–B1 40 B×B K×B 41 Q–K3 K–N2 42 N–B4 N–B1 43 N–Q3 N–Q2 44 N–N4 N–N1 45 P–N5 P–R4 46 Q–B3 Q×Q+ 47 K×Q K–B2 48 K–K3 K–K2 49 K–Q2 K–Q1 50 P–B4 NP×P 51 P×P K–B2 52 N–Q3 N–Q2 53 N–B4 N–B1 54 K–B3 K–N2 55 K–N4 K–N3 56 N–K2 N–Q2 57 N–B3 K–R3? 57 . . . P–B4+! 58 QP×P+**

N×BP 59 P×P N–Q6+ 60 K–B4
N×P+ 61 K–Q4 N–B6+= **58**
P×P BP×P 59 N×P P×N 60
P–K6 N–N1 61 K–B5 K–N2 62
P–K7 N–R3+ 63 K×P N–B2+ 64
K–Q6 K–B1 65 P–Q5 N–K1+ 66
K–B6 1–0

3220 AK–Harry Ennis:

Ruy Lopez

1 P–K4 P–K4 2 N–KB3 N–QB3
3 B–N5 P–QR3 4 B–R4 N–B3 5
0–0 B–K2 6 R–K1 P–QN4 7 B–N3
0–0 8 P–QR4 B–N2 9 P–Q3 P–N5
10 P–R5 P–Q4 11 P×P N×QP 12
N×P N–Q5?! 13 B–QB4 B–Q3
(A20)
14 N–Q2? 14 P–QB3 was best.
14 . . . N–B5 15 N2–B3 B3×N! 16
R×B N×N+ 17 P×N N–R6+
18 K–B1 Q–B3 19 P–B4 Q–KN3
20 B–K3 Q–N7+ 21 K–K1 B–B6?
21 . . . N–N8! e.g. 22 R–K7 N–B6+

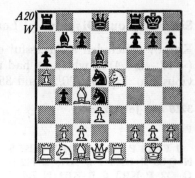

A20
W

23 K–K2 N–K4! 24 Q–KB1 Q–N5+
25 K–K1 B–N7 26 Q–K2 B–B6 27
Q–B1 N×B 28 P×N QR–Q1 and
Black wins easily. **22 Q–N1 Q×RP
23 Q–R2 N×P/5 24 K–Q2 N–R6 25
R–KB5 B–N5 26 R×P K–R1 27
R–KB1 Q–N7 28 R–K1 R×R 29
B×R R–KB1 30 Q–Q5 B–B6 31
Q–Q7 N×P 32 Q–K7 N–K5++
33 K–B1 R–B1 34 P×N P–N6 35
B×P 1–0**

Index of Openings

	+	=	−	+	=	−
13 N–N3 2515				.	1	.
13 P–Q5 *2907*	.	1	.			
13 N–B1 3205						
13 P×KP *0815*	.	1	.			
13 P×BP 1210, 2005				.	1	1
9 . . . N–N1 (Breyer):						
10 P–Q3 P–B4 1301				.	1	.
10 P–Q3 QN–Q2 11 QN–Q2 B–N2 1603,						
2408, 2506, 2602	2	1	.	.	1	.
10 P–Q4 QN–Q2:						
11 B–N5 *1915*	.	1	.			
11 P–B4 1806, 1912, 2703				1	2	.
11 QN–Q2 B–N2 12 B–B2:						
12 . . . P–B4 *2713*	1	.	.			
12 . . . R–K1 13 P–QN4 2708, 2803				.	2	.
12 . . . R–K1 13 N–B1 *1207, 1310, 1320*,						
2011, 2503, *3014*	1	3	.	.	2	.
1 P–K4 Other	**67**	**34**	**4**	**11**	**14**	**2**
Alekhine	**7**	**4**	**1**	**0**	**1**	**1**
2 N–QB3 0706				.	1	.
2 P–K5 N–Q4 3 P–Q4 P–Q3:						
4 P–QB4 N–N3 5 P×P BP×P 1315, *1703*	.	1	.	.	.	1
4 N–B3 (Modern):						
4 . . . B–N5 *1312, 1318*	2	.	.			
4 . . . P–KN3 5 B–K2 *0503, 0605, 0607*	.	2	1			
4 . . . P–KN3 5 P–B4 *0609, 0807, 0811*	2	1	.			
4 . . . P–KN3 5 B–QB4 P–QB3 *2404, 3214*	1	.	.			
4 . . . P–KN3 5 B–QB4 N–N3 *1805, 2717*,						
3219	2	.	.			
Caro Kann	**2**	**1**	**0**	**0**	**0**	**0**
Two Knights *3001*	1	.	.			
2 P–Q4 P–Q4 3 N–QB3 P×P 4 N×P:						
4 . . . N–Q2 *1103*	1	.	.			
4 . . . B–B4 *3009*	.	1	.			
Franco–Sicilian	**1**	**0**	**0**	.	.	.
1 P–K4 P–K3 2 P–Q4 P–QB4 3 P–Q5 *0404*	1					
French	**8**	**1**	**0**	**0**	**1**	**1**
Exchange *1216*, 2306	.	1	.	.		1
Winawer *2015, 3215*	1	.	.			
3 P–K5 P–QB4 4 P–B3 B–Q2 2805				.	1	.
Tarrasch:						
3 . . . P–KB4 *2311*	1	.	.			
3 . . . N–KB3 *0101*, 2502	2	.	.			
3 . . . P–QB4 *1102, 2512, 2707, 3012*	4	.	.			

Queen's Gambit Declined

Semi–Tarrasch:

Slav:

Catalan:

	+	=	−	+	=	−
Grünfeld:	1	1	0	1	1	0
Fianchetto 2012					1	
4 N–B3 B–N2 5 B–N5 *2510*	1					
Exchange 2109, *2206*		1		1		
Nimzo–Indian	1	0	0	7	8	1
Sämisch (4 P–QR3) 0504, 3210				1		
4 B–N5 0109				1		
4 P–KN3 0608					1	
4 Q–B2 0212, *1203*, 1319	1			2		
4 P–K3 0–0 5 KN–K2 2705					1	
Main Line (4 P–K3 0–0 5 B–Q3 P–Q4 6						
N–B3 P–B4 7 0–0):						
7 ... QN–Q2 0510, 0606				2		
7 ... P×P 8 B×BP:						
8 ... QN–Q2 1213, 2409				1		1
8 ... N–B3 9 P–QR3 B–R4:						
10 B–Q3 2009, 3101					2	
10 B–R2 2902, 3103, 3105, 3107					4	
Queen's Indian	1	0	0	1	14	3
4 P–QR3 1001						1
4 N–B3 0111						1
4 B–N5 3201						
4 P–K3 0604, 2407, 2908, 3208				1	1	1
4 P–KN3 B–N5+ *3003*	1					
4 P–KN3 B–N2 5 B–N2 B–K2:						
6 N–B3 N–K5 7 B–Q2 1206, 1910, 2107					3	
6 0–0 0–0:						
7 P–N3 2403					1	
7 N–B3 P–Q4 0208					1	
7 N–B3 N–K5:						
8 N×N 1815, 2507					2	
8 B–Q2 1303, 1909					2	
8 Q–B2 1819, 2001, 2914, 3004					4	
King's Indian	4	0	1	1	0	0
London System 1204				1		
1 P–Q4 N–KB3 2 P–QB4 N–KB3 3 P–KN3						
4 B–N2 0–0 5 N–KB3 P–Q3 6 0–0:						
Kavalek *1503*	1					
Hungarian *0901*			1			
Lesser Simagin *1104*	1					
Yugoslav *0817*, *2508*	2					

1 N–KB3 N–KB3 2 P–KN3 P–QN4 2401, 2906   2 · · ·
King's Indian Attack (1 P–K4 P–QB4):
2 P–KN3 P–Q4 3 P–Q3 *0204*   · 1 · ·
2 N–KB3 P–KN3 *0804*   1 · · ·
2 N–KB3 P–K3 3 P–Q3 N–QB3 4 P–KN3:
4 ... P–KN3 1813, 2505   · 2 ·
4 ... P–Q4 5 QN–Q2 B–Q3 6 B–N2 KN–K2
   2307, 3013   2 · ·

Index of Opponents

Italics indicate that Karpov was White

Name	+	=	−
Gofstein	1	.	.
Gouveia 2204	1	.	.
Grigorian K 1805, 2915	1	1	.
Gufeld 1605	.	1	.
Hartston 2004	1	.	.
Hase 2314	.	1	.
Hatlebakk	1	1	.
Hecht 2501, 2805	.	2	.
Holmov 1321	.	1	.
Hort 1911, 2412, 2502, 3009	2	2	.
Hostalet 0207, 0212	1	1	.
Hramtsov	1	.	.
Hübner 2208, 2702	1	1	.
Hug 0802, 2201	.	2	.
Ignatiev	1	.	.
Ivkov 1208	.	.	1
Jacobsen 0305, 0306	.	1	1
Jansa 2310	.	1	.
Jocha 0203, 0213	.	2	.
Juhnke 0812	1	.	.
Kapengut 1811	.	1	.
Kaplan 0816, 2413, 3011	1	2	.
Karasev 1303, 1812	1	2	.
Kärner 2103	.	.	1
Katalimov	1	.	.
Kavalek 1210	.	.	1
Keene 2007	1	.	.
Keres 2414, 2914	.	2	.
Kiprichnikov 0506	1	.	.
Kirillov 1404	1	.	.
Klovan 1401, 1602	1	.	1
Kogan E 0704	1	.	.
Konikowski 0703	1	.	.
Kopilov I	.	1	.
Korchnoi 1309, 1914, 2014, 2704, 2906	2	1	2
Kornasiewicz	1	.	.
Krasnov 0403	.	1	.
Krogius 1102, 1815	1	1	.
Kudishevich 0108	1	.	.
Kudriashov 2101	1	.	.
Kupka	.	1	.
Kupreichik	1	.	.
Kurajica 2010	1	.	.
Kuzmin 2104, 2707, 2909	2	1	.
Lapenis (2105)	.	1	.
Larsen 2403, 2710	.	2	.
Lein 1803	.	1	.
Lengyel 1903, 2506	1	1	.
Lepeshkin	.	1	.
Lerner	1	.	.
Lewi 0210	1	.	.
Liberzon 1307	.	1	.
Ligterink 0204, 0214	.	2	.
Lilein 0102	.	1	.
Lisenko 0507	1	1	.
Ljubojević 3006	.	1	.
Lukin 0109	.	1	.
Maeder 0202	1	.	.
Markevsky	1	.	.
Markland 2015, 2209	2	.	.
Markula	1	.	.
Maroszczyk	.	1	.
Matanović 2803	.	1	.
McKay 0805, 0811	1	1	.
Mecking 2006, 2415	1	1	.
Mikenas 1318	1	.	.
Miklyaev 0511	1	.	.
Mnatsakanian	1	.	.
Moiseyev 1306	.	1	.
Moles 0209	1	.	.
Najdorf 2013	.	1	.
Nebolsin 0705	.	.	1
Neckar 0807	1	.	.
Nikolayevsky 1814	1	.	.
Nisman 0504	1	.	.
Noakh 0104	2	1	.
Nowak E	.	1	.
Nowak V	1	.	.
O'Kelly 1207	1	.	.
Olafsson 1902	.	1	.
Orekhov 0101	1	.	.
Padevsky 2306	.	.	1
Panno 1209, 3002	.	2	.
Parma 1203, 1901	1	1	.
Pavlyutin	1	.	.
Payrhuber 0804	1	.	.
Peresipkin 1702	1	.	.
Peshina 0505	1	.	.
Petrosian A 1703	.	1	.

	+	=	−			+	=	−
Velimirović 2515	.	1	.	Wirtensohn *2309*	1	.	.
Veselovsky 1704	1	.	.	Wittmann *1503*	1	.	.
Vibornov	1	.	.	Yepez 1213	1	.	.
Villaroel *1212*	1	.	.	Zaitsev A *1103*	1	.	.
Visier *2313*	1	.	.	Zaitsev I 0107,			
Vogt *0813*	1	.	.	*1314*	1	3	.
Vujaćić 0808	1	.	.	Zara 0205, 0208	.	2	.
Vujaković 0301, *0302*,				Zhelyandinov *1002*	1	.	.
0303, *0304*	3	1	.	Zhukhovitsky	.	1	.
Walica	1	.	.	Zhuravlev V 1403	1	.	.
Whiteley *2801*	1	.	.	Zilbert	1	.	.

Appendix Games

Antoshin 3203

Balashov *3211*

Bronstein 3208

Chekhov *3217*

Ennis *3220*

Gipslis *3214*

Gufeld *3207*

Korchnoi 3206

Lutikov *3212*, 3213

Petrosian 3201

Polugayevsky *3209*, 3210

Sokolov 3216

Suetin *3202*

Tukmakov *3204*, 3205

Vaganian *3215*

Wills *3219*

Yeo *3218*

Index of Annotations

Parma 2006
Petrosian 2102, 2103
Portisch 2409
Radashkovich 1802
Shamkovich 1820, 2903
Shmit 1602
Smyslov 1809
Suetin 0511, 1703
Tal 1911, 1917
Tseitlin 2709
Tukmakov 2912, 3003, 3012

Uhlmann 1907
Vaganian 1001
Vasyukov 3106
Vatnikov 1917
Vasiliev 1810
Velimirović 2503, 2504
Vladimirov 0606
Yudovich 1802, 1809, 1816
Zaitsev I 2109, 2601, 2704, 2706, 2709, 2712, 2716, 2903, 2904, 2906, 2909

Sources

British Chess Magazine 2305, 3003.
Central Chess Club Bulletin 0511, 2002, 2006, 3207.
Chess 1805, 2014, 2409.
Chess Life and Review 1210, 1809, 1917, 2408.
The Chess Player **1**: 1501, 1503, 1801, 1802, 1805, 1806, 1807, 1808, 1809, 1810, 1814, 1816, 1817, 1818, 1819, 1820, 1901, 1903, 1904, 1906, 1907, 1911, 1912, 1914; **2**: 2003, 2004, 2006, 2007, 2010, 2011, 2014, 2015, 2107; **3**: 2206, 2208, 2302, 2308, 2311, 2312, 2315, 2409, 2411, 2413, 2502; **4**: 2510, 2702, 2713, 2717; **5**: 2801, 2802, 2805.
Deutsche Schachzeitung 2805.
Informator **5**: 0201, 0212; **9**: 1102, 1103; **10**: 1202, 1203, 1208, 1211; **11**: 1315, 1317, 1401; **12**: 1601, 1701, 1702, 1703, 1801, 1802, 1809, 1816, 1904, 1911, 1913, 1914, 1916, 1917; **13**: 1814, 1903, 1907, 2003, 2004, 2005, 2006, 2009, 2014, 2102, 2103; **14**: 2401, 2402, 2403, 2406, 2407, 2410, 2411, 2414; **15**: 2502, 2503, 2504, 2510, 2512, 2601, 2701, 2702, 2704, 2706, 2707, 2708, 2709, 2712.
Magyar Sakkelet 0903, 0904, 1917, 2502, 2508.
Sahs 0106, 0108, 1002, 1102, 1602, 1911, 1917, 2315.
Shakhmatisti Rossii 0809, 0812.
Shakhmatny Bulletin 1703, 1917.
Shakhmaty v. *SSSR* 0401, 0606, 1002, 1104, 1207, 1801, 1809, 1911, 1917, 2014, 2106, 2408, 3215;
64, 0801, 1001, 1201, 1203, 1207, 1208, 1213, 1816, 2109, 2208, 2302, 2311, 2312, 2511, 2514, 2601, 2602, 2703, 2706, 2709, 2712, 2716, 2901, 2903, 2904, 2906, 2907, 2909, 2912, 3003, 3012, 3101, 3102, 3103, 3104, 3105, 3106, 3108.
The Times 3012.
Schack VM Juniorer, Stockholm 1969 0811, 0812.
Skopje 72 Chess Olympiad, Matanovic 2301, 2302, 2304, 2305, 2306, 2307, 2308, 2309, 2310, 2311, 2312, 2314, 2315.
Chess Olympiad Skopje 1972, Keene, Levy 2302, 2305, 2306, 2308, 2311, 2312, 2315.
Leningrad 1973, USSR bulletins 2702, 2704, 2707, 2709,
USSR Ch 1973 bulletins 2903.
First published the notes by Ghizdavu, de Villiers, and the authors.